Studien zu Ritual und Sozialgeschichte im Alten Orient /
Studies on Ritual and Society in the Ancient Near East

Beihefte zur Zeitschrift für die alttestamentliche Wissenschaft

Herausgegeben von
John Barton · Reinhard G. Kratz
Choon-Leong Seow · Markus Witte

Band 374

Walter de Gruyter · Berlin · New York

Studien zu Ritual und Sozialgeschichte im Alten Orient / Studies on Ritual and Society in the Ancient Near East

Tartuer Symposien 1998 – 2004

Herausgegeben von / Edited by
Thomas Richard Kämmerer

Walter de Gruyter · Berlin · New York

∞ Gedruckt auf säurefreiem Papier,
das die US-ANSI-Norm über Haltbarkeit erfüllt.

ISBN 978-3-11-019461-6
ISSN 0934-2575

Bibliografische Information der Deutschen Nationalbibliothek

Die Deutsche Nationalbibliothek verzeichnet diese Publikation in der Deutschen Nationalbibliografie; detaillierte bibliografische Daten sind im Internet über http://dnb.d-nb.de abrufbar.

Printed in Germany

Einbandgestaltung: Christopher Schneider, Berlin

Vorwort

Nachdem im Herbstsemester 1997 und Frühjahrssemester 1998 die ersten Vorlesungen und Seminare in „Altorientalischen Sprachen und Kulturen“ sowohl bei den Kollegen der Theologischen Fakultät der Universität Tartu, Estland, als auch bei den Studierenden ganz unterschiedlicher Fächer auf großes Interesse gestoßen waren, entwickelte sich die Idee, an der Theologischen Fakultät zusätzlich eine Fachtagung im Bereich der interdisziplinären Ostmittelmeerforschung durchzuführen. Es gelang im darauffolgenden Herbstsemester 1998, eine Eröffnungstagung zu organisieren, deren Erfolg dazu führte, zu dieser Tagung nun jährlich einzuladen. Seit 1999 ist dieser Kongress fester Bestandteil des akademischen Angebotes der Theologischen Fakultät der Universität Tartu. 2006 beteiligte sich darüber hinaus auch die Abteilung Geschichte der Philosophischen Fakultät, und mit dem nächsten, bereits in Planung befindlichen Kongress wird sich auch die Abteilung der Klassischen Philologie der Philosophischen Fakultät anschließen, so dass nun die Organisation dieses Kongresses bei den zwei oben genannten Fakultäten mit ihren drei Fachbereichen Altorientalistik, Geschichte und Klassische Philologie liegen wird.

Für das Gelingen der Kongresse richtet sich der Dank an die Studierenden des Lehrstuhls für Altorientalische Sprachen und Kulturen der Theologischen Fakultät, die mitgeholfen haben, die Kongresse zu ermöglichen: Herr Kahrut Eller, Herr Peeter Espak, Frau Helena Liigi, Frau Ave Paulus, Frau Ave Põlenik, Herr Vladimir Sazonov, Frau Jaana Strumpe, Frau Marie Umming, Herr Raul Veede und Herr Ivo Volt. Besonderer Dank gilt Frau Aira Võsa und Herrn Dr. Amar Annus für die Übersetzung wie auch für die Zusammenstellung der Artikel und dem Verlag de Gruyter, dort besonders Frau Sabina Dabrowski, die es ermöglicht haben, die Drucklegung dieses ersten Bandes vorzunehmen. Ein ganz besonderer Dank gilt den Herausgebern von BZAW, die diesen ersten Tartuer Kongressband in ihre Reihe mit aufgenommen haben. Nicht unerwähnt bleiben darf die finanzielle Unterstützung der Universität Tartu und ihrer Theologischen Fakultät, sowie der Botschaft der Bundesrepublik Deutschland in Tallinn.

Tartu, 10.04.2007 Thomas R. Kämmerer

Einleitung

Dem Herausgeber ist es Freude und Genugtuung, nun unter dem Titel „Interdisciplinary Studies of the Ancient East-Mediterranean" einen ersten Band vorlegen zu können. Dieser Band enthält die überarbeiteten Versionen von Vorträgen, die während der ersten fünf internationalen Symposien in den Jahren 1998 bis 2004 in Tartu gehalten wurden.

Diese Symposien wurden vom Lehrstuhl für Altorientalische Sprachen und Kulturen der Theologischen Fakultät der Universität Tartu organisiert.

Der Teilnehmerkreis setzt sich vorwiegend aus Wissenschaftlern zusammen, die aus Deutschland, England, den USA und Finnland kommen. Kollegen aus Russland haben sich inzwischen ebenfalls angeschlossen. Ihnen allen gilt besonderer Dank, da sie mit ihrer Einwilligung zur Veröffentlichung ihrer Vorträge das Entstehen dieser neuen Reihe zur Ostmittelmeerforschung ermöglicht haben.

So liegt der Wert der Tartuer Symposien zusammen mit ihrem nunmehr entstandenen Publikationsorgan vor allem darin, dass sich in Tartu Kollegen vor allem aus West- und Osteuropa zusammenfinden, zum einen um über fachspezifische Probleme der Religionsgeschichte, Medizingeschichte, Linguistik des Antiken Ostmittelmeerraumes sowie der dazugehörigen Archäologie zu sprechen, zum anderen aber auch Fragen zu erörtern, die speziell in der Lage der jeweiligen Institute und Organisationen in Osteuropa begründet liegen. Die Ergebnisse dieser Forschungen der Fachwelt zugänglich zu machen, fördert ganz allgemein die Akzeptanz einer in Estland neu gegründeten, wissenschaftlichen Disziplin und erschließt nicht zuletzt gerade dadurch bei der jüngeren, estnisch-sprachigen Generation zusätzliche Interessensgebiete neu.

Es gilt grundsätzlich, dass die Artikel des vorliegenden Bandes alphabetisch nach Autorennamen sortiert sind und nicht dem tatsächlichen Ablauf der jeweiligen Symposien entsprechen. Die einzelnen Symposien hatten bis 2007 folgende Themenschwerpunkte, wobei in diesem ersten Band nur die Manuskripte Aufnahme fanden, die in der Zeit von 1999–2004 als Vorträge gehalten wurden:

1. Eröffnungssymposium: „Zur Einführung in die Altorientalistik" (Herbst 1998),

2. Symposium: „Mesopotamien und dessen Beziehungen zu den Nachbarregionen" (26. April – 28. April 1999),

3. Symposium: „Gesellschaftliche Beziehungen im Alten Vorderen Orient" (24. April – 27. April 2000).

Das für das Jahr 2001 geplante Symposium wurde mit dem internationalen Assyriologenkongress (RAI), der gemeinsam von den Universitäten Helsinki (Finnland) und Tartu (Estland) organisiert wurde, zusammengelegt.

4. Symposium: „Kunst und Magie im Alten Vorderen Orient" (22. April – 25. April 2002),

5. Symposium: „Zur Geschichte der Naturwissenschaften des Alten Vorderen Orients: Sektion Medizingeschichte" (28. April – 01. Mai 2003),

6. Symposium: „Magie und Religion" (26. April – 28. April 2004),

7. Symposium: „Mesopotamien und die Mittelmeerregionen" (25. April – 27. April 2005),

8. Symposium: „Zur Geschichte des Transfers von Techniken im Mittelmeerraum" (22. Mai – 24. Mai 2006),

9. Symposium: „Ideologien im Antiken Ost-Mittelmeerraum: vergleichende Annäherungen" (04. Juni – 07. Juni 2007).

Auf Grund des Erfolges und der neuen, interdisziplinären Ausrichtung des neunten und der zukünftigen Symposien, bedingt durch die Gründung des „Baltic Branchs of the Fondazione Mediterraneo (BBFM)" an der Universität Tartu werden die Publikationen des „International Congress for East-Mediterranean Studies (ICAEM)" unter dem Zeitschriftennamen „Acta Mediterranea Tartuensia" (AcMT) erscheinen.

Inhalt

The Soul's Ascent and Tauroctony:
On Babylonian Sediment in the Syncretic Religious Doctrines of Late Antiquity

Amar Annus, Tartu

Introduction

This paper tries to investigate some important concepts in the syncretic world of the religions of late antiquity with respect to its Mesopotamian heritage.[1] These features include the origin of Gnostic archons, the doctrines of fate, the soul's ascent and descent and its clothing, and some concepts especially pertinent to Mithraism such as grade systems, Mithras' rockbirth, and the tauroctony. Before giving an account of the Mesopotamian sediments in the religions of late antiquity perhaps a justification of the endeavour is in order. Apart from the pan-Babylonian school, there were some other scholars in the first half of the 20th century who admitted Mesopotamian influence on the late antique religions, most notably W. Anz (1897), F. Cumont (1912; 1949) and G. Widengren (1946). For example, according to the famous dictum of Franz Cumont, the mysteries of Mithras derived its origins from ancient Persia, and subsequently were deposited in Babylonia with "a thick sediment of Semitic doctrines" (*un sédiment épais de doctrines sémitiques*).[2]

In the second half of the 20th century, the Mesopotamian influences on the religions of late antiquity have for a quite long time been out of fashion, and the "Babylonian sediments" have never been systematically

1 The publication of this paper was supported by Estonian Science Foundation grant, number 6625. The materials used for it were gathered during 2003–2005, when I was working as the assistant of the Internet Database *Melammu* for the Intellectual Heritage of Assyria and Babylonia in East and West, under the Institute of Asian and African Studies, University of Helsinki, see http://www.aakkl.helsinki.fi/melammu/.

2 F. Cumont, *Les mystères de Mithra*, 3rd edition, 1913, p. 27.

studied. This has led many scholars to think that Cumont's verdict was mistaken and any similar endeavour is probably based on a misapprehension. For example, a recent account of the genesis of the mysteries of Mithras, which postulates a founding group at the end of the first century AD among the dependents of the dynasty of Commagene,

> looks again to Anatolia and to an Anatolian group steeped in an Iranian religious tradition. These, however, are not the Hellenized Mazdean magi, the *Magousaioi*, to whom Cumont remained so attached as Mithraism's putative ancestors. They are a less diffuse group and one whose devotion to Mithras may be inferred directly from the much heralded devotion of their dynastic patrons to that god. In an economy that is surely a desirable feature of any such account, this group also becomes the origin of another component of the Mysteries, the astrologically based cosmology, which Cumont located more distantly in space and time, in Babylon as the Semitic 'stratum' and contribution to Mithraism (Beck 1998: 125).

The present paper diverges from this stream of scholarship that refrains from recognition of any genuinely ancient elements in the syncretic religions of late antiquity, but rather tries to investigate some key concepts in these religions from a point of view of continuity of the ancient Mesopotamian ones. In the following pages, I will try first to show that the concept of Hellenistic astrology, which assumed the determination of mundane affairs from the influences of the movements of the seven planetary gods, derived quite obviously from Mesopotamian divination. Secondly, it will be my concern to show that the grade systems, so characteristic of the mystery religions, and especially of Mithraism, were also current in ancient Mesopotamia. The soul's gradual descent or genesis and its ascent or apogenesis in the late antique religions have several antecedents in the Mesopotamian myths and rituals, most prominently in the myth of the descent and ascent of the goddess Inanna/Ištar. The seven grades of the soul's ascent and descent can be shown to be related to the stations of the seven planetary gods in Mesopotamia. The investment and divestment of the soul with seven different kinds of qualities during its descent into bodily existence and ascent to the heavenly realm can be seen as parallel to the clothing and stripping metaphor in the Mesopotamian myth. Finally, I find parallels of the most important iconographic symbol of Mithraism, that of Mithras killing the bull, to the episode in the Epic of Gilgamesh, where Gilgameš and Enkidu kill the Bull of Heaven. Although I am not the first to put forward this connection, deeper analysis has been still lacking. The Bull of Heaven as the name of the constellation Taurus in Mesopotamia may have a relevance to the astrological interpretation of the main iconographic symbol in Mithraism, and other details in the Epic of Gilgamesh can point to a possibility of later astronomical interpretation. The late antiquity evidence quoted or referred to comes from a variety of sources, assuming that these doctrines of ultimately Mesopotamian origin were syncretically represented in several schools of late antiquity, including Mandeanism and Syrian Christianity.

The Seven Gods of Destinies

The gods fixing destinies for the king and his people is a pivotal theme in Mesopotamian literature. The royal fates were fixed in the assembly of the gods, and the most important decisions were made in the main temple of the religious centre of the land, in Nippur, or Babylon (see Annus 2002: 21-61). In the Sumerian composition "Enlil and Ninlil", which can be with certainty dated to the 21st century BCE, the gods who determined the destinies in Nippur are referred to as "the fifty great gods and the seven gods who decide destinies".[3] Exactly the same configuration is mentioned in the much later composed Babylonian Creation Epic VI 80–81, in the context of decreeing Marduk's lofty status: "The fifty great gods took their seats; the seven gods of destinies were confirmed for rendering judgement."[4]

In the Sumerian texts, the decreeing of royal destiny appears frequently in the context of enthronement of a new king. In the first millennium BCE, an assembly of gods decrees the destinies of the king, who represents Marduk (or Bēl "the Lord"), and of the Babylonian people at the New Year festival, and the passage cited from the Creation Epic refers to this occasion. The New Year festival *akītu* was the most important

3 In Sumerian, lines 56–57: dingir gal-gal 50-ne-ne dingir nam tar-ra 7-na-ne-ne. See the edition of the text in the home page of the *Electronic Text Corpus of the Sumerian Literature* (ETCSL), http://etcsl.orinst.ox.ac.uk/ under 1.2.1. From this electronic database are extracted all English translations of Sumerian texts in present paper.

4 In Akkadian: *ilāni rabûti hamšatsunu ušibu-ma ilāni šīmāti sebûšunu ana purussê uktinnu*. See the latest edition by Talon 2005. There is no consensus in dating the composition of this epic – the present writer opts for the middle of the second millennium BCE, see Annus 2002: 37–39.

religious festivity in Babylonia, and it continued to be celebrated until Roman times. From the Hellenistic period onwards, an *akītu* festival was celebrated in honour of these several Bēls, and not necessarily in the month of Nisan:

> Cults of Bel continued to flourish during the Parthian period both within and outside areas controlled at times by Rome: at Palmyra, Dura, Apamea-on-Orontes and Hatra the cult or at least its buildings appear to be newly emerged, but at Ashur, Arbela, Harran and Babylon powerful traditions of great antiquity have survived into the Roman period. The language in which the epic of creation was recited began as Babylonian, but creeping Aramaicisation may have resulted eventually in an all-Aramaic version. (Dalley 1995: 150–51.)

The mythological concept of the seven gods forming an assembly for decreeing the destinies for the whole world and writing them down on the Tablet of Destinies formed the backbone of the later practice of horoscopy, which emerged only in the Achaemenid period. The planets were associated with the gods already in the second millennium BCE Mesopotamian celestial omen texts. The planetary gods were treated as persons, because the protases of celestial omens refer to the actions or appearances of the planets and stars not appropriate to inanimate objects, but rather as anthropomorphic beings with agency and feeling. Furthermore, the anthropomorphic references in the celestial omens are to gods. For example, instead of simply stating, that there was a lunar eclipse, normally expressed by the Babylonian term *attalû* "eclipse", the moon, in anthropomorphic guise, is described as "mourning" or "feeling distress". The lunar eclipse was understood in terms of the distress of the moon god (Rochberg 1996: 478). The heavenly bodies were quite often personified as gods, and the metaphorical terms of description refer in each case to the particular deity of which the heavenly body was considered to be a manifestation (Rochberg 2004: 72, 167-73).

The seven gods were associated with the planets as follows – Šamaš with Sun, Sin with Moon, Jupiter with Marduk (= Bēl), Saturn with Adad, Mercury with Nabû or Ninurta, Venus with Ištar, and Mars with Nergal. According to the canonical Babylonian texts of the first millennium BCE, listing cultic topography, the Marduk's temple in Babylon, called Esagil, contained the Dais of Destinies where the two assemblies of the gods convened for making decisions on the 8th and 11th of Nisan, and which was equipped with seats for the seven destiny-decreeing gods (see Annus 2002: 76-81).

An aspect of the Mesopotamian gods, who formed an assembly to determine heavenly and mundane affairs, was revealed in planetary orientations (Rochberg 2004: 187-90). The decisions of fate were read from the night sky by learned men, who composed and used compendia of celestial omens. The assembly of Mesopotamian gods was thought to rule over the society and to be represented on earth by the Assyrian or Babylonian state council. The functional relationship in Mesopotamian divination was between the deities, the givers of signs, and humankind, for whose benefit the signs were given. The predictions given for the signs, the apodoses of the omens were sometimes called *purussû*, "(divine) decisions" (Rochberg 2004: 53, 59). In the Mesopotamian system of divination, agency is placed in the gods, who decide what events will happen on earth in association with ominous celestial phenomena (*ibid*: 266-67).

The notion of the gods' assembly also forms the ideological background for the cuneiform horoscopes, which are based on the idea of ascribing the planetary alignment at the moment of birth to the life and fortune of an individual. Surviving Babylonian horoscopes all date to the second half of the first millennium (see Rochberg 1998). From this branch of Babylonian astrological practice developed Hellenistic Greek genethlialogy that is at the base of later astrological doctrines. The evidence for Babylonian influence on Greek astrology:

> derives largely from the later periods of cuneiform tradition, i.e., the Achaemenid and Seleucid periods. The most fundamental tool for Greek astrology, the zodiac, is of Babylonian origin in the fifth century. Not only is the Babylonian origin of the zodiac assured on the basis of cuneiform documentation, but, as Neugebauer has demonstrated from the deviation (= 5^0) between modern longitudes and those given in Greek horoscopes, the astrological literature of hellenistic and Roman period continued to use the norming point of the Babylonian zodiac (Aries 8° or 10°). In two cases, the exaltations (hypsomata) and the forerunners of trine aspect, textual evidence traces the origins of these doctrines to the seventh century and even earlier traditions in the celestial omens of Enūma Anu Enlil. The Babylonian elements which can be pinpointed as direct contributions to Greek astrology, specifically, the planetary exaltations, the dodekatemoria, and trine aspect, represent significant features of the later system." (Rochberg-Halton 1988: 61.)

The Babylonian horoscopes represent a significant departure from the earlier Babylonian celestial divination, as represented by the omen series *Enūma Anu Enlil*, which always retained its concern with public matters – king and state. Babylonian horoscopy combines this with the tradition of birth omens, in which the birth had mantic significance in the way of any action occurring on a certain month and day, just as is seen in menologies and hemerologies, and finally, the personal divination such as is represented by the physiognomic omen series. In this way, the Babylonian "horoscopy" grew out from a complex foundation of interrelated mantic forms: the date of birth omen, the personal omen, the celestial omen and the nativity omen (Rochberg 1999-2000: 240–241).

Given the overwhelming evidence which we have for the influence of Babylonian celestial sciences on Hellenistic astrology and astronomy, it is not difficult to believe that the seven planetary gods involved in the late antique science of the celestial spheres were of Mesopotamian origin.[5] Deities or angels as planets or planetary spheres were considered in late antiquity as the divine powers who rule the physical universe and as such they corresponded to gnostic archons. In a fashion characteristic to Gnosticism, both the Jewish creator god and the Mesopotamian gods were demonized as evil beings. The number of archons was seven like the number of gods, who were involved in astral fatalism. In the gnostic texts the former Mesopotamian gods were transformed into evil archons, governing the physical universe under the service of the evil creator god. The term *kosmokratores* was frequently used for planets in the Greek magical papyri, personified as rulers of the heavenly spheres, sometimes regarded as evil.[6]

Thus the Mesopotamian religion and literary works must be considered as one of many resources for the developing branches of Gnosticism. In the Nag Hammadi treatise *The Hypostasis of the Archons* (92, 4ff) there is a passage which curiously resembles the Mesopotamian account of the Flood, the only difference being that instead of the "great gods" there are "archons", and the god Ea is represented as "the ruler of the

5 Another case is the recently published astronomical papyri from Oxyrrhyncus, which show that some types of Hellenistic astronomical texts are partially very similar to those extant in cuneiform. See Jones, A. *Astronomical Papyri from Oxyrhyncus (P. Oxy. 4133–4300a).* Memoirs of the American Philosophical Society, Vol. 223. Philadelphia: American Philosophical Society, 1999. See also Rochberg 2004: 34–35, 237–44.

6 See D. E. Aune in *Dictionary of Deities and Demons in the Bible*, (E.J. Brill, 1996) col. 154.

forces". The passage, however, is by no means a rewording of the biblical flood story:

> Then mankind began to multiply and improve. The rulers took counsel with one another and said, "Come, let us cause a deluge with our hands and obliterate all flesh, from man to beast." But when the ruler of the forces came to know of their decision, he said to Noah, "Make yourself an ark from some wood that does not rot and hide in it - you and your children and the beasts and the birds of heaven from small to large - and set it upon Mount Sir."[7]

This is a legacy of the Mesopotamian notion of the divine assembly, consisting of seven destiny-decreeing gods and their irrevocable decisions. The religions of Hellenistic and Roman periods witnessed a high point of astrological determinism, astrology was an element of general education in that period, and astronomy as a science was more developed than ever before. Also in the Hellenistic world, the planets were associated with gods:

> The acceptance of astrology led to a growing belief that the dwelling place of the gods was in the realm of the stars. For example, it was during the Hellenistic period that it became the standard practice to call the planets by the names of various Greek gods, such as Zeus (Jupiter) and Ares (Mars). Astrology also encouraged a new conception of life after death, according to which the soul did not go to the underworld, as had earlier been believed, but rather rose through the planetary spheres to the sphere of the fixed stars and then to the paradise that lay beyond the outermost sphere. In time this journey came to be imagined as difficult and dangerous, with secret passwords required to cross each planetary threshold (Ulansey 1989: 133).

One may conclude that in the Hellenistic and Roman periods, stars as gods virtually formed the divine government over the events of the cosmos. While for large masses of people this was a welcome device for explaining the world, still by others, consisting of the limited number of devotees of salvation religions, this acknowledged truth was regarded as calamitous. The rule of astral bodies over the society was probably better approved by upper classes and more fortunate ones in life, while hostility to the *status quo* can be associated with lower classes and the victims of

---

7 Translation by R. A. Bullard and B. Layton, see Robinson 1996: 166. For the Babylonian Flood Story in the Epic of Gilgamesh, see George 2003: 508ff. and 700ff. The name of the mountain Sir probably derives from the name Nisir in Babylonian source, where Utnapištim's boat landed, although the name can also be read Nimuš.

social or religious persecution.[8] For the second group of people the religion of astral fatalism, whose earliest forms ultimately originated in the Mesopotamian world view, became a prison of this-worldly powers. Opinions certainly varied to what extent the astral powers govern the universe, but it was only rarely denied altogether before the fourth century. The notion of soul's redemption from planetary powers became very important on the basis of these assumptions. The following statement by Culianu is certainly true in the context of Gnostic world-view, where

> the whole universe becomes an abode for evil. The seven planetary spheres, whose influence upon human affairs has become overwhelming thanks to astrology, are viewed as seats of vicious astral Rulers or archons, who, on the one hand, confer their own vices to all the souls entering the world, and, on the other hand, forbid heavenly passage to souls that attempt to leave the world. Fortunately, a saviour descends from heaven to earth, and reveals to his disciples the watchwords they must utter before the archons, in order to get free passage through the heavenly customs." (Culianu 1983: 2.)

In addition, the Neopythagorean Nicomachus of Gerasa (2nd century AD) reports in his *Theology of Arithmetic* that "the best-qualified among the Babylonians and (the famous sage) Ostanes, and Zoroaster" call the seven planetary spheres "herds" or "flocks" (*agélai*). The standard way of referring to the seven planets in Babylonian religious and astronomical texts was as "the seven sheep" (*bibbi*). In the seventh tablet of *Enūma Eliš* the planetary gods are once compared to a "flock", line 131.[9] The conversion by Greeks of the Babylonian flock of planetary sheep into planetary flocks is clearly related to the forced parallel, emphasized by Nicomachos, between the word *agelai* "flocks" and *aggeloi* "messengers, angels" (Kingsley 1995: 202).

Heavenly Grades in Ancient Mesopotamia

Even as in the theologies of the mystery religions of late antiquity, there is evidence for grade systems in ancient Mesopotamia. It is not surprising to

---

8 My interpretation has nothing in common with the notion of "cosmic pessimism", allegedly present in Roman world of third and fourth centuries AD, according to some prominent scholars, e.g. F. Cumont and E. Dodds. See N. Denzey, "'Enslavement to fate', 'cosmic pessimism' and other explorations of the Late Roman psyche: A brief history of a historiographical trend." *Studies in Religion* 33 (2004) 277–299. My understanding can perhaps be used as a starting point for sociology of Gnosticism.

9 See Talon 2005: 75, and *Chicago Assyrian Dictionary,* s.v. *sēnu.*

find it in the seven-fold grade structure of the ziggurat, the edifice for communication between men and gods. The textual evidence comes already from about 2115 BCE, when the ruler of the city-state Lagaš, Gudea, built a new temple for his god Ningirsu, called Eninnu "the house of fifty (powers)". The account of his building is written on clay cylinders. According to an improved reading of the crucial sign, the following passage can be shown to contain a reference to the seven-fold stucture of his temple under construction (Gudea Cylinders 562-577):

> Gudea, in charge of building the house, placed on his head the carrying-basket for the house, as if it were a holy crown. He laid the foundation, set the walls on the ground. He marked out a square, aligned the bricks with a string. He marked out a second square on the site of the temple, (saying,) "It is the line-mark for a topped-off jar of 1 ban capacity (?)". He marked out a third square on the site of the temple, (saying,) "It is the Anzud bird enveloping its fledgling with its wings". He marked out a fourth square on the site of the temple, (saying,) "It is a panther embracing a fierce lion". He marked out a fifth square on the site of the temple, (saying,) "It is the blue sky in all its splendour". He marked out a sixth square on the site of the temple, (saying,) "It is the day of supply, full of luxuriance". He marked out a seventh square on the site of the temple, (saying,) "It is the E-ninnu bathing the Land with moonlight at dawn".[10]

The seventh level of the building can be associated with the Moon-god, the Sumerian Su'ena. The sixth contains the word "day" which can be a reference to the Sun-god, as the two words are written with the same sign in Sumerian (Utu, or ud). The "blue sky" in the fifth level can be a reference to the sky-god An or to the storm-god Iškur. The panther and lion in fourth can be associated with Inanna, and the Anzud bird on the third with the owner of the temple himself, with Ningirsu, whose bird Anzud was.[11] The two uppermost levels can be quite certainly associated with the Moon on top and the Sun next to it.

---

10 For the reading of the sign, see Suter 1997. The translation here is taken from ETCSL website. There is supporting evidence for this translation from another inscription of Gudea, the Statues of Gudea G i 1–18 and E i 1–17 which read "For his king Ningirsu, the powerful warrior of Enlil, Gudea, ensi of Lagaš, who had built Eninnu of Ningirsu, built Epa, the temple of seven stages (é-ub-7), (and) his king Ningirsu decreed good fate for the temple, whose PA (é pa-bi) rose foremost" (Lapinkivi 2004: 147).

11 Simo Parpola, personal communication. See J. Black and A. Green, *Gods, Demons and Symbols of Ancient Mesopotamia* (London, 1992), *s.v.* Imdugud, lion.

The famous ziggurat of Marduk's temple in Babylon, É-temen-anki, also consisted of seven storeys, perhaps with an eighth roof-top structure above it, according to Babylonian metrological texts and where, according to Herodotus, only the god-chosen women could spend the night with the deity (1.181).[12] There is some evidence that the Christian heretic Bardaisan of Edessa (154-222 AD) situated the Paradise on the top of the ziggurat. Ephrem, the Syrian, wrote, while criticizing the views of Bardaisan that "the top of the building (*rēšâ d-benyānâ*), whose gates open to the Mother at command – in a shameful place he situated paradise" (*Hymns against Heresies* 55:7). The "top of the building" here quite certainly refers to what is the mythological equivalent to the top of the ziggurat as the divine bed-chamber (Babylonian *kissu elû*). The shamefulness of Bardaisan's paradise for Ephrem is, that there takes place a sexual union between the Father and the Mother, in his words:

> He also hated the blessed paradise of the Holy One and believed in another paradise of shame, (saying:) "Gods measured it and laid it out, that is the Father with the Mother, by their sexual union they founded it, they planted it with their descendants" (*ibid.* 55:8.).

The strophe 10 finally tells who the Father and the Mother were according to Bardaisan – viz. Sun and Moon: "He considered Sun and Moon; with the Sun he compared the Father, with the Moon he compared the Mother, male and female gods and their children" (Drijvers 1966: 147-48). Thus the sun and moon are here associated with "the top of the building" as they were in ancient Mesopotamia.

Similarly, as pertains to silver, associated with moon, and gold, associated with the sun in the ancient Mesopotamia, Herodotus describes a very similar seven-fold structure in his discussion of the seven concentric walls of Ecbatana (1.98):

> [Dioces, the king of Medes] built the great and mighty circles of walls within walls which are now called Ecbatana. The fortress is so planned that each circle of walls is higher than the next outer circle by no more than the height of its battlements; to which end the site itself, being on a hill in the plain, somewhat helps, but chiefly it was accomplished by art. There are seven circles in all; within the innermost circle are the king's dwellings and the treasuries; and the longest wall is about the length of the wall that surrounds

12 See A. R. George, *Babylonian Topographical Texts* (Leuven, 1992) pp. 117, 430–33, on the terminology of divine bed-chamber see p. 432–33.

> the city of Athens. The battlements of the first circle are white, of the second black, of the third circle purple, of the fourth blue, and of the fifth orange: thus the battlements of five circles are painted with colours; and the battlements of the last two circles are coated, these with silver and those with gold (translation by Godley, Loeb edition).

Simo Parpola has argued that the remains of the colouring on the ziggurat of Dur Šarruken, the Assyrian capital of Sargon II, show that each of its stages was painted in different colour, and the sequence of colours corresponded to the colouring of the seven concentric walls of Ecbatana in the Herodotus passage – white, black, purple, blue, orange, gold, silver. These colours symbolized the seven planetary spheres in the ord11er Venus, Saturn, Mars, Mercury, Jupiter, Sun, and Moon.[13] Through its seven-staged colouring, the ziggurat was associated with descent and ascent of the goddess Inanna or Ištar, as related in the Sumero-Akkadian myth. "Ziggurat" occurs as the epithet of Ištar of Nineveh in Assurbanipal's hymn to her, and the colours of the ziggurat's levels correspond to the seven garments or powers of the goddess, which she removes during her descent to the netherworld and subsequently puts on again during her ascent (Lapinkivi 2004: 146-47). The descent from the ziggurat's silver-coloured top (= the Moon) would symbolize undressing, while ascending it would symbolize putting on these coloured garments (Parpola: xcii, n. 114). The goddess in the myth can be plausibly interpreted as referring to the human or cosmic soul (see Lapinkivi 2004).

Planets and metals are associated with a Mithraic "ladder of seven gates" through which the soul passes in ascension, according to Origen, *Contra Celsum* 6.22:

13 Parpola 1997: xcii, n. 114. V. Place, *Ninive et l'Assyrie*, Paris 1870, Vol. II, 79: "Chacun des sept étages de l'Observatoire était peint d'une couleur particulière. La peinture des quatre premiers étages se voyait encore sur la ruine; celle des trois autres a été restituée, avec les étages eux-mêmes, et suivant les données que nous avons déjà fait connaître. Les sept couleurs, blanche, noir, rouge, bleu, vermillon, argent et or, sont de larges teintes plates, hautes chacune de 6 mètres; leur étendue, qui va en diminuant, selon l'étendue des étages, commence à la base par une longueur de 43 mètres et finit au dernier étage par une longueur de 17 mètres. Ces surfaces monochromes n'eussent produit qu'un effet assez médiocre, si elles n'avaient pas été habilement accidentées par les saillants et les rentrants dus à l'invention du constructeur. La monotonie disparaissait ainsi par suite des accidents d'ombre et la lumière. D'un autre côté, la variété des teintes, se différenciant d'étage en étage, devait accuser avec plus d'energie les proportions du monument." See also C. L. Woolley, *Ur Excavations,* Vol. 5, *The Ziggurat and its Surroundings* (1939), pp. 125, 142–43.

> Celsus also describes some Persian mysteries, where he says: 'These truths [= celestial ascent] are obscurely represented by the teaching of the Persians and by the mystery of Mithras, which is of Persian origin. For in the latter there is a symbol of the two orbits in heaven, the one being that of the fixed stars and the other that assigned to the planets, and of the soul's passage through these. The symbol is this. There is a ladder with seven gates and at its top an eighth gate. The first of the gates is of lead, the second of tin, the third of bronze, the fourth of iron, the fifth of an alloy, the sixth of silver, and the seventh of gold. They associate the first with Kronos (Saturn), taking lead to refer to the slowness of the star; the second with Aphrodite (Venus), comparing her with the brightness and softness of tin; the third with Zeus (Jupiter), as the gate that has bronze base and which is firm; the fourth with Hermes (Mercury), for both iron and Hermes are reliable for all works and make money and are hard-working; the fifth with Ares (Mars), the gate which as a result of the mixture is uneven and varied in quality; the sixth with the Moon as the silver gate; and the seventh with the Sun as the golden gate, these metals resembling their colors.' He next examines the reason for this particular arrangement of the stars which is indicated by means of symbols in the names of the various kinds of matter. And he connects musical theories with the theology of the Persians which he describes. (translation by H. Chadwick in Meyer 1987: 209).

A ladder or a staircase leading to the upper levels of heaven is also attested in Mesopotamian sources. Thus Namtar, the vizier of the netherworld goddess Ereškigal, "ascended the length (?) of the stairs of heaven" to visit the gods of heaven.[14] Also Šamaš is addressed as "you opened the bolt of heaven's door, you ascended the stairs of pure lapis lazuli".[15]

The sequence of planets in Origen's passage is summarized in the fifth column in the table below. It is interesting to note in comment that the sequence of planets listed by Origen corresponds exactly to the order of weekdays in Greek horoscopes, only in inverted order.[16] Why is the order

---

14 *Chicago Assyrian Dictionary,* s.v. *simmiltu*, p. 274: *ēl? Namtar arkat sisimmelat šamā*[*mi*] (STT 28 V 13 and 42).

15 *ibid.*: *sik*[*kūri*] *dalat šamê teliam simmila*[*t*] *uqnîm ellim.* On ladders leading to the stars in late antiquity, see K. Volk, "'Heavenly Steps': Manilius 4.119–121 and Its Background", in: R. S. Boustan and A. Y. Reed (eds.) *Heavenly Realms and Earthly Realities in Late Antique Religions* (Cambridge: University Press 2004), especially 40–46.

16 The weekday order of the planets is Mars – Mercury – Jupiter – Venus – Saturn – Sun – Moon, which became the standard order of the planets in Indian astronomy.

inverted? My answer is that the ordinary weekday sequence corresponds to birth or genesis, but because the Origen passage deals with the backward movement, namely, the ascent of souls to their heavenly home, the normal weekday order of the planets is inverted.

There is one more difference – the heavenly ascent in Origen begins with Saturn and attains its summit with the Sun, while the weekday order usually begins with Mars and ends with the Moon. As Neugebauer notes, in some Greek magical papyri the weekday sequence also begins with the Sun, and in a papyrus from the 4th century AD this sequence is called *hellenikon*.[17]

The Greek weekday order beginning with the Sun is also maintained in Mandean astrology, where all weekdays are governed by beings bearing names of ancient Mesopotamian gods. Sunday, which is governed by Šamaš, is the first day of the week and associated with the personified Habšaba, "First-Day-of-the-Week", a saviour spirit, who takes the souls to the seat of the Polar Star, Awathur. Sunday is associated also with ascent of the souls, as Lady Drower was informed, thus it is the holiest of the weekdays:

> "[Habšaba] takes purified souls in his ship to Awathur and to the World of Light. The Gate of the World of Light is ajar on this day and Hoshaba (Habshaba) takes the souls by means of electricity into the midst of the world of light." I was told that "Hoshaba" descends into Maṭaratha (Purgatories) on Sunday, returning with seven Mandaean souls to the world of light. "The revolving wheels of light whirl more swiftly on this day, thus assisting the souls in their ascent." (Drower 1937: 74-75.)

According to Mandeans, the second day of the week, Monday, is governed by Sin, the name of the ancient Mesopotamian Moon-god. Tuesday is governed by Nirig or Mars, which name derives from the Mesopotamian Nergal. Wednesday is governed by Nbu = Mercury = Mesopotamian Nabû, and Thursday by Bil or Bel = Jupiter = Babylonian Marduk (= Bēl). Friday is the day of Libat or Liwet, which name derives from Sumerian writing of Ištar's planet Venus, *Dilbat.* Saturday is the day of Kiwan, a name deriving from the Akkadian epithet of Saturn, *kajjamānu* "the steady one". Thus the order of planets in the Greek horoscopes which Mandeans still used in the 20th century is Sun – Moon – Mars – Mercury – Jupiter – Venus – Saturn, which corresponds exactly to the order listed by Origen,

17 O. Neugebauer, *History of Ancient Mathematical Astronomy* (Berlin, 1975), Vol. 2, p. 691.

only beginning from the other end. It is also important to note that in both systems the Sun is associated with the ascent of the soul.

There are two orders of the planets that occur in cuneiform texts, the older is listed in the first column below, and the later, in common use during the Persian-Hellenistic period, in the second column. Neither order occurs in the astrological compendium *Mul Apin*, nor is there any consistent order in that text (Hunger and Pingree 1989: 147). The third column lists the order according to the passage of Herodotus, supported by the evidence of ziggurat colouring in Dur Šarruken. The fourth column lists the order according to supposed distance from the earth, from the most distant planet inwards. This was the first and primary order in Greek astrology, it was known already to Cicero (*De divinatione* II, 43) and later it became the sequence of the deferents in Ptolemy's system. The weekday order was derived from it (Beck 1988: 4). The last column lists Origen's order, which in turn inverts the weekday order:

CT older	CT later	Herodotus	Acc. to distance	Origen
Jupiter	Jupiter	white (Venus)	Saturn	Saturn
Venus	Venus	black (Saturn)	Jupiter	Venus
Saturn	Mercury	purple (Mars)	Mars	Jupiter
Mercury	Saturn	blue (Mercury)	Sun	Mercury
Mars	Mars	orange (Jupiter)	Venus	Mars
		gold (Sun)	Mercury	Moon
		silver (Moon)	Moon	Sun

The unique grade system of Mithras' Mysteries also had seven tutelary deities for each of the seven grades. Origen's "ladder with seven gates" appears to be connected with the seven levels of Mithraic initiation, and the symbols for these initiatory stages are found associated with symbols of the seven planets in the mosaics found in the mithraeum at Ostia (Ulansey 1989a: 18-19). As shows the mosaic pavement of the Mithraeum of Felicissimus at Ostia, the gods for each rank were the seven planetary deities which are found presiding over the days of the week, thought not in the same order. The symbols of the grades are juxtaposed with symbols of the tutelary planets in a sequence of squares extending ladder-like up the aisle, beginning from the bottom of the slide to the top, in the following order (Beck 1984: 2011-13):

1. Corax – Mercury – "the Raven"
2. Nymphus – Venus – "the Male-bride"
3. Miles – Mars – "the Soldier"
4. Leo – Jupiter – "the Lion"
5. Perses – Moon – "the Persian"
6. Heliodromus – Sun – "the Sun-runner"
7. Pater – Saturn – "the Father"

This Mithraic order of planets does not correspond to any of these which were discussed above. It is confusing that it does not coincide by any reasonable measure with planetary stages of Mithraism reported by Origen. It may be inferred that many different planetary orders were simultaneously used in the mystery cults, therefore

> the order of the *Contra Celsum* was *but one* of the orders which the Mysteries used to explore, and to conduct the *mystes* through, the mystery of the celestial voyage. ... Celsus has given us neither the full truth, nor a distortion of the truth, but a *partial* truth. (Beck 1988: 76.)

Porphyry wrote about the mysteries of Mithras as follows: "Thus the Persians, as mystagogues, initiate the *mystes* by teaching him the downward way of the souls and their way back, and calling the place a grotto" (*De antro nympharum* 6). Thus the main teaching of the mysteries was the descent and ascent of the human soul from the world above and its return to the heavenly origins. The "place" is a grotto, "an image of the cosmos that Mithras created" (*ibid.*). Calling the visible world a grotto was most probably influenced by Plato's allegory of the Cave (*Rep.* 6-7). In towns, the temples of Mithras, or at any rate the cult-room itself was accordingly constructed below ground-level, so that one entered it by means of steps, sometimes seven in number (Clauss 2001: 44).

The teaching of upward and downward way of the souls was not confined to Mithraism.[18] In the eras of late antiquity, the earth was postulated as the center of the cosmos, and the other realms in spherical levels above it. The most significant cosmological divisions were either tripartite, distinguishing the material, heavenly, and hypercosmic realms, or sevenfold, dividing it into seven planetary spheres. In a tripartite system, the sun and the moon as luminaries tended to play a more important role than in a

18 See V. D. Arbel, *Beholders of Divine Secrets: Mysticism and Myth in the Hekhalot and Merkavah Literature* (State University of New York, 2003), chapter 4, "Mystical Journeys in Mythological Language."

sevenfold system, in which they are included with the other planets. The importance of these divisions in the cosmological system lies in the descent of the soul into the material world during the process of genesis (Edmonds 2004: 277-79).

Despite the undisputably inventive spirit, a "sheer creativity that gave rise to the mystery-cult" (Clauss 2001: 7), and the creation of the basic tenets of the mystery religions, it seems unreasonable to suggest that the conception of the planetary spheres and orders, and the doctrine of the soul's descent and ascent were invented all anew by these new religious movements without any recourse to previous Oriental traditions. The gods and planets were associated with the levels of ziggurat in ancient Mesopotamia, which as a model of cosmos also represented the order of universe. Therefore it is not valid to say, as Culianu does, that according to Babylonians, the seven planets moved on the same plane, at the same distance from the earth, and there was never a link between the vaults of heaven and the planets (Culianu 1983: 27-28). Thus the teaching of seven heavens in Jewish and Christian apocalypticism indeed originates in Babylonian tradition (cf. Yarbro-Collins 1995).

Garments and Faculties associated with Descent and Ascent

There are some details which help us to point out the Babylonian sediments in the mystery religions. The themes of descent and ascent are also found in the Sumerian and Akkadian myth *Inanna's/ Ištar's Descent to the Netherworld.* The first half of the story presents the soul's heavenly origin and the defilement of the soul in the material world (= the Netherworld), and the latter half presents her way back to her heavenly home. In the Sumerian version, the goddess abandons heaven and earth and goes to the Netherworld as the queen, dressed in her royal garments, holding the seven divine powers (*me* in Sumerian) in her hand. At each of the seven gates of the Netherworld, Inanna is stripped of her ornaments, equated with the seven divine powers, from top to bottom. At every gate the goddess enters into a dialogue with the gatekeeper, asking finally the purpose of the removal of her clothes, and getting the answer, "Be silent, Inanna, a divine power of the underworld has been fulfilled." When she arrives at her sister's, Ereškigal's throne, she is completely naked and dead (Lapinkivi 2004: 189-90).[19]

Before she leaves heaven, she instructs her minister to make a lament for her after she has gone, and go to her fathers Enlil, Nanna-Su'ena, and Enki to ask them not to let their "precious metal be alloyed there in the dirt of the underworld." After Inanna has spent three days in the Netherworld, her minister goes to her fathers, who all refuse to help his daughter, except Enki, who creates the two helpers so that they might sneak into the Netherworld and make the goddess alive by sprinkling the life-giving plant and water over her. In her ascent, the goddess is given back her clothing, thus making her complete and able to return to heaven. The drawback of her release is that the goddess must give someone to the Netherworld as her substitute, and finally she proceeds to Dumuzi. She decides to give Dumuzi as her substitute but regrets his fate and begins to weep. Finally she allows his sister Geštinanna to release him by taking his place after six months (Lapinkivi 2004: 190).

There has been much recent discussion of this myth and its parallels in Jewish mysticism, Gnostic myths, and Chaldean Oracles. The corresponding figures of Matronit-Shekhinah, Sophia and Hekate can be shown to play a very similar role in corresponding cosmologies (Lapinkivi 2004). A Nag Hammadi text, the *Exegesis on the Soul* (NHC 2.6), portrays the fall of the originally androgynous soul (= Sophia = Wisdom) from her "Father's house" in heaven into the earthly world, and her subsequent return to her original position. This text has been taken as a rephrasing of the Valentinian myth of Sophia, but its narrative much more closely follows that of the *Descent of Ištar to the Netherworld*, to the extent that it could be considered a running commentary or a paraphrase of the latter (Parpola 1997: xxxi). The nature of the soul is feminine – she has a womb – but as long as she is in heaven with her Father, she is virginal and androgynous. After her fall to this world, she is trapped in a body and loses her virginity; she falls into the hands of "robbers" and defiles herself. Soul's defilement is compared to dirty garments:

> So when the womb of the soul by the will of the father, turns itself inward, it is baptized and is immediately cleansed of the external pollution which was

19 The Mesopotamian goddess of the Netherworld Ereškigal frequently occurs in later Greek defixions and magical papyri. This is one of the most exact transcriptions from Sumerian into Greek. Ereškigal occurs still only on the texts of imperial era, but the period of borrowing may well have been much earlier (see Burkert 1992: 68).

> pressed upon it, just as [garments, when] dirty, are put into the [water and] turned about until their dirt is removed and they become clean. And so the cleansing of the soul is to regain the [newness] of her former nature and to turn herself back again. That is her baptism.[20]

She is helped by the will of the Father, who sends her Christ as her bridegroom, her brother, the "first-born", who can be compared to salvatory role of Tammuz in the myth of Ištar, who was "her childhood lover" (*Ištar's Descent*, l. 127). The soul cleanses herself, and sits in the bridal chamber filled with perfume waiting for her consort. But because of her fall, she has lost her memory of the time in her Father's house in heaven, and consequently she does not remember that she was once married to her brother. When the bridegroom arrives, he first decorates the bridal chamber, and there they unite with each other. She gets from him the seed that is the life-giving spirit, in order to be able to bear healthy children. Now she is also able to return to her Father's house with him: by her ascent to heaven, she is resurrected from death, i.e., from the state of ignorance (Lapinkivi 2004: 168). It is not my task here to give a full account of this and other comparisons made by Parpola (1997) and Lapinkivi (2004), I will only supplement their data from the point of view of this paper's interest.[21]

The first parallel which I want to add comes from a song in the Mandean Ginza, from the left part (52), which is entirely concerned with death

---

20 Translation is by W. C. Robinson and M. Scopello in Robinson 1996: 194. A lay Mandean explained to Lady Drower the dissolution of the soul as follows: "When it leaves the body the soul is in the shape of a person, wearing clothes, but it is of air and not substantial. We cannot see it. If an evil-doer, the garments it wears are black, and if it asks, "Why I am clothed in black?" the two angels answer it, "Are there not sacred books, given to man since the time of Adam? Hast thou not beheld sun, moon, and stars?" (Drower 1937: 197.) According to Maruta of Maipherkat (4th century AD) the followers of Bardaisan "wear and wrap themselves in white clothing, because they say that who wears white clothes belongs to the followers of Good, and who wears black, to the followers of Evil" (Drijvers 1966: 106–7.)

21 For example, the allegorical theme of soul's descent occurs also in Hrotswitha of Gandersheim's (10th century AD) play *Abraham*, where Abraham, the aged holy man, after much searching, finds his adopted daughter, Maria, in a inn/brothel, some years after she has run away. He acts the part of a customer and hires Maria's services, brings her back to the cloister and after much repentance, Maria purifies through fasting, weeping and praying. See *The plays of Hrotswitha of Gandersheim*. Translated by Larissa Bonfante, with the collaboration of Alexandra Bonfante-Warren. (New York, 1979).

and the fate of the soul in the next world (Drower 1937: 185). The Mandeans, both a people and a gnostic sect, preserved in their writings all of the more important god names of ancient Mesopotamia and a large portion of its culture until modern times. The seven planetary gods often occur in Mandean texts and are called by their ancient Mesopotamian names. In the song in question "a soul" makes its upward journey through the heavenly spheres and their watch-houses (*maṭarta*), each ruled by a planetary spirit. The song is repetitive, and there are only minor variants in the description of how the soul proceeds from the first planet to the seventh:

> Meine Seele verlangte in mir nach dem Leben, in meinem Innern blühte mir das Wissen auf. Meine Seele verlangte in mir nach dem Leben, nach dem Orte des Lebens war mein Gang. Ich flog und zog hin bis ich zum Ersten (der Planeten) kam. Die Diener des Ersten kamen mir entgegen: "Auf, wir wollen den Mann gefangen nehmen und ihn fragen, woher er gekommen ist: Genosse, woher kamest du hierher, wohin gehst du denn?" – "Ich komme aus der Tibil, aus dem Hause, das die Planeten gebauet. Meine Seele verlangte in mir nach dem Leben, nach der Orte des Lebens ist mein Gang." – "Dies ist das Haus des Lebens. Hierher! Wohin gehst du denn? Wenn du dich unter sie begiebst, tun sie (dir) alles Erdenkliche an." – "Das ist nicht, was ich wünsche, das ist nicht, was meine Seele begehrt" (Lidzbarski 1925: 578–82).

Quite obviously, the text describes the ascension of the soul through the planets, and corresponds to the goddess' ascent in the Mesopotamian myth. The dialog of the soul with heavenly customs inspectors is very reminiscent of the scenes in the Mesopotamian myth. After entering the seventh level, we can find a clothing metaphor in the song as well:

> Ich flog und zog hin, bis ich zum Hause des Lebens kam. Als ich am Hause des Lebens anlangte, ging das Leben mir entgegen. [Das Leben] ging mir entgegen, es kleidete mich in Glanz, brachte Licht und bedeckte mich damit. Es schloss mich in seine Rechnung ein, und in seiner Mitte kamen auch die Guten heraus: "Zwischen den Lampen des Lichtes sollen deine Lampen emporgezogen werden und leuchten." (Lidzbarski 1925: 582.)

The importance of the theology of clothing, can be seen in the writings of the Syrian Church fathers (Brock 1992: XI). The salvation history is described by some Syrian Christian writers as consisting of four main scenes. All four scenes are rarely presented together, but there is no doubt that the entire scenario was familiar to all Christian Syriac writers during the 4th to 7th centuries. In the first scene, Adam and Eve are together in Paradise, viewed as a mountain, and clothed in "robes of glory/light". In the second scene the fall takes place, Adam and Eve are stripped of their "robes of glory/light". In order to remedy the naked state of Adam and mankind, brought about by the Fall, in the third scene the Divinity himself "puts on Adam" when he "puts on a body", and the whole aim of incarnation is to "reclothe mankind in the robe of glory". The Nativity, the Baptism, the Descent or Resurrection are the three central "staging posts" of the Incarnation that are separate in profane time, but intimately linked in sacred time. All three are seen as descents of the Divinity into successive wombs, the womb of Mary, the womb of the Jordan, and the womb of Sheol. It can be remembered here that the womb of soul also played a decisive role in the *Exegesis on the Soul.*

Divinity's descent into the Jordan is of central importance, for it is then that Christ deposits the "robe of glory/light" in the water, thus making it available to the mankind for the second time to be put on in baptism. In the fourth scene the baptism of Christ is the foundation and source of Christian baptism: by descending into Jordan, Christ sanctified in sacred time all bapismal water; at Christian baptism it is the invocation to the Holy Spirit in the prayer of consecration of the water which effectually makes the water of the individual source identical in sacred time and space with the Jordan waters (Brock 1992: XI). This compares favourably with the role of life-giving water in resurrecting the fallen goddess from the Netherworld in the Mesopotamian myth.

In baptismal sacrament the Christian himself goes down into the Jordan waters and thence he picks up and puts on the "robe of glory" which Christ left there. Baptism is a reentry to Paradise, but this final stage of mankind is seen as far more glorious than the primordial Paradise, and God will bestow mankind with divinity that Adam and Eve tried to assume by eating from the Tree of Life.[22] It is important to note here that the descent or fall in the schemes of Syrian Church Fathers is not associated with putting on the garments, as in Genesis 3:7, but with loss of the original "robe of glory".

According to some other religious doctrines of late antiquity, in each of the seven planetary realms through which the soul descends on its way to incarnation it picks up some element of its mortal composition. In

22 Brock 1992: XI 11–13. Examples of clothing metaphor may also be found in Jewish literature, see G. Scholem, *Jewish Gnosticism, Merkabah Mysticism, and Talmudic Tradition* (New York: Jewish Theological Seminary 1960), 56–64.

other words, the soul acquires some characteristic of every planetary ruler as it passes through its sphere of influence (Edmonds 2004: 279). This doctrine partly derives from an astrological interpretation of Mesopotamian myth of Goddess' descent. And not only – it is also an astrologized and democratized version of the prominent element in ancient Mesopotamian royal ideology. According to royal inscriptions and some myths, the king received a package of regalia during his enthronement and determination of his destiny from the assembly of gods. Many royal hymns and inscriptions, both in Sumerian and Akkadian, refer to this occasion. There is also a myth called "The Creation of Man and King" where the creation of ordinary man is followed by the creation of the king. This myth refers to gods giving their attributes to the king as gifts – crown (Anu), throne (Enlil), weapons (Nergal), radiance (Ninurta), physical beauty (Bēlet-ilī) (see Mayer 1987). The gods bestowing the gifts are sometimes numbered seven in these texts, sometimes more and sometimes less. The objects given to the king include both concrete royal insignia and abstract abilities, and among the latter both physical and mental faculties (see Dietrich 1998: 171-79). In Sumerian these gifts are described by the word *me*, which is also used for Inanna's clothes in the myth of her descent to the netherworld.

In a very clear description of soul's incarnation process by Macrobius, in the *Commentary on the Dream of Scipio* 1.11-12, the characteristics received from the planetary spheres are called with a general term *obvolutio*, "envelopment" which are "put on" by the soul. According to a Neoplatonic group,

> [T]he blessed souls, free from all bodily contamination, possess the sky; but the soul that from its lofty pinnacle of perpetual radiance disdains to grasp after a body and this thing that we on earth call life, but yet allows a secret yearning for it to creep into its thoughts, gradually slips down to the lower realms because of the very weight of its earthly thoughts. It does not suddenly assume a defiled body out of a state of complete in corporeality, but, gradually sustaining imperceptible losses and departing farther from its simple and absolutely pure state, it swells out with certain increases of a planetary body: in each of the spheres that lie below the sky it puts on another ethereal envelopment (*aetheria obvolutione vestitur*), so that by these steps it is gradually prepared for assuming this earthly dress. Thus by as many deaths as it passes through spheres, it reaches the stage which on earth is called life (1.11.10–12). … Now if souls were to bring with them to their bodies a memory of the divine order of which they were conscious in the sky, there would be no dis-

> agreement among men in regard to divinity; but, indeed, all of them in their descent drink of forgetfulness, some more, some less. Consequently, although the truth is not evident to all on earth, all nevertheless have an opinion, since opinion is born of failure of the memory (1.12.9). … By the impulse of the first weight of the soul, having started on its downward course from the intersection of the zodiac and the Milky Way to the successive spheres lying beneath, as it passes through these spheres, not only takes on the aforementioned envelopment in each sphere by approaching a luminous body, but also acquires each of the attributes which it will exercise later. In the sphere of Saturn it obtains reason and understanding, called *logistikon* and *theoretikon*; in Jupiter's sphere, the power to act, called *praktikon*; in Mars' sphere, a bold spirit or *thymikon*; in the sun's sphere, sense-perception and imagination, *aisthetikon* and *phantastikon*; in Venus' sphere, the impulse of passion, *epithymetikon*; in Mercury's sphere, the ability to speak and interpret, *hermeneutikon*; and in the lunar sphere, the function of molding and increasing bodies, *phytikon*" (1.12.13-14, Stahl 1952: 132-36).

In Macrobius' description of the descent we find a clothing metaphor (*vestitur*), when the heavenly soul "takes on the aforementioned envelopment (*obvolutio*) in each sphere by approaching a luminous body". Here we can see the clothing metaphor as leading the soul to imprisonment and death, but the characteristics obtained by the soul are still positive attributes, useful to a productive life. In the Hermetic tractate *Poimandres*, the soul sheds the negative characteristics at each planetary station as it makes its way out of incarnation (Edmonds 2004: 280):

> Poimandres said: "First, in releasing the material body you give the body itself over to alteration, and the form that you used to have vanishes. To the demon you give over your temperament, now inactive. The body's senses rise up and flow back to their particular sources, becoming separate parts and mingling again with the energies. And feeling and longing go on toward irrational nature. Thence the human being rushes up through the spheres, at the first zone surrendering the energy of increase and decrease; at the second evil machination, a device now inactive; at the third the illusion of longing; at the fourth the ruler's arrogance, now freed of excess; at the fifth unholy presumption and daring recklessness; at the sixth the evil impulses that come from wealth, now inactive; and at seventh zone the deceit that lies in ambush. And then a human is stripped naked of what the spheres had effected on him

> (during the descent of the soul) and enters the region of the ogdoad, possessing his own power, and along with the blessed he hymns the Father."[23]

The process of physical descent is not described here, but the planetary influences are certainly presupposed. The soul arrives at the last heavenly region in a pure state as naked. So the stripping metaphor has here a positive connotation and clothing a negative one, as in this case descent of the soul is associated with clothing and ascent with stripping off the material qualities. Also in Porphyry, *De Abstinentia* 1.31.3, stripping is associated with the ascent of the soul:

> We have to strip off our many garments, both this visible one made of flesh, and the inner ones we have put on, which resemble 'those of skin'. Let us ascend to the stadium naked and without a garment to contest the soul's Olympic Games (Brock 1992: XI 33-34).

In spite of this inversion, descent still means sinking into materiality and ascent liberation from it, as in the Mesopotamian myth. So also according to Proclus:

> The vehicle of every particular soul descends by the addition of vestures (*chitōnes*) increasingly material; and ascends in company with the soul which makes use of it: for the soul descends by the acquisition of irrational principles of life; and ascends by putting off all those faculties tending to temporal process with which it was invested in its descent, and becoming clean and bare of all such faculties as serve the uses of the process.[24]

In all the cosmologies of late antiquity the material world was acknowledged to be inferior to the realm of gods, so each system had to deal with the question of why human beings lived in an inferior condition. There existed plentiful attitudes toward genesis and the world, ranging from the most positive Platonic celebrations of the cosmos' beauty to the most negative rejections of the world as the prison and the torture chamber of evil archons (Edmonds 2004: 282). For example, in the *Pistis Sophia* (131) each of the planetary archons contributes to the binding of the soul with its counterfeit spirit, causing it to become bound up in

---

23 Corpus Hermeticum I 24–26, translation according to Copenhaver 1992: 5–6, slightly modified. There is a partly parallel vision in the Nag Hammadi tractate *The Discourse on the Eighth and Ninth*: "For the entire eighth, my son, and the souls that are in it, and the angels, sing a hymn in silence" (Robinson 1996: 325).

24 Proclus, *Elements of Theology*, proposition 209, from Culianu 1983: 12, translation by Dodds. See also Proclus, *In Tim.* 3.355.13; Servius, *In Aen.* 6.714, 11.51.

forgetfulness and the passions of the world (Edmonds 2004: 280). Therefore the "qualities" obtained by the soul during its descent into the material world were not clothes or powers, but rags and vices (Culianu 1983: 51).[25] The hostile attitude towards planetary powers and the material world comes in my view from the dominant position that astrology had in the contemporary science and religion, which justified the current world order by astrological fate, exemplified in the words of Vettius Valens (5.9), "no one is free; all are slaves of Destiny (Heimarmene)" (Edmonds 2004: 291).

If one looks, for example, at how much space the Father Ephrem dedicates to refusal of astrology in his "Hymns against Heresies", the scope of popularity of the celestial sciences among the general population becomes evident.[26] Ephrem's *Prose Refutations* also contain an intermediate form of the ancient Mesopotamian and Neoplatonic versions of soul's incarnation myth. According to the heretic Bardaisan, Ephrem says, "the soul was mixed and set up of seven parts" (Mitchell 1912: xxxii). This is confirmed by Bardaisan's own words in *The Book of the Laws of Countries*:

> For that which is called Fate, is really the fixed course determined by God for the Rulers and Guiding Signs. According to this course and order the spirits undergo changes while descending to the soul, and the souls while descending to the bodies. That which causes these changes is called Fate and native horoscope of that mixture which was mixed and is being purified to the help of that which, by the grace and goodness of God, was and will be helped till the termination of all (Drijvers 1966: 86).

In Ephrem's *Prose Refutations* we find a different version – the followers of Mani and Bardaisan assumed that the human body received its "arrangement" from the Archons through female agency:

> [T]hey suppose that its nature is from evil, and its workmanship from the Archons, and the cause of its arrangement is from wisdom, (saying:) "And she (= Wisdom) showed an image of her own beauty to the Archons, and to the Governors, and she deceived them thereby so that when they were stirred

25 Concerning the teachings of Basilides and his son Isidorus, see Alexandrian Clement *Strom.* 2.20.112–113. Irenaeus, *Against the Heresies* 1.30.9 reports the doctrine of Ophites that from Seth and Norea were begotten multitude of people and driven into every wickedness by the lower Hebdomad – that is, the seven stars or planets. Cf. Origenes, *Ccels* 6.31.

26 See E. Beck *Des Heiligen Ephraem des Syrers Hymnen contra Haereses.* Corpus Scriptorum Christianorum Orientalium, Vol. 170 (Louvain, 1957). Cf. also Plotinus 2.3.1.

> up they effected (something) according to what they saw. Each of them gave from his treasure whatever he had; and for that reason their treasures were emptied of what they had snatched away" (Mitchell 1912: xc).

In another place we learn more of this female being and her actions. Ephrem asks: "Can it have been that Virgin of the Light about whom they say that she manifested her beauty to the Archons, so that they were ravished to run after her?" (Mitchell 1912: lxii.) Here the qualities derived from the planetary forces are not mechanically attached to the soul under genesis, but are acquired through the female intermediary from the planetary Archons. Although there is no mention of descent or ascent in the *Prose Refutations*, the passage cited is entirely parallel to the ascent motif in Mesopotamian myth where the goddess gains back her clothes, which were "snatched away" during her descent. The motif of ascent is removed by Ephrem, thus making his account quite illogical.[27] In Neoplatonic accounts cited above the female intermediary figure was eliminated, but she is silently present in the descending soul itself. In summary, we can find similar concepts of soul's fate, clothing, and composition throughout the late antique world. Under these circumstances it is not surprising to find the teaching of soul's ascent and descent as currents in many late antique doctrines, including in the branches of Gnosticism and Neoplatonism:

> in much of their respective cosmologies, anthropologies and soteriologies Neopythagoreanism and Neoplatonism on the one side and the Mysteries of Mithras of the other *converged.* There is no reason why the doctrine on the soul's celestial voyage should not have been *both* Neoplatonic *and* Mithraic. (Beck 1988: 81-82.)

The grade systems and sun's crossing-place

The Mithraic grade system is essentially comparable to the hierarchy of contemporary Christian Church, which also sought to correlate its hierarchy with the celestial one, in words of Alexandrian Clement (*Strom*

---

27 One more corrupted variant report of Bardaisan's teaching comes from Michael Syrus: "he who spoke with Moses and the prophets was an archangel and not God himself. Our Lord was clothed with the body of an angel, and Mary clothed a soul from the world of light, who enveloped himself in the shape of a body. The rulers (shaped) the man: the superior gave him his soul and the inferior his limbs." (Drijvers 1966: 189).

6.13.107): "the advancements pertaining to the Church here below, namely those of bishops, presbyters and deacons, are imitations of the angelic glory." The first level of cosmic hierarchy in Clement's system constituted of the seven celestial entities *prōtoktistoi*, "first created", whose subordinates were the angels and archangels. They are the bearers of divine name and are called "gods", but have no association with planets. The promotion from one level of the hierarchy to the next reflects the spiritual progress, and the church hierarchy is an imitation of the celestial hierarchy (see Bucur 2006). These "first created beings" in Clement's system are certainly remnants of underlying polytheistic system, which may well have been Babylonian. In the poetry of Ephrem the Syrian, even Paradise consists of different levels. He pictures the mountain of paradise with terraced levels, which he relates to different states of life in the Church. It is most probably the ziggurat image that is behind that picture:

> When He made this intricate design He varied its beauties, so that some levels were far more glorious than others. To the degree that one level is higher than another, so too is its glory the more sublime. In this way He allots the foothills to the most lowly, the slopes to those in between and the heights to the exalted. When the just ascend its various levels to receive their inheritance, with justice He raises up each one to the degree that accords with his labors; each is stopped at the level whereof he is worthy, there being sufficient levels in Paradise for everyone: the lowest parts for the repentant, the middle for the righteous, the heights for those victorious, while the summit is reserved for God's Presence (= Shekhinah).[28]

The Mithraic grade system gives an opportunity for some comments from the point of view of its Babylonian sediment. The grade Nymphus, which is sacred to Venus, is a paradoxical term with the meaning "male bride", and is associated primarily with marriage and light, but with a paradoxical association to androgyny and the assimilation of the female in an assertively masculine system (Beck 1984: 2092). This fits with the description of the Mesopotamian goddess Inanna/Ištar as androgyne, often described as wearing a beard in the texts and iconography (Groneberg 1986). Both for the ancient Mesopotamians and Gnostics,

28 Translation by S. Brock, *St. Ephrem the Syrian: Hymns on Paradise, Introduction and Translation* (St Vladimir's Seminary Press, 1990), Hymn II 10–11, pp. 88–89. For the interpretation, see R. Murray, *Symbols of Church and Kingdom: A Study in Early Syriac Tradition* (Cambridge: University Press 1975), pp. 306–310.

androgyny or bisexuality was an expression of perfection (see Parpola 1997: lxxxix, n. 97).

Additionally, the highest grade in the Mithraic mysteries, the Father, is associated with Saturn, while the cult of Mithras is a manifestly solar cult of the invincible Sun, who occupies only the sixth place in Mithras' hierarchy. The most likely and convincing answer to this seeming paradox is:

> Saturn can be set at the head and the Sun relegated to second (or penultimate) place *because Saturn is the Sun.* Therefore, where we see Saturn we also see the Sun (and vice versa): and so, arcanely and by paradox and enigma, it is still the Sun that we find at the head. (Beck 1984: 2049.)

It was widely attested in Mesopotamian astronomy and astrology that Saturn was the star of the Sun, and this association may be the prototype of Mithraic concept of "two Suns".[29] According to Hunger and Pingree (1989: 147) the name "Star of the Sun" arose from the fact that the Sun's *hypsoma* sets as Saturn's rises (see *Mul Apin* II I 19-21). According to Parpola, Saturn's association with the Sun probably had its basis in the planet's slow and steady motion, but it was also forcefully backed by linguistic and mythological speculation. The association of the two heavenly bodies was explained by two puns, one based on homophony of Akkadian *salmu* "black" and *salmu* "statue". Šamaš was called "statue" because the Sumerian epithet of the Sun-god in Sumerian was *an-dùl*, meaning both "statue" and "protection" – as a judge, the sun was looked upon as the protection of gods and men. The other pun was a play with the meanings of the verb *kwn* – "to be steady". Saturn's name *kajjamānu* "the steady one", derived from this root, is also once attested as the epithet of the Sun-god (4 R 28, 1:8), and also provided an etymological connection with *kittu* "truth, justice" (< **kintu*), the principal attribute of Šamaš. A further link between Saturn and the sun, according to Parpola, was provided by the fact that Saturn had its hypsoma or house in the constellation Libra, the cosmic scales of life and death where the sun stayed during the autumnal equinox (Parpola 1983: 343). The observation of Saturn and Sun had a special relevance for the state of affairs of the king, as attested in a letter to an Assyrian king: "Tonight Saturn approached the moon. Saturn is the star of the sun, the relevant

29 *Mul Apin* II I 39,64 MUL.dUTU "(Saturn is) the star of the Sun".

interpretation is as follows: it is good for the king. The sun is the star of the king" (Hunger 1992: text 95, rev.).

The association of Saturn with the Sun was also known to Greek and Roman authors.[30] Besides, Saturn was identified as Lord of Sabbath and the demiurge Sabaoth, based on etymological speculations on the Hebrew words "hosts" (*ṣ*^{e}*ba'ōt*) and "seven" (*šeba*ʿ), see Tacitus, *Histories* 5.4. Diodorus' account on the Chaldean priests that they consider Saturn "the most conspicuous and it presages more events and such as are of greater importance than the others" (2.30.3) has a parallel in Mandean texts, where Kewan is sometimes considered as the leader of planets (Fauth 1973: 101-3). Very important testimony comes from Ptolemy's *Tetrabiblos* 2.3.64, which explicitly equates Mithra with Saturn (Beck 1984: 2049):

> Of the second quarter, which embraces the southern part of Greater Asia, the other parts, including India, Arriana, Gedrosia, Parthia, Media, Persia, Babylonia, Mesopotamia, and Assyria, which are situated in the south-east of the whole inhabited world, are, as we might presume, familiar to the south-eastern triangle, Taurus, Virgo, and Capricorn, and are governed by Venus and Saturn, in oriental aspect. Therefore one would find that the natures of their inhabitants conform with the temperaments governed by such rulers; for they revere the star of Venus under the name of Isis, and that of Saturn, as Mithras Helios. Many of them likewise foretell future events; and they consecrate to the gods some of their bodily members, to which superstition they are induced by the nature of the figuration of the planets before mentioned (translation by Robbins, Loeb edition).

Thus we have strong evidence suggesting Mesopotamian ancestry of Saturn's association with the Sun.[31] More importantly, the omens of Saturn were related to the king, who was an incarnation of the Sun-god, expressed in the cuneiform writing by occasional use of the sign MAN for writing the word "king" (Akkadian *šarru*), with the sacred number of the Sun, 20. The Roman Mithras was also the solar god, but the fact is contradictory to the nature of Persian Mithra, who was no solar deity.

30 For Saturn as the star of the Sun, see in Epinomis 987c; Eudoxus Papyrus (col. 5); Diodorus 2.30.3; Hyginus, *De astron.* 2.42, 4.18; Servius *In Aen.* 1.729; Simplicius *De Caelo* p. 495.28–29 (ed. Heiberg).

31 Saturn as "star of the Sun" is also "reflected in the Indian conception of Saturn as the "son of the Sun". In Indian mythology also Mercury is the son of the Moon. The Sun is associated with Saturn and the Moon with Mercury also in a Mesopotamian text K. 148 r. 27–28 (Hunger and Pingree 1989: 147).

Some have assumed that the solar elements of Mithra may derive from Mesopotamian Šamaš:

> non-solar god of contract familiar from the Avesta may have acquired the solar features apparent in the Western Mithraism through Mesopotamian influence. But if this were so, it is difficult to understand why the god of that cult bears the Avestan Mithra's name, with whom he otherwise shares as little, instead of being called, say, Šamaš (Gnoli 1979: 731).

The most probable solution to that problem is that Mithras of the Roman Mysteries owes quite much to a kind of widespread Irano-Mesopotamian syncretism that must have emerged during the Achaemenid empire and later. This period, the fifth century BCE, was a formative period in the history of Babylonian celestial science when also the horoscopes emerged. The celestial divination expanded to a new branch of astrology whose concern was the individual rather than the king and state, and the astronomical data were regularly recorded in the horoscopes (Rochberg 2004: 100–101).

Some scholars have pointed to the similarity of the iconographical motif of Mithra born from a rock attended by his *paredroi* with the Mesopotamian motif of Šamaš rising over the mountains likewise attended by attendants.[32] We have also textual evidence of Šamaš rising from the great mountains, attended by the Anunna-gods, which comes from the incantation in the third house of the series concerning purification magic, called *Bīt rimki*, "The house of cleansing":

> O Šamaš, when you come forth from the great mountain, when you come forth from the great mountain, the mountain of the deep, when you come forth from the holy hill where destinies are ordained, when you [come forth] from the back of heaven to the junction point of heaven and earth, the great gods attend upon you for judgement, the Anunna-gods attend upon you to render verdicts (lines 1-5).[33]

In the Mesopotamian anti-witchcraft magic series *Maqlû*, the mountain of the same function appears as the city Zabban, which has two gates – one for the rising of the sun and the second for the setting of the sun. The name of the city can also be read Sappān, and be connected with Northwest Semitic Sapān, biblical Sāphôn, the cosmic abode of the deities El and Baal in Ugaritic texts (Abusch 2002: 263-64). In this cosmic locality

32 See Beck 1984: 2071, n. 103; Gnoli 1979: 733–34; Will 1955: 206f.

33 For the edition of this text, see Borger 1967; translation is from Foster 1996: 644.

on the horizon are the cosmic gates through which the sun and other heavenly bodies pass when they enter and leave the sky and return to the netherworld. It is situated on a cosmic shore where its quay and pass (*nēbiru*) serve as entry points through which cosmic travellers and ghosts pass without hindrance from the netherworld into the heavens, and where witches may be temporarily imprisoned (Abusch 2002: 275). This crossing-place of the souls is also found among Bardaisan's christianized doctrines, called in Syriac *maʿbartâ*, thus exactly matching the Akkadian *nēberu*. According to Ephrem's *Prose Refutations* Bardaisan believed that Christ was the first to cross that place:

> According to the doctrine of Bardaisan the death that Adam brought in was a hindrance to souls – in that they were hindered at the crossing-place, because the sin of Adam hindered them. "And the life", he (says), "that our Lord brought in, is that he taught verity and ascended, and brought them across into the kingdom. Therefore", he says, our Lord taught us that "every one that keeps my word, he shall not taste death for ever", that his soul is not hindered when it crosses at the crossing-place like the hindrance of old, wherewith the souls were hindered, before our Saviour had come. (Drijvers 1966: 155.)

In the opening incantation of *Maqlû*, the speaker stands on a rooftop and invokes the gods of the night sky to assist in the judgement and render decisions. The "rooftop" probably corresponded to the top of the ziggurat, at least when the king performed the ritual. He sprinkles water towards heaven and asks them to purify him in turn. This is a preparation for assuming the identity of an astral body and for entering the world of gods so that he may be incorporated into the court of the gods of the night sky. Now the speaker is stationed in a cosmic locale or area that connects heaven and the netherworld, he can ascend from Zabban into heaven and descend to the netherworld. He becomes a member of the company of the stars, the heavenly host of the gods of heaven (Abusch 2002: 276). The task of this main actor in the ritual is to make harmless the witches both in heaven and netherworld. Thus we find the motif of heavenly journey also in the Mesopotamian magic, where the participant joins the company of the stars.

In the Epic of Gilgamesh, the mountain "which daily guards the rising [of the sun]" (IX, 39) is specified as the Mount Māšu, "the Twin (mountains)", whose tops [abut] the fabric of heavens and whose bases (lit. 'their breast') reach down to Hades (*arallû*). There are scorpion-man and the scorpion-female guarding its gate and the sun at both sunrise and sunset (IX, 37-45, George 2003: 669). Twin-mountains' gate and their guards, the scorpion-men, may have had an astrological interpretation in ancient Mesopotamia corresponding to the constellation Scorpius. This double mountain is also attested in Mandean mythology as the birth-place of the Sun (see Lidzbarski 1925: 116 n. 4).

The rite of bull-killing

The mysteries of Mithras were one of the greatest mystery cults of late antiquity, with enormous popularity and spread all over the Roman Empire. Mithra of the ancient Iranian mythology is much different from the Mithras of the Roman mystery cult. Much speaks in favour of a reinvention of the cult in the West rather than continuity of ancient Persian, that is, Avestan doctrines. As was shown above, some elements in Mithraic Mysteries and other mystery cults as well as in Neoplatonic philosophy may still derive from the East in their original form, if a phenomenon I term Irano-Mesopotamian syncretism will be accepted. By assuming power in the Near East, the Achaemenid empire took over much of ancient Mesopotamian doctrines and religion, gave to them a Persian overlay and propagated them with a lasting impact in the Empire (see Panaino 2001). At the same time, the locus of astronomical activity shifted from the palace to the temple (Rochberg 2004: 117-18). The invention of horoscopy can be seen as the fabrication of a new staple by Babylonian priests under this new economical situation. Accordingly, it was during the Persian Empire that a priestly class of professional astrologers emerged.

Without assuming such a syncretism and its long-lasting influence, it would be difficult to explain, why the originally ethnic term "Chaldeans" survived in the Roman Empire as denoting "astrologers" and "soothsayers" (see Cumont 1949: 144f.). In a fourth-century AD Latin inscription (V 522) we even find a reference to "Babylonian priest of Mithras" in Rome:

> High-born descendant of an ancient house, pontifex for whom the blessed Regia, with the sacred fire of Vesta, does service, augur too, worshipper of reverend Threefold Diana, Chaldean priest of the temple of Persian Mithras (*Persidiciq(ue) Mithrae antistes Babilonie templi*), and at the same time leader of the mysteries of the mighty, holy taurobolium (Clauss 2001: 30).

A young man killing a bull was the central icon of Mithraism, scattered across the territory of the Roman Empire from England to Syria in hundreds of underground temples. Mithras killing the bull is his primary act, and it is depicted in the most prominent location in virtually every Mithraic temple. It is clear that this icon holds the key to the central secret of the Mysteries, but in the absence of any written explanation, deciphering it has proved a notoriously difficult task. F. Cumont argued that deciphering the tauroctony was a matter of finding parallels to its symbolic elements in ancient Iranian mythology. But there is no known Iranian myth in which Mithra has anything to do with killing a bull (Ulansey 1989: 131). In Beck's words:

> It is a somewhat embarrassing fact that the Eastern Mitra/Mithra kills no bulls (though in his Iranian form he is the god of herds and pastures). The Vedic Mitra participates (reluctantly) in a killing – the killing of Soma, the personification of the life-giving drink (Iranian *haoma*); and in the Iranian tradition (at least in that of the 'Bundahišn', ch. 6 ed. Anklesaria) a bull is killed – the primal bull from whose marrow sprang the useful plants and from whose sperm, purified in the Moon, sprang the useful beasts – but it is killed not by Mithra but by the evil Ahriman. Also in the Iranian tradition (Bd. 34), in the final days a second bull is to be killed – this time by a saviour figure, Sōšyant – and from its fat mixed with *hōm* (i.e. *haoma*) a drink of corporal immortality will be prepared. Most would agree that some of this material lies behind the bull-killing Mithras of the Mysteries, but in fitting the god to the act it has clearly undergone a sea change. Cumont's view was a rather inclusive one: somewhere in the transmission Mithras as bull-killer has been substituted for Ahriman as the perpetrator of a necessary evil in the process of creation; at the same time, he has assimilated the function of Sōšyant in an act which is also eschatological ... This view at least accepts at face value the differences between Eastern and Western forms. (Beck 1984: 2068-69.)

It seems reasonable to try to find in other parts of the Orient a divine person who fits to the act of bull-killing without a "sea change". I propose that the famous episode in the Babylonian Epic of Gilgamesh (tablet VI), where the hero with his friend Enkidu kills the Bull of Heaven, is to be seen as a more suitable model for the Mithraic icon. The story has a long history in Mesopotamia, the bull-killing episode in the standard Babylonian version derives from the more ancient Sumerian tale "Gilgamesh and the Bull of Heaven". The sixth tablet of the standard

Babylonian version begins with the scene of Gilgamesh's return from his expedition to the Cedar Forest, cleaning himself and putting on his kingly attire. The lady Ištar looks covetously on the hero's beauty and asks him for her husband. Gilgamesh insults her by enumerating the goddess' previous lovers, each of whom has had a miserable destiny as a result of having dealt with the goddess. Ištar becomes deeply offended by Gilgamesh's speech, then goes to heaven to ask her father Anu to give her the Bull of Heaven:

> O father, give me, please, the Bull of Heaven, that I may slay Gilgameš in his dwelling. If you will not give me the Bull of Heaven, I shall smash the underworld together with its dwelling place, I shall raze the nether regions to the ground. I shall bring up the dead to consume the living, I shall make the dead outnumber the living. (VII 94-100, George 2003: 625.)

This speech of Ištar is intertextually related to a passage in the Akkadian version of Ištar's Descent. At the gate of the Netherworld, Ištar says to the gatekeeper:

> Gatekeeper! Open your gate for me! Open your gate for me that I may enter, if you will not open the gate that I may enter, I will break down the door, I will smash the bolt, I will break down the frame, I will topple the doors, I will raise up the dead to devour the living, the dead shall outnumber the living! (lines 14-20, Foster 1996: 403.)

It is clear from this comparison that Ištar's descent can bring the dead to life. When we study the older Sumerian version of these lines, we find again a Bull of Heaven in connection with the goddess' entering into the Netherworld. Inanna says that the reason of her travel to the Netherworld is the death of Ereškigal's husband, the Great Bull of Heaven (*gud-gal-an-na*).

> Lines 78-89: Neti, the chief doorman of the underworld, answered holy Inanna: "Who are you?" – "I am Inanna going to the east." – "If you are Inanna going to the east, why have you travelled to the land of no return? How did you set your heart on the road whose traveller never returns?" Holy Inanna answered him: "Because lord Gud-gal-ana, the husband of my elder sister holy Ereškigala, has died; in order to have his funeral rites observed, she offers generous libations at his wake – that is the reason."

In other words, the death of the Bull of Heaven initiates the descent of the soul. In the Epic of Gilgamesh, this process is represented by the illness and death of Enkidu, which ensues directly after the victory over the

Bull of Heaven and subsequent assembly of the gods. Inanna says that her journey is directed "toward where the sun rises", that is, to the east. Neti's answer suggests that she is actually not going to the east, but rather that Inanna's journey represents descent to the Netherworld. Also in the *Mithras Liturgy* (694-704), whose connection with Mithraism may be doubted, the god is depicted as *descending* with a part of a bull on his shoulder, that he had probably slain:

> Now when they (= the seven gods) take their place, here and there, in order, look in the air and you will see lightning-bolts going down, and lights flashing, and the earth shaking, and a god descending, a god immensely great, having a bright appearance, youthful, golden-haired, with a white tunic and a golden crown and trousers, and *holding in his right hand a golden shoulder of a young bull*: this is the Bear which moves and turns heaven around, moving upward and downward in accordance with the hour. Then you will see lightning-bolts leaping from his eyes and stars from his body (Meyer 1987: 218, emphasis added).

The tauroctony in the Mithraic iconography was certainly related – directly or indirectly – to the contemporary ritual practice called taurobolium. Taurobolium was a ritual, mostly in honour of the Phrygian Great Goddess, in which a bull was sacrificed over a pit containing the initiand; through whose blood he was reborn for eternity (*in aeternum renatus* CIL VI 510, Clauss 2001: 31). According to Latin inscriptions, "dedicators desired to be purified by receiving the *taurobolium*" (Duthoy 1969: 72). Prudentius in the 4th century AD described the taurobolium in his poem *On the Martyrs' Crowns* (10, 1011-50), where the high priest (*summus sacerdos*) descended into the pit in order to receive the consecration (*consecrandus*). In Vermaseren's words:

> He is in full ceremonials, his head and temples are decorated with woollen fillets and ribbons, in his hair he wears a gold crown and he is attired in a silken toga. Over the pit a wooden platform has been constructed. The blood of the bull, which has been killed by means of a sacred spear (*sacrato venabulo*), drips down through holes, drilled in the boards. The priest lifts his face, and even licks up the blood (*linguam rigat*). When the animal has been dragged away the priest comes out, a gruesome sight (*pontifex visu horridus*), and he is hailed and saluted by the crowd, and worshipped from a distance (*adorant eminus*). (Vermaseren 1977: 103.)

Also in the Epic of Gilgamesh, the pits open in the ground when the Bull of Heaven arrives Uruk on the nose-rope of Ištar:

> At the snort of the Bull of Heaven a pit opened up, a hundred men of Uruk all fell into it. At its second snort a pit opened up, two hundred men of Uruk all fell into it. At its third snort a pit opened up, Enkidu fell in up to [his] waist. Enkidu sprang out and seized the Bull of Heaven by [its] horns; the Bull of Heaven spat slaver at his face, with the tuft of its tail […] … […]. (VI, 119-27, George 2003: 627.)

A number of altars related to the taurobolium inform us that during the rite the powers (*vires*) of the bull were removed (*excipere*), dedicated (*consecrare*), and finally buried (*considere*) – this last probably in the spot where the memorial stone was afterwards erected (Duthoy 1969: 74). The "might" (*dunnu*) and "strength" (*emūqu*) of the Bull of Heaven are also mentioned by Enkidu in his speech to Gilgameš:

> My friend, we vaunted ourselves [… in our] city, how shall we answer the dense-gathered people? My friend, I have experienced the might of the Bull of Heaven, [… its] strength [and] learning [its] mission. I will once again [experience] the might of the Bull of [Heaven,] behind [the Bull] of Heaven I shall […,] I will seize [it by the tuft of its tail.] (VI, 130–36, George 2003: 627.)

Many scholars interpret the sacred powers (*vires*) in the taurobolium as referring to the bull's genitals, basing the assumption on a myth related by Clement of Alexandria, who was once himself an initiate of Phrygian mysteries. Clement says that the myth was associated with Attis' passion for Cybele (*Protreptikos Logos* 2.15.2):

> The mysteries of Demeter commemorate the amorous embraces of Zeus with his mother Demeter, and the wrath of Demeter … on account of which she is said to have received the name Brimo (= the Grim one); also the supplication of Zeus, the drink of bile, the tearing out the heart of the victims, and unspeakable obscenities. The same rites are performed in honour of Attis and Cybele and the Corybantes by the Phrygians, who have spread it abroad how that Zeus tore off the testicles of a ram, and then brought and flung them into the midst of Demeter's lap, thus paying a sham penalty for his violent embrace by pretending that he had mutilated himself (translation by Butterworth, Loeb edition).

In the emasculation rite, the offer of the substitute genitals of bull or ram forms the enactment of the myth. Thus one identifies oneself with Attis and enters into a firm alliance with the Goddess. By offering procreative organs to the Goddess one hoped to obtain from her a similar power and special protection.[34] Bearing this in mind, one can understand the following passage from the Gilgamesh Epic, where the heroes offer the heart of the bull to Šamaš, and Enkidu throws a "haunch" (Akkadian *imittu*) of the Bull to enraged Ištar:

> Then Gilgameš like a butcher [(...)], brave and skilful, [pressed home] his knife between the yoke of the horns and the slaughter-spot. After they had slain the Bull of Heaven, they took up its heart and set it before Šamaš. They stepped back and prostrated themselves before Šamaš, both of them (then) sat down together. Ištar went up on the wall of Uruk-the-Sheepfold, she hopped and stamped, she uttered a woeful wail: "Woe to Gilgameš, who vilified me, (who) killed the Bull of Heaven!" Enkidu heard this speech of Ištar, he tore a haunch off the Bull of Heaven and threw it down before her. "You too, had I caught you, I would have treated you like it! I would have draped its guts on your arms!" (VI, 145-57, George 2003: 627-29.)

The tauroctony is almost always accompanied by a banquet scene in Mithraic iconography. The banquet is second in importance to the tauroctony, to which it is the complement, and it takes place on the bull's hide (Beck 1984: 2081). In the S. Prisca Mithraeum there is a depiction of Sol and Mithras banqueting together in a cave, attended by two servants, one of whom has a raven's head and claws for feet (*ibid.*: 2028). In other depictions, we find the torchbearers as attendants, and raven- and lion-headed servitors. The mythic feast is somehow repeated in the actual festivities of the cult (*ibid.*: 2083). A banquet scene is also described in the Epic of Gilgamesh, following the killing of the Bull of Heaven and prostration before Šamaš. After Gilgamesh has given the horns of the Bull to the craftsmen, the Babylonian version says laconically: "Gilgameš made merry in his palace" (VI, 179, George 2003: 631). The Sumerian version of "Gilgamesh and the Bull of Heaven" from Me-Turan describes in its final lines the wealth of bull's raw stuff, including its hide:

> As he (= Gilgameš) spoke, he consigned its hide to the streets, he consigned its intestines to the broad square, and the widows' sons of his city each took their share of its meat in baskets. He consigned its carcass to the knacker's, and turned its two horns into flasks for pouring fine oil to Inanna in Eanna. For the death of the Bull of Heaven: holy Inanna, it is sweet to praise you![35]

34 Vermaseren 1977: 105–6; see also Parpola 1997: xlvii n. 140.

35 See ETCSL (as in fn. 3), section 1.8.1.2.

Given the centrality of the bull-killing episode in the Mithraic representation, it must have been supremely relevant to the lives of the initiates. The tauroctony itself can be interpreted as an act of creation, or an act of salvation, or an eschatological act of consummation at the world's end – it may even be two or all three of these (Beck 1984: 2080–81). The S. Prisca Mithraeum has a couple of painted texts in verse which may be the openings of liturgical hymns or self-contained *symbola*. One of these may refer to the salvific act of bull-killing by Mithras: "us too you have saved by blood eternally shed" (*et nos servasti eternali sanguine fuso*), but the reading of the first part of the line is quite uncertain (*ibid.*: 2029).

The episode in the epic of Gilgamesh, where the hero kills the Bull of Heaven is reflected in the royal bull hunt descriptions in the royal inscriptions of ancient Mesopotamia. Already the king Šulgi killed "the big wild bull, the Bull of Heaven" (Šulgi B 85) during his hunting expedition. The prey of the royal hunt is called the 'Bull of Heaven' which places Šulgi's hunt in a cosmological context. As a deified ruler of the Ur III dynasty, his account of the bull hunt thus deliberately alludes to the episode in the Gilgamesh epic (Watanabe 2002: 74-75). Similar accounts of the royal bull hunting are attested also in the Assyrian royal inscriptions (see Watanabe 2002: 72-75). Theologically, the Assyrian king is acting as the counterpart of a divine saviour during the royal bull or lion hunt, saving his people and cattle (see Annus 2002: 102-8).

The Mithraic icon of tauroctony contains some standard elements, which include the metamorphosis of the tip of the bull's tail into an ear or ears of wheat, the presence of moon and torchbearers, a crater; and several animals: dog and snake, who are precisely on a par; a scorpion, a lion, and a raven (Beck 1984: 2080). Some prominent scholars of Mithraism would like to see the icon of tauroctony as a map of the heavens, the composite elements corresponding to a particular set of constellations – bull to Taurus, dog to Canis Major and/or Canis Minor, snake to Hydra, lion to Leo, crater to Crater, raven to Corvus, scorpion to Scorpius, and the wheat-ear at the tip of the bull's tail to the star Spica (*ibid.*: 2081, Ulansey 1989a: 24). This view is quite speculative, but can be supported by comparative data, including the Mesopotamian sources that are not taken into account by Roger Beck.

It may be relevant that the Bull of Heaven, Sumerian *gud-an-na* and Akkadian *alû*, was also the name of the constellation Taurus in Sumero-Babylonian astronomy. According to a Sumerian version of the tale, the

Bull of Heaven grazed where the sun rises before the battle with Gilgamesh:

> Great An replied to holy Inanna: "My child, the Bull of Heaven would not have any pasture (on the earth), as its pasture is on the horizon. Maiden Inanna, the Bull of Heaven can only graze where the sun rises. So I cannot give the Bull of Heaven to you!" (Version B 46-49.)

If the epic tale(s) of Gilgamesh served as a model or some kind of source for creative Mithraic reinterpretations under the circumstances of a Irano-Mesopotamian synthesis, then it may also be relevant that we have a nearly full set of animals occurring in the Epic of Gilgamesh that also appear on the Mithraic icon. A raven (*aribu*) occurs in the story of the Deluge as the last bird brought out by Utnapištim from his ark (XI, 154-56, George 2003: 713). The snake has an important role to play by stealing the wondrous herb given by Utnapištim to Gilgameš (XI, 305-7, George 2003: 723). The bull is present as the Bull of Heaven, and the tip of its tail is also mentioned in the passages quoted above. The scorpion-men occur in the epic as the guardians of the gate, whence the sun rises (tablet VII). A lion is mentioned as a lover of Ištar (VI, 51) to which the goddess dug "seven and seven pits"; and a set of lions is frequently mentioned as an epithet of Gilgameš, "who killed lions in the mountain passes". The dogs are mentioned in VI, 63 and XI, 116. Even if these parallels cannot help to better understand the Mithraic icon, it is still possible that there are historical links between the two traditions by means of later astrological interpretation.

Mithras is attended on the icon of the tauroctony, and sometimes also in other scenes, by two figures similar in dress to himself. Most likely they are twins, and are usually differentiated by the carrying of a raised torch by one and a lowered torch by the other. Their names are known from dedications – Cautes (raised torch) and Cautopates (lowered torch), and they were represented separately on pairs of statues. There is general agreement that they represent opposites to each other (Beck 1984: 2084). The kindling of lights was associated in standard Mesopotamian calendar with the time of festivals for the dead during the fifth month Abu. This month is described by the Assyrian Astrolabe B as follows:

> The month Abu, arrow of Ninurta, braziers are kindled, a torch is raised to the Anunna-gods, Girra comes down from the sky and rivals the sun, the month of Gilgameš, for nine days men contest in wrestling and athletics in their city quarters.

The torches were rised in Abu to help the deceased to find their way from the netherworld and the fire-god Girra to burn the witches and to convey them to the netherworld (Abusch 2002: 70). The traffic of souls in the month of Abu was intense, and the ritual series *Maqlû* was performed in order to ensure its safety to mortals.[36] *Maqlû* incantations contained the motif of heavenly journey of the soul, which is also the background Mithraic torch-bearing figures, as is shown below.

In the icon of tauroctony Cautes and Cautopates flank symmetrically the bull-killing Mithras on both sides, in some ways reminiscent of Mesopotamian depictions of Enkidu and Gilgameš killing the Bull of Heaven, with the difference being that Cautes and Cautopates do not kill the bull in the Mithraic icons. In Italy Cautes is usually on the left flank and Cautopates on the right from the spectator's point of view, but *vice versa* on the Rhine and Danube. According to Roger Beck the distinction relates to the torchbearers' different celestial associations (1984: 2084):

> The icon is aligned as a south-facing *templum* with east to the left and west to the right. Consequently, when the torchbearers represent the rising and setting of the Sun Cautes is on the left and Cautopates on the right. However, the torchbearers are also associated, through their occasional attributes, with the constellation Taurus (Cautes) and Scorpius (Cautepates). With these associations their position will be reversed, for in the celestial map of which the tauroctony is an expression Taurus is on the right (west) and Scorpius of the left (east). (Beck 1984: 2084-85.)

Cautes with raised torch is associated with the east, the rising sun, day, summer and the constellation Taurus. Cautopates with lowered torch signifies the west, the setting sun, night, winter and the constellation Scorpius (*ibid.*). The associations of the torchbearers certainly extended beyond the natural phenomena and encompassed the concerns inherent in the Mysteries as a religion of salvation. Porphyry, *De antro* 24, if read with an important emendation of the text (Beck 1984: 2053), links the torchbearers also

> … to the mechanisms and routes of genesis and apogenesis for the human soul, the processes which are ultimately controlled by Mithras in his median position whithin the cosmos, his "seat of the equinoxes." Significantly, it is Cautopates who is placed at the gate of genesis (north and cold) and Cautes

36 See M. E. Cohen, *Cultic Calendars of the Ancient Near East* (Bethesda: CDL Press 1993), pp. 319–21.

> at the gate of apogenesis (south and hot). With Cautopates one enters life, with Cautes one leaves it. (Beck 1984: 2085.)

The gates of souls, according to Porphyry's account (21-24) are situated in Cancer and Capricorn. According to Beck, this was justified by the logic of planetary houses. Cancer was the gate of descent because the Moon has Cancer as her house. Moon, as a manifestly genetic power, is the closest to the earth, the locus of our mortality. Capricorn was the gate of ascent and apogenesis because it is the house of Saturn, the most remote of the planets in the cosmology of late antiquity. The god Saturnus also presides over the Roman feast of liberation, the Saturnalia, celebrated in the season of Capricorn (Beck 1988: 96). Cautopates also became associated with Cancer and Cautes with Capricorn, the constellations which rose on the summer and winter solstices respectively. Thus the full set of associations in the Mithraic mysteries is: Cautopates – Moon – Cancer – Scorpius – cold – descent – mortality; and Cautes – Sun – Capricorn – Taurus – heat – ascent – immortality (Beck 1988: 94). The descent and ascent of souls through the gates in Cancer and Capricorn was described by Macrobius as follows (1.12):

> 1. At this point we shall discuss the order of the steps by which the soul descends from the sky to the infernal regions of this life. The Milky Way girdles the zodiac, its great circle meeting it obliquely so that it crosses it at the two tropical signs, Capricorn and Cancer. Natural philosophers named these the "portals of the sun" because the solstices lie athwart the sun's path on either side, checking farther progress and causing it to retrace its course across the belt beyond whose limits it never trespasses. 2. Souls are believed to pass through these portals when going from the sky to the earth and returning from the earth to the sky. For this reason one is called the portal of men and the other the portal of gods: Cancer, the portal of men, because through it descent is made to the infernal regions; Capricorn, the portal of gods, because through it souls return to their rightful abode of immortality, to be reckoned among the gods. (Stahl 1952: 133-34.)

Thus based on the previous discussion I assert that the Mithraic associations of Cautes and Cautopates with Taurus and Scorpius derive from an astrological interpretation of the Epic of Gilgamesh. The Bull of Heaven episode corresponds to the symbolism of the constellations Taurus and Cancer in Mithraism – it is the "portal of men" through which "descent is made to the infernal regions". The death of the Bull of Heaven also brings about the death of Enkidu, a mortal. In the Sumerian version of the goddess' descent, the reason of her descent is similarly the death of the Great Bull of Heaven. Thus the death of the Bull in both systems sends the soul down the path of mortality, eventually leading to immortality. In the Babylonian Gilgamesh Epic, Ištar does not descend, but assembles the courtesans and harlots, and institutes a mourning over the Bull of Heaven's haunch (VI, 158-59, George 2003: 629).

The turning-point on the path of mortality, which eventually leads to immortality in the Epic of Gilgamesh is the mountain Māšu, which is guarded by the scorpion-men. In Babylonian witchcraft series *Maqlû* this crossing place (*nēbiru*) was called Zabban, and corresponds to Bardaisan's "hindrance of souls" (see above). The gurdian scorpion-men are still seen in the presence of constellation Scorpius (or Capricorn) in the Mithraic and Neoplatonic systems, where according to Macrobius situates "the portal of gods, because through it souls return to their rightful abode of immortality, to be reckoned among the gods". On tablet IX, Gilgamesh sets out on the journey to Utnapištim, who symbolizes the "life" that Gilgameš seeks.[37] The scorpion-men correspond to the constellation Scorpius, and their gate is the gate of the night, the west, winter and genesis of the soul. After entering the gate, it is said of Gilgameš that "he [took] the path of the sun" towards the east (IX, 138 George 2003: 671) and enters the land of darkness, consisting of twelve double-hours.[38] From the point of view of the Mithraic mysteries:

> Now Taurus and Scorpius occupy diametrically opposite positions on the celestial sphere and on the zodiac, and part of the purpose of assigning their symbols to Cautes and Cautopates is to signify that the scene whose margins the torchbearers define corresponds to that semicircle of the zodiac, that half of the heavens, which lies between those two signs ... the tauroctony is celestially aligned, corresponding to a view of the heavens by a south-facing observer, so that west is to the right of the scene and east to the left (Beck 1988: 20).

37 It is highly interesting to note that the Yazidi mythological story of soul's voyage to Paradise after death has many parallels with Gilgameš's journey to Utnapištim in the Babylonian Epic. See M. Dietrich, "Die 'Teufelsanbeter' in Nord-Iraq und ihre historischen und religionsgeschichtlichen Beziehungen zum Alten Orient." *Jahrbuch für Anthropologie und Religionsgeschichte*, Band 2 (1974), pp. 139–68, esp. 158–61.

38 Gilgameš's travel on the path of the sun has a parallel in the Parmenides' fragment B1, see W. Burkert "Das Proömium des Parmenides und die Katabasis des Pythagoras." *Phronesis* 14 (1969) pp. 1–30, esp. 18–19.

The Moon and Goddess

From Porphyry, *De antro nympharum* (18, 29), we learn that the moon was a gate of the descending soul: "the theologians make the gates of souls the sun and the moon, the ascent taking place through the sun and the descent through the moon". The ascent through the sun's rays is well attested not only in classical antiquity, but also in ancient Mesopotamia. The Pythagoreans believed that the glittering particles of dust which moved themselves in a sunbeam (*xýsmata*) were souls descending from ether, borne on wings of light. They added that this beam, passing through the air and through water down to its depths, gave life to all things here below (Cumont 1912: 188). The idea is also found in the Hermetic Corpus (16, 16): "if by way of the sun anyone has a ray shining upon him in his rational part … the demons' effect on him is nullified. For none – neither demons nor gods – can do anything against a single ray of god" (Copenhaver 1992: 60–61). Recently R. Edmonds has argued that this apogenetic function of the sun's ray had also a place in Mithraism (Edmonds 2001).

And a similar idea is already present in the Akkadian great hymn to Šamaš, where the Sun-god lifts up the fallen soul: "You lift up him who goes down to the deep, you provide him with wings" (*tušelli ārid anzanunzê tušaškan kappa*, l. 70).[39] The Sun's association with ascent in Mesopotamia is also reflected on Tablet VII of the Gilgamesh Epic, where the dying Enkidu enters into a dialogue with Šamaš.

The moon is related to the genesis of the soul, and as a female being she was called the "Mistress of genesis" in some mystery religions. The Moon, as the latest sphere and the lowest boundary before the earth, was held to be responsible for birth and reproduction. The lunar phenomena were also of paramount importance in Babylonian horoscopy. The first astronomical datum provided in a horoscope was the position of the moon on the date of the birth, and significant moments in the lunar cycle occurring in proximity to the birth were viewed as having an impact on the birth (Rochberg 2004: 105-115). In the Neoplatonic descent theories, the lunar sphere is of prominent importance, for example according to Macrobius 1.12.15:

39 See *Chicago Assyrian Dictionary*, A/2, 153. The word *anzanunzû* means "subterranean water, abyss, deep water". Note that descent of the soul is associated with water also in the Mystery religions (cf. Lapinkivi 2004: 153).

> This last function, being the farthest removed from the gods, is the first in us and all the earthly creation; in as much as our body represents the dregs of what is divine, it is therefore the first substance of the creature. (translation from Stahl 1952.)

The doctrine of the moon's association with "life" also helps to explain some passages in the Epic of Gilgamesh. When the hero has duly buried his friend, in the beginning of tablet IX, he is said to pray to the moon-god Sîn and having a revelatory dream from him:

> I arrived one night at the mountain passes, I saw some lions and grew afraid. I lifted my head, praying to Sîn, to [..., the] light of the gods, my supplication went: "O [Sîn and ...,] keep me safe!" [Gilgameš] arose, he awoke with a start: it was a dream! [... in the] presence of the moon he grew happy to be alive. (IX 8-14, George 2003: 667.)

Gilgameš is here approaching the gate of the scorpion-men, and one can see here two powerful symbols of genesis: night, and the moon granting life to the hero. Usually it is Šamaš who assists Gilgameš and Enkidu during their travels and marches with them, he has a leading role in the epic. He even says a word of favour for Enkidu in the divine assembly, a scene which is preserved only in the Hittite translation.[40] When Enlil says that Enkidu must die,

> Celestial Šamaš began to reply to the hero Enlil: "Was it not at your word that they slew him, the Bull of Heaven – and also Humbaba? Now shall innocent Enkidu die?" Enlil was wroth at celestial Šamaš: "How like a comrade you marched with them daily!"

The descending Ištar in the Akkadian version is called "daughter of the Moon" (lines 2-3), and is relevant to the story. Calling Ištar with such epithet refers to her as descending into genesis. Since the Mesopotamian goddess was the daughter of the moon, the full moon with its perfect shining disc became one of her symbols: the full moon symbolized Ištar, as indicated by her mystic number 15 that coincides with the number of days in the lunar cycle, while the moon god was symbolized with the number 30 (Lapinkivi 2004: 155). The Moon was associated with the topmost stage of the Mesopotamian ziggurat, the first "gate" in the descent of the goddess, and there the sacred marriage rite took place. As some passages from the Sumerian hymn *Iddin-Dagan A* show, Inanna is

---

40 Text: *KUB* VIII 48; see the edition by E. Laroche, *Revue hittite et asianique* 26 (1968) 17.

associated with the phases of the moon, and the bed is set up for sacred marriage on the day of its disappearance (Lapinkivi 2004: 120):

> Monthly, at the new moon, the gods of the land gather around her so that the divine powers are perfected (l. 27f.) … At the New Year, on the day of the rites, in order for her to determine the fate of all the countries, so that during the day (?) the faithful servants can be inspected, so that on the day of the disappearance of the moon the divine powers can be perfected, a bed is set up for my lady (l. 173-77).

Parpola asserts that the loss of purity of the waning moon symbolized the gradual defilement, and descent of the Mesopotamian goddess, and its total disappearance symbolized corruption, or spiritual death. The waxing of the moon symbolized increasing purity, and after the conjunction, ascent and return to the original state (1997: xc-xci n. 111). A similar view is found in the teachings of Bardaisan who regarded moon as the Mother of Life, who had sexual union with the Father "on the top of the building". He also associated this sexual communion with the new moon, as do the Sumerian sources. The biography of Bardaisan, as transmitted by Agapius of Mabbug and Bar Hebraeus mentions that

> … according to Bardaisan the Mother of Life every month discards her clothing and goes in to the Father of Life, who has communion with her. She then bears seven sons. All the authors state, that this happens by analogy with the moon, who every month 'discards' her light and goes to the sun. The idea is, therefore, that the moon is impregnated by the sun. Bar Hebraeus in the Chronicon ecclesiasticum goes even further, and says that the Moon is the Mother of Life and the Sun the Father of Life. The Moon receives from the Sun the 'spirit of preservation', which she sends into the world. (Drijvers 1966: 149.)

No doubt that the goddess descended and ascended in the Mesopotamian myth for mankind's sake. She descended "to us", and from the point of view of mortals, her descent means "birth" or "life". From the point of view of divinity, her descent means "death". The ascent of the goddess means death to a mortal and his physical body, but "rebirth" to the goddess and her luminous body. This truth is expressed in the Mesopotamian dream omen series *ziqīqu*, Tablet IX, col. I, which says "If (a man) ascends to heaven: his days will be short" and "If he descends to the netherworld: his days will be long" (Rochberg 2004: 57). As was put by Macrobius,

> The difference between terrestrial and supernal bodies (I am speaking of the sky and stars and the other components) lies in this, that the latter have been summoned upwards to the abode of the soul and have gained immortality by the very nature of that region and by copying the perfection of their high estate; but to our terrestrial bodies the soul is drawn downwards, and here it is believed to be dead while it is shut up in a perishable region and the abode of mortality. Be not disturbed that the reference to the soul, which we say is immortal, we so often use the term 'death'. In truth, the soul is not destroyed by its death but is overwhelmed for a time; nor does it surrender the privilege of immortality because of its lowly sojourn, for when it has rid itself completely of all taint of evil and has deserved to be sublimated, it again leaves the body and, fully recovering its former state, returns to the splendor of everlasting life. (1.12.16-17, Stahl 1952: 136-37.)

As we can see, the generative power brought forth by the descending goddess was viewed positively in ancient Mesopotamia. In the Greek world, the positive reasons for the descent of the soul were primarily derived from Plato's *Timaeus* 39e and 41b. Some argued that the soul descends into genesis to fill out the cosmos, bringing all possible entities into existence or bringing divine benefits to the lower realms. The benefits of the upper realms may be viewed as the care and administration, or the soul's purpose may be described as the purification, perfection, and salvation of the lower realms (Edmonds 2004: 283).[41] This was also the Mesopotamian view. Accordingly, in the philosophical doctrines of late antiquity, the moon was viewed either positively or negatively depending of the evaluation of genesis in that particular doctrine or school. If the physical world was regarded as an abode of evil, as in many philosophical doctrines of late antiquity, the moon was regarded as a dangerous entity. In the *Mithras Liturgy*, the magician times the ritual preparations carefully to avoid the presence of the moon in the sky, and he does not see the moon during the ascent to a meeting with the supreme god (Edmonds 2004: 275):

> The theurgists, however, are not the only testimony to the moon's terrifying face. Clement relates [*Strom.* 5.49] that Orpheus called the moon Gorgonian because of its terrifying face, a face like that which Odysseus feared Perse-

41 See *Asclepius* 1.8, and Iamblichus quoted in Stobaeus 1.49.40.22–27, cf. Plotinus 4.8.5. Concerning the various reasons of soul's descent, see J. Dillon, "The Descent of the Soul in Middle Platonic and Gnostic Theory." In: *The golden chain. Studies in the development of Platonism and Christianity*. London: Variorum 1990.

> phone would send up to him in the underworld when he was consulting the shades. Plutarch too knows of this frightening face [*Fac.* 944bc], which terrifies souls coming out of incarnation, although he rationalizes it as merely a cliff formation on the surface of the moon (Edmonds 2004: 276).

According to Xenocrates and Plutarch (*Obsolescence of Oracles* 416c-f) the moon was the proper home of the demons. These demons, which occupied the middle world of the moon and the lunar air, acted as mediators between the two worlds of gods and humans. Due to their position, demons were similar to both gods and humans. Hekate, who was both an earthly and a heavenly goddess, was also the goddess of the moon (Seneca, *Medea* 790), and subsequently she was the queen of demons, both good and bad, who occupied the moon (Lapinkivi 2004: 178). Hekate was also associated with evil chthonic demons, called "dogs."

> Since the Chaldean system depicted Hekate as a savior figure, helping the theurgist, she had to be disassociated from these dogs. In order to achieve this, the Chaldean doctrine followed the Middle Platonic view of the double Soul: the upper part of the Soul that remained secluded from the Sensible World (Cosmos) became Hekate, whereas the lower part of the Soul that was involved with men and the matters of the material world became known as Physis. Physis was not evil but simply hylic, but because the dog-demons lived in her sublunar sphere, it was she that became their controller. Physis was closely related to Hekate since Physis was derived from her. (Lapinkivi 2004: 178.)

As Lapinkivi shows, the Mesopotamian goddess in her earthly form was also associated with dogs, and the conception of higher and lower souls can be compared with the sororal relationship of Ištar with Ereškigal. While the former is more involved in heavenly matters, the latter is involved in the matters of "down below", or with the matters of the material world. If Physis in the *Chaldean Oracles* originated from Hekate, the Soul, so also the netherworld queen Ereškigal can be seen deriving from the queen of heaven, Inanna/Ištar as a different hypostasis, the sinful soul versus the purified soul. In fact, a Middle Assyrian version of the first eleven lines of Descent of Ištar identifies Ereškigal as "Ištar (*ištaru*) who resides in the midst of Irkalla" (Lapinkivi 2004: 178-79).

There are very many intermediary principles between the higher powers and the realms below in the cosmological doctrines of the late antiquity, and they are all feminine. There is also a tendency to separate the two functions – one of giving and joining together (positive) and the other of division (negative). This tendency to separate leads to the multiplication of mediating principles, who may be imagined either as personifications of abstract principles or identified with divine figures from the mythic tradition (Edmonds 2004: 286-87). The higher, maternal aspect of this feminine principle was often called Sophia, Pronoia, Isis etc; and the lower and demonic aspect called Physis, Heimarmene, Anagke, among others.

> Systems with an optimistic view of genesis emphasize the higher principles that convey the benefits of the divine to the world below, whereas more pessimistic systems may multiply the entities that separate mortals from the divine and emphasize their absolute domination of human life. ... Indeed, philosophers and theologians meditating on the problems of fate and free will devised a vast number of different configurations of the relations of Physis and Pronoia, Anagke, Tyche, Heimarmene, and the Moirae, but all these powers are feminine principles that impose order on the lower world from their intermediary position. Although divine Providence is generally positively evaluated, Necessity, Fortune, the Fates, and Destiny are more often negatively viewed by the mortals whose fates they determine. In particular, the lowest level of fate (whether called Heimarmene, Anagke, or another name) becomes, in a cosmology with a pessimistic view of genesis, the power responsible for keeping souls imprisoned and miserable in matter. (Edmonds 2004: 287, 288-89.)

This intermediary feminine power in the Mesopotamian religion was Ištar, the goddess *par excellence*. Previously in this paper I have explained the myth of the goddess' descent as relating to the destiny of the soul, and it was believed in ancient Mesopotamia that the natural processes of birth and death were mediated through her. Through her association with the moon, the Mesopotamian goddess can be viewed as a model for the feminine intermediary figure in these late antique doctrines. The goddess is frequently seen in the Mesopotamian texts as acting for determining the king's power and well-being, and consequently the well-being of his subjects. In this function she corresponds to what the Greeks called the Tyche of the king (see Drijvers 1980: 69-70). Thus the system of continuities in the Near Eastern and Mediterranean worlds appears to be highly complex, but the impression that various late antique schools received and developed the religious ideas of Mesopotamian origin seems more and more likely.[42]

Conclusion

Are these proposals concerning the "Babylonian sediment" in late antique religious doctrines simply a new manifestation of the much-feared pan-Babylonism, allegedly an obsolete approach and a totally disproved theory? This paper asserts that some of the interpretations presented above stand on more solid ground, whereas some others are nothing more than proposals. Given a notoriously complicated subject with a lack of written sources as Mithraism, at present it appears quite inconceivable to offer a universally accepted theory. Scholars of different background may be more or less convinced of various aspects of the theories offered, but there is often more than one plausible explanation.

The approach of this paper has been to try to make a case for continuity rather than invention in the formation of the Mithraic and other prominent religious doctrines of Late Antiquity. There is a continuity of narratives and motifs, but the context of these Babylonian sediments in the religious systems Late Antique can only be recognized as motifs. This paper does not deny the invention, and indeed, the rich symbolism of the mystery religions, and Gnosticism can not be reduced to derive from only one part of the ancient world. Given the syncretic and mobile character of religious literature and imagery in the ancient Mediterranean world, it is not helpful to insist that the religious concepts and texts originate from one and only one tradition. As Karen King rightly notes: "Instead, we ought to be exploring the field of late antique cultural hybridity in order to illuminate their overlapping themes, strategies, and discourses, as well as their distinctive practices" (2003: 169). Thus, this paper asserts that we must acknowledge that ancient Mesopotamian sources played a part in the formation of many these Late Antiquity religious movements. Assyrian and Babylonian sources must be returned their honour of being in some sense the ancestors of the West. But not in the naïvely categorical manner as it was propagated by the pan-Babylonian

42 In this sense I would agree with J. Cooper's criticism of Parpola 1997 that "A more cautious reader would explain the similarities in the myths as the persistence of old Near Eastern patterns of myth into the Hellenistic period, and the similarities Parpola adduces between the figures of Ištar and Sophia can likewise be understood as the persistence of ancient aspects of the great goddess of the Orient" (JAOS 120 [2000] 440).

school, but as one of many resources of the developments of Late Antiquity. R. Beck wrote a quarter of century ago:

> It is perhaps no coincidence that as credence in the thoroughly Iranian structure of the Mysteries has been weakened over the past decade, so a new theory which postulates a doctrinal content drawn in very cosiderable part from astronomy and astrology of antiquity has come into play. A certain vacuum has been filled. However, whether this represents altogether a shift from Eastern to Western data … is in fact still an open question. For Babylon had of course its astronomy, and it may be that certain elements in the astronomy of the Mysteries derive from Mesopotamian sources, though I believe that its framework can be shown to be essentially Graeco-Roman. (Beck 1984: 2061-62.)

In addition to astrological doctrines, one also finds a concept of the soul's ascent and descent in mystery religions and in Neoplatonic schools very similar to the ancient Mesopotamian one. The metaphor of stripping and redressing of the soul as the means of salvation appears in the doctrines of the Syrian Chuch, Neoplatonists, Mithraism and Hermetic literature. Despite the divergencies and the richness of images that can be seen in various treatments of the clothing metaphor, the Mesopotamian heritage can definitively be seen as one source. In addition, the Epic of Gilgamesh can be shown to have been an ancient resource for the reinterpretation of the mystery religions of Late Antiquity (see also Dalley 1994). This thus establishes that the mythological and epic texts of ancient Mesopotamia were not simply stories of gods and heroes without any particular 'philosophy', but also had spiritual dimensions, even if by means of later reinterpretation, as the Homeric cave of nymphs became a source of inspiration for Porphyry.

References

Abusch, Tzvi 2002 Mesopotamian Witchcraft: Toward a History and Understanding of Babylonian Witchcraft Beliefs and Literature. Ancient Magic and Divination, Vol. 5. Leiden – Boston – Köln: Brill, Styx.

Annus, Amar 2002 The God Ninurta in the Mythology and Royal Ideology of Ancient Mesopotamia. State Archives of Assyria Studies 14. Helsinki: The Neo-Assyrian Text Coprus Project.

Anz, W. 1897 Zur Frage nach dem Ursprung des Gnostizismus: Ein religionsgeschichtlicher Versuch. Texte und Untersuchungen 15, 4. Leipzig: Hinrichs.

Beck, Roger 1984 "Mithraism since Franz Cumont". In: H. Temporini and W. Haase (eds.) Aufstieg und Niedergang der römischen Welt: Geschichte und Kultur Roms im Spiegel der neueren Forschung 17, 4. Berlin: de Gruyter, 2002-2115.

Beck, Roger 1988 Planetary Gods and Planetary Orders in the Mysteries of Mithras. Études préliminaires aux religions orientales dans l'empire romain, t. 108. Leiden – New York – Kobenhavn – Köln: E. J. Brill.

Beck, Roger 1998 "The Mysteries of Mithras: A New Account of their Genesis". Journal of Roman Studies 88, pp. 115-28.

Borger, R. 1967 "Das dritte Haus" der Serie Bīt Rimki (VR 50–51, Schollmeyer HGŠ NR. 1)". Journal of Cuneiform Studies 21, pp. 1-17.

Brock, Sebastian 1992 "Clothing Metaphors as a Means of Theological Expression in Syriac Tradition". Studies in Syriac Christianity, history, literature and theology. Variorum Reprints 1992.

Bucur, Bogdan G. 2006 "The Other Clement of Alexandria: Cosmic Hierarchy and Interiorized Apocalypticism". Vigiliae Chistianae 60, pp. 251-268.

Burkert, Walter 1992 The Orientalizing Revolution. Near Eastern Influence on Greek Culture in the Early Archaic Period. Cambridge, Mass.

Clauss, Manfred 2001 *The Roman Cult of Mithras. The God and his Mysteries.* Translated by Richard Gordon. New York: Routledge.

Copenhaver, Brian P. 1992 *Hermetica: The Greek* Corpus Hermeticum *and the Latin* Asclepius *in a new English translation with notes and introduction.* Cambridge: University Press.

Culianu, I. P. 1983 *Psychanodia I: A Survey of the Evidence Concerning the Ascension of the Soul and its Relevance.* Études préliminaires aux religions orientales dans l'empire romain 99. Leiden: E. J. Brill.

Cumont, Franz 1912 *Astrology and Religion among the Greeks and Romans.* American Lectures on the History of Religions. New York and London: G. P. Putnam's Sons.

Cumont, Franz 1949 *Lux perpetua.* Paris: Librairie orientaliste Paul Geuthner.

Dalley, Stephanie 1994 "The Tale of Buluqiya and the Alexander Romance in Jewish and Sufi Mystical Circles". In: J. C. Reeves (ed.) *Tracing the Threads. Studies in the Vitality of Jewish Pseudepigrapha.* Atlanta: Scholars Press, pp. 239-269.

Dalley, Stephanie 1995 "Bel at Palmyra and elsewhere in the Parthian Period". ARAM 7, pp. 137-51.

Dietrich, Manfried 1998 *bulṭ bēlī* "Lebe mein König!" Ein Krönungshymnus aus Emar und Ugarit und sein Verhältnis zu mesopotamischen und westlichen Inthronisationslieder". *Ugarit Forschungen* 30, pp. 155-200.

Drijvers, Han J. W. 1966 *Bardaisan of Edessa.* Assen: Van Gorcum & Comp.

Drijvers, Han J. W. 1980 *Cults and Beliefs at Edessa.* Études préliminaires aux religions orientales dans l'Empire Romain 82. Leiden: E. J. Brill.

Drower, Ethel Stefana 1937 *The Mandaeans of Iraq and Iran: their cults, customs, magic, legends, and folklore.* London: Clarendon Press.

Duthoy, Robert 1969 *The Taurobolium: Its Evolution and Terminology.* Études préliminaires aux religions orientales dans l'empire romain, 10. Leiden: E. J. Brill.

Edmonds, Radcliffe G. 2001 "Did the Mithraists Inhale? A Technique for Theurgic Ascent in the Mithras Liturgy, the Chaldaean Oracles, and some Mithraic Frescoes". *The Ancient World,* Vol. 32, 1, pp. 10–24.

Edmonds, Radcliffe G. 2004 "The Faces of the Moon: Cosmology, Genesis, and the *Mithras Liturgy".* In: R. S. Boustan and A. Y. Reed (eds.) *Heavenly Realms and Earthly Realities in Late Antique Religions.* Cambridge: University Press, 275-95.

Fauth, Wolfgang 1973 "Seth-Typhon, Onoel und der eselsköpfige Sabaoth: Zur Theriomorphie der ophitisch-barbelognostischen Archonten". *Oriens Christianus* 57, pp. 79-120.

Foster, Benjamin 1996 *Before the Muses: An Anthology of Akkadian Literature.* Bethesda, MD: CDL Press. Second Edition.

George, Andrew R. 2003 *The Babylonian Gilgamesh Epic: Introduction, Critical Edition and Cuneiform Texts.* Oxford: University Press.

Gnoli, Gherardo 1979 "Sol Persice Mithra". In U. Bianchi (ed.) *Mysteria Mithrae.* EPRO 80. Leiden: E. J. Brill, 725-40.

Groneberg, B. 1986 "Die sumerisch-akkadische Inanna/Ištar: Hermaphroditos?" *Die Welt des Orients* 17, pp. 25-46.

Hunger, Hermann 1992 *Astrological Reports to Assyrian Kings.* State Archives of Assyria, Vol. 8. Helsinki: University Press.

Hunger, Hermann and David Pingree 1989 *Mul Apin: An Astronomical Compendium in Cuneiform.* Archiv für Orientforschung, Beiheft 24. Horn: Verlag Ferdinand Berger & Söhne.

King, Karen L. 2003 *What is Gnosticism?* Cambridge, MA – London: The Belknap Press of Harvard University Press.

Kingsley, Peter 1995 "Meetings with Magi: Iranian Themes among the Greeks, from Xanthus of Lydia to Plato's Academy". *Journal of the Royal Asiatic Society Series* 3, 5, 2, pp. 173-209.

Lapinkivi, Pirjo 2004 *The Sumerian Sacred Marriage in the Light of Comparative Evidence.* State Archives of Assyria Studies, Vol. 15. Helsinki: The Neo-Assyrian Text Coprus Project.

Lidzbarski, Mark 1925 *Ginzā, der Schatz oder das grosse Buch der Mandäer übersetzt und erklärt.* Göttingen: Vandenhoeck & Ruprecht. Leipzig: J. C. Hinrichs.

Mayer, Werner R. 1987 "Ein Mythos von der Erschaffung des Menschen und des Königs". *Orientalia* NS 56, pp. 55-68.

Meyer, Marvin W. 1987 (ed.). *The Ancient Mysteries. A Sourcebook. Sacred Texts of the Mystery Religions of the Ancient Mediterranean World.* San Francisco: Harper 1987.

Mitchell, C. W. 1912 *S. Ephraim's Prose Refutations of Mani, Marcion, and Bardaisan. The Discourses Addressed to Hypatius.* Vol I. London: Williams and Norgate.

Panaino, Antonio 2001 "The Mesopotamian Heritage of Achaemenian Kingship". In: S. Aro and R. M. Whiting (eds.). *The Heirs of Assyria.* Melammu Symposia I. Helsinki: The Neo-Assyrian Text Corpus Project, 35-49.

Parpola, Simo 1983 *Letters from Assyrian and Babylonian Scholars.* Vol. 2. Commentary and Appendices. AOAT 6/2. Neukirchen: Kevelaer.

Parpola, Simo 1997 *Assyrian Prophecies.* State Archives of Assyria, Vol 9. Helsinki: University Press.

Robinson, James M. (ed.) 1996 *Nag Hammad Library in English.* Leiden: Brill.

Rochberg-Halton, Francesca 1988 "Elements of the Babylonian Contribution to Hellenistic Astrology". *JAOS* 108, pp. 51-62.

Rochberg, Francesca 1996 "Personifications and Metaphors in Babylonian Celestial *Omina*". *JAOS* 116, pp. 475-85.

Rochberg, Francesca 1998 *Babylonian Horoscopes.* Transactions of the American Philosophical Society, Vol. 88. Philadelphia.

Rochberg, Francesca 1999-2000 "The Babylonian Origins of the Mandaean Book of the Zodiac". *Aram*, vol. 11-12, pp. 237-47.

Rochberg, Francesca 2004 *The Heavenly Writing: Divination, Horoscopy, and Astronomy in Mesopotamian Culture.* Cambridge: University Press.

Stahl, William Harris 1952 *Macrobius Commentary on the Dream of Scipio.* New York: Columbia University Press.

Suter, Claudia E. 1997 "Gudeas vermeintliche Segnungen des Eninnu". *Zeitschrift für Assyriologie* 87, pp. 1-10.

Talon, Philippe 2005 *The Standard Babylonian Creation Myth Enūma Eliš*. State Archives of Assyria Cuneiform Texts, Vol. IV. Helsinki: The Neo-Assyrian Text Corpus Project.

Ulansey, David 1989 "The Mithraic Mysteries". *Scientific American*, December 1989 (vol. 261, #6), pp. 130–135.

Ulansey, David 1989a *The Origins of the Mithraic Mysteries: Cosmology and Salvation in the Ancient World*. Oxford: University Press.

Vermaseren, Maarten J. 1977 *Cybele and Attis: The Myth and the Cult*. London: Thames and Hudson.

Watanabe, Chikako E. 2002 *Animal Symbolism in Mesopotamia: A Contextual Approach*. Wiener Offene Orientalistik, Band 1. Wien: Institut für Orientalistik der Universität Wien.

Widengren, Geo 1946 *Mesopotamian Elements in Manichaeism*. Studies in Manichaean, Mandaean and Syrian-Gnostic Religion. Uppsala Universitets Årsskrift 1946, 3.

Will, E. 1955 *Le relief cultuel gréco-romain: contribution à l'histoire de l'art de l'Empire romain*. Bibl. des Éc. franç. d'Athènes et de Rome 183. Paris.

Yarbro-Collins, Adela 1995 "The Seven Heavens in Jewish and Christian Apocalypses". In J. J. Collins, M. Fishbane (eds.) *Death, Ecstasy, and Other Worldly Journeys*. New York: SUNY, 59-93.

Ugarit und seine Beziehungen zu Zypern und zur ägäischen Inselwelt

Manfried Dietrich, Münster

Einleitung: Ugarit – der vorderorientalische Partner Zyperns und Festlandstützpunkt eines thalassischen Handelsimperiums im östlichen Mittelmeerraum

Die Beziehungen zwischen Ugarit und seinen ‚überseeischen' ostmediterranen Nachbarn Zypern, Kreta und den ägäischen Inseln sind vielfältig und werden in den verschiedenen Epochen der ostmediterranen Geschichte des 2. Jt. v.Chr. unterschiedlich intensiv bezeugt. Einen umfassenden Überblick über die neuesten Forschungsergebnisse zu Fragen des Austauschs von Luxus- und Gebrauchsgütern, von Lebensmitteln und von kultur- und religionsgeschichtlichen Traditionen bietet das epochale Werk von H.-G. Buchholz: *Ugarit, Zypern und Ägäis. Kulturbeziehungen im zweiten Jahrtausend v.Chr.*[1] Im folgenden sollen ergänzend dazu einige Aspekte der Beziehungen zur Sprache gebracht werden, die sich aus den Texten der Spätzeit Ugarits ableiten lassen.

Nach einer knappen Einführung in die Gegebenheiten des Handels, die für die Zeit zwischen dem 14. und 12. Jh. v.Chr. bekannt geworden sind (Punkt 1), sollen folgende beiden Themen ausführlicher behandelt werden:[2] die Verbindungen zwischen Ugarit, Zypern, Kreta und der Ägäis, die aus den Aussagen der Mythen und Epen einerseits (Punkt 2) und aus denen der Briefe und Wirtschaftstexte andererseits (Punkt 3) ableitbar sind. Den Schluß bilden zusammenfassende Bemerkungen zum Verhältnis zwischen Ugarit und seinen ostmediterranen Nachbarn (Punkt 4).

---

1 H.-G. Buchholz 1999.

2 Ausgangspunkt für die nachfolgenden Ausführungen ist der Vortrag *Zypern und die Ägäis nach den Texten aus Ugarit*, der im Sommer 1997 gehalten und 2000 in überarbeiteter Form veröffentlicht worden ist (M. Dietrich 2000). Die hier vorgelegte Abhandlung berücksichtigt die nach 1997 geführte Diskussion zum Thema und bietet ergänzendes Textmaterial.

In der Mittel- und Spätbronzezeit, als die Rolle Zyperns als Schaltzentrale für den Handel im ostmediterranen Raum und als Kupferlieferant für die vorderorientalischen Nachbarn immer wichtiger wurde, war sein direkter Partner auf dem Festland gegenüber seiner östlichen Spitze, der Karpassos-Halbinsel, die Hafenstadt U g a r i t .[3] Hier hatte sich in der zweiten Hälfte des 2. Jt. v.Chr. ein Königshaus den politischen Gegebenheiten des Großraums Kleinasien-Syrien dadurch angepaßt, daß es die Oberhoheit der Könige des Neuhethitischen Reichs von Ḫattuša anerkannt und sich durch umfangreiche Tributlieferungen eine beträchtliche Entscheidungs- und Bewegungsfreiheit erkauft hat.[4]

Auf der Basis dieser Freiheit konnten die ugaritischen Könige vom ausgehenden 14. bis zum beginnenden 12. Jh. ein weitläufiges Handelsnetz unterhalten, das sich nicht nur auf die östlichen, im Binnenland beheimateten Partner, sondern auch auf die westlichen, die ‚überseeischen' erstreckte.[5]

Der Handel über See verlief nach den damaligen Möglichkeiten längs der Küste: In Tagesreisen zu den südlichen Partnern bis hin zum Sinai und nach Ägypten oder zu den nördlichen bis in die Bucht von Adana. Die kurze Entfernung an die Ostspitze von Zypern ermöglichte es den Seeleuten damals, den Sprung auf die Insel zu machen und von dort aus, nach der südlichen und westlichen Umrundung der Insel, den Golf von Adana in Richtung türkischer Südküste zu überqueren – eine Küstenfahrt längs der Buch von Adana westwärts war wegen der Winde und der Meeresdrift nur schlecht möglich und war stets mit größten Gefahren verbunden. Dementsprechend wurde sie selten in Angriff genommen. Die weitere Route in die ägäische Welt folgte zunächst der türkischen Südküste

3 M.C. Astour 1973, S. 21–22.

4 Siehe z.B. H. Klengel 1992, S. 132–133; M. Dietrich 2001, S. 118–120, mit Umschrift und Übersetzung des Briefs von Ibri-Addu an den König von Ugarit RS 34.150 – wichtig hier der Abschnitt Z. 6–16:

„(6) Herr: Soeben ist ein Bote (7) des Königs von Karkemiš (8) nach Qadeš aufgebrochen (9) wegen Wagen (und) Rekruten. (10) Auch nach Ugarit (11) wird er kommen. (u.Rd.: 12) Du aber, Herr, (13) darfst vor ihm (Rs.: 14) ja nichts zurückhalten! (15) Aber er darf (auch weder) Wagen (noch) Rekruten (16) (aus Ugarit) mitnehmen!"

Was gerne als militärische Schwäche Ugarits betrachtet wird, ist eher als ein Verzicht der Hafenstadt auf kriegerische Aktivitäten einzustufen: J. Vidal 2005, S. 657–662.

5 Vgl. u.a. M.H. Feldman 2006, S. 177–191: Representation and Negotiation in Between. Ugarit and the Northern Levant.

westwärts und benützte dann die Inseln Rhodos, Karpathos und Kreta als Sprungbretter.

An dieser Stelle ist darauf hinzuweisen, daß wir mit der Beschreibung dieser Route lediglich den nördlichen Teil des Netzes von Handelsrouten im ostmediterranen Raum angesprochen haben, zu dem die Route von der Ägäis ostwärts über Zypern an die Levante und nach Ägypten gehört. Mit dem Ziel Ägypten gab es aus dem Blickpunkt der Ägäis aber auch eine Route südwärts: die Direktpassage von der Südküste Kretas an die Nordküste von Afrika, in die Kyrenaika.[6] Von dort folgte die Route längs der nordafrikanischen Küste ostwärts, bis sie schließlich im Nildelta auf die Levante-Route stieß (siehe Karte 1).[7]

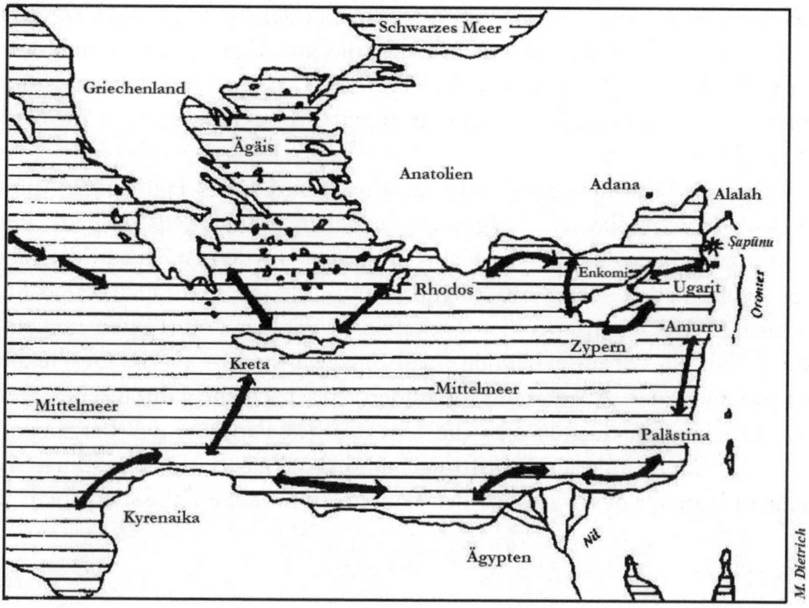

Karte 1
Ostmediterrane Handelsrouten

Wie die Karte verdeutlicht, bildeten die Handelsrouten im östlichen Mittelmeerraum unter Einbeziehung Ägyptens, schematisch gesehen, ein

6 Siehe z.B. H. Helck 1979, S. 39–40, oder M.C. Astour 1973, S. 17: „The earliest oversea links of Minoan Crete were with Libya and Egypt…"

7 Zum Thema siehe z.B. H. Helck 1979, S. 38–44.

Rechteck und nicht etwa, wie üblicherweise angenommen wird, einen rechten Winkel mit einer N- und einer S-Seite. Gleichzeitig führt die Karte vor Augen, daß Zypern auf der Nordroute ein Umschlagplatz für alle nur denkbaren materiellen und geistigen Güter seiner östlichen und westlichen Nachbarn war – die Voraussetzung dafür, daß Zypern gewissermaßen zu einer kulturellen Relaisstation im Östlichen Mittelmeerraum wurde.

Da sich nach Ausweis der jüngeren Ausgrabungsergebnisse hier wie auf dem benachbarten vorderorientalischen Festland bereits im Neolithikum eine mehr oder weniger eigenständige Kultur herausgebildet hatte, läßt sich für die Spätbronzezeit, die wir hier betrachten und in der auch der einheimische Kupferbergbau eine herausragende Bedeutung gewonnen hatte, ein höchst komplexes kulturelles Bild für die Insel zeichnen. Das bezeugen nicht nur die auf Zypern selber gemachten Funde, sondern auch, und zwar in besonderem Maße, die aus Ugarit, dem mindestens ebenso alten vorderorientalischen Partner Zyperns und Festlandstützpunkt eines thalassischen Handelsimperiums und Kulturraums im östlichen Mittelmeerraum.[8]

Die seit 1928 in Ras esh-Shamra/Ugarit und seiner Hafenstadt Minet al-Beida durchgeführten Ausgrabungen haben erbracht, daß Ugarit, von dem inzwischen mehr als die Hälfte freigelegt worden ist,[9] nach Maßgabe der einigermaßen sicher datierbaren Kleinfunde wie Gebrauchs- und Luxusartikel, vor allem aber der Tontafeln als Träger von Texten nur eine kurze Blüte in der ausgehenden Spätbronzezeit hatte – da die Geschichte Ugarits nach den Ausgrabungsbefunden jedoch etliche Jahrtausende weiter zurückreicht, dürften sich die Ugariter des Papyrus, des Pergaments oder der Baumrinde als Schriftträger und des Pinsels als Schreibmaterial bedient haben,[10] bevor sie sich der Tontafelkultur angeschlossen haben.

8 Zu diesem Thema gibt es zahlreiche Abhandlungen – aus dem Blickwinkel der Ägäis sei beispielsweise H.-G. Buchholz /V. Karageorghis 1971 oder J.L. Crowley, *The Aegean and the East. An Investigation into the Transference of Artistic Motifs between the Aegean, Egypt, and the Near East in the Bronze Age* (1989), aus dem Blickwinkel Zyperns beispielsweise V. Karageorghis 1982 und aus dem Blickwinkel Ugarits beispielsweise G.D. Young (Hrsg.), 1981 oder S. von Reden 1992 genannt. Hinzu kommen die ausführliche Dokumentation von C. Lambrou-Phillipson 1990 und die umfangreiche, den neuesten Kenntnissen und Funden entsprechende Monographie von H.-G. Buchholz 1999.

9 Siehe M. Yon 2006, Plan S. vi.

10 Zu diesen Fragen siehe M. Dietrich 1996.

Ca. 1320 tritt Ugarit unvermittelt ins Rampenlicht der Geschichte, weil sich sein damaliger Herrscher Niqmaddu II. (etwa 1350–1315 v.Chr.) dazu entschloß, seine Kanzlei, wie seinerzeit bei den Nachbarn üblich, sprachlich auf die mittelbabylonische Koine und, als Folge dessen auf die Tontafeln als Schriftträger umzustellen. Die von diesem Zeitpunkt an erhaltenen Texte – denkbar ist, daß die Ugariter die zuvor verwendeten Schriftträger auch weiterhin verwendet haben – zeichnen ein facettenreiches Bild des Geschehens für die Zeit zwischen ca. 1320 und 1190, als etwa acht Könige unter den neuhethitischen Großkönigen die *pax hethitica* zum Ausbau ihrer Aktivitäten genützt haben. Je nach der Reichhaltigkeit von priesterlichen, königlichen und privaten Bibliotheken und Tontafelarchiven erhalten wir ein buntes Bild von der Bevölkerung der vielbesuchten Hafenstadt sowie den inner-ugaritischen und überregionalen, ‚internationalen' Verbindungen seiner Regenten, Verwaltungsbeamten und Handelsherren. Die Informationen brechen 1192 v.Chr. abrupt ab, als Ugarit wohl infolge der unglücklichen Auseinandersetzung mit den über das Meer herandrängenden ‚Seevölkern' über Nacht zerstört wurde.[11] In der Folgezeit blieb die einst blühende Hafenstadt bis auf kleine Abschnitte auf der Akropolis ein Trümmerfeld, das unter der Ausgrabungsleitung von C.F.A. Schaeffer erst ab 1928/29 wieder zu neuem Leben erwachte.

Im Zusammenhang mit dem hier behandelten Thema *Ugarit und seine Beziehungen zu Zypern und zur ägäischen Inselwelt* sind es also die letzten ca. 130 Jahre der Stadt, die ein lebhaftes Miteinander zwischen Ugarit und Zypern sowie dessen westlichen Nachbarn Kreta und die ägäischen Inseln beschreiben.

Ugarit und seine ostmediterranen Nachbarn Zypern und die ägäische Inselwelt nach Aussage ugaritischer Mythen und Epen

Die Texte, die zum Mythenkranz um den Vegetationsgott Baʿal gehören (KTU 1.1-1.6[12]), unterbreiten den weitesten geographischen Horizont aller literarischen Texte aus Ugarit, weil sie direkte Bezüge bis hin zur ägäischen Inselwelt herstellen.[13] Die epischen Werke sind in dieser Hinsicht weniger

11 Zu einem Vorschlag, den Untergang der Stadt zu datieren, siehe M. Dietrich/O. Loretz 2003.

12 Den Zitaten liegt überall dort, wo im Folgenden Textpassagen angeführt werden, folgende Textausgabe zugrunde: M. Dietrich/O. Loretz/J. Sanmartín 1995 (KTU2); Ausgangspunkt für die Übersetzungen ist: M. Dietrich/O. Loretz 1997; vgl. auch D. Pardee 1997.

13 Zu den folgenden Ausführungen siehe auch M. Dietrich 2005, zum Baʿal-Mythos S. 13–18.

ergiebig: Das Keret-Epos (KTU 1.14-1.16) stellt keinen direkten Bezug zur Ägäis her,[14] und im Aqhat-Epos (KTU 1.17-1.19) werden die Blicke nur in der Szene auf die Ägäis gelenkt, in der der Kompositbogen für Aqhat angeliefert wird – die Rephaim-Texte (KTU 1.20–22), die zum Aqhat-Epos gehören dürften, scheinen in den erhaltenen Abschnitten nicht auf diese Region zu sprechen zu kommen.

Anspielungen auf Kreta und die Ägäis im Baʿal-Mythos

Der Baʿal-Mythos spielt auf die Ägäis im Zusammenhang mit dem angestrebten Bau eines Palastes für Baʿal an: Nach schweren Auseinandersetzungen mit seinem Widersacher Yam, dem Meeresgott (KTU 1.1-1.2), errang Baʿal zwar die Herrschaft über das Pantheon, besaß aber noch keinen eigenen Palast; zum Bau eines solchen mußte die Einwilligung des himmlischen Hochgotts El gewonnen werden, die die ‚Schwester' Baʿals, Anat, einzuholen zugesagt habe (KTU 1.3); Anat hatte den erwünschten Erfolg, so daß der Bau des Palastes durchgeführt werden konnte (KTU 1.4); kaum hatte Baʿal nach seinem Aufstieg an die Spitze der Götter seine Residenz bezogen, als sich schon sein Sturz ankündigte: Mot, der Todesgott, überwältigte ihn (KTU 1.5) und machte dadurch den Thron für den Gestirns-Gott Aṯtar frei (KTU 1.6).

Nachdem Anat und die ihr beistehende Gattin des El, 'Aṯirat, von El die Erlaubnis zum Palastbau für Baʿal erhalten hatten, wird der Auftrag innerhalb einer Botschaft an einen Baumeister mit westsemitischem Namen, Kōṯar-wa-Ḫasīs, wie folgt weitergegeben (KTU 1.3 VI 1-24):

> „[Tr]age [2][meine Botschaft in] deinem Kopf,
> [3][meine Worte] ‚zwischen deinen Augen',
> [4][und überquere] tausend [5][Längen im] Meer
> zehntausend [6][Län]gen in den beiden Strömen (:poetisch für „Meer").
>
> [7][Setze über] Berge, setze über [8]Hügel,
> setze über die Inseln 9am Horizont des Himmels (*iht np šmm*).
> Fahre dahin, [10]oh Fischer der 'Aṯirat,
> [11]komme an, oh Qidšu-Amurru (: der Botengott der 'Aṯirat)!

14 Der mit Kreta und Memphis verbundene Handwerkergott Kōṯar-wa-Ḫasīs ist in KTU 1.15 II 5 von Keret als Gast eingeladen.

[12]Dann wende dich [13]doch
nach dem göttlichen Memphis (ḥ{q}kpt) [14]in seiner Gesamtheit,
nach Kaphtor (kptr), [15]seinem Thronsitz,
nach Memphis (ḥkpt), [16]seinem Erbland!

[17]Über tausend Längen, zehntausend Längen hin
zu den Füßen des Kōṯar [19]verneige dich (dann) und fall nieder,
[20]wirf dich zu Boden und ehre ihn!

[21]Und sprich zu [22] Kōṯar-wa-Ḫasīs,
wiederhole dem He[23]yan mit den werkenden Händen:
'Eine Botschaft des 'Al['iyān Ba'al: …[15]]"

Die Passage zur Vorbereitung des Palastbaus für Ba'al ist nicht die einzige aus dem Ba'al-Mythos, die in Kōṯar-wa-Ḫasīs aus Kreta den kompetenten Baumeister sieht: Er sollte auch schon den Palast des Meeresgottes Yam, des Konkurrenten von Baʿal, errichten, wie der Befehl des El zu verstehen gibt (KTU 1.2 III 7-8):

„Kōṯar-wa-Ḫasīs, geh los!
Bau[e] ein Haus für Yam,
[err]ichte einen Palast für den Richter Fluß,
[8][ein Haus für den Fl]uß inmitten des [Meeres]!"

Diese Abschnitte aus dem Ba'al-Mythos weisen darauf hin, daß man sich in Ugarit dann, wenn es darum ging, einen Palast zu bauen, offensichtlich um einen Baumeister aus Kreta bemüht hat. Dieser scheint nach damaliger Meinung allein imstande dazu gewesen zu sein, den Bau eines königlichen Ansprüchen genügenden Palastes zu leiten. Auch wenn wir es hier mit Palästen für Götter zu tun haben, so dürfen wir dessen sicher sein, daß die ugaritischen Könige die göttlichen Bauten als Urbild für ihre irdischen angesehen und sich der Künste kretischer Baumeister zu deren Bau bedient haben dürften – daß auch ägyptische Auftraggeber dieser Ansicht waren, zeigt die oben zitierte Passage anläßlich des Palastbaus für Ba'al,

15 Da der Text ab hier verloren gegangen ist, kann man nur vermuten, daß die Auftragspassage vor den Ohren des Baumeisters wiederholt worden ist – die wörtliche Wiederholung garantierte dem Befehlsempfänger die Authentizität der Meldung.

der nach Z. 15/16 Memphis dem Wirkungsbereich des kretischen Baumeisters zurechnete.[16]

Betrachtet man die Ausgrabungsergebnisse aus allerlei Orten im ostmediterranen Raum, wozu auch Zypern mit seinen hervorragenden Relikten einer Großraumarchitektur à la Ugarit und Knossos gehört, dann zeigt sich tatsächlich eine erstaunliche Homogenität in der Struktur von Repräsentationsbauten, die nur damit erklärlich ist, daß ein übergreifendes Konzept als Ausdruck der „mykenischen Koine" (ca. 1400–1200 v. Chr.) existierte.[17] Die „mykenische Koine" läßt sich somit literarisch aufgrund der Palastbaupassagen des Baʿal-Mythos nachweisen, die ein klares Bild von übergreifenden kulturellen Verbindungen und Entwicklungen zeichnen.

In den Rahmen des Palastbaus für Baʿal mit kretischer Hilfe gehört auch die aufschlußreiche Passage über die Anfertigung von Gebrauchs- und Luxusartikeln, die die Muttergöttin ʾAṯirat als Geschenke für den Himmelsgott El brauchte, um ihn zum Bau des Baʿal-Palastes zu gewinnen (KTU 1.4 I 23-43):

> 23 Heyan (: ein Name des Kōṯar) stieg auf die beiden Blasebälge,
> 24 in der Hand des Ḫasīs (war) die Zange.
> 25 Er goß Silber, schmolz Gold:
> Er goß Silber 27 zu Tausenden (: Sekel),
> Gold schmolz er 28 zu Zehntausenden (: Sekel).
>
> 29 Er goß eine Wohnung, ein Ruhelager;
> 30 eine göttliche Kanne von 10.000 (Maßeinheiten);
> 31 eine göttliche Kanne bedeckt mit Silber,
> 32 überzogen mit Rotgold –
>
> 33 einen göttlichen Thron, einen Sitz 34 aus Obsidian;
> einen göttlichen Fußschemel, 35 der überreich versehen ist mit Marmor;
> 36 ein göttliches Podest, das höchst tragfähig ist,
> 37 daran seine Träger aus Gold –
> 38 einen göttlichen Tisch voll mit 39 Wesen,
> mit Getier von den 40 Grundfesten der Erde;

---

16 Hier haben wir einen literarischen Beleg für die engen kulturellen Verbindungen, die im 2. Jt. v.Chr. zwischen Kreta, der Ägäis und Ägypten bestanden haben, vgl. z.B. N. Lurz 1994.

17 Siehe S. Deger-Jalkotzy 1996.

41 eine göttliche Schale, die vollendet ist wie (eine von) Amurru,
42 deren Bearbeitung wie (eine) des Landes Yaman,
43 auf der zu zehntausenden Wildstiere sind!

Der Leser wird durch diese Passage ein zweites Mal in die Welt der Kunstfertigkeiten des Kōṯar-wa-Ḫasīs geführt, also auf Kreta in die ägäische Inselwelt. Der Kunsthandwerker hatte die Aufgabe, Gebrauchs- und Luxusgüter herzustellen, die des Hochgottes El würdig waren. Außer dem Mobiliar ist eine Schale Gegenstand der Fertigung. Letztere ist für heutige Recherchen von besonderem Interesse, weil sie zwei geographische Bezeichnungen in einem Atemzug nennt: Amurru und Yaman. Beide verleiten zu *ad hoc*-Assoziationen, weil sie an solche erinnern, die auch sonst geläufig sind: Amurru könnte den Nachbarn südlich von Ugarit meinen, mit dem Ugarit auch enge politische Beziehungen pflegte, und Yaman ein früher Beleg für das an sich erst Jahrhunderte später sicher nachweisbare Jonien.[18]

Angesichts der Bedeutung des Kōṯar-wa-Ḫasīs als Repräsentant der ägäo-kretischen Welt für den Palastbau ist es nicht verwunderlich, daß er auch dann zu Aktionen aufgerufen geworden ist, als es um die Ausstattung des von ihm geleiteten Baus ging: Nicht nur das Mobiliar, sondern auch die hier besonders ausführlich beschriebene Goldschale trägt seinen Stempel: Die Verzierung dieser Schale durch mythische Tiere, die kreisend aufeinander folgen, entspricht nämlich der auf zahlreichen Artefakten aus der kreto-mykenischen Welt bekannten.[19]

Anspielungen auf Kreta und die Ägäis im Aqhat-Epos

Im Aqhat-Epos steht der Kompositbogen im Mittelpunkt des Interesses,[20] den Danil für seinen Sohn Aqhat als Jagdwaffe durch den kretischen Handerwerkergott Kōṯar-wa-Ḫasīs hat anfertigen lassen. Da dieser Bogen wegen seiner besonderen Qualtität den Neid der Göttin Anat geweckt hat, sollte er Aqhat sogar zum Verhängnis werden: Anat bat um die Prunkwaffe und versprach Aqhat dafür übermenschlich-göttliches Leben. Aqhat

18 Ausführlich zu diesem Problemfeld: M. Dietrich/O. Loretz 1998. – Abweichend M.C. Astour 1995, der *Yman* als einen Ort im Herrschaftsgebiet Ugarits betrachtet (S. 60).

19 Siehe M. Dietrich/O. Loretz 1998, S. 355–357.

20 Zum Kompositbogen und zu seiner Beschreibung in KTU 1.17 VI 20–23 siehe U. Rüterswörden 1988, S. 253–255.

schlug das Ansinnen der Göttin unter Angabe guter Gründe aus und mußte das mit seinem Leben bezahlen.

Der Abschnitt mit der Ablieferung des Bogens durch Kōṯar-wa-Ḫasīs persönlich ist mit Ausnahme seines Anfangs und Endes – hier fehlen jeweils 11-12 Zeilen – gut erhalten und bietet nach den bruchstückhaft erhaltenen Resten einer Rede des Kunsthandwerkers folgenden Wortlaut – KTU 1.17 V 1-33:[21]

1 [Daraufhin[22]] antwortete[23] [Kōṯar-wa-Ḫasī]s:[24]

2 „Am [siebten Tag][25] werde ich bringen einen Bogen,
am achten[26] [Tag] 3 vierfach besorgen Pfeile.“
Und siehe, (es geschah) 4 am siebten (Tag) bei Tag(esanbruch):[27]

Dann erhob sich Danil, der Held des 5 Rāpi'u,
darauf der Mann, der Held des Harnamiten,
6 setzte sich nieder am Toreingang
unter die 7 Würdenträger auf dem Dreschplatz.

Er richtete 8 den Prozeßfall für die Witwe,
er entschied die Rechtsordnung für die Waise.[28]

21 Zu Übersetzung und Deutung von einzelnen Problemen siehe M. Dietrich/O. Loretz 1997: *Das Aqhat-Epos*, S. 1254–1305, hier: S. 1268–1270.

22 Hier könnte ein Adverb wie etwa *apnk*, o.ä., gestanden haben

23 Bemerkenswert ist die Konstruktion topikalisierendes-*w* + SK anstelle einer PK-Verbform, siehe J. Tropper 2000, S. 783–785: § 83.112.

24 Die Zeile läßt sich nach den erhaltenen Zeichenresten etwa folgendermaßen restaurieren: [xxxx . kṯr . w ḫs]s . w ʿ*n*yn.

25 Die Bruchkante am Anfang von Z. 2 folgt dem linken Diagonalkeil des *š*, von dem die Spitze des mittleren Senkrechten noch deutlich sichtbar ist. Die Zeitangabe wird offenbar mit dem adverbiellen Akkusativ konstruiert, wie aus den folgenden Formulierungen „achter" (Z. 2) und „siebter“ (Z. 3) klar hervorgeht.

26 Auf den Trenner nach dem schlecht erhaltenen *t* von *qšt* folgt eindeutig der untere Teil eines *ṯ*.

27 Unwahrscheinlich ist die Übersetzung des Ausdrucks *šbʿ b ymm* durch „am siebten Tag“ und das damit verbundene Postulat einer Inversion von Präposition und Zahlangabe.

28 Zum Abschnitt Z. 4b-8 und seine Relevanz für die ugaritische Rechtspraxis siehe O. Loretz 2003, S. 366.

[9] Beim Erheben seiner Augen sah er
über tausend Are, [10] zehntausend Are hin,
sah er fürwahr das Kommen des Kōṯar,
ja, sah das Heraneilen des Ḫasīs.

[12]Siehe da, er brachte den Bogen,
siehe, er [13]hatte vierfach Pfeile dabei.
Dann rief Danil, [14]der Held des Rāpiʾu,
    darauf der Mann, der Held des [15]Harnamiten
laut zu seiner Frau:

[16]„Höre, Dame Danatiya!
Richte her [17]ein Böcklein von der Herde
für den Hunger des Kōṯar-[18]wa-Ḫasīs,
für das Verlangen des Heyan, [19]des handwerklich Tüchtigen.[29]
Gib zu essen, gib zu trinken [20]dem Gott,
bediene, ehre ihn,
den Herrn [21]des göttlichen Memphis in seiner Gesamtheit!"

Es gehorchte [22]die Dame Danatiya.
Sie bereitete ein Böcklein [23]von der Herde
für den Hunger des Kōṯar-wa-Ḫasīs,
[24]für das Verlangen des Heyan, [25]des handwerklich Tüchtigen.

Daraufhin kam Kōṯar -[26] wa-Ḫasīs an.
In die Hände Danils gab er [27]den Bogen,
auf seine Knie legte er [28]die Pfeile.

Dann gab die Dame Danatiya [29]zu essen, gab zu trinken dem Gott,
[30]sie bediente, sie ehrte ihn,
den Herrn [31]des göttlichen Memphis in seiner Gesamtheit.

Kōṯar brach auf [32]zu seinem Zelt,
Heyan brach auf zu seiner Wohnstätte.

---

29 Zur Wendung *hyn d ḥrš yd* „Heyan, der handwerklich Tüchtige" siehe M. Dietrich/O. Loretz 2000.

Am Anfang der Kolumne V dürfte die Bitte um einen Kompositbogen – und möglicherweise auch seine Beschreibung wie in KTU 1.17 VI 20–23 – gestanden haben, mit der Danil an den ägäo-kretischen Handwerksgott herangetreten war. Der Wortlaut des Textes ist erst dort wieder erhalten, wo Kōṯar-wa-Ḫasīs zugesagt hat, den gewünschten Bogen nach seiner Herstellung persönlich zu bringen. Unmittelbar nachdem Danil, beflügelt von der Zusage des Kōṯar-wa-Ḫasīs, wieder an die Erfüllung seiner königlich-richterlichen Aufgaben gegangen war, sah er den Handwerkergott mit dem Bogen aus großer Ferne nahen. Da beauftragte er seine Gattin Danatiya, den Gast aus Memphis (*ḥkpt*) gleich nach seiner Ankunft mit den bestmöglichen Speisen zu versorgen. Bei der Begegnung mit Danil legte ihm Kōṯar-wa-Ḫasīs den Bogen und die Pfeile auf die Knie, nahm die vorbereiteten Speisen zu sich und begab sich gleich wieder auf die Heimreise.

Bei einer Gegenüberstellung der Traditionen des Baʿal-Mythos und des Aqhat-Epos fällt hinsichtlich der Angaben über die Heimat des Kōṯar-wa-Ḫasīs folgendes auf: Im Baʿal-Mythos (siehe oben zu KTU 1.3 VI 14-16) wird sie mit den beiden geographischen Größen „Kaphtor" (*kptr*) und „Memphis" (*ḥkpt*),[30] im Aqhat-Epos dagegen lediglich mit „Memphis" (*ḥkpt*) (Z. 21. 31) beschrieben.[31] Diese Differenz dürfte auf eine verkürzte Tradition im Aqhat-Epos zurückgehen, in der die kretische Heimat des Gottes ungenannt blieb. Der Schluß, daß die Differenz möglicherweise darauf zurückgeführt werden könnte, daß es sich im Aqhat-Epos um die Anfertigung und Lieferung des Kompositbogens ägyptischer Machart handelte und „Kaphtor" (*kptr*) deswegen bewußt weggelassen worden sei, weil Kreta und die Ägäis nichts mit diesem Bogen zu tun hatten, dürfte zu weit gehen.[32]

Zwischenergebnis

Auf den ersten Blick verwirren die geographischen Angaben dieser Texte: Die Boten der ʾAṯirat, Qidšu-Amurru (KTU 1.3 VI), und derjenige des

30 Vgl. die Parallele dazu in der Szene des Palastbaus für Yammu: KTU 1.1 III 1 und KTU 1.2 III 2.

31 Im Rahmen der Aufforderung Aqhats, Anat solle sich zwecks Herstellung eines ebensolchen Bogens direkt an Kōṯar-wa-Ḫasīs wenden (KTU 1.17 VI 20–25), nennt der Dichter keine Heimatregion: „… gib dem Kōṯar-wa-Ḫasīs, er soll herstellen einen Bogen für …!" (KTU 1.17 VI 24).

32 Zur Verbreitung des Kompositbogens ab der Akkad-Zeit in Mesopotamien und ab dem Neuen Reich in Ägypten siehe z.B. W. Mayer 1995, S. 467.

Danil, dessen Name nicht erhalten ist (KTU 1.17 V), sollten eine weite Reise – über Berge und das Meer – antreten, um dem in weiter Ferne residierenden Gott der Baukunst und des kunstvollen Handwerks den Auftrag zum Bau des Palastes für Ba'al, zur Fertigung der Gebrauchs- und Luxusgüter für El und zur Herstellung des Kompositbogens für Aqhat zu überbringen. Das Zielgebiet der Boten wird mit *Inseln am Horizont des Himmels, Memphis* und *Kaphtor* angegeben.

Von diesen Begriffen konnten die Interpreten die beiden letztgenannten problemlos einordnen: Nach ihrer Meinung konnte *Memphis* nur die unterägpytische Stadt mit dem Heiligtum für den Handwerkergott Ptaḥ, dem „ägyptischen Hephaistos", gemeint sein und *Kaphtor* nur die Insel Kreta.[33]

Schwierigkeiten bereitete jedoch die geographische Bestimmung *Inseln am Horizont des Himmels.* Da den geographiekundigen Ugaritern bekannt gewesen sein durfte, daß vor dem Nildelta ebensowenig Inseln lagen wie in dessen näheren Bereich, kann mit *Inseln am Horizont des Himmels* nur die Inselwelt der Ägäis gemeint gewesen sein.[34] Dazu paßt die Bemerkung, daß Kaphtor/Kreta der Sitz des Baumeisters sei; schwieriger ist die Erklärung der Bezeichnung „Erbland Memphis", in dem der Baumeister ein Erbe angetreten habe, hier nicht aber zu Hause gewesen sei. Das besagt, daß der Meister, der den Palast des Ba'al bauen sollte, auf Kreta Zuhause war und sein Können, gewiß im Verein mit Ptaḥ, auch schon in Memphis unter Beweis gestellt hatte – dasselbe dürfte auch die Passage aus dem Aqhat-Epos meinen, obwohl sie als Herkunftsregion des Kōṯar-wa-Ḫasīs nur *Memphis* nennt und *Kaphtor* nicht erwähnt –. Zusammen mit Ugarit in der nördlichen Levante bilden Kreta und Memphis, wie oben *sub* 2.1 schon hervorgehoben, das in der Literatur erfaßte ‚magische Dreieck' der Mykenischen Koine,[35] deren Relikte nach Ausweis der Ausgrabungsfunde vom Geist des kretischen Baumeisters auch einheitlich geprägt sind.

Bei alledem nimmt es Wunder, daß der kretische Baumeister und Kunsthandwerker den gutsemitischen Namen „Kōṯar-wa-Ḫasīs" trug, der

33 Siehe z.B. H. Helck 1979, S. 26–37: Die schriftlichen Erwähnungen Kretas in den ägyptischen und akkadischen Texten und die geographischen Fragen; M.C. Astour 1973, S. 19–20; C. Lambrou-Phillipson 1990, S. 121–124; S.P. Morris 1992, hier bes. Teil II: Daidalos and Kadmos, S. 73–194.

34 Zu einer detaillierten Interpretation dieser Passage siehe M. Dietrich/O. Loretz 1990.

35 S. Deger-Jalkotzy 1996.

mit „Künstler-und-Allwissender" übersetzt werden kann,[36] und nicht etwa einen mykenisch-minoischen wie etwa „Daidalos" oder „Hephaistos", die für Kreta und die Ägäis näherliegend gewesen wären.[37] Die Tatsache, daß nicht der mykenische Name des Baumeister und Handwerksgottes sondern der seines semitischen Pendants verwendet worden ist, wird gerne als Zeichen für einen intensiven Einfluß des Orients auf ägäo-kretische und altgriechische Welt angesehen.[38] Dies ist sicher der Fall, dürfte aber, für sich genommen, eine zu stark vereinfachte und einseitige Einschätzung sein, wenn man die nicht-orientalischen Strukturen und Formen der Architektur, Malerei und Kleinkunst bedenkt, die für die Funde der Ausgrabungen im Bereich der Mykenischen Koine typisch sind.[39]

Von daher wäre es vielmehr zu überliegen, ob der Patron der ägäo-kretischen Architektur und Handwerkskunst seinen angestammten Namen in Ugarit hat aufgeben müssen, weil die Dichter der ugaritischen Mythen und Epen – ob es nun Ilīmilku und/oder ein anderer war – ihrer Audienz zuliebe den einheimisch levantinisch-ugaritischen Namen dem ‚überseeischen' vorgezogen haben.

Die hier zur Sprache gebrachten Texte zeigen jedenfalls, daß Zypern in der mythologischen und epischen Literatur Ugarits offenbar keine be-

36 Zur Erklärung des Namensteils „Kōṯar" und seinen Verbindungen zur ägäo-kretischen Welt siehe S.P. Morris 1992, S. 73–93.

37 Sowohl „Daidalos" als auch „Hephaistos" sind in der Form nominaler Ableitungen schon auf den Tontafeln von Knossos bezeugt: *da-da-re-jo* bzw. *a-pa-i-ti-jo*, siehe S.P. Morris 1992, S. 75–78.

38 Vgl. demgegenüber M.C. Astour 1973, S. 21: „It was at that time, one may guess, that Kushar-wa-Khasis, the divine architect und artificer of Ugaritic mythology, was given Caphtor as one of his residences, along with Memphis … he was not a Cretan deity adopted by Ugaritians and Phoenicians but a West Semitic deity which came to be associated with a remote overseas country because of its artistic renown." – Eine vergleichbare Position nimmt S.P. Morris 1992 ein, die von einem orientalischen Ursprung des griechischen Handwerksgottes Daidalos spricht – S. 97–98: „For the name and qualities expressed by Homeric *daidala* duplicate the poetic relationship of *kṯr* and *mkṯr* as if Daidalos were a formation parallel to one or more of Kothar's appellations… Thus Daidalos would be an interpretatio *Homerica* of Kothar or his other names, perhaps the result of an epic collision with a craftsman already native to the Aegean and its poetic tradition."

39 Siehe z.B. A. Caubet/V. Matoian 1995, S. 110, das Zitat von P. Demargne (1964): « L'élargissement du monde mycénien: la naissance de civilisations composites »; N. Lurz 1994; S. Deger-Jalkotzy 1996; H.-G. Buchholz 1999, insbes. Kap. 9–13, S. 294–562; vgl. auch M. Yon 2006, Ch. 3, S. 125–171.

sondere Rolle gespielt hat – ob dieses Ergebnis auf die ugaritische Literatur insgesamt übertragen werden darf, sei dahingestellt. Der hieraus möglicherweise ableitbare Schluß, daß nach Auffassung der Literaten Ugarits die Nachbarinsel nichts Erwähnenswertes oder gar Eigenständiges zu Kultur Ugarits beigetragen habe, dürfte allerdings zu weit gehen. Denn es sind noch bei weitem nicht alle Begriffe der ugaritischen Literatur geklärt, die gegebenenfalls Auskunft über geographische und topographische Bezeichnungen geben könnten. Die Dokumente des täglichen Lebens, die Briefe und Wirtschaftsurkunden, geben auf jeden Fall ein anderes Bild ab.

Ugarit und seine ostmediterranen Nachbarn Zypern, Kreta und die ägäische Inselwelt nach Aussage ugaritischer Briefe und Wirtschaftstexte

Die zahlreichen Briefe und Wirtschaftsdokumente aus königlichen, priesterlichen und privaten Archiven, die auf Tontafeln entweder in der syllabischen Schrift der mittelbabylonischen Koine oder in der in Ugarit beheimateten alphabetischen Keilschrift niedergeschrieben sind, kommen auf Zypern vornehmlich unter der Bezeichnung „Alašia“[40] zu sprechen – es ist durchaus denkbar, daß auch noch andere, bisher nicht dahingehend erfaßte geographische Begriffe auf Zypern Bezug nehmen. Diese Dokumente konzentrieren sich vornehmlich auf die Praxis der politischen und wirtschaftlichen Verbindungen mit der Insel Zypern als dem direkten ‚überseeischem‘ Nachbarn und haben weniger die jenseits von Zypern gelegene Inselwelt der Ägäis und Kreta im Blick.

Vor der Darstellung besonderer Gegebenheiten, die sich aus ugaritischen Dokumenten mit Blick auf Zypern ableiten lassen, ist die Frage zu erörtern, auf welche geographische Größe die Texte konkret anspielen, wenn sie von „Alašia“ sprechen. Erst im Anschluß daran können Einzelfragen zur Sprache kommen.[41]

40 Alphabetisch normalerweise *a<u>t</u>ty(y)* „Alašier“ geschrieben, seltener *al<u>d</u>y* und einmal offensichtlich *alzy*. Die syllabische Wiedergabe ist (KUR) *A-la-ši-*(*i*)a/ia8 „Alašia”.

41 Von den zahlreichen Dokumenten können im folgenden nur wenige auf ihre zum Teil komplexen Aussagen besprochen werden. Ein gründliches Studium des Kontextes aller Belege wäre die Aufgabe einer Monographie.

Zypern – Alašia – Alassa

In der modernen Forschung besteht allgemeiner Konsens darüber, daß sich die Bezeichnung „Alašia“ dort, wo sie in den Keilschrifttexten – ob mit dem Landesdeterminativ KUR = *mātu* „Land“ oder dem Ortsdeterminativ URU = *ālu* „Ort, Stadt“ oder gar mit beiden gleichzeitig versehen ist – begegnet, die Insel Zypern meint.[42] Da im antiken Vorderen Orient eine Landschaft nur selten mit einem geographischen Namen versehen worden ist, ist es weniger wahrscheinlich, daß sich „Alašia“ auf die Insel als solche bezieht. Er dürfte damit vielmehr ein Ort auf der Insel mit seinem Hinterland angesprochen sein, der allenfalls, *pars pro toto*, auf die ganze Insel übertragen worden ist oder, ungeachtet einer ursprünglich sicher eindeutigen Zuordnung, je nach Blickpunkt des Briefabsenders auf irgendeinen Ort an jenem fernen, ‚überseeischen‘ Horizont anwendbar war.[43]

Bedauerlicherweise enthalten die vorderorientalischen Texte, die den Ort oder das Gebiet Alašia nennen, keinen Hinweis beispielsweise auf seine konkrete Lage beispielsweise in Bergen oder am Meer. Auch gibt es, soweit bislang erkennbar, keinen Text, der Nachbarorte von „Alašia“ aufführte – „Alašia“ steht für sich, sein Umfeld spielt für den, der auf es anspielt, keine Rolle.

Das führte beispielsweise C.F.A. Schaeffer zur Annahme, daß der Name Alašia nur für einen einzigen Ort gegolten habe, der als nennenswerte Größe das direkte Gegenüber, der unmittelbare Ansprech- und Handelspartner solcher levantinischen Hafenstädte wie Ugarit hätte sein können. Dafür bot sich nach seiner Meinung Enkomi, wenige Kilometer nördlich von Famagusta, an. Die topographische Lage, die Stadtanlage, die Großraumarchitektur auf der Basis von Steinquadern und zahlreiche

42 Siehe z.B. J.D. Muhly 1997, S. 92; J. Freu 2006, S. 209–212, u.a. – Die früheste bekannte Bezeugung von *Alašia* stammt aus den Texten von Babylon und Māri vom Ende des 18. Jhs., vgl. B. Groneberg 1980, S. 10; vgl. M.C. Astour 1973, S. 18–19. – Jüngst kam der wohl aufschlußreichste Beleg aus Māri hinzu: In dem bruchstückhaften Wirtschaftsdokument M 5572 + 14742 steht in zwei Zeilen untereinander: (4’) *i-na* URU.KI *A-la-ši-ia* […] (5’) *ù ki-ma* ZABAR x[…] „(4’) in/aus Alašia […], (5’) und gemäß dem Kupfer […]“ (D. Charpin 1990); hier wird, in welchem größeren Zusammenhang auch immer, die aus zahlreichen Dokumenten bekannte enge Verbindung zwischen Alašia und Kupfer zur Sprache gebracht.

43 Vgl. Y. Goren, et al., 2004, S. 70–71.

Kleinfunde wie Schriftdokumente und Statuetten waren für ihn Beweis genug dafür, daß Enkomi Alašia, das Pendant von Ugarit auf Zypern, gewesen sei. Nachdem er Enkomi mit Alašia verbunden hatte[44], etablierten sich in der Sekundärliteratur[45] rasch zwei eng mit einander verbundene Doppelnamen: der auf Syrien bezogene Ras Shamra-Ugarit und der auf Zypern bezogene Enkomi-Alašia.

Vor den Kampagnen von C.F.A. Schaeffer in Enkomi standen durchaus auch andere Orte für eine Gleichsetzung mit „Alašia" zur Sprache. Denn längs der Südküste Zyperns, zum Teil auch einwenig landeinwärts gelegen, finden sich antike Hafenstädte wie Perlen auf eine Kette gereiht und könnten durchaus in Konkurrenz zu Enkomi treten. Aufgrund der in ihnen durchgeführten Ausgrabungen konnte aber noch keine Enkomi verdrängen, das bislang als der ernsthafteste Kandidat für das nach den vorderorientalischen Texten so wichtige Alašia gelten könnte. Denn in ihnen sind nach dem heutigen Stand der Veröffentlichungen keine Funde gemacht worden, die eine stärkere Bindung an die Levante ausdrückten könnten als die von Enkomi.

Als Anfang des Jahrhunderts die Gleichsetzung zwischen Zypern und Alašia diskutiert wurde, zog man in Erwägung, ob sich im modernen Alassa, das wenig nordwestlich von Limassol und nördlich von Kourion an den Südhängen des Troodos-Gebirges liegt, den Namen des antiken „Alašia" herübergerettet haben könnte. Die Ausgrabungen von C.F.A. Schaeffer und die von ihm vertretene Ansicht, daß Enkomi das gesuchte Alašia sein müsse, haben alle andere Überlegungen verstummen lassen. Nun sind sie aufgrund der Erkenntnis wieder aufgeflammt, daß in den Mittel- und Spätbronzezeiten nicht nur Enkomi einen städtischen Charakter gehabt habe und damit ein geeigneter Kandidat für das „Alašia" der vorderorientalischen Texte sein könnte, sondern auch viele andere wie etwa Kition, Kalavassos oder Kouklia Palaepaphos.[46]

---

44 Vgl. etwa C.F.A. Schaeffer 1952, mit der am Ende des Bandes aufgeführten Reihe *Publications de la Mission Archéologique d'Enkomi-Alasia.*

45 Siehe beispielsweise J. Wiesner 1966, Sp. 2253: „... im 2. Jtd. v.Chr., als die Insel Alaschia hieß, nach der gleichnamigen Hauptstadt an der Ostküste, dem heutigen Enkomi"; oder J.D. Muhly 1997, S. 92–93: „Enkomi quickly became the most important site on Cyprus and is most probably to be identified as the capital of the kingdom of Alashiya."

46 Siehe z.B. O. Negbi 1986, S. 97–121 mit Pl. XXIV-XXV; A.B. Knapp 1996, S. 54–79; eine gute Übersicht über die bisherigen Diskussionen hierüber bietet Y. Goren, *et al.*, 2004, S. 70–71.

Ab 1983 haben sich zyprische Archäologen daran gemacht, das antike Alassa, das mit seinen Trabantenstädten Paliotaverna und Pano Mandilaris nahe einer der Kupferminen im Troodos Gebirge eine städtische Ruinenlandschaft aus dem Altertum bildet, zu untersuchen. Ihre Ausgrabungen haben ergeben, daß diese Orte einen städtischen Charakter hatten und zu den bedeutenden Verwaltungs- und Handelszentren der Spätbronzezeit gehörten.[47] Besonders ist dabei auf die Überreste von Bauten – seien sie einst Teile eines Palastes oder einer Residenz für Handelsherren gewesen – an breiten, gepflasterten Straßen hinzuweisen, für deren großen Räume die Bauherren, die ihren Wohlstand aus dem Kupferhandel geschöpft haben dürften, sorgsam behauene Quader als Verkleidung der mächtigen Mauern verwenden ließen. Wie die Veröffentlichungen zeigen, haben wir es hier mit den Relikten einer Stadt zu tun, die bis hin zur Bauweise durchaus mit denen von Enkomi, Kalavassos oder Ugarit verglichen werden können.

Dahingehende Überlegungen erfuhren jüngst eine Stütze durch die petrographische Analyse des Tons von Tontafeln unter anderen aus Amarna und Ugarit, die Y. Goren, I. Finkelstein und N. Na'aman innerhalb des SONIA AND MARCO NADLER INSTITUTE OF ARCHAEOLOGY der Tel Aviv-Universität durchgeführt haben.[48] Das Ergebnis ihrer Untersuchungen schließt nämlich die Herkunft der Tontafeln aus dem Raum Enkomi aus und legt die aus dem Raum Alassa-Kalavasos am Südhang des Troodos-Massivs nahe.[49]

Das Fehlen von Schriftdokumenten kann nur schlecht als ein Argument gegen die herausragende Bedeutung von Alassa und seiner Trabantenstädte im Altertum angeführt werden: Je weiter wir uns von der Ostküste mit ihren direkten Verbindungen zum vorderorientalischen Festland und der dort gängigen Tontafeltechnik und Keilschrift entfernen, desto

47 Siehe S. Hadjisavvas 1986, S. 62–76 mit Pl. XVI-XVIII; ders. 1994, S. 107–114 mit Pl. XIV-XXI; ders. 1996, S. 23: „After the first results, however, of the emergency excavations undertaken between 1984 and 1987 at Alassa, in association with the construction of the Kouris Dam, our late colleague Jean-Claude Courtois, an authority on the Cypriote LBA, expressed the wish that Alassa may one day be identified with Alasia" – Jean-Claude Courtois, der diese Äußerung getan hat, war immerhin der langjährige Ausgräber an der Seite von C.F.A. Schaeffer sowohl in Enkomi als auch in Ras Shamra-Ugarit –; ders. 2006.

48 Vgl. Y. Goren, *et al.*, 2004, S. 48–74.

49 Y. Goren, *et al.*, 2004, S. 60–65 – Karte S. 60; zu den Rückschlüssen auf die Interpretation der Amarna- und Ugarit-Briefe siehe S. 61–75.

eher ist damit zu rechnen, daß die Schreiberschulen an den ihnen geläufigen Schreibmaterialien und Schriftträgern wie etwa Baumrinde oder Papyrus festhielten, der die Jahrtausende nicht überstanden hat.

Kreta in einer Urkunde und Kreter im Onomastikon

Die Freistellungsurkunde RS 16.238[50] aus der Zeit von ʿAmmiṯtamru III. (ca. 1260–1230 v.Chr.),[51] S.d. Niqmepaʿ (ca. 1310–1260 v.Chr.), ist bisher das einzige Dokument, das Kreta[52] erwähnt – der schlechte Erhaltungszustand der Tafel hinterläßt Unsicherheiten:

> (1) Vom heutigen Tag an (2) hat ʿAmmiṯtamru, Sohn des Niqmepaʿ, (3) König von Ugarit, (4) (von Abgaben) freigestellt den Sinaranu, (5) Sohn des Siginu: Wie (6) die Sonne frei ist, so frei ist er: (7) Seine Gerste, sein Bier, sein Öl (8) müssen nicht (mehr) in den Palast kommen. (9) (Auch) sein Schiff ist frei (von Abgaben).
>
> (10) Wenn aus Kapturu (11) ein Schiff von ihm anlandet, (12) wird er sein Geschenk dem König (13) abliefern. Dann (14) wird sich seinem Haus kein Steuereintreiber (15) nähern. Gegenüber dem König, (16) seinem Herrn, ist Sinaranu devot …

Der Grund für die Befreiung des Sinaranu von Hafengebühren dürfte darin liegen, daß ein kretisches Schiff, wie diese einmalige Urkunde vor Augen führt, Ugarit nur selten angelaufen hat. Die Ware kretischer Schiffe dürfte normalerweise im Hafen von Alašia-Zypern auf kyprische oder levantinische umgeladen worden sein.[53]

Die Seltenheit kretischer Schiffe im Hafen und der dementsprechend wohl kleine Prozentsatz von Kretern in der Bevölkerung der Stadt führen zur Frage, ob das Onomastikon der ugaritischen Texte überhaupt Belege für Kreter bieten kann. Für die Gruppe von Namen, die auf den geogra-

50 Umschrift und Übersetzung: J. Nougayrol 1955, S. 107–108; Kopie: pl. LXIX; vgl. die neue Übersetzung bei S. Lackenbacher 2002, S. 310–311.

51 Für die Regierungsdaten der ugaritischen Könige siehe J. Freu 2006, S. 259–260 (Chronologie).

52 Kapturu in Z. 10 halbideographisch KUR.DUGUD-*ri* = KUR.*kabtu-ri* geschrieben; vgl. J. Freu 2006, S. 213.

53 Vgl. z.B. M.C. Astour 1973, S. 17; I. Singer 1999, S. 675.

phischen Begriff „Kreta" zurückgeführt werden können, ist dies vorstellbar. Diese seien nachfolgend auch auf die Gefahr hin aufgeführt, daß das damit gezeichnete Bild wegen der möglichen Mehrzahl von unerkannt gebliebenen ägäo-kretischen Namen einseitig ist:

— In der Urkunde KTU 4.371:18-19, die den ersten Monat des Jahres, *rišyn*, aufführt, wird ein *apn bn krty* „Apn, Sohne des/eines Kreters" genannt;
— in KTU 4.617:20 und 39 werden jeweils einem *krty* „Kreter" Familien und Gesinde zugewiesen;
— KTU 4.760 könnte eine Liste von Leuten sein, die einem *krty* „Kreter" (Z. 1) zugeordnet sind.

Diese wenigen Belege zeigen, daß auch in den Wirtschaftstexten auf den ersten Blick erkennbare Kreter in Ugarit selten sind.

Alašia, der direkte Nachbar

Anders verhält es sich, wie einleitend festgestellt, mit den Belegen für Alašia-Zypern. Diese sind wegen der engen politischen und wirtschaftlichen Beziehungen zwischen Ugarit und Alašia-Zypern zahlreich, so daß nur einige der aufschlußreichsten Texte zur Sprache gebracht werden können. Dabei seien die folgenden Themen in den Mittelpunkt gestellt: *Verbannungsort für unbotmäßige Prinzen aus Ugarit* (3.3.1), *Austausch von Handelsgütern mit Ugarit* (3.3.3), *Austausch von Schriftdenkmälern mit Ugarit* (3.3.2) und *Warnung vor kriegerischen Seefahrern* (3.3.4).

Verbannungsort für unbotmäßige Prinzen aus Ugarit

Für die Regenten des antiken Vorderen Orients bedeuteten aufbegehrende Prinzen eine latente Gefahr für die Ausübung ihrer Macht. Was mit solchen Prinzen geschah, ist selten schriftlich festgehalten. Dieses Schweigen durchbrechen einige Rechtsurkunden vom Hof des ugaritischen Königs ʿAmmiṯtamru III. (ca. 1260–1230 v.Chr.) mit überregionalem Charakter: Vor Ini-Teššub, dem in Karkemiš residierenden hethitischen Vizekönig, wurde ein Rechtsfall folgenden Inhalts festgehalten und die Tafel als Beweisdokument im Palast des ugaritischen Königs deponiert – RS 17.352:[54]

> (1) (Rechtsfall) vor Ini-Teššub, König von Kargamiš, (2) Sohn des Šaḫurunuwe, auch eines Königs von Kargamiš, (3) Enkel des Šarru-kušuḫ, ebenfalls eines Königs von Kargamiš, des Heroen:
>
> (4) Ḫišmi-šarrumma und ʿAbdi-šarrumma (5) haben gegen ʿAmmiṯtamru, den König von Ugarit, (6) eine schwere Verfehlung begangen. Aḫat-milku, ihre Mutter, (7) die Königin von Ugarit, hat ihren Erbanteil (8) an Silber, Gold und an ihren Gerätschaften (9) sowie an allem, was ihnen gehört hat, (10) (ihnen) gegeben und hat sie nach Alašia (11) geschickt. (12) Und bei ‚Ištar der Steppe'[55] hat sie einen Schwur (13) ihnen abgenommen: (14) „In Zukunft (15) darf weder Ḫišmi-šarrumma (noch) ʿAbdi-šarrumma, (16) auch nicht ihre Söhne, ihre Enkel, (17) wegen ihres Erbanteils (18) vor ʿAmmiṯtamru, dem König von Ugarit, (19) und vor seinem Sohn, seinem Enkel (20) Ansprüche anmelden." Niemals werden Ḫišmi-šarrumma (21) (und) ʿAbdi-šarrumma, sein Sohn, sein Enkel, (22) wegen ihres Erbanteils bei ʿAmmiṯtamru, (23) dem König von Ugarit, oder bei seinem Sohn, seinem Enkel, (24) um das Erbe Klage erheben! (25) Wenn sie Klage erheben, dann wird sie diese Tafel (26) zurückweisen. Von diesem Tage an (27) ist die Erbteilung ‚besiegelt'.[56]

Der hier festgehaltene Rechtsfall hat deswegen einen überregionalen und ‚internationale' Charakter, weil Aḫat-milku, die Mutter der schuldig gewordenen Prinzen und Brüder des Regenten von Ugarit, eine Prinzessin aus dem südlichen Nachbarland Amurru und Tochter des dortigen Königs Bentešina war, die ʿAmmiṯtamru zur Stabilisierung der wirtschaftlichen und politischen Verhältnisse zwischen Ugarit und Amurru geehelicht hatte. Es ist also klar, daß ein verschiedene Länder betreffender Konflikt als Rechtssache vor den Vizekönig des südlichen Teils des Neuhethitischen Reichs, der seinen Sitz in Karkemiš hatte, als höchster Instanz gebracht werden mußte – die Tatsache, daß sich nicht nur diese, sondern

---

54 Umschrift und Übersetzung: J. Nougayrol 1956, S. 121–122; Kopie: Pl. LV; vgl. die neue Übersetzung von S. Lackenbacher 2002, S. 107–108.

55 Zu dieser Göttin siehe S. Lackenbacher 2002, S. 107 Anm. 330, mit einer ausführlichen Diskussion der neueren Literatur. S. Lackenbacher stellt sogar die Frage, ob die Anrufung dieser Gottheit einen Hinweis darauf enthalte, daß die Bevölkerung Alašias zu jener Zeit hurritisch war.

56 Zur Problematik der Lesung und Deutung der Schlußbemerkung *ze-e-zu ba-as/ṣ/z-ru* siehe S. Lackenbacher 2002, S. 108 Anm. 331.

auch noch andere Urkunden (RS 17.35, RS 17.362 und RS 17.367)[57] mit diesem Thema befassen, zeigt dessen Brisanz an.[58]

Die Urkunde hat hintergründig die Thronfolge in Ugarit zum Thema, die zwischen drei Söhnen der Aḫat-milku ausgehandelt werden mußte. Daß die Mutter da ein gewichtiges Wort mitzusprechen hatte, zeigt der Text: In demselben Atemzug, in dem Aḫat-milku, die Mutter der drei widerstreitenden Brüder, einen, nämlich ʿAmmiṯtamru (III.) auf den Thron brachte, mußte sie die beiden Konkurrenten Ḫišmi-šarrumma und ʿAbdi-šarrumma aus dem Weg räumen – die ‚Verfehlung' der beiden dürfte also darin liegen, daß sie mit der Entscheidung ihrer Mutter bezüglich der Wahl des Thronfolgers nicht einverstanden waren und dagegen agierten. Die kluge Dame hat die Lage dadurch bereinigt, daß sie letztere nicht ins ‚Reich des Todes', sondern in die ‚Verbannung nach Alašia' geschickt hat. Damit folgte sie einem Brauch, der schon Jahrzehnte zuvor von hethitischen Herrschern befolgt worden war: Sowohl Ḫattušili III. (1283-1260 v.Chr.) als auch Arnuwanda (1240–1230 v.Chr.) haben Vasallen, die unbotmäßig waren, nach Alašia verbannt.[59]

Interessant wäre es, genauer zu wissen, welche Umstände die kleinasiatischen und vorderorientalischen Regenten dazu bewogen haben könnten, Alašia als einen guten Platz der Verbannung anzusehen. Möglicherweise war es nur die Insellage, die Alašia zu dieser Verwendung verhalf. Denn ohne die Benutzung eines seetüchtigen Schiffes dürfte es kaum möglich gewesen sein, irgendeinen Punkt auf dem gegenüberliegenden Festland zu erreichen; da die Schiffe unter der Flagge von Herrscherhäusern fuhren, die durch Verträge an einander gebunden waren – eine Änderung dieser Verhältnisse führten die ‚Seevölker' herbei, die am Anfang des 12. Jh. v.Chr. für das Ende der bis dahin gültigen Machtverhältnisse gesorgt haben –, wäre es für einen Verbannten immer schwer gewesen, eine Passage zum Festland zu erlangen.

Eine wichtige Frage im Zusammenhang mit den Überlegungen, ob Unbotmäßige nach Alašia verbannt werden konnten, ist sicher auch die nach dem rechtlichen Gegebenheiten zwischen dem Ort der Verbannung

57 Umschrift und Übersetzung der Texte: J. Nougayrol 1956, S. 123–124; Kopien: Pl. III und LVIII.

58 Ausführlich dazu J. Aboud 1994, S. 117–119; I. Singer 1999, S. 679–680; J. Freu 2006, S. 106–108; vgl. auch Ch. Lebrun 2004.

59 Vgl. hierzu die einschlägigen Erörterungen von A. Goetze 1957, S. 101; S. Lackenbacher 2002, S. 106.

und den verbannenden Königtümern: Konnten unbotmäßige Untertane in eine Gegend verbannt werden, zu der keine wie auch immer gearteten rechtlichen Verbindungen bestanden? Da es kaum denkbar ist, daß Unbotmäßige aus einem autarken Land in ein anderes abgeschoben worden sind, drängt sich bezüglich unseres Falles der unbotmäßigen Prinzen folgender Schluß auf: Die Hethiter und Ugariter pflegten mit Zypern intensive Handelsbeziehungen und unterhielten dort gegebenenfalls sogar Handelsniederlassungen, in die sie auch Leute schicken konnten, die sie in ihrer Umgebung nicht mehr dulden wollten; weil es sich hier um rechtlich an die Mutterstädte gebundene Territorien handelte, konnten sie dies offensichtlich auch ohne Belastung des zwischenstaatlichen Einvernehmens tun. Die Gestraften wurden dazu verurteilt, bei der Deckung des großen Kupferbedarfs der Mutterstädte mitzuhelfen, indem sie in Minen arbeiteten.

Die aufreibende Arbeit im Kupfer-Bergbau könnte nach allem durchaus ein Grund für die endgültige Verbannung unbotmäßiger Untertanen nach Alašia-Zypern gewesen sein. Denn die Arbeit in den Kupferminen dürfte durchaus mit einem Todesurteil vergleichbar gewesen sein.

In Weiterführung des Gedankens, daß der Kupferabbau auf Zypern mitunter durch verbannte Ausländer unterstützt oder gar getragen wurde, kann man zu folgenden weiteren Überlegungen gelangen:

– Der stets steigende Bedarf an Kupfer, wie ihn beispielsweise Ugarit als Handelsstadt hatte, mußte dazu führen, daß immer mehr Minenarbeiter auf Zypern gebraucht wurden.[60] Also liegt es auf der Hand, daß Ugarit stets auf der Suche nach Minenarbeitern für Zypern war und diesen Bedarf auf allerlei Weise zu erfüllen suchte. Dabei blieb wohl keine Bevölkerungsschicht aus der Stadt und ihrem Umland verschont.

– Der Einsatz zuverlässiger verantwortlicher Mitarbeiter in der Handelsniederlassung dürfte für die Herrscher von Ugarit stets ein besonders Anliegen gewesen sein. Möglicherweise haben angenehme Lebensbedingungen wie ein eigener Palast und Hofstaat Freiwillige zum leitenden Dienst in die Verbannung gelockt.

Der hier behandelte Rechtsfall über die Verbannung der beiden Prinzen Ḫišmi-šarrumma und ʿAbdi-šarrumma legt den Gedanken nahe, daß ʿAmmiṯtamru III. in die Lage gebracht wurde, eine glückliche Lösung für

60 Zum Thema des Bedarfs an Bergwerksarbeitern und Holz für den Stollenbau oder die Verhüttung siehe ausführlich H.-G. Buchholz 1999, Kap. 8: „Metallproduktion und -handel", S. 196–293; vgl. auch P.R.S. Moorey 1999, S. 242–250.

die Zeit seiner Regierung zu erleben: Die Auszahlung des reichen Erbteils verabschiedete sie zwar für immer aus Ugarit, bot ihnen aber gleichzeitig auch Gelegenheit, im Exil eine neue Existenz aufzubauen und für das Wohl ihrer Heimatstadt zu wirken.

Die Kenntnis von alledem verdanken wir dem glücklichen Umstand, daß im vorliegenden Fall die Prinzen Ḫišmi-šarrumma und ʿAbdi-šarrumma betroffen waren, die man nicht ohne ein ‚internationales' Gerichtsurteil von höchster Instanz und Hinterlegung einer entsprechenden Urkunde im heimischen Palast in die Arbeitsverbannung schicken konnte. Damit könnten sie Zeugen einer schweigenden Mehrheit geworden sein, von deren Verurteilung wir keine Aufzeichnungen haben.

Die Prinzen sind mit voll ausgezahltem Erbe auf die Insel verbannt worden und sollten keine Gelegenheit mehr bekommen, weitere Ansprüche an das Königshaus von Ugarit zu stellen. Über den weiteren Verlauf ihres Lebens liegt uns keine Meldung vor. Es ist durchaus denkbar, daß sie trotz allem die Sache ihrer Heimatstadt hochgehalten haben, wie es von Handelsvertretern in der Niederlassung erwartet wurde. Das führte zu engen wirtschaftlichen und politischen Bindungen zwischen Ugarit und Alašia, worauf nicht zuletzt die Anrufung der Götter von Alašia im Totenritual zu Ehren des Regenten ʿAmmiṯtamru III. spricht.[61]

Austausch von Handelsgütern mit Ugarit

Wiederholt ist in den Wirtschaftsdokumenten davon die Rede, daß Ugarit für Alašia die Basis für den Export- und Importhandel ist. Dabei geht es vornehmlich um Lebensmittellieferungen nach Alašia und Kupferlieferungen in umgekehrter Richtung. Stellvertretend für mehrere sei im folgenden auf die einschlägigen Passagen der beiden Wirtschaftstexte KTU 4.352 und KTU 4.390 hingewiesen, die beide in alphabetischer Keilschrift verfaßt und im Südarchiv des Palastes entdeckt worden sind:

---

61 Siehe M. Dietrich/W. Mayer 1997. Die hier S. 84–85 u.a. vertretene These, daß die Alašia-Götter in diesem Totenritual nur deswegen angerufen werden konnten, weil ʿAmmiṯtamru III. enge Beziehungen zu Alašia sowohl wegen der hierher verbannten Brüder Ḫišmi-Šarrumma und ʿAbdi-Šarrumma als auch wegen einer nicht direkt nachweisbaren Heirat mit einer Prinzessin aus Alašia hatte, bezweifelt S. Lackenbacher 2002, S. 106: „il est plus plausible que son rituel funéraire ait invoqué ses divinités ancestrales, des deux lignées, plutôt que ses dieux et ceux de ses épouses."

Handel mit Olivenöl nach KTU 4.352

In der Aufstellung für die Lieferungen von Olivenöl, das vielseitig – beispielsweise als Lebensmittel für die Zubereitung von Speisen, als Mittel der Körperpflege, als Brennmaterial für Lampen oder als Opfermaterie – gebraucht werden konnte, lauten die ersten Eintragungen in dem Wirtschaftstext KTU 4.352 (Z. 1-6):

> (1) 660 (Krüge zu je 10 Litern) Öl (2) für Abiramu, den Alašier.
> (3) 130 (Krüge) Öl (4) [für] Abiramu (nach) Ägypten.
> (5) 240 (Krüge) Öl (6) [für] die Bronzeschmiede …[62]

Bei den hier verzeichneten Öllieferungen fällt auf, daß es sich um verhältnismäßig große Mengen handelt. Da kaum anzunehmen ist, daß Ugarit und sein Hinterland genügend Plantagen von Olivenbäumen hatte, um Olivenöl des genannten Ausmaßes produzieren und exportieren zu können, dürfte Ugarit hier als Zwischenstation für den Olivenöl-Handel fungiert haben.

Einen Hinweis darauf könnte auch der zuerst genannte Empfänger geben, der interessanterweise zwei Lieferungen erhalten hat: Abiramu, ein Alašier, der je einen Posten wohl für seine Heimat und für Ägypten entgegengenommen hat. Dies legt den Schluß nahe, daß Abiramu ein am Palast akkreditierter Zwischenhändler war, dessen Schiffe Ladungen sowohl für Alašia auf Zypern als auch für Ägypten übernehmen konnten.

Der dritte Eintrag der Lieferliste hält fest, daß Kupferschmiede mit einer großen Lieferung Arbeitsmaterials bedacht worden sind. Da nicht angedeutet wird, wo diese Schmiede, die das zyprische Kupfer weiterverarbeiteten, tätig waren, dürfte es sich um solche handeln, die im Großraum Ugarit und Ras Ibn Hani[63] ihrem Handwerk nachgingen.

Handel mit Kupfer und anderen Metallgeräten nach KTU 4.390

Der Wirtschaftstext zählt die aus allerlei Handelsgut bestehende Ladung eines Schiffs aus Alašia auf:

---

62 Die nächstfolgenden Posten berücksichtigen Individuen aus unterschiedlichen Orten.

63 Hierzu siehe die neuesten Ausführungen: A. Bounni/É. et J. Lagarce 1998, S. 37–52, Fig. 68–73 (S. 142–143).

> (1) Ein Schiff aus Ala[šia], (2) das aus Atallig (kommend hier angelandet ist, hat folgende Ladung):
> (3) 15 (4) Talente Kupfer, (5) 2 Schilde,[64] (6) 2 Hämmer, (7) 1 Ziegelmodel aus Bronze, (8) 1 *krk*-Werkzeug für die Feinarbeit(?),[65] (9) 5 Lanzen, (10) 6 Säcke, (11) 11 (Sekel) (12) Purpurwolle, (13) 1 *krk*-Werkzeug [...].

Der erstgenannte Posten dieser Ladung handelt von 15 Barren („15 Talente") Kupfer, dem wichtigsten Exportgut Zyperns. Bei dem Begriff „Barren" wurde sicher die Form des „Vierzungen"-Typs eines Ochsenvlieses („oxhide", siehe dazu unten) mit dem Gewicht von je einem Talent (~ 30 kg) angespielt.[66]

Daneben werden noch andere Handelsgüter aufgeführt, von denen lediglich die beiden Eintragungen „6 Säcke" (Z. 10) und „11 (Sekel) Purpurwolle" (Z. 11-12) weniger gut zu den sonst zumindest teilweise aus Metall gefertigten Geräten und Waffen passen. Dies läßt darauf schließen, daß das Schiff, dessen Heimathafen Alašia gewesen sein dürfte, zur Aufnahme einer Beifracht von „Säcken" und „Purpurwolle" zuerst nach Atallig, einer der wichtigsten Hafenstädte südlich von Stadtstaat Ugarit, gesegelt war, um daran anschließend den Bestimmungshafen Ugarit anzusteuern.

Ob das Schiff außer den hier genannten Gütern, die für Ugarit bestimmt waren und darum hier registriert worden sind, auch andere geladen hatte, um sie an einem anderen Hafen abzuliefern, kann dem Text nicht entnommen werden.

Austausch von Schriftdenkmälern mit Ugarit

Die enge Verbindung zwischen Ugarit und Alašia läßt sich vortrefflich auch anhand des Transfers von Schriften und Schriftdenkmälern in beiden

---

64 Das Wort *ḫrt* „Schild" ist aus dem akk. *arītu* „Schild" (siehe AHw., S. 68; CAD A/2, S. 269f.) entlehnt (die Wiedergabe eines vokalischen Anlauts im Akk. durch ein *ḫ* in der ugar. Alphabetschrift entspricht der Regel) – zu anderslautenden Deutungsversuchen siehe DUL 347: *ḫrt* II „shield".

65 Die Wurzel KLY hat im G die Bedeutung „aufbrauchen, (samt und sonders) ausgeben", im D „ein Ende bereiten, vernichten, ausrotten". In Verbindung mit dem Nomen *krk*, das u.a. Werkzeug für Ziselierungen an Metallgeräten sein kann (vgl. z.B. J. Huehnergard 1987, S. 140–141; DUL, S. 455, *krk* I), könnte *kly* singgemäß mit „Abschluß-, Schlußarbeit; abschließende Feinarbeit" wiedergegeben werden.

66 Dazu siehe H.-G. Buchholz 1999, S. 195–293: Kap. 8.

Richtungen aufzeigen. Die Tatsache, daß wir es hier mit einer ganzen Reihe von Zeugnissen zu tun haben, unterstreicht die Intensität dieses Austauschs. Hervorzuheben ist allerdings, daß die Zeugnisse der hier zu erörternden Dokumente formal weder eindeutig auf Ugarit noch auf Alašia Bezug nehmen. Ihr Verhältnis zu der im vorigen Abschnitt namhaft gemachten Handelsniederlassung kann also nicht konkretisiert werden. Es sind nur allgemeine kulturelle Indizien der Schrift, die eine Verbindung zwischen den beiden geographischen Größen beschreiben.

Export der ugaritischen Alphabetschrift nach Zypern

Die schwedischen Ausgrabungen in Hala Sultan Tekke südwestlich von Kition/Larnaka haben 1981 eine Silberschale ans Tageslicht gebracht, in die eine Inschrift graviert ist, die alphabetische Zeichen in „Tropfenform" aufweist.[67] Die Inschrift (Abb. 1) hat folgenden Wortlaut:

Schale des Akkuya, des Sohnes des Yiptaḥ-Addu.

In der Forschungsgeschichte wurde die Schale wegen ihrer Inschrift zunächst als Importgut aus einem Ort der Levante angesehen. Als Argument dafür konnten die Alphabetschrift und die linksläufige Schreibrichtung angeführt werden, wie sie für levantinische Schriftdokumente geläufig ist. Dagegen spricht jedoch die Tropfenform der Zeichen mit einem nach unten oder oben spitz zulaufenden bauchigen Teil, die nur für Dokumente aus Zypern nachweisbar ist. Diese Form ist eine Nachahmung der kypro-minoischen Silbenschrift, die per Griffel mit rund-ovaler Spitze in den Ton gestochen worden und auf zahlreichen Tontafeln und anderen Schriftträgern zyprischen Ursprungs auf uns gekommen ist.[68]

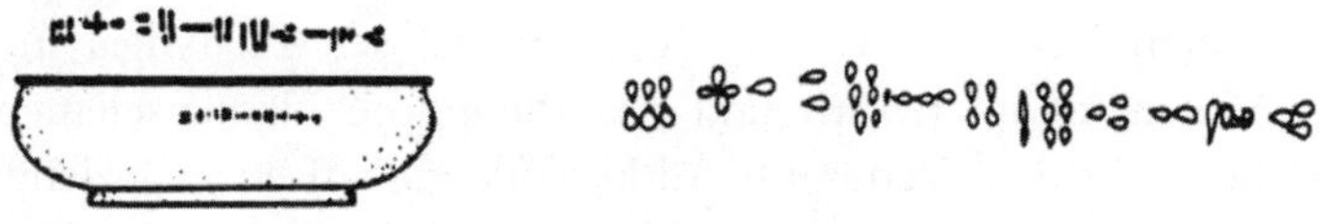

Abb. 1

Silberschale des Yiptaḥ-Addu von Hala Sultan Tekke

67 Siehe M. Dietrich/O. Loretz 1988, S. 206–214 (KTHST 6.1 = KTU 6.68).

68 Siehe unten 3.3.3.2.

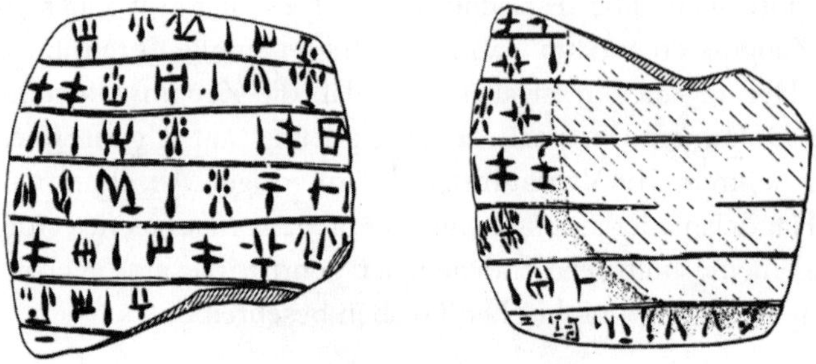

Abb. 2

Tontafel mit kypro-minoischer Schrift aus dem Archiv des Rašap-abu (RS 17.06)

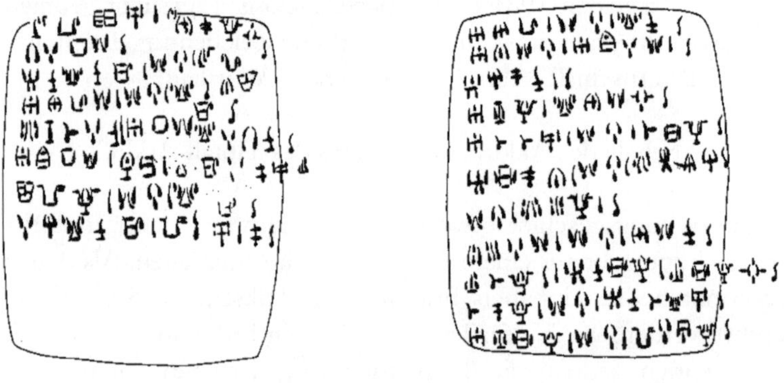

Abb. 3

Tontafel mit kypro-minoischer Schrift aus dem Archiv des Rap'ānu (RS 20.25)

Während die Alphabetschrift und die Schreibrichtung der Inschrift von links nach rechts nur vage für die Abhängigkeit von einer levantinischen Alphabettradition sprechen, deuten die Buchstabenformen, der Gebrauch des zweitletzten Buchstabens *ḥ* für den stimmlosen Pharyngal in dem Namen „Yiptaḥ-Addu" (*yptḥd*) und das theophore Namenselement an letzter Stelle *-d* für den Wettergott Addu eindeutig auf enge Beziehungen zu Ugarit und geben zur Vermutung Anlaß, daß der Träger des Namens sogar ein Ugariter gewesen sein könnte: Denn erstens erinnern die hier verwendeten Buchstabenformen und die Unterscheidung zwischen dem stimmlosen Pharyngal *ḥ* und dem stimmlosen Uvular *ḫ* an das ugaritische Langalphabet und weist zweitens die Nennung des Wettergottes Addu als theophores Namenselement auf den Wettergottkult Baʿal von Ugarit.

Import zyprischer Schriftdokumente nach Ugarit

In Ugarit wurden etliche Fragmente von Tonkrügen ausgegraben, die Vermerke in kypro-minoischer Schrift bieten. Auf mehr als das Zeichen für einen intensiven Handel zwischen Ugarit und Zypern konnte man daraus nicht schließen, weil die meist einzeilig-kurzen Vermerke sichere Lesungen und Deutungen nicht zulassen. Das änderte sich letztlich auch dann nicht, als 1953 und 1956 in Archiven der Handelsherren Rašap-abu und Rap'ānu die Tontafeln RS 17.06 (Abb. 2) und RS 20.25 (Abb. 3) mit Zeichen gefunden wurden, die denen der Vermerke entsprechen. Deren Text ist zwar umfangreich und gut erhalten, sperrt sich aber nach wie vor ebenso einer Deutung wie der anderer zyprischer Dokumente mit kypro-minoischer Schrift beispielsweise aus Enkomi, Kition, Kalavassos.[69] Es spricht also alles dafür, daß die Ugarit gefundenen Tafeln aus einer über ganz Zypern verbreiteten Schrifttradition stammen und mit zyprischer Handelsware nach Ugarit gelangt sind.

An dieser Stelle sind folgende Bemerkungen zur Entwicklung der kypro-minoischen Keilschrift angebracht: Der Ursprung der Keilschrift dürfte in der Notwendigkeit gelegen haben, die genuin zyprische Schrift, die mit dem Pinsel auf vergängliches Material gemalt wurde, für die Beschriftung von Tontafeln aufzubereiten. Das ist sicherlich nach dem Schema geschehen, das auch in Ugarit im 14. Jahrhundert angewandt wurde, als die dortige alphabetische Strichschrift aufgrund der Einführung der Tontafel in Keilschrift umgesetzt werden mußte. Während man in Ugarit den in Mesopotamien üblichen Griffel mit einer dreieckigen Spitze verwendete und die Buchstaben stark stilisierte,[70] bediente man sich auf Zypern eines Griffels mit rund-ovaler Spitze, die dafür geeignet war, den zyprischen Pinselstrich beizubehalten. Von daher erklärt sich die längliche Tropfenform der Zeichen mit einem rund zulaufenden bauchigen Teil.

Der traditionelle Schriftträger für die kyprisch-minoische Schrift könnte, wie beim genuin ugaritischen Alphabet, beispielsweise Papyrus oder Rinde gewesen sein. Der Grund für die Einführung eine Keilschrift auf Zypern ist weniger klar als der für die Umstellung des linearen Alphabets auf Tontafeln als Schriftträger in Ugarit. Hier gab eindeutig die Ausbreitung der babylonischen Koine während der Spätbronzezeit bis in die Levante den Anstoß. Warum wurde auf Zypern eine Keilschrift geschaf-

69 Zuletzt hat F.C. Woudhuizen 1994 einen Versuch mit dem Luwischen gemacht.

70 Siehe M. Dietrich/O. Loretz 1988, S. 99–127.

fen, wo doch, wie die Ausgrabungsfunde zeigen, die Ausbreitung der mesopotamischen Schriftkultur Zypern nicht in ihren Bann gezogen hat? Wollten dortige Regenten oder Handlungsträger mit Partnern auf dem Festland korrespondieren, dann konnten sie Gelehrte der Keilschrift in Dienst nehmen – das geschah, wie die wenigen Alašia-Briefe aus dem Amarna-Archiv vor Augen führen, offenbar am Anfang des 14. Jahrhunderts. Also scheint es den Verantwortlichen Zyperns gegen Ende der Spätbronzezeit, aus welchen Gründen auch immer, als unausweichlich erschienen sein, sich dem Festlandbrauch der Tontafeltechnik wenigstens teilweise anzuschließen. Die seltenen Belege für zyprische Tontafeldokumente auf der Insel und auf dem Festland zeigen an, daß sich Zypern gegenüber der Keilschrift letztlich doch verschlossen gehalten und an seinen Traditionen festgehalten hat.

Da die Entzifferung der kypro-minoischen Texte trotz intensiver Bemühungen noch nicht gelungen ist, fehlen uns noch Angaben zu der Bevölkerung der Insel und zu ihren sich immer intensiver darstellenden Verbindungen zum Festland, beispielsweise nach Ugarit.

Warnung vor kriegerischen Seefahrern

In dem Haus des Rap'ānu, des Handlungsbevollmächtigten und ‚Staatssekretärs' der letzten ugaritischen Könige, fanden sich drei etwas vor 1190 v. Chr. in babylonischer Koine verfaßte Briefe, die von zerstörerischen Umtrieben feindlicher Flottillen und ihrer kriegerischen Besatzungen berichten und deswegen Warnungen zur Achtsamkeit aussprechen.[71] Ein Brief rührt von Ešuwara, einem Verwaltungsbeamten in Alašia, an den König von Ugarit, ein zweiter von einem König von Alašia an seinen Kollegen Ḫammurapi, den letzten König von Ugarit, und ein dritter von dem König von Ugarit an den König von Alašia, seinen ‚Vater'. Alle drei Briefe erwecken den Eindruck, daß angesichts der Angreifer übers Wasser Panik herrscht.

Im folgenden sei der Brief des Ešuwara, eines königlichen Beamten in Alašia, in vollem Wortlaut wiedergegeben – bei den beiden anderen, die

71 Siehe dazu: M. Dietrich/O. Loretz 1985. – Zur historischen Auswertung siehe u.a. G.A. Lehmann 1970.

Zeugen für die ‚internationale' Korrespondenz sind, mögen hier die obigen Bemerkungen zum Inhalt genügen – RS 20.18:[72]

(1) Mitteilung des Ešuwara, (2) des Generalquartiermeisters von Alašia:
(3) Zum König von Ugarit (4) sprich:
(5) Dir, deinem Lande ebenso, (6) ergehe es wohl!
(7) Bezüglich der Tatsache, daß Feinde (8) den betroffenen Bewohnern deines Landes, (9) deinen Schiffen ebenso, (10) diese Schmach (11) angetan haben: (12) Sie haben einen Überfall auf die betreffenden (13) Bewohner deines Landes gemacht!
(14) Bei mir (15) darfst du dich deswegen nicht beklagen!
(16) Nun aber (folgendes): (17) 20 feindliche Schiffe (18) sind an den Bergen (offensichtlich) nicht[73] (19) angelandet - (20) sie haben nicht angehalten, (21) sondern sind eilig (22) weitergefahren. (23) Wo sie nun auftauchen werden, (24) wissen wir nicht.
(25) Dir zur Kenntnisnahme, (26) dir zum Schutz (27) schreibe ich dir (dies) hiermit.
(28) So seist du informiert!

Im ersten Abschnitt seines Schreibens wehrt sich Ešuwara offensichtlich gegen den Vorwurf des Königs, ihn und seine Leute auf See nicht rechtzeitig vor einem möglichen feindlichen Überfall gewarnt zu haben – er sei auch überrascht worden. Dieser Passus gibt einen vielsagenden Hinweis auf die Rolle Alašias, mit ihm sicher auch Zyperns insgesamt, als Relaisstation für den ostmediterranen Handel: Alašia war die Anlaufstation für alle, die vom Westen in Richtung Levante unterwegs waren. Wer hier angelandet ist und auf dem Weg in den Osten war, gab sein Ziel und seine Absichten bekannt. Da diese weitergemeldet wurden, bevor er seine Fahrt wieder aufgenommen hat, waren die nächste Anlaufstelle und der Zielhafen offenbar informiert. Angesichts der vielfach beklagten Piraterie konnte dieses Verfahren der Avisierung vor unangenehmen Überraschungen schützen. Da man bei einer ‚weiten' Strecke, wie die von der Karpassos-

72 Umschrift und Übersetzung: J. Nougayrol 1968, Nr. 22, S. 83–84; Kopie: S. 382; siehe die weiterführende Neubearbeitung von P.R. Berger 1969, S. 217–218; neuere Übersetzungen: M. Dietrich/O. Loretz 1985, S. 508–511; S. Lackenbacher 2002, S. 192. – Neuerdings bietet G. Steiner 2002 teilweise erheblich abweichende Lesungen und Deutungen des Schreibens.

73 la-a-ma ist als Negation lā mit -ma-Verstärkung und nicht als lāma „bevor" zu deuten.

Halbinsel oder Enkomi nach Ugarit, in der Bronzezeit sicher sein konnte, daß die Schiffe sich zuvor mit Proviant versorgten, war die Möglichkeit einer Vorwarnung gegeben.

Wenn der König von Ugarit überraschenderweise aus Richtung Meer überfallen wurde, mußte er angesichts dieser Gegebenheiten annehmen, daß das ‚Frühwarnsystem', das er mit seiner Handelsniederlassung und seinen Proviantstationen unterhalten hat, nicht funktioniert und die entsprechenden Meldungen nicht (rechtzeitig) weitergeleitet hat. Ešuwara stellt daher betroffen fest, daß ihm in diesem Fall keine Schuld bewußt sei: Er habe keine Gelegenheit zu einer Meldung gehabt; der Überfall sei auch für ihn überraschend gekommen, da er sich offenbar jenseits seines Horizonts auf dem offenen Meer ereignet habe.

Im zweiten Teil des Briefes macht Ešuwara dem König eine andere alarmierende Meldung: 20 feindliche Schiffe hätten keinen Stopp „an den Bergen" eingelegt, sondern seien sofort mit unbekanntem Ziel weitergefahren. Der Briefschreiber konnte also feststellen – ob durch eigene Beobachtung oder durch Fernmeldung –, daß die besagten Schiffe eine Stelle passierten, an der die Schiffe zwecks Ausstattung mit Proviant normalerweise nochmals festgemacht hatten. Da er aus Alašia schreibt, kann es sich bei den „Bergen" nur um eine ohne weiteres auszumachende Landschaftsmarke (an der Südküste) der Insel handeln, hinter der die Reisenden schließlich verschwanden. Das unterstützt die Annahme, daß Alašia am Hang des Troodos-Gebirges lag und daß seine Verantwortlichen die Schiffe beobachten konnten, die die Landzunge südwärts entlangfuhren, um an deren Ende nach erneuter Versorgung mit Proviant nach Osten abzubiegen. Ab diesem Moment waren sie für den Beobachter aus dem Blick.

Es ist anzunehmen, daß diese Meldung den König nicht vor der Ankunft der besagten 20 Schiffe erreicht hat.

Zwischenergebnis

Die Verbindungen Ugarits mit den ‚überseeischen' Nachbarn Zypern, Kreta und die ägäische Inselwelt konzentrierten sich nach allem vornehmlich auf den direkten Nachbarn Alašia-Zypern. Kreter waren offenbar seltene Gäste, die dann, wenn sie sich überhaupt in Ugarit eingefunden haben, unter dem Schutz des Palastes standen. Kreta und seine Häfen scheinen außerhalb des geographischen Horizonts der Ugariter gelegen zu haben. Von daher könnte man sich fragen, ob sich die Ugariter Kretas als eines konkreten Partners überhaupt bewußt waren.

Hinsichtlich Alašia-Zyperns herrschten andere Verhältnisse, wie die zahlreichen Dokumente vor Augen führen, die Alašia in allen Farben ausmalen. Auf der einen Seite sahen die Ugariter in Alašia den bedeutendsten Handelspartner und benützten es als Stützpunkt für ihren Überseehandel. Unterstützt wurden sie dabei durch Handelsniederlassungen, in denen Vertreter ihrer Interessen residierten. Auf der anderen Seite war Ugarit für die Alašiäer der wichtigste Stützpunkt in der Levante.[74]

Ergebnis: Verhältnis zwischen Ugarit und seinen ostmediterranen Nachbarn Zypern und der ägäischen Inselwelt im Spiegel der ugaritischen Texte

Die Dokumente des praktischen Lebens, Briefe und Wirtschaftstexte, haben von der westlichen Inselwelt vornehmlich Alašia-Zypern im Blick, die Ägäis, Kreta und die ägäische Inselwelt liegen außerhalb ihres Horizonts. Die Themen, die diese Dokumente berühren, sind vielfältig. Das lag vor allem daran, daß das – noch nicht einwandfrei lokalisierbare – Alašia eine Handelsniederlassung Ugarits gewesen sein oder unterhalten haben dürfte, die einerseits selbst versorgt werden mußte und andererseits stets darum bemüht war, gegenüber der Mutterstadt den wirtschaftlichen Nutzen zu beweisen. Dies führte zu einem regen Austausch von materiellen und ideellen Gütern.

In Ergänzung zu den Dokumenten des praktischen Lebens haben die der mythologischen Literatur einen sehr viel weiteren geographischen Horizont: Auf der Basis der im 2. Jt. v.Chr. herrschenden „mykenischen Koine“ in Architektur und Kunst, die im ganzen ostmediterranen Raum einschließlich Ägyptens nachweisbar ist, sprechen sie davon, daß dann, wenn ein Palast gebaut und eingerichtet werden sollte, der auf Kreta beheimatete Künstler Kōṯar-wa-Ḫasīs in Aktion trat. Damit bestätigen die literarischen Texte das Bild einer Kultur, die sich über den gesamten ostmediterranen Raum erstreckt hat und von der die modernen Ausgrabungen immer neue Zeugen ans Tageslicht bringen.

74 Vgl. z.B. F. Malbrant-Labat 2004; I. Singer 1999, S. 675–678; J. Freu 2006, S. 209–213.

Literatur

Aboud, J., 1994. *Die Rolle des Königs und seiner Familie nach den Texten von Ugarit.* Forschungen zur Anthropologie und Religionsgeschichte, 27, Münster.

ders., 1973. *Ugarit and the Aegean.* In: J. H.A. Hoffner (Hrsg.), *Orient and Occident. Essays presented to Cyrus H. Gordon on the Occasion of his Sixty-fifth Birthday.* AOAT 22, Münster, S. 17-27.

Astour, M.C., 1995. *La topographie du royaume d'Ougarit.* In: M. Yon et al. (Hrsg.), *Le pays d'Ougarit autour de 1200 av. J.-C.* Ras Shamra-Ougarit, Paris, S. 55-71.

Berger, P.R., 1969. *Die Alašia-Briefe Ugaritica 5, Noug. Nrn. 22-24.* Ugarit-Forschungen (Münster), 1: 217-221.

Bounni, A., Lagarce, É. und Lagarce, J., 1998. *Ras Ibn Hani, I. Le palais nord du Bronze Récent. Fouilles 1979-1995, synthèse préliminaire*, Beyrouth.

Buchholz, H.-G., 1999. *Ugarit, Zypern und Ägäis. Kulturbeziehungen im zweiten Jahrtausend v. Chr.* AOAT 261, Münster.

Buchholz, H.-G. und Karageorghis, V., 1971. *Altägäis und Altkypros*, Tübingen.

CAD, *Chicago Assyrian Dictionary*, Glückstadt/New York/Winona Lake.

Caubet, A. und Matoian, V., 1995. *Ougarit et L'Égée.* In: M. Yon et al. (Hrsg.), Le pays d'Ougarit autour de 1200 av. J.-C. Histoire et archéologie. Ras Shamra-Ougarit XI, Paris, S. 99-112.

Charpin, D., 1990. *Une mention d'Alašiya dans une lettre de Mari.* Revue d'Assyriologie (Paris), 84: 125-127.

Crowley, J.L., 1989. *The Aegean and the East. An Investigation into the Transference of Artistic Motifs between the Aegean, Egypt, and the Near East in the Bronze Age.*

Deger-Jalkotzy, S., 1996. *Ägäische Koine B 4 Die mykenische Koine, Der neue Pauly* I, Stuttgart/Weimar, S. 150–154.

Dietrich, M., 1996. *Aspects of the Babylonian Impact on Ugaritic Literature and Religion.* In: N. Wyatt et al. (Hrsg.), *Ugarit, religion and culture.* UBL 12, Münster, S. 33-48.

ders., 2000. *Zypern und die Ägäis nach den Texten aus Ugarit.* In: S. Rogge (Hrsg.), *Zypern – Insel im Brennpunkt der Kulturen.* Schriften des Instituts für Interdisziplinäre Zypern-Studien, Münster, S. 63-89.

ders., 2001. *Der Brief des Šumiyānu an den ugaritischen König Niqmepa® (RS 20.33).* Ugarit-Forschungen (Münster), 33: 117-192.

ders., 2005. *Der kult(ur)geographische und zeitliche Horizont ugaritischer und hurritischer Priester.* Ugarit-Forschungen (Münster), 36: 12-39.

Dietrich, M. und Loretz, O., 1985. *Historisch-chronologische Texte aus Alalah, Ugarit, Kamid el-Loz/Kumidi und den Amarna-Briefen.* In: O. Kaiser (Hrsg.), *Texte aus der Umwelt des Alten Testaments I/5*, Gütersloh, S. 508-511.

dies., 1988. *Die Keilalphabete. Die phönizisch-kanaanäischen und altarabischen Alphabete in Ugarit.* ALASPM 1, Münster.

dies., 1990. *Die Wurzel NŪP „hoch sein" im Ugaritischen.* Ugarit-Forschungen (Münster), 22: 67-77.

dies., 1997. *Mythen und Epen in ugaritischer Sprache.* In: O. Kaiser (Hrsg.), *Texte aus der Umwelt des Alten Testaments.* Band III, Lieferung 6: Mythen und Epen IV, Gütersloh, S. 1091-1316.

dies., 1998. *Amurru, Yaman und die ägäischen Inseln nach den ugaritischen Texten.* In: S. Izre¬el et al. (Hrsg.*), Past Links. Studies in the Languages and Cultures of the Ancient Near East.* Israel Oriental Studies, Winona Lake (IN). S. 335-363.

dies., 2000. *Das ugaritische Gottesattribut hrš „Weiser, handwerklich Tüchtiger. Eine Studie über die Götter El, Ea/Enki, Kṯr-w-Ḫss und Hyn.* Ugarit-Forschungen (Münster), 31: 165-173.

dies., 2003. *Der Untergang von Ugarit am 21. Januar 1192 v.Chr.? Der astronomisch-hepatoskopische Bericht KTU 1.78 (= RS 12.061).* Ugarit-Forschungen (Münster), 34: 54-74.

Dietrich, M., Loretz, O. and Sanmartín, J., 1995. *The Cuneiform Alphabetic Texts from Ugarit, Ras Ibn Hani and Other Places (KTU: second, enlarged edition).* ALASPM 8, Münster.

Dietrich, M. und Mayer, W., 1997. *Ein hurritisches Totenritual für ʿAmmištamru III. (KTU 1.125).* In: B. Pongratz-Leisten et al. (Hrsg.), *Ana šadî Labnāni lū allik. Beiträge zu altorientalischen und mittelmeerischen Kulturen. Festschrift für Wolfgang Röllig.* AOAT 247, Münster, S. 79-89.

DUL: G. del Olmo Lete und J. Sanmartín, 2004. *A Dictionary of the Ugaritic Language in the Alphabetic Tradition.* Handbuch der Orientalistik. I 67, Leiden - Boston.

Feldman, M.H., 2006. *Diplomacy by Design. Luxury Arts and an „International Style" in the Ancient Near East, 1400–1200 BCE*, Chicago.

Freu, J., 2006. *Histoire politique du royaume d'Ugarit.* KUBABA Sér.Ant., XI, Paris/Louvain-la-Neuve.

Goetze, A., 1957. *Kulturgeschichte Kleinasiens.* Handbuch der Altertumswissenschaft, 3/2, München.

Goren, Y., et al., 2004. *Inscribed in Clay. Provenance Study of the Amarna Letters and other Ancient Near Eastern Texts.* Monograph Series, 23, Tel Aviv.

Groneberg, B., 1980. *Die Orts- und Gewässernamen der altbabylonischen Zeit.* Répertoire Géographique des Textes Cunéiformes, 3, Wiesbaden.

Hadjisavvas, S., 1986. *Alassa. A New Late Cypriote Site. Report of the Department of Antiquities, Cyprus 1986*, Nicosia.

ders., 1994. *Alassa Archaeological Project 1991-1993. Report of the Department of Antiquities, Cyprus 1994*, Levkosia.

ders., 1996. *Alasa: A Regional Centre of Alasia?* In: P. Åström und E. Herscher (Hrsg.), *Late Bronze Age Settlement in Cyprus: Function and Relationship*, Jonsered, S. 23-38.

ders., 2006. *Aspects of Late Bronze Age Trade as seen from Alassa-Pano Mandilaris.* In: E. Czerny et al. (Hrsg.), *Timelines. Studies in Honour of Manfred Bietak*, Vol. II. Orientalia Lovaniensia Analecta, Leuven, S. 449-453.

Helck, H., 1979. *Die Beziehungen Ägyptens und Vorderasiens zur Ägäis bis ins 7. Jahrhundert v.Chr.* Beiträge der Forschung, 120, Darmstadt.

Huehnergard, J., 1987. *Ugaritic Vocabulary in Syllabic Transcription.* Harvard Semitic Studies, 32, Atlanta, GA.

Karageorghis, V., 1982. *Cyprus. From the Stone Age to the Romans*, Nicosia.

Klengel, H., 1992. *Syria 3000 to 300 B.C. A Handbook of Political History*, Berlin.

Knapp, A.B., 1996. *Settlement and Society an Late Bronze Age Cyprus: Dynamics and Development.* In: P. Åström und E. Herscher (Hrsg.), *Late Bronze Age Settlement in Cyprus: Function and Relationship*, Jonsered, S. 54-79.

Lackenbacher, S., 2002. *Textes akkadiens d'Ugarit.* Littératures anciennes du Proche-Orient, 20, Paris.

Lambrou-Phillipson, C., 1990: *Hellenorientalia. The Near Eastern Presence in the Bronze Age Aegean, ca. 3000–1100 B.C. Interconnections based on the material record and the written evidence.* Studies in Mediterranean Archaeology. Pocket-book 95, Göteborg.

Lebrun, C., 2004. *Lingai- et māmītu: réflexions sur les expressions communes dans les textes de Boĝazköy et d'Ougarit.* In: M. Mazoyer und O. Casabonne (Hrsg.), *Antiquus Oriens. Mélanges offerts au Professeur René Lebrun*, vol. II. KUBABA Sér. Ant., Paris/Louvain-la-Neuve, S. 29-40.

Lehmann, G.A., 1970. *Der Untergang des hethitischen Großreiches und die neuen Texte aus Ugarit.* Ugarit-Forschungen (Münster), 2: 39-73.

Loretz, O., 2003. *Götter - Ahnen - Könige als gerechte Richter.* AOAT, 290, Münster.

Lurz, N., 1994. *Der Einfluß Ägyptens, Vorderasiens und Kretas auf die Mykenischen Fresken. Studien zum Ursprung der Frühgriechischen Wandmalerei.* Europäische Hochschulschriften Reihe, XXXVIII/48, Frankfurt.

Malbrant-Labat, F., 2004. *Alašiya et Ougarit.* Res Antiquae (Bruxelles), I: 365-377.

Mayer, W., 1995. *Politik und Kriegskunst der Assyrer.* ALASPM, 9, Münster.

Moorey, P.R.S., 1999. *Ancient Mesopotamian Materials and Industries.* (Nachdruck: Winona Lake, IN).

Morris, S.P., 1992. *Daidalos and the Origins of Greek Art*, Princeton (NJ).

Muhly, J.D., 1997. *Cyprus.* In: E.M. Meyers (Hrsg.), *The Oxford Encyclopedia of Archaeology in the Near East*, Oxford, S. 89-96.

Negbi, O., 1986. *The Climax of Urban Development in Bronze Age Cyprus. Report of the Department of Antiquities, Cyprus 1986*, Nikosia.

Nougayrol, J., 1955. *Le palais royal d'Ugarit III, Mission de Ras Shamra VI*, Paris.

ders., 1956. *Le palais royal d'Ugarit IV, Mission de Ras Shamra IX*, Paris.

ders., 1968. *Textes suméro-accadiens des archives et bibliothèques privées d'Ugarit.* In: C.F.A. Schaeffer (Hrsg.), *Ugaritica V. Mission de Ras Shamra* XVI, Paris.

Pardee, D., 1997. *1. Ugaritic Myths. The Baʿlu Myth (1.86).* In: W.W. Hallo (Hrsg.), *The Context of Scripture. Volume I: Canonical Compositions from the Biblical World*, Leiden – New York – Köln, S. 241-274.

Reden, S. von, 1992. *Ugarit und seine Welt. Die Entdeckung einer der ältesten Handelsmetropolen am Mittelmeer*, Bergisch Gladbach.

Rüterswörden, U., 1988. *Der Bogen in Genesis 9. Militärhistorische und traditionsgeschicht-liche Erwägungen zu einem biblischen Symbol.* Ugarit-Forschungen (Münster), 20: 247-263.

Schaeffer, C.F.A., 1952. *Enkomi-Alasia. Nouvelles missions en Chypre, 1946-1950*, Paris.

Singer, I., 1999. *A Political History of Ugarit.* In: W.G.E. Watson und N. Wyatt (Hrsg.), *Handbook of Ugaritic Studies.* Handbuch der Orientalistik, Leiden, S. 603-733.

Soden, W. von, 1965. *Akkadisches Handwörterbuch: Unter Benutzung des lexikalischen Nachlasses von Bruno Meissner (1868-1947) / bearb. von Wolfram von Soden.* Harrassowitz, Wiesbaden.

Steiner, G., 2002. *Der Brief des Ešuwara (R.S. 20.18).* In: O. Loretz et al. (Hrsg.), Ex Mesopotamia et Syria Lux. Festschrift für Manfried Dietrich zu seinem 65. Geburtstag. AOAT, Münster, S. 723-734.

Tropper, J., 2000. *Ugaritische Grammatik.* AOAT 273, Münster.

Vidal, J., 2006: *Ugarit at War (I). The Size and Geographical Origin of the `rd-militia.* Ugarit-Forschungen (Münster), 37: 653-672.

Wiesner, J., 1966. *Zypern.* In: B. Reike und L. Rost (Hrsg.), Biblisch-historisches Handwörterbuch, Göttingen. Sp. 2252-2254.

Woudhuizen, F.C., 1994. *Tablet RS 20.25 from Ugarit. Evidence of Maritime Trade in the Final Years of the Bronze Age.* Ugarit-Forschungen (Münster), 26: 509-538.

Yon, M., 2006. *The City of Ugarit at Tell Ras Shamra*, Winona Lake (Ind).

Young, G.D.H., 1981. *Ugarit in Retrospect. Fifty Years of Ugarit and Ugaritic.* Winona Lake (IN).

Enki / Ea und El – Die Götter der Künste und Magie

Manfried Dietrich, Münster

Einführung

Das Thema „Art and Magic in the Ancient Near East“ übt auf den Altorientalisten eine besondere Anziehungskraft aus – gleichgültig, ob er auf dem Gebiet der Kunstgeschichte, der Religionsgeschichte oder der Philologie arbeitet. Die folgenden Darstellungen konzentrieren sich auf philologische und religionsgeschichtliche Fragen zum Thema „Kunst und Magie“ nach Maßgabe der religiösen Literatur. Hier fallen die Blicke des Betrachters spontan auf den mesopotamischen Schöpfergott Enki, *alias* Ea, und sein syrisches Pendant El. Von ihnen läßt sich ein Bild zeichnen, in dem sich die Bereiche „Kunst“ und „Magie“ eng berühren.

Die „Kunst“ der beiden altorientalischen Götter besteht vornehmlich in der Erschaffung des Lebens, dessen Kulminationspunkt der Mensch ist. Die Menschenschöpfung ist der Endpunkt der Kosmogonie und gewinnt dadurch an Gewicht, daß die Götter diese Kunst durch die Verleihung der Kraft zur anthropogenetischen Regeneration mittels Zeugung und Geburt sowie durch die Erhaltung des menschlichen Lebens in Notsituationen tagtäglich unter Beweis stellen mußten. Aus dem Blickfeld des Menschen liegen sowohl die Kunst der Erschaffung als auch die der Erhaltung des Lebens auf der transzendenten Ebene, der sich der Mensch mithilfe der von ihm entwickelten Kunst des Gebets[1] und der Beschwörung nur magisch nähern kann. Während er mit dem Bitt- und Preisgebet den Göttern Spielraum zum Handeln läßt, will er sie mit der Beschwörung verpflichten. Also zeichnen sich die Schöpfergötter nach dem Verständnis der Antiken Orientalen sowohl aktiv als auch passiv aus, indem sie einerseits die

1 Zu dem hier angesprochenen Komplex siehe das richtungweisende Werk A. Zgoll 2003.

Schöpfungskunst repräsentieren und andererseits seitens des Geschöpfes durch die Magie zum Handeln beschworen werden.[2]

Im ersten Punkt der folgenden Ausführungen sollen Texte zur Sprache gebracht werden, die einerseits von der göttlichen Kunst der Erschaffung und Erhaltung des menschlichen Lebens handeln und andererseits die menschliche Kunst vor Augen führen, die Götter mit Hilfe von Magie, Gebet und Beschwörung zur Lebenserhaltung zu bewegen: *Schöpfung und Erhaltung des menschlichen Lebens nach syro-mesopotamischen Texten* (2.). Von den wichtigsten Texten werden jene Passagen in vollem Wortlaut zitiert, die das Tagungsthema beleuchten.

Wie der Titel *Enki/Ea und El: Götter der Kunst und Magie* zu erkennen gibt, werden dabei nicht nur Texte aus Mesopotamien herangezogen, sondern auch solche aus Syrien, genauer aus Ugarit. Damit erhöht sich zwar die Zahl der zu befragenden Texte beträchtlich, die breitere Basis bietet aber auch die Möglichkeit, ein für die syro-mesopotamische Religionsgeschichte zentrales Thema aus mehr als einer Perspektive zu beleuchten.

„Kunst" und „Magie" wirken bei den Göttern Enki/Ea und El besonders deutlich nach Aussage derjenigen Texte zusammen, die die CREATIO AD USUM („Schöpfung von Wesen zur Erfüllung eines bestimmten Zwecks") oder CREATIO AD USUM („Schöpfung von Wesen zur Erfüllung eines bestimmten Falles") beleuchten. Die einschlägigen Texte führen uns vor Augen, daß die Götter die bestehende Schöpfung mitunter um neue, Zweckbestimmte Wesen – CREATURAE AD USUM/CASUM „Geschöpfe für besondere Gelegenheiten" – ergänzen mußten, weil die vorhandenen für anstehende Aufgaben der Magie nicht eingesetzt werden konnten. Diese Texte, die das Thema „Kunst und Magie" besonders deutlich werden lassen, werden im zweiten Punkt vorgestellt: *CREATIO AD USUM/CASUM nach syro-mesopotamischen Texten* (3.).

In *Schlußbemerkungen* (4.) seien schließlich die Ergebnisse zusammengefaßt.

2 Der Begriff „Magie" wird im Sinne von Bronislaw Malinowski verwendet: Magie besteht aus Handlungen, „die einen praktischen Nutzwert haben und wirksam sind nur als Mittel zu einem Zweck" (H.G. Kippenberg 1998, S. 85). Demnach hat sie keine Eigendynamik und soll im Einzelfall als Grundlage für ein Zusammenwirken zwischen Mensch und Gott bilden, um ein konkretes Ergebnis zu erreichen; – Zu einer instruktiven und übersichtlichen Darstellung der in der Moderne verbreiteten Vorstellungen und zur Begriffsabgrenzung zwischen „Religion" und „Magie" siehe R. Schmitt 2001; ders. 2004, S. 5–66.

Schöpfung und Erhaltung des menschlichen Lebens nach syro-mesopotamischen Texten

Die Menschenschöpfung nach der Nippur- und der Eridu/Babylon-Mythologie

Nippur-Mythologie

Die kultisch-religiösen Texte Altmesopotamiens, die auf die Schöpfung zu sprechen kommen, spiegeln für die Urzeit zwei Phasen wider: Eine frühere, in der der Kosmos aus einer nicht gegliederten Urmaterie bestand und in der die Hochgötter präexistent innerhalb einer u r u - u l - l a „uranfänglichen Stadt“ wirkten, und eine spätere, die dadurch entstand, daß die Urmaterie in die beiden Ebenen Himmel und Erde aufgeteilt wurde. Die Texte sehen diese Phasen, von denen wir den Äon der früheren Phase die *Vorwelt* und den der späteren die *Jetzt-Welt* nennen, in einem genetischen Zusammenhang.[3]

Die Erschaffung des Menschen soll nach der Vorstellung der Bewohner Mesopotamiens auf der Schwelle zur *Jetzt-Welt* stattgefunden haben. Dabei konkurrieren zwei Vorstellungen[4]: Die eine geht von Nippur aus, der Heimat der Ellil-Theologie, und die andere von Eridu und Babylon aus, wo die Hochgötter Enki/Ea und Marduk ihren Sitz hatten.

Sie seien knapp skizziert: Die Schule von Nippur vertrat im Blick auf die Entwicklung des Kosmos und der Welt die These der *autogenetischen Entfaltung*. Nach ihr hat sich eine Größe ohne Eingriff von außen autogenetisch aus einer anderen entfaltet. Sie meint also, daß die Kräfte, die dem Himmel und der Erde innewohnten und nach dem Umbruch zur *Jetzt-Welt* freigesetzt wurden, dazu in der Lage waren, sich bis zur aktuellen Welt des Dichters und Denkers in Eigengesetzlichkeit zu entwickeln – dazu bedurfte es keines erneuten Eingriffs einer Gottheit.[5]

Für die Vorstellung von der Entstehung des Menschen hat das zur Folge, daß auch er als ein natürliches Produkt der Erdentfaltung in der Frühzeit angesehen wurde: Der erste Mensch wuchs anthropogenetisch an

---

3 In der älteren Literatur wird die *Vorwelt* auch *Embryonale Welt* genannt, siehe u.a. J. van Dijk 1964–65, S. 1–59; ders. 1971, S. 449–452; ders. 1976, S. 126–133; M. Dietrich 1984, S. 155–184, hier bes. S. 156.

4 Siehe M. Dietrich 1984, S. 178–182.

5 Siehe M. Dietrich 1984, S. 168–169.

einem gottgewollten, heiligen Ort wie eine Pflanze aus dem Erdboden heraus, weswegen diese Vorstellung EMERSIO[6] genannt wird – als Kronzeuge sei der *Initiationsritus für die Spitzhacke*[7] angeführt, der auf Sumerisch verfaßt ist und vom Anfang des 2. Jt. stammt:

> [1]*Der Herr hat wahrlich das, ‚was sich geziemt', leuchtend aufgehen lassen,*
> [2]*der Herr, dessen Schicksalsentscheidungen unabänderlich sind:*
> [3]*Ellil, damit der Same des Landes aus der Erde hervorgehe,*
> [4]*beeilte sich wahrlich, den Himmel von der Erde zu entfernen,*
> [5]*beeilte sich wahrlich, die Erde vom Himmel zu entfernen,*
> [6]*Damit Uzumua die Erstlinge (: Gewächse) hervorsprießen lasse,*
> [7]*legte er am Boden von Duranki eine Spalte an.*
> [8]*Er setzte (: schuf) die Spitzhacke – der Tag ging auf –,*
> [9]*er gründete die Arbeitsaufgaben (: für die Spitzhacke), das Schicksal wurde bestimmt.*
> [10]*Während er den Arm zur Spitzhacke und zum Tragkorb ausstreckte, pries Ellil seine Spitzhacke.*
> …
> [18]*Er brachte die Spitzhacke ins Uzuea („Ort, an dem das Fleisch Sprießt") hinein.*
> [19]*Er legte die Erstlinge der Menschheit in die Spalte,*
> [20]*(und) während sein Land (: die Menschen) vor ihm (wie Gras) die Erde durchbrach,*
> [21]*schaute Ellil wohlwollend auf seine Sumerer.*

Dieser Abschnitt aus einem längeren Gedicht behandelt die Initiation der Spitzhacke, des für die Irrigationskultur wichtigsten Geräts. In demselben Zusammenhang wird der Tragkorb erwähnt, der für die künstliche Bewässerung neben der Spitzhacke das meistgebrauchte Arbeitsgerät war: Mit der Spitzhacke wurde der trocken-harte Alluvialboden aufgelockert, der Aushub anschließend mit dem Tragkorb weggetragen, um Bewässerungskanäle zu schaffen. Da diese landwirtschaftlichen Tätigkeiten die Basisarbeiten für die Stadtkultur waren, setzt dieser Text die Stadtkultur voraus.

Wie schon hervorgehoben, entstand der Mensch gemäß dieses Textes nach dem Prinzip der EMERSIO im Rahmen der kosmischen Entfaltungs-

---

6 G. Pettinato 1971, S. 39–46; M. Dietrich 1991, S. 70.

7 S.N. Kramer 1961, S. 52–53; G. Pettinato 1971, S. 82ff.

automatik: Der erste Mensch durchbrach wie eine Pflanze den Fruchtboden eines heiligen Ortes als Naturprodukt und erneuerte sich dann durch Autogeneration.

Im Blick auf das Tagungsthema „Art and Magic in the Ancient Near East“ kann die Nippur-Mythologie also allenfalls etwas für den Begriff „Magie“ beitragen, wenn wir davon ausgehen, daß der Automatismus der Weltentfaltung und der Anthropogenese, der Menschwerdung, auf göttlicher Magie beruht. Ein Akt göttlichen „Kunstwirkens“ wird hier nicht angesprochen.

Eridu-Babylon-Mythologie

Die Erschaffung des Menschen beschreiben die einschlägigen Texte der Eridu- und Babylon-Mythologie gänzlich anders. Hier treten der Hochgott Enki/Ea und dessen ‚Sohn‘ Marduk in Aktion. Nach der in Eridu und Babylon beheimateten Mythologie hat der Schöpfergott die Weiterentwicklung der Welt im Anschluß an den Umbruch von der *Vorwelt* zur *Jetzt-Welt* fest in seinen Händen gehalten: Alles, was in der aktuellen Welt existiert, ist am Anfang dieser Erdenphase einzeln und konkret erschaffen worden. Nichts war einer noch so gut funktionierenden Autogenese, also einem Zufall, überlassen. Ob Materie oder Leben: Ein Schöpfungsakt hat zu seiner Existenz geführt und das ‚tadellose‘ Urbild mit einem ihm vom Schöpfer zugedachten Aufgabenbereich geschaffen.[8]

Es war für die Eridu/Babylon-Mythologie also unvorstellbar, daß der Mensch das Endprodukt der Schöpfung nach einer Entfaltungsautomatik war. Wenn im Laufe der Zeit die Handschrift des Schöpfers verwischt, sein ursprünglicher Plan also weniger deutlich erkennbar oder gar verschüttet war, dann lag es am Ritualmeister, die Urzeit wachzurufen und das entstellte oder gar verfälschte Jetzt-Bild nach dem Ur-Bild neu auszurichten – dieser Vorgang ist magisch und gilt sowohl für die Materie[9] als auch für das Leben des Menschen, wie die medizinischen Texte angesichts eines Kranken lehren.

Die Erschaffung des Menschen wird in der Eridu/Babylon-Theologie dementsprechend auch auf einen speziellen Schöpfungsakt zurückgeführt, in dem vom Schöpfergott Enki/Ea ein Embryo nach seinen Vorstellungen vorgefertigt und der Muttergöttin zur Geburt anvertraut wird. Das

8 M. Dietrich 1984, S. 177–178.

9 Vgl. die Rituale anläßlich der Tempelrenovierung, z.B. M. Dietrich 1984, S. 173–175.

mag der folgende Text illustrieren, der den Titel *Enki und Ninmaḫ* trägt[10] – die Niederschrift des Textes geschah am Anfang des 2. Jt. v.Chr. in (neu)sumerischer Sprache:

> [14]*Damals lag Enki, der überaus weise Gott, der Schöpfer, der die zahlreichen Götter ins Dasein gerufen hatte,* [15]*im Engur, dem Trog, aus dem das Wasser fließt, dem Ort, dessen Inneres kein anderer Gott (mit dem Auge) durchdringen kann,* [16]*in einem Schlafgemach (und) stand vom Schlaf nicht auf.* [17]*Die Götter weinten und klagten: „Er hat das Elend geschaffen!"* [18]*Sie wagten (jedoch) nicht, gegen den Schlafenden, gegen den Liegenden, in dessen Schlafgemach einzudringen.*
> [19]*Nammu aber, die Mutter, die allen vorangeht, die Gebärerin der zahlreichen Götter,* [20]*überbrachte ihrem Sohn die Klage der Götter:* [21]*„Mein Sohn, du liegst, ja, du schläfst.* [22]*…* [23]*die (oberen) Götter schlagen den Leib deiner Geschöpfe!* [24]*Mein Sohn, steh' aus deinem Schlafgemach auf, du, der du aus (der Fülle) deiner Weisheit jede Kunst versteht:* [25]*Mache einen Ersatz für die Götter, damit sie ihren Tragkorb wegwerfen können!"*
> [26]*Enki stand auf das Wort seiner Mutter Nammu hin aus seinem Schlafgemach auf.* [27]*Der Gott ging in dem heiligen Raum auf und ab, schlug sich dann bei seinem Überlegen (spontan) auf die Schenkel:* [28]*Der Weise, der Wissende, der Umsichtige, der alles Erforderliche und Kunstvolle kennt, der Schöpfer (und) der, der alle Dinge formt, ließ das sigensigšar-Modell erstehen –* [29]*Enki bringt ihm die Arme an und formt seine Brust;* [30]*Enki, der Schöpfer, läßt in das Innere seines eigenen (Geschöpfes) seine Weisheit eindringen.*[11]

War nun das Modell des Menschen nach sorgfältiger göttlicher Planung geschaffen und trug es schon den göttlichen Verstand in sich, so mußte es doch noch zum Leben erweckt werden. Dafür, so berichtet der Text, übergibt Enki das Werk seiner Mutter Nammu und überträgt ihr die Aufgabe, dieses durch Geburt zu bewerkstelligen. Da die Formung eines Menschen vor der Geburt und die Geburt selbst einen komplexen Vorgang bilden, wird diese Vorstellung die der FORMATIO-GNATIO genannt.[12]

---

10 J. van Dijk 1964–65, S. 24ff.; G. Pettinato 1971, S. 69ff.; M. Dietrich 1994a, S. 8.

11 G. Pettinato 1971, S. 69–71: 14–30. Zu einer vielfach abweichenden Übersetzung gelangt W.H.Ph. Römer 1993, S. 389–391.

12 Diese Vorstellung wird üblicherweise FORMATIO genannt, vgl. G. Pettinato 1971, S. 54–56; M. Dietrich 1991, S. 70; da FORMATIO nur einen Teilaspekt des Vorgangs der Menschwerdung beschreibt, sollte er durch den der FORMATIO-GNATIO ersetzt werden, siehe M. Dietrich 1994b, S. 46.

Für das Selbstverständnis des Menschen, das aus den Texten der FORMATIO-GNATIO-Überlieferung abgelesen werden kann, ist das Bekenntnis zur Weisheit und Kunstfertigkeit des Schöpfergottes von größter Wichtigkeit. Mit diesen Gaben fühlt er sich beschenkt, sie bilden die Basis dafür, daß er mit seinem Schöpfer und Erhalter ins Gespräch kommen, zu ihm beten oder gar Einsichten in die Wege Gottes erhalten kann. Das findet seinen Ausdruck beispielsweise in der Semantik der Wörter *emēqu* „weise sein"[13] und *emqu* „weise, klug"[14], von denen ein *šutēmuqu* „inbrünstig flehen"[15] abgeleitet ist, oder *nakālu* „künstlich, kunstvoll sein, werden"[16] und *nikiltu* „kunstvolle, listige Gestaltung"[17] .

Nachfolgend sei von vielen möglichen Beispielen für die epische Überlieferung der Eridu-Babylon-Mythologie der einschlägige Bericht aus dem *Enūma eliš* angeführt, der für den Zeitpunkt, den Anlaß und die Art und Weise der Menschenschöpfung besonders aufschlußreiche Anhaltspunkte bietet und am Ende des relevanten Abschnitts Ee VI 1-38 zudem hervorhebt, daß die Menschenschöpfung ein Akt war, der über jedes Verstehen hinausragt.

Das *Enūma eliš*[18], dessen Textzeugen ins 8./7. Jh. v.Chr. zurückreichen und wohl auch im 1. Jt. in der uns bekannten Form ausgestaltet worden ist,[19] schildert den Aufstieg des Marduks, des Stadtgottes von Babylon, an die Spitze des sumero-mesopotamischen Pantheons.[20] Dieser Weg Marduks war nur mit einem Sieg über die vor ihm herrschende Götterwelt möglich. Also stellte der Dichter diesen Sieg in den ersten vier Tafeln des breit angelegten Epos dar. Danach habe Marduk seine Widersacherin *Tiāmat* getötet und sie als Basis für seine neue Welt[21] verwendet: Zerteilt bildete sie hinfort die beiden Ebenen Himmel und Erde als Grundelemente seines neuen Kosmos. Wie die fünfte Tafel vor Augen

---

13 AHw. 213f.; CAD E 151–152.

14 AHw. 214; CAD E 151–152.

15 AHw. 214; CAD Š/3 400–401.

16 AHw. 717; CAD N/1 155–156.

17 AHw. 788; CAD N/2 220–221.

18 Trotz der neuen Edition und Übersetzung von Ph. Talon 2005 steht eine abschließende Bearbeitung des Epos noch aus. Die nachfolgenden Zitate stammen aus einer eigenen Textzusammenstellung: M. Dietrich 1994a, S. 120–123.

19 Vgl. M. Dietrich 2006, bes. S. 157–161.

20 Siehe W. Sommerfeld 1982, S. 174–182.

21 Siehe M. Dietrich 1991, S. 51–61.

führt, mußte Marduk nun Hand anlegen, seinen Kosmos auszustatten. Dann hielt er seine programmatische Rede, die in dem Wunsch endete, auf der Erde ein Heiligtum einzurichten – Ee V 119 - 130:

119 *„Über dem Apsû, dem Wohnsitz, den ihr aufgeschlagen habt,*
120 *dem Gegenstück zum Ešarra-Tempel, den ich für euch gebaut habe,*
121 *unter dem Himmelszelt, dessen Boden ich gefestigt habe,*
122 *will ich ein Haus bauen–dies soll die Residenz meiner Allmacht sein!*
123 *Mitten hinein will ich ihre Kultstadt gründen,*
124 *ich will heilige Räume anlegen, will die Herrschaft dauerhaft machen!*
125 *Wenn ihr vom Apsû zur Versammlung heraufsteigt,*
126 *sei dieser Ort euer Übernachtungsort vor der Versammlung–*
127 *wenn ihr vom Himmel zur Versammlung herabsteigt,*
128 *sei dieser Ort euer Übernachtungsort vor der Versammlung!*
129 *Ich will seinen Namen* KÁ.DINGIR.RA.KI *nennen,*
„Haus der großen Götter“[22] –
130 *wir werden dann darin unsere Feste feiern!“*

Zweifelsohne haben seine Göttergenossen und Mitsieger diesen Plan zwar begeistert aufgenommen, haben aber gleichzeitig darauf hingewiesen, daß sie, um ihr Gottsein voll erleben zu können, den Menschen vermissten – der Text dazu ist weitgehend verloren gegangen. Dort, wo der Text in der sechsten Tafel wieder einsetzt, reagiert Marduk auf ihre Rede – Ee VI 1-38:[23]

1 *Wie Marduk die Worte der Götter hört,*
2 *trägt er sich mit dem Plan, Kunstvolles zu schaffen.*
3 *Sein Wort sagt er dem Ea,*
4 *was er sich in seinem Herzen überlegt hat, gibt er als Rat weiter:*
5 *„Blut will ich ballen, Gebein hervorbringen,*
6 *den lullû-Urmenschen*[24] *will ich auf die Beine stellen, amēlu-Mensch sei sein Name!*

22 É.MEŠ DINGIR.MEŠ GAL.MEŠ ist eine freie Übersetzung des KÁ.DINGIR.RA.KI und nimmt Bezug auf den Abschnitt Ee V 125–128, in dem den Göttern des Apsû und des Himmels zugesichert wird, daß sie bei ihrer Wallfahrt ins Heiligtum Marduks hier eine Herberge finden könnten.

23 Vgl. zu diesem Abschnitt auch M. Dietrich 2006, S. 149–150.

24 Der Begriff *lullû* (wohl dem sumerischen LÚ.U18/U19.LU entlehnt) wird, vergleichbar etwa dem biblischen Adam, für den von den Göttern ins Dasein gerufenen Ersten Menschen verwendet; AHw. 562: „ursprünglicher Mensch“, CAD L 242: „man“.

7 *Ich will schaffen den lullû-amēlu!*
8 *Ihm werde die Mühsal der Götter auferlegt: Sie sollen Ruhe haben!*
9 *(Fürs) Weiter(e) will ich die Wege der Götter kunstvoll gestalten,*
10 *Gemeinsam mögen sie verehrt werden, in zwei (Gruppen) seien sie gegliedert!"*
11 *Ea antwortete ihm, indem er ihm (folgendes) Wort sagte,*
12 *um den Göttern Ruhe zu verschaffen, teilte er ihm seinen Plan (zur Ausführung) mit:*
13 *„Ein Bruder von ihnen werde mir ausgeliefert,*
14 *der möge vollends vernichtet werden, daß Menschen geformt werden können!*
15 *Die großen Götter mögen sich zu mir versammeln,*
16 *der Schuldige werden ausgeliefert, die anderen mögen Bestand haben!"*
17 *Marduk versammelte die großen Götter,*
18 *(mit) freundlich(er Stimme) gibt er Befehl, erteilt Weisungen.*
19 *Seinem Wort lauschen die Götter–*
20 *der König spricht (folgendes) Wort zu den Anunnakū:*
21 *„Wahr sei gleich eure erste Namensnennung,*
22 *wahrheitsgemäß sprecht ein Wort zu mir!*
23 *Wer ist es, der den Kampf inszeniert,*
24 *der die Tiāmat aufgebracht, die Schlacht organisiert hat?*
25 *Ausgeliefert werde, der den Kampf begann!*
26 *Ich will ihm seine Strafe aufbürden, ihr werdet dann in Ruhe wohnen!"*
27 *Da antworteten ihm die Igigū, die großen Götter,*
28 *dem ‚König über die Götter des Himmels und der Erde', dem Ratgeber der Götter, ihrem Herrn:*
29 *„Kingu war es, der den Kampf inszeniert hat,*
30 *der die Tiāmat aufgewiegelt, die Schlacht organisiert hat!"*
31 *Sie fesselten ihn und hielten ihn vor Ea fest,*
32 *sie erlegten ihm die Strafe auf, indem sie sein(e) Blut(adern) durchtrennten.*
33 *Aus seinem Blut schuf er die Menschheit,*
34 *erlegte (ihm) die Mühsal der Götter auf, den Göttern gab er (dadurch) freien Lauf.*
35 *Nachdem Ea, der Weise, die Menschheit geschaffen hatte,*
36 *erlegte er ihr die Mühsal der Götter auf.*
37 *Dieses Werk kann man nicht verstehen,*
38 *nach dem kunstverständigen Vorschlag des Marduk hat Ea geschaffen."*

Wie diesem Abschnitt des *Enūma eliš* zu entnehmen ist, wird der Mensch, dessen Konzeption so kunstvoll und großartig ist, daß sie jede Vorstellung sprengt, in eine voll entwickelte, intakte Welt gestellt und hat die Aufgabe, den Göttern, ob ehedem Dienende oder Bediente, durch Übernahme der Arbeitslasten in der Schöpfung zu ihrem Gottsein zu verhelfen:

> 34 *(Ea) erlegte (ihm) die Mühsal der Götter auf, den Göttern gab er (dadurch) freien Lauf.*

Aber auch hier ist die Übernahme der Arbeitslasten nur ein Teilaspekt der menschlichen Tätigkeiten: Ein anderer, der wohl wichtigere, war der des Feierns von Festen in eigens dafür errichteten Kultbauten, wie aus der Rede Marduks herausklingt. Denn er hatte seine Schöpfertätigkeit nach der Schaffung des Kosmos als abgeschlossen betrachtet und mußte erst von seinen Mitgöttern dazu aufgefordert werden, auch den Menschen ins Dasein zu rufen.[25]

Wie alle Texte, die auf die Menschenschöpfung zu sprechen kommen, führt auch der relevante Abschnitt aus dem *Enūma eliš* vor Augen, daß dann, wenn davon die Rede ist, daß der Mensch geschaffen werden soll, immer Enki/Ea, der Gott der Weisheit, eingreift. Dies gilt nicht nur für die Texte aus dem mesopotamischen Kernland, sondern auch für die aus Syrien, in denen Enki/Ea zur Sprache kommt. Als Beispiel sei zum Schluß jener Weisheitstext zitiert, der Bestandteil von Gelehrtenbibliotheken von Ugarit in der nördlichen Levante und von Emar am Euphratknie war[26] – das einleitende Bikolon, das eine Überschrift darstellt, gibt das Thema an, mit dem sich der Dichter in seiner Komposition auseinanderzusetzen gedenkt und hat folgenden Wortlaut:

> 1*Durch Ea sind die Geschicke (des Menschen vor)gezeichnet,*
> 2*auf Geheiß des El sind zugeteilt die Lose.*

Als Geschöpf des Gottes Ea trägt der Mensch das Los eines Lebens, das den üblichen Gesetzen für Freude und Tod unterliegt. Diese Aussage ist nur auf dem Hintergrund der mesopotamischen Anthropogonie erklärbar. Bemerkenswert ist schließlich die hier bezeugte Gleichsetzung zwischen Ea und El, die sich aus dem Parallelismus des Bikolons ergibt und auch aus anderen Ugarit-Texten bekannt ist.[27]

---

25 Siehe oben: Ee V 119–130.

26 Siehe M. Dietrich 1994a; ders. 1994b.

27 Zur Bedeutung der Parallelsetzung von Ea und „der Gott" ohne weitere Angaben gegenübersteht, siehe M. Dietrich 2003.

Die Erhaltung des menschlichen Lebens

Da es nach den Vorstellungen der Mesopotamier als beklagenswerte Selbstverständlichkeit galt, daß das ursprüngliche makellose Geschöpf durch Krankheit belastet und damit vom heilen Urbild entfernt sein konnte, trat die Kunst der Erhaltung des menschlichen Lebens an die Seite der seiner Erschaffung. Damit rückte Enki/Ea erneut ins Zentrum des Interesses: So wahr Enki/Ea für die Erschaffung der Menschen verantwortlich war, so wahr mußte er auch dessen Stärken und Schwächen kennen. Also wandte sich der betroffene Bittsteller, wenn er sein Leben bedroht sah, direkt an ihn um Hilfe und Rettung.

Beispiele dafür gibt es in der umfangreichen Gebets- und Beschwörungsliteratur viele. Ich zitiere nachfolgend eines aus dem 1. Jt. v. Chr., das Modellcharakter hatte und in einem beliebigen Notfall eingesetzt werden konnte[28] – dann nannte sich der Betende mit Namen und gab zudem an, welchem Ortsnumen er sich von Hause aus verantwortlich sah:

[1]Beschwörung: *Ea, Šamaš und Asalluḫi, große Götter:*
[2]*Ihr seid es, die ihr das Land richtet, das Schicksal festlegt,*
[3]*die Geschicke vorzeichnet, die Lose zuteilt* [4]*im Himmel und auf Erden.*
[5]*Das Schicksal zu bestimmen, die Geschicke vorzuzeichnen, ist euer Hände Werk.*
[6]*Ihr seid es, die das Schicksal des Lebens bestimmen,*
[7]*ihr seid es, die die Geschicke des Lebens vorzeichnen,*
[8]*ihr seid es, die die Urteile über das Leben fällen.*
[9]*Euer Zauber bedeutet Leben,*
euer Wort Heil,
[10]*euer Ausspruch bedeutet Leben!*
[11]*Ihr seid es, die ihr das Land richtet,*
die weite Erde unter den Füßen habt,
[12]*den ausgedehnten Himmel unter den Füßen habt, wohin er sich auch erstrecken mag,*
[13]*die das Übel bekämpfen, das Gute einführen,*
[14]*die schlechten Zeichen und Vorzeichen –* [15]*wirre, schlechte, böse Träume – auslöschen,*
[16]*das Band des Übels entwirren, den Bann auflösen* [17]*wo auch immer die Zeichen und Vorzeichen auftreten mögen:*

28 R. Caplice 1971, S. 157–158; siehe M. Dietrich 1994a, S. 9–10.

> [18]*Ich, der NN, Sohn des NN, dessen Gott NN und Göttin NN ist,*
> [19]*gegen den böse Zeichen und Vorzeichen aufgetreten sind,*
> [20]*ich fürchte mich, ich habe Angst und ich bin verschreckt.*

Die beiden Gottheiten, die hier außer Ea beschworen werden, gehören in dessen Entourage: Šamaš, der Sonnengott, der Gott des Rechts und der Gerechtigkeit, sowie Asalluḫi, *alias* Marduk, Sohn des Ea. Alle drei sollten dafür Sorge tragen, daß der Befallene nicht zuschanden wurde und zur Unzeit das Leben verlor.

Diese formularhafte Gebetsbeschwörung stammt aus dem 1. Jt. Zur Demonstration dessen, daß derartige Gebetsbeschwörungen zum mesopotamischen Alltag auch früherer Zeiten gehörten, können die Beschwörungen des ‚Marduk-Ea-Typs'[29] angeführt werden, deren Tradition in die Ḫammurapi-Zeit (18./17. Jh. v.Chr.) zurückreicht.[30] Hier wird der Schöpfergott Enki/Ea durch die Vermittlung Asalluḫis um Hilfe gebeten: Die erste enthält die Bitte um Beseitigung einer Krankheitsnot und die zweite um Bewahrung vor Todesfolgen von Gift.

Zur ersten: Asalluḫi, der Sohn des Enki/Ea, wurde bei seinem Vater vorstellig und bat diesen, ihm das Rezept zu überlassen, das seinem Geschöpf helfen könnte:

> *Der böse Udug, der die stillen Straßen schwer (zu begehen) macht,*
> *der insgeheim einhergeht, der die Straßen bedeckt,*
> *der böse galla-Dämon, der in der Steppe losgelassen ist, der schonungslose Räuber,*
> *die dimme-Dämonin, der dim(me)-Dämon,*[31] *die den Menschen (mit Geifer) bespritzen,*
> *die Herzkrankheit, die Eingeweidekrankheit, die ...-Krankheit*[32]*,*
> *die Kopfkrankheit, der* u_{18}*-lu-Geist*[33]*, der den Menschen zudeckt,*
> *haben den rastlos hin- und hergehenden Menschen wie ein Sturm gelähmt, ihn in seine Galle getaucht,*
> *der besagte Mensch geht ‚jenseits seines Lebens' herum, wie eine Wasserflut wogt er,*
> *kann weder Speise essen noch Wasser trinken, verbringt in ‚Weh und Ach!' die Tage.*

---

29 Siehe W.H.Ph. Römer 1987, S. 189–191.

30 Siehe M. Dietrich 1997, S. 64–66.

31 Zwei Dämonen, von denen die erstere die Neugeborenen wegrafft und der zweite Krankheiten bewirkt.

32 Der Name läßt auf keine besondere Krankheit schließen.

33 Eine mentale Krankheit.

Asalluḫi sah (es), trat zu seinem Vater Enki ins Haus ein (und) spricht zu Ihm.
– Es werden alle Symptome wiederholt –
Nachdem er es wiedererzählt hatte, (fuhr er fort:)
„Was ich [dagegen tu]n soll, weiß ich nicht, was wird ihn dabei beruhigen?"
[Enki] antwortet seinem [Soh]ne [As]alluḫi:
„Mein Sohn, was weißt du nicht, was könnte ich dir hinzufügen?
Asalluḫi, was weißt du nicht, was könnte ich dir hinzufügen?
Das, was ich weiß, weißt auch du,
gehe, mein Sohn Asalluḫi!"
Hierauf folgt ein Rezept mit der Anweisung zur Anwendung –
Möge sich der namtar-Dämon, der sich im Körper des Menschen befindet, entfernen!
…[34]

Dieser Abschnitt der Beschwörung besagt, daß die Krankheitsnot eines Menschen dem Asalluḫi bekannt ist und er die Not vor seinen Vater bringt, der als Schöpfer am ehesten weiß, wie dem Geschöpf geholfen werden kann. Asalluḫi – mit ihm ist Marduk, der Stadtgott Babylons, seit seinem Auftreten Anfang des 2. Jt.s gleichgesetzt worden[35] – tritt also als Mittler zwischen dem Kranken und Enki/Ea auf, weil offenbar nur er befugt ist, von seinem Vater Rat und Vollmacht zur Heilung einzuholen. Damit erfüllt Asalluḫi eine Doppelfunktion: Einerseits ist er als Sohn des Hochgottes Enki/Ea eine selbständige Gottheit, andererseits übernimmt er bei seinem Vater Enki/Ea die Botenrolle der *sukkallu*-Götter.

Der zweite Texte zeigt, daß Asalluḫi/Marduk in den ‚Marduk-Ea-Beschwörungen' nicht immer selbst als Bote vor seinen Vater tritt, sondern seinerseits auch einen Sendboten haben kann. Der Text vom Anfang des 2. Jt. bietet eine Bitte um Bewahrung vor Todesfolgen bei einer Vergiftung:[36]

Den Menschen hat eine Schlange gebissen, hat ein Skorpion gestochen, hat ein rasender Hund gebissen, ihr Gift haben sie in ihn hineingebracht.
Asalluḫi schickte einen Boten zu seinem Vater Enki (mit den Worten:)
„Mein Vater, den Menschen hat eine Schlange gebissen, hat ein Skorpion gestochen, hat ein rasender Hund gebissen, ihr Gift haben sie in ihn hineingebracht.
Was ich dagegen machen soll, weiß ich nicht!"

34 Zitiert nach W.H.Ph. Römer 1987, S. 196–198.

35 W. Sommerfeld 1989, S. 362.

36 Zitiert nach W.H.Ph. Römer 1987, S. 210–211.

(Enki antwortet:) „Mein Sohn, was weiß er nicht, was könnte ich ihm hinzufügen?
Nachdem er mit seinem reinen Wassergefäß gereinigt hat, über das betreffende Wasser die Beschwörung gesprochen hat, das betreffende Wasser den gebissenen Menschen hat trinken lassen, möge das betreffende Gift von selbst aus ihm herausgehen!"

Bis auf die Tatsache, daß Asalluḫi/Marduk einen ‚Boten'[37] sendet und nicht selbst vor seinen Vater tritt, können die Aussagen dieser Beschwörung mit denen der vorangehend zitierten parallel gesehen werden.

Den ‚Marduk-Ea-Beschwörungen' ist gemeinsam, daß Asalluḫi sich eines Menschen in seiner Not annimmt und als Mittler vor seinen selbst für Götter unerreichbaren Vater Enki/Ea tritt. Das unterstreicht die für Asalluḫi/Marduk sonst nicht bekannte *sukkallu*-Botenrolle, die es ihm im vorliegenden Zusammenhang ermöglicht hat, eine Brücke zwischen den Welten der Immanenz und der Transzendenz zu schlagen.

Derartige Beschwörungen sind auch in Ugarit in der nordsyrischen Levante belegt, wie beispielsweise die Beschwörung KTU 1.128[38] bezeugt, die bei Weihrauch gebetet worden ist. Sie ist in hurritischer Sprache abgefaßt und richtet sich an den ugaritischen Hochgott El, das syrische Pendant von Enki/Ea – hier wird *Ilabrat* als Mittler und *sukkallu*-Götterbote angerufen:

Weihrauch-Erhöhung:
El, der befehligt die Erde,
El, der das Wort führt im Himmel.
Bei den hohen Göttern bist du erhöht, oh Fähiger,
bei den niederen Göttern bist du erhöht, oh Gott!
Komm schnell El, komm schnell, oh König El!
Den Thron nimm ein, zum Gabentisch komm schnell, oh El des Gebirges!
Nimm an das Begrüßungsgeschenk vom Tablett,
aus dem Topf, aus dem Becher, aus dem kaddale-Gefäß!
Schenk' Liebe, oh El, (er ist) der Helfer!
Da (ist) El, da (ist) Kušuḫ, da (ist) Kumarbi, da (ist) Ellil
– Ilabrat (ist) der Bote(, der) von El (kommt):
Löse, El,
der du mit deinen Händen bei Wasser (und) Weihrauch löst!
Göttlicher, nimm das auf mir Liegende weg!

37 Hier schlicht LÚ „Mensch; jemand bestimmter".

38 M. Dietrich/W. Mayer 1994, S. 87–94.

Sprich, Herr!
Ich will weihräuchern (und) schlachten!
Dadurch, daß es von dir angenommen ist, werden immerzu Heil und Lösung bewirkt!

Zwischenergebnis

Die Texte, die hier aus den Kulturbereichen Mesopotamiens und Ugarit-Syriens zur Sprache gebracht wurde, heben zwei Aspekte des Tagungsthemas „Art and Magic in the Ancient Near East" hervor: einerseits die göttlich-magische Kunst der Erschaffung und Erhaltung des menschlichen Lebens und andererseits die menschliche Kunst der Magie, die die Götter mit Hilfe von Gebeten und Beschwörungen zur Kunst der Lebenserhaltung bewegen soll. Voraussetzung für die damit verbundenen Vorgänge ist, daß der Mensch das Produkt eines Schöpfungsaktes ist, wie sie die FORMATIO-GNATIO-Vorstellung der Eridu-Babylon-Mythologie in Verbindung mit den Schöpfungsgöttern Enki/Ea, Marduk und El von Ugarit vorsieht.

CREATIO AD USUM / CASUM nach syro-mesopotamischen Texten[39]

Wie in der Einführung ausgeführt, kommt in Texten, die von einer CREATIO AD USUM/CASUM handeln, die Kunst der Lebenserschaffung und -erhaltung und die damit verbundene Magie besonders deutlich zum Ausdruck. Der Schöpfergott griff nach Aussage dieser Texte auf seine schöpferischen Fähigkeiten zurück und rief ein kurzzeitig wirkendes, übernatürliches Wesen ins Leben, das zur Durchführung einer besonderen Aufgabe gebraucht wurde – die CREATURAE AD USUM/CASUM: Die vorübergehende Aufgabe solcher Wesen hatte er an der Schwelle von der *Vorwelt* zur *Jetzt-Welt*, als die Schöpfung der Lebewesen stattfand, nicht im Blick. Denn damals wurden nur Lebewesen erschaffen, die mit der autogenerativen Kraft der Zeugung und Geburt ausgestattet waren, nicht aber solche, die aus gegebenem Anlaß gebraucht waren und nur kurzzeitig wirken sollten.

In der syro-mesopotamischen Mythologie sind aus den Texten, die eine CREATIO AD USUM/CASUM bezeugen, folgende drei CREATURAE AD

39 Zu diesem Abschnitt vgl. auch M. Dietrich 2004, S. 5–17.

USUM/CASUM, Geschöpfe für besondere Gelegenheiten, besonders gut bekannt:

1. *Ṣaltum* – die Göttin „Zwietracht, Streit“ wurde im 18. Jh. v. Chr. als Kontrahentin der übermächtigen Ištar, *alias* Agušaya, in Babylon besungen,
2. *Aṣû-šu-namir* – der Lustknabe „Sein Aufgehen ist glänzend“ befreit Ištar aus der Unterwelt, wie der sumero-akkadische Mythos von *Ištars Höllenfahrt* im 2. und 1. Jt. v. Chr. berichtet, und

Šaʿtiqat – die Göttin „Vortreffliche“ wurde gebraucht, um den ugaritischen König Keret von seinem Leiden zu heilen.

Ṣaltum – die Göttin „Zwietracht, Streit“

Vorbemerkung

Unter dem Namen *Agušaya* besingt ein Dichter der Zeit des Königs Ḫammurapi von Babylon, des Nestors der babylonischen Literatur im 18. Jh. v. Chr., die Göttin Ištar in einem hochpoetischen und darum sprachlich schwer verständlichen Gesang, dem Agušaya-Lied. Ihr steht in diesem Lied die Ṣaltum gegenüber, die als ihre Kontrahentin geschaffen worden ist. Von dem Lied der Auseinandersetzung zwischen Ištar und Ṣaltum sind bislang zwei Tontafeln leider nur bruchstückhaft auf uns gekommen, die wir mit den Buchstaben A und B auseinanderhalten.[40]

Das Agušaya-Lied hat der Initiation des jährlich in Babylon gefeierten Sommerfestes zu Ehren der Göttinnen Ištar und Ṣaltum gedient. Das Fest fand in der Mitte des babylonischen Jahres, also im Monat Elūlu (ca. Juli/August), statt – dieser Monat war der Festmonat der Ištar und hieß dementsprechend KIN.^{d}INANNA = *têrti Ištar* „Anweisung der Ištar“, d.h., in ihm hat Ištar das Sagen. Das Fest war, wie das Lied am Ende her-

40 Zur letzten Edition und Diskussion philologischer und inhaltlicher Fragen siehe B.R.M. Groneberg 1997, S. 55–93: Kapitel III, *Ištar* und *Ṣaltum* oder das sogenannte *„Agušaya-*Lied"; vgl. auch K. Hecker 1989, S. 731–740. – Die hier zugrunde gelegte Übersetzung weicht in wesentlichen Punkten von den bisherigen ab und wird an anderer Stelle gerechtfertigt.

vorhebt, ein Straßenfest nach Art des Karnevals[41] und war von ausgelassenen Frauen bestimmt. In seinem Verlauf wurden göttliche Kampfspiele von männlich verkleideten Frauen ausgetragen, in deren Mittelpunkt Ištar und Ṣaltum samt ihren irdischen Vertreterinnen standen.

Das Lied weist den göttlichen Ursprung des Straßenfestes nach und stellt die Anführerinnen der beiden sich bekämpfenden Frauenparteien vor: Auf der einen Seite die kampflustige Ištar, auf der anderen die Ṣaltum, „Zwietracht, Streit", die geschaffen wurde, um als adäquates Gegenüber der Ištar aufzutreten.

Kontext

Text A beginnt mit der Beschreibung der Ištar als einer außerordentlichen Erscheinung am Himmel der Götter:

> [1]Preisen will ich die Größte [2]unter den Göttern, die Sieggewohnte,
> [3]die Erstgeborene der Ningal: [4]Ihre Stärke will ich hochpreisen, ihren Namen!
> [5]Ištar, die Größte [6]unter den Göttern, die Sieggewohnte,
> [7]die Erstgeborene der Ningal,
> [8]von ihrer Stärke will ich erneut berichten!

Ihre Ausstattung als Himmelskönigin kommt ausführlich in Kol. IV von Text A zur Sprache, gleichzeitig aber auch der Schrecken, den sie mit ihrem unbescheidenen, auftrumpfenden Verhalten in der Welt der Götter verursacht. Die von Ištar, *alias* Agušaya, verbreitete Unruhe dringt schließlich bis zum Schöpfergott Enki/Ea in den Apsû vor; dieser fühlt sich durch die Tochter des Himmelsgottes Anum gestört und grollt ihr – ein Thema, das in der 1. Tafel des *Enūma eliš* ausführlich zur Sprache kommt – :

> [14]Sie verbreitet mehr Zittern als ein Stier, [15]wenn ihr Schrei in Zorn (erschallt).
> [16]In Lumpen ist sie nie aufgetreten, [17]in (vollem) Ornat ist sie ausgezogen.
> [18]Bei ihrem Geschrei ist erschrocken [19]der weise Gott Ea.
> [20]Er wurde voll des Zorns über sie, [21]Ea grollte ihr.

41 B VII 19–20: „Sie (die Menschen) mögen auf den Straßen tanzen (*li-me-el-lu i-sú-qí-im*) – höre ihr Kreischen!"

Als die Götter nach einem Weg suchten, der Ištar jemanden entgegenzusetzen, der sie mit den ihr angeborenen Eigenschaften bändigen könne (A V 2-13), kamen sie auf den Schöpfergott Ea, der alleine dazu befähigt sei, einen Bändiger ins Leben zu rufen:

> [18]„Allein für dich ist es passend, [19]dieses zu tun! Wer sonst könnte
> [20]etwas Außergewöhnliches [21]in Gang setzen?"

So begann Ea erneut mit einem Schöpfungswerk, das in seinen Ausführungen ganz und gar an Formulierungen erinnert, die für die Erschaffung des Menschen gebraucht werden und, wie oben angedeutet, die Bilderwelt der FORMATIO/GNATIO von Eridu und Babylon spiegelt:

> [22]Er hegte die Worte, die sie ihm entgegneten, [23]der weise Ea.
> [24]Lehm kratzte mit seinen Fingernägeln [25]siebenmal zusammen,
> [26]nahm ihn in seine Hand (und) buk ihn.
> [27]Damit hat Ṣaltum geschaffen [28]der weise Ea.
>
> [30]Als der Gott Ea loseilte, [31]sich darauf konzentrierte,
> [32]schuf er die Ṣaltum [33]zum Streit mit Ištar.

Die anschließende Beschreibung der Eigenschaften der Ṣaltum heben ihre außergewöhnliche Statur hervor und gipfelt in der Feststellung:

> [41]Verschlagen ist sie, daß niemand [42]ihr gleicht, (und) ausdauernd.
> [43]Ihr Fleisch ist Kriegführen, [44]Streiten ihr Haar.

Kol. VI der Tafel A führt nun breit den Auftrag aus, für den Ea sie erschaffen hat: Sie solle losziehen und Ištar bekämpfen; sie brauche keine Angst zu haben, weil er sie mit allen Fähigkeiten ausgestattet habe, die sie für den Kampf brauche. Sie sei ihr keineswegs unterlegen, eher noch überlegen:

> [38]„Sie wird sich auf dich stürzen,
> [39](folgendes) Wort wird sie zu dir sagen, [40]wird dich fragen:
> „Mädchen, wohlan! [41]Tu mir kund deinen Weg!"
> [42]Du sei dann wirsch, [43]beuge dich nicht vor ihr!
> [44]Was das Herz beruhigt, [45]entgegne ihr mit keinem Wort!
> [46]Wann könnte sie dir schon etwas wegnehmen, [47]die du doch ein

Geschöpf meiner Hände bist!
[48]Herrisch sei jeder deiner Sprüche, [49]und zwar rede vor ihr
vollmundig!"

Obwohl die nächstfolgenden Abschnitte teilweise schlecht erhalten sind, geben sie zu verstehen, daß Ṣaltum ihren Auftrag bravourös erfüllt und Ištar, *alias* Agušaya, als gleichwertige Partnerin in die Knie gezwungen hat. Dies tritt besonders klar in der Bitte der Agušaya zutage, die das Lied abschließt – B VII[42] 1-4:

[1]„Nachdem du ihre Größe bestimmt hast,
[2]Ṣaltum ihr Geschrei [3]gegen mich ausgeführt hat,
[4]soll sie nun in ihr Loch zurückkehren!"

Denn diese Aufforderung besagt, daß Ištar, *alias* Agušaya, ihren Übermut im Kampf mit Ṣaltum abgebaut habe und dankbar wäre, wenn Ṣaltum wieder aus der Welt geschafft würde. Ea stimmt ihr zu:

[7]„Gewiß werde ich, wie du gesagt hast, [8]handeln!
[9]Du ermunterst mich, [10]du gibst mir Freude, (sie) für dich zu
entfernen!"

Zusammenfassende Bemerkungen zu Aufgaben und Charakter der Ṣaltum

Aus dem Blickpunkt der CREATIO AD USUM/CASUM ergeben sich folgende Beobachtungen:

— Ṣaltum („Zwietracht, Streit") war ein gleichwertiges Pendant zur Kriegs- und Liebesgöttin Ištar, der Tochter des Himmelsgottes Anum. Sie hatte die übermütige Ištar mit Sitz in Uruk gebändigt.
— Ṣaltum war ein Geschöpf des Enki/Ea und gehörte damit dem Götterkreis von Eridu und Babylon an.
— Ṣaltum wurde nach Erfüllung ihres Auftrags wieder entfernt – das jährliche Ištar-Straßenfest erinnert jährlich an ihre kurzzeitige Existenz.

---

42 Entgegen allen anderen Darstellungen handelt es sich hier um Kol. VII, weil die Kol. IV und V ganz weggebrochen sind.

— Ṣaltum war als Kontrahentin der Ištar/Agušaya eine Dame, wie das grammatische Geschlecht ihres Namens auch formal zu erkennen gibt.
— Ṣaltum hatte einen streitbaren Charakter.

Zum Tagungsthema *Kunst und Magie* trägt das Agušaya-Lied folgendes bei:

— Enki/Ea hat Ṣaltum nach den Prinzipien der FORMATIO/GNATIO erschaffen und damit seine Fähigkeiten als Schöpfer erneut unter Beweis gestellt. Darum führt der Text auch dort, wo er auf Ea zu sprechen kommt, dessen Attribute „Weisheit, Kunstfertigkeit" an.

Die Kunstfertigkeit der Schöpfung geschieht hier auf der transzendenten Ebene und dient der Initiation des jährlichen Ištar-Straßenfestes. Damit ist es ein Mittel der Magie.

Aṣû-šu-namir – der *assinnu*-Lustknabe „sein Aufgehen ist glänzend"

Vorbemerkung

Der Mythos vom Besuch der Himmelsgöttin Ištar, die Göttin für Liebe und Krieg, bei ihrer Kollegin Ereškigal, der Göttin des Todes, in der Unterwelt, die im Sumerischen kur.nu.gi4.a und im Babylonischen *qaqqar/erṣet lā târi* „Land ohne Rückkehr" heißt, bietet den Rahmen für das CREATIO AD USUM/CASUM-Geschöpf Aṣû-šu-namir. Dieses wurde ins Leben gerufen, um Ištar aus der Unterwelt zu befreien.

Der Mythos gehörte ab dem Beginn des 2. Jt. v.Chr. offenbar zum festen Bestandteil einer Keilschrift-Bibliothek. Seine Beliebtheit und seine lange Traditionsgeschichte haben zahlreiche, teils besser und teils schlechter erhaltene Exemplare auf uns gekommen lassen.[43] In der modernen Literatur trägt der Mythos den Titel „Ištars Höllenfahrt".

Kontext

Der Mythos beginnt mit folgenden Zeilen:

[1]Zum Kurnugia, dem Land [ohne Wiederkehr,]

43 G.G.W. Müller 1994, S. 760–766; für den Text siehe R. Borger 1979, S. 95–104.

[2]wandte Ištar, die Tochter des Sîn, ihren Sinn.
[3]Es wandte die Tochter des Sîn ihren Sinn
[4]nach dem finsteren Haus, der Wohnstatt von Erkalla,
[5]zum Haus, der, wer es betritt, nicht mehr verläßt,
[6]auf den Weg, dessen Beschreiten ohne Rückkehr ist,
[7]zum Haus, worin, wer es betritt, des Lichtes entbehrt,
[8]wo Staub ihr Hunger, ihre Speise Lehm ist,
[9]das Licht sie nicht sehen, sie in der Finsternis sitzen.

Es ist anzunehmen, daß Ištar durch ihr Handeln die Behauptung widerlegen wollte, daß die Unterwelt ein „Land ohne Wiederkehr“ sei. Nachdem sie sieben Tore durchschritten hatte, begegnete sie ihrer Kontrahentin Ereškigal:

[63]Sobald Ištar zum Kurnugia hinabgestiegen,
[64]erblickte Ereškigal sie und fuhr sie zornig an.
[65]Ištar, unbesonnen, stürzte auf sie zu.

Für ihren Übermut bestrafte sie Ereškigal mit dem Auftrag an ihren Wesir Namtar („Todesgeschick“), sie mit allen nur denkbaren Krankheiten zu belegen. Diese bewirkten bei ihr schließlich den Tod. Gleichzeitig erlosch auf Erden jegliches Liebesverlangen und der Wille zur Zeugung. Weil damit eine der Grundregeln des Kosmos außer Kraft gesetzt war, sanken die Götter in Trauer und wandten sich hilfesuchend an Ea. Er sollte offenbar entweder einen Ersatz für die verstorbene Ištar erschaffen oder ein Wesen kreieren, das Ištar aus der Unterwelt herausholen konnte:

[76]Nachdem Ištar, meine Herrin, [hinabgestiegen zum Kurnugia,]
[77]bespringt nicht mehr der Stier die Kuh, der Esel schwängert die
Eselin nicht mehr,
[78]das Mädchen auf der Straße schwängert nicht mehr der Mann,
[79]es liegt der Mann al[lei]n,
[80]es liegt das Mädchen al[lei]n.

[81]Papsukkal, der Wesir der großen Götter, gesenkt ist sein Haupt,
sein Gesicht [verdüstert,]
[82]mit einem Trauergewand bekleidet, mit ungekämmtem Haar,
[83]er geht ermattet zu Sîn, seinem Vater, er weint,
[84]vor König Ea fließen seine Tränen:

[85]„Ištar stieg in die Erde hinab und ist nicht mehr heraufgekommen.
[86]Seitdem Ištar hinabgestiegen zum Kurnugia,
[87]bespringt nicht mehr der Stier die Kuh, der Esel schwängert die
Eselin nicht mehr,
[88]das Mädchen auf der Straße schwängert nicht mehr der Mann,
[89]es liegt der Mann allein,
[90]es liegt das Mädchen allein."

Ea wählte die Variante, ein Wesen ins Dasein zu rufen, das Ištar aus der Unterwelt befreien konnte. Er erschuf einen *assinnu*-‚Lustknaben', also eine Person, die im antiken Mesopotamien als Geschlechtsneutraler Kultdienste erfüllte:

[91]Ea, in seinem weisen Herz, schuf einen Plan.
[92]Er schuf Aṣû-šu-namir, den Lustknaben (und sprach zu ihm):

[93]„Geh, Aṣû-šu-namir, wende dich dem Tor des Kurnugia zu,
[94]die sieben Tore des Kurnugia sollen geöffnet werden vor dir,
[95]Ereškigal soll dich sehen und sich freuen über deine Anwesenheit!

[96]Nachdem ihr Herz sich beruhigt, ihr Gemüt erheitert,
[97]lasse einen Eid sie schwören auf die großen Götter,
[98]erhebe dein Haupt und richte deinen Sinn auf den Wasserschlauch:
[99]‘He, meine Herrin, den Wasserschlauch soll man mir geben!
Wasser will ich daraus trinken!'"

[100]Als Ereškigal das hörte,
[101]schlug sie sich auf den Schenkel, biß sich in den Finger:
[102]„Du hast mich um etwas gebeten, worum man nicht fragt!
[103]Komm, Aṣû-šu-namir! Ich will dich mit einem großen Fluch verdammen!"

Aṣû-šu-namir gelang es tatsächlich, bis zur Ereškigal vorzudringen und sie auf ihre oberirdischen und himmlischen Götterkollegen einzuschwören. Nachdem sich ihr Interesse an ihm gelegt hatte, bittet er sie um ein Erfrischungsgetränk. Dieses konnte sie ihm, obwohl die Bitte gegen die Gesetze der Unterwelt verstieß, nach dem Schwur nicht mehr verwehren. Sie war also auf eine List hereingefallen und mußte grollend nachgeben: Als letztes Mittel gegen die Gesetze des Lebens belegte sie Aṣû-šu-namir mit einem Fluch. Da aber auch dieser in den Räumen der Unterwelt wirkungslos verscholl, erteilte sie ihrem Wesir Namtar den Auftrag, Ištar durch Besprengen mit Wasser wieder zum Leben zu erwecken:

> 109Ereškigal tat ihren Mund auf zu sprechen,
> 110sie sagte zu Namtar, ihrem Wesir:
>
> 111„Geh, Namtar, klopf an beim Egalgina,
> 112schmücke die Türschwellen mit Muscheln,
> 113laß die Anunnaki hinausgehen und auf goldenen Thronen sitzen:
> 114Besprenge Ištar mit dem Wasser des Lebens und bringe sie zu mir!"

Ištar konnte nun ihren Rückweg in die Oberwelt antreten und dafür sorgen, daß das Leben in den gewohnten Bahnen weiterging.

Zusammenfassende Bemerkungen zu Aufgaben und Charakter des Aṣû-šu-namir

Aus dem Blickpunkt der CREATIO AD USUM/CASUM ergeben sich aus der Höllenfahrt Ištars folgende Beobachtungen:

— Aṣû-šu-namir („sein Aufgehen ist glänzend") sollte als ‚grenzüberschreitendes' Wesen in die Unterwelt vordringen, um Ištar zur Rückkehr auf die Oberwelt zu verhelfen.
— Aṣû-šu-namir war ein Geschöpf des Enki/Ea und gehörte damit in den Götterkreis von Eridu und Babylon.
— Aṣû-šu-namir ist nach Erfüllung seiner Aufgaben verschwunden, wurde also offenbar wie Ṣaltum wieder entfernt.
— Aṣû-šu-namir war ein geschlechtsneutraler Lustknabe für Kultdienste.
— Aṣû-šu-namir wirkte auf Ereškigal verführerisch und konnte sie überlisten.

Zum Thema *Kunst und Magie* trägt der Mythos Ištars Höllenfahrt folgendes bei:

— Die Kunst der Schöpfung hat Enki/Ea mit der Erschaffung des Aṣû-šu-namir unter Beweis gestellt. Er hat Aṣû-šu-namir nach den Prinzipien der FORMATIO/GNATIO und nach einem entsprechen

Entwurf seines „weisen Herzens" (*i-na em-qí lìb-bi-šú*) erschaffen (*ibtani*).

Das Geschöpf Aṣû-šu-namir mußte aus der Oberwelt in die Unterwelt. Das konnte er nur mit Hilfe der Magie.

Šaʿtiqat – die Göttin „Vortreffliche"

Vorbemerkung

Die Heilkraft Šaʿtiqat, die „Vortreffliche"[44], kommt als drittes syro-mesopotamisches Beispiel für ein gut bekanntes Geschöpf der CREATIO AD USUM/CASUM zur Sprache. Sie tritt im ugaritischen Keret-Epos auf und wurde geschaffen, um den todkranken König Keret zu heilen.

Das Keret-Epos, von dem drei Tafeln (KTU 1.14-16) auf uns gekommen sind, schildert in der poetischen Sprache des 14.-13. Jh. v.Chr. den Leidensweg eines – historisch nicht mehr greifbaren – Königs von Ugarit. Obwohl sich Keret befleißigte, mit Recht und Gerechtigkeit zu regieren, durchschritt er die unendlichen Tiefen des familiären und persönlichen Leids: Seine Frauen starben, bevor sie ihm einen Thronerben schenken konnten, er selbst sah auf dem Krankenbett dem Tod in die Augen. Also ist das Epos über seinen Lebensweg ein literar- und religionsgeschichtlich einmaliges Beispiel für einen „gerechten Leidenden".[45]

Kontext

Das Epos scheint aus zwei Episoden zusammengesetzt zu sein, die vormals literarisch selbständig überliefert waren. Die erste Episode hatte den Verlust der Frauen des Keret und seinen Zug zur Einholung der Ḥuriya, die ihm den Thronerben Yaṣṣib geschenkt hat, zum Thema (erste und zweite Tafel, KTU 1.14 - 1.15). Mit dieser ist dann eine zweite verwoben worden, die sich mit dem Gelübde und seinen Folgen befaßt, das Keret auf seinem Weg nach Udum vor der Göttin ʾAṯirat in Tyrus abgelegt, dieses nach der Geburt des Thronerben aber nicht eingehalten hat. Die

44 Oder „die im Rang Erhöhte"; zur Diskussion über die unterschiedlichen Deutungen des Namens siehe J. Tropper 1990, S. 90–91; ders. 2000, S. 602; vgl. DUL 800: „DN, healing genie created by the god *il*".

45 M. Dietrich/O. Loretz 1999, S. 133–164.

Göttin hat daraufhin das Vergehen mit einer Krankheit geahndet, die den Brecher des Gelübdes an den Rand des Todes geführt hat – mit der Krankheit und dem näher rückenden Tod des Königs befaßt sich die dritte erhaltene Tafel, KTU 1.16.

In den ersten beiden Kolumnen von KTU 1.16 wird die Krankheit beklagt, die den König zum Todgeweihten gemacht hat. Hier steht die Frage im Mittelpunkt, wie es El zulassen könne, daß sein Sprößling dahingerafft werde:

> „Ach, ist Keret denn kein Sohn Els,
> nicht ein Sprößling des Gütigen und des Heiligen?!“
> (KTU 1.16 II 48-49)

Wie der schlecht erhaltenen Kolumnen III zu entnehmen ist, trauerte wegen des bevorstehenden Todes des Königs auch die Natur: die Saat auf dem Feld sei vertrocknet, alle Lebensmittel seien aufgebraucht. Ein letzter Versuch, die Hilfe Els zu beschwören, unterbreitet Kolumne IV: Denn es will sich niemand mit dem Tod des Königs abfinden.

Die Wende der Ereignisse führt Kolumne V aus. Da El seinen Diener Keret nicht im Stich lassen will, wendet er sich an den Götterrat und fragt seine Kollegen, ob sich jemand unter ihnen befinde, der bereit sei, die Krankheit Kerets zu beenden – KTU 1.16 V 9b-22:

> [Da rief] ^{10}der Gütige, El der Gemütvolle:
> „[Wer] ^{11}von den Göttern [treibt die Krankheit aus,]
> ^{12}verjagt das Siech[tum?]“
> [Keiner der Götter] ^{13}antwortete ihm.
>
> Ein zwei[tes Mal, ein drittes Mal] ^{14}rief er:
> „Wer von den [Göttern treibt] ^{15}die Krankheit [aus],
> verjag[t das Siechtum?]“
> ^{16}Keiner der Götter an[wortete ihm].
>
> [Ein viertes Mal], ^{17}ein fünftes Mal rief er:
> [„Wer von den Göttern] ^{18}treibt die Krankheit aus,
> ver[jagt das Siechtum?]“
> ^{19}Keiner der Götter ant[wortete ihm].
> Ein sechstes Mal, ^{20}ein siebtes Mal rief er:

„[Wer] von den Göttern [21]treibt die Krankheit aus,
verjagt das Siechtum?“
[22]Keiner der Götter antwortete ihm.

Angesichts der Hilflosigkeit seiner Kollegen sucht El nach einen neuen Weg, der Krankheit Herr zu werden: Er erschafft ein Wesen, das die Aufgabe der Heilung übernehmen kann – KTU 1.16 V 23-31a:

[23]Da antwortete der Gütige, El der Gemütvolle:
[24]„Kehrt zurück, meine Kinder, zu euren Wohnstätten,
[25]zu euren fürstlichen Thronen!

Ich selbst [26]werde zaubern und erschaffen,
[27]erschaffen eine, die austreibt die [Kran]kheit,
eine, die verjagt [28]das Siechtum!“
Er füllte [seine Han]dfläche mit [29]fester Masse,
[Lehm] kniff er ab [30]wie des Töpf[ers].
[Er formte] eine, die [31][Krankheit] beseitigt,
[…]
[37]In der Bru[st der Dame ʾAṯirat] [38]wurde sie gefor[mt],
[im Herzen Els gebildet.]

Nach Vollendung des heilbringenden Geschöpfes, dem er den Namen Šaʿtiqat, „Vortreffliche“, „die (alle Götter) übertrifft“, gibt, erteilt ihr El den Auftrag, Keret mit der Hilfe einer magischen Pflanze von seinem Leiden zu befreien – KTU 1.16 V 39 - VI 2a:

[39][El nahm] den Becher [in die Hand,]
[40]ein Trink[gefäß in seine Rechte:]

[41]„Du Šaʿ[tiqat, entferne,]
[42]entferne [die Krankheit K][43]erets,
en[tferne sein Siechtum!]“
[44][Er gab eine] ‚Primel‘ [in die Hand,]
[45]in den Mund der Šaʿ[tiqat eine Beschwörung:]

[46]„[Gehe in die St]adt,

> [47]durch die Stadt [laß deiner Beschwörung freien Lauf,]
> [48]es fliege [dein] B[lumenstengel durch die Stadt!]
>
> [49]Die Krank[heit …]
> [50]das Siech[tum …].
> …
> VI
> [1]Mot sei jener, der zerschlagen werde,
> Šaʿtiqat jene, die [2]überwältige!"

Šaʿtiqat geht los und handelt gemäß ihrem Auftrag. Unter höchster Anstrengung wird sie, mit ihrer magischen Pflanze wedelnd, zur Heilbringerin:

> Und Šaʿtiqat ging los.
> [3]In das Haus Kerets trat sie ein,
> [4]weinend öffnete sie und trat ein,
> [5]klagend ging sie ins Innere.
>
> [6]Durch die Stadt ließ sie ihrer Beschwörung freien Lauf,
> [7]durch die Stadt ließ sie fliegen den Stengel.
>
> [8]Sie rollte zu einem Stab die ‚Primel':
> Als [9]das Siechtum aus ihm herausgetreten
> und über seinem Kopf war,
> [10]wusch sie sich wiederholt den Schweiß ab.
> [11]Sie öffnete seinen (: Keret) Schlund zum Essen,
> [12]seine Kehle zum Speisen.
> [13]Mot war jener, der zerschlagen wurde,
> Šaʿtiqat jene, [14]die überwältigte.
>
> Da befahl [15]der edle Keret,
> er erhob seine Stimme [16]und rief:
> „Höre, oh Dame, [17]Ḥuriya!
> Schlachte ein Lamm, [18]denn ich will essen,
> eine Köstlichkeit, denn ich will speisen!"
>
> [19]Es gehorchte die Dame Ḥuriya.
> [20]Sie schlachtete ein Lamm, und er aß,

[21]eine Köstlichkeit, und er speiste.

Siehe, ein Tag [22]und ein zweiter:
da saß Keret auf seinem Thron,
[23]er saß auf seinem Königsthron,
[24]auf dem Ruhesitz, auf dem Thron der Herrschaft.

Nach der Genesung und einer kräftigen Mahlzeit wendet sich Keret wieder seinen Aufgaben als Regent zu.

Über den Verbleib der Heilbringerin Šaʿtiqat erfahren wir nichts mehr. Das Epos leitet unmittelbar auf die Episode über, die das oppositionelle Verhalten des Thronerben Yaṣṣib ausführt – dieser hatte während der Erkrankung seines Vaters offenbar schon alle Vorbereitungen für die Übernahme der Regierungsgeschäfte getroffen und war mit dessen Genesung nicht einverstanden.

Zusammenfassende Bemerkungen zu Aufgaben und Charakter der Šaʿtiqat

Im Blick auf die CREATIO AD USUSM/CASUM lassen sich folgende Beobachtungen formulieren:

— Šaʿtiqat („Vortreffliche") sollte mit einer magischen Pflanze durch die Straßen der Stadt Kerets ziehen und den König im Palast von seiner Krankheit befreien.
— Šaʿtiqat war ein Geschöpf des El.
— Šaʿtiqat ist nach Erfüllung ihrer Aufgaben aus dem Blickfeld des Erzählers verschwunden.
— Šaʿtiqat war, wie das grammatische Geschlecht ihres Namen anzeigt, eine Dame.
— Šaʿtiqat war selbst eine Magierin, die mit einer Pflanze die Krankheit besiegt hat.

Zum Tagungsthema *Kunst und Magie* trägt die Episode von der Heilung des ugaritischen Königs Keret folgendes bei:

— Die Kunst der Schöpfung hat El mit der Erschaffung der Šaʿtiqat bewiesen. Er befolgte dabei wie Enki/Ea die Prinzipien der FORMATIO/GNATIO-Schöpfung, die der Dichter mit Bildern der

Töpferei beschreibt: Er nahm Ton in die Hand und formte die Gestalt des Geschöpfes (V 28b-30a); die Übergabe an ʾAṯirat, die Gattin Els, symbolisiert die Geburt, die das Geschöpf zum Leben bringt (V 37-38). Also ist hier neben der FORMATIO auch die GNATIO angesprochen.

— Die Magie spielt bei der Krankenheilung erwartungsgemäß eine zentrale Rolle: El nennt die Erschaffung seines Wesens nicht nur „Zauberei" (V 26), sondern gibt seinem Geschöpf auch magische Kräfte mit: Eine Pflanze als *Concretum* legt sie ihm in die Hand und ein Wort der Beschwörung als *Abstractum* in den Mund (V 44-45).

Šaʿtiqat verkörpert also einen zweifach magischen Akt: Die Erschaffung eines Wesens zur Krankenheilung wird ergänzt durch die der Aktivitäten dieses Wesens.

Zwischenergebnis: Aufgaben und Charaktere der CREATURAE AD USUM/CASUM

Die syro-mesopotamische Mythologie weiß von der Erschaffung von Wesen zu berichten, die der Schöpfergott Enki/Ea und sein ugaritisches Pendant El für besondere Aktionen nach den Prinzipien der FORMATIO/GNATIO erschaffen haben und als CREATURAE AD USUM/ CASUM – Anklänge an die EMERSIO-Schöpfung liegen in keinem Fall vor. Nach der Durchführung ihrer diversen Aufgaben hatten diese Wesen keinen Grund, weiter zu existieren, und wurden darum wieder fallen gelassen: Ṣaltum sollte nach ihrer Auseinandersetzung mit Ištar „in ihr Loch" zurückkehren, Aṣû-šu-namir und Šaʿtiqat wurden nach dem Geleit der Ištar in die Oberwelt bzw. nach der Heilung des Keret vom Erzähler schichtweg totgeschwiegen, als hätte es sie nie gegeben.

Das Geschlecht der CREATURAE AD USUM/CASUM ist bei Ṣaltum und Šaʿtiqat formal weiblich, bei Aṣû-šu-namir dagegen männlich. Da es sich bei Aṣû-šu-namir jedoch um einen kultisch tätigen, geschlechtsneutralen Lustknaben handelt, darf bei ihm das grammatisch männliche Geschlecht nicht überbewertet werden. Entsprechend ist bei Ṣaltum und Šaʿtiqat, bei denen das grammatische Geschlecht ihrer Namen auf Damen schließen läßt, zu bezweifeln, ob es sich bei ihnen tatsächlich um weibliche Wesen gehandelt hat. Sie scheinen vielmehr, wie bei Aṣû-šu-namir mit umgekehrten Vorzeichen, geschlechtsindifferente, also neutrische Wesen gewesen sein. Diese Klassifizierung der CREATURAE AD USUM/CASUM, die aus einer CREATIO AD USUM/CASUM hervorgegangen sind, unterstreicht das syro-mesopotamische Konzept der Schöpfung, bei der die autogenerative Kraft von Zeugung und Geburt im Mittelpunkt steht. Diese kann es bei neutrischen Wesen nicht gegeben haben.

Die Charaktereigenschaften der CREATURAE AD USUM/CASUM, Geschöpfe für besondere Gelegenheiten, hingen davon ab, zu welchem Anlaß sie erschaffen wurden: Ṣaltum war kriegerisch, weil sie Ištar paroli bieten sollte, Aṣû-šu-namir war ein Buhlknabe, weil er Ereškigal mit List für sein Vorhaben gewinnen mußte, und Šaʿtiqat war mit magischen Heilkräften ausgestattet, weil sie den todkranken König zu neuem Leben bringen mußte.

Die CREATURAE AD USUM/CASUM haben die Schöpfergötter Enki/Ea und El anläßlich bestimmter Gegebenheiten erschaffen und zu deren Regelung eingesetzt. Also symbolisieren sie für göttliche Kräfte, die von ihrem Schöpfer gezielt eingesetzt werden konnten.

Für das Tagungsthema „Art and Magic" bietet die CREATIO AD USUM/CASUM nach allem zahlreiche Aussagen: Alle CREATURAE AD USUM/CASUM sind das Ergebnis der Schöpferkunst, wie die Anwendung Bilder und der damit verbundene Wortgebrauch aus der FORMATIO/GNATIO -Vorstellung beleuchten.

Gleichzeitig sind die CREATURAE AD USUM/CASUM nicht nur Hilfsmittel der Magie, sondern, wie im Falle der Šaʿtiqat aufgezeigt, auch selbst der Magie mächtig.

Schlußbemerkungen

Ausgangspunkt für obige Betrachtungen zum Thema *Enki/Ea und El : Götter der Kunst und Magie* waren Texte der syro-mesopotamischen Kulturregion, bei denen einerseits die göttlich-magische Kunst der Erschaffung und Erhaltung des menschlichen Lebens und andererseits die menschlich-magische Kunst, die Götter mit Hilfe von Gebeten und Beschwörungen zur Kunst der Lebenserhaltung zu bewegen, im Mittelpunkt standen.

Unterstrichen wird die Verbindung von Kunst und Magie bei den Schöpfergöttern Enki/Ea, Marduk und El in jenen Texten, die das Phänomen der CREATIO AD USUM/CASUM überliefern. Denn sie betonen, daß alle CREATURAE AD USUM/CASUM, Geschöpfe für besondere Gelegenheiten, das Ergebnis der Schöpferkunst sind, die uns aus der FORMATIO-GNATIO-Vorstellung geläufig sind. Gemäß dieser Vorstellung sind die Götter aktiv und erschaffen mit dem Menschen etwas höchst Kunstvolles, das jenseits jeder Vorstellungskraft liegt. Infolgedessen ist ihnen an seiner Erhaltung selbst mittels Magie gelegen.

Die Doppelfunktion des Schöpfergottes als Kunstschaffender und Magier, wie sie dem mesopotamischen Enki/Ea eigen ist, scheint in Ugarit aufgelöst worden zu sein: Die Rolle des Schöpfers und weisen Zauberers, wie wir beispielhaft bei dem Text über die Heilung des Keret sehen konnten, ist dem Hochgott El zugedacht worden, die des Kunstschaffenden und des Patrons des Kunsthandwerks jedoch dem Kōṯar-wa-Ḫasīs, dem im gesamten ostmediterranen Raum verehrten Kunst- und Handwerkergott – dem Hephaistos der griechischen und dem Ptaḥ der ägyptischen Mythologie.

Literatur

AHw, 1965. *Akkadisches Handwörterbuch*: Unter Benutzung des lexikalischen Nachlasses von Bruno Meissner (1868-1947)/bearb. von Wolfram von Soden, Harrassowitz, Wiesbaden.

Borger, R., 1979. *Babylonisch-assyrische Lesestücke.* Analecta Orientalia 54, Roma.

CAD, *Chicago Assyrian Dictionary*, Glückstadt/New York/Winona Lake.

Caplice, R., 1971. *Namburbi Texts in the British Museum.* V. Or., 40 (Roma): 133-183.

Dietrich, M., 1984. *Die Kosmogonie in Nippur und Eridu.* Jahrbuch für Anthropologie und Religionsgeschichte, 5 (Saarbrücken): 155-184.

ders., 1991. *Die Tötung einer Gottheit in der Eridu-Babylon-Mythologie.* In: D.R.D.et al. (Hrsg.), *Ernten, was man sät. Festschrift für Klaus Koch zu seinem 65. Geburtstag*, Neukirchen-Vluyn., S. 49-73.

ders., 1994a. *Ea hat die Geschicke des Menschen festgesetzt.* MARG, 8 (Münster): 1-24.

ders., 1994b. *„Wir wollen die Menschheit schaffen!" Der göttliche Ursprung des Menschenwegs nach der sumero-babylonischen Mythologie.* Mitteilungen für Anthropologie und Religionsgeschichte, 9 (Münster): 41-54.

ders., 1997. *Sukkallu – der mesopotamische Götterbote. Eine Studie zur „Angelologie" im Alten Orient.* In: G. Ahn und M.D. (Hrsg.) (Editors), *Engel und Dämonen. Theologische, Anthropologische und Religionsgeschichtliche Aspekte des Guten und Bösen.* Akten des 2. Gemeinsamen Symposiums der theologischen Fakultät der Universität Tartu und der deutschen Religionsgeschichtlichen Studiengesellschaft am 7. und 8. April 1995 zu Tartu/Estland. Forschungen zur Anthropologie und Religionsgeschichte, Tartu, S. 48-74.

ders., 2002. *Mesopotamische Gottheiten in der ugaritischen Literatur. Regionale Differenzierung und Transformation der mesopotamischen Vorstellungen über den Schöpfergott En-*

ki/Ea in Ugarit, IV. Internationales Colloquium der Deutschen Orient-Gesellschaft am 20.-22. Februar 2002 (i.D.).

ders., 2004. Creaturae ad casum. „Geschöpfe für einen besonderen Fall“. Temporärnumina in antiken syro-mesopotamischen Panthea. In: M.W. (Hrsg.), Gott und Mensch im Dialog. Festschrift für Otto Kaiser zum 80. Geburtstag, Berlin – New York, S. 3-21.

ders., 2006: Das Enūma eliš als mythologischer Grundtext für die Identität der Marduk-Religion Babyloniens. FARG 40 (Münster), S. 135-163.

ders., 2007. Ugarit und seine Beziehungen zu Zypern, Kreta und zur ägäischen Inselwelt, siehe die vorliegende Ausgabe von BZAW.

Dietrich, M. und Loretz, O., 1999. *Keret, der leidende „König der Gerechtigkeit“. Das Wortpaar ṣdq || yšr als Schlüssel zur Dramatik des Keret-Epos (KTU 1.14 I 12-21a)*. Ugarit-Forschungen (Münster), 31: 133-164.

Dietrich, M. und Mayer, W., 1995 *Hurritische Weihrauch-Beschwörungen in ugaritischer Alphabetschrift*. Ugarit-Forschungen (Münster), 26: 73-112.

Dijk, J. van, 1964-65. *Le motif cosmique dans la pensée sumérienne*. Acta Orientalia ediderunt Societates Orientales Danica, Norvegica, Svevica (Le Monde Orientale), 28 (Havniae): 1-59.

ders., 1971. *Sumerische Religion*. In: J.P. Asmussen and J.L. (Hrsg.), *Handbuch der Religionsgeschichte*, Göttingen, S. 431-496.

ders., 1976. *Existe-t-il un « Poème de la Création » sumérien?* In: B.L.E. (Hrsg.), *Kramer Anniversary Volume. Cuneiform Studies in Honor of Samuel Noah Kramer*. AOAT, Kevelaer / Neukirchen-Vluyn), S. 125-133.

DUL, Olmo Lete, G. del, und Sanmartín, J., 2004. *A Dictionary of the Ugaritic Language in the Alphabetic Tradition*. Handbuch der Orientalistik. I 67, Leiden, Boston.

Groneberg, B.R.M., 1997. *Lob der Ištar. Gebet und Ritual an die altbabylonische Venusgöttin*. Cuneiform Monographs 8, Groningen.

Hecker, K., 1989. *Aus dem Aguschaja-Lied*. In: O.K. (Hrsg.), *Texte aus der Umwelt des Alten Testaments* II/5, Gütersloh.

Kippenberg, H.G., 1998. *Magie, Handbuch religionswissenschaftlicher Grundbegriffe* IV, Stuttgart., S. 85-98.

Kramer, S.N., 1961. *Sumerian Mythology. A Study of Spiritual and Literary Achivement in the Third Millennium B.C.*, New York – London.

Müller, G.G.W., 1994. *Ischtars Höllenfahrt*. In: O.K. (Hrsg.), *Texte aus der Umwelt des Alten Testaments* III/4, Gütersloh, S. 760–766.

Pettinato, G., 1971. *Das altorientalische Menschenbild und die sumerischen und akkadischen Schöpfungsmythen*. Abhandlungen der Heidelberger Akademie der Wissenschaften. Philosophisch-historische Klasse, 1971/1, Heidelberg.

Römer, W.H.P., 1987. *Magische Rituale und Beschwörungen. Texte aus der Umwelt des Alten Testaments*, Bd. II/2, Gütersloh, S. 189-211.

ders., 1993. Enki und Ninmach, *Texte aus der Umwelt des Alten Testaments*, Gütersloh, S. 386-401.

Schmitt, R., 2001. *Magietheorien und die Religionen des Antiken Vorderen Orients*. Mitteilungen für Anthropologie und Religionsgeschichte, 13, 1998 (Münster): 309-332.

ders., 2004. *Magie im Alten Testament.* AOAT, 313, Münster.

Sommerfeld, W., 1982. *Der Aufstieg Marduks. Die Stellung Marduks in der babylonischen Religion des zweiten Jahrtausends v.Chr.* AOAT, 213. Kevelaer / Neukirchen-Vluyn.

ders., 1989. *Marduk*. In: D.O.H. Edzard (Editor), *Reallexikon für Assyriologie*, Berlin, S. 360–370.

Talon, P., 2005. *The Standard Babylonian Creation Myth Enūma Eliš.* State Archives of Assyria Cuneiform Texts, IV, Winona Lake.

Tropper, J., 1990. *Der ugaritische Kausativstamm und die Kausativbildungen des Semitischen. Eine morphologisch-semantische Untersuchung zum Š-Stamm und zu den umstrittenen nichtsibilantischen Kausativstämmen des Ugaritischen.* ALASP, 2 (Münster).

ders., 2000. *Ugaritische Grammatik.* AOAT, 273, (Münster).

Zgoll, A., 2003. *Die Kunst des Betens. Form und Funktion, Theologie und Psychagogik in babylonisch-assyrischen Handerhebungsgebeten an Ištar.* AOAT 308, Münster.

The Galgūla Family in South Judah and the Local Sanctuaries

Michael Heltzer, Haifa

Recently we published an article concerning the *Galgoula* large family (*byt 'b* – "father's house") that did live in the Babylonian exile, and which can be traced from the VIII century B.C.E. in the Arad *Ostraka* till the Greek documents from Judah at the time of the revolt of Bar Kochba.[1] It is important that on the name *bny glgl* – was on the Arad Ostracon (Aharoni, 1978: 82-86) among the priestly families of the local sanctuary, closed by the reform of king Heskiyāhu.

One of the central sources is there an ostracon, speaking about a field of *glgwl* – "Galgoula".[2] Now we know about new publications of ostraca, originating from the same kind of place or vicinity, dated by the IV century B.C.E., according to the dates on the ostraca from 362-312 B.C.E.[3] So, they come from late Persian times and the very beginning of the Hellenistic period.

The exact place of provenance of these hundreds of ostraca is not known, but according to all hints in the text they are from Maqqeda in the

1 M. Heltzer, the South Judean Family *bny Glg(w)l* between the VII century B.C.E. and the II Century A.D.; *AOF*, 28, 2001, pp. 185–189. The same Sh. Ahitub, An Edomite Ostracan from Maqqeda, Studies in the History of Eretz-Israel, presented to Yehuda Ben-Porat, Jerusalem 2003, pp. .

2 Sh. Aḥiṭuv, An Edomite Ostracon, in Michael, Historical, Epigraphical and Biblical Studies in Honor of Prof. Michael Heltzer, Tel Aviv, 1999, pp. 33–37; also J. Efa'l, J. Naveh, Aramaic Ostraca of the Fourth Century B.C. from Idumaea, Jerusalem, 1996, pp. 92–93, Nos. 200 and 201.

3 A. Lemaire, Nouvelles inscriptions araméennes d'Idumée, Tome II, Paris 2002, pp. 199–200, nos. 1–104 on pp. 11–63.

vicinity of Khirbet el-Kom, South Judah, 14 km southwestwards from Hebron.[4]

In the recent edition of A. Lemaire we find again *glgwl.* So, on the ostracon No. 258[5] we read 1) *ḥlq ʻrq* "parcellation" or "distribution" of land(plots). Despite the fact that the text is partly broken, we can understand that the land was measured by the "rope of the soil (earth, land)" *'šl'rq'*, but also according to the quantity of the *séah* measures, needed for sowing on the plot(?).

In line 3 of the text we read: *mšt……gl[?]gl sX plg šbr'sX*

"[….?...] Gilgal (s(éahs) X, half of the month Shabirā, X s(éahs) (Possibly the last number belongs to the almost destroyed line 4).

And line 6: *[ ]glgwl tḥṭy s X III III I q II*

"[ ] Galgoul the lower s(éahs) 17.qabs 2."[6]

By all means we see that the Galgoul(a) were also landowners (peasants), but the size of their field is not known. The quantity of the cereals, measured in s(éahs), shows that the fields were not very large. From the other side we read about the "(measuring) rope of land" (*'šl 'rq'*), which in the I. millennium B.C.E. had the length of 120 cubits. If we take even a minimal short cubit of 42 cm, so the land-plot measured by the rope had the length of ≈2500 m². But here we do not know the exact measuring system in this area in the Persian period.[7]

More important is here the ostracon No. 283 in the recent publication of A. Lemaire. We give it here according to the reading of A. Lemaire, it reads:[8]

1) *tl' zy tḥt mn byt ʻz'*
2) *whybl' zy byt yhw*

4 Lemaire, Nouvelles inscriptions, pp. 197–198; D.A. Dorsey, the Location of the Biblical Maqqedah", Tel Aviv 7, 1980, pp. 185–193.

5 Lemaire, Nouvelles inscriptions, pp. 133–135.

6 Séah, = 7–7, 5 liters; qab = 1,2 liters.

7 *'šl* "rope" akk. *ašlu*; *ḥbl* "rope" akk. *eblu.* Acording to AHW, pp. 81b and 183a-b the square *eblu* could have the size of 6 *ikū*, i.e., 2 hectares. And we cannot accept; cf. also M. Powell, Masse und Gewichte, RlA, VI, pp. 488 ff. where the author equals the square rope to 3 *ikū*; cf. also Zach. 2:5 *wehinnē 'īš ūbeyādō ḥebel middā* "and there is a man with the measuring-rope in his hand". Despite the fact that Zacharia is a prophet of the Persian period and he speaks about a measuring-rope, we do not receive information about the size of the rope.

8 Plate XLVII, 283.

3) *zbr zby rpyd' zy bṭn'*
4) *bz' s'rw kpr glgwl*
5) *rqq zy byt nbw (?)*
6) *kpr ynqm*

1) "The hillock, which is under the House of 'Uzza', (The expression *zy tḥt mn* seems to show that "the House (temple, shrine) of the Goddess 'Uzzā' covers the tel (*tl'*)).
2) And the district (area, land-plot)[9] which (is) of the House of Yahō.
3) An unproductive plot[10] of Zabi, the terrace(?)[11] of the terebinth tree.
4) The devastated land[12] of Sa'dou,[13] the tomb[14] of the Galgoula family.
5) A basin (pool)[15](?); which (belongs) to the House (temple, shrine) of Nabou(?).[16]
6) The tomb of the Yinqam (family)"

The text seems to be a cadastrial. But it does not deal with agricultural soil or peasants, but gives other information. First of all, we read here above the burial caves of the Galgoula family and the Yinqam family. So, these families were rich and prominent possessing their family burial places.

It is also interesting that at this period, i.e., 360 B.C.E. and later, the population was mixed. Most personal names are Edomite, where we see a lot of theophoric names, with the component *qws* (*qaus or qōs), designating the national god of Edom. We have to add that even in the area of Hebron a small altar was found with the Greek inscription *κως*, and this

9 *ḥybl'*, var. of *ḥbl* "rope" (also *ḥbwl, ḥbl* graphic variants). Cf. Lemaire, Nouvelles inscriptions, p. 248.

10 *Zbr* is a *hapax legomenon.* The translation is contextual. Cf. Lemaire, Nouvelles, p. 130.

11 Lemaire, p. 150, but the word is unclear.

12 Lemaire, p. 151 takes *bz'/byz'*; cf. DNWSI, p. 149, *bz'* to destroy" and *bzz2* "plunder".

13 We prefer the name Sa'dou reading the third letter as *d* (*daleth*).

14 *Kpr* can also be "village", but in Nababean Aramaic *kpr'* a family tomb (possibly burial cave) DNWSI *kpr'* of a wealthy family.

15 The translation of Lemaire (p. 151) is a contextual one.

16 As we see, Lemaire doubts about the reading and reads *k/nbd/r/w* but possibly *nbw.*

tells us that even in the Hellenistic period there was an Edomite element of the population.[17]

But the ostracon No. 238 gives us additional information. We see here (line 31), that there was a *byt 'z'* "sanctuary of the goddess 'Uzza." This deity is well-known in South-Arabia in Sabean, Qatabanian, Minean and other inscriptions.[18] The deity is also known in North-Arabian, i.e., Liḥyanite inscriptions.[19]

This deity was also worshipped by the aramaized Arabs, i.e., in Palmyrene[20] and nearer geographically to Judah in the Negev by the Nabateans.[21] The Edomites worshipped also 'Uzza. But more interesting is here the fact, that "the House of 'Uzza" and "the House of Yahō" were proximate one to another and this thing was considered as a normal feature.[22] We can add here about the mentioning of tombs in the same place, i.e., that it was considered as a holy one. Till now we knew concerning the Persian period only about temples of Yaho (*Yhwh, Yhw, Yhh*) of the Samaritans on Mount Gerizim, built at the time of Nehemiah,[23] and the temple of Yaho in Southern Egypt – Elephantine, which existed quite in the VI cent. B.C.E., and where *byt Yhw* (var. *byhw* etc.) are known from papyri and ostraca.[24] Important is the fact that this *byt Yhw* was outside the limits of the Yehud province of the V satrapy of the Persian Empire. And

17 E. Mader, Mambre. Die Ergebnisse der Ausgrabungen im heiligen Bezirk Râmet el-Ḫalil in Südpalästina 1926–1928, Fribourg 1957, p. 137, pl. 76.

18 J. Ryckmans, 'Uzzā et Lāt dans les inscriptions Sud-Arabes: a propos de deux amulettes méconnues, JSS, 25/2, 1980, pp. 193–204.

19 W. Caskel, Lihyan und Lihyanisch, Köln, 1954, p. 141, *han-'Uzzay*. Not entering especially to an exhaustive review about this deity we can add that 'Uzza was also known in early Islam: M.C.A. Macdonald et L. Nehme, 'al 'Uzzā, Encyclopedia of Islam, X Leiden, 2000, pp. 967–968.

20 J.K. Stark, Personal Names in Palmyrene Inscriptions, Oxford, 1971, p. 105.

21 J. Patrich, 'Al-'Uzzā Earrings, IEJ, 34, 1984, pp. 39–41; Ph.C. Hammond, D.J. Johnson, R.N. Jones, A Religio-Legal Nabatean Inscription from the Atargatis/Al-'Uzza Temple at Petra, BASOR, 263, 1986, pp. 77–80.

22 We do not enter here the dubious question about the shrine of Nabu, for the reading of this line of the ostracon is far from being certain.

23 J. Naveh, Y. Magen, Aramaic and Hebrew Inscriptions of the Second Century B.C.E. at Mount Gerizim, 'Atiqot, 32, 1997, pp. 9–18; J. Frey, Temple and Rival Temple. – The Cases of Elephantine Mt. Gerizim and Leontopolis, Community without Temple (ed. B. Ego, A. Lange et al.), Tübingen, 1994, pp. 171–204.

24 TADAE, II, B3.2:2; 3.3:2; 3.4:25; 3.5:2; 3.10:2; 3.11:2 etc., IV D 7.18:13:35:1, etc.

we learn in general from the ostraca from Idumea of the IV cent. B.C.E. a lot about Jewish presence in the area. We have here also a good illustration to the passage in the Book of Nehemia 4:6 where we read about the "Jews, which dwell among them"[25] and where the Jews dwelling in the other provinces of the V satrapy are meant.

This brings us to the Story of Susanna, added to the book of Daniel, and where we read in the version of Theodotian and LXX about the gathering-place of the Jews, where they had their internal self government and possibly also their "House of god." We will see in the future, can we speak about additional local Jewish sanctuaries.

Abbreviations

AHW	W. von Soden, Akkadisches Handwörterbuch, Wiesbaden, I-III, 1959-1981.
AOF	Altorientalische Forschungen
BASOR	Bulletin of the American Schools of Oriental Research
DNWSI	J. Hoftijzer, K. Yongeling, Dictionary of the North-Westsemitic Inscriptions, Leiden, 1995.
IEJ	Israel Exploration Journal
JSS	Journal of Semitic Studies
RlA	Reallexikon der Assyriologie
TADAE	B. Porten, A. Yardeni, Textbook of Aramaic Documents from Ancient Egypt, I-IV, Jerusalem 1986-1999.

25 *hayehūdīm hayyošbīm 'eṣlām.*

Infektionskrankheiten: ihre keilschriftliche Überlieferung und molekularbiologische Bewertung*

Thomas R. Kämmerer, Tartu

Vor etwa 10 Jahren fing ich damit an, keilschriftliches Textmaterial zu untersuchen, das von unseren Kollegen zum Teil bereits schon und letztmals vor nunmehr 45 Jahren bearbeitet worden war. Es ging mir weniger um die vollständige philologische Neubearbeitung dieser Texte, sondern vielmehr um die Feststellung, daß diese Texte u.a. eine nicht unbedingt zusammenhängende Aufzählung von Krankheitssymptomen, Beschwerden und nach heutigen Begriffen kaum definierbare Krankheiten enthielten, ohne daß man den Versuch gemacht hatte, mit den vorhandenen Lexemen *eine* oder mehrere *bestimmte* Krankheiten zu identifizieren. Diese Texte erschienen mir trotz ihrer anfänglichen Unverständlichkeit so interessant, daß ich es für sinnvoll hielt, mich daraufhin *medizinisch* beraten zu lassen.

Es ergab sich auf Anhieb, daß hier die Symptome einer Infektionskrankheit beschrieben wurden. Darüber hinaus machte es keine große Mühe, diese Symptome und das damit verbundene Umfeld zu einem Krankheitsbild zusammenzufügen, bei dem es sich um die *Pocken* handeln mußte. Es wurde dann eine Art Checkliste (d.h. ein Epikrisenmuster)[1] aufgestellt, die alles medizinisch esentliche enthielt. Mit ihrer Hilfe ließ sich der medizinische Inhalt dieser Texte übersichtlich darstellen und erfassen.

---

* Ich möchte mich hiermit bei meinem Vater, Prof. Dr. med. Heinz Kämmerer, für seine wissenschaftliche Beratung bei meinen medizin-historischen Studien bedanken.

1 Welche Bedeutung hat ein Epikrisenmuster *medizinisch aus heutiger Sicht*? Unter einer Epikrise versteht man die Kurzzusammenfassung aller für eine Krankheit eines bestimmten Patienten erheblichen Parameter. Bei einem Epikrisenmuster wird dann diese Zusammenfassung verallgemeinert und auf ein ganzes Kollektiv Erkrankter übertragen. Damit kann man dann aus eine großen Menge Kranker die evtl. vorhandene gemeinsame Erkrankung herausfiltern.

Epikrisenmuster:

1. Ursache der Krankheit (damals unbekannt, Gottheit, Dämon),
2. Ursprung der Krankheit (Himmel),
3. Krankheitsträger (Lämmer, Zicklein, Mensch),
4. Alter der Krankheitsträger (Jungtiere, Kleinkinder),
5. Symptome (Hochfieberhafte Erkrankung mit Befall der Haut),
6. Leitsyndrom (typische Hautausschläge),
7. Heilmittel (symptomatische[2] Behandlung),
8. Verlauf (typisch, Spontanheilung oder Tod),
9. Erkrankungstypus (angedeutet durch gleichzeitigen Krankheitsausbruch mehrerer Tiere und Menschen (Seuche)),
10. Fehlende Spezifiztät in Bezug auf Mensch und Tier.

An dieser Stelle ist noch festzuhalten: Es handelt sich hier um die ersten erkennbaren Textbelege zum Thema Pocken im mesopotamischen Raum überhaupt. Sie sind an den Beginn des 2. Jahrtausends v.Chr. zu datieren und stammen aus *Māri*. Weltweit gibt es darüber hinaus aus der vorchristlichen Zeit einige wenige *andere* Belege, die aber später datieren.

Vor 5 Jahren konnte man sich darüber freuen, hiermit einen weiteren Beitrag zur Entstehung der Infektionskrankheiten erbracht zu haben, nicht nur für die Region des Alten Orients, sondern ganz allgemein für die zeitliche und geopathologiosche Lokalisierung im weitesten Sinne.

Auch Molekularbiologen dürften nicht umhin können, Ergebnisse einer derartigen Spurensuche anerkennend zu Kenntnis zu nehmen; wir jedoch müssen zur Kenntnis nehmen, daß sich ihre Vorstellungen in ganz anderen Zeiträumen vollziehen. Damit wird ein kleiner Exkurs eben in diese *Molekularbiologie* notwendig. Ich bin weder Molekularbiologe noch Genetiker und kann mich daher nur auf mein Schulwissen und die Kenntnisse meiner medizinischen Berater stützen. Es dürfte aber ausreichen, um zumindest in groben Zügen, die Zusammenhänge zu verstehen, die ja heute zur Allgemeinbildung gehören.

Was für die Entstehung, Fortentwicklung und Ausbreitung durch Fortpflanzung des menschlichen Erbgutes gilt, gilt auch für das Erbgut von Bakterien und Viren. Es ist bekannt, daß die Chromsomen Träger der einzelnen Gene sind und daß diese Gene wiederum Träger des sogenannten genetischen Code sind. Dieser Code wird von vier chemisch genau definierten Substanzen, den Purinbasen, kurz auch DNA genannt, ge-

2 D.h. nicht auf die Krankheitsursache ausgerichtet, die ja unbekannt ist.

schrieben, vergleichbar mit den vier Buchstaben A,B,C und D. Nach den Regeln der Kombinatorik würden bereits 3 Buchstaben genügen, um aus 20 anderen Substanzen die richtige Auswahl zu treffen. Und diese 20 anderen Substanzen sind dann die Aminosäuren, die in richtiger Reihenfolge und Häufigkeit zu Einweißkörpern anzuordnen sind. Wie dies funktioniert und was das im Einzelnen bedeutet, kann uns hier nicht interessieren.

Diese 4 Buchstaben, eben die DNA-Moleküle, liegen in Form langer Ketten oder Fäden in den Chromosomen und bilden dort die Helix, bzw. Doppelhelix, die es ermöglicht, Erbgut an die nächste Zelle weiterzugeben. Gerade in diesem Frühjahr wurden überall in den Medien die beiden Molekularbiologen *Watson* und *Crick* herausgestellt, die vor 50 Jahren für ihr Denkmodel den Nobelpreis erhielten, eben weil sich dieses Denkmodel als zutreffend erwiesen hatte.

Molekularbiologen haben in den letzen Jahren herausgefunden, daß bestimmte, gut lokalisierbare Abschnitte eines Gens in Abhängigkeit von ihrem Alter Veränderungen unterworfen sind. Diese Veränderungen unterliegen bestimmten Gesetzen, die sich mathematisch-statistisch erfassen lassen. Dadurch kann das Alter eines Gens, bzw. der Zeitpunkt zu dem sich seine Codierung herausgebildet hat, in guter Näherung errechnet werden. Auf ein paar 1000 Jahre kommt es dabei natürlich nicht an. So haben Molekularbiologen unter der Leitung von *Malcolm Gardener* vom Institut für Genomforschung in Rockville (US-Staat Maryland) jetzt errechnet, daß das Genom des Malariaerregers (Plasmodium falciparum), ein Bakterium, und übrigens auch das seines Überträgers, der Mücke *anopheles gambiae*, vor 100 000 bis 180.000 Jahren entstanden sein muß, also in einer Zeit, in die nach *G. Bräuer* vom Institut für Humanbiologie der Uni Hamburg der „spätere archaische homo sapiens" (200.000–120.000) datiert. Diese Datierung entspräche ungefähr den Funden aus *Singa* in Ostafrika die um 150.000 datieren. Dagegen besitzen wir aus Vorderasien bislang lediglich Funde, die mit dem *homo sapiens sapiens* aus *Qafzeh* in Israel älter als 100.000 Jahre und aus *Skhul* ebenfalls in Israel 100.000 Jahre alt sind.

Bei dem Fund von 1969 aus Qafzeh IX handelt es sich um das Skelett einer Frau, die ungefähr mit 20 Jahren starb und in einem Doppelgrab beigesetzt worden war. Das Skellet wurde von C. Howell der „Proto-Cro-Magnon" Population zugerechnet. Mittels des Thermoluminiszenverfahrens konnte dieser Fund zuerst auf 92.000 Jahre, schließlich aber mit der Elektronenspinresonanzmethode auf 120.000 bis 100.000 Jahre geschätzt werden. Durch die geographische Nähe zu Afrika ergibt sich ein unmittelbarer Bezug. Da sich dieses Skelett andererseits deutlich von denen eines Neandertalers unterscheidet, mit dem der heutigen Menschen aber deutlich übereinstimmt, besitzen wir mit diesem Fund ein Bindeglied zwischen den Funden in Afrika und dem Jetztmenschen. Zusammen mit den Bewohnern der Skhul-Höhle stellen die Menschen der Qafzeh-Höhle anscheind die Urbevölkerung der heutigen Menschen dar.

Diese Funde sind somit deutlich älter als der *homo neanderthaliensis* aus *Shanidar* I-V, der zwischen 40.000 – 70.000 datiert. Medizinhistorisch bedeutsam ist das Skelett Shanidar I, das deutliche Verletzungen am Schädel und am rechten Arm aufweist. E. Trinkaus erklärt die Ursache dieser Verletzungen folgendermaßen: „Entweder wurde der Arm knapp über dem Ellbogen amputiert oder aber er brach am Ellbogen, ohne zu verheilen, so dass der Unterarm samt Ellbogen abfiel.“[3]

Die Methodik der mathematisch-statistischen Erfassung von Veränderungen eines Gens ist eben erst aus der Taufe gehoben worden. So ist am Institut für Mikrobiologie der Universität Göttingen unter der Leitung von *G. Gottschalk* jetzt das Genom des Wundstarrkrampferregers *clostridium tetani* bestimmt worden. Berechnungen seines Entstehungsalters liegen noch nicht vor. In diesem Zusammenhang wurden mir von Mikrobiologen zwei Literaturstellen mitgeteilt, nach denen es Berichte über Tetanus von vor 2500 Jahren gegeben habe. Leider steht in den zitierten Artikeln nichts darüber.

Auch gibt es in der aktuellen Literatur zum Alter des Pockengenoms noch keine Untersuchungsergebnisse. Bei dem derzeitigen allgemeinen Interesse an Pockenviren dürfte dies aber nur noch eine Frage der Zeit sein. In jedem Falle zeigt die molekularbiologische Altersbestimmung beim Malariaerreger, was die Forschung heute zu leisten vermag.

Ohne der Sache Gewalt anzutun, darf unterstellt werden, daß in Analogie für das Genom der Pockenviren das gleiche gilt wie für Malariabakterien. Wir dürfen in naher Zukunft in zunehmendem Maße mit derartigen Forschungsergebnissen rechnen.

Immerhin wird von Seiten der Bioarchäologen die Ansicht vertreten, daß am Ende der Eiszeit der (zweiten Periode der Menschhheitsgeschichte), also am Ende des Pleistozens, etwa 11.000 bis 10.000 Jahre vor Chr. alle wesentlichen Entstehungsprozesse in der Menschheitsentwicklung und der der belebten Natur schlechthin abgeschlossen waren. Es ist der Beginn der Seßhaftwerdung und Produzierung von Nahrungsmitteln.

Die Bioarchäologie stellt ein ganz neues Forschungsgebiet dar, das u.a. eben mit Hilfe von DNA-Analysen überdauerter Eiweißmoleküle in Knochen und mumifiziertem Gewebe phylogenetische Zusammenhänge auf-

---

[3] Solecki, Ralph, Shanidar, The first flower people, New York 1971.

klärt. Mit den gleichen Methoden beginnt man heute den Entstehungszeitpunkt des menschlichen Genoms einzugrenzen.

Wir Altorientalisten haben sicherlich keinen Grund zur Resignation, müssen aber erkennen, daß unsere eigenen originären Forschungsergebnisse an keilschriftlichen Überlieferungen aus *molekularbiologischer* Sicht in Hinblick auf zeitliche Bestimmungen doch sehr in den Hintergrund treten.

Nach wie vor fügen sie sich aber in das wissenschaftliche Gesamtkonzept ein und geben nach wie vor Aufschluß über die *lokale* Verbreitung bestimmter Viren, was *molekularbiologisch* wiederum kaum zu bestimmen ist. Hinzu kommt, daß die philologischen Belege einen Beitrag liefern, erkennen zu können, wie die Menschen damals unter ihren Bedingungen mit einzelnen nunmehr genauer zu bestimmender Erkrankungen fertig geworden sind.

So hat der Versuch, die Entstehungsvorgang von Infektionskrankheiten, damit von einzelnen Krankheitserregern, ihr Eindringen und ihre Ausbreitung in die menschliche Bevölkerung zu erklären und zu datieren, *kultur-* und *menschheitsgeschichtliche* Bedeutung. *J. Diamond*, einer der führenden Wissenschaftler auf dem Gebiet von Humangenetik und Phylogenie nähert sich diesem Problem, indem der die *Domestizierung* von Pflanzen und Tieren in ihrer Evolution zugrunde legt. Seine Schlußfolgerungen sind folgende:

„Die hauptverantwortlichen Killer der Menschen seit Entwicklung der Landwirtschaft sind akute, hochinfektiöse epidemische Krankheiten, die auf den Menschen beschränkt sind. Entweder töten sie ihre Opfer schnell oder aber sie überleben und sind für ihr Leben immunisiert." (Lit.-Zitate). Derartige Krankheiten waren nicht existenzfähig zu einer Zeitperiode ohne Landwirtschaft, denn sie können sich nur in einer sehr dichten Population aufrecht erhalten. Vor einer Entstehung von Landwirtschaft waren sie nicht existenzfähig und werden deshalb oft auch als Massenerkrankungen bezeichnet. Das Geheimnis der Entstehung vieler dieser Krankheiten ist in den letzten Dekaden durch *molekularbiologische Untersuchungen* gelöst worden. Dabei ist gezeigt worden, daß sie sich aus ähnlichen epidemischen Erkrankungen unsrer domestizierten Herdentiere entwickelt haben, mit denen wir etwa vor 10 000 Jahren in engen Kontakt gekommen sind. Damit hing die Entwicklung dieser Krankheiten von zwei verschiedenen Domestikationserscheinungen ab:

1) Die Herausbildung sehr viel dichterer, menschlicher Populationen.
2) Eine viel häufigere Übertragung von Tiererkrankungen unserer Haustiere als von erjagten Wildtieren.

Bedenken wir, daß sich nach heutigem Wissenstand das AIDS-Virus in bestimmten Affen irgendwo in Afrika in einer bestimmten Affenart herausgebildet hat und 1959 erstmals in unser medizinisches Bewusstsein kam. Oder der jüngste furchtbare Virus SARS aus einer asiatischen Katzenart.

Wie gesagt, wird die Entstehung epidemischer Infektionskrankheiten von *J. Diamond* mit den Anfängen der Landwirtschaft gleichgesetzt, also mit den aufkommenden Kulturen von u.a. *Jericho, Çatalhüyük, Qal'at Ǧarmo, Haçilar.*

Sie, d.h. die Landwirtschaft, ermöglicht eine Zunahme und Verdichtung der Population und schafft somit die Voraussetzungen für Massenerkrankungen: „Such diseases could not have existed before the origins of agriculture, because they can sustain themselves only in large dense populations that did not exist before agriculture, hence they are often termed ‚crowd diseases'".

Dabei verweist *J. Diamond* auf molekularbiologische Untersuchungen an unseren domestizierten Herdentieren, mit denen wir vor etwa 10.000 Jahren in Kontakt gekommen sind.

So sind *Masern* und *Tuberkulose* vom Weidevieh (Schafe: *immeri ritti*, Wildschaf: *atūdu*, Ziegen: *enzu(m), ṣenu(m) III*, Rinder: *alap ritti*, *puṭāru(m),* Weidetier: *sādīu*) auf den Menschen übertragen worden, *Influenza* von Schweinen (*šaḫû(m)* und Enten (*paspasu, usu(m) II*). Es sind ausnahmslos Erreger, die sich aus Krankheiten von Tieren entwickelt haben und sind – wie Diamond herausstellt – paradoxerweise in den meisten Fällen nur noch auf den Menschen beschränkt oder für Tiere nur ganz schwach pathogen.

Völlig offen dagegen sei die Herkunft der *Pocken.* Als deren Überträger werden wiederum Weidevieh und vor allem Kamele bzw. Dromedare (*gamallu*, *ibilu, udru*) diskutiert. Überlegungen dieser Art beziehen sich allerdings im eigentlichen Sinne auf die Ausbreitung vorhandener Erreger in der menschlichen Population und nicht auf die Entstehung des Krankheitserregers.

Damit kommen wir zu einem weiteren, für uns interessanten Aspekt, nämlich zu der Frage:

Wurden die Pocken auf den Menschen vom *Kamel*, bzw. *Dromedar* oder vom Weidevieh, also Rindern, Schafen oder Ziegen übertragen?

Gesichert ist, daß es Schafe und Ziegen und auch die beiden Kamelsgattungen *Kamel* und *Dromedar* bereits am Ende der großen Eiszeit, somit um 10.000 vor Chr., gegeben hat. So besitzen wir Knochenfunde aus *Sihi* an der Südküste des Roten Meeres, die auf Grund einer Radio-Carbon Untersuchung 8.200 v.Chr. datieren. Sicher ist auch, daß Schafe und Ziegen die ersten Weidetiere waren, die domestiziert wurden. Das Wissen um Kamele ist für den Vorderasiatischen Raum nach *Bilddokumenten* jedoch erst mit ca. 2500 v.Chr. anzusetzen. So besitzen wir neben zahlreichen Kamelknochen als älteste Darstellung eines Kamels ein Wandrelief von der Insel *Umm an-Nar* in *Oman*. Allerdings sind keinerlei Anzeichen wie zum Beispiel Zaumzeug zu erkennen, die darauf schließen lassen könnten, daß es sich bereits um ein domestiziertes Tier gehandelt habe. Auch dort und in *Ras Ghanada* an der Golf-Küste der Vereinigten Arabischen Emirate gefundene Knochenreste vom ausgehenden 3. Jahrtausend belegen keine Domestizierung. Die Begleitfunde deuten eher darauf hin, dass diese Tiere gejagt wurden.

Lediglich die aus dem 3. Jahrtausend stammenden Belege für gesponnenes Kamelhaar und Kameldung in Verbindung mit Kamelknochen aus *Jericho*, den *Küstengebieten* rund um die *Arabische Halbinsel* und aus *Shar-i-Sokhta* in *Ost-Iran* weisen *möglicherweise* auf Domestizierung hin. Zu den wenigen vielfach als solche verstandenen Belege aus *Mesopotamien* sagt *R.W. Bulliet*:

„To be sure, one or two representations of camels from early Mesopotamia have been alleged, but they are all either doubtfully camelline, as the horsy looking clay plaque from the third dynasty of ur (2345-2308 B.C.), or else not obviously domestic and hence possibley depictions of wild animals, as ins the case with the occasional Ubaid and Uruk period (4000–3000 B.C.) examples".[4]

„There are no sound grounds for doubting Albright's contention that camel domestication first became a factor of importance in the Syrian and north Arabian deserts around the eleventh century B.C., and, as will be seen, there is much to support the contention besides the absence of camelline remains in Holy Land archaeological sites of earlier date, which was Albright's primary datum. On the other hand, this date need not be taken as the beginning date of camel domestication in an absolute sense.

4 Bulliet, Richard W., The Camel and the Wheel, Columbia: 1990 (orig. ed. 1975), S. 46.

Closer attention to the process of domestication indicates that the camel was actually domesticated long before the year 1100 B.C."[5]

Die ersten *Textbelege* – dann als Belege *für* die *Domestizierung* von Kamelen – datieren ab 1500 v. Chr. Ebenso ein von *Salonen* in Hippologica Accadica 54 zitierter Text aus *Ugarit*, der: „anše-⌜a-ab⌝-ba" belegt, zu deutsch: „anše von jenseits des Persischen Golfes" oder mit *W.G. Lambert* „donkey of the sea = dromedary". Er weist daraufhin:

„There can be no dispute that these lexical texts from Ugarit go back eventually to Old Babylonian originals from Southern Mesopotamia". „Here then is evidence that the dromedary was known in Southern Mesopotamia in Old Babylonian times." „Perhaps then East Arabia is the region to which we should look for the domestication of the camel."[6]

Punkt 3 des oben erwähnten Epikrisenmusters listet Weidevieh, Schafe und Ziegen auf. Auf ein und derselben Tafel wird eine Krankheit beschrieben und beschworen, die für Menschen und Tier (Lämmer, Zicklein, Steppengetier) offensichtlich als die gleiche Krankheit verstanden wurde. Ätiologische Ursachen und Zusammenhänge waren natürlich damals noch nicht bekannt.

Wenn also von naturwissenschaftlicher Seite die Frage noch offen ist, ob es Ziegen, Schafe oder etwa *Kamele* oder *Dromedare* waren, in denen sich das Pockenvirus herausgebildet hat und dann auf andere Tiere und Menschen übergegangen ist, erlauben unsere philologischen Befunde doch gewisse Denkanstöße. Natürlich wissen wir nicht, was sich vor den Anfängen der Landwirtschaft tatsächlich abgespielt hat. In jedem Fall begegnen wir aber in unseren Texten Ziegen und Lämmern und eben *keinen* Kamelen oder Dromedaren.

Folgt man den oben beschriebenen Überlegungen *J. Diamonds*, so unterstützt unser Befund die These, daß die Pocken ihren Ursprung vom Weidevieh genommen haben. Mögen sie wo immer auch entstanden sein, ihre Erscheinung als menschliche Infektionskrankheit könnte von daher viel eher auf das beschriebene Weidevieh zurückgeführt werden als auf Kamele und oder Dromedare. Fassen wir noch einmal in einer Übersicht zusammen:

---

5 Ders., ebd., S. 36.

6 Lambert, W.G., BASOR 160, S. 43.

Zunächst das allgemeine Schema der Domestizierung von Tieren:

Tier	Name der Wildform	domestiziert seit ±	Fundort
Hund	Wolf	11.000	Mittlerer Osten
Ziege	bezoar Ziege	8.500	Mittlerer Osten
Schaf	Mufflon	8.000	Mittlerer Osten
Schwein	Eber	7.500	Mittlerer Osten
Rind		7.000	Mittlerer Osten
Katze	Wildkatze	7.000	Mittlerer Osten
Huhn	Geflügel	6.000	China
Esel	Wildesel[7]	4.000	Mittlerer Osten
Pferd	Tarpan	4.000	Vorderes Schwarzes Meer
Kamel	Wildkamel	3.000	Südarabien, Indien
		2.500	Umm an-Nar (Oman)
		1.500	Syrien, Mesopotamien
Kaninchen	Wildkaninchen	1.000	Spanien

Es zeigt sich, daß die Domestizierung der Kamele in Arabien stattgefunden hat, zumindest mit hoher Wahrscheinlichkeit.

Des Weiteren können heute Molekularbiologen ganze Virenfamilien beschreiben, deren Einzelviren genetisch sehr ähnlich oder verwandt sind. Dabei stößt man auch auf das Pockenvirus, das neben dem Menschenpockenvirus und dem Kuhpockenvirus eine enge Verwandtschaft mit dem Kamelpockenvirus besitzt. Also auch virologisch gesehen, ist eine Übertragung vom Kamel auf den Menschen möglich. Hierzu die nächste Übersicht:

7 aus Umm Dabaghijja, südlich von Mosul: Wandmalerei mit Onagerjagd, 7. Jahrt. v.Chr.).

Entwicklung und Übertragung des virus orthopox variola vom Tier zum Mensch:

1.8 Milionen Jahre 180.000–100.000	Wildtiere (akk. *atūdu(m), sappāru(m), akannu, ḫarādu(m), paraḫu, mesukku, ...*)	←	Auftreten von Viren orthopox variola (variola vera) (variola haemorrhagica)
	↓		
9.000–6.000 v.Chr. sum. Belege: seit 3200 v.Chr.; akk. Belege: seit 2500 v.Chr.	Erstmals domestiziertes Weidevieh (sum. udu, ùz, usduḫa, gu4) (akk. *immeri ritti, enzu(m), ṣenu(m), alap ritti, puṭāru(m), sādīu, ...*)	→	Erwachsene (Seßhafte Bauern) ↓ (tödlich oder Immunisation) Kinder
2.500–1.800 v. Chr. sum. lex. Belege: seit aB akk. Belege: seit JB	Erstmals domestiziertes Kamel / Dromedar (camelus dromedarius, camelus bactrianus) (sum. anše-a-ab-ba) (akk. *gammalu(m), udru, ibilu, ...*)	→	Erwachsene (Nomaden, Mütter) ↓ (tödlich oder Immunisation) Kinder

Fasst man die verstreuten Hinweise zusammen, so dürften etwa in der Mitte des 2. Jahrtausends v.Chr. an verschiedenen Orten der damaligen Welt eine Krankheit aufgetreten und beschrieben worden sein, bei der es sich mit großer Wahrscheinlichkeit um Pocken gehandelt hat. *G. Seifert* sieht die Verbreitung der Pocken folgendermaßen: „So kann man mit gewisser Vorsicht den Schluß ziehen, daß der Urherd der Pocken in zentralasiatischen Gebieten, vielleicht auch, wie Wu Lien Teh annimmt, nicht fern vom Kaspischen Meer liegt. Man kann annehmen, daß sie von hier über dem südlichen Wege nach Indien, auf dem östlichen Wege zu Mongolenstämmen und von ihnen nach China, und auf dem westlichen Wege über Persien, Arabien nach Europa verbreitet wurden. Die Pocken wären dann ähnliche Wege wie die Pest gewandert."

Aber auch G. Seifert merkt an, daß alle diese Berichte aus den verschiedensten Gründen mit Zurückhaltung zu bewerten sind. Es ist deshalb von gewisser Bedeutung, daß für den Kulturraum des Alten Vorderen Orients Keilschrifttexte gefunden wurden, die bei der auch hier gebotenen kritischen Zurückhaltung doch klarere Aussagen erlauben. So existiert eine altbabylonische Beschwörung, die nach Vorarbeiten anderer A. Goetze als „A incantation against diseases" vorgestellt hat. Von dieser Beschwörung gibt es verschiedene Textduplikate sowie eine weitere neubabylonsiche Version. Ihr Alter ist in die ausgehende altbabylonische Sprachperiode zu datieren. Ergänzend existiert eine weitere Beschwörung, die A. Cavigneaux (Nr.15289, Tafelkatalog von Māri) publiziert hat, die das gleiche Thema behandelt.

Sieht man von einigen ersten Bearbeitungen ab, die im Vorfeld dieser Textanalysen erfolgten, haben sowohl A. Goetze als auch A. Cavigneaux aus diesen Texten lediglich eine undifferenzierte Aneinanderreihung von Krankheiten herausgelesen und die etymologische Analyse der einzelnen Lexem weitgehend unabhängig vom Gesamtkontext vorgenommen. Damit hatte man aber, wohl unbewusst den gedanklichen Ansatz außer acht gelassen, die einzelnen Krankheiten eben nicht als Krankheiten sondern als Symptome ein und derselben Krankheit zu verstehen. Das Bild ändert sich, wenn man versucht, den Inhalt dieser Texte einer ganzheitlichen Betrachtung zu unterziehen. Dann stellt man überraschend fest:

1. es werden Symptome beschrieben, die der Pockenerkrankung zuzurechnen sind.
2. es treten bei Tieren Symptome auf, die denen beim Menschen gleichen.
3. Die Krankheitssymptome treten bei Tier und Mensch zeitgleich auf.
4. Sie deuten auf eine Infektion hin.
5. Offensichtlich besteht zwischen Tier und Menschen eine Brücke. Es wird das Auftreten der Symptome (hier Krankheiten) in der medizinisch richtigen Reihenfolge beschrieben.

Die molekularbiologische Rückdatierung der Entstehung des Pockenvirus, die noch aussteht, ist die eine Sache, der Nachweis ihres tatsächlichen Auftretens unter Menschen und Tieren die andere Sache. Dabei würde es sich allerdings ohnedies um Zeiträume handeln, aus denen nur sehr wenige Zeugnisse in Form von Artefakten auf uns gekommen sein können.

Wie das Beispiel des Malariagenoms zeigt, hat es den Erreger und seinen Überträger, die Anophelesmücke, schon gegeben ohne daß es seinen späteren Träger der Krankheit schon gab. Es ist das Vorhandensein von Krankheitserregern also nicht notwendigerweise an die Existenz seines späteren Erkrankungsopfers gebunden. Erst sehr viel später tritt die Krankheit mit dem Auftreten ihres Substrates, des Menschen, aus der Verborgenheit heraus und bildet mit ihren Symptomen ein reproduzierbares Krankheitsbild. Und als nächster Schritt muß dann dieses Krankheitsbild von den Betroffenen auch perzipiert werden. Dies herauszufinden ist dann Aufgabe des Medizinhistorikers.

Insgesamt wird man auf Schriftzeugnisse angewiesen sein. Schrift gibt es seit Ende des 4. Jahrtausends. Und dabei nimmt die Schreibtechnik auf Tontafeln nach und nach den ersten Platz ein und liefert schließlich bleibende Dokumente. Hier ergeben sich für den medizinhistorisch versierten Altorientalisten entsprechende Ansatzpunkte.

Mit der hier vorliegenden, erneuten Aufarbeitung der Pockenerkrankung können zu den bisherigen Kenntnissen zwei neue Gesichtspunkte hinzugefügt werden:

1. Der Bioarchäologie gelingt es mit einer Auf- und Entschlüsselung der Genome eines Erregers, Entstehung des Genoms und damit des Erregers zu datieren. Dies ist für die Erreger von Masern und Tuberkulose bereits geschehen. Als Überträger gilt das Weidevieh.

2. Auch wenn die Genomanalysen nichts über das Auftreten von Pocken und die Wahrnehmung und Einordnung durch die erkrankten Menschen aussagen, so konnte doch in dieser Studie u.a. ein philologischer Ansatz gefunden werden, der zeigt, daß auch der Pockenerreger vom Weidevieh übertragen wurde und nicht von Kamelen bzw. Dromedaren. So erweist sich die philologische Aufarbeitung überlieferter Keilschrifttexte als unbedingt notwendig. – Philologie und Naturwissenschaft ergänzen sich.

Bibliographie

AHw., 1965. *Akkadisches Handwörterbuch*: Unter Benutzung des lexikalischen Nachlasses von Bruno Meissner (1868-1947)/bearb. von Wolfram von Soden., Harrassowitz, Wiesbaden.

Bräuer, G., Das Out-of-Africa-Modell und die Kontroverse um den Ursprung des modernen Menschen. In: Conard, N.J. (Hg.): Woher kommt der Mensch? Tübingen : Attempto Verlag, S. 164–187.

Bulliet, Richard W., The Camel and the Wheel, Columbia: 1990 (orig. ed. 1975).

CAD, *Chicago Assyrian Dictionary*, Glückstadt/New York/Winona Lake.

Diamond, J., Guns, Germs, and Steel: The Fates of Human Societies, 1997.

Gardener, M., The evolutionary origin of the 35 kb circular DNA of *Plasmodium falciparum*, Molecular and General Genetics MGG, 1994.

Gottschalk, G., Characterization of a heme oxygenase of Clostridium tetani and itspossible role in oxygen tolerance. Arch. Microbiol. 182, 2004, 259–263.

Kämmerer, Th.R., About the emergence and spreading of smallpox in the Ancient Near East - it reaches us from camels or cattle?, Le Journal des Médecines cunéiformes, Paris 2004(2), 16–25.

Ders., Pathologische Veränderungen an Leber und Galle, Das Krankheitsbild der Gelbsucht, Revue d'Assyriologique 94, Paris 2000, 57–93.

Ders., Die erste Pockendiagnose stammt aus Babylonien, UF 27, Neukirchen-Vluyn 1995, 129–168.

Ders. – Schwiderski, D., Deutsch-Akkadisches Wörterbuch, AOAT 255, Münster 1998.

Lambert, W.G., The Domesticated Camel in the Second Millennium – Evidence from Alalakh and Ugarit, BASOR 160, 1960, 42–43.

Salonen, A., Hippologica Accadica, eine lexikalische und Kulturgeschichtliche Untersuchung über die Zug-, Trag- und Reittiere 54, 1955.

Seifert, G. – Dscheng-Hsing DU, Zur Geschichte der Pocken und Pockenimpfung, in: SudArch 30, 1937/38.

Solecki, R., Shanidar, The first flower people, New York 1971.

Watson, J.D., The Double Helix: A Personal Account of the Discovery of the Structure of DNA, 1968.

Wu Lien Teh, Plague Fighter, The Autobiography of a Modern Chinese Physician, W. Hefer & Sons, Cambridge 1959.

Arthur Vööbus – ein Forscher des christlichen Orients

Kalle Kasemaa, Tartu

Arthur Vööbus wurde am 28. April 1909 im Dorf Vara im Kreis Tartu geboren in der Familie eines Schullehrers. 1926 absolvierte er cum laude das Hugo Treffner-Gymnasium in Tartu, das für die Ausbildung der estnischen Intelligenz seit langem verdienstvoll war. Manche spätere Dozenten der Universität und Pfarrer der Estnischen Ev.-Luth. Kirche waren seine Klassenkameraden. Schon in der Schule war A. Vööbus ein fleißiger und ernster Junge. 1932 absolvierte er die Theologische Fakultät der Universität Tartu und wurde zum Geistlichen der Estnischen Ev.-Luth. Kirche ordiniert. 1933–1940 war A. Vööbus einer der Pfarrer in der Paulus Gemeinde in Tartu. 1934 verteidigte er seine Magisterarbeit an der Theologischen Fakultät der Universität Tartu unter dem Thema „Der wahre Christ, das wahre christliche Leben und die wahre christliche Kirche nach Sören Kirkegaard" und bekam den Grad des magister theologiae. Danach begann er sich für die Arbeit vorzubereiten, die ihn später weltweit berühmt gemacht hat. In den Jahren 1934–1940 konnte er in den namhaften Bibliotheken und Handschriftensammlungen in Rom, Paris, London, Berlin und Leipzig arbeiten; in diesen Jahren publizierte er in der Zeitschrift der Akademischen Theologischen Gesellschaft in Tartu einige Aufsätze über die Askese bei den Judenchristen, d.h. bei den Christen, die früher des jüdischen Glaubens gewesen waren, und über die Judenchristen in Syrien und Mesopotamien. Seine Zeitgenossen haben diese Zeit im Leben A. Vööbus als eine außerordentlich arbeitsame und zielstrebige gekennzeichnet. A. Vööbus besaß einen unbeugsamen Willen und ließ keinen Augenblick ungenutzt, wobei er unter keinem physischen Hindernis litt wie Taha Hussein. Als A. Vööbus die Universität absolviert hatte, begann er unter der Leitung von Uku Masing das Studium der semitischen Sprachen, nämlich des Syrischen und des Arabischen, die später für ihn so wichtig wurden. Der Lehrbeauftragte U. Masing schrieb in seinen Berichten an die Theologische Fakultät, dass die Zahl der Teilnehmer beim syrischen Sprachunterricht 2–3 betrug, einer davon war immer A. Vööbus (eine andere war die spätere Frau von U. Masing). Im Sommer, als die Absolventen der Universität einen militärischen Lehrgang durchmachten und alle einen ermüdenden Tag hinter sich hatten, laß A. Vööbus nach dem Zapfenstreich, als die Lichter in der Kaserne gelöscht wurden, im Vorraum noch ein Paar Stunden, indem er auf einem Stuhl stand und das Buch gegen die schwache Glühbirne hielt. Ebenso haben die Zeitgenossen erzählt, dass nach seiner Hochzeit 1936 A. Vööbus seinen Freunden erzählte, dass für ihn dieser Tag als ein Arbeitstag verloren gegangen ist, obwohl sonst alles schön und gut war.

Bei der Machtergreifung der Kommunisten 1940 flüchtete Vööbus nach Deutschland. In Deutschland geriet er mit seiner Frau wegen seiner kritischen Einstellung zum Naziregime in den Interessenkreis der Gestapo, mit der er als Christ natürlich nicht einverstanden sein konnte. Direkte Schuldbeweise wurden allerdings nicht gefunden und so kannte er nach Estland zurückehren, doch erst 1942, als Estland von der deutschen Wehrmacht okkupiert worden war. 1943 verteidigte A. Vööbus an der theologischen Fakultät der Universität Tartu seine Dissertation „Das Mönchtum in Syrien, Mesopotamien und Persien bis zum 10. Jahrhundert: seine Entstehung, geschichtliche Entwicklung und kulturgeschichtliche Bedeutung“ (in der Maschinenschrift 475 Seiten), die später zur Grundlage seiner „History of the Ascetism in the Syrian Orient“, Bd. I–III (Louvain, 1958, 1960, 1980) wurde.

1944 flüchtete A. Vööbus zum zweiten Mal vor der sowjetischen Okkupation nach Deutschland und wirkte 1944–1948 als Pastor in Flüchtlingslagern in Deutschland. 1946–1948 war A. Vööbus als Professor für die ältere Kirchangeschichte an der baltischen Universität in Pinneberg bei Hamburg tätig. Als die baltische Universität unter dem Druck der Sowjetmacht ihre Tätigkeit aufgeben musste, ging A. Vööbus nach England, um auf Grund eines Stipendiums des LWB im Britischen Museum Forschungsarbeit zu betreiben. Von dort wurde er nach den USA berufen, wo er von 1948 bis zu seiner Emeritierung 1977 als Professor der Wissenschaft des Neuen Testaments und der älteren Kirchengeschichte in Chicago an der Lutheran School of Theology gearbeitet hat. Er starb in Chicago am 25. September 1988. A. Vööbus war Mitglied mehrerer Akademien und wissenschaftlichen Gesellschaften in Amerika, Europa und Asien. Der Tätigkeit von A. Vööbus ist gewidmet die Festschrift „Tribute to Arthur Vööbus. Studies in Early Christian Literature and its Environment, Primarily in the Syrian East“, ed. by Robert H. Fischer, Chicago 1977, ebenso das Werk „The Professor Arthur Vööbus Collection of Syrian Manuscripts on Film and The Institute of Syrian Manuscript Studies“, Chicago 1982. Eine Biographie von A. Vööbus hat der Bischof der Estnischen Ev. Luth. Kirche (im Exil) Karl Raudsepp geschrieben: „Arthur Vööbus 1909–1980“, Toronto 1990.

Wenn der Talmud sagt, dass Gott alles gibt, nur nicht zu gleicher Zeit, dann gilt es offensichtlich nicht ganz für Arthur Vööbus. Bei ihm haben sich mehrere günstige Umstände vereinigt, die sich selten in einem Menschenleben zusammenfügen. Man kann natürlich spekulieren, ob das Leben fern von der Heimat ein Glück sein kann, aber andererseits ist es sicher, dass unter der sowjetischen Okkupation in seiner Heimat A. Vööbus - wenn er überhaupt am Leben geblieben wäre - ein kümmerliches Leben hätte führen müssen wie viele Intellektuelle in Estland, und wäre nicht zu einem weltweit anerkannten Wissenschaftler und einer führenden Autorität in der Syrologie geworden. Dank seiner Ehe mit der Tochter eines reichen Kaufmanns und seiner Pfarrstelle in einer grossen Gemeinde konnte A. Vööbus sich frühzeitig die notwendige wissenschaftliche Literatur beschaffen (die Universitätsbibliothek in Tartu, so wie die meisten Universitätsbibliotheken in Europa sind wenig geeignet für die syrologische Forschung). Nach Aussage eines Zeitgenossen besass A. Vööbus am Ende der 1930-er Jahre alle Publikationen der syrischen Texte und andere Fachliteratur, ausgenommen von 3 Druckwerken, die er sich nicht beschaffen konnte. In der Dissertation von A. Vööbus trifft man zwar nicht viel Sekundärliteratur, weil über das Mönchtum in Syrien nicht viel geschrieben worden ist, aber dafür verwendet er weitläufig syrische Quellentexte und es entsteht der Eindruck, dass der Autor sich in dieser Literatur heimisch fühlt.

Man kann vermuten, dass auch dann, wenn die Geschichte Estlands sich anders gestaltet hätte, der richtige Ort für Arthur Vööbus im Westen gewesen wäre. Die Syrologie nämlich ist immer ein sehr begrenztes Forschungsgebiet gewesen und ist an den meisten Universitäten nicht vertreten. In Chicago aber konnten die Voraussetzungen von A. Vööbus eine vollständige Verwendung finden.

Aus den USA hat er – meistens im Sommer – wenn keine Lehrveranstaltungen stattfanden, mehr als 40 Forschungsreisen in die Türkei, den Libanon, nach Syrien und in den Irak unternommen. In christlichen Klöstern des Orients hat er mit einer gewöhnlichen Handkamera – denn der Transport spezieller Filmaufnahmetechnik hätte ein Zusätzliches Lasttier erforderlich gemacht – syrische Handschriften verfilmt, die ihm gezeigt wurden, nachdem er das Vertrauen der Klosterinsassen gewonnen hatte. Meistens ging es dabei um seltene Handschriften, die in einer feindlichen islamischen Umwelt sorgfältig aufbewahrt und versteckt waren. In den Briefen an seine Frau beschreibt er die Umstände, unter denen seine Reisen stattfanden. Die Temperatur war öfters 40 Grad C, und zweimal hat er wegen der Hitze das Bewusstsein verloren. Das andere Problem war der Mangel an Trinkwasser. Man trank Regenwasser, das nach ein Paar Monaten stinkend wurde; nur in grösseren Städten konnte man Coca-Cola kaufen, und seine Frau bezeugt, wie er einmal in einen Restaurant vor dem Essen 10 kleine Flaschen ausgetrunken hat. Ein Problem war auch das Essen: alles war schmutzig und man musste ständig um seine Gesundheit fürchten; nur in Klöstern gab es mehr Sauberkeit; doch war das Essen der Mönche karg und bestand meistens aus Früchten. Auch hat er sich in mehreren Briefen über das Ungeziefer und den Lärm in den Hotels beklagt. Als Folge seiner Forschungreisen kam zustande eine einzigartige Filmsammlung meistens bisher unbekannter syrischer Handschriften im Umfang von 150000–200000 Seiten. 1979 wurde auf Grund dieser Sammlung in Chicago ein Institut für die Erforschung der syrischen Handschriften begründet.

Gleichzeitig mit der Entdeckung der syrischen Handschriften hat A. Vööbus diesen Stoff bearbeitet, die Texte und ihre Übersetzungen veröffentlicht (in der Serie „Corpus Scriptorum Christianorum Orintalium“, 27 Bände) und wissenschaftliche Monographien geschrieben. Von dem umfangreichen und weitläufigen literarischen Nachlass von A. Vööbus machen das Publizieren der syrischen Handschriften und die syrologische Forschungsarbeit den Hauptteil aus. Er hat mehr als 80 Abhandlungen bzw. Bücher und mehr als 240 Aufsätze in verschiedenen estnischen, englischen, deutschen, französischen und arabischen Ausgaben veröffentlicht, darunter solche wie z.B. „Encyclopaedia Britannica“, „Lexikon für Theologie und Kirche”, „Encyclopaedia Persica“ u.a.

1951 hat A. Vööbus die Serie der „Abhandlungen der Estnischen Theologischen Gesellschaft im Exil“ gegründet (Papers of the Estonian Theological Society in Exile = PETSE); im Rahmen dieser Serie hat er 49 Werke auf Englisch und Deutsch veröffentlicht. Darunter sind Publikationen über syrische Texte, über das Neue Testament, über die altaethiopischen Evangelientexte, über die altgeorgischen Evangelientexte, aber auch über die Geschichte von Estland in den letzten Jahrzehnten (The Department of Theology at the University of Tartu: its Life and Work, 1, Martyreom and Annihilation“, PETSE 14, 1963; The Kommunist Menace, the Present Chaos and our Christian Responsibility”, PETSE Popular Series 1, 1955; „Christian Consciousness in the Face of the Current Confusion: The Dignity of the Christian vis-à-vis the Sovietization of the Mind“, PETSE Popular Series 1982; „the Martyrs in Estonia: the Suffering of the Bloodwitnessing Churches in Estonia“, PETSE 29, 1977), in diesem Rahmen erschien auch sein monumentales Werk Studies in the History of the Estonian People“ in 14 Bänden 1969–1985. Dieses Werk ist ein sprechendes Beispiel für den Fleiss und das Gründlichkeitsstreben von A. Vööbus. Man sagt, dass das Werk als Antwort auf die öfters unausgesprochene Frage der amerikanischen Kollegen des Verfassers geschrieben wurde: wer sind die Esten, und warum kann man sie überall in der Welt anzutreffen? waren dem Autor in Amerika nicht alle Quellen für die Geschichte Estlands erreichbar (immerhin konnte er die Materialien in schwedischen Archiven verwenden, die für die Forscher in Sowjetestland unzugänglich waren), aber er wollte auch keine erschöpfende Darstellung bieten: im Untertitel des Werkes ist vermerkt, dass der Hauptaugenmerk auf Fragen des Geistes und geistlichen Lebens, der Volksbildung und Kultur gerichtet ist. In besonderen Bänden wurde der Befreiungskrieg 1918–1920 behandelt (VI. Band, 1980), die Universität Tartu (der VIII. Band erschien zum 350. Jahrestag der Universität 1982), die estnische Literatur während der Estnischen Republik 1916–1940 (IX. Band, 1983), die estnische Musik (X. Band, 1984), die estnische Kunst (XI. Band, 1984), die erste sowjetische Okkupation 1940–1941 (XIII. Band, 1984) und die Zeit der deutschen Besatzung 1941–1944 (XIV. Band, 1985). Zu den mehr als 240 Aufsätzen von A. Vööbus sind nicht gerechnet unzählige Aufrufe, Briefe, Proteste zum Schutz der Menschen unter dem kommunistischan Regime, die in verschiedenen Ausgaben in Europa und in den USA veröfftentlicht worden sind.

Arthur Vööbus war einer der eifrigsten Befürworter der Freiheit für das estnische Volk, aber gleich den anderen wurde seiner Stimme kein Gehör geschenkt – weder in der Sowjetunion noch im Westen. Wohl aber hat sein Lebenswerk die syrologische Forschung im Westen und anderswo richtungsgebend beeinflusst. Dank seiner zahlreichen sensationellen Handschriftenfunde beabsichtigte A. Vööbus eine neue „Geschichte der syrischen Literatur“ zu schreiben (die letzte von Anton Baumstark stammt von 1922). Leider weiss ich nicht, ob er sein Vorhaben verwirklichen konnte (der I. Band sollte im Rahmen der Serie PETSE erscheinen). Doch konnte er eigenartigerweise den 1800. Geburtstag des grossen christlichen Theologen Origenes feiern: er veröffentlichte 1935 die syrische Übersetzung des Hauptwerkes von Origenes, das bisher als spurlos vermisst galt. A. Vööbus ist heutzutage einer der führenden Syrologen in der Welt und einer der weltweit bekanntesten estnischen Wissenschaftler.

Cimmerians in the Western Anatolia: A Chronological Note

Mait Kõiv, Tartu

The Cimmerians – a people whom the Greek accounts depict as immigrating from the north of the Black sea[1] into the western Asia, and terrorising the region during the 7th century BC[2] – are well known besides from the Greek historical tradition also from the Assyrian records. Both these strains of evidence give some indications for dating their invasion. In the case of the intrusion into the western parts of Anatolia, where the Cimmerians are told to have conquered Midas the king of Phrygia and ravaged Sardeis the capital of Lydia, this chronology has been usually reconstructed by combining the data of the Greek tradition, the Assyrian documents and the archaeological evidence from Gordion, the capital city of Phrygia. But it seems that when juxtaposing the Greek and Assyrian evidence the scholars have not wholly taken into consideration the nature of the Greek accounts, particularly their chronographical works. The purpose of the present paper is to point to some inconsistencies in the previous discussion of the problem of dating the Cimmerians' attack against Phrygia and Lydia, with the hope that a more adequate evaluation of the Greek evidence will allow some correction of the chronology of these events.

The summary version of the Cimmerians' invasion known to the Greek authors runs as follows.[3] The Cimmerians were a people dwelling in the steppes north of the Black sea. They were attacked by the invading Scythians, left their country, crossed the Caucasian hills and moved into Anatolia, where settled down in the region of the future Greek city Sinope

---

1 But see for example Kristensen 1988 and Sauter 2000 arguing for the Near Eastern origins of the Cimmerians. For recent criticism of these and other 'anti-traditional' theories of the Cimmerians' origins see Lebedynsky 2004.

2 All the following dates are BC.

3 For the summary and discussion of the Greek evidence see especially Lehmann-Haupt 1921, 412–419; Ivantchik 1993, 69–73, 105–114; and Sauter 2000, 82–93, 166–173.

in the Black sea's southern coast.[4] They attacked the famous Phrygian king Midas, who committed suicide after the defeat.[5] They moved against the Lydians, ravaging their capital Sardeis, except acropolis, at the time when the Lydians were reigned by King Ardys the son of Gyges.[6] They also attacked the Greek cities Magnesia and Ephesos, sacking the first and burning the famous sanctuary of Artemis in the latter,[7] and forced a part of the Greek population to take refuge on the islands of the Aegean see.[8] Their leader Lygdamis, who had lead them into Asia and conducted the destruction of both Sardeis and the Ephesian Artemision, next invaded Kilikia (south-eastern Anatolia) and perished there.[9] The Cimmerians were driven out from Asia by the Lydian king Alyattes the grandson of Ardys.[10] The Cimmerians' invasion into the western Asia was soon followed by that of the Scythians. The Scythians attacked the Medians, were about to invade Egypt, and acquired hegemony over Asia for 28 years, as is reported by Herodotos.[11]

The Greek account depicts the principal events of the Cimmerian invasion as taking place during a relatively short period: the Cimmerians are told to have invaded Asia under the leadership of Lygdamis – the chief who also led them against Lydia and the Greek cities. This demonstrates

4 The best account is given by Herodotos IV 11–12; I 15, 103; but see also Ps-Scymn. 947–952; Eustath. ad *Od.* XI 14.

5 Strab. I 3. 21; Eustath. ad *Od.* XI 14.

6 Hdt. I 15; Kallisthenes *FGrHist* 124 F 29 (= Strab. XIII 4. 8); Strab. I 3. 21; Eustath. ad *Od.* XI 14.

7 The attack was mentioned by Hdt. I 6. More details in Strab. XIV 1. 40; Callim. *Hymn. Artem.* 251–258; Athen. XII 525c. Aristotle mentioned Cimmerian occupation of Antandros on the Aegean coast opposite to the island Lesbos (fr. 478 Rose).

8 This is mentioned in an inscription containing a letter of King Lysimachos to the citizens of Samos dating from 283/2 (Welles 1966, 46–51).

9 Lygdamis as the leader of the Cimmerians in their intrusion into Asia: Plut. *Mar.* 11; the sack of Sardeis and the attack of the Ionian cities by Lygdamis: Strab. I 3. 21; the destruction of the Ephesian Artemision by Lygdamis: Callim. *Hymn. Artem.* 251–258; Hesych. s.v. Λύγδαμις; the death of Lygdamis in Kilikia: Strab. I 3. 21.

10 Hdt. I 16. 2; Polyaen. VII 2. 1.

11 Hdt. IV 12; I 73, 103–105. According to Justinus II 3. 4 and Orosius I 14 the hegemony of the Scythians lasted for 15 years.

that the Greek authors imagined all these events as parts of one great invasion accomplished in course of a single generation.[12]

In the western Anatolia we hear about one more invading tribe – the Treres, who were labelled by the Greeks as a 'Cimmerian people' (*kimmerikos ethnos*), and were believed to have been of Thracian provenance, immigrating from Europe.[13] According to the 4th century historian Kallisthenes, these Treres also sacked Sardeis, slightly later than the Cimmerians.[14] They were believed to have been defeated and expelled from Asia by the Skythian leader Madys, apparently at the same time when the Cimmerians were thrown out by Alyattes.[15] Nothing is told about the exact relationship between the Cimmerians and the Treres, but a report of Arrianos about a defeat inflicted to the Cimmerians by the Thracians (a possible correlate for the Treres, when considering their alleged Thracian origins)[16] suggests the possibility that according to the Greeks' point of view the Cimmerians were expelled from the western part of Anatolia by the victorious Treres – an act which could well have been considered the reason for Lygdamis' move to Kilikia – before the Lydians and the Scythians threw both of these people definitely out from the region.

Most of this story is recorded already by Herodotos, who probably relied mostly on the oral tradition current in Greek cities of Asia Minor in the 5th century. This evidence comes thus from the time about two centuries after the events. But Herodotos and later sources quote also some earlier evidence. We know that Cimmerians' expulsion from their home-

12 When Kallisthenes noted that Sardeis had been sacked twice (*FGrHist* 124 F 29: Φησὶ δὲ Καλλισθένης ἁλῶναι τὰς Σάρδεις ὑπὸ Κιμμερίων πρῶτον, ἔθ' ὑπὸ Τρηρῶν καὶ Λυκίων) and Strabo mentioned the frequency of the attacks (I 3. 21: πολλάκις δέ καὶ οἱ Κιμμέριοι καὶ οἱ Τρῆρες ἐποιήσαντο τὰς τοιαύτας ἐφόδους) they clearly kept in separate ventures of Cimmerians and Treres (see below) – see Jacoby 1930, 426–427; Ivantchik 1993, 106–107. It is therefore not justified to view the Greek sources as ascribing both these attacks against Sardeis to the Cimmerians, placing the first at the time of Gyges and second at the time of Ardys (so Sauter 2000, 180–181).

13 Strab. I 3. 21; XIV 1. 40 (ὑπὸ Τρηρῶν ..., Κιμμερικοῦ ἔθνους). Treres are described as a Thracian people in Thuc. II 96. 4–5; Strab. XIII 1. 8; Steph. Byz. s.v. Τρῆρος; cf. Keil 1937.

14 Kallisthenes *FGrHist* 124 F 29; see n. 12.

15 Strab. I 3. 21. Herodotos synchronised Madyas with the Median king Kyaxares, whose reign overlapped, in his view, with that of Lydian Alyattes, the king expelling the Cimmerians from Asia (compare Hdt. I 16. 2, 73 and 103).

16 Arrianos ap. Eustath. ad *Dion. Per.* 332 and 791.

land by the Scythians was mentioned by an Archaic epic poet Aristeas of Prokonnesos,[17] that the sack of Sardeis both by the Cimmerians and the Treres was mentioned by the contemporary Ephesian poet Kallinos, and that the Cimmerians' attack on the Greek cities was, in all likelihood, alluded to by Archilochos – another Greek poet of the same time.[18] We cannot say how extensive exactly was the information that Herodotos and the later writers could deduce from the verses of these and perhaps some other early poets,[19] but as the eventual comparison of their data with the Assyrian sources (see below) demonstrates, they have preserved the main course of the events (but not necessarily the details) fairly reliably.

Concerning the date of these events, Herodotos, as said, placed the sack of Sardeis to the time of the Lydian king Ardys, an opinion followed by later Greek chronographers.[20] In Herodotos' counting the reign of Ardys fell roughly to the years from 679/8 – 630/29,[21] and the attack against Sardeis consequently in between of these years. Later Greek chronographers dated Ardys slightly later (664/3 – 627/6 according to the Canon of Eusebios and 653/2 – 616/5 according to Eusebios' Armenian version),[22] and there are reasons for suggesting that the sack of Sardeis was synchronised with Ardys' seventh year, which falls to ca. 672 according to the counting of Herodotos, and to ca. 657 according to Eusebios'

17 Hdt. IV 13. According to Herodotos, Aristeas composed his epics more than 240 years before Herodotos' own time, which suggests a date not later than the early 7th century making Aristeas virtually a contemporary of the Cimmerians' invasion. Suidas (s.v. 'Aristšaj) synchronised Aristeas with the Lydian last king Kroisos (around the middle of the 6th century).

18 Kallinos ap. Strab. XIV 1. 40 (Cimmerians) and ap. Steph. Byz. s.v. Τρῆρος (Treres); see also Strab. XIII 4. 8. Archilochos ap. Strab. XIV 1. 40 (the sack of Magnesia).

19 It is possible that the Cimmerians were mentioned by a mid-seventh-century poet Terpandros (see below, with n. 58). In addition, we are told that the 6th century poets Mimnermos and Xenophanes composed poems about the past of Smyrna and Kolophon (for *Smyrnaeis* of Mimnermos and *Kolophonos ktisis* of Xenophanes see Podlecki 1984, 58, 165–166) which both could have mentioned the attacks of the Cimmerians.

20 See n. 23.

21 Herodotos does not establish the absolute dates for the Lydian kings. But he presents the lengths of the reigns of every ruler, which allows to calculate the absolute dates by counting back from the last year of the last Lydian king Kroisos – 547/6. Later Greek chronographers certainly knew this date, perhaps from the Babylonian history of Berossos, as suggested by Mosshammer 1979, 262.

22 For the full evidence and discussion of the Greek sources on the dating of Lydian kings see, above all, Gelzer 1875, 299–244; Kaletsch 1958, 1–25.

Canons.[23] The defeat and death of the Phrygian king Midas, and thus the Cimmerians invasion against Phrygia, was dated by Eusebios to the year 696/5.[24] In addition, there is circumstantial evidence suggesting that some other Greek scholars dated Midas' death to the year 676.[25]

---

23 The sack during the reign of Ardys was established by Herodotos (see n. 6); the evidence for the seventh year, a precision of later chronographers, is circumstantial: The foundation of Istros in the Black sea, which according to Ps.-Skymnos (767) took place when the Cimmerians invaded Asia, was dated by Eusebios to the year 656 (Euseb. *Chron.* II 86–87 Schoene), which suggests that this year was, in some dating system followed by Eusebios, considered as a suitable date for the Cimmerians' invasion. Eusebios' date for Alkman, a poet of supposedly of Lydian origin, was established at the previous year 657, the seventh year of King Ardys. In the Suidas (s.v. Ἀλκμάν) Alkman's date was explicitly connected with the reign of Ardys and established at the Olympiad beginning with the year 672, the seventh of Ardys according to the chronology of Herodotos. In sum, all this suggests that for some reason unknown to us the seventh year of Ardys was believed to have marked the invasion of the Cimmerians, the date of Alkman was established according to this event, and this set of synchronisms was simply dated according to two different chronologies: to 672 according to Herodotos and to 657/6 according to Eusebios (see Rhode 1878, 199 ff; Kaletsch 1958, 26–27 and Mosshammer 1979, 222–225; according to the belief of Rhode, Kaletsch and Lehmann-Haupt [1921, 418], the dating to the seventh year of Ardys is a reliable reflection of the historical reality, while Mosshammer regards the date to this particular year as an occasional coincidence).

24 Euseb. *Chron.* II 84–85 Schoene. The accession of Midas was dated by Eusebios to 738 (*Chron.* II 82–83 Schoene). There is no reason to follow Ivantchik (1993, 72–73) who suggests that Eusebios rejected the synchronism between Midas and the Cimmerians' invasion. Eusebios clearly stated that Midas died drinking bull's blood (Jerome in Euseb. *Chron.* II 85 Schoene: *Mida cum apud Frygas regnante sanguine tauri potato extinctus*), which was generally known to have been the result of the defeat by the Cimmerians (Strab. I 3. 21: οἵ τε Κιμμέριοι ... τοτὲ μέν ἐπὶ Παφλαγόνας τοτὲ δέ καὶ Φρύγας ἐμβαλόντες, ἡνίκα Μίδαν αἷμα ταύρου πιόντα φασὶν ἀπελθεῖν εἰς τὸ χρεών; Eustath. ad *Od.* XI 14: τοὺς Κιμμερίους, ... ἐμβαλεῖν δέ καὶ ἐπὶ Παφλαγόνας καὶ Φρύγας, ὅτε καὶ Μίδας λέγεται αἷμα ταύρου πιὼν). There is therefore every reason for believing that Eusebios recorded the usual story of Cimmerians defeating Midas. When Eusebios dated a Cimmerian invasion also to the year 1087/6 (Euseb. *Chron.* II 60–61 Schoene) he in all probability simply kept in mind another invasions of the Cimmerians together with the mythical Amazons about 100 years after the Trojan war, and 400 years before the second at the time of Midas. In any case, Eusebios often gave different dates for the same events (the cases are amply discussed by Mosshammer 1979, 169–319).

25 The date 676 for Midas fall is never recorded in the sources, but it can be firmly conjectured (see Gelzer 1875, 252 n. 6): Midas was dated to the time of Judean Amos (Leo Grammaticus ap. Cramer *Anecd. Paris.* II 264; Gregor. Hamartol. 170 Muralt.; Kerdenos

In the Assyrian sources the Cimmerians (Gimirrai) first appear in a set of texts from the time of Sargon II (721–705),[26] the most important of them concerning a defeat of a king of Urartu at Gamir, which has been localised either north of lake Sevan in the central Transcaucasia, or in the Mannean land in the region of Zagros, south-east of Urartu.[27] Though neither the identity of the defeated Urartian king nor the exact date of the battle is ever made explicit in the sources, the event is usually associated with Rusas I and dated to ca. 714, that is almost to the same year as the eight campaign of Sargon, culminating with the defeat of the Urartian forces at Mount Waush and the destruction of the towns of Urartu.[28] Few years later – in 705 – Sargon perished in a campaign against certain Eshpai the Kulummean, either in Tabal (eastern part of central Anatolia) or in Media. Moderns have often identified these adversaries of Sargon as the Cimmerians, although this is not clearly stated in the sources.[29]

Roughly simultaneously to these Cimmerian exploits, the King Mita of Mushki (probably Midas of Phrygia)[30] appears in several Assyrian texts as a mighty Anatolian dynast, an ally of Rusas I of Urartu, instigating disloyalty of the Assyrian vassals in the south-eastern Anatolia and northern Syria. In 709, however, Mita gave up his previous opposition towards the Assyrians and formed an alliance with Sargon.[31] It has been suggested that

195 Bekker), the first year of Amos was dated exactly 100 years after that of Ahas (Cramer *Anecd. Paris.* II 263), and the first year of Ahas was equalized with Ol. 1 in 776 (Synkellos 372; Cramer *Anecd. Paris.* II 265; Georg. Hamartol. 180 Muralt). It is believed this evidence reflects the chronology of Julius Africanus which may, in turn, derive from the chronicle of Apollodoros (see Mosshammer 1977, 117, 126–127).

26 For recent discussion of the Assyrian evidence see especially Kristiansen 1988; Lanfranchi 1990, 11–125; Ivantchik 1993, 19–125; Sauter 2000, 217–248; Lebedynsky 2004, 26–34.

27 Near lake Sevan: Sulimirski and Taylor 1991, 558; Ivantchik 1993, 26–28; Lebedynsky 2004, 28–29. In the Mannean district: Kristensen 1988; Sauter 2000, 223–224.

28 So already Lehmann-Haupt 1921, 402. But see especially Barnett 1982, 355–357; Sulimirski and Taylor 1991, 558–559; Kristensen 1988; Lanfranchi and Parpola 1990, XX; Ivantchik 1993, 21–26; Parker 1995, 11–19; Sauter 2000, 219–222; Lebedynsky 2004, 28–30.

29 The identification is uphold by Barnett 1982, 356; Hawkins 1982, 422; Sulimirski and Taylor 1991, 559; Drews 2004, 111; see also Kuhrt 1995, 499. But note the skepticism of Kristensen 1988, 101 n. 339; Ivantchik 1993, 53–55; Sauter 2000, 224–225; Lebedynsky 2004, 30.

30 The identification of this Mita of Mushki with Midas of Phrygia is generally accepted by the scholars. But see the doubts of Sevin 1991, 97.

31 The evidence comes from the years 718–709. See especially Hawkins 1997 and Fuchs 2001.

his change of policy was caused by the Cimmerian threat,[32] but there is no explicit evidence to support this suggestion.[33] Another Mita, a city lord in Anatolia, is know from the time of Assarhaddon (680–669), but his identity or his connection with Mushki and/or Phrygia cannot be clearly established.[34]

The next time after the defeat of Urartu (in 714) we encounter the Cimmerians in the Assyrian sources, is the year 679, when a governor of Assarhaddon defeated Teushpa, the chief of Gimirrai (the Cimmerians), in Khubushkia in Tabal (in Anatolia). At this time the Cimmerians were allied with Rusa II of Urartu.[35] This is the first time when the Assyrian sources clearly locate the Cimmerians in Anatolia, albeit giving no indication of their intrusion into the western part of Anatolia. Few years later, in 676/675, Assarhaddon again fought against the Cimmerians in Anatolia, where the latter had apparently concluded an alliance with Phrygia (Mushku). Mita the city lord from Anatolia is also mentioned in connection with these events.[36] There is no indication of any hostility between the Cimmerians and Phrygia, and the case clearly demonstrates that Phrygia was still a considerable power at this time.

The first clear indications in the Assyrian texts about the Cimmerians' attacks against the western Anatolia date from the time of Ashurbanipal (668 – ca. 630). We learn that in some time between 668–665 the Lydian king Gugu (Gyges of the Greek accounts) sought Assyrian support against the Cimmerian pressure, that he thereafter defeated the Cimmerians and renounced the Assyrian protection allying himself instead with the Egyptian king Psamtik I, perhaps because in 657 the Cimmerians had invaded Syria and Palestine making the alliance with the Assyrian king useless for Gugu, that in the time between 650–644 Gugu perished in a new mighty attack of the Cimmerians against his country, and that his son and successor once again sought Assyrian protection. Slightly later – ca. 640 or thereafter – a Cimmerian leader Dugdammi (probably identical with Lygdamis of the Greek sources) formed an anti-Assyrian alliance with Tabal

32 Barnett 1982, 356; Hawkins 1982, 420–421.

33 Note the skeptical attitude of Kristensen 1988, 101 n. 339.

34 Starr 1990, 15; Ivantchik 1993, 68; Röllig 1997, 494; Fuchs 1999, 756.

35 For the defeat of Teushpa see Hawkins 1982, 427; Kristensen 1988, 104; Sulimirski and Taylor 1991, 559; Ivantchik 1993, 57–61; Parker 1995, 30; Sauter 2000, 226–228; Lebedynsky 2004, 30–31; Drews 2004, 111.

36 Starr 1990, LVII and no. 1; Ivantchik 1993, 65–68; Parker 1995, 30; Röllig 1997, 494; Lebedynsky 2004, 31. On Mita see n. 34.

but soon died, whereupon both his Tabalite allies and his son Sandakshatru concluded alliance with Assyria.[37]

The Assyrian sources, thus, clearly support the Greek accounts, as far as the Cimmerian attacks against the Lydians are concerned, and even make it clear that Greek tradition has fairly correctly preserved the name of a principal Cimmerian leader – Lygdamis/Dugdammi. On the other hand, they demonstrate that the Greek accounts, when depicting the Cimmerians attacking Phrygia and Lydia immediately after their crossing of Caucasus, have compressed the story in a way characteristic for oral tradition. From the Assyrian sources we know that the Cimmerians were in Asia already by ca. 714 while there is no indication of the attacks against the western Anatolia prior to the time of Assurbanipal and Gyges in the 660ies (or perhaps the late 670ies). Rather on the contrary, they suggest that in 676-5 Phrygia was still a great power and had good relations with the Cimmerians. Therefore, there is no support in the Assyrian sources for the destruction of Phrygia and the defeat of Midas in either 696/5 or 676 as the Greek chronographers believed.

The traces of the Cimmerians' attacks have been, naturally enough, sought also from the archaeological record. As far as the Phrygian capital Gordion is concerned,[38] this tradition has been thought to be confirmed archaeologically, since a layer of destruction has been in the city dated to the early 7th century, which corresponds with the date of the defeat and death of Midas at 696 as recorded by Eusebios.[39] A great burial mound near the city, containing a richly furnished burial chamber with a body of a 60–65 years old man, probably dating from the early 7th century, has been considered as the burial of Mita/Midas, despite the fact that, according to the Greek tradition, Midas perished in a disaster, which should make a magnificent burial rather surprising.[40] However, new investigations in

37 For the full account of the evidence see Lehmann-Haupt 1912, 1960–1965; 1921, 416–419; Kaletsch 1958; Cogan and Tadmor 1977; Spalinger 1978; Mazetti 1978; Ivantchik 1993, 95–115; Aro-Valjus 1999; Sauter 2000, 232–237; Drews 2004, 107–109; Lebedynsky 2004, 32–34. Although the sources do not identify Dugdammi explicitly as a Cimmerian, there seems to be little doubt that he was (see Ivantchik 1993, 118–120).

38 On the archaeological evidence from Gordion see Prag 1989; Mellink 1991, 628–634; Kuhrt 1995, 562–564, 566–567; Voigt and Henrickson 2000.

39 First suggested by Young 1955, 16. See especially Mellink 1991, 628–629.

40 The excavator, R. Young, doubted whether the tomb was that of the most famous Phrygian king because his reign ended, according to the tradition, with the destruction of the city. But K. DeVries, who edited the excavation report, favored the identification (Prag

Gordion have made it clear that the destruction layer must be much earlier, presumably from the early 8th century and thus cannot be connected with Mita the contemporary of Sargon or with the Cimmerian invasion.[41] We are therefore deprived of any archaeological evidence for dating the sack of Gordion by the Cimmerians. This change in the interpretation of the archaeological record has however not affected the date of the great burial mound, which can be constantly ascribed to Mita active in the end of the 8th century. But the archaeological record gives no reason for associating the burial with any catastrophe – on the contrary, the magnificent burial suggests rather prosperous conditions at the time of the death. A destruction layer has been discovered also in Sardeis, but this again seems to be considerably earlier than the dates suggested for the invasion by the Assyrian sources, and its connection with the Cimmerians is therefore hardly possible.[42]

Thus we can see that the Greek and Assyrian evidence agree in general lines, except in the dating of the events, the first suggesting that Phrygia was invaded already at the very beginning of the 7th century and the second allowing this only from the late 670ies onwards. The archaeological record is not of much help for resolving the question of chronology. This apparent contradiction of the Greek and Assyrian evidence proves however to be rather illusory when we consider the nature of Greek chronological record. It is clear beyond any reasonable doubt that the dates in the early Greek history mostly were not based on any documentary data but were calculated by the relatively late chronographers who combined the evidence from the ultimately oral tradition with what they were able to deduce from the verses of the early poets, and were, compelled to date the early events relying on counting according to generations. The dates they arrived at are therefore the results of their research, often quite hypothetical, and cannot be taken at face value.[43] But they can

1989, 159). The tomb belongs to the period when the Phrygians had adopted alphabetic writing (Hawkins 1997, 273), thus not before the last decades of the 8th century. For K. De Vries, the style of the finds in the tomb as well as of the burial ritual suggested rather an early 7th than late 8th century dating (Prag 1989, 159).

41 Voigt and Henrickson 2000, 48, 51–52.

42 See Drews 2004, 109 and 185 n. 28. A royal tomb at Karniyarik Tepe, probably robbed already in antiquity, has been ascribed to Gyges.

43 See especially Rhode 1881; Jacoby 1902, Burn 1936; Mosshammer 1979; Fehling 1985; Shaw 2003. In the case of the discussion of the dates of the Cimmerian invasion it has been well noted by Ivantchik 1993, 70.

still convey valuable information, possibly leading us to the evidence according to which they were calculated and which may derive from a reliable tradition.

In the present case it is clear that the dates of the Lydian kings given by the Greek writers do not exactly correspond to the truth. For example, Gyges was dated either to 717/6 – 679/8 (according to Herodotos), to 700/699 – 664/3 (in the Canon of Eusebios) or to 679/8 – 653/2 (in Eusebios' Armenian version),[44] all of which are too early for the real Gyges who almost certainly was still alive at ca. 650 and died shortly afterwards.[45] It is clear that the Greek dates were calculated back from 547/6 (the date of the fall of the last Lydian king Kroisos), and that the differences were caused by the use of the different lengths of reigns for the kings. Whence these lengths were taken from by the Greek chronographers cannot be established,[46] but they certainly did not correspond exactly to the historical truth.

So, in the case of Lydia, the comparison with the Assyrian sources proves that the dates of the Greeks are not exactly true, for which reason they are justly disregarded by the scholars. But in the case of the dates of the fall of Midas and the Phrygian kingdom the Assyrian sources, being silent about any Cimmerian involvement in the western Anatolia prior to Ashurbanipal and Gyges, do not afford possibilities for a clear proof. Therefore, the Greek dates 696 or 676 for the destruction of Gordion are constantly relied upon in the discussion of the Cimmerian invasion and the end of the Phrygian power, the scholars being divided in two camps in the question of which of them should be preferred.[47] Indeed, the date 696

---

44 See n. 22.

45 Cogan and Tadmour 1977, 78–79 n. 25; Spalinger 1978, 405. Ivantchik 1993, 104–105; Lebedynsky 2004, 33. Earlier writers (Gelzer 1875, 262–263; Lehmann-Haupt 1912, 1964; 1921, 416; Kaletsch 1958, 30) settled upon the date 652, given for Gyges' death by the Armenian version, which is relatively close to the date suggested by the Assyrian evidence (this dating is uphold by Sauter [2000, 234] basing on the Assyrian evidence). But there is no reason to suggest that the editor of Eusebios' Armenian version had better evidence than his predecessors and thus regard the closeness of his date of Gyges' death to the reality as anything but an occasional coincidence.

46 For the discussion of the reason of Herodotos' datings see, for example, Strasburger 1956, 140–151; Miller 1963, 118–127; Den Boer 1967, 53–57; Drews 1969; Mazetti 1978, 175; Ivantchik 1993, 108–113; Burkert 1995.

47 For 696: Kroll 1932, 1539; Barnett 1982, 356; Hawkins 1982, 422; 1997, 272; Mellink 1991, 624, 626; Van de Mieroop 2004, 257. For 676: Lehmann-Haupt 1921, 413–414; Kammen-

has been used for dating the archaeologically attested destruction of Gordion.[48] This date also forms a part of argument for the assumption of the Cimmerian pressure against Phrygian Mita at the time of Sargon, as well as for the identification of the adversaries of Sargon in his fatal battle as the Cimmerians – all this fits perfectly together, if the date 696 for Midas' final defeat could be accepted as reliable.[49] The date 676 on the other hand has been used for assuming an attack of the Cimmerians against Mushki (Phrygia) in connection with Assarhaddon's campaign in Anatolia in 676-5,[50] although there is no confirmation for this in the Assyrian record which suggests that there was an alliance between Mushki and the Cimmerians in this time.[51]

But there is no *a priori* reason to trust dates 696 and 676 for the defeat of the Phrygians any more than the dates of the Lydian kings, and there is no warrant that they can be relied on as exact evidence. The dates for the defeat of Midas are, similarly to these of the Lydian kings, in all likelihood also secondary constructions the reasons of which cannot be strictly established, but can still be reasonably guessed.[52]

We know that the year 676 was according to a Hellenistic Spartan antiquarian and chronographer Sosibios the date of the establishment of Karneian festival at Sparta.[53] Hellanikos, a Greek historian of the late 5th century, stated that the first winner in this festival was a famous Lesbian poet Terpandros, a contemporary of Midas of Phrygia.[54] It was therefore quite natural for the later Greek chronologists to synchronise the establishment of the first Karneia at the time of Terpandros with the King Midas. There can be scarcely any reasonable doubt that the dating of both the fall of Midas and the establishment of Spartan Karneia to the same

huber 1976–1980, 594; Kristensen 1988, 104–105; Ivantchik 1993, 73–74; Röllig 1997, 494 (dating the destruction to 674/3); Lebedynsky 2004, 31.

48 Mellink 1991, 629.

49 The wish to adjust the Greek dates with the Assyrian evidence about Mita and the death of Sargon has been, in turn, the reason to prefer the date 696 to that of 676 (Mellink 1991, 624; but see also Hawkins 1982, 422; Barnett 1982, 356).

50 Ivantchik 1993, 73–74; Lebedynsky 2004, 31.

51 See above, with n. 36.

52 For a good discussion of the problem see Ivantchik 1993, 69–74.

53 Sosibios *FGrHist* 595 F 3.

54 Hellanikos *FGrHist* 4 F 85 a (Terpandros as the first winner in Karneia; note also [Plut.] *Mus.* 9, ascribing to Terpandros the first 'establishment' of music in Sparta) and F 85 b (the synchronism of Terpandros and Midas).

year 676 resulted from the synchronisation of these events.[55] The question can be only in which way this exact date was arrived at.

It has been suggested that the establishment of the major Spartan festival was simply placed 100 years after the celebration of the first Olympic games in 776,[56] and that the date calculated in such a simplistic way became, consequently, to mark the fall of Midas as well. Or alternatively, Sosibios might have used some local Spartan evidence for dating the Karneian festival.[57] In both cases the date of the first Karneia, and thus of Terpandros, was the primary one, the date for Midas resulting from the rough synchronisation of the king with the Lesbian poet and thus with the Spartan festival. In the first case there is obviously no slightest possibility to accept the date 676 as reliable (the hundred years assumed between the first Olympic games and the first Karneia can hardly be anything but a suitably round number). In the second case much depends of what kind of evidence did Sosibios have for establishing the date of the first Karneia. Indeed, it is quite probable that Hellanikos was correct in regarding Terpandros as a contemporary of Midas (some indication of this fact might have been preserved in the verses of the Lesbian poet),[58] and that Midas, consequently, reigned when Karneian festival was established at Sparta. But even if Sosibios' evidence for dating the establishment of the festival was solid and his calculations were sound, something we cannot be certain about, this could still give us only a vague date for Midas death, because there is no reason to assume an exact synchronism between the first Spartan festival and the Cimmerians' attack against Phrygia. As far as our evidence goes, Hellanikos mentioned only a general synchronicity of Midas and Terpandros; the rest is a result of deduction.[59]

But there is also the possibility that the date of the Karneian festival was determined according to the supposed date of Midas' fall, not vice

55 This has been noted already by Gelzer 1875, 252; but see also Lehmann-Haupt 1921, 413–414; Mosshammer 1977, 116–118; Ivantchik 1993, 71. Whether or not the evidence of Hellanikos about the synchronism Midas–Terpandros–Karneia and the exact dating of the first Karneia to 676 by Sosibios were first put together by Apollodoros (as suggested by Mosshammer 1977, 128–129 and Ivantchik 1993, 71) cannot be established.

56 Mosshammer 1977, 126.

57 As implied by Jacoby 1902, 148, and Forrest 1963, 172.

58 As it is suggested by Ivantchik 1993, 73.

59 About the date of Terpandros we can say scarcely more than that he flourished around the middle of the 7th century: besides to the time of the first Karneia (676) he was dated also to 645 (*Marm. Par.* ep. 34) or 641 (Euseb. *Chron.* II 89 Schoene).

versa: that Sosibios believed he knew the date of the fall of Midas, and consequently dated the first Karneia in the same year. If the ancient Greeks tried to establish the date for Midas according to some Asian evidence, it was natural for them to follow Herodotos, whose evidence suggested that the last year of Lydian Gyges was 679/8 and placed the sack of Sardeis to the time of his son Ardys. And if the later Greek authors roughly synchronised the Cimmerian attacks against Phrygia and Lydia, which they where wholly entitled to do given their belief that in both cases the blow was affected by Lygdamis, it was wholly natural for them to date Midas' suicide a couple of years after the death of Gyges – hence to ca. 676. There is thus a good reason for suggesting that the date 676 was established according to Herodotos' chronology of the Lydian kings. We have seen that this chronology did not render correct datings (Gyges, dated by Herodotos to the years 717/6 – 679/8, was probably still alive in the early 640ies and should be dated rather to ca. 680–645). There could have been no chance of arriving at a correct dating by building on this evidence. Of course, if our considerations are right, the date of Midas' death was calculated to fall after that of the death of Gyges, to the early years of his son Ardys, which would give us no reason for using this date for reconstructing the events during the early years of Gyges' reign in the 670ies.

The date 696/5 was probably calculated by assuming a different juxtaposition of Midas and Gyges. Herodotos stated that Midas was the first barbarian ruler making dedications at Delphi, and that he did it earlier than Gyges the Lydian.[60] Herodotos could have relied here on the Delphic tradition.[61] This statement obviously suggests that Midas preceded Gyges. And the chronology of Eusebios, in fact, dates these rulers accordingly: the accession of Gyges in 700/699 and the death of Midas in 996/5, one Olympiad later.[62] The rough synchronisation of Midas' death with Gyges' accession could well have been the very reason for Eusebios' dating of the Cimmerians' attack against Phrygia to the year 696/5.[63]

Admittedly, none of the possibilities demonstrated here can be considered as certain. But conversely, there is no evidence suggesting or any reason for believing that the ancient Greeks' datings of Midas' death were

60 Hdt. I 14. 2.

61 As suggested by Sauter 2000, 91.

62 Euseb. *Chron.* II 84–85 Schoene.

63 Ivantchik 1993, 72, who keeps in mind only the date of death of Midas without regarding this as a date of the Cimmerians' invasion (see n. 24).

based on authentic documentary data. The varying chronologies of the Lydian king, none of which does exactly correspond to the truth, clearly do not suggest that the Greeks used a reliable record for the early Anatolian chronology. A reliable date for the Cimmerians' defeat of the Phrygians could have derived only from the Assyrian sources, which means that the Greeks of the Hellenistic period should have had an access to the Assyrian chronological record. Perhaps this possibility cannot be absolutely ruled out,[64] but there is not much evidence for it. It is much more probable that both dates of Midas death are the result of the reconstruction of Greek chronographers, similarly to the whole chronology of the early Greek history.[65]

What the Greek tradition actually tells us is that there was a great wave of invasion into the western Anatolia, led by Lygdamis who troubled Phrygia, Lydia, and the Greek cities on the Anatolian western coast during several years, causing the defeat and suicide of Midas and the sack of Sardeis at the time of Ardys. The Assyrian sources clearly suggest a rather prosperous Phrygia in the 670ies, place the Cimmerians invasion of the western Anatolia to the time of Ashurbanipal and Gyges in the 660ies – 640ies, and show that the son of Gyges (Ardys) was also pressed enough by the Cimmerians to compel him to renew the alliance with Assyria, concluded and renounced by his father. The most obvious divergence of the Greek and Assyrian accounts is that the Greek tradition has not recorded the wars and the defeat of Gyges who so prominently figures in the Assyr-

64 The Hellenistic Greeks certainly knew the work of Babylonian Berossos, from whom they might have learnt the date 547/6 for Kroisos' fall (see n. 21) and possibly also the date of the famous battle between the Lydian king Alyattes and the Median king Kyaxares in 585, which was interrupted by the solar eclipse predicted by Thales the philosopher (Hdt. I 74; the date is given in Euseb. *Chron.* II 94–95 Schoene; the eclipse in Anatolia took place in Mai 28. 585). Both these dates were probably known correctly by the Greek chronographers (but see the doubts of Parker 1993, 393–395 about the dating of the battle to 585), which suggests an access to the Near Eastern chronological evidence. But these dates of comparatively recent and epochal events of the Median and Persian history, which were of highest importance for Mesopotamia, can hardly be compared with the date of the defeat of Phrygia, an event which took place much earlier, in the periphery of the Assyrian realm, and is therefore less likely to have been recorded in the Mesopotamian chronicles which could have been accessible for the Greeks of the Hellenistic period.

65 This has been briefly noted by Parker 1995, 29 n. 85. Ivantchik 1993, 73–74, although understanding the nature of the Greek chronography, still accepts the date 676 as basically reliable.

ian record, but we cannot tell the reason for this neglect.[66] The Greek tradition proper, in contrast to the secondarily deduced dates, contains nothing to suggest that Midas of Phrygia was defeated considerably earlier than Lydia was attacked. Consequently, the combination of the Assyrian and Greek data proposes that the destruction of Gordion took place in the late 670ies at the earliest, and that the whole set of attacks against the western Anatolia – the sack of Phrygian, the attacks against Lydia and the Greek cities from the 660ies onwards – were all probably different phases of one great wave of invasions led by the formidable chief Lygdamis/Dugdammi who died in ca. 640, probably in Kilikia as related by the Greek story.[67]

In this case Mita the contemporary of Sargon clearly cannot be identified with Midas defeated by the Cimmerians, unless we assume a very long reign of this ruler (at least from ca 720 to ca 670). But here the Greek tradition might have compressed the evidence (as it certainly did when depicting the Cimmerians' attack against Phrygia and Lydia immediately after the crossing of Caucasus) by merging different Phrygian kings into one legendary figure. There is a possibility of postulating two homonymous kings – perhaps grandfather and grandson – and identifying the latter with the second Mita known from the Assyrian sources, who may

66 Ivantchik (1993, 112) suggests that Herodotos was led to place the Cimmerians' invasion to the time of Ardys by synchronizing this event with the invasion of the Scythians pursuing the Cimmerians, and juxtaposing the Lydian and Median chronologies – the reign of the Median king Kyaxares, in whose time the Scythians overrun Asia according to Herodotos' belief, happened in his counting to be the contemporary of Lydian Ardys, which forced him to date the invasion of the Cimmerians in Ardys' reign. However, this would have been impossible if the Greek tradition had preserved the connection of the invasion with Gyges. I would rather suggest that, despite Gyges' defeat and death, Sardeis was sacked slightly later, during the reign of Ardys, when the also Greek cities on the coast were under attack, which was the reason why the Greek tradition connected the invasion with Ardys not Gyges.

67 It must be conceded that the Greek tradition, being ultimately oral one, cannot be considered as completely reliable, and could, in principle, have erroneously contracted the events from a wide range of time by telescoping them into a single great event. But since the Assyrian evidence, revealing the Cimmerian attacks against the western Anatolia only from the time of Gyges and his successor, partly supports and by no means contradicts the Greek account, it would be reasonable to admit this story as basically trustworthy.

well be considered as the Midas perishing in the hands of the Cimmerians.[68]

If the chronology of the events outlined here is accepted, then the date 676 for the fall of Midas happens to be not far from historical truth. But as the previous discussion should have revealed, this coincidence must not encourage us to accept it as reliable. Very probably it was a guesswork of the later Greek scholars, like the rest of the Greek dates of the early Anatolian history, which simply happens to fall close to the historical truth. The Greek evidence only allows us to state that the Cimmerian invasion against Phrygia and Lydia took place at the time of the poets Kallinos, Archilochos and Terpandros, who all probably flourished around the middle of the 7th century.

References

Aro-Valjus, S. (1999), Gugu. In: The Prosopography of the Neo-Assyrian Empire. Vol. 1. Part II, 427–428.

Barnett, R. D. (1982), Urartu. In: CAH Vol. III Part 1, 314–371.

Burkert, W. (1995), Lydia between east and west or how to date Trojan war: a study in Herodotus. In: Carter, J. B. and Morris, S. P. (Ed.), The Ages of Homer. Austin, 139–148.

Burn, A. R. (1935), The dates in the early Greek history. In: JHS 40, 130–146.

Cogan, M. and Tadmor, H. (1977), Gyges and Ashurbanipal. A study in literary transmission. In: Orientalia 46, 65–85.

Deb Boer, W. (1967), Herodot und die Systeme der Chronologie. In: Mnemosyne 20, 30–60.

Dickie, M. (1995), The geography of Homer's world. In: Andresen, Ø. and Dickie, M. (Ed.), Homers World. Fiction, Tradition, Reality. Bergen, 29–56.

Drews, R. (1969), The fall of Astyages and Herodotus' chronology of the eastern kingdoms. In: Historia 18, 1–11.

Drews, R. (2004), Early Riders. New York, London.

Forrest, W. G. (1963), The date of the Lykourgan reforms in Sparta. In: Phoenix 17, 157–179.

Fehling, D. (1985), Die Sieben Weisen und die frühgriechische Chronologie. Eine traditionsgeschichtliche Studie. Bern, Frankfurt am Main, New York.

Fuchs, A. (2001), Mita. In: The Prosopography of the Neo-Assyrian Empire. Vol. 2. Part. II, 755–756.

68 So Parker 1995, 28–32, whose general view of the course of events is fairly similar to that suggested here.

Gelzer, H., Das Zeitalter des Gyges. In: RhM 30, 230–262.

Hawkins, J. D. (1982), The Neo-Hittite states in Syria and Anatolia. In: CAH Vol. III Part. 1, 372–441.

Hawkins, J. D. (1997), Mita. In: RlA VIII, 271–273.

Huxley, G. L. (1966), The Early Ionians. London.

Ivantchik, A. I. (1993), Les Cimmériens au Proche-Orient. Göttingen.

Jacoby, F. (1902), Apollodors Chronik (Philologische Untersuchungen 16). Berlin.

Jakoby, F. (1930), Die Fragmente der griechischen Historiker II D (Kommentar zu Nr. 106–261). Berlin.

Kaletsch, H. (1958), Zur Lydischen Chronologie. In: Historia 7, 1–47.

Kammenhuber, A. (1976–1980), Kimmerier. In: RlA V, 594–596.

Kiel, J. (1937), Treres. In: RE Hb. 12 (NR), 2291.

Kristensen, A. K. (1988), Who were the Cimmerians and where did they come from? Sargon II, the Cimmerians, and Rusa I. Copenhagen.

Kroll (1932), Midas. In RE Hb. 30, 1526–1540.

Kuhrt, A. (1995), The Ancient Near East c. 3000–330 BC. London and New York.

Lanfranchi, G. B. (1990), I Cimmeri. Emergenza delle élites militari iraniche nel Vicino Oriente (VIII – VII sec. a.C.). Padova.

Lanfranchi, G. B. and Parpola, S. (1990), The Correspondence of Sargon II. Letters from the Northern and Northeastern Provinces. Helsinki.

Lebedynsky, I. (2004), Les Cimmériens. Les premiers nomades des steppes européennes IX – VII siècles av. J.-C. Paris.

Lehmann-Haupt, C. (1912), Gyges. In RE Hb.14, 1956–1966.

Lehmann-Haupt, C. (1921), Kimmerier. In: RE Hb. 21, 397–434.

Mazetti, C. (1978), Voprosy Lidiyskoi chronologii. In: Vestnik Drevnei Istorii, 2, 175–178.

Mellink, M. (1991), The native kingdoms of Anatolia. In: CAH Vol III Part 1, 619–665.

Miller, M. (1963), Herodotus as chronographer. In: Klio 46, 109–128.

Mosshammer, A. A. (1977), Phainias of Eresos and chronology. In: CSCA 10, 105–132.

Mosshammer, A. A. (1979), The Chronicle of Eusebius and Greek Chronographic Tradition. Lewisburg and London.

Parker, V. (1993), Zur griechischen und vorderasiatischen Chronologie des sechsten Jahrhundertes v.Chr. unter besonderer Berücksichtigung der Kypselidenchronologie. In: Historia 42, 385–417.

Parker, V. (1995), Bemerkungen zu den Zügen der Kimmerier und der Skythen durch Vordenasien. In: Klio 77, 7–34.

Podlecki, A. J. (1984), The Early Greek Poets and Their Times. Vancouver.

Prag, A. J. N. W. (1989), Reconstructing Midas: a first report. In: Anatolian Studies 39, 159–165.

Rhode, E. (1878), *Gegone* in den Biographica des Suidas. In: RhM 33, 161–220, 620–622, 638.

Rhode, E. (1881), Studien zur Chronologie der griechischen Litteraturgeschichte. In: RhM 36, 380–434, 524–575.

Röllig, W. (1997), Muški, Muski. In: RlA VIII, 493–495.

Sauter, H. (2000), Studien zum Kimmerierproblem. Bonn.

Sevin, V. (1991), The Early Iron Age Elaziğ region and the problem of the Mushkians. In: Anatolian Studies 41, 87–97.

Shaw, P.-J. (2003), Discrepancies in Olympiad Dating and Chronological Problems of Archaic Peloponnesian History. Stuttgart.

Spalinger, A. J. (1978), The date of the death of Gyges and its historical implications. In: JOAS 98, 400–409.

Strasburger, H. (1956), Herodots Zeitrechnung. In: Historia 5, 129–161.

Starr, I. (1990), Queries to the Sungod. Divination and Politics in Sargonid Assyria. SAA 4, Helsinki.

Sulimirski, T. and Taylor, T. (1991), The Scythians. In: CAH Vol III Part 1, 547–590.

Van de Mieroop, M. (2004), A History of the Ancient Near East ca. 3000–323 BC. Malden, Oxford, Carlton.

Voigt, M. M. and Henricson R. C. (2000), Formation of the Phrygian state: the Early Iron Age at Gordion. In: Anatolian Studies 50, 37–54.

Welles, C. B. (1966), Royal Correspondence in the Hellenistic Period. No. 7. Roma.

Young, R. S. (1955), Gordion: preliminary report – 1953. In: AJA 59, 1–18.

The Social Meaning of Greek Symposium

Anne Lill, Tartu

This paper discusses the development in classical scholarship concerning symposium.[1] It could also be of interest for Oriental studies. My main idea in the approach to this question is that different societies can be better understood if we observe them in comparison and especially concerning the way people spend their time free from everyday obligations. In classical Greek culture symposium was one of these characteristic social activities that reflected the political principles of the *polis*.

General theoretical basis: dining in classical literature

Any society is characterised best by the way how its members spend their leisure time, i.e. the time spent away from the official and communal obligations. It relates to the question how members of society spend their time and means that have left over from the immediate needs. One of the indicators how spare time was spent in Greece and Rome leads us to consider the consumption of wine. In Greece, wine was drunk at the ceremonial drinking party that was named symposium (*symposion* i.e. drinking together), in Rome known as convivium. In this paper symposium is defined as an organization of all-male groups, aristocratic and egalitarian at the same time, which affirm their identity through ceremonialized drinking under the control of established rules and a master of ceremonies.

Symposium was a dominating form of social interaction from archaic times to the late Hellenistic period. Further, I will discuss the following themes: 1) the general theoretical basis of the topic related to symposium, 2) scholarly study on Greek symposium, 3) Greek and Roman authors on ceremonial drinking, 4) the philosophy of drinking and the political philosophy, and 5) a comparison of Greek and Oriental symposia.

---

1 I am grateful to The Earl of Carlisle for his friendly help in correction of my English.

The problem of symposium is regarded as one of the major themes for research into the civilization of ancient Greece. Symposium has been defined as a social phenomenon that contains the most characteristic traits of Greek society. This was one of the occasions when Greeks differ from other cultures, and symposium carries a special flavour of 'greekness' in itself. Especially in classical time it was considered that *to hellenikon* was created by blood and language, by the common religion and offering and by the common life style (Herod. *Hist.* 8.144).

It is true to say that symposium was an important part of this life style. Greek and Roman authors describe this kind of ceremonial drinking-party in various times and in various literary genres: poetry, epic, prose. In philosophical texts we find discussion of the philosophy of drinking and its importance in social life, thus, drinking wine even became a political question.[2]

In Greek and Greek-influenced Roman literature one aspect which was stressed in extolling 'our culture' that of others ('barbarians') was in reference to drinking habits: especially wide spread was the contrast between the Greek and Persian (or Scythian) way of drinking.[3] Greek historians refer to the Scythian habits of excessive drinking of wine unmixed with water (Herod. *Hist.* 6.84). Thus, when we deal with the question of drinking party it means not only observation of history of customs and habits but in a wider context we touch also upon the philosophical problem of 'we' and 'them' (or the others), i.e. we deal with the political philosophy. From this point of view we may ask how ceremonial drinking habits in Greece reflected the values and attitudes in the society. My aim is to observe Greek symposium from the psycho-ethical aspect: to analyse it as the event where personal feelings appear in the social context and to answer the question how the values of the society and of the group at a banquet were related. The question will be raised whether there exits a connection between different attitudes towards symposium and the different social forms in different countries.

---

2 Plato began his description of the laws in the ideal state with the rules of symposium (see *Nomoi*, book 1).

3 Roman poet Horace expressed the similar idea : *Persicos odi, puer, apparatus, /…/ me sub arta vite bibentem* (Hor. *Carm.* 1.38.1–8: 'I hate the Persian elegance /…/ me as I drink beneath the close-leafed vine').

Theoretical assumptions based on anthropology

The main initiative in the development of this field of research came from an anthropological study. In the 1970s, Dwight Heath published several papers concerning the patterns of thought and action in relation to drink.[4] This anthropological view of alcohol differed from the earlier medical and sociological approach where stress was laid on the abuse of alcohol and its negative influences. The different approach of the anthropologists was more concentrated on the cultural patterns. Mary Douglas proposed the main ideas in a quite figurative way as follows.

First, drinks give the actual structure of the social life as surely as if their names were labels affixed upon expected forms of behaviour; second, the ceremonials of drinking construct an ideal world which reflects the values of the society; third, drinking act as marker of personal identity and of boundaries of inclusion and exclusion.[5]

Drunkenness expresses culture, as it takes the form of highly patterned, learned comportment that varies from one culture to another. In most cultures drinking is a normal adjunct of celebration, and it is a social act, performed in a recognized social context under fixed rules.[6] Drinking reveals sensitive mechanisms for redefinition of the social roles. Serving as a relaxation, drinking party can take the task of ritual: it creates a new intelligible, bearable world, a kind of ideal world with the attitudes, values and actions in society which are directly or indirectly connected with drinking, and especially with the ceremonial drinking.

Dwight Heath formulates the conclusions of the most significant generalizations that have been derived from cross-cultural study of the subject: 1) in most societies, drinking is essentially a social act embedded in a context of values, attitudes, and other norms, 2) these norms constitute important socio-cultural factors that influence the effect of drinking, regardless how important biological, physiological a.o. factors may be, 3) the drinking of alcoholic beverages is regulated by the rules concerning who may drink, how much of what, in the company of whom etc. These rules focus on strong emotions and sanctions, and 4) the

4 e.g. Heath 1976a, 1976b, 1978.

5 Douglas 1988: 8.

6 Ibid., 4.

function of alcohol for promoting relaxation and sociability is emphasized.[7]

The idea of the systematic research on the topic in classical philology was formed in the 80s and after later a number of works were published.[8] For the Greek and Latin authors symposium was an important topic in their works. Already in Homer we can see that this kind of banquet was a part of the Greek civilisation from the archaic times.[9] One of the most obvious ways to explain it is to relate the question to the striving for personal pleasure by the ancients. This aspect is, in fact, uppermost in lyric poetry and in a number of drinking songs. In this case we lay stress on the 'drinking'-part of the expression. But if we concentrate on the prefix 'sym-' ('together'), then the very meaning of symposium provides us with with another flavour: it enables us to look beyond the pleasure principle and stress the aspect of togetherness. Indeed, drinking parties contributed to the principles of living together in Greek polis more than in other forms of society.

The sources from the ancient authors

One of the Greek authors of later Hellenism who gave the most comprehensive description of the principles and philosophy of symposium was Plutarch (A.D. 43-120) in his work on moral questions, *Moralia.* It contained seven books of Table-talk, *Quaestiones convivales*

7 Heath 1988: 46.

8 The symposium on symposia organised by Oswyn Murray in September 1984 in Balliol College, Oxford, see Murray 1994. Main works on the subject: Slater, William J. (1991) *Dining in Classical Context*, Ann Arbor: The University of Michigan Press, here symposium and dining is discussed from various angles: from the point of view of participants, social customs, the arrangement of a dining room etc. This book contains also the article of Walter Burkert (1991) 'Oriental Symposia: Contrasts and Parallels', pp. 7–24; Gowers, Emily (1993) *The Loaded Table. Representations of Food in Roman Literature.* Oxford: Clarendon Press; Griffin, Jasper, *Latin Poets and Roman Life*, London: Bristol Classical Paperbacks 1994. Murray, Oswyn (ed.) (1994) *Sympotica. A Symposium on the Symposion.* Oxford: Clarendon Press; Pellizer, Ezio (1994) Outlines of a morphology of sympotic entertainment, In Murray, Oswyn (ed.) *Sympotica. A symposium on the Symposion*, Oxford: Clarendon Press; Tecuşan, Manuela (1994) *Logos Sympoticos*: patterns of the irrational in philosophical drinking: Plato outside the Symposium, In Murray, Oswyn (ed.) *Sympotica. A symposium on the Symposion,* Oxford: Clarendon Press; Vernant, Jean-Pierre (1991) *L'Uomo Greco*, Roma: Editori Laterza. This book is important as a contribution to the subject in the wider context of Greek culture.

9 Burkert 1991: 7.

(Συμποσιακῶν βίβλια). There he discussed the questions connected with banqueting and drinking wine from moral, social and individual aspects. Plutarch referred in his book also to the earlier traditional views concerning symposium. The other author who gathered treasurestore knowledge about banqueting is Athenaeus who wrote the book *Deipnosophistae* ('Learned men at the banquet', beginning of the 3rd century). It is a compendium of 15 books and containing the table talk of 30 men on various cultural and literary subjects all in some way connected with dining. Although the book was written in Greek, Athenaeus' banquet took place in Rome and the participants were of Roman and Hellenic background. The Roman and Greek realia are mixed but the quotations are mainly from Greek authors. The work of Athenaeus contains an enormous amount of material about drinking and dining habits, drinking songs and other literary and cultural matters. Thus, Plutarch and Athenaeus are the main authors who describe the nature of symposium together with its technical and spiritual characteristics.

The other aspect of the problem is addressed in the works of philosophers. Plato and Aristotle mention in their works the ethical and political background of symposium. Sometimes also a literary discussion is held during a drinking party.[10]

In the first book of Plato's *Nomoi* (Laws) a question is raised of the importance of the drinking party in the society. There, an Athenian defended the view of the great significance of symposium while the representative of the oligarchic Sparta hold a contrary opinion: in their state drinking was despised and considered as harmful (*Nomoi* 1.637a). The discussion about wine and drunkenness was based on the assumption that in different states laws and attitudes (i.e. *nomoi*) were different. Symposium was considered to be one of the several social activities with its own law and order which reflected the rules and habits in society. In the first two books of *Nomoi* Plato's discussion dealt with the regulations during symposium and restrictions in the drinking of wine.

Of the Roman authors there are descriptions of banquets in Horace's odes and satires, in the epigrams of Martial, in the novel of Petronius *Satyricon*. The latter gives a vivid picture of the Roman drinking party with description of the attitudes and social relations during it.

---

10 In Plato's *Symposium* and Xenophon's *Symposium* we meet the atmosphere of the learned banquet where philosophical questions are discussed.

Symposium and polis

Symposium has been juxtaposed with the state (polis) by the ancients from the archaic times. Didactic poetry and elegy, especially the poems of Solon and Theognis were the first literary works to express the connection between these two. Later, the same idea was discussed in the political philosophy of Plato and Aristotle. We become aware that the organisation of Greek symposium reflected the principles of Greek states: the members in both were all male and inside this group, an egalitarian code of behaviour ruled. A selected group of citizens (adult, male and Greek) was active in both occasions on terms of equality. But in different periods, symposium was understood in Greek society in different ways: from the aristocratic club in the archaic period to the model of the democratic polis in classical times in Athens (5th and 4th cent. B.C.). In all periods there prevailed a common aspect: symposium was the occasion where personal pleasure and social significance were interrelated. Symposium was a party among friends and there was often a specific reason for celebration: victory on theatrical and sporting competitions, political and military victory a.o.

Therefore it had a social function intended to highlight by a collective consensus, exceptional moments in an individual's life and in that of the community. life.[11] The topic in Pericles' *Funeral Oration* (in Thukydides 1.22.1) gives a short and concise synopsis of entire philosophy of the Athenian character and government. It declares the principles on which the Athenian democracy was built. The main point of the speech was to make a distinction between Athenian democracy and Spartan oligarchy: the latter being the rule of the few, restricting eligibility for office to one section of citizens. Pericles may have exaggerated in opposing the governmental systems of Athens and Sparta and much of his speech is political propaganda but, nevertheless, the main message of his speech remains valid. It is the openness of the Athenians and the tolerance toward one another which made the main distinction in the social attitudes these two states.[12] All these attitudes were reflected in the organization of symposium.

11 Pellizer 1994, p. 178. The sympotic gathering may sometimes ignore the social norms which regulate the public life in the wider civic community but the members commit themselves to accepting the laws which the gathering itself imposes.

12 Harris 1992, pp. 162–163.

The role of the leader of the symposium, symposiarchos (συμποσίαρχος), is especially prominent during the party. In his case, the parallel between a banquet and society becomes explicit. A symposiarchos was elected *ad hoc* and he controlled the disciplined use of wine. As in all social institutions, symposium functioned better and gave the feeling of pleasure under the leader who supervised the conduct during the drinking party and determined the customs in drinking: order, strength and the amount of wine. There existed certain requirements for such a man. He had to be himself a moderate drinker, also an older and a temperate man. He had to conduct himself like a head of the democratic state in fixing the rules of the gathering which would be in accordance with the expectations of its members. Plutarch in *Table-talk* compares a president of symposium and a leader of the democratic polis. Pericles, the leader of democratic Athens was constantly reminding himself of his obligations in such a way: "Keep in mind, Pericles, you govern free men, you govern Greeks, you govern Athenians."[13] A good symposiarchos must act in a similar way: to make sure that the correct rules are agreed previously and good order prevails at the banquet and friendly relations between symposiasts last throughout the event. The ideal of this kind of leader had to be a wise man who carried out his duty with moderate constraint, taking into consideration the circumstances. Thus, the ideals of the symposium were both political and cultural, and the well organised and successful symposium was the vehicle to express these relations.[14] Both the society and symposium had to function correctly. In symposium, there were rules which regulated drinking and were directed towards moderate drinking of wine. In the ideal symposium, both drunkenness and with its consequences and complete abstinence were avoided. The idea resembled the principle of measured balance praised by Aristotle in his ethical and political theory.[15]

---

13 See Plutarchus *Moralia* 1.4, 620d.

14 Slater 1991, p. 3.

15 In *Nicomachean Ethics* Aristotle praised the middle way (*mesos, mesotes* and *metron*) in moral character (*ēthos*) which means an intermediate state between two possible extremes. It is connected with the rational reasoning (*phronesis*) that will help to choose correct conduct. The excellence of character (virtue, *aretē*) is according to Aristotle a state of character concerned with choice (*hexis proairetikē*) to strive moderation in all things, this being determined by rational principle (*logo*) and by that principle by which the man of practical wisdom (*phronimos*) will determine it (*EN* 2.6.1106b36–1107a2). Further, the second book of *Nicomachean Ethics* contains a discussion on various virtues and their opposing vices (ch. 7–9).

Logos sympotikos

Communication in symposium (λόγος συμποτικός) was considered to be most important. It consisted of a learned talk that promoted intellectual aims together with a poetical performance of solo or choral singing. These drinking songs performed at banquets (scolia) included heroic and love motives. Scolia give moral examples and ethical maxims, providing positive or negative models, praising an excellent, virtuous man and blaming a vicious one. The ethical principles common to the state and to the drinking party refer to symposium as the preparation of citizens for public life. The educational aim relates the goals of polis to these of symposium: convivial gathering, when rightly conducted, is an important element in education (*paideia*, Plato *Nomoi* 1.641d). Plato's concern is to prescribe an ethical rule for the symposium.[16] The requirements for a member of polis and of drinking party resemble each other: moderation, temperance, peace, harmony, order and obedience to the rules. In Greek ethics, these principles of symposium were expressed by the concepts of temperance, cheerfulness, ease, order and respect (σωφροσύνη, εὐφροσύνη, ἡσυχίη, εὐνομία, χάρις). This moral code of private and civic virtue was valued not only for the pleasure of the individual but more because of their importance to the common body of the participants.

Symposium belonged to the socially important events where civic behaviour of a certain kind was expected and misconduct criticised.[17] To be accepted as a member of the society one had to meet the expectations of one's fellow members. Drinking wine had its role in testing political, moral, public and private values.[18] We know of these values and of the rules of symposium in the Athenian context. It seems that there were certain aspects in the Athenian *politeia* that had their counterpart in the organisation of symposium. The main common denominators were: freedom, equal rights for the members and the dominance of speech (λόγος, παρρησία, ἰσηγορία, see e.g. Herodotus 5.77-78).

The guaranteed freedom of speech made Athenians feel superior to the other states in Hellas. In the democratic polis it meant freedom to

16 Tecuşan 1994, p. 260.

17 The other places of public meetings where similar social expectations existed were the theatre, markets, law-court, baths and *gymnasia* (sporting grounds).

18 Bowie 1997, p. 2.

participate, to speak and to listen to the others. This was highly valued.[19] With regard to the same principle in the symposium we can see that it had to be organized in such a way that all could speak and all had an opportunity to listen to the other members of the banquet. From this principle, the concept of the sympotic unity arose (Plut. *Mor.* 1.1.615a) which was based on the feeling of togetherness. The subject of conversation had to be of common interest to all: it varied from the historical to contemporary events and was often connected with ethical questions – piety, courage, magnanimity, kindness and benevolence.[20]

Table-talk and wine complemented each other. According to Plutarch, in symposium wine must be common and so must be the conversation (*Mor.* 1.1.614e, 615f). It would be worse, nevertheless, to take away the pleasure of conversation at the table than to run out of wine, but stuffing themselves with food would be absolutely swinish (*Mor.* 1.716e). The function of wine was to contribute to the friendly feelings among the participants of symposium. Friendly relations and wine belong together in the good symposium. Wine makes one's attitude mild, compassionate and gentle (*Mor.* 1.4.620 d-e). Describing the excellent drinking companion, Plutarch uses the word *philologos* (i.e. a man with the skill of speech, *Mor.* 1.1. 613d) which sounds like an echo from the Platonic discourse about laws in polis and in symposium. Plutarch draw many close parallels between talkativeness and drinking wine: *Just as wine, discovered for the promotion of pleasure and good fellowship, is sometimes misused to produce discomfort and intoxication /.../ so speech, which is the most pleasant and human of social ties, is made inhuman and unsocial by those who use it badly and wantonly* (*Mor.* 504e). According to the old proverb cited by Plutarch: 'What is in a man's heart when he is sober is in his tongue when he is drunk' (*Mor.* 503f).

The religious basis of the drinking party supported openness and freedom of conduct: these were also the key words in the cult of Dionysus, the god of wine who was named a Liberator (*Lyaios*, e.g. Plut. *Mor.* 7.10.716b-c). Dionysus the Liberator of all things unbridled the tongue, thus, the idea of wine revealing the truth was created. It also supported the assumption that wine was a pain-alleviating drug.

19 See Aristotle *Politics* 4.1291b30–38, 6.1317a40–1318a3.

20 εὐσέβειαν, ἀνδρικῶν πράξεων, μεγαλοθύμων, χρηστῶν, φιλανθρώπων, see Plutarchus *Moralia* 1.1. 614b where these principles belong to the virtuous conduct.

Philia

The concept of philia, i.e. closeness and friendly co-operation may be considered one of the most important characteristics of the drinking party.[21] In sympotic poetry we can see how friendship was a central theme at a Greek and also at a Roman banquet. Although, we see in the ancient epics how a common convivial feast cements ties of friendship between men.

Here also, the inside world of symposium resembled the outside world of the polis.[22] In symposium, as in the state, a friendly co-operation was greatly respected. Mutual friendship supported unity of feelings and sentiments among the members of the party (συμπόται), their spirits were harmoniously and profitably stirred (Plut. *Mor.* 1.1.614e). The function of wine was to create friendly attitudes while symposium created an atmosphere of sociability (Plut. *Mor.* 1.1.612d). Wine enhanced a feeling of compassion, benevolence, gentleness, friendship and affection (*Mor.* 1.4.620 d-e). Shared emotions and talk dispelled hard feelings (*Mor.* 7.10.715f).

The organisation of the party and even the room itself must contribute to it. Too large a room and too big a party were thought to be unsociable and unfriendly (*Mor.* 5. 5. 679b). It made a general conversation difficult, and a talk between two or three was inappropriate in a symposium.

Sympotai were described in terms of *us*. Athenaeus, when talking of various forms of drinking cups quoted words of different poets as to how

21 The concept of *philia* (φιλία) signifies various types of interpersonal bonds from political loyalty to erotic affection. In the ancient texts we can see how this kind of love-friendship functions as an institutional phenomenon, the bonds of this kind referring to the relations between the members of a certain group. *Philia* exists between the members of various groups: family, companions in political, professional and the military sphere a.o. All were held together by common interests and goals. *Philia* was the ethical corner-stone which determined the way how the relations between the members of society functioned at the informal level. In this case not so much the written law and the official order but the conventions and customs were important. *Philia* was the obligatory part of the good life in Aristotle's sense. During the time of the flourishing of the Athenian democracy the ties of *philia* were mostly honoured. Friendship in this sense is not a typical for the royal virtues. Also, a ruler's capacity for *philia* or *amicitia* is almost absent from the later legacy, except the imitations of classical authors (Konstan 1997, p. 128). The rise of the democratic activity in the state made it possible to consider *philia* as the part of the political system, *politeia.*

22 Donlan 1985, pp. 236–237.

wine should be poured. Wine was meant not for every single person separately, not only for 'me' or for 'you', but also for all members, for us, thus what we hear is a characteristic invocation – let us drink (πίνωμεν, Ath. 11. 463c). In symposium, it is we who become fellow drinkers (Ath. 10.426f), we drink, we are thirsty and we pray, (ibid, see also 11. 496b-c; 11. 497c). This feeling of mutual relatedness was equally important also in the wider context, in polis, and played an educational role in society.[23] Both Greek and Roman banquet were based on social relations which focused on the qualities of true friends.[24] Even the Roman high-class convivium retained some atmosphere of the Greek symposium, including also a wide social range of participants and provided a socially egalitarian setting.[25]

Political and poetical philosophy of wine

Greek poets and philosophers have discussed from two aspects the role and the influence of wine as a mirror of soul and a test of character. First, there is a personal and beneficial effect: wine relieves tension, brings joy and happiness into the soul. On the other hand, the influence can be disastrous when drunks to excess and the wine is too strong.[26] A sharp distinction was always made between drinking and being drunk. The Greeks compared their habits in relation to other nations and especially with those of barbarians.[27]

Wine and the atmosphere of the symposium was in the minds of archaic poets a remedy against grief and depression. In their poems wine was first of all important in connection with personal feelings: *we should not*

---

23 Jaeger 1947, p. 300.

24 Nappa 1998, p. 393 where Catullus 12 is discussed. In this context the convivial culture becomes a way of showing the poet's personality in the face of a social milieu.

25 John D'Arms 1994, p. 318–319 where a picture of the Roman *convivium* is given as a place where persons of various rank were linked together creating a social and a cultural cohesion.

26 We can recall what happened to Cyclops in Odyssey 9 (and the same event in the satyric play of Euripides *Cyclops*).

27 Bowie 1997, p. 2 discusses the question in the context of Attic comedy. Although the formal symposium belonged largely to the wealthier classes it was not inimical to a democracy. Idealised sympotic practice was of balance and restraint (*ibid.* 3–4).

surrender our hearts to the troubles /.../ the best of remedies is to bring wine and get drunk.[28]

In the poems of Theognis, symposium took the form of an aristocratic drinking party. The banquet with drinking wine became a place where men's intentions, their mind and thoughts were revealed.[29] We meet the development of similar ideas later in Plato.

Before the period of the Athenian democracy, symposium and wine were related more to personal relations and emotions. The influence of wine on the soul was of major interest and few connections were made with the society at large. Later, the personal element remained but there appeared a new emphasis to the social aspect of symposium in Athens. In Plato we find the first lengthy discussion on the moral effect of symposium and wine in society. He argues that the influence of wine is worthy of a thorough philosophical discussion. In *Nomoi* (1.649b-50b) he describes how wine is related to human nature and his habitual character (*ēthos*, ἦθος). In symposium the hidden side of the soul and the state of mind is revealed. According to Plato, wine may become a touchstone (βάσανος) for learning the traits of men's character. Wine reveals both positive and negative side of the soul. Drinking affects one's mind in many respects: sensations, memory, opinions, rational thinking.[30] Wine makes one act and talk out of the ordinary. As a result, it can be considered as a cheap, easy and harmless character test which reveals personal traits which are usually hidden. This makes the convivial gathering an important element in education (*Nomoi* 1. 641d).

Plato looked at the triad – moral character, emotions and wine – from the aspect of practical philosophy that was concerned with the question how and under which conditions society could function best. Connecting emotions and wine, Plato made it clear that wine had an important role in social relationship. Fellow drinkers become friends and wine confirms mutual relationship (*Nomoi* 1. 671e). During a drinking party, the emotions, including those of pleasure, pain, passion and lust (ἡδονὰς, λύπας, θυμοὺς, ἔρωτας, ibid., 645d) are intensified and revealed. The beneficial influence of wine reveals itself as a remedy against fear while it inspires confidence (ibid., 647a, 649a).

---

28 Alcaeus fr. 335: οὐ χρῆ κάκοισι θῦμον ἐπιτρέπην,/ ... φαρμάκων δ᾽ ἄριστον / οἶνον ἐνεικαμένοις μεθύσθην.

29 Donlan 1985, p. 237.

30 *Nomoi* 1. 645e: αἴσθησις, μνήμη, δόξα, φρόνησις.

The system of polis had to resolve in its organisation the similar problem as in the symposium: to find a reasonable balance between liberty and order. Greek symposium helps to understand the need to find a middle way between the extremes. Bringing together various characteristics of the symposium, the emotional, intellectual and social aspects could observed out which made the symposium an important institution in Athenian civic life. First of all, it was the educational potential of the banquet to promote the values which were considered to be the most important: the convivial gathering, when rightly conducted, was an important element in the education of the citizens. In its logocentric character, the symposium developed the skill to talk and to listen to others, which contributed to the way the Athenian political and cultural life functioned. Drinking together in symposium and living together in polis required from the citizens, to a great extent, the similar ability to cooperate. The ethical principles common to the state and to the drinking party refer to symposium as the preparation of citizens for public life, e.g. to find a proper relation between their own wishes and the rules established by the symposiarch, to practice moderation and to master the emotions.

Greek and Oriental symposia

Some forms of drinking parties may be expected to occur everywhere according to the socializing function of alcohol. There are, nevertheless, differences in the customs between various nations and states. Walter Burkert examins the the similarities and the differences between the Greek symposia and the Oriental drinking party (Mesopotamia, Anatolia, Syria, Palestine, Egypt). Greek symposium in the circle of friends differed from the banquets of the Oriental kings in the number and in the arrangement of the event. In the Orient we find a greater number of participants who were arranged in the hierarchical order.[31] There is not a great difference in personal feelings, if we compare these two kinds of festivities. We can find similar motives of joy and relaxation in the Oriental drinking songs as in the Greek. One of the oldest Sumerian drinking songs goes:

31 Later, in the Hellenistic times in Greece in the regal banquets the number of the participants could reach two hundred. In such a huge gathering the common conversation bewteen all the participants is of course impossible.

Our liver is happy, our heart is joyful ... while I feel wonderful.

The oldest evidence in the Orient is the ceremonial drinking party in the old Mesopotamian tradition. An iconographic type from the 3rd millennium shows a seated couple, male and female, drinking together, drawing the beverage from the vessel with a tube. The scene should refer to the ceremonial evening meal at the temple held by the royal couple on the occasion of a harvest festival. The drink is evidently beer: Xenophon witnessed such a form of drinking in Armenia (*Anabasis* 4.5.26 ff., 32). The scene constitutes some form of social control, bringing the rulers close to the gods.

The important difference from Greece concerned the drinks: beer was common in Mesopotamia and in Egypt while in Greece a common drink was wine. Although, we learn from Herodotus of wine imported from Greece and from Phoenicia to Egypt (*Historia* 3.6).[32]

As a whole, in Orient, we shall find more contrasts than parallels with the Greek symposium. The main differences are as follows: in the Orient women participated at the party, and drinking was not arranged as among equals but represented a monarchic system. In the Orient, there seems to be not much evidence of the mixing bowl – *kratēr*, while in the Greek symposium, mixing wine with water was essential for civilised drinking.[33] But the question of mixing wine in Oriental regions remains unresolved. In the Ugaritic texts the word 'to mix' is used frequently in the formulaic descriptions of banquet scenes: to serve wine means to mix the drink.

Beer drinking and mixing wine are comparable. Mixed wine was generally as strong as beer. The amount of wine that was drunk could be compared then to the amount of beer. But nevertheless, from Biblical examples we can find that mixing wine means a degradation of it (*Isaiah* 1.22).

From Ugaritic and Hebrew sources we learn about the negative influence of excessive drinking. A marza'u at Ugarit is somewhat an analogue to the Greek *thiasos*: it is a social organisation where men meet for ceremonial feasts, including heavy drinking, in the worship of a

32 Herodotus discusses in his work the problem of wine-jars that were afterwards sold to Syria, although not for holding wine but water.

33 Mixing wine occurs already in *The Iliad* 9.203, and in *The Odyssey* 9.5–11 which may be the earliest description of symposium. *Kratēr* stood in the centre of the room around which *sympotai* were situated. Thus, the mixing bowl in Greek symposium had also a unifying function similar to the role that a hearth played in the house.

specific god. There are texts in Ugarit that introduce the gods' feasting and consuming huge amounts of wine. In the mythological text the God El was giving a banquet in his palace and drank too much wine and consequently lost his strength. His daughters gave him a certain herb which restored his strength and healed him. This enfeebling effect of wine resembles the Cyclops episode from *The Odyssey* but with less serious consequences. But drunkenness has become a metaphor for catastrophe in the prophetic text (*Isaiah* 51.17 ff.).

In conclusion, we can say that by observing the way wine was consumed we can understand better both the character of the individual and of the society. Poetic descriptions of drinking and feasting in company are an essential part of ancient Greek and Roman literature. But the representation of symposium in ancient literature goes beyond the literary and an aesthetic sphere. It widens our view of society and brings forth the most characteristic traits of how it functioned.

Bibliography

Bowie, A.M. (1997) "Thinking with drinking: wine and the symposium in Aristophanes". In: Journal of Hellenic Studies, 117, 1-21.

Burkert, Walter (1991) "Oriental symposia: contrasts and parallels". In: Dining in a classical context. Ann Arbor: The University of Michigan Press.

D'Arms, John (1994) "The Roman convivium and the idea of equality". In: Murray, Oswyn (ed.) Sympotica. A symposium on the symposion. Oxford: Clarendon, 308-320.

Donlan, Walter (1985) "Pistos Philos Hetairos". In: Figuera, Thomas J. and Nagy, Gregory (eds.). Theognis of Megara. Baltimore: The Johns Hopkins University Press 1985, pp. 223-244.

Douglas, Mary (1988) "A distinctive anthropological perspective". In: Douglas, Mary. Constructive drinking. Perspectives on drink in anthropology. Cambridge: Cambridge University Press.

Harris, Edward M. (1992) "Pericles' praise of Athenian democracy Thucydides 2.37.1". In Harvard Studies in Classical Philology, 94, 157-167.

Heath, Dwight B. (1976a) "Anthropological perspectives on alcohol. An historical review". In: Everett, M., Waddell, J. and Heath, D. (eds.) Cross-cultural approaches to the study of alcohol: an interdisciplinary perspective. Hague: Mouton.

Heath, Dwight B. (1976b) "Anthropological perspectives on the social biology of alcohol: an introduction to the literature". In: Kissin, B. and Begleiter, H.

(eds.) The biology of alcoholism, vol. 4. Social aspects. New York: Plenum Press, pp. 37-76.

Heath, Dwight B. (1978) "The sociocultural model of alcohol use". In: Journal of Operational Psychiatry, 9, pp. 55-66.

Heath, Dwight B. (1988) "A decade of development in the anthropological study of Perspectives on drink in anthropology alcohol use: 1970–1980". In: Douglas, Mary (ed.) Constructive drinking. Cambridge: Cambridge University Press.

Jaeger, Werner (1947) Paideia. Die Formung des griechischen Menschen. Berlin: Walter de Gruyter & Co.

Konstan, David (1997) "Friendship and Monarchy: Dio of Prusa's Third Oration on Kingship". In Symbolae Osloenses 72, 124-143.

Levine, Daniel B. (1985) "Symposium and the Polis". In: Figuera, Thomas J. and Nagy, Gregory (eds.). Theognis of Megara. Baltimore: The Johns Hopkins University Press, pp. 178-196.

Murray, Oswyn (1994) "Sympotic history". In: Murray, Oswyn (ed.) Sympotica. A symposium on the symposion. Oxford: Clarendon, 3-13.

Nappa, Christopher (1998) "Place settings: convivium, contrast and persona in Catullus 12 and 13". In: American Journal of Philology, 119, 3, 385-397.

Pellizer, Enzio (1994) "Outlines of a morphology of sympotic entertainment". In: Murray, Oswyn (ed.) Sympotica. A symposium on the symposion. Oxford: Clarendon, 177-184.

Slater, William J. (1994) "Sympotic Ethics in the Odyssey". In: Murray, Oswyn (ed.). Sympotica. A symposium on the symposion. Oxford: Clarendon Press, pp. 213-220.

Slater, William J. (1991) Dining in a classical context. Ann Arbor: The University of Michigan Press.

Tecuşan, Manuela (1994) "Logos sympotikos: patterns of the irrational in philosophical drinking: Plato outside the Symposium". In: Murray, Oswyn (ed.). Sympotica. A symposium on the symposion. Oxford: Clarendon Press, pp. 238-260.

The Babylonian Almanac in the West

Alasdair Livingstone, Birmingham

The subject of the relationship between Babylonian literature in Mesopotamia and literature in Babylonian in the West, that is to say Anatolia, Syria, the Levant, is at the very least as complicated as the subject of the evolution, spread and transmission of Babylonian literature in Babylonia and Assyria, matter that still requires investigation. Earlier and long known finds such as the library at Hazarina (Sultantepe) had already demonstrated that there were provincial centres of scribal excellence [Gurney and Finkelstein 1953]. The finds at Me-Turan (Tell Haddad) show that there was not only scribal excellence outside the heartland but that there were also scribes in the provinces producing sophisticated material not present in the well known Babylonian and Assyrian corpora [Cavigneaux and al-Rawi 1993]. What is at issue here is not only the question of variation within one or more textual traditions, but the actual spread and individual location of centres that produced original literary composition.

Outside Assyria, Babylonia and Elam the Babylonian Almanac[1] is textually represented at Emar, Ḫattuša and Ugarit. At Emar there are four relevant text witness of the Babylonian Almanac.[2] At Ḫattuša were found five fragments of the Almanac, which were probably once part of the same tablet.[3] At Ugarit were excavated two as yet unpublished fragments of the Almanac,[4] on one of which text of the literary calendar series *iqqur īpuš* was included.[5] As will be discussed below each of these western

1 Unless otherwise stated, information given in this paper about the Babylonian Almanac and other hemerologies stems from the present writer's forthcoming edition of these texts. See Livingstone 1999.

2 *Emar* VI/2 165, 413–4, 584 and 585.

3 *KUB* IV 42–45.

4 I am grateful to W. von Soldt for this information. The excavation numbers of the two fragments are RS 25.141 + 454F and RS 25.440A. For Babylonian literature at Ugarit see Malbran-Labat 1999.

5 R. Labat, 1965, Un calendrier babylonien des travaux, des signes et des mois. Paris 1965.

forms of the Almanac deviates in some manner from the text as known in Mesopotamia. First, these matters will be placed in their immediate context of recent investigation.

The phenomenon of the appearance of Babylonian literature in Egypt, Syria and the Levant has been the subject of recent and detailed study by Izre'el [1997] and Kämmerer [1998]. Various linguistic matters concerning the western Akkadian have been taken up recently by Gianto [1999], while Ikeda [1999] and Hess [2004] have each respectively concerned themselves with scribes and ritual calendars, in particular at Emar.

The Babylonian Almanac is particularly instructive for a number of reasons. The manuscript fragments from Ugarit mainly represent integrity of transmission, in so far as one can tell from the twenty-four lines that have been preserved. However, for the 8th of Tašrīt the entry replaces the expected UZU.ŠAḪ UZU.GU$_4$ NA.AN.KÚ.E I.BÍ.ZA IGI, 'He should not eat pork or beef, or he will experience loss!' known from two exemplars from Babylon and Sippar with a phrase containing the word *šuḫarr*[*iš*]. If correctly restored, as is likely, from the point of view of published texts this word is a *hapax legomenon*; it is represented in the relevant volume of *CAD* (Š/III, p.203) only by the attestation [*ā*]*durma mūtu ana tāḫāzi uk a'ir atūra arkiš* [x-x]-x-*ta-ma ana* GN *attašab šuḫarriš*, I feared death. I did not advance in battle (but) turned back, I [...]-ed to GN and stayed (there) in numbed silence.' Given this attestation and the probably etymology from *šaḫurru* (*AHw* p.1133b, 'erstarrt') the translation given by *CAD* seems secure. The point here is that the vocabulary of the Almanac within Babylonia and Assyria comprises a closed system with a total number of 115 attested expressions, varying permutations of which are distributed over the ideal year of 360 days, and these do not include the word *šuḫarriš*, although it could clearly be appropriate enough in a cultic context within the prohibitions and interdictions of the Almanac.

Turning to the Almanac at Ḫattuša one finds a situation that is in some respects similar to that at Ugarit but in others significantly more divergent from the Babylonian traditions. Two of the fragments commence with the usual UD.x.KÁM date formula followed by selections from the closed system of the Almanac referred to above. It is not however possible to place them within the Almanac on the correct days as known from Assyria and Babylonia, so that one is forced here to see a separate tradition with respect to the distribution of the admonitions and prohibitions over the day and months. Two of the fragments, however, are truly striking in their lack of indication of calendar days. The notion of calendar days being individually associated with the admonitions and prohibitions is so fundamental to the genre 'hemerology' that one might initially doubt whether these fragments belong to the Babylonian Almanac at all. The sheer density of phrases that belong to the Almanac's closed system of vocabulary belie any such doubt: *dāṣātu*, 'treacheries'; ŠE, 'favourable' and NU ŠE, 'unfavourable'; DÙ *ṣibûti*, 'achieving a goal'; DAM-*su ana* É-*šú* KU_4 É-*šú* DAGAL-*iš*, 'He should bring his wife into his house, his house will expand!'; *ṭēm busurrāti*, 'news of good tidings'; DAM NU TUK *giḫlû* GIG, 'He should not marry a wife, mourning, sickness'. Whatever purpose, it is clear that the terminology of the Babylonian Almanac is the subject of these two fragments and that this terminology is being presented in a format not to be found in the substantial number of exemplars of the Almanac known from Assyria and Babylonia.

Turning now to Emar one finds a situation that replicates that at Ḫattuša but adds a new twist. Two of the fragments (Msk 731085e and Msk 74266a), for which both the numbers of the days and sufficient text to pass a judgement are preserved, cannot be fitted into scheme well known from Assyria and Babylonia. The terminology is that of the Babylonian Almanac, but the fragments represent a different tradition of the distribution of the phrases over the months and days of the ideal calendar. In the case of the two other fragments (Msk 74266c and Msk 74163a), however, there is a new situation. They fit into the scheme of the Babylonian Almanac known in Assyria and Babylonia, but with one proviso. The first of these fragments fits into the scheme for the 4th to 13th days of the third month, the 3rd to 9th days of the fourth month and the 2nd to the 9th days of the fifth month, while the second fits for the 3rd to 20th days of the fifth month. The proviso that these matches depends on is that the admonition or prohibition at Emar, while otherwise agreeing with the text of the Babylonian Almanac, is consistently one day later. In a real sense the well-known hemerological tradition of Mesopotamia is being followed, but a local alteration has been introduced, whether initiated at Emar itself or copied from elsewhere. In common with many other aspects of the spread of Babylonian literature westwards this requires more investigation. Remaining within the realm of cult observances and practices, but turning to official rather than private religion one could compare the different dates of the *taklimtu* ritual of Dumuzi in Assyria in Neo-Assyrian times [Livingstone 1986, p.140]. The *taklimtu* or 'showing the display' involved 'screaming' and 'releasing' and took place a day later at Calaḫ and Arbēla than it did at Aššur and Nineveh.

Bibliography

Cavigneaux, A. and F. al-Rawi, New Sumerian Literary Texts from Tell Haddad (Ancient Meturan): A First Survey. *Iraq 55* (1993), 91-105.

Gianto, A., Amarna Akkadian as a Contact Language. Languages and Cultures in Contact: At the Crossroads of Civilizations in the Syro-Mesopotamian Realm. Proceedings of the 42th RAI. K. Van Lerberghe and G. Voet (eds.), Orientalia Lovaniensia Analecta 96 (Leuven, Uitgeverij Peeters en Departement Oosterse Studies: 1999): 123-132.

Gurney, O.R. and Finkelstein J.J., The Sultantepe Tablets. (London, British School of Archaology at Ankara: 1957)

Hess, R. S., Multiple-Month Ritual Calendars in the West Semitic World: Emar 446 and Leviticus 23. The Future of Biblical Archaeology: Reassessing Methodologies and Assumptions. The Proceedings of a Symposium August 12-14, 2001 at Trinity International University. J. K. Hoffmeier and A. R. Millard (eds.) (Grand Rapids, Michigan/Cambridge, William B. Eerdmans Publishing Company: 2004): 233-253.

Ikeda, J., Scribes in Emar. Priests and Officials in the Ancient Near East: Papers of the Second Colloquium on the Ancient Near East - The City and its Life held at the Middle Eastern Culture Center in Japan (Mitaka, Tokyo), March 22-24, 1996. K. Watanabe (ed.) (Heidelberg, Universitätsverlag C. Winter: 1999): 163-185.

Izre'el, S., Hatti and the Kingdom of Amurru: Linguistic Influences. La circulation des biens, des personnes et des idées dans le Proche-Orient ancien: Actes de la XXXVIIIe Rencontre Assyriologique Internationale (Paris, 8-10 juillet 1991). D. Charpin and F. Joannès (eds.) (Paris, Éditions Recherche sur les Civilisations: 1992): 227-230.

Izre'el, S. The Amarna Scholarly Tablets (Gronningen, Styx: 1997).

Kämmerer, Th.R., Šimâ milka: Induktion und Reception der mittelbabylonischen Dichtung von Ugarit, Emar and Tell el-'Amarna. (Ugarit Verlag, Münster: 1998).

Livingstone, A., Mystical and Mythological Explanatory Texts of Assyrian and Babylonian Scholars. (Oxford, OUP 1986 and 1987, Winona Lake, Eisenbrauns, 2007).

Livingstone, A. The Magic of Time. In Mesopotamian Magic. Textual, Historical, and Interpretative Perspectives, ed. Tzvi Abusch and Karel van der Toorn. (Styx, Gronningen: 1999).

Malbran-Labat, F., Les textes akkadiens découverts à Ougarit en 1994. Languages and Cultures in Contact: At the Crossroads of Civilizations in the Syro-Mesopotamian Realm. Proceedings of the 42th RAI. K. Van Lerberghe and G. Voet (eds.), Orientalia Lovaniensia Analecta 96 (Leuven, Uitgeverij Peeters en Departement Oosterse Studies: 1999): 237-244.

„Der Ursprung des größten Leids für die Juden" (Josephus Ant. 19.366)

Ronald Mayer-Opificius, Münster

Das Verhältnis zwischen römischen Truppen und jüdischer Zivilbevölkerung in Palästina 44–66 n. Chr.*

in memoriam Dr. iur. Joseph Mayer (1905–95)

Am Ende des 19. Buchs seiner *Jüdischen Altertümer* geht Flavius Josephus kurz auf das Verhältnis zwischen Juden und römischen Soldaten ein. Im Rahmen der Umwandlung Judäas in eine procuratorische Provinz nach dem Tod des Herodes Agrippa befahl Kaiser Claudius, „die Ala der Caesarener und Sebastener und die 5 Kohorten [*die bisher in Judäa gestanden hatten*] nach Pontus zu transferieren, damit sie dort ihren Dienst versähen. Eine entsprechende Anzahl Soldaten aus den römischen Legionen Syriens sollte ausgewählt werden, um deren Stelle einzunehmen."[1] Hinter diesem Beschluß des Kaisers steckte die Absicht, so Josephus, die heidnische Bevölkerung dieser Städte für ihr Verhalten nach dem Tod des Herodes Agrippa zu bestrafen. Der verstorbene König und seine Familie waren nämlich wegen ihrer vermeintlichen Begünstigung der Juden aufs äußerste geschmäht worden. Bemerkenswert ist, daß Claudius durch die Versetzung der Auxiliareinheiten die städtische Bevölkerung treffen wollte, der Kaiser also die Truppen und die Stadtbevölkerung als eine Gemeinschaft sah. Josephus fährt fort, daß eine Gesandtschaft es vermochte, Claudius umzustimmen – dies ist auch interessant als Information darüber, wie beispielsweise Gesandschaften oder kaiserliche Freigelassene den Prozeß der imperialen Entscheidungsfindung beeinflußten.[2] Claudius' ursprüngliche Anordnung wurde also nicht ausgeführt, und Josephus schreibt: „Die Truppen waren in der Folgezeit der Ursprung des größten Leids für die

* Ich möchte mich bei Jochen Walter, Christian Grewe und Ruth Mayer-Opificius bedanken für Anregungen und Korrekturen.

1 Jos. *Ant.* 19.365.

2 Hingewiesen sei an dieser Stelle nur auf F. Millars Studie: Millar 1993.

Juden, da sie die Saat des Krieges unter Florus säten, weshalb Vespasian sie, sobald er herrschte, (...) aus der Provinz herausführte."[3]

Im Folgenden will ich der Frage nachgehen, was Josephus dazu veranlaßte, das Verhältnis zwischen römischen Truppen und jüdischer Zivilbevölkerung, zweier wichtiger Gruppen der Gesellschaft Palästinas, so düster zu charakterisieren. Dabei sollen nicht nur die Ereignisse unmittelbar vor Ausbruch des Jüdischen Krieges berücksichtigt werden, sondern auch die Zeit vom Tode Herodes des Großen bis zum Ausbruch des Krieges.

Wichtig ist es, sich zunächst die Quellenlage und ihre Begrenzungen vor Augen zu führen. Für eine Untersuchung des Verhältnisses zwischen den römischen Besatzungstruppen in Palästina und der jüdischen Zivilbevölkerung sind wir im Wesentlichen auf zwei literarische Quellen angewiesen. Die Schriften des Neuen Testaments, und dort vor allem die Apostelgeschichte, enthalten Informationen zu den römischen Soldaten in Palästina.[4] Wichtiger ist jedoch das Werk des jüdischen Historikers Flavius Josephus, der keineswegs ein unbeteiligter Chronist der Geschichte Palästinas im ersten Jh. n.Chr. war, sondern vielmehr selbst als Akteur an den Geschehnissen beteiligt war.[5] So versucht er in seinen Schriften einerseits, seine eigene fragwürdige Rolle während des jüdischen Aufstandes von 66 n.Chr. zu rechtfertigen, andererseits ist er aufs äußerste bemüht, seinen Patronen, also dem flavischen Kaiserhaus, zu schmeicheln – daher auch das Lob für Vespasian in der eingangs zitierten Passage *Ant.* 19, 366. Gleichzeitig sucht er die Schuld für die Katastrophe der Zerstörung des Tempels sowohl der römischen Administration als auch radikalen jüdischen Gruppen zuzuschreiben. Mit dieser Absicht schildert er Judäa als einen konstanten Unruheherd – die Geschichte der römischen Herrschaft über Judäa erscheint bei Josephus als eine einzige Reihe von Katastrophen mit dem unausweichlichen Endpunkt der Zerstörung des Tempels 70 n. Chr.[6] Dies ist jedoch, wie J. McLaren gezeigt hat, Josephus' Interpretationsmuster. Für unsere Fragestellung nach der sozialen Beziehung zwischen den römischen Besatzungstruppen und der jüdischen Zivilbevölkerung bedeutet dies, daß Josephus Konflikte zwischen den beiden Gruppen

3 Jos. *Ant.* 19.366.

4 Z.B. *Apg.* 23,23ff.

5 Allgemein zu Josephus: Schürer I, 43–63; Rajak 1983; Bilde 1988.

6 Eine Zusammenstellung der Ursachen des Jüdischen Krieges, wie sie sich bei Josephus finden, bei Bilde 1979.

möglicherweise besonders betont, da dies sein interpretatives Gesamtkonzept unterstützt.[7]

Doch zurück zur eingangs zitierten Josephus-Stelle. Wenn der Autor hier von großem Leid spricht, so meint er den großen Jüdischen Krieg von 66–70 n.Chr. Ganz spezifisch denkt er hier an die Ereignisse, die zur stetig eskalierenden Spirale der Gewalt im unmittelbaren Vorfeld des Krieges gehören. Der Procurator Cessius Florus stand vor dem Dilemma, daß das Steueraufkommen Judäas nicht der imperialen Maßgabe entsprach, d.h., daß die Juden nicht in ausreichendem Maße ihre Abgaben an Rom bezahlt hatten. Er entschied sich, diese Lücke mit Mitteln aus einer äußerst unglücklich gewählten Quelle zu füllen, nämlich aus dem Schatz des Jerusalemer Tempels. Dieses Vorgehen, als Provokation verstanden, verlangte geradezu nach nach einer Reaktion seitens der Juden Palästinas. Bereits unter Florus' Vorgänger Pontius Pilatus war es zu ähnlichen Ereignissen gekommen, als dieser versucht hatte, Mittel aus dem Tempelschatz für den Bau eines Aquäduktes zu verwenden.[8] Florus' Entscheidung, den Tempelschatz anzutasten, rief Protestaktionen hervor, deren Ironie vielleicht besonders ins Schwarze traf – es wurde nämlich Geld für den „armen“ Florus gesammelt.[9] Florus führte daraufhin Truppen aus Caesarea heran, um die Ordnung wiederherzustellen. Josephus behauptet, daß Vermittlungsversuche von Seiten der lokalen Elite Judäas bei dem Procurator auf taube Ohren stießen. Er befahl vielmehr, so Josephus, seinen Truppen, den oberen Markt in Jerusalem zu plündern und zu töten, wen auch immer sie anträfen. Besondere Beachtung für unsere Fragestellung nach der Beziehung zwischen Soldaten und Zivilisten in Palästina verdient die folgende Behauptung von Josephus, daß die Auxiliare geradezu auf die Ausführung dieses Befehls brannten und mit ungekannter Brutalität vorgingen. Die Auxiliare drangen, so Josephus, sogar in Häuser ein und veranstalten eine Hetzjagd auf die jüdische Zivilbevölkerung. Sogar vor Berenike, der Tochter Herodes' Agrippas, machten sie nur zögernd halt – geradezu eine Ironie des Schicksals, war es doch die Beleidigung

7 McLaren 1998, passim. Zu Josephus' Darstellung der Gründe des Jüdischen Krieges: Bilde 1979. Die wissenschaftliche Literatur zu den Ursachen des Jüdischen Krieges sind zahlreich und beinahe unüberschaubar. Wichtigste Beiträge sind Goodman 1987, Hengel 1988.

8 Jos. *BJ* 2. 293. Und *BJ* 2.403 Josephus impliziert, daß Florus sich selbst bereichern wollte. Die Rede Agrippas jedoch verdeutlicht, daß das Steueraufkommen unzureichend war. Daher ist davon auszugehen, daß durch Florus' Zugriff auf den Tempelschatz das Steuerdefizit ausgeglichen werden sollte.

9 Jos. *BJ* 2.295.

Berenikes und ihrer Schwestern, die mehr als 20 Jahre früher Claudius beinahe zur Versetzung eben dieser Einheiten ans Schwarze Meer veranlasst hätte.[10]

Dieses Massaker war jedoch noch nicht das Ende der von Josephus geschilderten gewaltsamen Vorfälle. Erneut intervenierten bei Florus Vertreter der Führungsschicht, um die Situation zu entspannen. Der Procurator bestand aber darauf, daß die Jerusalemer Bevölkerung zwei weitere aus Caesarea anrückende Kohorten vor der Stadt begrüßen sollte. Dies war eine eindeutige Unterwerfungsgeste, da die Bevölkerung so symbolisch die römische Herrschaft willkommen heißen sollte. Diese Begrüßung der Truppen führte jedoch zu einem erneuten Desaster: Die Soldaten reagierten nicht auf das Willkommenheißen. Josephus schreibt, daß dies auf Florus' Anordnung geschah. Bald kam es zu Schmährufen und die Reaktion der Auxiliare darauf – sie griffen an – war erneut durch äußerste Brutalität gekennzeichnet.[11] Dies sind die Ereignisse, auf die Josephus in *Ant.* 19.366 anspielte. Sie stehen jedoch nicht vereinzelt da. Immer wieder hören wir in Josephus' Berichten von Zusammenstößen zwischen den römischen Truppen und der jüdischen Bevölkerung. Bereits für die Statthalterschaft des Pontius Pilatus vermeldet Josephus mehrfach solche Konflikte. So gingen die Auxiliare mit großer Brutalität gegen die jüdische Zivilbevölkerung vor, als es zu Protesten kam, nachdem Pilatus für den Bau eines Aquäduktes Silber aus dem Tempelschatz entnommen hatte. Obwohl die Soldaten Befehl hatten, keine Schwerter einzusetzen, sondern ‚nur' Knüppel, kamen zahllose Juden um.[12] Erneut zeichneten sich also die römischen Truppen durch ihre Erbarmungslosigkeit aus.[13] Dies kann als weite-

10 Jos. *BJ* 2.305–15. Durch die Darstellung dieser unerhörten Respektlosigkeit will Josephus zeigen, wie verdorben Florus und seine Truppen waren, da sie nicht einmal mehr soziale Rangstellungen respektierten. Ein Thema, das sich wie ein roter Faden durch diese Passage zieht – berichtet Josephus doch auch von Kreuzigungen jüdischer *equites*, deren sozialer Status eine angesehenere Hinrichtungsart verlangte. Generell sind solche Verletzungen der sozialen Rangordnung in der Antike aufs äußerste mißbilligt worden.

11 Jos. *BJ* 2. 318–29.

12 Jos. *BJ* 2.175–8; *Ant.* 18.60–2; vgl. dazu Bond 1998, 85–9; Demandt 1999, 90f.; K. Jaroš vermutet, daß es sich nicht um einen Neubau, sondern nur um Instandsetzung eines bereits von Herodes gebauten Aquäduktes handelte, von der Pilatus persönlich profitierte, Jaroš 2002, 60–8.

13 A. Demandt weist darauf hin, daß diese Darstellung in Josephus' Interpretationsschema paßt. So will er zeigen, daß gewaltsamer Widerstand gegen Rom nur Leid und Tod bringt. Dagegen zeigt er, daß gewaltloser Widerstand Erfolg verspricht, wie in *BJ* 2.169–74 und

res Anzeichen gewertet werden, daß sie den Juden gegenüber ausgesprochen feindlich eingestellt waren. Dem muß jedoch entgegen gehalten werden, daß die römische Armee nie besonders human vorging. Im Gegenteil: Römische Kriegsführung war durch eine ungehemmte Brutalität gekennzeichnet, die letztendlich auch zur Verrohung des individuellen Soldaten führen mußte.[14] Mehrfach hören wir auch außerhalb militärischer Auseinandersetzungen von erstaunlicher Härte und rücksichtslosen Provokationen im Umgang mit bereits Unterworfenen. Römische Soldaten besaßen umfangreiche Requirierungsrechte. Dabei ist den Quellen zu entnehmen, daß römische Soldaten diese Rechte häufig mißbrauchten und darüberhinaus auch die Zivilbevölkerung mißhandelten. Nur als Beispiel sei auf den Rat Epiktets verwiesen, sich über eine Requisition nicht zu beschweren, da der Besitz sowieso verloren sei, und man, wenn man still hielte, mindestens nicht verprügelt würde.[15] Einer Passage des Lukas-Evangeliums können wir entnehmen, daß das Verhalten römischer Soldaten in Palästina nicht anders war, steht doch dort, daß Soldaten sich des Raubes und falscher Anschuldigungen enthalten und mit ihrem Sold zufrieden sein sollten.[16] Tacitus berichtet, daß die in der Colonia Claudia Vitricensis angesiedelten Veteranen die Trinovanten, in deren Gebiet die Kolonie lag, rücksichtslos behandelten. Er erwähnt auch, daß die Veteranen die Trinovanten enteigneten und Sklaven oder Kriegsgefangene nannten. Dieser Stamm aber war, soweit wir wissen, nicht mit Rom verfeindet gewesen. Im Gegenteil waren die Trinovanten ursprünglich mit Caesar verbündet gewesen. Darüber hinaus waren sie kurz vor der römischen Eroberung Britanniens von den Catuvellauni, den Hauptgegnern Roms, unterworfen worden. Somit hätten sie allen Grund gehabt, die römische Herrschaft willkommen zu heißen – Kriegsgefangene und Sklaven Roms im herkömmlichen Sinn waren sie nicht.[17] Das Verhalten der Veteranen und der sie unterstützenden Legionäre war höchst unsensibel, arrogant und provokant. Es läßt sich jedoch festhalten, daß diese Feindseligkeit gegenüber der Zivilbevölkerung eher durch Unkenntnis und Arroganz

---

Ant. 18.55–9, als Standarten mit Kaiserbildern aus Jerusalem wieder abgezogen wurden; Demandt 1999, 91. Von daher mag Josephus die Brutalität und den Verlust an Menschenleben besonders betonen, um sein Interpretationsschema besser zu vermitteln.

14 Vgl. dazu auch Campbell 2002.

15 Epiktet *Disp.* 4.1.79. Weitere Beispiele: Ulpian *Digest.* 1.18.6.5–7. Plin. *Ep.* 10.77f.; Select Papyri (Loeb) 2, nr. 221; vgl. Campbell 2002 mit weiterführenden Literaturhinweisen.

16 *Lk.* 3.12–4.

17 Tac. *Ann.* 14.31.3; Caes. *BG* 5.20f.

hervorgerufen wurde und nicht spezifisch gegen die Trinovanten gerichtet war. Analog muß die Brutalität der Auxiliare in Palästina auch nicht unbedingt als spezifisch antijüdisch verstanden werden. Ihre bisher beschriebene gewalttätige Rücksichtslosigkeit gegenüber den Juden kann daher auch einem allgemeinen Verhaltensmuster der römischen Armee entsprechen.

Es gibt jedoch zwei Vorfälle in der Geschichte des römisch besetzten Palästinas, die gezielt antijüdische Provokationen seitens römischer Soldaten zeigen und von daher auch eine andere Qualität haben. Die großen religiösen Feste in Jerusalem waren vor allem wegen der gesteigerten religiösen Sensibilität der Teilnehmer ein Unruhepotential, auf das die römische Verwaltung Palästinas mit einer gewissen Nervosität schaute.[18] Als Konsequenz standen während dieser Feste römische Truppen bereit, um Ausschreitungen zu verhindern. Josephus berichtet sowohl im *Bellum Judaicum* als auch in den *Altertümern* von einem Vorfall, bei dem gerade eben die Präsenz der Auxiliarsoldaten einen gewaltsamen Zwischenfall verursachte.[19] Beiden Versionen ist gemein, daß eine Doppelzenturie auf der Säulenhalle des Tempels aufgestellt wurde. Im *Bellum Judaicum* schildert Josephus, daß einer der Auxiliarsoldaten sein Gewand hob, der versammelten Menge der Festteilnehmer sein Gesäß zudrehte, sich bückte und, so Josephus, ein entsprechendes Geräusch von sich gab. Daraufhin verlangte die aufgebrachte Menge die Bestrafung des Soldaten. Die Situation verschärfte sich zusehends, als die römischen Soldaten mit Steinen beworfen wurden. Der Procurator Ventidius Cumanus reagierte, indem er die Truppenpräsenz verstärkte. Anstelle einer Deeskalation bewirkte er das Gegenteil, denn als die Verstärkung anrückte, brach unter den Festteilnehmern Panik aus. Josephus behauptet, daß über 30 000 von ihnen dabei gestorben seien. Obwohl es sich eindeutig um eine Provokation handelte, ist die Reaktion der Festteilnehmer in ihrer Heftigkeit doch überraschend. Die Parallelüberlieferung in den *Altertümern* weicht davon in einigen entscheidenden Punkten ab. Es ist von geringerer Bedeutung, daß Josephus die Zahl der zu Tode gekommenen mit 20 000 geringer angibt als im *Bellum*. Wichtiger jedoch ist, daß er die Provokation des Soldaten anders beschreibt: Dieser Soldat soll sich entblößt und der Menge seine Genitalien gezeigt haben. Nach Josephus verstand die versammelte Menge der Festteilnehmer dies nicht als eine an sie gerichtete Beleidigung, sondern als Schmähung ihres Gottes. Die Version in den *Altertümern* ist m. E. die plausiblere Darstellung der Ereignisse. Vermutlich entblößte sich der Sol-

18 Zu dem Phänomen religiöser Feste als Unruhefaktor vgl. Mayer-Opificius 2003.

19 Jos. *BJ* 2.223–7; *Ant.* 20.105–12.

dat, um den versammelten Juden provokativ zu zeigen, daß er nicht beschnitten war. Die Beschneidung war einer der definierenden Unterschiede zwischen Juden und Heiden. Gleichzeitig war sie eine der jüdischen Sitten, die von heidnischer Seite am heftigsten, vor allem als Verstümmlung, attackiert wurde und in vielen Fällen Gegenstand von Witzen und Vorurteilen war.[20] Daher kann davon ausgegangen werden, daß die Aktion des Soldaten äußerst provozierend war. Bei einem religiösen Fest so despektierlich darauf hinzuweisen, selbst kein Jude zu sein, mußte besonders kränkend empfunden worden sein. Festzuhalten ist, daß diese Provokation nicht zufällig von Seiten eines Soldaten geschehen ist. Vielmehr war sie in dieser spezifischen Form eine gezielt antijüdische Geste. Dies kann als ein erster eindeutiger Hinweis verstanden werden, daß unter den römischen Truppen in Judäa in dieser Zeit eine außerordentlich feindselige Einstellung gegenüber der jüdischen Zivilbevölkerung vorherrschte, die über das bekannte Maß römischer Rücksichtslosigkeit hinausging.

Direkt im Anschluß an diesen Vorfall berichtet Josephus wiederum im *Jüdischen Krieg* und in den *Altertümern*, wie provokantes Verhalten seitens der Auxiliareinheiten zu einer weiteren Eskalation der Gewalt zu führen drohte.[21] Ein kaiserlicher Sklave namens Stephanos wurde auf der Straße nach Bethoron überfallen und sein Gepäck (vermutlich eskortierte er kaiserlichen Besitz) geraubt. Josephus' Bericht deutet an, daß der Überfall politisch, also antirömisch motiviert war. Die Reaktion des Procurators Cumanus fiel heftig aus. Wiederum divergieren die von Josephus überlieferten Versionen. Im *Jüdischen Krieg* befiehlt der Procurator einer Einheit, die Bewohner der umliegenden Dörfer gefangen zu nehmen, da diese die Täter nicht dingfest gemacht hätten. In den *Altertümern* dagegen befiehlt Cumanus zusätzlich, die Dörfer zu plündern. In beiden Versionen fährt Josephus fort, daß ein Soldat eine Kopie der Thora an sich brachte. Er zerriß die Schriftrolle und verbrannte sie. In den *Altertümern* beschreibt der Autor zudem noch, daß der Soldat dies gezielt vor Zeugen tat und, während er die Rolle vernichtete, auch noch Verwünschungen ausstieß. Diese Provokation löste eine solche Protestbewegung in ganz Judäa aus, daß Cumanus sich am Ende gezwungen sah, diesen Soldaten hinzurichten.

Dieser Vorfall ist in mehrfacher Hinsicht aufschlußreich. Die Vernichtung der Thora war in der Tat eine schwerwiegende Provokation. Die physische Kopie der Thora, also die Schriftrolle, wird im Judentum stets mit Hochachtung behandelt und als heilig angesehen (und so z.B. bis auf

20 Philo *De Spec.Leg.* 1,1; Mart. 7,82; vgl. dazu Feldman 1993, 152–8; Schäfer 1997, 90–103.

21 Jos. *BJ* 2.228–31; *Ant.* 20.113–7.

den heutigen Tag kultisch bestattet). Die Zerstörung einer solchen Schriftrolle war dementsprechend ein gewaltiges Sakrileg und symbolisiert zugleich die Verachtung gegenüber den Juden und ihrem Gott. Daß der Auxiliarsoldat die Schriftrolle gezielt vor Zeugen zerstörte, deutet darauf hin, daß die Provokation beabsichtigt und nicht nur ein Akt blinder Zerstörungswut war. Gleichzeitig darf angenommen werden, daß sich der Täter bewußt gewesen ist, wie schwerwiegend diese Provokation sein mußte.

Die Feindseligkeit gegenüber der jüdischen Bevölkerung, wie sie sich in diesen beiden Vorgängen zeigt, ist bemerkenswert. Das Verhalten der Auxiliare in Palästina zeigt in der Tat antijüdische Tendenzen, und es unterscheidet sich damit auch von den sonst üblichen Übergriffen römischer Soldaten gegen die Zivilbevölkerung. Die Provokationen sollten offenbar gezielt den jüdischen Glauben verletzen.[22] Das Verhalten hat eine andere Qualität und ist nicht unbedingt typisch für die römische Armee.[23] Es muß folglich eine spezielle Erklärung dafür gefunden werden.

Zum besseren Verständnis der soeben beschriebenen Vorfälle ist es wichtig, sich einiges über die Natur und den Aufbau der römischen Armee vor Augen zu führen. Anders als die überwiegende Mehrzahl moderner Streitkräfte, die sich die meiste Zeit auf eine militärische Auseinandersetzung vorbereiten, nahmen die Truppen Roms vielfältige Aufgaben wahr. Beispielsweise war die Armee wirtschaftlich aktiv (wie auch heute noch die Volksbefreiungsarmee in der VR China).[24] Sie wurde aber auch – und dies ist für unsere Fragestellung wichtig – als Ordnungsmacht eingesetzt. Ein Statthalter mußte sich für die Ausführung seiner Politik im Wesentlichen auf die in seiner Provinz stationierten Truppen verlassen. Insbesondere aus der Apostelgeschichte können wir sehen, daß die römische Armee Polizeiaufgaben wahrnahm. In ihrer Organisation stützte sich die Armee Roms im Wesentlichen auf zwei Säulen.[25] Die eine Säule der Armee bilde-

---

22 Das Verhalten der Soldaten in *Mt.* 27. 27–31 mag ebenfalls von antijüdischen Provokationen geprägt gewesen sein, z.B. könnten zu den Demütigungen Jesu erzwungene Verstöße gegen Reinheitsgebote gehört haben.

23 Die Andersartigkeit der Provokationen ist jedoch auch durch die Quellenlage bedingt. Durchaus denkbar wären solch provokante Tabuverletzungen sowohl in anderen Provinzen als auch gegenüber anderen Religionen. Überliefert ist derartiges Verhalten nur für Palästina.

24 Vgl. zu diesem Aspekt Fischer 2000, 49–52.

25 Zur römischen Armee vgl. Webster 1998; Le Bohec 1993; gesondert für die Römische Armee im Vorderen Orient vgl. Isaac 1993.

ten in dem hier behandelten Zeitraum die ca. 28 Legionen schwerer Infanterie. Kommandiert wurden die Legionen von jeweils einem Legaten mit senatorischem Rang. Die Truppenstärke einer Legion lag theoretisch bei 5 280 oder 6 000 Mann, war in der Praxis jedoch erheblich niedriger, so daß man für die Gesamtstärke der Legionen im römischen Heer nicht mehr als 140 000 Mann annehmen sollte. Theoretisch zumindest war der Besitz des römischen Bürgerrechts Voraussetzung, um in den Legionen zu dienen. Ursprünglich wurden Legionen in Italien ausgehoben, jedoch entwickelte sich bald die Praxis, daß eine Legion aus dem Umfeld ihres Standortes rekrutierte. Obwohl in der Theorie jeder wehrfähige Bürger zum Dienst herangezogen werden konnte, scheint es so gewesen zu sein, daß sich die meisten Legionäre freiwillig zum langjährigen Dienst verpflichteten.

Die andere Säule der römischen Armee waren die Auxiliareinheiten. Diese ergänzten die Legionen in vielen Bereichen. Während die Legionen am besten als schwere Infanterie zu definieren sind, gab es unter den Auxiliareinheiten die verschiedensten Waffengattungen, wie Kavallerie, Bogenschützen, Schleuderer usw. Ihr Ursprung lag in den Kontingenten der Verbündeten Roms. Zunächst waren dies irreguläre Einheiten, aber bereits in den ersten Generationen des Prinzipats wurden die Auxilien reguläre Formationen. Von Tacitus wissen wir, daß den Legionen eine gleich große Anzahl an Auxilien zur Seite stand.[26] Für das 2. Jh. n.Chr. ergibt sich mit theoretisch 224 000 Mann sogar ein deutlich höherer Anteil an der Gesamtstärke des römischen Heeres.[27] Die Auxiliareinheiten waren in Kohorten und Alen mit einer Sollstärke von 500 oder 1 000 Mann organisiert. Im Gegensatz zu den Legionen wurden die Auxilien in den Provinzen ausgehoben. Der Dienst in ihnen war länger, und der Sold lag vermutlich unter dem der Legionäre. Gleichzeitig kann aus unseren Quellen geschlossen werden, daß die Auxiliarsoldaten nicht unbedingt freiwillig dienten, da wir mehrfach von unpopulären Aushebungen hören.[28] Zudem wurden die Auxilien häufig fern von ihrem Aushebungsort stationiert – ein Punkt, auf den noch zurückzukommen sein wird. Zwar winkte den Auxiliarsoldaten am Ende ihrer Dienstzeit die Erlangung des römischen Bürgerrechtes als Belohnung, es läßt sich aber trotzdem festhalten, daß die

26 Tac. *Ann.* 4.5. Zur Entwicklung der Auxiliareinheiten vgl. Cheesman 1914, Callies 1964, Saddington 1982.

27 Holder 1980.

28 Z.B. Tac. *Hist.* 4.14.1.

Legionen privilegiert waren und der Dienst in ihnen ebenso wie das Kommando über sie mit mehr Prestige verbunden war.

In Palästina waren in der Zeit vor dem Jüdischen Krieg keine Legionen stationiert. Vier Legionen standen jedoch in der benachbarten Provinz Syrien und konnten gegebenenfalls in Palästina eingreifen, so z. B. nach dem Tod Herodes des Großen, als Quinctilius Varus einen Aufstand in Jerusalem niederschlug.[29] Erst nach Beendigung des großen Aufstandes 70 n.Chr. hat Vespasian eine Legion permanent nach Jerusalem verlegt. Die Abwesenheit von Legionen kann zum Teil dadurch erklärt werden, daß die Römer mit wenigen Ausnahmen Legionen nur dort stationierten, wo eine auswärtige Gefahr drohte oder Gebiete noch nicht vollständig unterworfen waren. Wurden Klientelkönigreiche in direkte römische Verwaltung überführt, wie dies mit Judäa geschehen war, so wurden meist keine Legionen dorthin verlegt, vielleicht weil solche Bereiche bereits als gesichert galten. In Palästina standen zu dieser Zeit demzufolge nur Auxiliareinheiten, und zwar fünf Auxiliarkohorten und eine Ala, die alle in Caesarea stationiert waren. Eine Ala und eine weitere Kohorte lagen zudem in Askalon, und Josephus berichtet, daß zusätzlich noch kleinere Detachments über Palästina verteilt waren. Aus der *Apostelgeschichte* und Josephus' Beschreibung des Tempels im 5. Buch des Jüdischen Krieges geht zudem hervor, daß eine 1000 Mann starke Kohorte in der Festung Antonia lag.[30]

Josephus bezeichnet die Einheiten als Kohorten der Sebastener und Caesarener. Daraus läßt sich schließen, daß die römischen Auxiliartruppen lokal unter der heidnischen Bevölkerung Palästinas rekrutiert wurden. Die *Apostelgeschichte* berichtet zusätzlich noch von einer italischen Kohorte.[31] Wahrscheinlich handelte es sich dabei um eine Kohorte römischer Bürger. In der Tat ist aus dem 2. Jh. n.Chr. eine solche Einheit inschriftlich aus Syrien bekannt.[32] Möglicherweise war es die aus dem Neuen Testament bekannte Einheit, die unter Vespasian aus Palästina abgezogen wurde. Vielleicht war sie ursprünglich in Italien ausgehoben worden, vielleicht dienten aber auch zunächst nur römische Bürger Caesareas und Samarias/Sebastes in dieser Einheit. Auf jeden Fall darf davon ausgegangen werden, daß neue Rekruten aus der lokalen Bevölkerung kamen. Wichtig ist dabei festzuhalten, daß die Rekruten für alle römischen Auxiliartruppen

---

29 Jos. *BJ* 2.42–79; *Ant.* 17.252–98.

30 Schürer I 363ff.

31 *Apg.* 10.1ff.; vgl. Schürer I, 364f.; Speidel 1982.

32 CIL 3.13483a; 6.3528; 11.6117; 14.171; 16.106; AE 1948, 150.

ausschließlich aus der heidnischen Bevölkerung kamen. Die Ursachen dafür sind vielfältig. Zunächst hatten mehrere römische Feldherren in republikanischer Zeit den Juden das Privileg der Befreiung vom Militärdienst gewährt.[33] Dabei ist offen, wie weit dies nur für Juden mit römischem Bürgerrecht galt oder ob es automatisch aufgehoben wurde, als Judäa zur Provinz wurde. Jedoch läßt sich festhalten, daß bis 70 n.Chr. Juden nicht in der römischen Armee dienten. Abgesehen von dem Privileg scheinen vor allem auch religiöse Tabus dem Dienst in der römischen Armee entgegengestanden zu haben. Dies ist erstaunlich, da in den Armeen der hellenistischen Großreiche jüdische Söldner des Öfteren zu finden sind. Offensichtlich herrschte zunehmend Unklarheit darüber, wann z.B. das Sabbatgebot im Kriegsfall verletzt werden durfte und wann nicht. Dadurch, daß Militärdienst generell vermieden wurde, konnte diesem Problem aus dem Weg gegangen werden. Gleichzeitig stellte der Herrscherkult, dem die römische Armee in besonderer Weise verpflichtet war, ein Problem dar. Auch war koschere Verpflegung kaum zu gewährleisten, solange Juden nicht in ausschließlich jüdischen Einheiten dienten. Möglicherweise hatte sich auch in der Auseinandersetzung mit dem Hellenismus das Problembewußtsein hinsichtlich des Militärdienstes verschärft.[34] Somit war den führenden jüdischen Schichten auch eine Aufstiegsmöglichkeit innerhalb des römischen Reiches verschlossen, da gerade das Kommando über Auxiliareinheiten einen Einstieg in die Reichselite ermöglichte.[35]

Zurück zu der extremen Feindseligkeit der Auxiliare gegenüber der jüdischen Zivilbevölkerung: Wie wir gesehen haben, stammten die Soldaten, die in den Auxiliareinheiten dienten, aus den hellenisierten Städten Palästinas. Diese Städte lagen jedoch in einem steten Konflikt mit den Juden, wobei die religiöse Feindschaft auf alten Traditionen beruhte, da die griechischen Städte zumeist Neugründungen bereits seit kanaanäischer Zeit bestehender Siedlungen waren, die ihrerseits bereits seit langem mit den Juden in einem Konflikt gestanden hatten.[36] Zum einen war dies ein religiöser Konflikt zwischen hellenistischem Heidentum und Judaismus, gleichzeitig war es aber auch ein Konflikt zwischen Stadt und Land. Die Griechen lebten überwiegend in den urbanen Zentren, während die ländliche Bevölkerung überwiegend jüdisch war. In den Städten führten ge-

33 Jos. *Ant.* 14.204, 226–8, 232–40.

34 Goodman 1987, 47f.

35 Zu den Offizieren der Auxiliareinheiten vgl. Saddington 1980.

36 Kasher 1990, 313–5; Feldman 1993, 12.

mischte Nachbarschaften häufig zu Konflikten – insbesondere, wenn Sozialneid als Faktor hinzukam.[37]

Auch in der politischen Geschichte standen griechische Städte und jüdische Bevölkerung meist in entgegengesetzten Lagern. Die Städte verbanden sich häufig mit auswärtigen Mächten, die so in den Konflikt zwischen Juden und hellenisierten Städten hineingezogen wurden. Unter den Hasmonäern gerieten die griechischen Städte unter jüdischen Einfluß, was zur Folge hatte, daß jüdisches Recht eingeführt wurde, es teilweise zu Zwangsbekehrungen kam und heidnische Riten verboten wurden. Diese Expansion schürte auch den bereits bestehenden antijüdischen Diskurs in der griechischen Welt.[38] Die römische Eroberung Palästinas bedeutete eine Reversion des unter den Hasmonäern für die Juden Erreichten und das Ende der Judaisierung Palästinas. Unter Herodes d.Gr. wurden die entgegengesetzten Lager nicht zuletzt durch sein brutales Vorgehen unter Kontrolle gehalten. Die Herrschaft der römischen Statthalter brachte jedoch wiederum eine Verlagerung des Kräfteverhältnisses zugunsten der griechischen Städte, symbolisiert schon durch die Wahl Caesareas als Sitz des Statthalters.

Die religiöse Natur des Konfliktes bewirkte, daß Provokationen oft auf kultische Tabus zielten. So berichtet Josephus, daß heidnische Provokateure Tauben vor dem Eingang der Synagoge in Caesarea opferten.[39] Der Vorfall erinnert in der Art der Provokation an die zuletzt beschriebenen antijüdischen Aktionen der Soldaten, also Zerstörung der Thora und die Entblößung auf der Säulenhalle des Tempels. Wird berücksichtigt, daß die Einheiten lokal unter der heidnischen Bevölkerung Palästinas ausgehoben worden waren, liegt die Vermutung nahe, daß die Judenfeindlichkeit der Soldaten als Teil des Konfliktes zwischen hellenisierten Städten und Juden in Palästina gesehen werden sollte. Dadurch, daß die Römer die Garnisonstruppen Palästinas aus der Bevölkerung dieser Städte rekrutierten, wurden sie in einen Konflikt hineingezogen, der keineswegs im Interesse Roms war. Im Gegenteil, diese Truppen verschärften sogar noch die Auseinandersetzung. Zum einen mußte für die jüdische Bevölkerung die römische Herrschaft eng mit den ihnen verfeindeten hellenisierten Städten

37 Feldman 1993, 107–13.

38 Feldman 1993, 324–6 mit Quellenangaben. C. Habicht sieht in den gewaltsamen Konversionen gar die Initialzündung des antiken Antisemitismus; vgl. Habicht 1973, 97–110; Z. Yavaetz' kritisiert die überspitzten Formulierungen Habichts, jedoch kann er damit Habichts These letztendlich nicht vollkommen widerlegen, vgl. Yavaetz 1997, 29–32.

39 Jos. *BJ* 2.284–92.

assoziiert sein, da Rom die Bürger eben dieser Städte bewaffnete und sie so mit der Autorität des römischen Reiches ausstattete. Zum anderen war es den römischen Truppen in Palästina daher auch erschwert, ihre Funktion als Ordnungsmacht wahrzunehmen – waren sie doch durch ihren ethnischen Hintergrund eigentlich Teilnehmer des Konfliktes zwischen hellenisierten Städten und Juden.[40] In der Tat berichtet Josephus genau dies für die Auseinadersetzungen in Caesarea 60 n.Chr. Die Auxiliarsoldaten ergriffen eindeutig Partei für die heidnische Bevölkerung, die daraus Zuversicht für ihren Streit mit den Juden gewann.[41] Vier Jahre später, als der Konflikt wieder entbrannte, vermochte es der Präfekt der dort stationierten Ala nicht, die Spannung zwischen Juden und heidnischer Bevölkerung Caesareas zu deeskalieren – ganz offensichtlich wurde er nicht als unparteiisch gesehen.[42]

Den Konflikt in Palästina so zu verschärfen, kann aber keineswegs im Interesse Roms gelegen haben. Stand also hinter Claudius' eingangs diskutiertem Plan, die Auxiliare nach Pontus zu verlegen, mehr als nur die Absicht, die Einheiten für ihr ungebührliches Verhalten gegenüber dem Andenken und der Familie des Herodes Agrippa zu disziplinieren? Wollte der Kaiser, der auch in anderen Fällen zu Gunsten der Juden entschieden hatte, die Situation in Palästina entschärfen?[43] Mit Sicherheit läßt sich dies nicht beantworten. Es muß jedoch festgehalten werden, daß es römische Praxis war, Auxiliare fern ihres Aushebungsortes zu stationieren - besonders dann, wenn eine Einheit dort Probleme verursachen konnte. So wurde beispielsweise eine Kohorte der germanischen Sugambrer unter Augustus am unteren Lauf der Donau stationiert, und Dio berichtet, daß 5 000 sarmatische Reiter in Britannien stationiert wurden.[44]

Warum also änderte Claudius seine ursprüngliche Absicht, die Truppen ans Schwarze Meer zu versetzen? Der Erfolg der Gesandschaft, die

---

40 Eine zeitgenössische Parallele, wie alle solche Parallelen nur mit einem *caveat* zu sehen, wäre die prädominant protestantische Royal Ulster Constabulary. Sie wird von katholischer Seite kaum als unbeteiligte Polizei gesehen, sondern mit der protestantischen Konfliktpartei identifiziert. Einzelne ihrer Mitglieder haben auch loyalistischen Terror gegen Katholiken toleriert bzw. unterstützt. Hervorzuheben ist in diesem Kontext auch, daß der Patten-Report über die RUC gerade auch riet, den Anteil der Katholiken in dieser Polizeitruppe zu erhöhen.

41 Jos. *BJ*. 2.266–70.

42 Jos. *BJ*. 2.284–92.

43 Claudius entschied in einem Konflikt mit den Samaritanern zugunsten der Juden; Jos. *BJ* 2.245f.; *Ant*. 20.134–6.

44 Tac. *Ann*. 4.47.3; cf. Alföldy 1968, 84f.; Cass. Dio 72.16.

Claudius dazu bewog, sollte im Rahmen des antiken Diskurses über die Belastungen des Militärdienstes gesehen werden. Bereits Livius beschreibt, wie der lange Dienst in der römischen Armee fern der Heimat schon im 2. Jh. v.Chr. zu schweren Belastungen führte.[45] Beschwerden darüber waren jedoch römischen Bürgern in den Mund gelegt. Bei Tacitus finden sich Stellen, in denen Provinziale ähnlich über den Dienst in den Auxiliareinheiten klagen. Insbesondere Stationierung fern der Heimat wird bitterlich beklagt. Diese Klagen finden sogar Eingang in die Passagen der topischen Romkritik[46]. Es liegt die Vermutung nahe, daß die Gesandtschaft der Caesarener mit eben diesen Argumenten arbeitete, wie wir sie bei Tacitus und Livius finden. Daß Claudius die Einheiten nicht versetzte, läßt sich vielleicht teilweise auf die Überzeugungskraft der Argumente über die Beschwerlichkeit des Dienstes in den Auxiliareinheiten fern des Rekrutierungsortes zurückführen.

Hätte Josephus im beginnenden 21. Jh. gelebt, hätte er vielleicht geschrieben: Es war tragische Ironie, daß ein an Humanität appellierender Diskurs über die Belastungen des Militärdienstes den „Ursprung des größten Leid für die Juden" schuf, als Claudius sich entgegen römischer Praxis entschied, die judenfeindlichen Einheiten der Caesarener und Sebastener nicht zu versetzen.[47]

Bibliographie

Alföldy, G., 1968: Die Hilfstrupppen der römischen Provinz Germania Inferior, Epigraphische Studien 6, Bonn.

Bilde, P., 1979: The causes of the Jewish War according to Josephus, JSJ 10, 179-202. 1988, Flavius Josephus between Jerusalem and Rome, Sheffield.

Bond, H.K., 1998: Pontius Pilate in History and Interpretation, Society for New Testament Studies, Monograph Series 100, Cambridge.

45 Liv. 42.33.3–34.15.

46 So etwa in der Rede des Calgacus Tac. *Agr.* 31f., und in *Ann.* 4.46.

47 Ein vielschichtiges Thema konnte hier nur angerissen werden. Fragen, ob z.B. die Terroraktionen der Sikarier zu einer Brutalisierung der Auxiliare gegenüber Zivilisten führten, da sie nicht mehr zwischen Zivilisten und Sikariern unterscheiden konnten, oder wie weit die Stationierung in den Städten, wie sie im Osten des römischen Reiches praktiziert wurde, zu einer Gemeinschaft zwischen Städtern und Soldaten führte, oder wie weit lokale Rekrutierung den ethnischen Charakter von Einheiten veränderte, würden die Fragestellung sinnvoll ergänzen, jedoch auch den Rahmen dieses Beitrags sprengen.

Callies, H., 1964: Die fremden Truppen im römischen Heer des Prinzipats und die sogenannten Nationalen Numeri. Beiträge zur Geschichte des römischen Heeres, Bericht der römisch-germanischen Kommision 45, 130–227.

Campbell, B., 2002: Power without Limits: "The Romans always win", in: Chaniotis, A./ Ducrey, P. (Hrsg.), Army and Power in the Ancient World, Stuttgart.

Cheesman, G. L., 1914: The Auxilia of the Roman Army, Oxford.

Feldman, L. H., 1993: Jew and Gentile in the Ancient World, Attitudes and Interactions from Alexander to Justinian, Princeton.

Demandt, A., 1999: Hände in Unschuld, Pontius Pilatus in der Geschichte, Köln.

Fischer, T., 2000: Die römische Armee als Wirtschaftsfaktor, in: Wamser, L., Römer zwischen Alpen und Nordmeer, zivilisatorisches Erbe einer europäischen Militärmacht, Mainz, 49-52.

Goodman, M. D., 1987: The Ruling Class of Judaea, Cambridge.

Habicht, C., 1974: Hellenismus und Judentum, Heidelberger Akademie der Wissenschaften, 97-110.

Hengel, M., 1988: The Zealots, Investigations into the Jewish Freedom Movement in the Period from Herod I Until 70 A.D, Edinburgh.

Holder, P. A., 1980: Studies in the Auxilia of the Roman Army, BAR International Series 70, Oxford.

Isaac, B., 1993: The Limits of Empire, 2. Auflage Oxford.

Jaroš, K., 2002: In Sachen Pontius Pilatus, Mainz.

Kakar, S., 1996: The Colors of Violence, Cultural Identities, Religion, and Conflict, Chicago.

Kasher, A., 1990: Jews and Hellenistic Cities in Eretz-Israel : Relations of the Jews in Eretz-Israel during the Second Temple Period (332 BCE-70 CE), Tübingen.

Le Bohec, Y., 1993: Die römische Armee. Von Augustus zu Konstantin d. Gr., Stuttgart

Mayer-Opificius, R. F. R., 2003: Pilgerreisen und Feste als Unruhefaktoren im Pälastina des ersten nachchristlichen Jahrhunderts, MARG 15.

Millar, F., 1993: The Emperor in the Roman World, 2. Auflage London.

McLaren, J. S., 1998: Turbulent Times, Josephus and Scholarship on Judaea in the First Century CE, JSPS 29, Sheffield.

Rajak, T., 1983: Josephus, the Historian and his Society, London.

Saddington, D. B., 1980: Prefects and Lesser Officers in the Auxilia at the Beginning of the Roman Empire, The Proceedings of the African Classical Associations 15, 20–58. 1982: The Development of the Roman Auxiliary Forces from Caesar to Vespasian (49 B.C.-A.D. 79.), Harare.

Schäfer, P., 1997: Judaeophobia, Attitudes towards the Jews in the Ancient World, Cambridge MA.

Schürer, E., 1973-86: The History of the Jewish People in the Age of Jesus Christ (175 B.C.-A.D. 135), G. Vermes, F. Millar et al. (Hrsg.), 3 Bde, überarbeitete Auflage Edinburgh.

Speidel, M.P., 1982: The Roman Army in Judaea under the procurators, The Italian and the Augustan cohort in the Acts of the Apostles, Ancient Society 13-14, 233-40.

Webster, G., 1998: Roman Imperial Army of the First and Second Century, 3. Auflage, Oklahoma.

Yavaetz, Z., 1997: Judenfeindschaft in der Antike: die Münchner Vorträge, München.

Die Platane von Gortyna

Helmut Naumann, Münster

Ich suche die Anfänge Europas. Die Historiker sind sich darüber einig, dass sie auf der Insel Kreta liegen, dem Verbindungsglied zwischen Afrika, Asien und Europa. Dort hat es in früher Zeit, nach dem Ende der Steinzeit, eine mächtige Herrschaft mit hoher Kultur gegeben, die man seit Arthur Evans die minoische nennt, weil sie mit dem Namen des sagenhaften Dynastiegründers Minos verbunden ist. Die Archäologen haben inzwischen mehrere minoische Paläste von großartiger Architektur und eine Vielzahl kunstvoller Fundstücke ausgegraben, so dass an der Höhe dieser Kultur im dritten und zweiten Jahrtausend vor Christus nicht zu zweifeln ist. Darüber allerdings, wie sich diese Herrschaft gebildet, wann und wo sie ihren Anfang gehabt hat, vermögen uns die Ausgrabungen keine Auskunft zu gehen. Im Allgemeinen gilt das heutige Knossos bei Heraklion als der Mittelpunkt und vermutliche Ursprungsort dieses Königtums; darauf konzentriert sich das Augenmerk.

Die Entstehung der minoischen Kultur fällt in die vorschriftliche Zeit, aus der es keine Urkunden und sonstige Aufzeichnungen gibt, die es dem Historiker erlaubten, die Geschichte dieser Jahrhunderte zu erkennen. Nur eine Vielzahl mündlich überlieferter Sagen hat sich erhalten, die man in ihrer Gesamtheit den Mythos nennt. Was sie von Göttern und Menschen erzählen, erscheint dem heutigen Menschen als sagenhaft, einerseits farbig und anschaulich und bemerkenswert, andererseits wenig glaubwürdig. Wir kennen die vom Mythos erzählten Zusammenhänge, die den König Minos zum Mittelpunkt haben, recht genau; die in ihnen bewahrten geschichtlichen Erinnerungen aus den Handlungen der Götter herauszuschälen, hat noch niemand unternommen. Das Handeln der Menschen und der Götter ist so eng miteinander verbunden, dass es sich kaum unterscheiden lässt und daher für den Heutigen, dem die Götter der Alten keine geglaubte Wirklichkeit sind, unbrauchbar erscheint.

Der Mythos enthält Spuren, die nicht anders als aus geschichtlicher Erinnerung der frühen Menschen verstanden werden können. Diese Spu-

ren wollen ernst genommen werden; sie sind imstande, unsere Erkenntnis anzuleiten und uns zu neuen Einsichten zu verhelfen.
Wenn wir den Mythos fragen, was er von den Anfängen der minoischen Kultur weiß, dann antwortet er, indem er von den Anfangen ihres Beginners, eben des Königs Minos, erzählt. Dessen Anfang erzählt er nun aber auf den Punkt genau, indem er berichtet, wie Minos gezeugt worden ist.

Die Sage ist seit der Antike bis heute allgemein bekannt, dass der Gott Zeus Stiergestalt angenommen habe, dass sich an der phönizischen Küste die Königstochter Europe auf seinen Rücken gesetzt habe und er darauf mit ihr durch das Meer geschwommen und in Kreta an Land gegangen sei. Dort sei er mit ihr zu einer immergrünen Platane bei Gortyna geeilt und habe in deren Schatten oder sogar in ihrem Geäst die Vereinigung mit Europe vollzogen; daraus seien drei Söhne Minos, Rhadamantys und Sarpedon entsprungen, die ein kretischer König namens Asterios für den entschwebenden Gott aufgezogen habe[1].

An dieser Geschichte ist eine Einzelheit von solch konkreter Diesseitigkeit, dass in ihr anderes als religiöse Phantasie gegenwärtig sein muss; das ist die Ortsangabe Gortyna mit der Erwähnung der immergrünen Platane. Merkwürdigerweise hat die Erinnerung der dort wohnenden Menschen diesen Baum bis heute nicht vergessen: Noch heute zeigt man in Gortyna die sagenumwobene Platane, die nach Jahrtausenden eine Nachfolgerin der ersten sein muss; noch heute ist sie ein Exemplar der seltenen immergrünen Art.

Was die Botanik über diese spezifisch kretische Variation lehrt, macht die Sage nicht unglaubwürdig. George Sfikas gibt über die Platane als Pflanze an:[2]

> 1. Platanis orientalis: Großer, seine Blätter verlierender Baum, mit einem dicken Stamm und ausladenden Ästen. (...) Vorkommen: Flussbänke. Bäche und kühle Plätze von der Küstenzone bis zur Gebirgszone. 2. Platanus orientalis - var cretica: Der gleiche Baum wie Nr. 1, jedoch immergrün. Seltenes Vorkommen an verschie denen Plätzen im Flachland. Diese Variante gibt es nur auf Kreta.

---

1 Karl Kerenyi, Die Mythologie der Griechen I: Die Götter- und Menschheitsgeschichten, München 16. Auflage 1994. S. 88.

2 George, Sfikas, Die wilden Blumen Kretas, aus dem Englischen von Birgit Kienast. Athen 1995, S. 95f.

Hellmut Baumann[3] zählt die Platane unter die heiligen Bäume:

> Die Platane nahm aber unter den heiligen Bäumen auch sonst eine Sonderstellung ein. Mit ihrem hellgrünen Laub verkündet der Baum dem durstigen Wanderer bereits aus der Ferne die nahende Quelle und den kühlenden Schatten. Ist es da verwunderlich, dass die Alten die Platane als ein Geschenk der Götter ansahen, dem sie Verehrung schuldig waren? Im gewundenen Tal des lydischen Mäander war einst sogar der grausame Perserkönig Xerxes von der Schönheit und Geborgenheit ausstrahlenden Erscheinung einer Platane derart geblendet, dass er sie mit goldenem Schmuck behängte und einen Krieger bei ihr zurückließ, um sie zu bewachen (Herodot 7.31).

Besonders die Platane von Gortyna gehört dazu:

> In direkter Beziehung zum Mythos der Entführung Europas durch Zeus steht die bereits bei Theophrast (1.9.5) erwähnte Platane beim kretischen Gortyn, die in Erinnerung an die im Schatten ihrer dichten Laubkrone vollzogene göttliche Hochzeit nie mehr ihre Blätter verlieren sollte. Tatsächlich sind auf Kreta bislang 29 Exemplare einer immergrünen Platanenart bekannt, bei der es sich um eine möglicherweise aufs Altertum zurückgehende Mutation dieses sonst laubabwerfenden Baumes handelt.

Trotz des hohen Alters, das Platanen erreichen,[4] dürfte der heute in Gortyna zu sehende Baum keine viertausend Jahre alt sein. Man hat aber offenbar das nachfolgende Exemplar stets wieder an die Stelle des Vorgängers gepflanzt, so dass der Standort als derselbe gelten darf: Dieser Standort ist nun allerdings aufschlussreich. Er liegt unweit dem Ufer des Baches, der in der Antike Lethaios hieß und heute Mitropolianos heißt, an der Stelle, wo der Bachlauf aus der Enge der Hügel heraustritt und das Tal erweitert. Auf dem Hügel am gegenüberliegenden Ufer, dem Agios Ioannis, errichtete man zum Schutze des heiligen Baumes zwischen dem 10. und dem 6. Jahrhundert v.Chr. eine Akropolis, auf der Funde aus der Zeit

3 Hellmut Baumann, Die griechische Pflanzenwelt in Mythos: Kunst und Literatur München. 3. Aufl. 1993. S. 46; Baumann zeigt in zwei Abbildungen die Platane im sommerlichen und im winterlichen Zustand, ebd. S. 49 Abb. 70 und 72.

4 Ebd. S. 48.

um 3000 v.Chr. die frühe Besiedelung erweisen.[5] Seinen Charakter als Heiligtum wahrte der Ort offenbar Jahrhunderte hindurch. Dass der erste Bischof von Kreta, der Begleiter des Apostels Paulus, Titus, in unmittelbarer Nachbarschaft eine Kirche errichtete und dass Gortyna zum Zentrum der Christianisierung Kretas wurde, kann diese Bedeutung bestätigen.[6] Wenn man seit alters die Gründung der Stadt Gortyna dem König Minos oder einem seiner Nachkommen zuschreibt,[7] dann besagt das, dass die Platane, in der Minos gezeugt wurde, vor der späteren Stadt da war. Dieser Baum ist das Älteste an dieser Stelle; die Stadtgründung erfolgte später. Dass dieser heilige Baum im Bewusstsein der Menschen eine herausragende Stelle einnahm, ist daraus zu entnehmen, dass in unmittelbarer Nähe und in sechs Kilometern Entfernung noch zum erweiterten Bezirk von Gortyna gehörig, ein Dorf den Namen Platanos trägt und dass dieses Dorf im Totenkult des Landes eine Rolle gespielt hat.[8]

---

5 Antonis Vassilakis, Phaistos, Gortyn, u.a, deutsch von Martin Kroch, Athen o.J., nach 1978. S. 22. Sonnabend erwähnt die Platane nicht (Holger Sonnabend, Artikel Gortyn, in: Der Neue Pauly, 1998, IV. Sp. 1159–1161).

6 Klaus Gallas, Kreta, Köln, 8. Aufl. 1995, S. 313. Wie Theophrast bezeugt, wurde in Gortyna eine Göttin Hellotis verehrt: „Auf Kreta als Baum- und Erdgöttin im hlg. Platanenhain von Gortyn (...) der Europa verschmolzen.“ Ihre Feste (Hellotia) wurden mit Pflanzen- und Feuersymbolik begangen (Wolfgang Fauth, Artikel Hellotis. Der kleine Pauly II, 1967, Sp. 1012f. Hellotis war der „Name einer mit Europe identifizierten Göttin in Kreta“ (Fritz Graf, Artikel Hellotis, in: Der neue Pauly V, Sp. 326f.).“ Auf Kreta – namentlich genannt ist Gortyn, das urspr. H(ellotis) hieß (...) – ist H(ellotis) auch Name eines großen Kranzes aus Myrtenzweigen, der in der Prozession der Helena mitgeführt wird und in dem sich angeblich die Gebeine der Europe befanden; wohl deswegen gilt H(ellotis) als alter Name der Europa (...)“ (Graf ebd.). Schon Wilamowitz wusste von einem Fest Hellotia in Gortyn: „Ob Europa sonst mit ihm etwas zu tun hatte, wissen wir nicht“ (Ulrich von Wilamowitz-Moellendorff, Der Glaube der Hellenen, 2. Aufl., Berlin 1955, I, 382–384; Beilage 4, „Hellotis“). Harder fasst neuerdings zusammen: „Kultisch verehrt wurde E(urope) in Gortyn auf Kreta als E(urope) Hellotis, wo ihr zu Ehren alljährlich die Hellotia gefeiert wurden (...). Die Münzen von Gortyn zeigen ab dem 5. Jh. wohl Europas Bild.“ (Ruth E. Harder, Artikel Europe (2), in: Der neue Pauly IV, Sp. 293f.).

7 Vassilakis, a.a.0., S. 34; Gallas, a.a.0., S. 296. Nach Sonnabend ist Gortyn eine vordorische Gründung; seine eigentliche Geschichte beginne aber mit der dorischen Landnahme im 7. Jahrhundert v.Chr. (a.a.0., Sp. 1159).

8 Dort wurden 1915 zwei Rundgräber entdeckt, wie sie auf Kreta seit etwa 2600 v.Chr. gebaut wurden. Das eine davon ist mit 13 m lichtem Durchmesser das größte Rundgrab der ganzen Insel und war im dritten Jahrtausend v.Chr. in Gebrauch. „Das von Osten zugängliche Grab bei Platanos war ein Familien- oder Sippengrab, das über Jahrhunderte

Als der Kreter Zeus, von Phönizien kommend, in Matala an Land stieg und auf die Platane (beim späteren Gortyna) zueilte, kannte er diesen Baum und wählte ihn für seinen hieros gamos aus. Wahrscheinlich war die Platane das Heiligtum einer Fruchtbarkeitsgottheit; die drei Söhne des Gottes, die er dort zeugte, waren die Folge seiner Wahl.[9]

Gortyna liegt fünfzehn Kilometer von der Südküste entfernt. Die Vorstellung, dass Europe diese Strecke auf dem Rücken eines Stieres zurückgelegt haben sollte, war schon der Antike schwer nachvollziehbar; so erfand man die Version, der Gott habe sich in einen Adler verwandelt. Dieser Ausweg kann nur bestätigen, dass man von der Platane bei Gortyna nicht abzugehen gedachte. Auf diesen Schauplatz konnte man nicht verzichten: Dort ist die minoische Dynastie durch den kretischen Gott gezeugt worden. Dort hat Europas Kultur begonnen.

Diese Ereignisse, an die sich der Mythos erinnerte, sind ins dritte vorchristliche Jahrtausend zu datieren. Die Einwohner von Gortyna haben Jahrhunderte hindurch die besondere Bedeutung ihres Ortes nicht vergessen. Als sie nach 600 v.Chr. als erste Stadt Kretas – noch vor Knossos – Münzen zu prägen begannen und auf diesen Prägungen das zum Ausdruck brachten, was sie von sich selbst wussten, haben sie selbstverständlich die auf dem Stier reitende Europe auf der Vorderseite abgebildet.[10] Da der Stier in dieser Szene den Gott Zeus verkörperte, zeigen diese frühen Münzen auf dem Revers etwas anderes, nämlich den Kopf eines Löwen[11]. Nachdem spätere Münzen auf der Vorderseite nur noch Europe

---

hinweg ununterbrochen, bis ca. 2000 v.Chr. benutzt wurde; ja, das selbst um 1700 v.Chr. nochmals für kurze Zeit Tote aufnahm." (Gallas, a.a.O., S. 347f.).

9 Bis in unsere Zeit hat sich der Volksglaube erhalten, dass Frauen, die ein Blatt dieser Platane pflücken, drei Söhne gebären werden. Es kann dies ein Glaube sein, der auf die Sage von Zeus und Europa zurückgeht; es ist jedoch nicht auszuschließen, dass dem eine noch ältere Überzeugung voraufgeht.

10 Jean-N. Svoronos, Numismatique de la Crète Ancienne, Macon 1890 (Nachdruck Bonn 1972), S. 158–160, Nr. I-II. 24f. und Tafel XII Abb. 21–26. 34 und 35. Die Münzen von Gortyna werden immer wieder genannt und als Zeugnisse herangezogen; gründlich betrachtet hat sie, soviel ich sehe, bisher noch keiner - Die frühesten Darstellungen des Europe-Mythos in der antiken Kunst, die bisher bekannt sind, sind eine Metope des ältesten Tempels in Selinunt (Palermo, Museum), eine Metope vom Schatzhaus der Sikyoner in Delphi (Delphi, Museum) und eine Vasenmalerei auf einer attischen Amphora (Rom, Vatikan); die Metopen werden um 550 v.Chr. datiert, die Amphora ins 6. Jahrhundert v.Chr. (Herbert Hunger, Lexikon der Griechischen und Römischen Mythologie, Reinbek 1980, S. 133.) Die ältesten gortynischen Münzprägungen sind von vergleichbarem Alter.

11 Dieser formelhaft in ein Quadrat einbeschriebene Löwenkopf bedarf der Deutung.

allein abbildeten, wurden die Rückseiten lange Zeit vom Bild eines Stieres oder eines Stierkopfes beherrscht.[12] Man muss sich dessen bewusst sein, dass dieser Stier das Bild eines Gottes ist, dass also Zeus in Gortyna lange Zeit hindurch seinen Charakter als Stiergott gewahrt hat, bis er später anthropomorph als Kopf eines bärtigen Mannes erscheint.[13] Wenn zuletzt Zeus zweimal auf einer Münze erscheint, einmal als Kopf des Gottes und dann auf der Kehrseite nochmals als der Stier, auf dem Europe sitzt, dann ist die Vorstellung vom Stiergott dabei zu verblassen.[14]

Es ist nun in hohem Grade aufschlussreich, in welcher Situation Europe dargestellt wird, wenn sie nicht mehr auf dem Stier reitet: Sie sitzt in einem Baum.[15] Dieser Baum ist nichts anderes als die Platane, in der Zeus sie gefreit hat.[16] Wenn eine Version der Sage erzählte, dass der Gott die Gestalt eines Adlers angenommen habe, so kennen die Münzen von Gortyna auch dies. Auf einigen Prägungen sitzt der Vogel neben ihr im Baum[17], auf anderen bedrängt er sie heftig.[18] Man hat in Gortyna die Sagen von Zeus bis in die hellenistische Zeit hinein sehr genau gekannt und auf den von der Stadt geprägten Münzen wiedergegeben; denn sie begründeten den Ruf und den beanspruchten Rang dieser Stadt. Eines muss dabei festgehalten werden: Auf den gortynischen Münzen ist keine Spur vom Minotauros zu entdecken; dieses Motiv ist allein den Münzen von Knossos vorbehalten.

Wenn man die Münzprägungen als Dokumente des Mythos versteht, in denen die Bewohner eines Ortes das darstellen, was sie von sich selbst und ihrer Herkunft wissen, dann beginnen diese Bilder zu erzählen und über sonst unbekannte Zusammenhänge Auskunft zu geben.

---

12 Svoronos, a.a.O., S. 161–171, Nr. 26–106 und Tafel XIII Abb. 1–25. XIV Abb. 1–21, XV Abb. 1–18.

13 Ebd., S. 172, Nr. 113–131, 143–154, 156–177 und Tafel XV Abb. 21–28, XVI Abb. 8–12. 14–21.

14 Ebd., S. 177–174, Nr. 114–117, 120–127 und Tafel XV Abb. 22. 23, 26–28.

15 Ebd., S. 161–171, Nr. 26–31. 34–36. 51–53. 54–72. 75–78. 81–86, 98–106 und Tafel XIII, Abb. 1–5. 8–10. 22–25, XIV Abb. 1–19, XV Abb. 1–2. 5–8. 15–18.

16 So auch Baumann, a.a.0., S. 47, Abb. 68; Wilamowitz sieht in diesem Baum keine Platane (a.a.O., S. 124); „Die Göttin auf einem Baume (keiner Platane), die auf schönen Münzen von Gortyn erscheint, wird den Baumkult fortsetzen, so freilich, dass die hellenische Waise die in dem Baume lebende Gottheit als Nymphe fasst, selbst wenn man sie damals Europa genannt haben mag, was den Mythos ihrer Einführung durch den Gott in Stiergestalt voraussetzt."

17 Svoronos, a.a.0., S. 166–171, Nr. 69–71. 104f., Tafel XIV Abb. 16–18, XV Abb. 18.

18 Ebd., S. 167, Nr. 72. 76–78, 81–84, Tafel XIV Abb. 19, XV Abb. 1, 2, 5–7.

Der kultische Bezirk um die heilige Platane von Gortyna muss eine weite Ausdehnung gehabt haben, wie schon der Dorfname Platanos bezeugt. Auch der benachbarte Ort Phaistos muss in der Frühzeit einmal dazugehört haben. Eine frühe Münzprägung aus Phaistos ist auf Vorderseite und Revers vom selben Typ wie eine gortynische Münze:[19] Sie zeigt die auf dem Stier reitende Europe. Der gemeinsame Münzherr hat den gleichen Typ verwandt, aber die beiden Orte unterschieden und jeden für sich genannt. Eine weitere Prägung aus Phaistos stellt die dem Stier entgegensehende Europe dar.[20] Diese Szene der Begegnung des Mädchens mit dem Gott kehrt sonst niemals wieder. Auf zahlreichen Rückseiten seiner Münzen verwendet Phaistos den Stier als Kopf oder in ganzer Gestalt;[21] es folgt also der Nachbarstadt, wenn es Zeus als Stiergott beibehält.

In anderer Hinsicht geht Phaistos allerdings eigene Wege, so in der Verwendung des Talos[22], des Hermes[23], des Velchanos[24] und des Herak-

---

19 Ebd., S. 254, Nr. 1 und Tafel XXII, Abb. 34. Vgl. S. 158, Nr. 1 und Tafel XII Abb. 21. Beide Münzen zeigen auf der Vorderseite Europa auf dem Stier, die gortynische nach rechts, die phaistische nach links reitend. Das Revers hat beidemal den in ein Quadrat eingepassten Löwenkopf, der beidemal von einer ähnlich lautenden Umschrift umgeben ist. In Gortyna lautet sie - nach der Lesung von Svoronos S. 158 - gut lesbar, wenn auch in archaischer Schrift: Γόρτυνς το φαῖμα; auf der Münze aus Phaistos steht, weniger gut erhalten, doch deutlich erkennbar - wiederum nach der Lesung von Svoronos S. 154 - φαιστίων το φαῖμα. - Die Umschrift gibt Fragen auf. Die Wörterbücher weisen ein Nomen φαῖμα nicht aus; das Wort mir dem Suffix m dürfte untergegangen sein. Wahrscheinlich ist es als Verbaladjektiv an den Stamm φαει(νω) oder φαι(νω) ‚leuchten, glänzen' anzuschließen, so dass die Bedeutung sein könnte: ‚Gortynos (Phaistos) das leuchtende'. Von dem Adjektiv φαίμα lässt sich der Name Φαιστός als Superlativbildung verstehen, was den Ort sprachlich besonders herausheben könnte (Eduard Bornemann/Ernst Risch, Griechische Grammatik, Frankfurt am Main, 2. Auflage, 1978, S. 55 und S. 601.

20 Sovronos, a.a.0., S. 254f., Nr. 2 und Tafel XXII, Abb. 35. Die Münze trägt die schwer lesbare Inschrift φαιστιο in archaischer Schrift (so Sovronos S. 254).

21 Ebd., S. 255–265, Nr. 1. 6–73. 76f. und Tafel XXIII, Abb. 1. 3–19. 21–26. XXIV Abb. 1–10. 12–17. 19–24, XXV Abb. 1.

22 Ebd., S. 255, Nr. 4–6, S. 264f., Nr. 67–75 und Tafel XXIII, Abb. 2 und 3. XXIV Abb. 24–26.

23 Ebd., S. 754f., Nr. 7 und Tafel XXII, Abb. 35–37.

24 Ebd., S. 259, Nr. 79–31 und Tafel XXIII, Abb. 24–26. Die Münzen tragen in archaischer Schrift (mit erhaltenem Digamma) den Namen Vελχανος, was Sovronos als „Zeus Felchanos", Vassilakis (a.a.O., S. 651 als „Zeus Belchanos" liest. Gerhard Radke (Artikel Velchans in: Der kleine Pauly V, Sp. 1155f. nimmt ebenfalls einen kretischen Zeus Velchanos

les[25] als Münzbild. Ein Kopf des anthropomorphen Zeus findet sich auf Münzen aus Phaistos niemals, auch kein Minotauros. Nach anfänglicher Gemeinsamkeit mit dem Nachbarort Gortyna hat Phaistos seinen eigenen Münztyp gewählt und sich vor allem durch Herakles repräsentiert gesehen.

Mit den Prägungen in Gortyna und Phaistos sind die in Knossos zu vergleichen. Die Abfolge der Münzen zeigt deutlich, wie ein ursprünglich kretisch-knossisches Münzbild von anderen, z.T. fremdbestimmten abgelöst und überlagert worden ist. Das deutlichste Beispiel dafür ist die römische Fremdherrschaft seit der augusteischen Zeit, die nur noch Römerköpfe auf die Münzen prägt und jede Erinnerung an die heimische Überlieferung tilgt.[26] Die ersten Prägungen enthalten die Bilder, die als ursprünglich knossisch zu gelten haben: den Minotauros im Knielauf und auf dem Revers das Labyrinth[27]. Auf einer dieser Münzen erscheint auch der abgekürzte Ortsname KNOS(ION)[28]. Diese Münzen sind nach 600 v.Chr. geprägt worden: sie bewahren eine Erinnerung, die mindestens tausend Jahre alt ist. Das Wissen vom Minotauros gehört zum überlieferten Selbstbewußtsein dieser Stadt.

Erstaunlich ist, dass man das von Theseus erschlagene Ungeheuer auf die Vorderseite einer Münze setzt. Dort gehört nach dem, was bei den frühen Münzprägungen üblich ist, das Bild eines Gottes hin. Diese Tatsache zwingt zu der Annahme, dass der Minotauros für die Knosier kein Ungeheuer, sondern eine Gottheit war; ihre Tradition sah dieses Wesen - anders als die athenische Überlieferung, die dominant geworden ist - posi-

---

an; Dietrich Wachsmuth (Artikel *Zeus*, ebd., Sp.1516– 1525, dort 1520, Zeile 28) spricht im Unterschied zum indogermanisch-griechischen patriarchalischen Zeus Pater von dem „ganz heterogenen, weil matriarchal(ischem) Kontext zugehörenden ‚kretischen' Z(eus) Velchanos, Diktaios, Kretagenes". Wilamowitz spricht vom „Jungmann" Zeus, der kein Kind mehr ist und „als Zeus Velchanos auf gortynischen Münzen erscheint" (Wilamowitz a.a.0., I. 130). Auf gortynischen Münzen erscheint Velchanos nicht, sondern auf phaistischen; ob der auf einem Baumstamm sitzende, einen Hahn in der Hand haltende junge Mann als Erscheinungsform des Zeus aufzufassen ist, bezweifle ich. Auf den Prägungen aus Phaistos begegnet Zeus niemals anthropomorph; stattdessen ist auf dem Revers der drei Münzen der Gott jedesmal in Stiergestalt präsent. Diese Figur ist uns eben so rätselhaft wie Wilamowitz (ebd. S. 170 Anm. I).

25 Ebd., S. 256–263, Nr. 3–28. 32–44. 46–66 und Tafel XXIII, Abb. 5.

26 Ebd., S. 91–95, Nr. 192 - 217 und Tafel VIII, Abb. 17–27.

27 Ebd., S. 65–67, Nr. 1–12 und Tafel IV, Abb. 23–32, auch S. 364, Nr. 13 und 14 und Tafel Addenda II, Abb. 13 und 14.

28 Ebd., S. 65, Nr. 4 und Tafel IV, Abb. 25.

tiv, und zwar als den Gott Asterios[29]. Das ist auch der Grund dafür, dass die frühen Münzen in die Mitte des Labyrinthes einen Stern setzen[30] oder dass ein Stern im einrahmenden Quadrat überhaupt den Inhalt der Rückseite bildet.[31] Eine Münze ersetzt den Stern durch den Kopf eines bartlosen Heros im Mäanderquadrat, der aber kaum als Theseus oder Apollon bestimmt werden dürfte.[32] Nach diesen - offenbar frühen - Prägungen kommt der Minotauros als Stiermensch nicht mehr vor, wohl aber ein Stierkopf von vorn im Mäanderquadrat[33]. Der Stern kommt noch wiederholt vor;[34] später werden aus dem Stern fünf Punkte an dieser Stelle,[35] bis er schließlich wegfällt.[36] Das Labyrinth als solches aber bleibt als Revers-Bild, während die Vorderseite der Münze von weiblichen Köpfen besetzt wird, die den Minotauros ablösen.[37]

Das Labyrinth erscheint in vier verschiedenen Gestalten, von denen eine, nämlich die runde[38], als einmalige Ausnahme gelten muss und nicht repräsentativ sein kann. Das ist deshalb wichtig, weil dieses Bild offenbar als Grundriss eines Bauwerkes aufgefasst worden ist, wie es der Mythos von Daidalos ja auch erzählt. Die auf den Münzen zunächst vorkommende Form geht von einem Quadrat aus. Die nur einmal bezeugte Gestalt

---

29 Hans von Geisau, Artikel Asterion, in: Der kleine Pauly I, Sp. 658; Fritz Graf, Artikel Asterion, in: Der neue Pauly II, Sp. 118, vgl. S. 130, Anm. 29.

30 Svoronos, a.a.0., S. 65, Nr. 3 und 4 und Tafel IV, Abb. 24 und 25.

31 Ebd., S. 66, Nr.5–10 und Tafel IV, Abb. 26–30.

32 So Svoronos, S. 66 zu Nr. 11 und Tafel IV, Abb. 31. Eher hat man einen weiblichen Kopf zu denken, wie er in der Prägung Nr. 13 – ebenfalls im Mäanderquadrat – erscheint. (In dieser Gestalt will Svoronos Ariadne erkennen).

33 Ebd., S. 67, Nr. 16 und Tafel V, Abb. 1 und S. 365, Nr. 16 und Tafel Addenda 11, Abb. 16. Diesem Revers ist die Ortsbezeichnung KNOSI bzw. KNOSION beigegeben, die die Münze eindeutig als knossisch ausweist.

34 So in Nr. 20–24. 26–28 (=Tafel V, Abb. 3–8, dann noch Nr. 129–132 (=Tafel VII, Abb. 15–17).

35 Ebd., Nr. 37–39. 42. 45. 46 (=Tafel V, Abb. 12–16. 18).

36 Ebd., Nr. 34.

37 Svoronos vermutet darin außer Ariadne auch Persephone und Demeter; das ist nach Kopfschmuck und Haartracht kaum zu entscheiden, vor allem, da die Kränze auf den Münzen durchweg abgegriffen sind.

38 Ebd., Nr. 96 und Tafel VI, Abb. 18. Dass eine Neigung, sich das Labyrinth rund zu denken, auch andernorts bestand, zeigt die Zeichnung auf dem etruskischen Weinkrug von Tragliatella, ugf. 600 v. Chr. (John Kraft, The Cretan Labyrinth and the Walls of Troy. An analysis of Roman Labyrinth designs, Opuscula romana XV, Stockholm 1985, 79–86, dort S. 86, Abb. 13).

des in vier Viertel unterteilten Quadrates scheint das ursprüngliche zu sein.[39] Die Viertel sind jedes für sich mit Mäander ausgefüllt; dieses Motiv ist auch beim nächsten Typus beherrschend. Dessen Gestalt geht von 3 x 3 = 9 Feldern aus, deren vier Eckfelder vertieft werden[40] oder leer bleiben.[41] Die ans Mittelfeld angrenzenden Felder, die mit ihm zusammen ein Kreuz bilden, werden dann mit Mäander gefüllt. Es entsteht so ein swastika ähnliches Gebilde.[42] Dieser dritte Typus wird eines Tages durch eine neue Gestalt abgelöst, von der wir aus einem Linear-B Täfelchen aus Pylos wissen, dass sie schon um 1250 v.Chr. bekannt war,[43] die also aus unbekannten Gründen erst später übernommen worden ist. Die seitdem vorherrschende Form ist wiederum das Quadrat, dessen ganzes Innenfeld jetzt mit bis zu fünf umlaufenden Gängen angefüllt ist, zu denen meist oben, mitunter auch unten, ein Eingang den Zutritt ermöglicht.[44]

Der erste Typus des Quadrates war ein Muster an Übersichtlichkeit; wenn es den Grundriss eines Bauwerkes wiedergibt, so war dieses ein regelmäßig angelegter Bau mit vier Räumen, später dann mit einem Zent-

---

39 Svnronos, S. 364, Nr. 13 und Tafel Addenda 11, Abb. 13.

40 Ebd., S. 65, Nr. 1. 3. 4, S. 70, Nr. 39–43, S. 364 Nr. 14 und Tafel IV, Abb. 23–25. Tafel V, Abb. 15–18. 20 und Tafel Addenda 11, Abb. 14.

41 Ebd., S. 67, Nr. 12 und Tafel IV, Abb. 32. Auf der Münze S. 365, Nr. 18 und Tafel Addenda 11, Abb. 18 sind die vier Eckfelder mit einem Stern ausgefüllt.

42 Ebd., S. 68–72, Nr. 19–42. 43f., 51–55. 58 und Tafel V, Abb. 2–18. 20. 21. 23–25. 27; S. 365, Nr. 17 und Tafel Addenda 11, Abb. 17. Mehrfach ist in der Mitte des Kreuzes ein Stern abgebildet und in den leeren Winkeln ein Halbmond. In Abb. IV, 74 ist in den vier Flügelräumen ebenfalls ein Stern eingezeichnet; das könnte andeuten, dass der Asterios-Kult auch dort Räume hatte.

43 Abbildung bei Günther Kehnscherper, Kreta – Mykene – Santorin, 5. Auflage, Leipzig 1982. S. 17.

44 Svoronos, S. 71, Nr. 47f., 61–74. 88–93. 97–103. 105, 106–132. 174–179. 185f. 188; S. 365, Nr. 19 und Tafel V, Abb. 19 und 22; Tafel VI, Abb. 1–9. 15–17. 19–25. 27; Tafel VII, Abb. 1–17; Tafel VIII, Abb. 1. 2. 4. 5–7. 13. 14; Tafel XXXI, Abb. 25f.; Tafel Addenda 11, Abb. 19. - Bemerkenswert ist, dass eine Münze mir einem Frauenkopf auf der Vorderseite offenbar den Übergang kennzeichnet, weil sie auf dem Revers zweimal das alte Labyrinth zeigt (Svoronos, S. 71, Nr. 43 und 44 und Tafel V, Abb. 20 und 21) und zweimal das neue (ebd., Nr. 47 und 48 und Tafel V, Abb. 19 und 22). Die letzte Prägung enthält zu Seiten des Labyrinthes eine Pfeilspitze und ein in der Scheide steckendes Schwert; in der Mitte der Irrgänge zeigt sie ein kleines Gebilde, das Svoronos als K liest (ebd., S. 71, Nr. 48 und Tafel V, Abb. 22, in dem Traeger dagegen einen Stierkopf erkennt (a.a.O., S. 26, Typ C). Nach Traeger ist dieser Übergang ins Ende des 4. Jahrhunderts v.Chr. zu setzen; der Grund dafür ist bisher nicht bekannt.

ralraum und vier Flügeln, in dessen Mitte der Gott Asterion verehrt wurde. Um ihn zu betreten und zu verlassen, brauchte man keinen Ariadnefaden. Das Mäandermotiv in den vier Flügeln ändert daran nichts; es weckt nur den Eindruck, als wenn der Zugang zum Mittelraum durch gewisse Umwege verlängert worden sei. Unentrinnbar war dieses Labyrinth nur für diejenigen, die als Opfer hineingeführt wurden.

In den späteren Prägungen wird das Mäander zum reinen Schmuckmotiv.[45] Die Linien sind so verbunden, dass von den vier Flügeln her kein Zugang zum Mittelraum mehr offen ist; der ist von außen her unzugänglich.[46] Wenn wir heute mit dem Begriff des Labyrinthischen die Vorstellung des Verwirrenden und Unentrinnbaren verbinden, so entspricht der letzte Typus auf den Münzen dem um einiges mehr. In ihm gibt es nur noch einen verlängerten Zugang zum Raum in der Mitte; er ist durch mehrere Um- und Rückläufe mit zahlreichen für den Eintretenden nicht überschaubaren Ecken gestreckt worden; das Problem für den sich darin Bewegenden besteht darin, dass er Hin- und Rückweg nicht verwechselt und wieder hinausfindet. Der innerste Raum in der Mitte wird bei diesen Darstellungen kaum noch ausgespart und hervorgehoben;[47] das Ganze wird ein Weg ohne Ziel, an dessen Ende man nur noch in anderen Gängen zurückkehren kann. Zu welchem Zweck jemand diesen langen Gang betritt und durchläuft, ist schwer einzusehen; nichts erinnert mehr an den Minotauros = Asterios. In dieser Form war das oft mit der Beschriftung KNOSION gekennzeichnete Quadrat bis in die Römerzeit das Wahrzeichen von Knossos und galt den Zeitgenossen draußen in der Welt als das „Labyrinth".[48]

Der neue Typus des Labyrinthes ist zum Charakteristikum von Knossos geworden und hat die Rückseiten seiner Münzen bis in die Römerzeit

---

45 Über die symbolische Bedeutung des Mäanders vgl. Kerényi, Dionysos S. 69–73. In Nr. 11 (Tafel IV, Abb. 31) umgab das Mäander den Götterkopf in der Mitte: in Nr. 7 (Tafel IV Abb. 27) war es noch ein Stabornament gewesen.

46 So in Nr. 19. 20. 25. 26 und den folgenden (Tafel V Abb. 2. 3. 5. 6).

47 Nur in Nr. 61. 63. 64 und 65 (Tafel VI, Abb. 1–6). Die beiden letzten füllen den Innenraum mit einem Stern.

48 So um 1700 v. Chr. dem Schreiber des Linear-B-Täfelchens in Pylos auf dem Peleponnes, dem Zeichner des Graffitos im Hause des Lucretius in Pompeji (Kraft a.a.0., S. 86, Abb. 14) oder dem Mosaik in Hippo Regius um 150–200 v. Chr. (Kraft a.a.0., S. 80, Abb. 2). Vgl. Hans von Geisau, Artikel Labyrinthos, in: Der kleine Pauly, Band III, Sp. 433–435, dort 433, Zeile 18–38.

gekennzeichnet.[49] Wenn auf das letzte Vorkommen des Labyrinthes auf einer Münze des Augustus eine neue Prägung desselben Münzherrn folgt, auf deren Revers die eine Nike tragende Stadtgöttin Roma an diese Stelle getreten ist, so zeigt das anschaulich, wie die Autonomie von Knossos durch die siegreichen Römer beendet worden ist.[50]

Schon vor den Römern haben auswärtige Mächte auf die Gestaltung der Münzen von Knossos Einfluss genommen und ihnen ihren Stempel aufgeprägt, so die Athener. Die Tetradrachmen, die auf der Vorderseite den Kopf der Athene und auf dem Revers die ihr heilige Eule zeigen, die auf einer umgestürzten Amphore neben dem an den Rand gedrängten Labyrinth sitzt, sprechen eine deutliche Sprache.[51] Eine Gruppe von Münzprägungen zeigt den Einfluss der mit Knossos rivalisierenden Stadt Gortyna: Das Motiv der auf dem Stier reitenden Europe[52] ist dort beheimatet und auf Münzen bezeugt;[53] es hat ursprünglich mit Knossos nichts zu tun. Wahrscheinlich hat Gortyna seine Vorherrschaft während des mit Knossos geführten Krieges (um 220 v.Chr.) zu dieser Prägung benutzt.

* * *

Auf den Münzen von Gortyna ist nichts vom Minotauros und vom Labyrinth zu finden; diese Kennzeichen gehören allein Knossos an. Umgekehrt findet sich auf den knossischen Münzen niemals der Stiergott Zeus als

---

49 Eine Ausnahme bildet eine Periode, die erst den Adler des Zeus mit aufgespannten Flügeln und später den Köcher der Artemis an diese Stellt setzt; Svoronos, S. 82–86, Nr. 133–167, dann Nr. 167–172 und Tafel VII, Abb. 18–23 und 24–28.

50 Ebd., S. 90, Nr. 188. (Traeger gibt S. 31 an, das Labyrinth finde sich noch bis zur Zeit des Kaisers Nero; nach Svoronos ist das letzte unter Augustus festzustellen.) Augustus machte die Stadt zur Kolonie seiner Veteranen. Bei voraufgehenden Prägungen setzten die Römer einen Pflug auf die Vorderseite der Münze (ebd., Nr. 185 und 186) und duldeten das Labyrinth noch; doch damit ging es zu Ende.

51 Svoronos, S. 88, Nr. 174 und Tafel VIII, Abb. 1; Traeger ordnet diese Prägung als Typ H ein und datiert sie auf etwa 85 vor Christus (a.a.O., S. 32f.). Auch Kydonia (Svoronos, S. 109 und 110, Nr. 77–79 und Tafel X, Abb. 10 und 11). Gortyna (ebd., S. 179f., Nr. 181–186 und Tafel XVI, Abb. 23–25). Polyrhenion (ebd., S. 282f., Nr. 46 und Tafel XXVI, Abb. 25) und Priansos (ebd., S. 298, Nr. 26 und Tafel XXIX, Abb. 5) kennen diesen Münztyp.

52 Ebd., S. 80f., Nr. 117–125 und Tafel VII, Abb. 8–14.

53 Ebd., S. 158–160, Nr. 1–14. 24. 25 und Tafel XII, Abb. 21–27. 34. 35.

Revers.[54] Wenn Zeus dargestellt wird, dann anthropomorph als thronender Herrscher[55] oder später als bärtiger Kopf.[56] Während der Thronende möglicherweise an König Minos erinnert und damit eine direkt auf Knossos bezogene Überlieferung wahrt, scheint der Zeus-Kopf ein Zeichen dafür zu sein, dass in Kreta allgemeinere griechische Auffassungen um sich greifen. Ursprünglich hat in Knossos Zeus nicht im Vordergrund gestanden; er gehört nicht zum engeren Kreis der Motive, die diese Stadt auf ihre Münzen setzte.

Die Münzen entsprechen damit dem Mythos, der erzählt, das Daidalos im Auftrage des Minos das Labyrinth in Knossos zur Unterbringung des Minotauros errichtet habe.[57] Das bedeutet, dass Minos, der in Gortyna, dem Vorort des kretischen Südens, geboren sein soll,[58] einen großen Bauauftrag in den Norden Kretas erteilt und dort ein neues Heiligtum für den Gott Asterion gegründet hat. Sicher ist der König vom Süden der Insel in den Norden gezogen und hat in der Nähe seiner Stiftung gewohnt. Ob der Labyrinthos den Palast des Königs umfasste oder in der Nachbarschaft lag, ist nicht entscheidend; wichtig ist die Verlagerung seines Herrschaftsmittelpunktes.

Gleichzeitig mit der Erbauung des Labyrinths wurde die für Kreta neue Göttergestalt des Minotauros kreiert. Minos hatte aus Gortyna den Glauben an den theriomorphen Stiergott Zeus mitgebracht, der dort auch später noch Jahrhunderte lang die Münzbilder beherrschte. In Knossos schuf er auf dem Wege zu einem anthropomorphen Gott die Mischgestalt

54 Der Stierkopf im Mäanderquadrat kann ebenso den Minotauros bedeuten: ebd., S. 365, Nr. 16 und Tafel Addenda 11, Abb. 16.

55 Tafel IV, Abb. 33–35, ebd., S. 67, Nr. 13–15. Die Münze Nr. 14 trägt die Aufschrift MINOS, so dass Svoronos in dem Thronenden den König Minos erkennt. Das kann ebenso für die beiden anderen Münzen gelten. Den auf dem Labyrinth Sitzenden, der in der Rechten eine Nike trägt, spricht Svoronos ebenfalls als Minos an (ebd., S. 76 Nr. 88 und Tafel VI, Abb. 15).

56 Ebd., S. 77f., Nr. 97–101 und Tafel VI, Abb. 19–23. In diesen Köpfen sieht Svoronos Zeus oder Minos. Der gehörnte Kopf auf der Münze Nr. 102 (Abb. 24) ist als Zeus Ammon anzusprechen. Auf den Münzen Nr. 105f. (=Tafel VII, Abb. 27 und VII, Abb. 1). 109–116 (=Tafel VII, Abb. 4–7), Nr. 133–166 (=Tafel VII, Abb. 18–23) ist der Kopf des Zeus dargestellt, auf den letzten mit dem Adler auf dem Revers. Auf den Münzen Nr. 177–179 (=Tafel VIII, Abb. 4 und 5) hat dieser bärtige Kopf noch einmal das Labyrinth auf dem Revers; Svoronos (S. 88) sieht darin eher den König Minos als Zeus.

57 Daidalos war noch mit einem zweiten Auftrage in Knossos tätig; Er baute den Tanzplatz der Ariadne, wie Homer berichtet (Ilias 18. 590).

58 Vassilakis, a.a.0., S. 33.

des Menschenkörpers mit Tierkopf, die er Asterios nannte. Der Architekt Daidalos soll für seinen Bau ein ägyptisches Vorbild gehabt haben;[59] auch für den Stiermenschen sind ägyptische Götter wie Horus, Anubis, Hathor beispielhaft gewesen.[60] Außerdem ist phönizischer Einfluss anzunehmen; die phönizischen Götter Baal und Moloch wurden stierköpfig dargestellt.[61] Von Baal und dem ihm verwandten Moloch sind dem Minotauros die Menschenopfer zugekommen, die seinen Kult kennzeichnen.[62]

Minos hatte aus Gortyna sicherlich einen richtigen Stier nach Knossos mitgebracht, der dort im Mittelpunkt der Stierspiele stand und auf einem Fresco im Palast abgebildet wurde. In der künstlerischen Gestaltung wählte man den Stierkopf mit Menschenkörper, wie ihn ein in Phaistos gefundener Siegelstein aus der Zeit nach 1500 v.Chr. zeigt.[63] Den Götternamen Asterion nahmen die Griechen nicht an; ihre Bezeichnung war - bewusst ungläubig und abwertend - Mino-Tauros = ‚Stier des Minos'. Das war kein Name, sondern eine Kennzeichnung,[64] die den Kern des Phänomens traf. In den Augen der Griechen war dieses Wesen ein Ungeheuer, so wie es Plutarch später kennzeichnet,[65] und Minos der Despot, der Für diesen Pseudogott die Menschenopfer eintrieb. Die Athener vergaßen das nicht.

Nachdem in der Nähe der heiligen Platane die Stadt Gortyna gegründet worden war, und zwar möglicherweise durch Minos selbst, schickte sich dieser Ort am Rande der Messara-Ebene an, zum Vorort Südkretas, ja

59 Vgl. ebd., S. 108.

60 Heinz Mode, Fabeltiere und Dämonen, Die phantastische Welt der Mischwesen, Leipzig 1973, 3. Auflage, 1983, S. 56–58.

61 Ebd., S. 251 und 259. In Mesopotamien gab es im dritten Jahrtausend v.Chr. Ebenfalls einen Stiermenschen: im Gilgameš-Epos hat der Held einen Gefährten Enkidu, der als Stiermensch dargestellt wurde (Mode S. 34f. und 254).

62 Die Jahwe-gläubigen Israeliten eifern gegen die Brandopfer für Baal und Moloch (2. Kön. 13, 10; 2. Chron. 33, 3–6; Jer. 19, 5 und 32, 35). Dazu Herbert Haag, Artikel Baal, in: Herbert Haag (Hrsg), Bibel-Lexikon, 2. Auflage 1968, Sp.157; Walter Kornfeld, Artikel Moloch, in: ebd., Sp. 1163; M. J. Muider, Artikel Baal, III, in: Theologisches Wörterbuch zum Alten Testament I, Stuttgart 1973, Sp. 718–727, dort 723f.

63 Hans-Günter Buchholtz/Vassos Karageorghis, Altägäis und Altkypros, Tübingen 1971, S. 116 und 392, Nr. 1401. Vgl. das kretische Siegel bei Mode, a.a.0., S. 50.

64 Wilamowitz, a.a.0., I, 110.

65 Plutarch kennzeichnet in seiner Theseus-Biographie (15) den Minotauros unter Berufung auf Euripides: „Der Minotauros soll, wie Euripides sagt, ‚ein missgestaltetes Tier, gemischt aus zwei Gestalten –' gewesen sein, und ‚aus einem Stier und halb aus einem Mann gebildet'." (Zitiert nach: Erich Lessing, Die Griechischen Sagen, München 1977, S. 183f.

der ganzen Insel, aufzusteigen. Die Neugründung Knossos musste bei diesem Streben Gortynas Rivale sein; die Jahrhunderte währende Feindschaft der beiden Städte, die bis zum Krieg gegeneinander führte, hat hier ihren Grund.[66]

Gortyna war mit seinen Häfen Matala, Kommos und Lendas zum lybischen Meer hin gerichtet; es war offen für Einflüsse von Süden her, vor allem von Ägypten und dessen phönizischen Vermittlern. Dass der Stiergott Zeus mit Europa in Matala aus dem Meere stieg, entsprach der Verkehrsverbindung. Die Südküste Kretas ist hafenarm, und die Häfen sind für den Schutz von Schiffen nicht gut geeignet, wie der Apostel Paulus im Jahre 59 n.Chr. erfahren hat.[67] Die Nordküste der Insel hat dagegen zahlreiche Buchten mit guten Häfen; in der Nähe von Knossos liegt der minoische Hafen von Amnisos, den schon Homer nennt.[68]

Wenn Minos Knossos zu seinem Mittelpunkte wählte, so vollzog er eine Blickwendung von Süden nach Norden; er wandte sich der griechischen Ägäis zu und bereitete seine Seeherrschaft in diesem Raume vor. Der kretische Einfluss ist in Thera (Santorin) zu beobachten; die Verbindung mit dem Peloponnes und den Mykenern ist die Folge dieser Öffnung nach Norden. Der Hörneraltar, den Theseus auf Delos errichtete, war nach kretischem Vorbild gebaut. Bei seinem Ausgriff nach Norden stieß Minos dann auch auf die aufsteigende Seemacht in Attika, auf Athen. Dessen Königssohn drang im Gegenstoß in den Labyrinthos ein und beendete den Asterios-Kult. Die Gegnerschaft Athens zu Kreta hat neben den politischen auch religiöse Gründe.

Im Asterios-Kult von Knossos gab es Menschenopfer. Der Tribut von Jungfrauen und Jünglingen, den Athen dem Mythos zufolge an Minos leisten musste, erfolgte zu diesem Zweck. Den Athenern war dieser Gottesdienst ein Greuel; ihnen galt Minos als bösartiger Tyrann, weil er diesen Tribut von ihnen forderte. Dieses Minos-Bild und das entsprechende Bild von den Kretern überhaupt wurden vor allem durch die attischen Tragiker verbreitet.

Ein Athener hat in diesem parteiischen Gegensatz einen klaren Kopf behalten und sich vom Vorurteil seiner Landsleute distanziert: Platon. Er

66 Als die Römer Kreta besetzten, verbündete sich Gortyna mit ihnen gegen Knossos und wurde von ihnen verschont. Sie machten das dem südlichen Meer zugewandte Gortyna oder, wie sie es nannten: Gortys, zur Hauptstadt ihrer Provinz Creta et Cyrene und damit für Jahrhunderte zur ersten Stadt Kretas.

67 Apostelgeschichte 27, 7–13.

68 Gallas, a.a.0., S. 273; Odyssee 19, 188f.

hat einen wenig beachteten Dialog mit dem Titel MINOS geschrieben und darin den kretischen König als Gesetzgeber gerühmt.[69] Platon gibt darin das folgende Zwiegespräch des Sokrates mit einem Schüler wieder:[70]

Sokrates: Und von welchem der alten Könige sagt man, dass er ein guter Gesetzgeber war, dessen Satzungen noch jetzt bestehen, da sie göttlich sind?

Der Schüler: Ich kann mich nicht entsinnen.

Sokrates: Weißt du nicht, welche die ältesten Gesetze unter den Hellenen in Gebrauch haben?

(...)

Der Schüler: Von Kreta, sagt man.

Sokrates: Besitzen also nicht diese die ältesten Gesetze unter den Hellenen?

Der Schüler: Ja.

Sokrates: Weißt du nun, wer deren treffliche Könige waren? Minos und Rhadamantys, die Söhne des Zeus und der Europa, von denen diese Gesetze stammen.

Der Schüler: Von Rhadamantys zwar erzählt man, lieber Sokrates, dass er ein gerechter Mann war, Minos aber soll ziemlich roh, hart und ungerecht gewesen sein.

Sokrates: Das ist eine attische Sage, mein Bester, und eine Tragödienfabel, die du da anführst.

Der Schüler: Wieso? Wird denn das nicht von Minos erzählt?

Sokrates: Jedenfalls nicht von Homer und Hesiod; und dabei sind diese glaubwürdiger als alle Tragödiendichter zusammen, von denen du das gehört hast, was du sagst.

Schließlich setzt Sokrates zum Preise des Minos an, indem er sich auf Homer und Hesiod beruft:

Sokrates: (...) Und so will ich auch deshalb jetzt von Minos erzählen, wie ihn Homer und Hesiod preisen, damit du dich nicht als Mensch und Sohn eines Menschen gegen einen Heros und Sohn des Zeus in Worten vergehst. Homer sagt nämlich von Kreta,

69 Platon, Minos, in: Gunther Eigler (Hrsg.), Platon, Werke in acht Bänden, VIII. 2. Auflage, Darmstadt 1977, S. 517–553. Dazu Ottomar Wichmann, Platon, Ideelle Gesamtdarstellung und Studienwerk, Darmstadt 1966, S. 129–132.

70 Platon, 318c-321b, (Eigler, a.a.0., S. 543–553).

> dass sich darauf viele Menschen und neunzig Städte befänden, und fährt dann fort:
> 'Unter diesen ist Knossos, die mächtige Stadt, in der
> Minos herrschte, der alle neun Jahre Vertrauter des
> mächtigen Zeus war.'
> Dies ist nun eine von Homer in wenigen Worten ausgedrückte Lobrede auf Minos, wie sie Homer auf keinen einzigen seiner Heroen gedichtet hat. (...) Darum behaupte ich, Minos sei von allen am meisten von Homer gepriesen worden; denn dass er ein Sohn des Zeus war und als einziger von Zeus unterrichtet worden ist, das kann durch kein anderes Lob überboten werden.

Platon lässt Sokrates noch einen Beleg aus Hesiod anführen, bevor er dem Schüler erklärt, weshalb Minos bei den Athenern in schlechtem Rufe steht. Er beweist dabei eine außerordentlich genaue Sachkenntnis; der Heutige kann das Phänomen nicht besser begründen:

> Der Schüler: Warum hat sich denn nun eigentlich, lieber Sokrates, dieser Ruf des Minos verbreitet, dass er ein ungebildeter und harter Mann gewesen sei?
>
> Sokrates: Aus demselben Grund, mein Bester, weshalb auch du, wenn du vernünftig bist, dich hüten wirst wie auch jeder andere, dem an einem guten Ruf liegt, euch jemals mit einem Dichter zu verfeinden. Denn die Dichter haben großen Einfluss auf den Ruf, je nachdem, was sie über die Menschen dichten, ob sie nun loben oder tadeln. Darin hat denn auch Minos einen Fehler begangen, dass er unsern Staat bekriegte, in welchem sich überhaupt viel Weisheit und namentlich Dichter aller Art sich finden, sowohl in andern Dichtungsgattungen als insbesondere auch in der Tragödie. (...) Von der Dichtung ist aber die Tragödie diejenige Gattung, die das Volk am meisten ergötzt und die Gemüter am stärksten beeindruckt; in dieser Dichtungsgattung bringen wir daher den Minos auf die Bühne und rächen uns so dafür, dass er uns gezwungen hatte, jenen Tribut zu zahlen.

Der Athener Platon sieht also in der Feindschaft Kretas gegen seine Stadt einen Fehler des Minos, der sich an seinem Rufe rächt. Andererseits bleibt er bei seinem Urteil über den großen Gesetzgeber:

> Sokrates: (...) Das war also der Fehler, den Minos begangen hatte, dass er sich uns verfeindete; dadurch also geriet er, wonach du ja gefragt hast, in einen ziemlich üblen Ruf. Denn dass er in der Tat ein tüchtiger und gesetzlicher Mann war, wie wir auch schon früher bemerkten, ein tüchtiger Hirt, dafür ist der stärkste Beleg, dass seine Gesetze unangetastet geblieben sind.

Platons Dialog geht der Frage nach, was ein Gesetz sei und woran sich eine gute Gesetzgebung erkennen lasse. Es ist sicher nicht zufällig, dass der fragende Schüler einen Einwand vorbringt, den Sokrates entkräften muss und der, ohne den Namen zu nennen, den Hauptvorwurf der Athener gegen Minos vorwegnimmt:[71]

> Der Schüler: (...) Zum Beispiel gibt es bei uns kein Gesetz, dass man Menschen opfern soll, sondern dies gilt als frevelhaft; die Karthager aber opfern sie, weil das für sie als fromm und gesetzlich gilt, ja einige von ihnen opfern sogar ihre eigenen Söhne dem Kronos, wie vielleicht auch du gehört hast. Und nicht nur, dass Barbaren völker andern Gesetzen folgen als wir, sondern auch die Bewohner von Lykaia und die Nachkommen des Athamas - was für Opfer bringen diese dar, obwohl sie Griechen sind!

Ob man des Sokrates Erwiderung für stichhaltig hält oder nicht, ist in diesem Zusammenhang unwichtig; hier interessiert uns Platons Zeugnis, dass man in Athen die Gerechtigkeit des Minos in Zweifel zog, weil er wie die Karthager (die auch Phönizier waren) Menschenopfer für fromm und gesetzlich hielt. Bei der guten Kenntnis Platons über die athenischen und die kretischen Verhältnisse kommt dieser Nachricht Beweiswert zu. Es hat also ein athenisches Minos-Bild gegeben, das von der früheren Feindschaft Athens gegen Kreta geprägt war und das Minos die unter seiner Herrschaft gesetzmäßigen Menschenopfer vorwarf. Platon musste mit Homer und Hesiod die stärksten Zeugen dafür aufbieten, dass der kretische König ein großer Gesetzgeber war, dessen Satzungen noch zu seiner Zeit Bestand hatten. Diese späte Rechtfertigung war die Folge davon, dass Minos, als er Knossos und das Labyrinth erbaute, sich der Ägäis und dem griechischen Raum zuwandte und dabei mit Athen zusammenstieß. Dass ein Athener sie aussprach, obwohl er den Fehler des Minos einsah, allerdings wohl nicht als notwendig erkannte, macht dieses Urteil besonders

71 Platon, 315b.c (Eigler, a.a.0., S. 531).

gewichtig. Platon zweifelt auch nicht am Mythos, der Minos zum Sohne des Zeus macht. Diese von Homer bestätigte Herkunft macht den Göttersohn besonders rühmenswert. König Minos war als Beginner der minoischen Kultur, als Bauherr des Labyrinths in Knossos und als Gesetzgeher einer durch Jahrhunderte beständigen Verfassung ein Heros, wie es keinen zweiten gab.

Der Ursprung dieses Großen um Anfang der europäischen Geschichte ist bei der heiligen Platane von Gortyna zu suchen. Nach seiner Mutter, die ihn dort von einem Gott empfing, nennt sich unser Kontinent.

Beobachtungen zur alttestamentlichen Weisheitsliteratur auf Grund der poetologischen Analyse (Kolometrie)[1]

Urmas Nõmmik, Tartu

Im Folgenden wird ein kurzer Rundgang durch die alttestamentliche Poesie vorgenommen. Dabei werden einige inhaltliche Merkmale und die Kolometrie der ausgewählten Texte beobachtet, um die Aufmerksamkeit auf zwei grundsätzliche form- und traditionsgeschichtliche Fragen zu richten. Die erste betrifft das Problem der Entwicklung der kolometrischen Gestalt der alttestamentlichen Poesie während mehrerer Jahrhunderte hauptsächlich im nachexilischen Zeitalter. Die andere Frage bezieht sich auf die These, daß in diesem Zeitalter kaum mehr von einheitlicher, sondern von parteiischer Entwicklung der alttestamentlichen Tradition(en) die Rede sein muß.

Im Gegensatz zur literar- und formkritischen Arbeit, in der poetologische Mittel manchmal tatsächlich ein Argument für die Schichtung der Texte bilden, ist eine Voraussetzung der rein poetologischen Analysen und der darauf aufgebauten Monographien und Aufsätze fast immer die Einheitlichkeit der alttestamentlichen Texte gewesen.[2] Es ist freilich schwierig, manchmal gar unmöglich, die Grundschichten der alttestamentlichen Texte festzustellen, aber es sind auch stets Textblöcke vorhanden, deren Einheitlichkeit nicht in Frage gestellt werden kann, oder deren Grundgestalt ohne Probleme festzustellen ist und deren Form und Gattung daher feste Anhaltspunkte bieten, um gewisse Entwicklungslinien zu

---

1 Bei diesem Beitrag handelt es sich um die stark modifizierte und ergänzte Fassung meines Vortrags bei der assyriologischen Tagung am 22. Mai 2006. Ich bedanke mich bei den Teilnehmern der Diskussion.

2 Das Festgestellte will nicht den Beitrag solcher schwerwiegenden Bücher wie W.G.E. Watson, Classical Hebrew Poetry. A Guide to its Techniques, JSOT.SS 26, 1984, L. Alonso Schökel, A Manual of Hebrew Poetics, Subsidia biblica 11, 1988, K. Seybold, Poetik der Psalmen, PSAT 1, 2003, u.a. keinesfalls in Frage stellen; es ist eher als Ausblick zu verstehen.

rekonstruieren.[3] Unten wird zuerst die kolometrische Form[4] einiger Belege der weisheitlichen Texte erörtert und nachher gefragt, ob nämlich in diesem Bereich von einer Entwicklung gesprochen werden kann, und auch, ob von der kolometrischen Gestalt her die „Weisheitlichkeit" eines gewissen Textes behauptet werden kann.[5]

Die Form- und Gattungsanalyse der alttestamentlichen Weisheitsliteratur spielt neben der den Inhalt betreffenden – an sich unbestritten wichtigen – Beobachtung, daß die entsprechenden Aussagen sich auf die Vergeltungslehre oder den Tun-Ergehen-Zusammenhang stützen[6], eine zweitrangige Rolle. Statt der Form wird oft auch von den Begriffsfeldern ausgegangen. Sind in einem Text gewisse, überwiegend aus den klassischen Vertretern der Weisheit – Sprüche, Hiob, Kohelet – bekannte Vokabeln vorhanden, wird nach seiner Weisheitlichkeit gefragt.[7] Zumal bei der Klassifizierung der Psalmen oder ihrer Teile bietet sich das Vokabular oft als das Hauptargument für den weisheitlichen Charakter an. So verhält es sich z.B. bei der Erwähnung oder Häufung der Begriffe צַדִּיק und רָשָׁע (Ps 1; 37; 73 usw.). Darüber hinaus wird von der Form der weisheitlichen Lehr- oder Mahnrede, die gewissen Aufbauelementen und bestimmter Rhetorik unterworfen ist, gesprochen.[8] Wie bei den anderen alttestament-

---

3 Eine Form, bei der die Forscher den Konsens erreicht haben, bildet das Akrostichon: hier wird fast immer literarkritisch operiert und die aus der Reihe fallenden Kola werden als sekundär beurteilt.

4 Zur Methode siehe O. Loretz / I. Kottsieper, Colometry in Ugaritic and Biblical Poetry. Introduction, Illustrations and Topical Bibliography, UBL 5, 1987.

5 Während die Psalmen bereits massiv von Oswald Loretz kolometrisch untersucht worden sind (z.B. Die Psalmen, Teil II. Beitrag der Ugarit-Texte zum Verständnis von Kolometrie und Textologie der Psalmen. Psalm 90–150, AOAT 207/2, 1979, und Psalmstudien. Kolometrie, Strophik und Theologie ausgewählter Psalmen, BZAW 309, 2002; vgl auch U. Nõmmik, Die Gerechtigkeitsbearbeitungen in den Psalmen. Eine Hypothese von Christoph Levin formgeschichtlich und kolometrisch überprüft, UF 31 [1999], 443–535), liegen für die Weisheitsdichtung keine vergleichbaren umfangreichen Studien vor.

6 Siehe allgemein dazu K. Koch, Gibt es ein Vergeltungsdogma im Alten Testament? ZThK 52 (1955), 1–42; H. Gese, Lehre und Wirklichkeit in der alten Weisheit. Studien zu den Sprüchen Salomos und zu dem Buche Hiob, 1958, 42–45; G. von Rad, Weisheit in Israel, 1970, 165ff.

7 Wie z.B. in einer charakteristischen Studie von R.N. Whybray, The Intellectual Tradition in the Old Testament, BZAW 135, 1974.

8 Z.B. C. Kayatz, Studien zu Proverbien 1–9. Eine form- und motivgeschichtliche Untersuchung unter Einbeziehung ägyptischen Vergleichsmaterials, WMANT 22, 1966; K.F.D.

lichen Büchern ist auch bei der Weisheitsliteratur z.B. der Strophenbau analysiert worden, in neueren Zeiten oft unter dem Blickpunkt der rhetorischen Kritik.[9] Generell ist aber festzustellen, daß die Forschung der Poetologie der alttestamentlichen Literatur oft unter der mangelnden diachronen Betrachtungsweise leidet und der ursprünglichen Gestalt der Texte eine regelmäßige oder strenge poetische Form nicht zutraut.

Außerdem herrscht in den letzten Jahrzehnten in der alttestamentlichen Wissenschaft immer mehr die Idee zahlreicher Fortschreibungen und der Spätdatierung. So entstehen aber neue prinzipielle Probleme, die noch wenig behandelt worden sind, z.B. wie sind sehr viele Fortschreibungen, deren theologische und kulturelle Voraussetzungen für ihre Entstehung Zeit brauchen, auf den engen nachexilischen Zeitraum zu verteilen? Um nur ein Beispiel aus vielen zu bringen, können die Schichten des Hiobbuches aufgezählt werden: der ursprüngliche Dichter, der Übergangsredaktor, der Verfasser der Elihureden, die Niedrigkeits-, Gerechtigkeits- und Majestätsredaktionen.[10] Sind entsprechende Anschauungen tatsächlich sukzessiv innerhalb einer engen Tradition entstanden? Hat man bisher ausreichend mit der logischen Möglichkeit gerechnet, daß es bereits in der persischen Zeit mehrere Schulen oder Entwicklungslinien gegeben hat, die eigene theologische Grundsätze besessen haben, die aber trotzdem so nahe miteinander gewirkt haben, daß einige Texte von einer in die andere Tradition übernommen und innerhalb relativ kurzer Zeit durch unterschiedliche inhaltliche Aspekte ergänzt worden sind? Falls so, geben auch formale Aspekte, z.B. die Kolometrie, davon Anzeichen?

Beobachtungen zum Hiobdialog

Der Rundgang durch die alttestamentliche (weisheitliche) Poesie kann mit dem ursprünglichen Hiobdialog angefangen werden, weil er trotz allen Bedenkens sich durch den ausgeprägten Strophenbau und Stil hervor-

Römheld, Die Weisheitslehre im Alten Orient, Elemente einer Formgeschichte, BN.B 4, 1989.

9 Z.B. P. van der Lugt, Rhetorical Criticism and the Poetry of the Book of Job, OTS 32, 1995, Ders., Strophes and Stanzas in the Book of Job. A Historical Survey, in: W. van der Meer / J.C. de Moor (edd.), The Structural Analysis of Biblical and Canaanite Poetry, JSOT.SS 74, 1988, 235–264.

10 Siehe dazu M. Witte, Vom Leiden zur Lehre. Der dritte Redegang (Hiob 21–27) und die Redaktionsgeschichte des Hiobbuches, BZAW 230, 1994, und O. Kaiser, Das Buch Hiob. Übersetzt und eingeleitet, 2006.

hebt.[11] Neben zahlreichen stilistischen und rhetorischen Figuren zeigt sich die kolometrische Grundgestalt der Hiobdichtung als extrem streng und regelmäßig. Der Hiobdichter hat nur Bikola benutzt[12] und die Länge der Zeilen durchgehend dem Ideal von 12–15, bzw. 11–17 Konsonanten pro Kolon angemessen. Als Musterbeispiel[13] bedienen wir uns der zwei ersten Strophen der ersten Elifasrede Hi 4,2–6.7–11. Aus zehn Bikola zählt nur ein Kolon weniger als 12 Konsonanten (3a) und nur drei mehr als 15 Konsonanten (5a; 7a; 8a). Dabei können alle überlangen Kola durch die besondere Position am Anfang der Strophe oder Unterstrophe (hier z.B. 5a; 7a; beide Strophen teilen sich in zwei Unterstrophen nach dem Muster 3+2)[14], die Verwendung der Anakrusis[15] (5a) oder durch die Betonung einer wichtigen Aussage erklärt werden (7a; 8a). Die Beobachtung muß dadurch ergänzt werden, daß der Hiobdichter die Sprache und die Bilder aus Weisheitsliteratur, Psalmen und Propheten sehr schöpferisch gemischt hat. Die strenge poetische Form wirkt vor diesem Hintergrund überraschend. Sie bleibt eindeutig einer bestimmten poetischen Schule treu.[16]

Beispiel 1: Hiob 4,2–11

2	hnsh dbr 'lyk tl'h	15
	w^{c}ṣr bmlyn my ywkl	15
3	hnh ysrt rbym	11
	wydym rpwt t ḥzq	13

11 Die Frage wird gründlich in meiner Dissertation über die Freundesreden des Hiobbuches behandelt.

12 So schon N. Peters, Das Buch Job, EHAT 21, 1928, 223. Das wird auch von Witte, Vom Leiden, 58, Anm. 8, angenommen.

13 Da die Darstellung der kolometrischen Analyse viel Raum einnimmt, können im Folgenden nur kurze Belege geliefert werden. Diese sind jedoch nicht zufällig gewählt, sondern wollen, erstens, repräsentativ sein und zweitens, die textkritischen Probleme vermeiden.

14 Zum Phänomen der Verlängerung, um die Abschnitte zu markieren, siehe Watson, Classical Hebrew Poetry, 164f.; Seybold, Poetik, 126f.; und Nõmmik, Die Gerechtigkeitsbearbeitungen, 453.468.

15 Zur Figur siehe Watson, Classical Hebrew Poetry, 110f.

16 Zum Vergleich kann man die kolometrische Analyse von Hi 3 von O. Loretz, „Schwarze Magie" des Tages in Hi 3,8 und KTU 1.6 VI 45b–53; 1.14 I 19–20; 1.4 VII 54–56. Zur Überlieferung der „schwarzen Magie" in Altsyrien-Palästina, UF 32 (2000), (261–287), 263f., heranziehen. Der Gesamteindruck ist sehr ähnlich.

4	kwšl yqymwn mlyk	14
	wbrkym kr^{c}wt t’mṣ	15
5	ky ^{c}th tbw’ ’lyk wtl’	17
	tg^{c} ^{c}dyk wtbhl	12
6	hl’ yr’tk ksltk	13
	tqwtk wtm drkyk	13
7	zkr n’ my hw’ nqy ’bd	16
	w’yph yšrym nkḥdw	15
8	k’šr r’yty ḥršy ’wn	16
	wzr^{c}y ^{c}ml yqṣrhw	14
9	mnšmt ’lwh y’bdw	14
	wmrwḥ ’pw yklw	12
10	š’gt ’ryh wqwl šḥl	15
	wšny kpyrym nt^{c}w	14
11	lyš ’bd mbly ṭrp	13
	wbny lby’ ytprdw	14

Beobachtungen zu den Proverbien

Die traditionsgeschichtliche Untersuchung zeigt, daß der Hiobdichter trotz der Sprach- und Motivmischung stets vom weisheitlichen Grundparadigma ausgeht. Die Freundesreden benutzen zwar die Sprache der Psalmen oder prophetischen Unheilsverkündigungen, vertreten aber die weisheitliche, theologisierte Vergeltungslehre. Hiob unterscheidet sich von den Freunden nicht durch seine Lehre, sondern nur durch den Kontext; seine Lage und nicht Hiob selbst spricht gegen die theologisierte Vergeltungslehre. Wird das festgestellt, muß der Frage nachgegangen werden, wie die kolometrische Gestalt der Literatur aussieht, in der die Vergeltungslehre am besten in Erscheinung tritt. Ein Beispiel aus den Proverbien 15,1–10 möge die Form dieser Weisheitsliteratur veranschaulichen. Es bildet einen Teil aus der älteren Salomonischen Spruchsammlung.[17] Wie es dem Text zu entnehmen ist, herrscht zwar nicht der aus den Lehrreden

17 Obwohl bei der Frage der Datierung der Spruchsammlungen oder ihrer Wachstumsetappen noch Vieles offen steht, scheint es naheliegen, daß in der Zeit des Hiobdichters größere Spruchsammlungen bereits existierten; siehe dazu O. Kaiser, Grundriß der Einleitung in die kanonischen und deuterokanonischen Schriften des Alten Testaments. Band 3. Die poetischen und weisheitlichen Werke, 1994, 59f.63ff.

bekannte synonyme oder synthetische Parallelismus, sondern der den Einzelsprüchen eigene antithetische Parallelismus. Der Text kann auch nicht in Strophen geteilt werden, aber die kolometrische Gestalt kann trotzdem als sehr regelmäßig und ähnlich dem oben angeführten Beispiel aus der Hiobdichtung bezeichnet werden. Der Text besteht nur aus Bikola und die Kolonlänge beträgt nicht weniger als 13 und mehr als 17 Konsonanten. Dabei ist zu merken, daß der Unterschied zwischen den Konsonantenzahlen beider Kola in einem Bikolon nicht mehr als 2–3 Konsonanten beträgt.

Beispiel 2: Proverbien 15,1–10

1	m^{c}nh rk yšyb ḥmh	13
	wdbr ^{c}ṣb y^{c}lh 'p	13
2	lšwn ḥkmym *ttyp*[18] d^{c}t	*16* (17)
	wpy ksylym yby^{c} 'wlt	17
3	bkl mqwm ^{c}yny yhwh	15
	ṣpwt r^{c}ym wṭwbym	14
4	mrp' lšwn ^{c}ṣ ḥyym	14
	wslp bh šbr brwḥ	13
5	'wyl yn'ṣ mwsr 'byw	16
	wšmr twkḥt y^{c}rm	13
6	*b*byt ṣdyq ḥsn rb	*13* (12)
	wtbw't rš^{c} n^{c}krt	*14* (15)
7	śpty ḥkmym yzrw d^{c}t	16
	wlb ksylym l' kn	13
8	zbḥ rš^{c}ym tw^{c}bt yhwh	17
	wtplt yšrym rṣwnw	15
9	tw^{c}bt yhwh drk rš^{c}	15
	wmrdp sdqh y'hb	13
10	mwsr r^{c} l^{c}zb 'rḥ	13
	śwn' twkḥṭ ymwt	13

Der so gewonnene Eindruck wiederholt sich bei der väterlichen Lehre in den ersten Kapiteln des Sprüchebuches 1–9, die vor dem Hintergrund der

[18] Zu den Konjekturen hier und in V.6 siehe BHS.

alttestamentlichen Literaturgeschichte gewöhnlich als der jüngste Teil des Buches eingeschätzt wird.[19] In der hauptsächlich aus Strophen mit vier Bikola bestehenden zehnten Lehrrede[20] ist die kolometrische Form sehr regelmäßig.

Beispiel 3: Proverbien 7,14–17

14	zbḥy šlmym ʿly	12
	hywm šlmty ndry	13
15	ʿl kn yṣʾty lqrʾtk	15
	lšḥr pnyk wʾmṣʾk	14
16	mrbdym rbdty ʿrśy	15
	ḥṭbwt ʾṭwn mṣrym	14
17	npty mškby mr	11
	ʾhlym wqnmwn	11

Beobachtungen zu den Psalmen

Die Form- und Gattungsanalyse der Psalmen ist oft mit viel größeren Problemen verbunden als die der Weisheitsliteratur, weil die Psalmen meistens viel intensiverer Redaktionsarbeit unterworfen worden sind. Daher ist ihre Kolometrie komplizierter und manchmal gar die Rede von der Grundgestalt unmöglich, weil sie aus verschiedenen umfangreicheren Textblöcken redaktionell zusammengesetzt worden sind. Eine beträchtliche Zahl der Psalmen ist für weisheitlich gehalten worden.[21] Diese sind

19 Siehe z.B. H. Ringgren, Sprüche, in: Ders., W. Zimmerli, O. Kaiser, Sprüche. Prediger. Das Hohe Lied. Klagelieder. Das Buch Esther, ATD 16, 31981, (1–120), 8; Kaiser, Grundriß, 64; G. Baumann, Die Weisheitsgestalt in Proverbien 1–9. Traditionsgeschichtliche und theologische Studien, FAT 16, 1996, 272.

20 Zur Einteilung der väterlichen Lehre siehe Kaiser, a.a.O.

21 Das Prädikat „weisheitlich" gehört heute zum Grundstock der Psalmenanalyse, vgl. z.B. die neueren Einleitungen E. Zenger, Das Buch der Psalmen, in: Ders. u.a., Einleitung in das Alte Testament, 42001, (309–326), 322f., und M. Witte, Schriften (Ketubim), in: J.C. Gertz (Hrsg.), Grundinformation Altes Testament, UTB 2745, 2006, (404–508), 417. Zum Problem siehe auch R.N. Whybray, The wisdom psalms, in: J. Day, R.P. Gordon, H.G.M. Williamson (edd.), Wisdom in Ancient Israel. Essays in Honour of J.A. Emerton, 1995, 152–160, und aus den Klassikern S. Mowinckel, Psalmen und Weisheit (=Psalms and Wisdom), in: P.H.A. Neumann (Hrsg.), Zur neueren Psalmenforschung, WdF 192, 1976, 341–366.

die nachkultischen, späten Psalmen, darunter auch die oben bereits erwähnten Akrosticha, deren ursprüngliche Gestalt sich relativ leicht feststellen läßt und die teilweise regelmäßige kolometrische Form haben. Z.B. besitzen die Kola mit der Länge von 11–16 Konsonanten in dem nur aus Bikola zusammengesetzten Psalm 112 die absolute Vorherrschaft. Anhand der Vergeltungslehre und des Begriffsfeldes wird er oft zu den Weisheitspsalmen gezählt.[22] Nimmt man die Lehre und zwei markante Termini צַדִּיק und רָשָׁע (112,4.6.10), wird man an weitere „weisheitliche" Akrosticha erinnert, darunter an die berühmten Psalmen 37 und 119. Blickt man diese an, kann eine vergleichbar strenge Einhaltung der Kolonlänge – auch falls die textkritischen Probleme beseitigt werden könnten – nicht festgestellt werden. Beide Psalmen verwenden zwar gleichmäßige Strophen und ursprünglich nur Bikola, aber die Kolonlänge variiert stark. Z.B. vermitteln die ersten Bikola V.1b–6 in Ps 37 den Eindruck der Regelmäßigkeit (12–16 Konsonanten pro Kolon), V.7 und 9f. sind aber entsprechend mit 8:9, 15:19 und 14:21 Konsonanten bereits problematisch. In Ps 119 bewegt sich die Kolonlänge oft zwischen 10–15 Konsonanten, wird aber ab und zu sehr kurz (z.B. V.4f.: 13:7 und 12:8) oder relativ lang (z.B. V.21.23: 8:18 und 17:13). Verläßt man die Akrosticha, muß der aus dem Gegensatz der צַדִּיקִים und רְשָׁעִים lebende „weisheitliche" Psalm 1 erörtert werden. Auch dort tritt die bikolonische Struktur in Erscheinung, die Kolonlänge variiert in der uns vorliegenden Gestalt des Psalms aber zwischen 7–20 Konsonanten, so daß manche Teile sogar als freie Dichtung oder prosaisch scheinen.[23] Überhaupt können die mit dem Begriffsgeld צַדִּיקִים // רְשָׁעִים in Verbindung stehenden Gerechtigkeitsbearbeitungen in den Psalmen oft durch die Verachtung der in dem zu ergänzenden Text vorhandenen poetischen Regeln charakterisiert werden.[24]

Verläßt man das besprochene Begriffsfeld, bleibt aber beim Grundsatz der Vergeltung, kann ein auffallender Abschnitt aus Psalm 7 dargestellt werden. In ihm ist die Kolometrie eines Abschnitts V.13–17 im Vergleich zum übrigen Psalm viel regelmäßiger und ähnelt wegen der Bikola, deren Kolonlänge 10–15 Konsonanten beträgt mit einer Ausnahme in V.13a (17 Konsonanten als Strophenmarker), den oben angeführten weis-

22 So z.B. K. Seybold, Die Psalmen, HAT 1/15, 1996, 441ff., L.C. Allen, Psalms 101–150, WBC 21, 2002, 128; vgl. auch E.S. Gerstenberger, Psalms. Part 2, And Lamentations, FOTL 15, 2001, 273.277.

23 Vgl. die Behandlungen von Ps 1 bei Nõmmik, Die Gerechtigkeitsbearbeitungen, 512–514, und Loretz, Psalmstudien, 11–29.

24 Siehe z.B. Ps 7,10a; 31,18f.; 146,9b und dazu Nõmmik, a.a.O.

heitlichen Belegen. Der Abschnitt unterscheidet sich auch inhaltlich vom übrigen Psalm und kann durchaus als weisheitlich eingestuft werden. Folglich bildet der Abschnitt entweder einen weisheitlichen Einschub oder ist vom Verfasser des Psalms aus der weisheitlichen Tradition aufgenommen worden.

Beispiel 4: Psalm 7,13–17

13	’m l’ yšwb ḥrbw ylṭwš	17
	qštw drk wykwnnh	14
14	wlw hkyn kly mwt	13
	ḥṣyw ldlqym ypʿl	14
15	hnh yḥbl ’wn	10 (14)[25]
	[whrh] ’ml wyld šqr	14 (10)
16	bwr krh wyḥprhw	13
	wypl bšḥt ypʿl	12
17	yšwb ʿmlw br’šw	13
	wʿl qdqdw ḥmsw yrd	15

Eine Anmerkung kann in Verbindung mit der ganz späten Psalmendichtung aus Qumran (Hodajot) gemacht werden. In der Qumran-Gemeinde hat man frühere Psalmendichtung, besonders Hymnen nachgebildet oder späte Nachdichtungen benutzt und bewahrt.[26] Dabei scheinen die Lieder die These zu bestätigen, daß spätere Poesie die strenge Form der Kolometrie nicht bewahrt hat und eher der Form von Ps 1 entspricht. Wegen der *matres lectionis* sind die Kola im Durchschnitt länger, aber die Variierung der Konsonantenzahl ist groß. Die Trikola scheinen generell die Bikola zu ersetzen, aber nicht konsequent.

Es kann jedoch nicht generalisierend behauptet werden, daß sich die strenge kolometrische Form der hebräischen Poesie sukzessiv abgelöst hat, weil trotz den Hodajot oder dem Ps 1 z.B. der oben erwähnte Ps 112 zeitlich nicht fern von Ps 1 liegen kann. Es muß mit mehreren parallelen Schulen oder Formen gerechnet werden.

---

25 Das Wort והרה ist vom Ende des ersten Kolons an den Anfang des zweiten zu verschieben.

26 Vgl. R.E. Murphy, A Consideration of the Classification ‚Wisdom Psalms‘, in: Congress Volume Bonn 1962, VT.S 9, 1963, (156–167), 161: „The Hodayot of Qumran as late as they are, still show an attempt to express praise in the traditional psalm forms.“

Eine Beobachtung zur Prophetenliteratur

Die große Gruppe der prophetischen Texte kann an dieser Stelle nur flüchtig besprochen werden. Sie ist so umfangreich und während so langer Zeit entstanden, daß sicherlich auch weisheitliche Texte in sie aufgenommen worden sind. Sie ist kolometrisch sehr wenig untersucht worden[27] und daher hat man entsprechendes Argument bei der Feststellung der „Weisheitlichkeit" eines gewissen Textabschnitts nicht benutzt. Unten wird ein Beleg dafür, daß die oben konstatierte kolometrische Regelmäßigkeit im Hiobdialog und den Proverbien auch in den Prophetenbüchern als zusätzliches Argument verwendet werden kann, dargestellt. Bekanntlich bilden die Prophetensprüche relativ kleine Einheiten, zwischen denen manchmal durch die umfangreiche fortschreibende Arbeit formelle Unterschiede entstanden sind. Gleich am Anfang des *Corpus propheticum*, in Jes 1,3 fällt ein Spruch (3a) und ein Kommentar dazu (3b) auf, deren Weisheitlichkeit anhand von Tiervergleichen und dem Paar ידע // בין behauptet worden ist.[28] Diese zwei Bikola fallen aber auch durch die relativ regelmäßigere Kolonlänge auf, was nicht unbedingt über die Nachbarversen gesagt werden kann. Die Kolonlänge variiert nicht so stark wie in V.2 und ist im Durchschnitt nicht so kurz wie in V.4a.

Beispiel 5: Jesaja 1,2–4a

2	šmʿw šmym	8
	whʾzyny ʾrṣ	10
	ky yhwh dbr	9
	bnym gdlty wrwmmty	16
	whm pšʿw by	9
3	ydʿ šwr qnhw	10
	wḥmwr ʾbws bʿlyw	14
	yśrʾl lʾ ydʿ	10
	ʿmy lʾ htbwnn	11

27 Eine beispielhafte Studie muß jedoch erwähnt werden: M. Nissinen, Prophetie, Redaktion und Fortschreibung im Hoseabuch. Studien zum Werdegang eines Prophetenbuches im Lichte von Hos 4 und 11, AOAT 231, 1991.

28 Z.B. von O. Kaiser, Isaiah 1–12. A Commentary, OTL, 21983, 13f.

4a	hwy gwy ḥṭʾ	9
	ʿm kbd ʿwn	8
	zrʿ mrʿym	8
	bnym mšḥytym	11

Ausblick

Welche Konsequenzen können aus diesem flüchtigen kolometrischen Rundgang gewonnen werden? Nicht bewiesen, aber naheliegend erscheint die These, daß die klassischen weisheitlichen Texte des ATs eine strenge kolometrische Form besaßen. Diese bestand aus relativ einheitlichen Bikola und die Kolonlänge betrug idealiter etwa 12–15 Konsonanten. Das Minimum von 10 und Maximum von 17 Konsonanten war erlaubt, aber die Variierung durfte innerhalb eines Bikolons nicht allzu groß sein. Diese Form stammte höchstwahrscheinlich aus der vorexilischen Zeit, wie Teile des Sprüchebuches beweisen, und ist aus der einfachen, aus zwei Kola mit ähnlicher Länge bestehenden Sentenz hergeleitet worden. In der nachexilischen Zeit ist die Form intensiv vom Hiobdichter und den Autoren der jüngeren Teile des Proverbienbuches gepflegt worden.[29] Sind weisheitliche Abschnitte oder Sprüche in die Psalmen oder in die Prophetenliteratur übernommen worden, können auch sie manchmal von der strengen kolometrischen Form zeugen. Vielleicht kann die kolometrische Form der weisheitlichen Sprüche und Reden als Anzeichen einer bestimmten Tradition oder Schule angenommen werden, die zwar das Experimentieren mit der Sprache und den Bildern aus mehreren Gattungen zugelassen hat (wie die Hiobdichtung zeigt), es aber in eine bestimmte Form gießen ließ. Die Tradition ist sehr konsequent gewesen, da sie bis in die apokryphe Literatur gereicht hat. Als Beweis bedienen wir uns des hebräischen Sirachbuches. In seiner ältesten und wegen der Nähe zur Verfassungszeit sehr wichtigen hebräischen Handschrift aus Masada[30] sind Teile aus den Kapiteln 39–44 enthalten. Ein relativ gut erhaltenes Fragment 42,1–4 vermittelt den Gesamteindruck von extrem einheitlicher kolometrischer Form des Textes.

29 Qohelet ist von uns bisher nicht erwähnt worden, weil aus seinem Text zu wenige von den text- und literarkritischen Problemen freie Abschnitte zu finden sind. Bei mehreren Teilen ist die ursprüngliche kolometrische Einheitlichkeit jedoch nicht ausgeschlossen.

30 Laut P.C. Beentjes, The Book of Ben Sira in Hebrew. A Text Edition of All Extant Hebrew Manuscripts and A Synopsis of All Parallel Hebrew Ben Sira Texts, VT.S 68, 2006, 6, sich auf die Meinung von Y. Yadin stützend, aus der ersten Hälfte des 1. Jh.s n.Chr.

Beispiel 6: Sirach 42,1–4[31]

1	mšnwt d[b]r tšmʿ	[12]
	wmḥšp kl dbr ʿṣh	13
	[whyy]t byyš bʾmt	[13]
	wmṣʾ ḥn bʿyny kl ḥy	14
	[ʾk] ʿl ʾlh ʾl tbwš	[13]
	wʾl tšʾ pnym wḥṭʾ	14
2	ʿl twrt ʿlywn wḥq	14
	wʿl mšpṭ lhṣdyq ršʿ	16
3	ʿl ḥšbwn šwtp wdrk	15
	wʿl mḥlqt nḥlh wyš	15
4	ʿl šḥqy mznym wpls	15
	w[ʿ]l tmḥy ʾyph wʾbn	[15]

Das Sirachbuch gilt als einer der jüngsten Vertreter der alttestamentlichen Weisheitstradition und der Weisheit auf Hebräisch (etwa 190–180 v. Chr.)[32]; so sind wir mit der besprochenen kolometrischen Form in das 2. Jh. gelangt.

Im Lichte der von einer weisheitlichen Schule verwendeten einheitlichen Form fallen die oft für weisheitlich gehaltenen Psalmen wie Ps 1; 37 oder 119 u.a. aus der Reihe. Sie pflegen ähnliche Themen wie die Weisheitsliteratur, aber sind nicht mehr durch die strenge kolometrische Form bezeichnet. Sie können auch nicht mehr in den wenigen Jahrzehnten zwischen Jesus Sirach und Hodajot gedichtet sein, sondern immerhin schon im 4. oder 3. Jh. So bleibt die Annahme, daß sie aus einer anderen Schule oder Tradition stammen, die parallel mit der weisheitlichen Schule existiert hat.[33] Trotz der ähnlichen Thematik und des verwandten Wortfelds sind inhaltliche Unterschiede vorhanden, die zur Idee führen, ob diese parallele Tradition eher als fromme Tradition bezeichnet werden darf, weil sie von der Thora-Frömmigkeit und dem Ideal eines Gerechten vor Gott durch-

---

31 Text aus Beentjes, a.a.O., 117, in Klammern die Rekonstruktion anhand von Manuskript B (a.a.O., 167).

32 So O. Kaiser, Die alttestamentlichen Apokryphen, Eine Einleitung in Grundzügen, 2000, 83f.

33 Vgl. Whybray, The wisdom psalms, 158: „To use the term 'wisdom' to cover all types of religious thought in ancient Israel would be to deprive it of all specific meaning".

drungen ist. Arbeitet die fromme Tradition meistens in optimistischer Schwarz-weiß-Technik, sind der weisheitlichen Schule pessimistischere Zwischentöne erlaubt. So müssen alle alttestamentlichen Texte nicht mehr auf eine Zeitlinie gestellt werden und können nebeneinander entstanden sein. Während die Verfasser der weisheitlichen Texte noch viele Berührungspunkte mit den außerisraelitischen Traditionen gehabt haben und universal dachten, verstanden die frommen Autoren sich vollkommen im Rahmen des gerade entstehenden Judaismus mit der Thora-Frömmigkeit im Mittelpunkt. Während die Weisen mehr mit den theologischen Ideen und mit der alttestamentlichen Sprache experimentierten, haben sich die Frommen der formellen Sprache bedient, sich aber viel freier gegenüber den traditionellen Formen und Gattungen gefühlt. Da aber die alttestamentliche Weisheit genauso in die israelitische Tradition gehört wie die fromme Tradition und trotz der Parteienbildung nicht von allzu vielen unterschiedlichen religiösen Taditionen im nachexilischen Juda gesprochen werden kann, sind auch die Grenzen zwischen unterschiedlichen „Schulen" bestimmt fließend gewesen. Trotzdem kann durch die genannten Beobachtungen ein zusätzliches Argument gewonnen werden, um in den bunten und komplizierten Werdegang der alttestamentlichen Texte in der nachexilischen Zeit Licht zu bringen.

Die Hiobdichtung – ein überregionaler Dialog? Am Beispiel der drei Freunde Hiobs[1]

Urmas Nõmmik, Tartu

Vor dem Hintergrund der fast unübersichtlich gewordenen Forschung und Literatur am Hiobbuch bietet die Frage der Beziehungen der Hiobdichtung zu den altorientalischen Traditionen keine Neuigkeit. Trotz zahlreicher Erörterungen zur Herkunft des Hiob und seiner drei Freunde sowie zur Lokalisierung des Dialogs fehlt eine systematische Studie hinsichtlich der möglichen Hinweise auf die eine oder andere altorientalische Tradition, die zugleich von der unterschiedlichen Gestaltung der Dialogparteien ausginge.[2]

Die drei Freunde als ursprünglich unterschiedliche Gestalten

Ohne auf die drastische Eingrenzung der literarischen Gestalt der Reden in Anknüpfung an die wichtigen Thesen von Markus Witte über die umfangreichen Niedrigkeits-, Majestäts- und Gerechtigkeitsredaktionen[3] einzugehen, werden im Folgenden die inhaltlichen und stilistischen Hauptunterschiede der ursprünglichen Freundesreden kurz aufgezählt:

(1) Sowohl die Freunde als auch Hiob erörtern dasselbe weisheitliche Prinzip der theologisierten Vergeltungslehre. Am deutlichsten fällt aber die Lehre des Elifas auf, weil sie fein und seelsorgerisch auf die Idee der Hoffnung und des Glaubens vor Gott aufgebaut worden ist (4,6; 15,4;

---

1 Der Vortrag stützt sich auf die gründlichere Analyse, die einen Teil meiner Dissertation über die Form und den Inhalt der Reden der drei Freunde Hiobs bildet.

2 Wenigstens ist mir im Moment keine solche bekannt. Zur Forschungssituation siehe H.-P. Müller, Das Hiobproblem. Seine Stellung und Entstehung im Alten Orient und im Alten Testament, EdF 84, [3]1995, und J. van Oorschot, Tendenzen der Hiobforschung, ThRu 4 (1995), 351–388.

3 M. Witte, Vom Leiden zur Lehre. Der dritte Redegang (Hiob 21–27) und die Redaktionsgeschichte des Hiobbuches, BZAW 230, 1994. Man muß vor allem mit größeren sekundären Textblöcken in 4,12–21; 5,9–17; 15,11–16 und 25 rechnen.

22,4f.). Bildad stellt sich als ein Rechtsanwalt dar, der die Gerechtigkeit Gottes verteidigt und den Ankläger mit kompromisslosen und düsteren Bildern warnt (8,2f.; 18,4). Zofar dagegen legt Wert auf die universale Lehre selbst und auf deren Richtigkeit seit Anfang der Welt (11,7; 20,2–5). Er reflektiert am meisten die Lippensünde Hiobs (11,2–4; 20,2f.), nicht so sehr die Taten wie bei Elifas (22,6–9).

(2) Deutlich unterschiedlich erweisen sich die Legitimationen der Lehren. Bei Elifas handelt es sich um einen erfahrenen Mann und Seelsorger, der das mit eigenen Augen Gesehene (vgl. 4,7f.; 15,2f.9f.17) unterstreicht. Bildad tritt als ein Vorkämpfer der Tradition auf, weil er seine Lehre auf die der Väter gründet (8,8.10–13). Die Legitimierung der Lehre des Zofar gründet darin, daß die gerechte Ordnung seit Anfang der Welt gilt (20,4f.) und daß alle gebildeten Männer es wissen sollten.

(3) Die Aufbau- und rhetorische Analyse zeigt, daß die Elifasreden entsprechend ihrem seelsorgerischen Charakter neben den konstitutiven Redebauteilen wie Anrede, Lehre und Zusammenfassung viel Mahnung und Rüge, Aufforderungen zur Umkehr und Verheißungen beinhalten. Der Aufbau der Bildad- und Zofarreden besteht in größerem Maße aus Lehre und daher aus Bildern; der Anteil der anderen Aufbauelementen umfasst weniger Raum als bei Elifas.

(4) Stilistisch hat der ursprüngliche Hiobdichter die Freunde gegeneinander ausgespielt. Sie unterscheiden sich z.B. durch das Tempo, den ausgeprägten künstlerischen Strophenbau, die Verwendung der komplizierten konditionalen und kausalen Fügungen, der Anakrusis, der Partikel und Deiktika, der bemerkenswert umfangreichen Klangfiguren und der charakteristischen Schlüsselwörter und vor allem durch die Metaphorik.

(5) Um aus den zuletzt genannten Merkmalen nur einige zu nennen, seien bei Elifas der programmatische Begriff ‚Gottesfurcht' (4,6; 15,4; 22,4) und die Löwenmetapher (4,10f.), bei Bildad die umfangreiche Vegetations- (8,11f.16–19; 18,16) und Jagdmetaphorik (18,7–11) und die dämonischen Personifikationen der Krankheit (18,13f.), bei Zofar die Metaphorik in Bezug auf Rede- und Verdauungsorgane (20,12–15) und die Kriegsbilder (20,24f.) hervorgehoben.

Anmerkungen zu den Freunden laut der Rahmenerzählung

Dank der Angabe in der Rahmenerzählung des Hiobbuches 2,11 wissen wir, daß Elifas ein הַתֵּימָנִי, Bildad ein הַשּׁוּחִי und Zofar ein הַנַּעֲמָתִי sein sollen. Diese drei Herkunftsnamen haben für ein Florilegium der unterschiedlichen Hypothesen den Boden bereitet, ohne daß sich bis heute ein Konsens abzeichnet.

Während man die Herkunft des Elifas generell unter den Temanitern, bzw. Edomitern sucht,[4] scheint das keilschriftlich belegte *Sûḫi* oder *Šûḫi* am mittleren oder oberen Euphrat[5] wegen der zu großen Entfernung nicht unbedingt einleuchtend, so daß manche Ausleger stattdessen an einen nordarabischen Stammesname denken,[6] ganz zu schweigen von der sehr spekulativen Lokalisierung von *Na'ama*.[7] So wird oft für alle eine edomitische Herkunft unterstellt,[8] während viele im Anschluß an Georg Fohrer davon ausgehen, Elifas entsprechend im Süden, im edomitischen Teman, Bildad im Osten, am oberen Euphrat, und Zofar im Norden, z.B. in Verbindung mit dem Ortsnamen *ᶜAin Ṣôfar* in heutigen Libanon zu lokalisieren.[9] Für eine arabische Lokalisierung des Hiobdialogs (nicht des Verfassers) ist Ernst Axel Knauf eingetreten: im Gegensatz zu dem Araber Hiob kämen die Freunde aus Schuach am mittleren Euphrat (dem Nordosten), Tema (dem Nordwesten) und mit Na'ama (wohl für Ra'mah = Nagran) dem Süden.[10]

Ungeachtet der Frage, ob das hiobsche Land עוץ auf dem edomitischen, aramäischen oder arabischen Boden zu suchen ist,[11] gehen wir der Frage

4 Zu den Einzelheiten und zur Diskussion siehe G. Fohrer, Das Buch Hiob, KAT 16, 1963, 105.

5 So z.B. Fohrer, a.a.O., 105f.

6 So z.B. A. de Wilde, Das Buch Hiob, OTS 22, 1981, 93; vgl. K. Budde, Das Buch Hiob, GHK 2/1, 21913, 11; A. Weiser, Das Buch Hiob, ATD 13, 71970, 37.

7 Zu den meist in Richtung der edomitisch-arabischen Gegend tendierenden Varianten siehe de Wilde, a.a.O., und E. Dhorme, A Commentary on the Book of Job, (1967) 1984, xxvii.

8 Vgl. z.B. B. Duhm, Das Buch Hiob, KHC 16, 1897, 15; R.H. Pfeiffer, Edomitic Wisdom, ZAW 44 (1926), (13–25), 18; de Wilde, a.a.O., 94.

9 Zur Diskussion siehe Fohrer, a.a.O., 105f.; vgl. auch F. Delitzsch, Das Buch Iob, BC 4/2, 65. Hierbei spielt es keine Rolle, ob die Redeeinleitungen samt den Freundesnamen 4,1; 8,1; 11,1 usw. von dem Hiobdichter selbst stammen oder nachträglich bearbeitet worden sind wie W.-D. Syring, Hiob und sein Anwalt. Die Prosatexte des Hiobbuches und ihre Rolle in seiner Redaktions- und Rezeptionsgeschichte, BZAW 336, 2004, 168, vermutet. Der Bearbeiter, der Prolog und Dialog miteinander verbunden hat, konnte möglicherweise bereits dem Dialog entnehmen, daß die Freunde aus unterschiedlichen Orten stammen.

10 E.A. Knauf, Ijobs multikulturelle Heimat, *BiKi* 59 (2004)G18, (64–67), 65.

11 Zur Diskussion siehe N.H. Tur-Sinai (H. Torczyner), The Book of Job. A New Commentary, (1967) 1981, 2ff., und O. Kaiser, Grundriß der Einleitung in die kanonischen und deuterokanonischen Schriften des Alten Testaments. Band 3. Die poetischen und weisheitlichen Werke, 1994, 79f.: zur aramäischen, bzw. nördlicheren Gegend neigen weniger Wis-

nach, ob sich die von der Rahmenerzählung nahegelegte unterschiedliche Herkunft der Freunde in irgendeiner Weise in ihren Reden spiegelt. Selbstverständlich dürfen dabei nicht automatisch fremde Einflüsse unterstellt werden, weil sich zeigen läßt, daß die Freundesreden vor allem eine unmittelbare Verbindung mit der alttestamentlichen Tradition besitzen.[12]

Der Hiobdichter geht mit der biblischen Tradition relativ frei um; daher ist nicht zu erwarten, daß sich in den außerbiblischen Weisheitstraditionen direkte Parallelen finden lassen. Wenn überhaupt, dann läßt sich am ehesten hinter der Häufung bestimmter inhaltlicher und formaler Gesichtspunkte eine gewisse Nähe der Freundesreden zu der einen oder anderen Tradition feststellen. Dabei sind die Aussichten für die Elifasreden, im Gegensatz zu denen seiner Kollegen, außerisraelitische Parallelen zu finden, wesentlich geringer, weil bei ihm die Bildhaftigkeit der Sprache zugunsten der Lehre in den Hintergrund tritt.

Die aramäischen Aḥiqarsprüche und ihre Parallelen zumal in den Zofarreden

Die aramäischen Aḥiqarsprüche aus der zweiten Hälfte des 8. oder der ersten Hälfte des 7. Jh. v.Chr., die in der Tradition der Aramäerstaaten des südsyrischen Raumes stehen[13], erregen zunächst wegen ihrer zeitli-

senschaftler, z.B. Delitzsch, Das Buch Iob, 44ff.; A. Dillmann, Hiob, KeHAT, 41891, 2; Fohrer, Das Buch Hiob, 73; F. Horst, Hiob. 1. Teilband: 1–19, BK 16/1, 1968, 8f.; J.E. Hartley, The Book of Job, NICOT, 1988, 66, Anm.9; Kaiser, a.a.O.; vgl. aber J. Day, How Could Job Be an Edomite?, in: W.A.M. Beuken (Hrsg.), The Book of Job, BEThL 114, 1994, 392–399.

12 Vgl. auch H. Gese, Lehre und Wirklichkeit in der alten Weisheit. Studien zu den Sprüchen Salomos und zu dem Buche Hiob, 1958, 31: „Wenn wir daher im folgenden von der „Aufnahme“ der Weisheitslehre in Israel sprechen, so meinen wir primär nicht die historische Übernahme einer bestimmten Denkart, sondern die eigene Ausbildung dieser Denkart innerhalb der israelitischen Gedankenwelt, mit der nachweislich die Ausbildung dieser Denkart in den umliegenden Kulturen in einem geistesgeschichtlichen Zusammenhang steht."

13 So das sachgemäße Urteil von I. Kottsieper, Die Sprache der Ah□iqarsprüche, BZAW 194, 1990, 241.246 u.a.; K.F.D. Römheld, Die Weisheitslehre im Alten Orient. Elemente einer Formgeschichte, BN.B 4, 1989, 113f., hat sich mit ähnlichem Ergebnis an J.M. Lindenberger angeschlossen. Zur Sache vgl. auch W. McKane, Proverbs. A New Approach, OTL, 1970, 156–182; H. Niehr, Die Weisheit des Achikar und der *musar lammebin* im Vergleich, in: C. Hempel, A. Lange, H. Lichtenberger (Hrsg.), The Wisdom Texts from Qumran and the Development of Sapiential Thought, BEThL 159, 2002, (173–186), 174ff.

chen, geographischen und kulturellen Nähe unsere Aufmerksamkeit. Neben den Parallelen zu den biblischen Proverbien könnten sich die Sprüche des weisen Aḥiqar für einen Vergleich als ebenso fruchtbar erweisen.[14] Dies trotz der unterschiedlichen Form der Streit- und Mahnreden der Freunde und der aus relativ lose verbundenen Sentenzen, Lehren und Fabeln des Aḥiqar.[15]

Eines der Haupttopoi der Aḥiqarsprüche bildet die Erörterung des falschen Zeugnisses, der falschen Lehre oder nicht angemessenen Rede und des Geschwätzes. Es erinnert sehr an die Worte des Zofar, deren Schwerpunkt auf der Betonung der Lippensünde liegt und der Hiob daher als „Mann der Lippen" rügt (11,2). Zofar fühlt sich als ein Weiser, der richtige Lehre und törichtes Reden zu unterscheiden meint (11,2–5; vgl. 20,12):

> Soll dies' Wortschwall ohne Antwort bleiben,
> oder der Schwätzer {אִישׁ שְׂפָתַיִם}[16] Recht behalten,
> dein Geschwätz Männer zum Schweigen bringen,
> sollst du spotten, unwiderlegt?
> Du sagtest: „Rein ist meine Lehre,
> lauter bin ich in deinen Augen."
> O möge Gott mit dir reden
> und seine Lippen {שְׂפָתָיו} auftun gegen dich!

Vgl. dazu in den Aḥiqarsprüchen V (56 I) 7; X (54) 5 (vgl. VI [56 II] 15):[17]

> Denn: Die Beliebtheit eines Mannes liegt in seiner Zuverlässigkeit,
> aber seine Ablehnung in der Unzuverlässigkeit seiner Lippen {*špwth*}.

Zu den Beziehungen mit dem AT siehe I. Kottsieper, Die alttestamentliche Weisheit im Licht aramäischer Weisheitstraditionen, in: B. Janowski (Hrsg.), Weisheit außerhalb der kanonischen Weisheitsschriften, VWGTh 10, 1996, (128–159), 131ff.

14 Es ist heute allgemein anerkannt, daß z.B. Prv 23,12–14; 27,3.7 ihre Parallelen in den Aḥiqar-Sprüchen besitzen; vgl. z.B. Kaiser, Grundriß, 53; D. Römheld, Wege der Weisheit. Die Lehren Amenemopes und Proverbien 22,17–24,22, BZAW 184, 1989, 47ff.; H.F. Fuhs, Sprichwörter, NEB 35, 2001, 10.

15 Vgl. auch die Beurteilung von Niehr, Die Weisheit, 178, daß es sich bei den Aḥiqarsprüchen um eine sekundäre Sammlung von Einzelsprüchen handelt.

16 Hier und weiter in Klammern Wörter, die ihre Parallele im Aramäischen oder Akkadischen besitzen oder im Text behandelt werden.

17 Beide Rekonstruktionen und Übersetzungen nach Kottsieper, Die Sprache, 9.12.15.20.

Be[sei]tige die Fallen deines Mundes {*pmk*},
danach laß [dein Wort] zu seiner Zeit herausge[hen],
denn größer als eine Kampfeslist ist die List des Mundes {*pm*}.

In den Aḥiqarsprüchen generell ist ein produktives Wortfeld mit ‚Mund' verbunden: „die Fallen deines Mundes", *ʾḥdy pmk* (X [54] 5), „die List des Mundes", *ʾrb pm* (X [57] 5), „Böses kommt aus ihrem Mund", *lḥyh tnpq [mn] pmhm* (XII [55] 14), „Gutes kommt aus dem Mund", *npqh ṭbh mn pm* (XII [55] 13). Der Hiobdichter baut auch in den Zofarreden umfangreiche Bilder mit Hilfe der Metaphorik in Bezug auf den Mund auf. Dazu gehören charakteristisch die metaphorischen Vorwürfe der Maßlosigkeit in der zweiten Zofarrede, die sich auf Fressgier und daher auf entsprechende Organe stützen; vgl. 20,12ff.:

Schmeckt süß {מתק Hif.}[18] das Böse in seinem Munde {פֶּה},
und verbirgt er es unter seiner Zunge {תַּחַת לָשׁוֹן},
hütet er es ängstlich und läßt nicht los,
und hält es {מנע} in seinem Gaumen {חֵךְ} zurück,
verwandelt sich {הפך Nif.} die Speise {לֶחֶם} in seinem Gedärm,
zu Schlangengift {מְרוֹרָה} in seinem Innern.
Das Gut {חַיִל}, das er verschlang {בלע}, muß er ausspeien,
aus seinem Bauche {בֶּטֶן} treibt es Gott heraus.

Ein ähnliches Bild kehrt mehrmals als feste Mahnung in den Aḥiqarsprüchen wieder, vgl. VI (56 II) 7 (ferner V [56 I] 11f.):[19]

Nicht sei süß {*ʾl tḥly*}, damit man dich nicht [verschlucke] {*[ybl*ʿ*]wk*};
nicht sei bitter {*ʾl tmr*}, [damit man dich nicht ausspeie!]

---

18 Alle hebräisch angegebenen Vokabeln begegnen auch im Aramäischen, entweder in den Aḥiqarsprüchen oder in den sehr erwähnenswerten Beschwörungen und Gebeten aus Uruk (ausgehendes 3. Jh. v.Chr.; siehe C.H. Gordon, The Aramaic Incantation in Cuneiform, AfO 12 [1937–39], 105f.) und aus Papyrus Amherst 63 (7. Kolumne; etwa 4. Jh. v.Chr.; siehe R.C. Steiner / C.F. Nims, You Can't Offer Your Sacrifice and Eat It too: A Polemical Poem from the Aramaic Text in Demotic Script, JNES 43 [1984], 89–114).

19 Rekonstruktion und Übersetzung nach I. Kottsieper in TUAT III, 330; ähnlich auch A. Cowley, Aramaic Papyri of the Fifth Century B.C., 1923, 225.

Darüber hinaus wird in der zweiten Zofarrede (20,23b–25*) ein Kriegsbild verwendet, in dem Gott in der Schlacht den Bogen (קֶשֶׁת) gegen den Frevler benutzt:

Er (Gott) sendet auf ihn (Frevler) seines Zornes Glut
und läßt auf ihn regnen *Feuer seiner Wut*.[20]
Entflieht er vor der eisernen Rüstung,
durchbohrt ihn der eherne Bogen {קֶשֶׁת}.
Der Spieß durchbohrt dann seinen Rücken,
ein Blitz *tritt* aus seiner Galle {מְרֹרָה}[21] *hervor.*

Wie in der Zofarrede lenkt Gott auch in Aḥiq. V (56 I) 1 und 3 den Bogen (ebenfalls *qšt*) und Pfeil gegen den Bösewichter zurück:[22]

[Nicht bespanne deinen B]ogen {*qšt*}
und le[g]e deinen Pfeil auf einen Gerechten an,
damit nicht (sein) Gott als sein Helfer auftrete
und ihn auf dich zurücklenke.
[Warum] hast du deinen Bogen {*qšt*} [gespa]nnt
und deinen Pfeil auf einen, der gerecht vor dir ist, angelegt?
Eine Sünde ist dies vor den Göttern!

An dieser Stelle können aus zahlreichen weiteren Beobachtungen nur noch zwei genannt werden. Erstens begegnen von den Freunden nur bei Zofar Wendungen wie „frevelhafter Mensch" (אָדָם רָשָׁע 20,29), „der Widerspenstige" (conj. אִישׁ מְרִי 20,29), „hohler Mensch" (אִישׁ נָבוּב 11,12), denen in den Aḥqarsprüchen Wendungen wie „guter" (*gbr ṭb*) oder „böser Mensch" (*gbr lḥh* z.B. VII [57 I] 5f.; V [56 I] 5.13) und „Mann ohne

20 Zu den kursiv angegebenen Textänderungen und Streichungen in diesem Passus siehe BHS, Fohrer, Das Buch Hiob, 324ff.; Tur-Sinai, The Book of Job, 319f.; H. Bobzin, Die ‚Tempora' im Hiobdialog, 1974, 286ff.; Witte, Vom Leiden, 68, u.a.

21 Die dem Wort מְרֹרָה zugrundeliegende Wurzel מרר ist sowohl in den Zofarreden als auch in den Aḥiqarsprüchen produktiv: vgl. Hi 20,14.25 und das gerade oben angeführte Beispiel Aḥiq. VI (56 II) 7; ferner VIII (57 II) 15 (*mrrwt'*), X (54) 11 (*mrrt'*, *[m]ryr*); so Kottsieper, Die Sprache, 12.

22 Rekonstruktion und Übersetzung nach Kottsieper, Die Sprache, 9.15.

Verstand" (*gbr l' l[bb]* X [57] 4) ähneln.[23] Zweitens fällt angesichts der besonderen Vorliebe des Zofar zu den konditionalen Gefügen mit der Konjunktion אִם auf, daß sich auch die Aḥiqarsprüche oft konditional mit Hilfe der Konjunktion *hn* äußern (vgl. z.B. V [56 I] 2.4f.; IX [53] 3f.9; X [54] 9 u.a.).

Die Weisheit der Väter in den Bildadreden und in der mesopotamischen Weisheitsliteratur

Als Einleitung zum Folgenden bedienen wir uns eines weiteren Passus aus den Aḥiqarsprüchen, weil dort (XV [58] 7b.8a) der Verfall eines Bösewichtes mit dem Fall des Triebs (*'b'*) verglichen wird.[24] Das hebräische Äquivalent אֵב begegnet im AT nur in Cant 6,11 und Hi 8,12. In der ersten Bildadrede gehört das Wort zur sehr umfangreichen Pflanzenmetaphorik, die bei Bildad insgesamt sieben Verse umfaßt. Dabei sind die Verse 11f. besonders gewichtig, weil sie den Kern der Lehre der Väter bilden:

> Kann denn Papyrus {גֹּמֶא} wachsen, wo kein Sumpf ist,
> das Riedgras {אָחוּ} ohne Wasser sprießen?
> Noch ist es im Triebe {אֵב}, nicht abgeschnitten,
> schon aber ist es dürr vor allem Gras {חָצִיר}.

Die ebenfalls in diese Reihe gehörenden Wörter für Papyrus und Riedgras, גֹּמֶא und אָחוּ, haben die Forscher stets veranlaßt, an das Ägyptische (*ḳm3*; *i̓jḥ*, *i̓ḥj*) zu denken.[25] Da diese Pflanzen aber fast überall im Nahen Osten bekannt sind[26] und das Bild selbst nicht unbedingt aus Ägypten stammen

---

23 Vgl. außerdem „Mensch, dessen Wandel gefällig und dessen Herz gut ist" (*'yš [šp]yr mrd[h] wlbbh* VII [57 I] 1), „Mann, der Böses tut" (*'yš zy y'bd lḥyt'* V [56 I] 9), „Betrüger" (*kdb* V [56 I] 8) und „Dummkopf" (*rt'* VIII [57 II] 5).

24 Rekonstruktion nach Kottsieper, a.a.O., 12.22. Er übersetzt ‚Frucht' statt ‚Trieb', doch siehe G.H. Dalman, Aramäisch-Neuhebräisches Handwörterbuch zu Targum, Talmud und Midrasch, [3]1938, 1a, und Ges[18] 2b.

25 So KBL 28a.187b und Ges[17] 23a.143b und die Mehrheit der Exegeten.

26 Z.B. ist das Wortpaar אחו / חציר auch aus den aramäischen Sefire Inschriften I A:28f. (*ḥṣr* / *'ḥwh*; siehe dazu Y. Avishur, Stylistic Studies of Word-Pairs in Biblical and Ancient Semitic Literatures, AOAT 210, 1984, 469f.), bekannt. Vgl. auch laut Ges[17] 23a und N. Peters, Das Buch Job, EHAT 21, 1928, 91, den Versuch von Sarowski, אָחוּ aus ass. *aḫu* ‚Küste' anzuleiten. Im Ugaritischen ist das Wort *'ḫ* ‚Wiese' ebenso belegt (KBL 28a; Foh-

muß,[27] kann seine Herkunft auch in anderen Traditionen gesucht werden. Da das Vergänglichkeitsbild in den Aḥiqarsprüchen in Verbindung mit dem allwissenden und richtenden Gott Šamaš steht, erweckt Mesopotamien unsere Aufmerksamkeit. Im Akkadischen ist das Wort *inbu* (ein Gegenstück zu אֵב) tatsächlich bekannt gewesen, noch mehr aber das Schilfrohr, dabei auch in der sehr populären Vegetationsmetaphorik und den Pflanzenfabeln. So kann eine Metapher aus der Beschreibung der Flut von Tigris und Euphrat in einer Fabel vom Ochsen und Pferd (K 3456 + DT 43, Vs., Z.17f.) als geradezu landeskundlicher Kommentar zu Hi 8,11 gelesen werden:[28]

The unworked [land] became a bog.
In reed-bed [and thicket] the plants grew.

Mittels weiteren Belegstellen erhält man Beweise dafür, daß das Bild von den Früchten oder Blüten in der Tat auch metaphorisch für Lebenskraft oder Nützlichkeit eines Menschen gebraucht werden konnte.[29] Aber auch für die Schilderung der Beeinträchtigung der Lebenskraft oder des Sterbens eignen sich die aus der Pflanzenwelt entnommenen Bilder von der die Früchte oder Wurzeln ausdörrenden Dürre sowie von der gewaltsamen Beschädigung der Pflanzen, ähnlich wie der Verfasser des Hiobdialogs es durch die bildhafte Sprache Bildads zusammen mit dem oben zitierten Vers (8,12) in mehreren Gängen ausführt (8,16–18; 18,16):

Er steht voll Saft im Sonnenschein {לִפְנֵי־שָׁמֶשׁ},
durch seinen Garten rankt sich sein Sproß.
Über Steinhaufen verflechten sich seine Wurzeln {שָׁרָשׁ},

rer, Das Buch Hiob, 185; M.H. Pope, Job. Introduction, Translation, and Notes, AncB 15, ³1985, 66).

27 Pope, a.a.O., und R. Gordis, The Book of Job: Commentary, New Translation, and Special Studies, Moreshet series 2, 1978, 90, halten die ägyptische Herkunft des Bildes nicht für unbestritten.

28 Rekonstruktion und Übersetzung nach W.G. Lambert, Babylonian Wisdom Literature, 1960, 177.

29 Z.B. durch eine babylonische Sentenz (Bo 4209+4710, Z. 7f.): „Prematurely ripe fruit {*inbu* !} is produce (bringing) grief" (Lambert, a.a.O., 279); oder durch eine assyrische Variante der Fabel von der Tamariske und der Palme (VAT 8830, Z. 22f.): „You, Tamarisk, are a useless tree. What are your branches? Wood … without fruit {*inbu* !}" (Lambert, a.a.O., 162f.).

zwischen Steinen *hält er sich fest.*[30]
Reißt man ihn aus von seinem Ort,
verleugnet der ihn: „Ich kenn' dich nicht".
Unten verdorren seine Wurzeln {שֹׁרֶשׁ}
und oben verwelken seine Zweige.

Neben einem Passus aus *Ludlul bēl nēmeqi* (II, 69f.), in dem die Krankheitsdämonen das Schilfrohr brechen und verstümmeln, liefert eine akkadische Gebetsbeschwörung an Ea, Šamaš und Marduk (VAT 8237) ein weiteres anschauliches und für unseren Vergleich ergiebiges Bild (Z. 23):[31]

Wie eine ausgerissene Tamariske kehre er nicht zum (alten) Ort zurück!

Das in der Pflanzenmetaphorik geläufige akkadische Äquivalent *šuršu* für שֹׁרֶשׁ „Wurzel" führt zu einer ganzen Reihe von Pflanzenvergleichen, die es als Metapher für menschliches Schicksal verwenden. Als Prototyp dazu können Aussagen wie die auf den Tafeln 5–6 der Beschwörungsserie Šurpu aus Ninive dienen, in der Verbrennungsriten zur Reinigung des Klagenden von den unbekannten zerstörerischen Einflüssen eingesetzt werden. In den Zeilen 64f. wird zu der im Mittelpunkt der Handlungen stehenden und zu verbrennenden Zwiebel unter anderem gesagt:[32]

... sie im Erdboden nicht mehr Wurzel fassen kann,
kein Trieb mehr aus ihr sprossen und das Sonnenlicht sehen kann.

Halten wir nach weiteren einschlägigen Parallelen zu den Bildadreden Ausschau, richtet sich die Aufmerksamkeit sogleich auf die altbabylonische Šamaš-Hymne[33]: der Kontext der Wächterrolle des Gottes über Recht und Gerechtigkeit, das metaphorische Spiel mit Licht und Finsternis und die Beschreibung des unvermeidbaren Untergangs der Frevler wirkt vor dem Hintergrund der Bildadreden (18,5f.18) beeindruckend:

---

30 Konjiziert nach Budde, Das Buch Hiob, 38f., Fohrer, Das Buch Hiob, 184f., u.a.

31 Übersetzung von W. von Soden in SAHG, 341; siehe zu derselben Beschwörung auch unten.

32 Übersetzung nach W. Farber in TUAT II, 266. Des Weiteren vgl. das akkadische Erra-Epos, in dem die Wurzel (*šurussu*) verwendet wird, um auszusagen, daß der Baum durchgeschnitten ist und seine Frucht (*piri'šu*) nicht wachsen kann (IV 125; siehe Avishur, Stylistic Studies, 520, und K. Hecker in TUAT III, 798).

33 Text in Lambert, Babylonian Wisdom, 126–138.

Allein des Frevlers Licht erlischt
und die Flamme seines Feuers leuchtet nicht.
Das Licht in seinem Zelt ward dunkel
und über ihm verlöschte seine Leuchte {נֵר}.

Er wurde vom Licht in die Finsternis gestoßen
und vom Festland verjagt.

Vgl. in der Šamaš-Hymne Z. 149f.:[34]
You grant revelations, Šamaš, to the families of men,
Your harsh *face* and fierce light {*nūru*} you give to them!

Auf das zweite Beispiel treffen wir im Vasallenvertrag des assyrischen Königs Asarhaddon, in dem die Funktion des Sonnengottes als gerechter Richter und Herr über Licht und Finsternis erneut bestätigt wird:[35]

Möge Šamaš, das Licht {*nu-úr*} des Himmels und der Erde, euch billiges und gerechtes Gericht versagen, möge er euch das Augenlicht nehmen; wandelt (dann) in Finsternis!

In einem Abschnitt der Šamaš-Hymne tritt der Gott als Garant des Rechts und Vollzieher seiner eigenen gerechten Urteile auf (vgl. z.B. Z. 95–100). In dem Zusammenhang werden viele verschiedene Arten von Fallen, Fallstricken, Schlingen, Netzen und Fesseln gegen den Frevler instrumentalisiert (Z. 74, 83, 84, 87, 90, 94, 97). Eine ähnliche und im AT auffallende Häufung dieser Metaphern spielt wiederum in der zweiten Bildadrede (18,8–10) eine Rolle, wo sie unmittelbar auf die Schilderung der erloschenen Lichter in den Zelten der Frevler folgen und den Sturz der Bösewichter schildern:

Kurz wurden seine kräftigen Schritte
und *wanken machte ihn*[36] sein eigener Rat.
Denn er geriet mit seinen Füßen in ein Netz

34 Übersetzung a.a.O., 135; Kursiv ebenso von Lambert.

35 Übersetzung nach H. Schmökel, Mesopotamische Texte, in: Walter Beyerlin (Hrsg.), Religionsgeschichtliches Textbuch zum Alten Testament, ATD.E 1, ²1985, 95–168, 154; ferner vgl. eine Gebetsbeschwörung an Šamaš in SAHG, 318ff., Z. 11, und in *Ludlul bēl nēmeqi* II, 119f.

36 Zu beiden Konjekturen siehe BHS.

und lief über Flechtwerk hinweg.
Es hielt die Schlinge die Ferse fest,
der Fallstrick *packte* ihn.
Seine Schlinge {חֶבֶל}[37] lag verborgen auf der Erde
und seine Falle auf dem Pfad.

Noch eindeutiger werden das Fangnetz und die Falle als Instrumente des Gerichtsvollzugs dem Richter Šamaš in dem sehr alten mesopotamischen Mythos vom Himmelsflug Etanas zugeschrieben. In dessen Rahmen wird eine Fabel mit einer kurzen Beschwörung an Šamaš beendet:[38]

Dein Fangnetz ist die weite Erde,
deine Falle der fe[rne Himmel]:
Deinem Fangnetz [entkomme] der Adler nicht,
der Böses [und] Abscheuliches tat
und Böses für seinen Freund bereitete.

Darüber hinaus sind von mehreren Auslegern die anthropomorphisierten Krankheitsbilder in Hi 18,12–14 hervorgehoben worden, weil sie an Krankheitsdämonen in der mesopotamischen Tradition erinnern. Dieser reichen Quelle der Metaphorik bedient sich der Dichter des *Ludlul bēl nēmeqi* besonders ausführlich in der Schilderung der physischen Leiden des Duldenden (II, 49–111). In der Bildadrede lassen gerade „der Erstgeborene des Todes" בְּכוֹר מָוֶת (Hi 18,13) und „der König des Schreckens" מֶלֶךְ בַּלָּהוֹת (Hi 18,14)[39] sowie die Metapher von den gefressenen Haut und Körpergliedern (Hi 18,13) einen ähnlichen Eindruck entstehen, wie er

37 Die Wurzel חבל wird mit assyrischem *naḫbalu* und *ḫâbilu*, mit akkadischem *eblu* und *naḫlabu* in Verbindung gesetzt (KBL³ 274, Ges¹⁸ 318f.). Vgl. *na-aḫ-bal* in *Ludlul bēl nēmeqi* II, 84.

38 Diese Übersetzung stammt aus der altbabylonischen Fassung (Textzeuge S, Rs., Z. 20'–24') nach K. Hecker in TUAT.E, 37. Vgl. aber auch die mittelassyrische Fassung, II', Z. 1–2 (a.a.O., 38) und die späte Fassung aus Bibliothek des Assurbanipal, II, Z. 22, 46f., 67–72 (a.a.O., 44f.), und darüber hinaus die einleitenden Anmerkungen a.a.O., 34ff.

39 Die Frage, ob es sich hier um die „dichterischen Personifikationen" handelt (zur Diskussion siehe G. Fuchs, Mythos und Hiobdichtung. Aufnahme und Umdeutung altorientalischer Vorstellungen, 1993, 110–113) oder welche genauen Analogien sie in der mesopotamischen oder kanaanäischen Mythologie besitzen könnten, spielt keine große Rolle, weil sich die Beobachtung, daß überhaupt allein Bildad unter den Freunden personifizierte Mächte neben Gott und Mensch auf die Bühne stellt, als wichtiger erweist.

sich aus der Reihe von Dämonen in Z. 53–55, 71 und 102 ergibt. Bildad sagt in V. 13f.:

> *Seine Haut wurde* von Krankheit *gefressen*[40],
> der Erstgeborene des Todes fraß seine Glieder.
> Ausgerissen wurde er aus seinem Zelte, seinem Zufluchtsort,
> und hingetrieben zum König der Schrecken.

Dabei erweist es sich als wichtig, daß in der akkadischen Gebetsbeschwörung an Ea, Šamaš und Marduk[41] Šamaš eindeutig mit dem Krankheitsdämon und mit dessen Entmachtung in Verbindung gebracht wird.

Angesichts der gezeigten Parallelen kann man jedenfalls mit einigem Recht die Frage stellen, ob es ein Zufall ist, daß im gesamten Hiobdialog allein in der ersten Bildadrede (8,16) das Wort שֶׁמֶשׁ begegnet? Es ist immerhin auffällig, daß die Formel לִפְנֵי שֶׁמֶשׁ aus der Bildadrede ihre akkadische Parallele in dem Ausdruck *la-pa-an* ^{d}*Šamaš* eines babylonischen Spruchs besitzt.[42] So ist es nicht ausgeschlossen, daß die augenfälligen Häufungen der Pflanzenmetaphern (8,11f.16–18; 18,16) und der Wörter für Fanginstrumente (18,8–10), das Spiel mit Licht und Finsternis (18,5f.18) und die Personifikationen der Krankheit (18,13f.) von dem Verfasser der Bildadreden eingesetzt worden sind, um dem vom oberen Euphrat stammenden Schuchiten sein Lokalkolorit zu geben.

Besitzen die Elifasreden Parallelen in der außerbiblischen Weisheit?

Von den Freunden stützt sich Elifas im Gegensatz zu dem idealistischeren Gepräge der Bildad- und Zofarreden auf die praktische Lebenserfahrung und behauptet die Nützlichkeit der Gottesfurcht, um den Forderungen der Gesellschaft gerecht zu werden (vgl. den Sündenkatalog in 22,6–9) und die sich daraus ergebenden guten Lebensverhältnisse zu genießen. Obwohl ein ähnlicher Grundsatz auch vielen Sprüchen aus dem aramäischen Aḥiqar und der mesopotamischen Weisheit zugrunde liegt, muß der allgemeine Tonus der ägyptischen Lebenslehren seit Amenemope den Elifasreden in dieser Hinsicht viel naheliegender sein. Besonders eine

40 Konjiziert nach BHS.

41 Die Beschwörung (VAT 8237) ist oben bei der Pflanzenmetaphorik bereits betrachtet; für uns sind Z. 4–11 und 17ff. wichtig.

42 In diesem losen Proverb (Lambert, Babylonian Wisdom, 282) handelt es sich um den Fuchs, der nicht ausgehen kann, ohne daß Šamaš es nicht wüßte.

Stelle aus der demotischen Lehre des Anchscheschonqi (26,9) könnte ohne Probleme eine These des Elifas bilden:[43]

> Jede Krankheit ist traurig; aber der Weise versteht es, krank zu sein.

Weiterhin fällt bei den Elifas- im Vergleich zu den Bildad- und Zofarreden besonders die Berufung auf die eigene Lebenserfahrung auf. Sie gilt auch in den ägyptischen Lehren als die wichtigste Legitimation.[44] Dagegen fehlen einschlägige Parallelen in den mesopotamischen Lehren oder in den Aḥiqarsprüchen. Darüber hinaus finden sich zumal zu den Pflanzenmetaphern der zweiten Elifasrede im metaphorischen Gedicht zur Schilderung des Schicksals des „Heißen" und des „Schweigers" aus dem vierten Kapitel der Lehre des Amenemope (6,1–12) gewisse Ähnlichkeiten.[45] Es fällt jedoch auf, daß bei Amenemope zwei Vergleiche von gleicher Länge, ein negativer und ein positiver, einander gegenübergestellt werden, in den Freundesreden fehlen dagegen positive Beispiele völlig.[46] Obwohl in der babylonischen Weisheit vorhanden, bilden in ihr die positiven Vergleiche oder Metaphern gegenüber den negativen, soweit uns bekannt, eine Minderheit. Darüber hinaus zeichnet sich der stilistische Unterschied zwischen Metapher und Vergleich ab; denn im Amenemope handelt es sich ausschließlich um den zweiteren, in den Bildad- und Elifasreden um die erstere. Außerdem werden unsere Beobachtungen durch die Tatsache unterstrichen, daß die Stelle in der ägyptischen Weisheitslehre eher eine Ausnahme bildet und weitere Pflanzenvergleiche sehr selten, bzw. uns

---

43 Übersetzung nach H. Brunner, Altägyptische Weisheit. Lehren für das Leben, 1988, 290, Z. 446.

44 Siehe N. Shupak, Where can Wisdom be found? The Sage's Language in the Bible and in Ancient Egyptian Literature, OBO 130, 1993, 242; Brunner, a.a.O., 19. Vgl. z.B. in der Lehre des Cheti: „ich habe Geprügelte gesehen" oder „ich habe aber auch die beobachtet..." (Z. 10; Übersetzungen nach Brunner, a.a.O., 159); ferner zählen zur Lebenserfahrung die Beschreibung in der Lehre für Kagemni, daß sein Vater der Menschen Wesen durchschaut hatte (Z. 39–41), oder die Lehre an den Sohn in Ptahhotep, daß die Alten aus ihrer Erfahrung sprechen (Z. 502).

45 Siehe den Text z.B. bei Brunner, Altägyptische Weisheit, 240f., und seinen Kommentar, S. 476.

46 Auf die positiven Pflanzenvergleiche stoßen wir im AT in den einschlägigsten Parallelen zum 4. Kap. von Amenemope in Jer 17,8 und Ps 1, ferner auch in Ps 52,10; 92,13–15; Jer 11,16f. und Ez 17,5ff. Diese Stellen sind auch meistens von den Forschern hervorgehoben (z.B. H. Brunner, Ägyptische Texte, in: Beyerlin [Hrsg.], Religionsgeschichtliches Textbuch, [29–93], 77, Anm. 239).

nicht bekannt sind. Wie wir gesehen haben, bilden sie im Zweistromland ein literarisches Allgemeingut. Darüber hinaus bleibt in keiner der Metaphern in den Freundesreden von den Pflanzen etwas übrig, dagegen baut der Verfasser von Amenemope auf das Holz der Bäume sogar ein weiteres Vergleichsbild auf und fügt das den alten Ägyptern so wichtige Schicksal nach dem Tode vor Augen.

Es erweist sich als wesentlich einfacher, die Argumente zusammenzustellen, die gegen die These möglicher Anspielungen auf die ägyptische Weisheit in den Elifasreden sprechen[47]: schon die Tatsache, daß wir aus dem mesopotamischen Raum und nicht aus Ägypten zahlreiche Belege für „Hiobdichtungen" besitzen, mag darauf hindeuten, daß auf den Vergleich mit der ägyptischen Weisheitsliteratur keine allzu großen Erwartungen zu richten sind.[48] Da der Hiobdichter nach dem Exil gelebt hat, kommen entsprechend eher die babylonischen, aramäischen und persischen Einflüsse in Frage. Das dritte Gegenargument verbirgt sich in der viel pragmatischeren Kolorierung der ägyptischen Lebensweisheit, die außerdem generell nicht in dem Maße theologisiert worden ist wie die israelitische und zumal die Hiobdichtung. Als ein Beispiel möge hier die Gegenüberstellung von Weisen und Toren dienen, die in Ägypten kaum auf die göttliche Ordnung bezogen worden ist. Wenn überhaupt, so konnte solche Kontrastierung vornehmlich im Horizont der kosmischen *Ma3at* und erst sekundär durch den göttlichen Willen erfolgen. Elifas betont zwar die logischen Folgen der Taten von einem אֱוִיל, aber doch deutlich in einem theologisierten Kontext (vgl. 5,2).[49]

Ein Hinweis auf das mögliche Lokalkolorit der Elifasreden kann sich in der Bezeichnung הַתֵּימָנִי verbergen. Die Weisheit der Edomiter ist in

47 Vgl. auch J. Day, Foreign Semitic influence on the wisdom of Israel and its appropriation in the book of Proverbs, in: J. Day, R.P. Gordon, H.G.M. Williamson (edd.), Wisdom in Ancient Israel. Essays in Honour of J.A. Emerton, 1995, (55–70), 63f.66f., daß die Gegenüberstellung der Gerechten und Frevler nicht der ägyptischen Weisheit eigen ist, dagegen aber in den Aḥiqarsprüchen vertreten ist, und die „graded numerical sayings" (z.B. Hi 5,19–22; 33,14–22.29; 40,5) nicht in Ägypten vorkommen, dafür aber in Ugarit und in Aḥiqar; außerdem kommt die „Gottesfurcht" nicht in der ägyptischen Weisheitsliteratur vor Anchscheschonqi vor.

48 Vgl. auch J. Day, a.a.O., 57.

49 Vgl. J. Hausmann, Studien zum Menschenbild der älteren Weisheit (Spr 10ff.), FAT 7, 1995, 33.36, die den Schluß zieht, daß die Toren und Weisen in Prv 10ff. gegenüber der ägyptischen Weisheit und trotz ähnlicher Themen eher die „ethische Dimension" darstellen und keine intellektuelle.

den alttestamentlichen Zeiten berühmt gewesen (Jer 49,7; Ob 8). Leider ist ein Vergleich mit den aus Edom stammenden Weisheitstexten unmöglich, weil sie bisher nicht vorliegen. Doch können der Wortschatz und die Wendungen der Freundesreden gelegentlich im AT sehr selten sein oder überhaupt keine Parallelen besitzen. Solche Stellen können sich entweder auf eine uns unbekannte Tradition stützen oder die vorhandene im eigenen Interesse umprägen. Als ein Beispiel erweist sich die Löwenmetapher in der ersten Elifasrede 4,10f., deren seltene Wortwahl, beispiellos im AT, eine gewisse Nähe zu den mesopotamischen (semitischen) Sprüchen ihre nördliche, östliche oder südöstliche Abstammung nicht ausschlösse. Elifas verwendet auffallender Weise nicht das Wort אֵב wie Bildad, obwohl die Früchte, Sprosse oder Blüten bei ihm in 15,30b.32f. auch sechsmal genannt werden (יוֹנֵק; פֶּרַח; זְמוֹרָה[50]; כִּפָּה; בֹּסֶר; נִצָּה). Nur ein Wort (יוֹנֵק) stimmt mit dem Wortschatz Bildads überein (8,16). Dies mag dafür sprechen, daß der Hiobverfasser möglicherweise Elifas doch von Bildad auch durch ein Lokalkolorit unterscheiden wollte, aber ihn nicht weit weg von Juda ansetzte.[51]

Fazit

Aufgrund der nachgewiesenen Unterschiede inhaltlicher, stilistischer und metaphorischer Art in den Freundesreden und gestützt auf einen Vergleich mit den Weisheitstexten des Alten Nahen Ostens und Ägyptens hat sich der Verdacht erhärtet, daß Sprache und Vorstellungswelt des Verfassers des Hiobdialogs nicht nur durch die ihm bekannten biblischen Traditionen geprägt worden ist, sondern er sich auch darum bemüht hat, durch ein bestimmtes Vokabular und Motive aus der Weisheitsüberlieferung Vorderasiens den Freundesreden ein gewisses Lokalkolorit zu geben. So zeigt der Vergleich die Nähe der Zofarreden zumal zur aramäischen und die der Bildadreden zu den mesopotamischen Traditionen. Die Frage nach einer entsprechenden Kolorierung der Elifasreden kann dagegen nicht beantwortet werden, weil wir über kein entsprechendes Textgut verfügen. Eine ganze Reihe von Beobachtungen spricht gegen eine Verbindung mit der ägyptischen Weisheit. Elifas in Edom anzusetzen, wie es heute weithin angenommen wird, wird auch durch unsere Untersuchung nicht ausgeschlossen.

---

50 פֶּרַח und זְמוֹרָה sind konjiziert, so die meisten Kommentatoren.

51 Zu Elifas als Edomiter siehe J.R. Bartlett, Edom and the Edomites, JSOT.SS 77, 1989, 40.89.

The Neo-Assyrian Ruling Class*

Simo Parpola, Helsinki

Despite its crucial role in the administration of the empire, the Neo-Assyrian political elite has never been adequately studied as a social class. This paper assembles the basic facts relevant to the subject and preliminarily charts the distinctive features of the elite against other segments of the Neo-Assyrian society. It will be shown that while Assyrian ethnic nobility continued to form an important component of the ruling class, in the mature imperial period (late eighth-seventh centuries BC) the elite as a whole was multi-ethnic and international in composition. Despite its heterogenous background, it constituted a culturally and linguistically homogenous whole, which derived its identity from Assyrian imperial culture and jealously guarded its privileges against other social classes, including ethnic Assyrians not forming part of the elite.

At the beginning of its history, Assyria was a city-state engaged in long-distance overland trade rather than in military exploits. It had grown into statehood first as part of the Akkadian Empire and then as a province of the Sumerian Ur III Empire. The first kings of Assur came from families that had previously ruled the city as governors of the emperors of Akkad and Ur; in their inscriptions they perpetuate the traditions of their predecessors, and in due course they clearly regarded themselves as heirs to the imperial legacy of Akkad.[1] They ruled with the help of a city council com-

* An earlier version of this paper was presented on April 26, 2000, at "Social Relations in the Countries of Ancient Near East", the 3rd Symposium of the Estonian Assyriological Society, Tartu. The present version was submitted to press in 2001 and the bibliographical references have not been updated since.

1 On the adherence of the first independent Assyrian kings to Akkadian rather than Ur III imperial traditions and on the evolution of their titulary from "governor of (the city) Aššur" [title of a provincial governor] to "governor of (the god) Aššur" [title of a regional ruler with imperialistic claims] see Hannes D. Galter, "Textanalyse assyrischer Königsinschriften: Die Puzur-Aššur-Dynastie", *SAAB* 12/1 (1998), 1–38. That the Puzur-Aššur dynasty (like the contemporary dynasty in near-by Ešnunna) with the growth of its power began to regard itself as the heir of the Akkadian empire is evident from the names of two of its later kings, Sargon and Naram-Sîn, which certainly not accidentally evoked the names of the two most powerful kings of Akkad. The title *šar kiššati*, "king of the universe", by

posed of a local aristocracy, a good part of which came from rich merchant families. Apart from numerous trade colonies in Anatolia and upper Syria, their sphere of influence was confined to the immediate surroundings of Assur, whose population must have been relatively homogeneous ethnically.[2]

The city of Assur and the regions close to it retained their status as the heartland of Assyria until the fall of the Empire. The Assyrian royal line continued almost unbroken through the centuries, and the native aristocracy and the old influential families seem to have kept their place in the Assyrian power structure until very late times. A well-known letter from the year 666 BC addressed to Assurbanipal quotes the king as saying to the heads of the old families of Nineveh: "Bring me your sons, let them stay in my entourage."[3] Lists of priests in the Assur temple,[4] scribal genealogies found in colophons of Neo-Assyrian literary texts,[5] and other similar evidence confirm that there indeed was remarkable continuity in the ruling class of the Empire, many important offices passing from father to son in the same family line.

Nevertheless, important changes had taken place in the composition of the imperial power elite. In the letter just quoted, the summoning of the sons of the old families to court is presented as a token of the king's love towards Nineveh; the writer thus reveals that the court positions, which the old family aristocracy traditionally held, were no longer automatically renewed or self-evident. This is made even clearer by another contemporary letter. The writer tells us that when he recently saw the goddess Ištar being carried in procession to her temple, he found no members of the old families of Nineveh among the carriers; all of them

---

which the Assyrian kings expressed their claim to universal hegemony, is attested in Assyria only since Šamši-Adad I (c. 1813–1781), but appears in Ešnunna already at the time of the Puzur-Aššur dynasty (in inscriptions of Naram-Sîn), see M.-J. Seux, *Épithètes royales akkadiennes et sumériennes* (Paris, 1967), 308.

2 On the Old Assyrian city-state see, fundamentally, Mogens Trolle Larsen, *The Old Assyrian City State and Its Colonies* (Mesopotamia 4, Copenhagen: Akademisk forlag, 1976).

3 *ABL* 2 = SAA 10 226 r.6–9. On the date of the letter see the commentary in *LAS* II (no. 121).

4 See *KAV* 26 and *KAR* 215 r. VI 5–12 (= B. Menzel, *Assyrische Tempel* [Studia Pohl, Series Maior 10, Rome, 1961], Bd. II, T 79); cf. *ABL* 43 and *CT* 53 149 (= SAA 10 96–97), and *CT* 53 899 (= SAA 13 207).

5 See H. Hunger, *Assyrische und babylonische Kolophone* (AOAT 1, Neukirchen-Vluyn, 1968). Cf. my remarks on the family of Adad-šumu-uṣur in LAS II (1983), p. XVIIIf.

were *homines novi* from Calah.[6] The reason behind such changes in the Assyrian power structure was the growth of the royal power, which leads to the creation of an aristocracy of high officials dependent on the king alone, and ultimately to the internationalization of the royal court and the entire ruling elite class.

The Middle Assyrian royal court already had a markedly international character. Foreign ambassadors and envoys frequented the royal palace,[7] the king had numerous foreign wives and concubines,[8] members of the Mitannian aristocracy (such as the *tartānu* and the *sartennu*) had been incorporated into the royal administration,[9] and a deposed and exiled Kassite king even served as a year eponym,[10] to mention only the most obvious examples. In the Neo-Assyrian period, the process of internationalization continued hand in hand with the expansion of the empire.

6 *ABL* 1103 = SAA 13 152.

7 See, e.g., C. Kühne, "Ein mittelassyrisches Verwaltungsarchiv und andere Keilschrifttexte", in W. Orthmann et al., eds., *Ausgrabungen in Tell Chuera in Nordost-Syrien* I (Saarbrücken, 1995), 216–219 referring to the arrival of diplomats from Sidon, Egypt, Hatti, and Amurru; E. Cancik-Kirschbaum, *Die mittelassyrischen Briefe aus Tall Šēḫ Ḥamad* (Berlin: Dietrich Reimer, 1996), 147–149 (letter no. 10). For the international correspondence of the Middle Assyrian kings see W.L. Moran, *The Amarna Letters* (Baltimore: Johns Hopkins, 1992), EA 15 and 16; H. Freydank, "Zum mittelassyrischen Königsbrief KBo XXVIII 61–64", *AoF* 18 (1991), 23–31; H. Otten, "Ein Brief aus Hattuša an Babu-aḫu-iddina", *AfO* 19 (1959/60), 39–46; E. Weidner, *Die Inschriften Tukulti-Ninurtas I. und seiner Nachfolger* (AfO Beih. 12, Graz, 1959), pp. 40 no.36 (KUB 3 76), 48 no. 42 (*ABL* 924), 53 no. 56 (and 64–68 (KUB 3 74; 23 88, 99, 102, 109); idem, "Aus den Tagen eines assyrischen Schattenkönigs", AfO 10 (1935/6), 2–8; W. von Soden, "Drei mittelbabylonische Briefe aus Nippur", *AfO* 18 (1957/8), 368–371; idem, "Weitere mittelassyrische Briefbruchstücke aus Hattusas", in E. Neu and C. Rüster, eds., *Documentum Asiae Minoris Antiquae. Festschrift H. Otten* (Wiesbaden, 1988), 333–346.

8 See E. F. Weidner, "Hof- und Harems-Erlasse assyrischer Könige aus dem 2. Jahrtausend v.Chr.", *AfO* 17 (1954–56) 257–293. A Middle Assyrian queen named Kurṣiptu "Butterfly" is mentioned in S. Franke and G. Wilhelm, "Eine mittelassyrische fiktive Urkunde zur Wahrung des Anspruchs auf ein Findelkind", *Jahrbuch des Museums für Kunst und Gewerbe Hamburg* 4 (1985), 19–26.

9 On the Mitannian origin of the Assyrian ministers *tartānu* and *sartennu* see G. Wilhelm, "*ta/erdennu, ta/urtannu, ta/urtānu*", *UF* 2 (1970) 277–282.

10 See E. Weidner, "Studien zur Zeitgeschichte Tukulti-Ninurtas I.", *AfO* 13 (1939/41), 118 and 122–123.

Large contingents of foreign troops were added to the imperial army and the royal bodyguard with every new conquest.[11] Foreign princes and aristocrats seeking asylum in Assyria were permanent guests at the court along with exiled and deported foreign royalty and nobility.[12] Egyptian dream interpreters, Hittite augurs and Babylonian scholars served as royal advisors beside Assyrian scribes and scholars.[13] Foreign musicians and dancing girls performed at royal banquets.[14] At least twice every year, vassal rulers and government officials gathered in the capital for the royal New Year's reception.[15] From the early 9th century on, men with non-Assyrian names start to make their way into the imperial elite as year eponyms and holders of important state offices.[16] The royal practice of marrying foreign wives continued and was taken further than ever: the principal queens of at least three Neo-Assyrian kings (Tiglath-Pileser III, Sargon and Sennacherib) were West Semites, Aramean or Israelite.[17]

What is significant in this development is the fact that the foreign elements evidently were being absorbed into the ruling class quite deliberately and systematically. We know that noble youths of foreign origin, detained as hostages or exiles at the seventh-century Assyrian royal court,

11 See B. Oded, *Mass Deportations and Deportees in the Neo-Assyrian Empire* (Wiesbaden: Reichert, 1979), 48–59 and 108–109; note also S. Dalley and J. N. Postgate, *The Tablets from Fort Shalmaneser* (CTN 3, London, 1984), 35–43 and 173, referring to chariot troops from Samaria.

12 See S. Parpola and K. Watanabe, *Neo-Assyrian Treaties and Loyalty Oaths* (SAA 2, Helsinki, 1989), XX-XXI.

13 *ADD* 851 = SAA 7 1; SAA 10 (1993), XIV and XXVI.

14 See J. V. Kinnier Wilson, *The Nimrud Wine Lists* (CTN 1, London, 1972), 76–78.

15 See SAA 7 148–157 (cf. p. XXXI-XXXIV) and R. Mattila, "Balancing the Accounts of the Royal New Years Reception", *SAAB* 4 (1990), 7–22; cf. S. Parpola, LAS

16 The first of these was Aia-ḫalu (Yaḫalu), who held the office of state treasurer (*masennu*) in 833 and of commander-in-chief (*turtānu*) in 824 and 821; see R. Mattila, The King's Magnates: *A Study of the Highest Officials of the Neo-Assyrian Empire* (SAAS 11, Helsinki, 2000), 14f and 108f. Aia-ḫalu's name is Aramean, see PNA s.v. Most non-Akkadian names of later high officials are likewise Aramean; however, high officials with names of unknown linguistic affiliation are also known, e.g. Banbâ, the deputy prime minister (*sukkallu šaniu*) of 676, and Uarbis, the chief judge (*sartennu*) of 656 BC.

17 On Sennacherib's queen with the Aramean name Naqya („Pure, innocent") see S. Melville, *The Role of Naqia/Zakutu in Sargonid Politics* (SAAS 9, Helsinki, 1999); for Tiglath-Pileser III's queen Yabâ and Sargon's queen Atalya, the latter of whom almost certainly was a Samarian princess, see Ahmed Kamil in Muayad S. Damerji, *Gräber assyrischer Königinnen aus Nimrud* (Jahrbuch des römisch-germanischen Zentralmuseums 45, Mainz, 1999), 13–17 and *PNA* s.vv.

were routinely educated there in Mesopotamian scientific and religious lore, in exact the same way as Daniel and his companions a century later at the court of Nebuchadnezzar.[18] The purpose of this education probably was not so much to introduce these youths into the fine points of Assyrian culture as to permanently integrate them into the imperial elite; having been thoroughly imbued with Assyrian values, religion and ideology, they were sent back to their native countries as administrators or vassal rulers totally devoted to the imperial cause.[19] We possess several letters from such Assyrianized foreign aristocrats, which eloquently testify to the degree of completeness by which their Assyrianization had been accomplished.[20]

Side by side with the internationalization of its elite, Assyria as a whole was transformed from an ethnically homogeneous city-state into a multinational empire. In its primitive form, the empire was but a loose conglomeration of tributary vassal kingdoms bound together by oaths of loyalty to the Assyrian king. From the ninth century on, however, it was gradually converted into a much more durable and homogeneous whole through a ruthless but highly successful policy of social, economic and linguistic integration. From the reign of Tiglath-Pileser III on, rebel vassal states were systematically converted into Assyrian provinces. Their ethnic and cultural identities were obliterated through extensive deportations, their capitals were reorganized and rebuilt after Assyrian models, and a uniform system of taxation and conscription was imposed along with imperial standards, measures, calendar, and cults, as well as an imperial *lingua franca*, Aramaic. Deportees transplanted into central Assyria became completely Assyrianized in the course of a few generations,[21] while those deported to

18 See S. Parpola, "A Letter from Šamaš-šumu-ukīn to Esarhaddon", *Iraq* 34 (1973), 21–34, esp. 33f.

19 Parpola and Watanabe, *Neo-Assyrian Treaties* (n. 12 above), XXI.

20 E.g., *ABL* 756 (from Kudurru, the son of Šamaš-ibni of Bit-Dakkuri); *ABL* 755+ = SAA 10 179 (from the same[?] Kudurru); *ABL* 943, 1148 and 1400 (from the Elamite prince Tammaritu); *ABL* 390 (from Bel-iqiša of Gambulu); *ABL* 992 and *CT* 53 16, 148 and 289 (from a Babylonian named Itti-Šamaš-balāṭu, now an imperial official in Phoenicia). All except one of these letters are written in Neo-Assyrian but exhibit various orthographic and linguistic peculiarities which betray the non-Assyrian origin of their writers.

21 Cf., e.g., the case of the two *ḫunduraya* families in Assur, both orginally deportees from the Iranian city of Hundur but entirely Assyrian in their names by the 7th century (see O. Pedersén, *Archives and Libraries in the City of Assur, Part II* [Uppsala, 1986], 85–95, or the Egyptian colony of Assur, whose leaders bore names such as Urdu-Aššur "Servant of Aššur",

peripheral areas spread the Aramean language and culture there. By the end of the eighth century BC, the Assyrian provincial system with its uniform imperial culture already covered most of the ancient Near East, and in the course of the following century it was expanded further.[22]

The cornerstone of this process of integration and assimilation was the imposition of Aramaic as the *lingua franca* of the empire, which must be viewed as carefully calculated government policy. While Assyrian royal inscriptions of the ninth century still refer to Arameans in negative terms,[23] by the end of the next century the ethnicon "Aramean" had completely lost its negative connotation. The Aramaic language and script were now commonly used in administration beside Akkadian and the cuneiform script.[24] By the beginning of the seventh century, most official records seem to have been drawn up in both Akkadian and Aramaic, and a generation later the administrative correspondence of the empire seems to have been carried out in Aramaic only.[25] This implies that Aramaic had by then become an essential part of Assyrian identity, to the extent that in

Kiṣir-Aššur "Host of Aššur", and La-turammanni-Aššur "Do not forsake me, O Aššur!" (ibid. 125–129).

22 See in more detail my article "Assyria's Expansion in the 8th and 7th Centuries BCE and Its Long-Term Repercussions in the West", forthcoming in W. Dever and S. Gitin, eds., *Symbiosis, Symbolism and the Power of the Past: Canaan, Ancient Israel and their Neighbors*, Proceedings of the Centennial Symposium of The W. F. Albright Institute of Archaeological Research and the American Schools of Oriental Research, Jerusalem, 2000.

23 See RIMA 2 p. 150:53 (Adad-narari II) and 261:93–95 (Ashurnasirpal II); RIMA 3 p. 19:38 (Shalmaneser III).

24 See P. Garelli, "Importance et rôle des Araméens dans l'administration del l'empire assyrien", in H.-J. Nissen and J. Renger, eds., *Mesopotamien und seine Nachbarn. Politische und kulturelle Wechselbeziehungen im Alten Vorderasien vom 4. bis 1. Jahrtausend v.Chr.* (Berlin: Dietrich Reimer, 1982), 437–447; H. Tadmor, "On the Role of Aramaic in the Assyrian Empire", in M. Mori, ed., *Near Eastern Studies Dedicated to H.I.H. Prince Takahito Mikasa on the Occasion of His Seventy-Fifth Birthday* (Bulletin of the Middle Eastern Culture Center in Japan 5, Wiesbaden: Harrassowitz, 1991), 419–426.

25 See S. Parpola, *The Correspondence of Sargon II, Part I: Letters from Assyria and the West* (SAA 1, Helsinki, 1987), XV-XVI. Revealingly, already under Sargon (721–705), the governor of Ur, with the Akkadian name Sîn-iddin, wanted to write to the king not in Babylonian on clay tablets, but in Aramaic on letter-scrolls (*CT* 54 10)!

later Greek usage, Aramaic language and script were commonly referred to as "Assyrian language and script."[26]

In summary, the Neo-Assyrian society markedly differed from the Old Assyrian one. Instead of an ethnically uniform society where both the ruling class and the bulk of the population spoke Akkadian, we now have a situation where Akkadian had become a minority language and spoken only in the Assyrian heartland and by an elite of mixed origin, while the bulk of the population, also of mixed origin, spoke a different language, Aramaic.[27] The ruling class and the masses differed in other respects, too.

The elite owned or controlled most means of production and most of the land.[28] It had the exclusive access to high state offices and enjoyed numerous privileges that added to its wealth, such as shares of taxes, tribute, audience gifts and spoils of war.[29] It distinguished itself from the masses by its distinctive and expensive dress, jewellery and insignia,[30] as well as by its Akkadian personal names and the use of the Akkadian language and the cuneiform script. As its fortunes were dependent upon the largesse and whimsies of the king, it shared a heavily emperor-centered ideology and world view, which regarded Assyria as a sort of "kingdom of heaven" upon earth and the king as the sole earthly representative of god.[31]

---

26 See R. C. Steiner, "Why the Aramaic Script was Called 'Assyrian' in Hebrew, Greek, and Demotic", *Orientalia* n.s. 62 (1993), 80–82; S. Parpola, "Assyrians after Assyria", *Journal of the Assyrian Academic Society* 12/2 (2000), 1–16, esp. 8–13.

27 See J N. Postgate, "Ancient Assyria - A Multi-Racial State", *ARAM Periodical* 1/1 (1989), 1–10.

28 V. A. Jakobson, "The Social Structure of the Neo-Assyrian Empire", in I. M. Diakonoff, ed., *Ancient Mesopotamia: Socio-economic History* (Moscow, 1969), 277–295; J. N. Postgate, "Ownership and Exploitation of land in Assyria in the 1st Millennium B.C.", in M. Lebeau and P. Talon, eds., *Reflets des deux fleuves: Mélanges offerts à André Finet* (Leuven, 1989), 141–152.

29 J. N. Postgate, "The Economic Structure of the Assyrian Empire", in M. T. Larsen, ed., *Power and Propaganda* (Mesopotamia 7, Copenhagen: Akademisk forlag, 1979), 193–221.

30 J. N. Postgate, "Rings, Torcs, and Bracelets", in P. Calmeyer et al., eds., *Beiträge zur Altorientalischen Archäologie und Altertumskunde. Festschrift für Barthel Hrouda* (Wiesbaden: Harrassowitz, 1994) 235–24. Cf. Xenophon's Cyropaedia 1.3.2–3 and Anabasis 1.2 and 1.8, showing that the Median and Persian elites inherited their way of distinctivc dressing from the Assyrians.

31 See S. Parpola, "The Assyrian Cabinet", in M. Dietrich and O. Loretz, eds., *Vom Alten Orient zum Alten Testament. Festschrift für Wolfram Freiherrn von Soden zum 85. Geburtstag*

The bulk of the population, by contrast, owned little, carried the burden of military service, taxation and forced labor,[32] and was entitled to only the basic education at best. It was in practice, though not by law, also excluded from high state offices and held no privileges, except in a few cult centers, which had been exempted from taxation. It did, however, have in common with the elite the imperial culture and ideology, which were propagated to it by all possible verbal and visual means.[33] Giving the children Akkadian names also seems to have been common even among people of non-Assyrian origin (see Appendix).

With such deeprooted differences between the rulers and the ruled, it hardly needs to be pointed out that the elite was highly exclusive in character and jealously guarded its privileges. While instruction in Mesopotamian religious and scientific lore was, as we have seen, freely poured upon foreign newcomers to the establishment,[34] it was withheld from native Assyrians who did not belong to the ruling class. Revealingly, an anonymous letter to the king denounces a wealthy goldsmith from Assur who had hired a Babylonian scholar to teach his son exorcism, astrology and extispicy, arts that were considered by the writer to be the royal prerogative only.[35] Restricting access to higher education to the elite certainly strengthened its cohesion as a social class and added to its sense of superiority, which was further strengthened by its other distinctive features, such as dress and language. There cannot be any doubt that Akkadian enjoyed the status of a high language vis-à-vis Aramaic, and it is no wonder that the foreign nobility who joined the elite readily assumed Assyrian names consonant with imperial ideology, such as *Šarru-lū-dāri*, "May the king live for ever."[36]

(AOAT 240, Neukirchen-Vluyn, 1995), 379–401; idem, "Sons of God: The Ideology of Assyrian Kingship", *Archaeology Odyssey* 2/5 (1999), 16–27.

32 See J. N. Postgate, *Taxation and Conscription in the Assyrian Empire* (Studia Pohl, Series Maior 3, Rome: Biblical Institute Press, 1974).

33 See S. Parpola, "Monotheism in Ancient Assyria", in Barbara N. Porter, *One God or Many? Conception of the Divine in Ancient World* (Casco Bay, 2000), 165–209.

34 See nn. 18–19 above.

35 See *ABL* 1245 discussed in S. Parpola, "The Man Without a Scribe and the Question of Literacy in the Assyrian Empire", in B. Pongratz-Leisten et al., eds., *Ana šadî Labnāni lū allik. Beiträge zu altorientalischen und mittelmeerischen Kulturen. Festschrift für Wolfgang Röllig* (Neukirchen-Vluyn, 1997), 315–324, n.18.

36 At least four nobleman of foreign origin are known to have borne this name between 701 and 664: 1. a Philistine, son of Rukibtu, appointed as king of Ashkelon by Sennacherib, see

On the other hand, it must not be overlooked that with all their differences, the elite and the masses also shared many common features. After all, they lived in the same country, participated in the same wars and conquests, frequented the same temples and festivals, and communicated, intermarried[37] and intermingled in a myriad of different ways. As a result, the elite must have been largely bilingual and eventually may even have largely spoken Aramaic as its first language.[38] This was certainly true of the scribe who used the cuneiform sign "lord" for writing the word "son" in a beautiful copy of the first tablet of the Epic of Gilgamesh, which he contributed to the library of Assurbanipal.[39] Such a mistake could only have been made by an Assyrian speaking Aramaic as his first language: Aramaic

---

H.-U. Onasch, Die assyrischen Eroberungen Ägyptens, Teil I: Kommentare und Anmerkungen (Ägypten und Altes Testament 27/1, Wiesbaden, 1994), 41; 2. an Egyptian accused for conspiring against Esarhaddon in the letter *CT* 54 22 = SAA 10 112 r.11, datable to 676, see Onasch, ibid.; 3. an Egyptian appointed as king of Ṣinu/Pelusium by Esarhaddon after the conquest of Memphis, see Onasch, ibid. pp. 36 and 40. It is almost certain, as pointed out by Onasch, that all these individuals had previously sojourned at the Assyrian royal court. In addition, an individual called Muṣrayu („Egyptian"), son of Šarru-lū-dāri *(Mṣry br Srldr)* occurs as a witness in an Aramaic legal document from Assur dating from mid-7th century (M. Lidzbarski, *Altaramäische Urkunden aus Assur* [WVDOG 38, Leipzig, 1921], no. 6). The name was extremely common in the period, and it is likely that in most cases it was an assumed name. Note the frequency of the Aramaic phrase ***mlkʾ lʿlmyn ḥyy*** "may the king live forever!" as a salutation to the king in Dan. 2:4, 3:9, 5:10 and 6:7.22.

37 That marriages between the Akkadian and Aramean segments of population were actively encouraged by the government is made likely by NL 26 (*Iraq* 18 pl.10), a letter to Tiglath-Pileser III, which reads (obv. 4ff): "Concerning the Arameans of whom the king said, 'They should be married (MÍ.MEŠ *lu-šá-ḫi-zu-šú-nu*)', I have selected many women, but their fathers refuse to give them unless they get [money]. May money be given to them, so they can marry." A comparison with another letter from the same sender (NL 25) shows that the Arameans in question were professional soldiers equipped by the government for a campaign. Another letter (*ABL* 556 = SAA 15 54 r. 10–13) shows that it was standard government policy to provide such troops with wives along with other amenities; cf. also CT 53 128 = SAA 1 21, dealing with the widows of fallen soldiers.

38 This is true of the royal family as well; note that many Assyrian kings since Tiglath-Pileser III had Aramaic or Israelite queens (see above, with n. 17), so their children will have learned Aramaic as their "mother tongue." Note also the prominence of the theophoric element Sîn "Moon" in the names of the Sargonid dynasty (Sîn-aḫḫe-riba; Sîn-nadin-apli, Sîn-per'u-ukin; Sîn-šarru-iškun), doubtless reflecting the attention given by this dynasty to the cult of the Aramaic moon god of Harran.

39 See S. Parpola, *The Standard Babylonian Epic of Gilgamesh* (SAACT 1, Helsinki, 1997), p. 74, line 242 (ms. D) // line 265 (ms. A2).

maraʾ (st. det. *marʾā*) "lord" was homophonic with Assyrian *marʾu* (st. constr. *mara*) "son."[40]

It is hence clear and worth emphasizing that the differences between the elite and the masses were *social*, not ethnic. Both were equally Assyrian and, like citizens of the United States of America, shared the same national and political identity. The distinctive features of the elite served to lift it above the masses; but while certainly important to their identity as a social class, they did not constitute the *totality* of Assyrian identity, which in Neo-Assyrian times must have essentially resided in the Aramaic language as well – a language spoken all over the empire by the broad masses and the elite alike, but nowhere outside of it. Of course, beside their primary identity as citizens of Assyria, the masses also had a number of other identities corresponding to their diverse ethnic origins. But so did also the members of the ruling elite.

A modern analogy may help bring home the point. My own native country, Finland, is a bilingual state where a Swedish-speaking minority has for centuries exploited a Finnish-speaking majority.[41] The language of the elite continues to be essential to its cultural and social identity but is secondary from the viewpoint of its national identity. Like the Assyrian ruling class, the Swedish-speaking elite is largely bilingual; in many cases, its members speak Finnish as their first language. Its ethnic background is mixed; it largely consists of assimilated ethnic Finns, but it also includes ethnic Swedes and assimilated ethnic Germans, Russians, Danes, Poles, Dutch and other nationalities. In earlier times (until the end of the 19th century), higher education was possible only to members of the elite, and for joining the elite, it was necessary to assume a Swedish name, master the Swedish language, and embrace the Swedish culture and values. Today, of course, Finland is constitutionally a bilingual country where both languages theoretically have an equal status. However, in practice Swedish

40 A similar revealing slip is also attested in *ABL* 1201 = SAA 1 220:3, a letter concerning Israelite deportees, where the sign DUMU "son" (*marʾu*) is conversely used for writing the word "lord" (*marʾu* in Aramaic, but *bēlu* in Akkadian). The DUMU sign is also used for Aramaic *marʾu* "lord" in spellings of the personal names Maraʾ-biʾdi (*ADD* 720:4) and Maraʾ-suri (*ADD* 479:5).

41 Finland was annexed to Sweden in 1155 and remained under Swedish rule until 1809. The dominant position of the Swedish-speaking elite was not significantly affected by the period of the Russian rule (1809–1917), because Finland then was an autonomous duchy under the direct rule of the Czar. Information on the Swedish-speaking minority of Finland can be found e.g. at the Internet address http://www.folktinget.fi/info_uk.htm.

still retains the status of high language, and mastering it is still a must for anyone who aspires for a high government office or acceptance within the Establishment. The Swedish-speaking minority still controls most of the economy[42] and enjoys several privileges within the educational system. Speakers of Swedish are still instinctively associated with the elite, while those *unable* to speak it are instinctively associated with the uneducated masses.

Yet both language groups unquestionably share the Finnish identity. The Swedish-speaking minority refuses to identify with the Swedes of Sweden, even though it does sympathize with them. The Swedish culture in Finland has been deeply influenced by the Finnish culture and vice versa; correspondingly, the Swedish and Finnish languages have deeply influenced each other, so that they share numerous common words, idioms and syntactic features, and even the same intonation.

The situation was very similar in Assyria, where the cultural and linguistic assimilation and convergence process was additionally helped by the structural similarity of Akkadian and Aramaic, both being Semitic languages.

Of course, the analogy is not perfect: Finland is a small country with a political system totally different from that of imperial Assyria. In Assyria, the ruling class constituted a highly centralized power structure that inevitably generated recurrent power struggles comparable to those of imperial Rome. The internationalization of the ruling class, surely calculated to contribute to the cohesion and durability of the empire, ultimately proved fatal to Assyria.

As is well known, the fate of Assyria was sealed by the Mede Cyaxares and the Chaldean Nabopolassar, who, after a prolonged civil war, divided the empire between themselves. For all that we know, both were members of the Assyrian ruling class, who had received an Assyrian education at the royal court and then served as trusted governors and generals in their home countries.[43] Having triumphed in the internal power struggle, they

---

42 Until very recently, much of Finnish economy was controlled by the so-called "ten families", all but one of them Swedish-speaking. There is a recent monograph on the subject by the Finnish Euro-Parliamentarian Esko Seppänen (see E. Seppänen and H. Taanila, *Ken on maassa rikkahin*, Jyväskylä: Gummerus, 1983).

43 A Berossus fragment quoted by Eusebius entitles Cyaxares "satrap of Media", see P. Schnabel, *Berossus und die babylonisch-hellenistische Literatur* (Leipzig: Teubner, 1923), 270: 47 and 47a, and cf. S. M. Burstein, *The Babyloniaka of Berossus* (SANE 1/5, Malibu: Undena Publications, 1978), 25f.

reorganized their home courts, ousting Assyrians from it and replacing them by the ethnic groups who constituted their power base. Their Assyrian education, however, guaranteed that the empire they inherited, though now split in two, and remained essentially the same as before.[44]

As for the masses, the change of power had little effect on their identity or daily life. They were and remained Assyrians, as shown by the communities of modern Assyrians that still survive in many parts of the Near East. With the rout of the Akkadian-speaking elite, the Assyrian culture in Upper Mesopotamia lost its cuneiform dimension, but its Aramaic form has survived, albeit with modifications, into the present day.[45]

APPENDIX: Bilingual Patronymics[46]

A. Father: Akkadian name, Son: Aramaic/foreign name

1. Abâ son of Buṭunaiu A 1804:4 (630*)

(The text erroneously has "Astyages/Azdahak" for Cyaxares.) Again according to Berossus, Nabopolassar („Bupalassaros") was a general of Sîn-šarru-iškun („Sarakos"), who was sent to Babylon to fight rebellious sea people but turned against his master, allying himself with the chief of the Medes („Azdahak"); see Schabel, *Berossus*, p. 271, and Burstein, *Babyloniaka,* p. 26. According to Ktesias, both Cyaxares and Nabopolassar were Assyrian generals; the former, "a Mede by race, and conspicuous for his bravery and nobility of spirit, was the general of the contingent of Medes which was sent each year to Nineveh"; the latter was "the general of the Babylonians", who learnt to know the former "during this service" (i.e., his sojourn at Nineveh) and subsequently incited him to overthrow the empire of the Assyrians (Diodorus of Sicily, 2.23.4; in this account, the names of the two conspirators appear in the garbled forms "Arbakes" and "Belesys", but there cannot be any doubt as to their identity). Nabopolassar's title as an Assyrian official is not known from cuneiform sources, but it is very likely that he had been the Assyrian governor (*šaknu*) of Sealand, like his treacherous predecessors Nabû-zēr-kitti-lišir and Nabû-bēl-šumāti under Esarhaddon and Assurbanipal; see G. Frame, *Babylonia 689–627 B.C.: A Political History* (Leiden, 1992), 211–212, and cf. R. Borger, *Die Inschriften Asarhaddons, Königs von Assyrien* [AfO Beiheft 9, Graz, 1956], p. 46:40, and M. Streck, *Assurbanipal* (VAB 7, Leipzig 1916), 142 viii 47ff; for a letter sent by Nabû-bēl-šumāti to Assurbanipal while still a loyal Assyrian official see *ABL* 839.

44 Cf. Parpola, "Assyrians after Assyria" (n. 26 above), 5–7.

45 See Parpola, "Assyrians after Assyria", 13–16.

46 See above. The great majority of the non-Akkadian names in the list are Aramaic. The numbers following the references (in parentheses) are dates. For the bibliographical abbreviations and the system of dating the (asterisked) post-canonical eponyms see PNA.

2. Abdunu son of Kukkullanu	ADD 311:7 (627*)
3. Abi-salamu son of Ḫambussu	PSBA 30 2:2
4. Adda-sakâ son of Kazallaiu	ADD 055:4
5. Addî son of Kenî	Rfdn 17 4r.13 (631*)
6. Aḫ-abû son of Kaldaiu	ND 2684 r.2
7. Aḫ-abû son of Nabû-balti-ili	O 3685 r.19 (682)
8. Aḫi-nasi son of Aššur-aḫu-ereš	A 3201 r.10 (732)
9. Aḫi-nasi son of Nabû-naṣir	A 3201 r.7 (732)
10. Aḫi-immê son of Kanunaiu	Rfdn 17 16:2 (615*)
11. Aḫi-Milkati son of Šumu-kenu	SAAB 1 18:2
12. Aḫunu son of Sapiku	ADD 891 r.8
13. Am-dukuru son of Uḫabbi-ilu	SAAB 7 1 r.20 (602)
14. Arnabâ son of Se'-aplu-iddina	ADB 1 102
15. Arwas-maàdi son of Bi-Nanaia	STT 406 r.24
16. Aširê son of Aḫu'a	ADD 446 r.12 (630*)
17. Barik-il son of Marduk	CT 54 582:3
18. Barikî son of Remanni-ilu	ND 3435:2, 3435B:4 (650)
19. Bariku son of Ra'iu	A 2551:5
20. Bibiia son of Aḫu-lešir	A 2693:2
21. Bibî son of Iddin-aḫḫe	SAAB 2 11 r.8
22. Dadi-aba son of Kanunaiu	ADD 780:5 (616*)
23. Dadia son of Aššur-eṭiranni	A 3201 r.9 (732)
24. Dadî son of Nergal-naṣir	ADD 16:4 (638*)
25. Dadî son of Bel-remanni	ADD 1241 r.12 (659), ABL 152:3
26. Al-Našḫu-milki son of Ilu-ittiya	ADB 2 111
27. Erisu son of Mannu-ka-Dadi	ADB 5 210
28. Geiâ son of Bel-ali	ADD 415 r.5 (734)
29. Giritu son of Qurdi-ilani	CTSHM 30:13
30. Ḫamputi son of Urdu-Gula	SAAB 2 7:2 (631*), 9 r.8
31. Ḫan-ṣaruru son of Nanaia	A 1806 r.7
32. Ḫanana son of Bel-dan	SAAB 7 1:2 (602), DeZ 6223 r.16
33. Ḫanana son of Ḫarranaiu	O 3702b:2
34. Ḫannanu son of Adad-riba	DeZ 10459 r.5 (676)
35. Ḫanunu son of Purattaiu	O 3685 r.15 (682)
36. Ḫawnanu son of Mannu-ki-aḫḫe	Ass 11634a:4 (622*)
37. Ḫati-Adda son of Nabû-šallim	DeZ 10459 r.8 (676)
38. Ḫuddaia son of Muṣuraiu	ADD 250:1 (639*)

39. Ḫulaiu son of La-teggi-ana-Issar	CTN 3 9:2 (613*)
40. Il-idri son of Arbailaiu	VS 1 88 r.15 (629*)
41. Luqu son of Aššur-šarrani	Ass 2282f:8
42. Mar-liḫia son of Ṭab-šar-Issar	ND 3426 r.21
43. Mati'-il son of Mannu-ki-ili	VS 1 87:6 (613*)
44. Mati'î son of Ṣil-Aššur	SAAB 9 96:5 (645*)
45. Milki-il son of Sin-aḫu-uṣur	SAAB 9 69:2 (629*)
46. Nasi' son of Nergal-ašared	Ass 9661b:4 (671)
47. Nanî son of Ululaiu	BT 128:4, 128a:2 (682)
48. Palṭi-Iau son of Sangi-[...]	PSBA 30 2 r.18 (617*)
49. Pašî son of Ibašši-ilani	ADD 373:2 (634*)
50. Pipia son of Šamaš-naṣir	A 1863 r.10 (762)
51. Ququa son of Aḫu-lamur	SAAB 9 73 r.9 (698)
52. Ququa son of Šelubu	Ass 1408 r.8 (708)
53. Samsi-idri son of Babilaiu	ZA 73 10 r.15, AfO 32 38 r.15 (636*)
54. Saqapâ son of Ubru-Issar	VAT 21538:4
55. Sasî son of Aḫulamma	MAss 29:11
56. Sauli son of Apladad-salim	VS 1 93:2 (613*)
57. Se'-ma'adi son of Asalluḫi-uṣur	STT 406+ r.22
58. Se'-rapê son of Sîn-zaqip-keni	AnSt 7 139:7
59. Se'-riḫimu son of Remutu	ND 2684:5
60. Ṣan'uru son of Sîn-na'di	ADD 22:5 (626*)
61. Ṣiṣianu son of Damu-ibni	ND 2750:6
62. Šer-nuri son of Adi-mat-ili	SAAB 9 124:2 (636*)
63. Tammeš-natan son of [...]du-Zababa	ND 2479 r.3
64. Ušinni son of Šumu-ṭabu	A 1911:2 (657)
65. Zabinu son of Ubru-Ninuwa	Muscarella Ladders 126:18 (633*)
66. [...]-ḫutni son of Sîn-aḫu-iddina	ADD 589:4

B. Father: Aramaic/foreign name, Son/Daughter: Akkadian name

1. Abi-ul-idi son of Zabdî	STT 406+ r.23
2. Adad-bani son of Zabdî	ADD 384+:4 (634*)
3. Adad-milki-ereš son of Menassê	SAAB 7 1 r.13 (602)
4. Adad-riba son of Masî	O 3682:2 (737)
5. Adad-šallim son of Attara	ADD 237 r.13 (665)
6. Aḫu-dur-enši son of Ḫuru	A 1882:4 (644*)

7. Aḫu-lamur son of Kisî	GPA 9:1
8. Aḫu-lamur son of Ṭua	GPA 82 r.14
9. Apladad-danninanni son of Rapi'	VS 1 100:2 (616*)
10. Apladad-killanni son of Riṣâ	ADD 153:3, 154:4 (663)
11. Aplu'a son of Iaqiru	SAAB 5 35 r.26 (625*)
12. Arbail-ḫammat daughter of Bisua	MAss 24:6
13. Aššur-balassu-iqbi son of Bibî	SAAB 9 73 r.25 (698)
14. Aššur-balassu-iqbi son of Abi-suri	Ass 1408 r.14 (708)
15. Aššur-iqbi son of Bessu'a	MAss 20:4, MAss 24 r.9
16. Aššur-iqbi son of Kurê	SAAB 5 44 r.4 (630*)
17. Aššur-mudammiq son of Susu	MAss 29:14
18. Aššur-mudammiq son of Buṣaiu	KAJ 270:2
19. Aššur-nadin-aḫḫe son of Didu	BaM 16 31:5 (620*)
20. Aššur-nadin-aḫḫe son of Abdî	VAT:9764 r.11 (723)
21. Aššur-šarru-uṣur son of Arbaiu	A 1857:2
22. Bel-šallim son of Iadi'-il	ADD 880 113
23. Dilil son of Buadi-Iau	ADD 311 s. i 3 (627*)
24. Eriba-Aššur son of Zabatâ	Ass 14231f:5 (652)
25. Ḫadi-lipušu son of Rauzu	GPA 82 r.3
26. Ḫarranaiu son of Ḫandî	O 3662:7, 3685 r.2
27. Ilu-uṣur son of Bir-Attar	O 3687:2
28. Inurta-aplu-uṣur son of Zabunu	Ass 10804:15
29. Kalbi-Aia son of Pisaniši	CTN 3 41:2 (616*)
30. Kenî son of Adda-lakusu	DeZ 5662:2 (622*)
31. Kiṣir-Aššur son of Ḫanṭasu	TCL 9 57 r.12 (658)
32. Kiṣir-Aššur son of Kunnanu	KAV 124 r.7
33. Kiṣir-ili son of Ḫa-bašti	Ass 2282l:19 (648*)
34. Kusaiu son of Zabad	TH 108:4 (625*)
35. Kutaiu son of Se'-DI	ABL 502:8
36. La-teggi-ana-Aššur son of Meiaṣabutu	Rfdn 17 9:2.9 (639*)
37. La-turammanni-Aššur son of Iašanimu	SAAB 9 68:2 (625*)
38. Lipḫur-ilu son of Zizî	ADD 446 r.9 (630*)
39. Lu-šakin son of Sariuni	NALK App I:1 (623*)
40. Lu-šakin son of Abši	ADD 331:2 (666)
41. Mannu-[ki-a]ḫḫe[?] son of Takiuanu	SAAB 2 12 r.9 (627*)
42. Mannu-ki-Arbail son of Puḫutana	A 1902:4 (645*)
43. Mannu-ki-Arbail son of Abdâ	SAAB 2 11 r.5

44. Mannu-ki-Issar son of Il-immi	SAAB 5 31A:2, 31B:4 (658)
45. Mannu-ki-Ninuwa son of Se'-dalâ	O 3685 r.16 (682)
46. Mannu-ki-šarri son of Zabinu	Fs Garelli 1:25 (650)
47. Marduk-nadin-aḫḫe son of Bar-ili	GPA 103 r.6 (788)
48. Marduk-šarru-uṣur son of Gabbê	ADD 116 r.11, 418 r.15, 439 r.2, 611 r.4 (all 664), ABL 1106:12
49. Mullissu-ḫammat daughter of Pabbau	A 2527:3 (675)
50. Mušallim-aššur son of Ḫarbiṣaṣu	SAAB 5 35 r.28 (625*)
51. Nabû'a son of Aḫ-abû	ND 3479 r.19 (671)
52. Nabû-malik son of Aḫ-Iau	SAAB 7 1 r.17 (602)
53. Nabû-reḫtu-uṣur son of Aḫarṭeše	ADD 307:2 (623*)
54. Nabû-sagib son of Parruṭu	ABL 847:3 (Ash)
55. Nabû-šarru-uṣur son of Adda-rapi	DeZ 5663 r.7
56. Nabû-šulmu-iqabbi son of Aširâ	DeZ 10459 r.7 (676)
57. Nabû-ušabši son of Šilani	Tadmor Tigl Summ:7:15
58. Nadinu son of Zammanišše	Rfdn 17 4:2 (631*)
59. Nergal-sakip son of Baua	Rfdn 17 7 r.17 (613*)
60. Nupsati son of Zabaqa	Ass 2282l:22 (648*)
61. Nur-Šamaš son of Kur'e-ila'i	ND 3426 r.14, 3429 r.11
62. Nusku-aḫu-iddina son of Atar-suri	TCAE 360 r.21 (702)
63. Pan-Aššur-lamur son of Bua	MAss 24:12, 29:2
64. Qibit-Aššur son of Bel-asuri	A 1866:4, 1866*:2 (639*)
65. Qibit-Aššur son of Meiaki	Rfdn 17 4 r.12 (631*)
66. Qibit-Issar son of Šatuṣu	A 2510:6 (648*)
67. Qurdi-Adad son of Isputu	SAAB 5 43:2 (628*)
68. Qurdi-Gula son of Busasu	SAAB 9 127:8 (636*)
69. Qurdi-Issar son of Il-ma'adi	A 1899:5
70. Qurdi-Issar son of Aṣidu	DeZ 10459 r.4 (676)
71. Remanni-Illil son of Iatana	ADD 621:2 (623*)
72. Remut-ilani son of Adda-idri	Ot 29 9 3:3
73. Remut-ili son of Ḫari-[...]	ADD 356:2
74. Sangi-Issar son of Ḫanda-riṣi	ADD 1241:2 (659)
75. Sebetti-aḫu-uṣur son of Nabudi	Ass 21548c:4
76. Sîn-na'di son of Muṣuraiu	SAAB 7 4 r.6 (600)
77. Sîn-nammir son of Ḫarranaiu	Fs Garelli 1:7 (650)
78. Sukki-Aia son of Parna-uari	TIM 11 2:1.13 (638*)
79. Sukki-Aia son of Muṣuraiu	MAss 19:7

80. Ṣil-Issar son of Baḫianu	ND 3486 109
81. Ša-Nabû-šû son of Šamaš-idri	Fs Garelli 1:2 (650)
82. Šamaš-abu'a son of Kaki	ADD 337:2
83. Šamaš-ibni son of Tammeš-natanu	ABL 454:15 (Asb)
84. Šamaš-kenu-uṣur son of Samaku	ADD 321:4
85. Šamaš-na'di son of Ḫandidî	Assur 2/4 no. 10:8
86. Šamaš-šarru-uṣur son of Kur[...]	SAAB 5 53 r.11
87. Šarru-lu-dari son of Ariḫu	ADD 815 R310
88. Šarru-lu-dari son of Rukibtu	AGS 141:5, OIP 2 C_1 :40, OIP 2 H_{1a} :265
89. Šarru-nuri son of Nani	Muscarella Ladders 126:1 (633*)
90. Šep-Aššur-aṣbat son of Ḫanda-sanu	SAAB 9 73 r.19 (698)
91. Šep-šarri son of Nabuti	DeZ 5663 r.2
92. Šulmu-aḫḫe son of Uadi	ADB 3 r.i 12
93. Šulmu-aḫi son of Zizuli	A 3201 r.12 (732)
94. Šumaia son of Ninê	CT 54 215:9
95. Šumma-Aššur son of Parnâ	SAAB 5 8:5 (639*), 35:4 (625*)
96. Tabši-lešir son of Quia	GPA 24:2 (746)
97. Tukulti-Aššur son of Assî	Ass 9573bc r.15, SAAB 5 52 r.1 (616*)
98. Turṣi-Issar son of Ḫaruwi	ND 2335B:3
99. Ubbuku son of Zabunu	VAT:9742 r.6
100. Ubrî son of Ḫala-iddi	ADD 345:2
101. Ubru-[...] son of Baia	SAAB 9 102:2 (644*)
102. Ubru-Aia son of Tira	A 1863 r.17 (762)
103. Ubru-Aššur son of Ḫazuqu	A 60 r.11
104. Ubru-Mullissi son of Atî	ADD 307 r.11 (623*)
105. Ubru-Nabû son of Iaḫuli	ND 2088:2 (625*)
106. Ubru-Sî son of Sa'ilu	DeZ no. 23 r.1
107. Ululaiu son of Se'-[...]	Ass 11682o:2
108. Ululaiu son of Ḫaza-il	AnSt 7 144:2 (674)
109. Urdu son of Aḫi-iabu	Ass 2282:2 (629*)
110. Urdu-Aššur son of Puṭi-ḫutapiša	A 1841:13.17 (618*)
111. Urdu-Belet son of Ḫallabeše	A 1881:4 (646*)
112. Urdu-Issar son of Ḫariruri	ADD 311 s. i 1 (627*)
113. Urdu-Nabû son of Abdi-Kura	TIM 11 6:2 (622*)
114. Urdu-Nanaia son of Sasû	ND 3420 r.15 (730)

115. Zar-Issar son of Ḫanbî	SAAB 2 11 r.3
116. Zarî son of Tata	SAAB 9 127:2.6 (636*)
117. Zarutî son of Gugî	ADD 44:6 (670)
118. Zer-[...] son of Burallaia	ADD 1242 r.8
119. [...]-aḫḫe-šallim son of Adda-atar	O 3664 r.4
120. [...]-Aššur son of Ḫarwaṣi	A 314 r.5 (625*)
121. [...]-iqbi son of Kurê	Ass 9661c r.4 (621*)
122. [...]-šumu-ibni son of Iadâ	VAT 10696:7

Krankheit – ein Makel an heiliger Vollkommenheit. Das Urteil altisraelitischer Priester in Leviticus 13 in seinem Kontext

Henning Graf Reventlow, Bochum

1. „Ehre den Arzt, weil man ihn braucht. Denn auch ihn hat Gott erschaffen. Von dem Höchsten kommt Heilkunst und vom König empfängt er Geschenke."

Dieser Weisheitsspruch steht im Buch des Jesus Sirach (Sir 38, 1-2), einer Schrift, die in das hebräische Alte Testament nicht mehr aufgenommen wurde, weil sie erst aus dem zweiten Jahrhundert vor Christus stammt. Aber selbst der Siracide läßt bald darauf den Spruch folgen: „Wer gegen seinen Schöpfer sündigt, fällt in die Hände der Ärzte" (Sir 38, 15). Gegen den anfangs deutlichen Einfluß der hellenistischen Kultur macht sich hier doch wieder das alttestamentliche Erbe bemerkbar. Obwohl das Alte Testament in seiner hebräischen Sprachform das einzige ununterbrochen und vollständig überlieferte altorientalische Dokument darstellt, ist dort bemerkenswerter Weise von Ärzten kaum, und dann negativ, die Rede, und in unserem Sinne medizinische Heilverfahren werden nicht geschildert. Vergleichende Darstellungen betonen,[1] daß sich dieses Ergebnis deutlich von unseren Erkenntnissen über Ägypten und Mesopotamien abhebt. Daher liegt das Urteil nicht fern, die Heilkunst sei, mit diesen alten Kulturen verglichen, in Israel ziemlich primitiv gewesen.[2] „Medicine as a profession was held in low esteem", lautet der Schluß.[3] Dieses Urteil scheint

---

1 Wie J. V. Kinnier Wilson, Medicine in the Land and Times of the Old Testament, in: T. Ishida, Hg., Studies in the Period of David and Salomo and Other Essays (Winona Lake, IN, 1982), 339–365; P. J. King / L. E. Stager, Life in Biblical Israel (Louisville / London 2001), 68–84, 69.

2 King / Stager, Life, 69. Another opinion with R. North, Medicine and Healing in the Old Testament Background, in ders., Medicine in the Biblical Background and Other Essays on the Origins of Hebrew (Analecta Biblica 142) (Rom 2000), 9–34, 32.

3 King / Stager, Life, 77.

allerdings einen wesentlichen Gesichtspunkt zu übersehen. Charakteristisch ist etwa der in dem späten 2. Chronikbuch (2. Chron 16, 12) gegen den judäischen König Asa erhobene Vorwurf, in seiner tödlichen Krankheit habe er sich nicht an Jahwe, sondern an die Ärzte gewandt. Aber das hängt nicht damit zusammen, daß in der biblischen Welt Ärzte und ihre Kunst für ineffektiv gehalten wurden,[4] sondern an der für die Verfasser der alttestamentlichen Schriften alles beherrschenden Voraussetzung, daß allein Jahwe die Macht hat, Krankheit zu schicken und auch zu heilen. Deshalb wird verschiedentlich Jahwe selbst metaphorisch als „Arzt" für das Volk Israel bezeichnet,[5] und an anderen Stellen[6] als derjenige angesprochen, von dem auch der einzelne Heilung erwarten kann. Diese vollständige Ausrichtung des gesamten Lebens auf die Religion, die erst für moderne westliche Beobachter, deren Kultur durch die Aufklärung hindurchgegangen ist, befremdlich ist, unterscheidet das alttestamentliche Israel nicht wesentlich von den übrigen altorientalischen Kulturen, doch die monotheistische Prägung wenigstens des offiziellen Glaubens an den einen Gott Jahwe hat offensichtlich in kanonischen Schriften wenigstens dem äußeren Anschein nach einen für Israel eigentümlichen ideologischen Gegensatz zwischen Religion und ärztlicher Kunst geschaffen. Untersuchungen, die sich vom modernen medizinhistorischen Blickpunkt aus mit dem Stand der Heilkunst im alten Israel befassen,[7] müssen einigermaßen

4 King / Stager, Life, 81.

5 Jer 8, 22; Ex 15, 26. Verbal: Dt 32, 39; Jes 6, 10; 57, 18.19; Jer 30. 17; 33, 6 (Jerusalem); Hos 6, 1; 7, 1; 11, 3; für Ägypten Jes 19, 22.

6 Jer 17, 14; Hi 5, 18; Ps 103,.3; 147, 3.

7 Vgl. bes. H. Avalos, Illness and Health Care in the Ancient Near. The Role of the Temple in Greece, Mesopotamia, and Israel (HSM 54) Atlanta, GA 1995; C. J. Brim, Medicine in the Bible (New York 1936); G. Fohrer, Krankheit im Licht des Alten Testaments, in: ders., Studien zu alttestamentlichen Texten und Themen (1966–1972) (BZAW; 155) (Berlin-New York 1981), 172–187; ders., Man and Disease according to the Book of Job, in: ders, Studien zum Alten Testament (1966–1988) (Berlin - New York 1991), 80–84; H. F. J. Horstmanshoff (ed.), Magic and Rationality in Ancient Near Eastern and Graeco-Roman Medicine Leiden/Boston 2004; P. Humbert, Maladie et médicine dans l'Ancient Testament, in: RHPhR 44 (1964), 1–29; Kinnier-Wilson, Medicine [o. Anm. 1]; J. Preuss, Biblisch-Talmudische Medizin (Berlin 1911; Nachdruck u. a. Wiesbaden 1992); K. Seybold /Ulrich Müller, Krankheit und Heilung (BiKon; 1008) (Stuttgart 1978); M. Sussman, Diseases in the Bible and the Talmud, in: D. Brothwell / A. T- Sandison, Hg., Diseases in Antiquity. A Survey of the Diseases, Injuries and Surgery of Early Populations (Springfield, IL, 1967), 209–221; E. Testa, Le malatie e il medico secondo la Bibbia, in: RivBib 43 (1995), 253–267;

mühsam im Alten Testament verstreute Spuren suchen, die etwa das Auftreten bestimmter Krankheiten, das Auftauchen von Seuchen und sehr selten auch Vorformen medizinischer Behandlungen erkennen lassen. Einige der erwähnten Fälle von Heilung oder gar Totenerweckung (wie die Taten Elias, 1. Kön 17, 19–22, bzw. Elisas, 2. Kön 4, 32–35 – es handelt sich um eine Wundertradition) tragen magischen Charakter. Im Gegensatz zu dem breiten Ausmaß, das Beschwörung und Magie bei dem Umgang mit Krankheit in anderen Kulturen des Alten Orients einnahmen, berühren diese in der volkstümlichen Überlieferung über die Vorschriftpropheten erhaltenen Darstellungen allerdings nur einen Randbereich.[8] Das Feigenpflaster, das der Prophet Jesaja nach der Erzählung von König Hiskias Krankheit und Genesung dem König auf sein Geschwür legt, so daß dieses abheilt und der König entsprechend der von Jesaja übermittelten göttlichen Botschaft noch fünfzehn Jahre am Leben bleibt (Jes 38, 21), kann als Volksheilmittel betrachtet werden. Seine Wirkung beruht nach der Erzählung aber nicht auf der Behandlung selbst, sondern darauf, daß Hiskia zuvor unter Tränen zu Jahwe gefleht und um Errettung gebeten hatte. Die Klagelieder des Psalters, in denen häufig nie genau diagnostizierbare Krankheitssymptome genannt werden[9], sind ganz von der Voraussetzung beherrscht, daß eine Rettung aus diesen und anderen Nöten allein von Jahwe zu erwarten ist.

2. Beim augenblicklichen Stand der Forschung ist festzustellen, daß die einschlägigen Beobachtungen über Erwähnungen von Krankheit und Heilung im Alten Testament ziemlich vollständig in der Sekundärliteratur erfaßt[10] und im inneralttestamentlichen Text neue Funde kaum zu erwarten sind. Meine heutigen Ausführungen sollen sich deshalb mit einem speziellen Textzusammenhang befassen, der die Rolle der Priester und damit insbesondere bisher wenig gewürdigte Aspekte im Umgang mit Krankheit im alten Israel beleuchten kann. Zwar hat das Kapitel Lev 13, von dem ich ausgehen möchte, in einer bestimmten Hinsicht durchaus Beachtung gefunden. Doch ging das erkenntnisleitende Interesse dabei fast ausschließlich von dem medizinhistorischen Gesichtspunkt aus he-

---

8 Zu Ägypten und Mesopotamien vgl. Kinnier Wilson, Medicine (o. Anm. 1), 338–349; Avalos, a.a.O.

9 Dazu besonders K. Seybold, Das Gebet des Kranken im Alten Testament (BWANT; 99) (Stuttgart u. a. 1973). - Ob allerdings eine solche besondere Gruppe von Krankheitspsalmen als eigene Gattung auszusondern ist, ist umstritten.

10 Eine ausführliche Bibliographie bei R. North, Medicine, 35–68, in welcher auch die Standardartikel der Lexika enthalten sind.

rauszufinden, welche Krankheit denn mit dem vorwiegend in diesem und dem folgenden Kapitel auftretenden hebräischen Begriff צרעת(Lev 13, 2.3.8.9.11–13.15.20.25.27.30.42.43; 14, 3.7.32.54.57) gemeint sei.[11] An der Antwort auf diese Frage waren auch kirchliche Fachleute interessiert, die mit der Aufgabe betraut waren, neue moderne Bibelübersetzungen herzustellen. Das Problem entstand historisch vor allem dadurch, daß schon die Septuaginta den Begriff צרעת regelmäßig mit λεπρα wiedergab – was dazu führte, das spätere Tochterübersetzungen darin die Wiedergabe der medizinisch als morbus Hansen bezeichneten Erkrankung sahen. Das trifft in Wahrheit offenbar nicht zu, weil in der klassischen Antike für diese Krankheit die Bezeichnung ελεφαντιασις gebräuchlich war. Der Begriff λεπρα ist offensichtlich von dem Adjektiv λεπρος abzuleiten, das mit „uneben, rauh" wiederzugeben ist.[12] Die LXX hat einfach das damals einzig geeignet erscheinende Wort für eine solche Hautkrankheit gewählt, durchaus sachentsprechend, weil auch im Urtext keine eindeutige Krankheitsdiagnose vorliegt.[13] Außerdem gibt es gegen die Gleichsetzung von צרעת mit dem heute Lepra genannten Leiden chronologische und symptomatische Bedenken. Umstritten ist chronologisch, ob die heutige klinische Lepra in der fraglichen Periode überhaupt schon in den Raum Palästinas vorgedrungen war. Eine möglicherweise zutreffende Überliefe-

11 Vgl. bes. S. G. Browne, Leprosy in the Bible (London 1970, 1979^{3}); R. G. Cochrane, Biblical Leprosy: A Suggested Interpretation (London 1961 / Glasgow 1963); K. P. C. A. Gramberg, Melaatsheid, Lepra of Morbus Hansen. Hoe moet de juiste benaming luiden?, in: Nederlands Tijdschrift voor Geneeskunde 96 (1952), 3157–3159; ders., Over de melaatsheid in de Bijbel, in: Geloof en Wetenschap 56 (1958), 172–203; ders., 'Leprosy' and the Bible, in: BT 11 (1960), 10–23; R. K. Harrison, Art. Leprosy, in: IDB 3 (1988^{3}), 103–106; E. V. Hulse, The Nature of Biblical 'Leprosy' and the Use of Alternative Medical Terms in Modern Translations of the Bible, in: PEQ 107 (1975), 87–105; Ludwig Köhler, Aussatz, in: ZAW 678 (1955), 290–291; Margareth Lloyd Davies, Levitical Leprosy: Uncleanness and the Psyche, in: ET 99 (1988), 136–139; E. Nida, The Translation of Leprosy, in: BiTr 11 (1960), 80–81; J. Pilch, Biblical Leprosy and Body Smbolism, in: BTB 11 (1981), 108–113; J. F. A. Sawyer, A note on the etymology of ṣaraʿat, in: VT 26 (1976), 241–245; J. L. Swellengrebel, 'Leprosy' and the Bible. The Translation of 'Tsara'at' and 'Lepra' in: BiTr 11 (1960), 69–80; D. H. Wallington, 'Leprosy' and the Bible. Conclusion, in: BT 12 (1961), 75–79; J. Wilkinson, Leprosy and Leviticus, in: SJTh 30 (1977), 153–160; 31 (1978), 153–166.

12 Vgl. Menge-Güthling, Griechisch-deutsches und deutsch-griechisches Hand- und Schulwörterbuch (Berlin-Schöneberg 1910), s. v.

13 Vgl. dazu auch J. Milgrom, Leviticus 1–16 (AB; 3) (New York u. a. 1993), 816–820.

rung[14] besagt, daß die mycobakterielle Lepra erst mit den aus Nordindien zurückkehrenden Truppen Alexanders des Großen 324 v.Chr. ins Land gekommen sei. Ob die Erkrankung des Königs Uzzia (Asarja) von Juda (773–736) Symptome aufweist, die auf Lepra deuten, kann nicht eindeutig festgestellt werden. Der späte Text 2. Chron 26, 19f. dürfte der solcherart ermittelten Datierung kaum im Wege stehen. Er spricht von einem Ausbruch von צרעת auf des Königs Stirn; die ältere Vorlage 2. Kön 15, 5 gebraucht, ohne Symptome zu nennen, wie 2. Chron 26, 20 den Begriff מצרע: Das einzige Motiv, das für die klinische Lepra spricht, wie wir sie aus dem Neuen Testament kennen, ist der Umstand, daß die Erkrankung zu Absonderung und dauernder Regierungsunfähigkeit des erkrankten Herrschers führt. Die symptomatischen Bedenken richten sich dagegen, daß die für die schwere Form der Lepra charakteristischen Verstümmelungen ganzer Gliedmaßen oder Entstellungen im Gesicht in Lev 13 gar nicht erwähnt werden. Zumindest die Bildung von Knoten gehört zu den Erscheinungen dieser Form von Lepra. Eine mildere Form (die sog. „nervöse“ Lepra) zeigt sich allerdings im Auftreten weißer Hautflecken, wie sie in Lev 13 erwähnt werden, ohne daß es zu einer Verstümmelung kommt.[15] Man hat jedoch mit Recht dagegen eingewandt, daß eine an jedem siebenten Tag durch den Priester durchgeführte Inspektion mit der Erwartung möglicher Besserung des Aussehens der Haut bei einer chronischen Erkrankung wie der klinischen Lepra sinnlos gewesen wäre.[16]

Eine genaue Durchsicht von Lev 13 ergibt, daß sich die Symptome eher als Psoriasis (Schuppenflechte) oder andere, teils leichtere Hautkrankheiten erklären, manche möglicherweise als Vitiligo oder Favus.[17] Insgesamt werden sechs verschiedene Hauterscheinungen beschrieben, die mit dem Namen צרעת bezeichnet werden und vorübergehend oder auf Dauer dazu führen, daß die betreffende Person von den Priestern für unrein erklärt wird. Wahrscheinlich ist, daß das Kapitel allmählich zu seinem jetzigen Umfang herangewachsen ist, indem in der Praxis neu auftretende Fälle hinzugefügt wurden. Es findet also eine priesterliche Inspektion statt; ihr Ziel ist festzustellen, ob ein Gemeindemitglied kultisch rein ist, d. h. am Gemeindeleben in gesellschaftlicher wie gottesdienstlicher Hinsicht teilnehmen kann. Wie sorgfältig ein solches Verfahren durchge-

14 Vgl. dazu Davies (vorige Anm.), 136f.

15 Vgl. dazu Kinnier Wilson (o. Anm. 1), 354.

16 Sussman, Diseases (o. Anm. 1), 217.

17 Besonders die Arbeiten von Hulse und Gramberg (o. Anm. 10) sind in dieser Hinsicht einflußreich gewesen.

führt wird, zeigt sich in der Bestimmung in V. 4–8, wo für das Auftreten eines weißen Hautfleckens vorgeschrieben wird, daß der Priester mögliche Veränderungen zweimal hintereinander im Abstand von je einer Woche überprüfen muß, bis ein endgültiges Urteil getroffen werden kann.[18] Maßstab dafür ist, ob sich die Krankheit ausgebreitet hat oder nicht. Die Formel, mit der ein solches Urteil ausgesprochen wird, ist stereotyp; sie lautet: צרעת הוא (V.8); umgekehrt, wenn keine Unreinheit vorliegt: „er ist rein“: ורטה הוא (V. 17). Die Feststellung, mit der das geschieht, ist ein deklaratorischer Akt; schon G. von Rad hat dafür die Bezeichnung „deklaratorische Formel“ geprägt.[19]

Auf den ersten Blick sieht es in Lev 13 so aus, als ob sich die Priester in keiner Weise darum bemühen, irgendwie zu einer Heilung der Krankheiten beizutragen, deren Auswirkungen auf die Haut sie feststellen. Im Text ist jedenfalls kein Hinweis darauf zu finden. Es scheint, daß der Erkrankte zwischen einer ersten und zweiten Inspektion der Haut zunächst nach Hause („in Quarantäne“)[20] geschickt worden war. Ob man sich dort um eine Behandlung gekümmert hat, davon ist im Text nicht die Rede, weil es die priesterlichen Handlungen nicht berührt. Wenn, wie die Erörterungen der Symptome durch Hulse[21] nahelegen, es sich teilweise um weniger gravierende, schnell von selbst abheilende Hautreizungen oder Ekzeme gehandelt haben mag, ist eine Behandlung in den gutartigen Fällen vermutlich auch nicht nötig gewesen. Ausdrücklich scheint das bei einer bereits abgeheilten Narbe von einem Geschwür (V. 23) oder von einer Brandwunde (V. 28) der Fall zu sein.

Damit ist allerdings die grundsätzliche Frage noch in keiner Weise beantwortet. Einen genaueren Einblick in die Probleme des Textes kann vermutlich ein Vergleich mit den keilschriftlichen Zeugnissen aus Mesopotamien bieten. Während wir über Heilverfahren im Israel der alttestamentlichen Periode so gut wie gar nichts wissen, sind wir über die dortigen Verhältnisse besser unterrichtet.[22]

18 Manche Ausleger sehen in der zweiten Prüfung das Ergebnis einer Weiterarbeit am Text, doch ist das nicht eindeutig zu beweisen.

19 G. von Rad, Die Anrechnung des Glaubens zur Gerechtigkeit: ThLZ 76 (1951), 129–132 = ders., Gesammelte Studien zum Alten Testament (I) (ThB; 8) (München 1958), 130–135.

20 E. Gerstenberger, Das 3. Buch Mose, Leviticus (ATD; 6) (Göttingen 1993), 145 u. ö.

21 Vgl. o. Anm. 10.

22 Vgl. bes., H. Avalos, Illness and Health care in the Ancient Near East. The Role of the Temple in Greece, Mesopotamia, and Israel (HSM; 54) (Atlanta, GA 1995); D. Goltz, Studien zur altorientalischen und griechischen Heilkunde, Therapie, Arzneimittelbereitung –

Lange Zeit war die besonders von Edith Ritter[23] vertretene These in der Fachwelt herrschend, daß zwischen den Aufgaben zweier bei einem Heilverfahren in Mesopotamien beteiligten Amtspersonen, dem åçipu „Beschwörer" und dem eigentlichen Arzt asû zu unterscheiden sei. Der erstere sei nur für die eigentliche Beschwörung zuständig gewesen, während der zweite ausschließlich ärztliche Aufgaben ausgeübt habe. Auch diese Aufgabenteilung hätte die ausschließlich auf kultrechtlichte Maßnahmen beschränkten Inhalte von Lev 13 erklärt. Der hier agierende Priester wäre für fachärztliche Heilbehandlungen nicht ausgebildet und nicht zuständig gewesen, sondern habe nur mit vorwissenschaftlichen (magischen, apotropäischen und exorzistischen) Methoden zu heilen versucht. Neuerdings hat jedoch S. M. Maul[24] darauf hingewiesen, daß man in dem Haus des Beschwörers des Asssurtempels Kiṣir-Aššur in dem im Jahre 614 v.Chr. von den Medern zerstörten Assur zahlreiche medizinische Rezepturen gefunden habe, die ausweisen, daß dieser auch umfangreiche ärztliche Fähigkeiten besessen habe. „Hiermit fällt die These Ritters."[25] Offensichtlich wurden die magisch-religiösen und die vor allem auf Kräutermedizinen beruhenden, durchaus wirksamen[26] ärztlichen Heilverfahren von einem und demselben Fachmann ausgeführt. Wenn also von Heilung in Lev 13 mit keinem Wort die Rede ist, so hat dies ausschließlich den Grund, daß der Text nur die Ordnungen enthält, die für die kultische Funktion des Priesters bei der Reinheits- und Unreinheitserklärung von Hautkranken gültig sind. Daß er daneben auch ärztliche Behandlungen durchgeführt hat, ist damit keineswegs ausgeschlossen.

Rezeptstruktur (Sudhoffs Archiv, Beiheft 16; Wiesbaden 1974); H.F.J. Horstmannshoff and M. Stol (eds.), Magic and Rationality in Ancient Near Eastern and Graeco-Roman Medicine (Studies in Ancient Medicine; 27). Leiden/Boston 2004. Darin bes.: S. M. Maul, „Die ‚Lösung vom Bann': Überlegungen zu altorientalischen Konzeptionen von Krankheit und Heilkunst, 79–95 (94–95: Lit.)."

23 E. K. Ritter, „Magical Expert (=āšipu) and Physician (=asû). Notes on two complementary professions in Babylonian medicine, in: Studies in Honor of Benno Landsberger (AS 16) Chicago 1965, 299–321."

24 ‚Lösung vom Bann', 81.

25 Ebd. –Vgl. auch J. Scurlock, Physician, Exorcist, Conjurer, Magician, in: T. Abusch/K.van der Toorn (eds.), Mesopotamian Magic: Textual, Historical, and Interpretative Perspectives (Groningen 1999), 69–79.

26 Vgl. u.a. M. Haussperger, Die mesopotamische Medizin und ihre Ärzte aus heutiger Sicht, in: ZA 87 (1997), 196–217.

Aus dem Text geht auch klar hervor, daß die Aussonderung einer Person keine hygienischen Gründe hat. In für uns befremdlicher Weise wird nämlich verfügt, daß, wenn צרעת so ausbricht, daß der Ausschlag den gesamten Körper bedeckt, der betreffende Kranke für rein erklärt wird, weil er jetzt ganz weiß geworden sei (V.12-13). In diesem Fall scheint nicht die Krankheit als solche, sondern der optische Eindruck, den die Haut des Kranken erweckte, den Ausschlag zu geben. Offenbar ist die einheitlich weiße Oberfläche entscheidend: ein Ideal optischer Ganzheit, die nach den priesterlichen Grundsätzen als Reinheit zu beurteilen ist. Störend sind Flecken oder Vertiefungen (V. 3. 20. 25–26. 30–31), teilweise auch mit Verfärbung der Haare an bestimmten Stellen des Kopfes oder Bartes verbunden. Physische Ansteckungsgefahr scheint keine Rolle zu spielen – obwohl generell das Auftreten von Epidemien eine durchaus bekannte Erscheinung war. Aber sie wurden religiös gedeutet: Als z. B. im Heer der zur Zeit des Königs Hiskia (um 700 v.Chr.) die Stadt Jerusalem belagernden Assyrer eine verheerende Seuche ausbrach, welche die Belagerer zum plötzlichen Abzug nötigte, sah man darin das Werk eines Engels Jahwes (2. Kön 19, 35). Die natürlichen Ursachen waren noch nicht bekannt.

3. Im nächsten Schritt müssen wir unseren Horizont etwas erweitern. Im weiteren Kontext von Kap. 13 wird nämlich der Begriff צרעת in verblüffender Weise ausgedehnt. War bis einschließlich V. 46 von menschlichen Hauterscheinungen die Rede, geht es nun (V. 49–58) um Stoffe von Kleidern, um Gewebe und aus Leder hergestellte Gegenstände. Wenn eines dieser Dinge Flecken bekommt und dieser Flecken grell grün oder rötlich aussieht (V. 49), ist es ein „Befall von צרעת“ (נגע צרעת). Das Verfahren ist dann zunächst analog zu dem bei menschlichem צרעת angewandten: Der Priester muß das fragliche Stück besehen und für sieben Tage einschließen. Ist danach der Flecken größer geworden, ist es ein bösartiger צרעת. Die Konsequenz ist in diesem Fall, daß das Stück verbrannt wird. Bei einem leblosen Gegenstand kann die Ausmerzung de Schadens radikaler durchgeführt werden als beim Menschen. Blieb er aber unverändert, wird wiederum eine analoge Prozedur vorgenommen: Nachdem das Stück zuerst gewaschen worden ist, schließt es der Priester erneut für sieben Tage ein. Ist der Stoff danach unverändert, ist er dennoch unrein, auch wenn der Schaden nicht weiter um sich gegriffen hat. Die Anweisung ergeht jetzt dahin, die entsprechende Stelle auszubrennen (V. 55). Ist er aber abgeblaßt, soll der Priester die entsprechende Stelle aus dem Stück herausreißen – offenbar eine weniger rabiate Methode, weil ein

minder schwerer Fall von Unreinheit vorliegt. Tritt danach erneut צרעת an demselben Kleidungsstück auf, hilft nichts: Es muß als ganzes verbrannt werden (V. 57). Ein gegensätzlicher Fall steht am Schluß (V. 58): Wenn der Flecken beim Waschen verschwindet, muß man es nur noch einmal waschen, dann ist das Stück wieder rein.

Die weitgehende Parallelität, die sich in beiden Fällen zeigt: bei Hauterkrankungen von Menschen und dem Auftreten von Flecken an Stoffen oder Leder, im Ablauf der Inspektion durch die Priester und den von ihnen je nach ebenfalls paralleler Entwicklung des Schadens (Ausbreitung, Gleichbleiben oder Verschwinden), nur mit den durch die unterschiedlichen Objekte gebotenen Unterschieden, getroffenen Maßnahmen deutet darauf hin, daß die gesamte Perspektive eine ausschließlich rituelle ist: Es geht darum, den geschützten Lebensraum der Gemeinde (im Sinne der Stadtbevölkerung) vor Störungen der Harmonie, die durch den Anblick von mit Flecken auf der Haut behafteten Gemeindeangehörigen oder durch befleckte Kleidung und Stoffe entstehen würden, zu bewahren. Bei Stoffen und Kleidungsstücken genügt, wenn sie nicht teilweise oder ganz verbrannt werden müssen, daß das beschmutzte Stück herausgerissen wird. Ein Loch ist anscheinend unschädlich, nur Flecken gelten als unrein. In diesem Zusammenhang gilt die alte Einsicht, daß die Wiedergabe des kultischen Begriffs טמא mit „unrein“ nur eine Notlösung ist, weil die adäquate Umschreibung des Wortsinns etwa lauten müßte: Im kultischen Raum nicht zugelassen, ihn entweihend.

4. Die Perspektive weitet sich noch aus, wenn wir den nächsten Schritt tun und einen ebenfalls parallelen Abschnitt in Augenschein nehmen, der sich, nach einer Unterbrechung durch Vorschriften für die Reinigungszeremonie eines von צרעת Geheilten (14, 1–32) im zweiten Teil von Kap. 14 findet. Man hat den Eindruck, daß er ursprünglich unmittelbar an Kap. 13 anschloß. Hier geht es um ein Haus, an dem ebenfalls ein נגע צרעת entstehen kann. Ein kleiner Nebenzug (V. 36) ist, daß der vom Hausbesitzer, welcher den Schaden in der Wand seines Hauses bemerkt hatte, herbeigerufene Priester zuerst alle Gegenstände aus dem Haus ausräumen läßt, ehe er es betritt, „damit nicht alles, was im Hause ist, unrein werde“. Das ist ein Hinweis darauf, daß nicht bereits der Tatbestand als solcher: die bloße Nähe zu der mit einem נגע צרעת verunreinigten Hauswand den Hausrat kultisch unrein werden läßt, sondern erst der ausdrückliche priesterliche Bescheid, daß ein נגע צרעת vorliegt, eine solche Wirkung hat. Warum das so ist, wäre einer Überlegung wert, aber wir müssen uns Ausführungen darüber an dieser Stelle ersparen. Auffällig ist

die Entsprechung zum Fall der Stoffe bei 14, 37 im Vergleich mit 13, 49, indem es auch bei der verfleckten Hausmauer auf die gleichen Farben grün oder rötlich ankommt, wenn ein נגע צרעת festgestellt wird, und zu den Beispielen von צרעת am Menschen, daß die Flecken tiefer aussehen als die übrige Wand. Das Verfahren geht dann parallel weiter: Wieder wird nicht sofort entschieden, sondern der Priester tritt wieder aus dem Haus heraus, verschließt die Tür und kommt nach sieben Tagen wieder. Nun gelten die gleichen Grundsätze für die Beurteilung: Wenn sich der Schaden während der Woche vergrößert hat, soll die entsprechende Schadenstelle entfernt werden, in diesem Falle sachgemäß, indem der Priester die Steine herausbrechen und durch neue ersetzen läßt. Hier ergeht zusätzlich die Anweisung – weil man Steine nicht verbrennen kann – daß die ausgebrochenen Steine weggeschafft und an einem unreinen Ort außerhalb deponiert werden sollen. Auch soll der alte Putz von dem Haus abgekratzt und dieses mit neuem Mörtel beworfen werden. Wenn trotzdem der Schaden wiederkehrt, ist mit halben Maßnahmen nichts mehr zu machen: Jetzt muß das ganze Haus als unrein abgebrochen und die Steine aus der Stadt herausgeschafft werden (V. 45). Im Text folgt wieder der positive Fall: Wenn der Priester bei der Besichtigung findet, daß der Schaden nicht weiter um sich gegriffen hat, nachdem das Haus frisch verputzt ist, soll er es für rein erklären. Ähnlich wie am Anfang von Kap. 14 Vorschriften für die Reinigungszeremonie des von צרעת geheilten Menschen folgen, so stehen an seinem Ende noch kurze Regeln für ein Opfer zur Entsühnung des Hauses, das wieder rein geworden ist.

In den drei parallelen Beispielen: Verunreinigung von Menschen, von Stoffen und von Hausmauern waltet, wie wir gesehen haben, eine strenge Entsprechung. Das läßt nun auch die Frage nach der Bedeutung von צרעת in einem neuen Lichte sehen. Hat nicht die gesamte Auslegungstradition, die in Lev 13, 1–46 den Begriff צרעת als die Bezeichnung für eine Hautkrankheit zu identifizieren suchte, seit die LXX ihn mit λεπρα wiedergab, einen Irrweg eingeschlagen? Die Weiterverwendung in den beiden anderen Sparten von Schäden, die mit Hautkrankheit direkt nichts zu tun haben, deutet darauf hin, daß die Bedeutung des Wortes allgemeiner sein muß. Beachtenswert ist ein Vorschlag von Ludwig Köhler, der in seinem bekannten Büchlein „Der hebräische Mensch“[27] die Wiedergabe des Wortes mit „Schlag“ ins Gespräch brachte. Doch ist einzuwenden, daß damit besser das Wort נגע wiederzugeben ist, dass in Kombination mit צרעת

27 Göttingen 1953, 43 [ET: Hebrew Man. London 1956, 56].

vorkommt und als „Schlag, Befall“ übersetzt werden sollte. J. F. A. Sawyer, welcher der Etymologie des Wortes weiter nachging, wandte dagegen ein, in der Verbindung נגע צרעת würde dann eine Tautologie eintreten.[28] Eine Prüfung der Lexika[29] ergibt, daß die aus den Tochtersprachen abgeleitete Etymologie des Wortes durchweg von der irreführenden Übersetzung der LXX abhängig ist. Da nun aber die bereits abgewiesene Bedeutung ‚Lepra‘ oder als Alternative ‚Ausschlag‘ zwar auf menschliche Haut, nicht aber auf Stoffe, Leder oder eine verputzte Steinmauer anwendbar ist, scheint mir ernsthaft zu erwägen zu sein, ob nicht in einem kultischen Text eine rituelle Bedeutung angemessener erscheint. Mein Vorschlag wäre ‚Makel‘, denn mit einem Flecken, der die einheitliche Oberfläche der Haut eines Menschen, die Reinheit von Stoffen oder Leder wie auch einer weiß gekalkten Wand unterbricht, ist die Vollkommenheit beeinträchtigt, die nach priesterlichem Urteil die Gemeinschaftsfähigkeit von Menschen, von Stoffen, die sie als Bekleidung tragen und von Häusern, die sie bewohnen, stört.

Unter den Maßstäben, die dafür wichtig sind, scheint die Farbe eine hervorragende Rolle zu spielen: Sowohl bei Stoffen wie bei Wänden stört die Fehlfarbe „grün“ oder „rötlich“ eines Fleckes die notwendige Harmonie (13, 49; 14, 37). Umgekehrt wird eine Hauterkrankung, die dazu führt, daß der ganze Körper eines Kranken weiß erscheint (13, 12f.), nicht beanstandet, weil nun eine einheitliche, als rein betrachtete Farbe, auch wenn es nicht die natürliche Hautfarbe eines Gesunden ist, zu sehen ist.

5. Es ist nun an der Zeit, die Perspektive nochmals zu erweitern und nach den leitenden Gesichtspunkten zu fragen, die für die kultische Tora (14, 54) über Rein und Unrein maßgebend sind, wie wir sie in den besprochenen Abschnitten aus Lev 13–14 vor uns haben.

Ich hatte schon auf die Ortsangabe in 14, 45 (vgl. auch V. 53) hingewiesen, nach der die abgeräumten Steine und der abgekratzte Putz von dem befleckten und reparierten Haus „vor die Stadt“ herausgeschafft werden sollen. Daraus ergibt sich zunächst, daß die vorliegende kultische Gesetzgebung – trotz der fiktiven Situation vor der Landnahme mit der Anrede Gottes an Mose und Aaron in 14, 34 – in die Periode der Seßhaftigkeit gehört, in der die Bevölkerung in Städten lebt. Die Fiktion wird in anderen Teilen der Priesterschrift weiter getrieben, indem dort vom Lager der Israeliten während der Wüstenwanderung und entsprechend von der Wüste außerhalb des Lagers (מחוץ למחנה, Ex 29, 14; 33, 7; Lev 4, 12 u. ö.)

28 J. F. A. Sawyer, A note (o. Anm. 10).

29 Vgl. zuletzt HAL^3, s. v. צרעת.

die Rede ist. Die Wüste außerhalb des bewohnten Raumes bzw. des Kulturlandes rings um eine Stadt ist der „unreine" Ort, wo z. B. die verunreinigten Steine des abgebrochenen Hauses abgelagert werden können (14, 45), wohin aber auch am Großen Versöhnungstag (Lev 16) der Bock, der die Sünden der Gemeinde aufgeladen bekommen hat, hinausgetrieben wird. Hinter diesen Abgrenzungen wird die kultische Sicht der Priester sichtbar, die sich in der priesterlichen Tora niederschlägt. Sie ordnet die Welt in den bewohnten Bezirk, die Stadt, typologisch das Lager, und den unbewohnten, die umliegende Wüste, das Umland. Rein ist die Wohnheimat, in der Menschen zusammenleben und in der, kultisch gesehen, Harmonie herrschen soll. Störungen der Harmonie treten dann ein, wenn das Ideal einer Vollkommenheit beeinträchtigt wird. Diese ideale Vollkommenheit prägt sich, für uns anfänglich schwer begreifbar, ganz dinglich in scheinbaren Äußerlichkeiten aus: Zunächst in Krankheiten, die, wie Gerstenberger in seinem Leviticuskommentar betont,[30] damals noch nicht durch Blutproben und andere internistische Untersuchungen diagnostiziert werden konnten, sondern lediglich am äußeren Aussehen der Haut abzulesen waren. Ist die Haut nicht in Ordnung, ist der ganze Mensch krank. Ein Kranker aber muß, wenigstens zeitweise, von der Gemeinschaft der Reinen abgesondert werden, denn er bedeutet eine Störung der gottgewollten Harmonie, die in der Gemeinschaft herrschen soll. Wenn der Zustand behoben ist, bedarf es einer in 14, 1–32 ausführlich beschriebenen Kulthandlung mit Opfern, mit welcher der vorher Kranke wieder in die Gemeinschaft zurückgeführt wird. Diese Zeremonie läuft auf eine Sühnehandlung (כפר) hinaus, denn diese Gemeinschaft ist religiös begründet: Es geht nicht nur um das Zusammenleben der Menschen untereinander, sondern entscheidend um die Gemeinschaft mit Gott. Denn Krankheit wird als Folge einer Sünde, eines, wenn auch verborgenen, gestörten Verhältnisses zu Gott verstanden.[31] Etwa Ps 32 zeigt diesen Zusammenhang im Bekenntnis eines Beters, der sich zum Bewußtsein seiner Schuld durchgerungen und von Gott Vergebung erfahren hat (Ps 33, 5). Die priesterlichen Regulierungen, die den Kranken zeitweise von der Gemeinschaft trennen, ihm aber, wo immer möglich, auch den Weg zur Rückkehr öffnen, sind eine im Ansatz barmherzige Konsequenz aus dieser Grundauffassung. Die umfassende Sicht, die damit verbunden ist,

30 Das 3. Buch Mose (o. Anm. 16), 144.

31 Vgl. dazu u. a. F. Lindström, Suffering and Sin. Interpretations of Illness in the Individual Complaint Psalms (CB.OT; 37) (Stockholm 1994).

wird darin sichtbar, daß auch Gegenstände, die zum Leben des Menschen in enger Beziehung stehen – die Kleidung, die man trägt, das Haus, in dem man wohnt – mit einem Makel (צרעת) behaftet sein können, den es zu beseitigen gilt.

Die Festlegungen als Rein und Unrein dienen also aus priesterlicher Sicht durchaus einem theologischen Zweck: Auch das normale Zusammenleben von Menschen in einer Stadt (typologisch: dem Lager) hat einen kultischen Hintergrund, denn das menschliche Miteinander ist durch die Gemeinschaft mit Gott begründet. Ideal ist diese Gemeinschaft, wenn Vollkommenheit herrscht, die auch ganz äußerlich im Fehlen von Mängeln sichtbar wird. Treten sie auf, müssen sie in jeweils angemessener Weise beseitigt werden. Die Begriffe „rein“ und „unrein“ sind insofern eine nicht ganz adäquate Wiedergabe der entsprechenden hebräischen Begriffe, weil sie, des kultischen Gehalts entkleidet, als rein äußerliche Bezeichnungen mißverstanden werden können. Äußerliche Erscheinung und innerer Gehalt sind aber eng miteinander verbunden: Wie sich Krankheit im äußeren Anblick der Haut manifestieren kann, so haben auch Flecken an Stoffen oder Hauswänden hinweisenden Charakter auf eine grundlegende Störung.

An dieser Stelle genügt ein Hinweis darauf, daß die Thematik im Kontext noch damit zu Ende geführt wird, daß in Kap. 15 das Thema „Ausflüsse“ aus dem menschlichen (männlichen oder weiblichen) Körper behandelt wird. Dabei geht es um natürliche oder krankhafte Zustände, hauptsächlich aus dem Genitalbereich. Dieses Kapitel erforderte eine eigene ausführliche Behandlung, die an dieser Stelle unterbleiben muß. Unreinheit tritt in jedem Fall ein, auch wenn ein Ausfluß natürlich ist - dann aber weniger gravierend und kürzer als bei Erkrankungen. Auch hier werden neben Waschungen Opferhandlungen vorgesehen, die den unreinen Zustand beenden.

6. Unsere Überlegungen werden abgerundet, wenn wir zum Schluß noch einen Blick auf den Abschnitt Lev 21, 16–24 werfen, der zwar nicht im unmittelbaren Kontext steht und auch zu einer anderen Quelle, dem sogenannten Heiligkeitsgesetz, gehört, aber einen bisher noch nicht behandelten Aspekt hinzufügt. Dieser Abschnitt handelt nicht wie die bisher behandelten von Laien, sondern von der Zulassung von Priestern zum Dienst am Heiligtum.

Er ist geprägt von Regelungen, welche die Zulassung zum priesterlichen Dienst von vollständiger körperlicher Unversehrtheit abhängig machen. Voraussetzung ist, daß, wie bekannt, das Priestertum im alten Israel erblich, an die exklusive Zugehörigkeit zu wenigen priesterlichen Familien gebunden war. Wer diesen priesterlichen Familien angehörte, hatte grundsätzlich das Recht, das Priesteramt auch auszuüben. Die Praxis sah allerdings, besonders nach der Kultzentralisation zum Tempel in Jerusalem durch König Josia in spätvorexilischer Zeit, teilweise anders aus. In diesem Abschnitt geht es aber um die persönliche Qualifikation von geborenen Priestern zur Amtsausübung, speziell der Darbringung von Opfern am Heiligtum. Diese Erlaubnis wird nur erteilt bei vollkommener körperlicher Unversehrtheit. Hat jemand einen körperlichen Fehler (מום), ist er vom Dienst ausgeschlossen. Was als Fehler beurteilt wird, wird in einer längeren Liste (V.18–20) aufgezählt, die mit Lahmen und Blinden beginnt, aber auch Personen, die an einem Glied verstümmelt, entmannt, mit Knochenbruch behaftet, bucklig oder schwindsüchtig sind, und sogar solche, die einen Fleck im Auge haben, einschließt. Hier, wo es um den unmittelbaren Dienst im Heiligtum geht, ist eine vollständige körperliche Unversehrtheit die strikte Voraussetzung. In V. 22 wird einem solchen Priester allerdings zugesichert, daß er von den Speisen, die den Priestern beim Opfer zu ihrer Versorgung zustehen, sowohl dem Heiligen wie dem Hochheiligen, essen darf. Es geht allein um das Heilige, das nicht durch körperlich unvollkommene Diener entweiht werden darf.

Wir können den gesamten Zusammenhang erst richtig verstehen, wenn wir uns in das in höchstem Maße symbolträchtige priesterliche Denken des antiken Volkes Israel hinein versetzen. Kernpunkt ist dabei die Realität des Heiligen, wie sie Rudolf Otto in seinem berühmten gleichnamigen Buch[32] beschrieben hat. Für das kultische Denken des altisraelitischen Priestertums erscheint mir als neuere Arbeit die Untersuchung von P. P. Jensen, „Graded Holiness“[33] wichtig, deren Untertitel „A Key to the Priestly Conception of the World“ Absicht und Inhalt zutreffend beschreibt. Wie schon der Titel besagt, ist der Kern der Darstellung die Erkenntnis, daß das priesterliche Denken den Kosmos kultbezogen in konzentrische Kreise einteilt. Der äußere Umkreis ist der nach außen hin unabgeschlossene Bereich des Unreinen, Chaotischen, Wüsten, der Bereich, wo Dämonen wie Asasel (Lev 16) und wilde Tiere hausen. Die reale Steppe und Wüste, die an das Land Palästina grenzt, bietet für die Israeliten hierzu eine greifbare Verkörperung. Dorthin wird alles fortgeschafft, was die Ordnung in den inneren Bereichen stört. Weiter nach innen schließt sich der Bereich des Reinen an. In diesen Bezirk reicht schon die

32 1. Aufl. 1917 (München 196331–35).

33 SOTS.S; 106 (Sheffield 1992).

Herrschaft Gottes hinein; sie verlangt Harmonie, die in menschlicher und dinglicher Hinsicht immer wieder hergestellt werden muß, indem störende Unreinheit herausgeschafft wird. Dies zu bewirken, dient die priesterliche Tora, wie wir sie u. a. in Lev 13–14 antreffen. Auch andere Aspekte, wie die Speisegebote von Lev 11, gehören hierher. Weiter innen befindet sich der Bereich des Heiligen, der Bezirk, der dem Kult und damit dem priesterlichen Dienst gewidmet ist. Er ist geprägt durch das in seiner Mitte befindliche Heiligtum. Zwischen dem umrahmenden Temenos, dem äußeren Vorhof des Tempels und dem eigentlichen Tempelgebäude besteht nochmals ein gradueller Unterschied im Ausmaß von Heiligkeit. Das Tremendum im Sinne von Rudolf Otto hält im gleichen Augenblick die Verehrer des Göttlichen in Ehrfurcht fern (so können Laien zwar am Kultus teilnehmen, aber doch nur bis zu einem bestimmten Punkt in den Tempelvorhöfen heranschreiten) wie das Fascinosum sie anzieht (von daher die Sehnsucht nach dem Heiligtum, die sich in Psalmen wie Ps 42/43 oder Ps 84 ausspricht). In diesen inneren Bereich zum unmittelbaren Opferdienst dürfen nur die Priester aus wenigen, dazu durch altererbte Privilegien bestimmten Geschlechtern, hineinkommen. Unter diesen nach Lev 21 aber auch nicht alle geborenen Mitglieder, sondern nur diejenigen, die sich durch vollkommene körperliche Unversehrtheit ohne äußere vom Ideal abweichende Eigenschaften auszeichnen. Als Typos für dieses Ideal dient in der Priesterschrift die Lagerordnung, wie sie Num 2–3 beschrieben wird. Die künftige ideale Landverteilung, wie sie im Buch Ezechiel visionär für die Zeit nach dem Exil gefordert wird (Ez 45, 1–8; Kap. 48), sieht ebenso eine Aufteilung vor, in der das Heiligtum nun auch in der geplanten Raumordnung direkt im Mittelpunkt des Landes innerhalb des abgeteilten heiligen Bezirks liegen soll. Eine letzte Steigerung von Heiligkeit bedeutet dann im Inneren des Tempels selbst das Adyton, das Allerheiligste, das nur Aaron (der Hohepriester) nach Lev 16 einmal im Jahr am großen Versöhnungstag betreten darf. Diese Züge sind allerdings erst in der Spätphase der Israelitisierung des Stoffes hineingekommen. Die Grundanschauungen vom Heiligen waren dagegen schon in der Tradition seit Urzeiten vorhanden. Besonders liberal-protestantischen Forschern war die Symbolik des Heiligen immer etwas suspekt. Wir haben aber allen Grund sie ernst zu nehmen. Die Welt läßt sich nur in Zeichen verstehen, und die Gegenwart Gottes im Gottesdienst ist im tiefsten Grunde sakramental. „Gott ist gegenwärtig, lasset uns anbeten und in Ehrfurcht vor ihn treten“, dieses Lied des reformierten Dichters Gerhard Tersteegen steht noch heute in unserem Gesangbuch.[34] Ein Grundgedanke, der das ganze priesterliche System in den von uns betrachteten Abschnitten außerdem durchzieht, ist ebenfalls als wichtig festzuhalten: Das Ziel der priesterlichen Kontrollen und Reinigungsbemühungen liegt letztlich darin, Harmonie im Kosmos herzustellen, Unvollkommenheiten zu beseitigen, und da, wo das nicht möglich ist, wie bei nicht zu reparierenden körperlichen Gebrechen, die Träger solcher Makel zumindest vom Zutritt zum inneren Bereich des Heiligen auszuschließen. Dies alles ist symbolisch zu verstehen, als Hinweis auf eine bessere Welt, die zwar im Hier und Jetzt nicht zu realisieren, aber als Endziel des Wirkens Gottes in der Welt doch im Auge zu behalten ist.

34 EG Nr. 165.

Rituelle Überlieferungen in Lev 1-4 als kanaanäisches Erbe

Henning Graf Reventlow, Bochum

Im Rahmen des weitgespannten Themas unseres Symposiums wird es nicht fehl am Platze sein, wenn wir uns auch mit dem Import fremder Kultordnungen nach Israel beschäftigen. Die Kapitel 1–7 des Buches Leviticus, in denen solche Rituale zu finden sind, bieten dazu die geeignete Grundlage. Bereits literarkritische Untersuchungen hatten Uneinheitlichkeiten in diesen Kapiteln festgestellt und sie ihrer Methode entsprechend mit Redaktionsschichten und der Tätigkeit von Redaktoren gedeutet.[1] Eine traditionsgeschichtliche Sicht wird solche Brüche anders erklären.

Kap. 1 fängt in V. 1–2a mit einer Einleitung an, die JHWHs Anrede an Mose, das „Zelt der Begegnung“ und einen Auftrag an Mose zur Wortübermittlung enthält. Das sind Züge eines Rahmens, der dadurch als zur typisch priesterschriftlichen Gesamtdarstellung gehörig gekennzeichnet ist. Bereits in V. 2b beginnt eine ganz anders geartete Schicht. Mit כי אדם setzt eine Regel in unpersönlich-kasuistischer Formulierung und mit einem ganz allgemein gehaltenen Subjekt ein: „Gesetzt, ein Mensch ...“ „bringt ein Opfer dar“ – das „für JHWH“ ist sichtlich ergänzt, wie auch das „von euch.“ Die ursprüngliche Fortsetzung im gleichen Stil beginnt in V.3 mit dem für kasuistische Unterabschnitte charakteristischen אם „wenn“ und setzt sich in V.3a mit einer Vorschrift für das Opfer eines Einzelnen, eben dieses „Menschen“ fort: Wenn es ein Brandopfer ist, soll er ein fehlerloses männliches Rind darbringen. V. 3b füllt diese Anweisung mit zahlreichen Zügen der Zelttradition auf, wie auch dem charakteristischen לפני יהוה „Vor JHWH“. V. 4 setzt die Ritualvorschrift fort: Die Opferordnung beginnt mit der Anweisung, wonach der Opfernde seine Hand auf den Kopf des Opfertiers stemmen soll, und erklärt in einer ty-

1 Das bekannteste Beispiel ist K. Elligers Kommentar *Leviticus* (HAT I, 4) Tübingen 1966.

pisch passivisch-unpersönlichen Formel[2] die Gültigkeit des so vollzogenen Opfers.[3] V. 5a schließt sich unmittelbar mit der durch den Opfernden persönlich vorgenommenen Schlachtung an. Danach geht im jetzigen Text die Aktivität an die „Söhne Aarons" – über, die das Blut des Opfertiers an den Altar sprengen sollen. R. Rendtorff[4] hatte jedoch aus dem unpersönlich- passivischen Stil in dem Parallelvers Lev 7,2 und mit Verweis auf 2. Kön 16,13 geschlossen, daß auch der Akt der Blutbesprengung ursprünglich dem Opfernden selbst zustand. Zu beachten ist, daß auch der Altar nur ganz allgemein benannt wird. Sowohl ein bestimmtes Heiligtum ist nicht im Blick, wie auch der Altar nicht auf eine Funktion im Dienste eines bestimmten Gottes festgelegt ist. Das ist erst durch die Überarbeitung geschehen, welche die „Söhne Aarons" und den Ort an der Tür des „Zeltes der Begegnung" nachträglich in den Text eingefügt hat.In V.6 ist weiter der Opfernde an der Reihe: Er soll dem Opfer die Haut abziehen und es in Stücke zerlegen. V. 7 ist stärker überarbeitet:

Nach dem jetzigen Text sind es die Söhne Aarons, die aaronitischen Priester, welche die folgenden Akte vollziehen sollen, nämlich Feuer auf den Altar zu bringen und Holz auf dem Feuer zu arrangieren. Der ältere Text scheint jedoch auch hier durch: Erstens ist weiterhin allgemein von „dem Altar" die Rede, zweitens erscheint noch ein weiteres Subjekt הכהן „der Priester". Daß diese Bezeichnung ursprünglich sein muß,[5] wird durch ihr Wiederauftreten in V. 9 deutlich. Ursprünglich werden die Verben also im Singular verwendet worden sein. Die Anonymität der Bezeichnung verweist wiederum in den älteren Kontext, der nicht einem bestimmten Kult zuzuordnen ist. V. 8 bietet ein ähnliches Bild: Fleischstücke, Kopf und Fett des Opfertieres sollen auf die Holzstücke gelegt werden. Das tun

2 Zuerst beschrieben von G. von Rad, Die Anrechnung des Glaubens zur Gerechtigkeit, in: ThLZ 76 (1951), 129–132= ders., Gesammelte Studien zum Alten Testament (THB 8). München 1958, 130–135.

3 Wenn die Formel לכפר עליו ein Zusatz ist, wie R. Rendtorff, Leviticus 1,1–10,20 (BK III,1) Neukirchen-Vluyn 2004), 36–37, mit dem schlüssigen Hinweis darauf, daß in Kap. 1–3 gar nicht von Schuldopfern die Rede ist, gezeigt hat, fällt der Sühneaspekt hier fort.

4 R. Rendtorff, Die Gesetze in der Priesterschrift (FRLANT N. F. 44) Göttingen 1954 (19632), 8f. hat schon mit Verweis auf Lev 7,2 und 2. Kön 16,13 die Vermutung geäußert, daß auch das Blutversprengen zu den Aufgaben des Opfernden gehörte.

5 Die Peschitta hat in Plural geändert, vgl. BHS App. a-a z. St. Dieser Vorschlag wird auch in vielen Kommentaren gemacht. R. Rendtorff, Leviticus 1,1–10,20 (BK III, 2) Neukirchen-Vluyn 2004, 56f., bietet eine komplizierte Erklärung des Numeruswechsels, die sich aber erübrigt, wenn man ihn durch die redaktionelle Arbeit an dem Kapitel erklärt.

nach dem jetzigen Text die „Söhne Aarons", aber dahinter steht noch הכהנים. Die Pluralform läßt sich durch Angleichung an die voranstehenden „Söhne Aarons" erklären, besonders wenn man berücksichtigt, daß der folgende V. 9 wieder die Singularform aufweist. Das gilt bereits für V. 9a, wo die Singularform ירחץ „er soll waschen" sich nur auf *den* Priester als Subjekt beziehen kann. Das Waschen von Eingeweiden und Unterschenkeln zur Vorbereitung ihres Verbrennens sind wie dessen Durchführung Aufgaben des einzelnen Priesters. Am Schluß steht dann noch die förmliche Definition des Opfers, die den Anfang in V.3 wiederaufnimmt: Es handelt sich um ein Brandopfer.

Was noch folgt: die Glosse „ein Feueropfer"[6] und die auch sonst auftretende Formel ריח-נחוח ליהוה „ein angenehmer Geruch für JHWH" – ein typischer Bestandteil der JWH-Redaktion, gehört zur Bearbeitung.

Wenn wir das Ergebnis überblicken, stellt sich heraus, daß die Grundlage des Kapitels in einer vorjahwistischen, keiner spezifischen Religion zuzuordnenden Opferordnung besteht, die den Vollzug eines Brandopfers durch einen einzelnen regelt. Mitwirkende sind der Opfernde selbst, der die wichtigsten Handlungen des eigentlichen Opfers vollzieht, und ein einzelner Priester, der dabei mit ihm kooperiert. Der Ort ist ein einzelner Altar, der keinem bestimmten Heiligtum zugeordnet ist. Roy Gane nennt diesen Typ von Opfer „Outer Sanctum ... Offerings."[7]

Kap. 2 weist eine von Kap. 1 stark unterschiedene Struktur auf, läßt sich aber der gleichen Traditionsentwicklung zuordnen. Der Anfang gleicht noch stark der Form in Kap. 1. Statt אדם כי heißt es jetzt נפש כי, was etwa gleichbedeutend, nur noch allgemeiner ist: „Jede Person." Das geschieht vielleicht deswegen, weil es sich hier um vegetabile Opfer handelt, die von jedermann dargebracht werden können.[8] Auch hier ist der Hauptakteur der Opfernde, und er kooperiert mit dem Priester, der auch hier im Singular genannt wird. Wie in Kap. 1 hat dieser die Funktion, die Verbrennung des Opfers vorzunehmen, und erneut ist der Opferort ein offenbar freistehender Altar (V. 2b). Wieder stehen diese Aussagen in Spannung zu v.2a, wo von den Söhnen Aarons, den Priestern (im Plural) gesprochen wird. Zusätze sind außerdem die Formeln ליהוה „für

6 R. Rendtorff, Leviticus. Exkurs 2 (63–65) schlägt für אשה die Bedeutung „Gabe" (an eine Gottheit) vor.

7 Roy Gane, Cult and Character. Purification Offerings, Day of Atonement, and Theodicy. Winona Lake, IN, 2005, 71 (speziell von den Reinigungsopfern).

8 Die Kombination נפש כי oder נפש אשר findet sich im gleichen Formgebrauch noch Lev 4,2; 5,1.4.15.17.21; 7,20.21.27.

JHWH" (v. 1)", Feueropfer, angenehmer Geruch für JHWH" (V. 2, vgl. 3).

Im zweiten Teil des Kapitels ab V. 4 tritt ein Stilwandel ein. Jetzt begegnet die Anrede in der 2. pers. sg. an den potentiellen Opfernden, dem jetzt Vorschriften für den Vollzug des Opfers bei verschiedenen Unterfällen des vegetabilen Opfers gemacht werden. Es handelt sich also um einen ursprünglich von dem ersten unabhängigen Abschnitt. Die Formen des kasuistischen (Sakral-) Rechts begegnen aber auch hier: Der Abschnitt beginnt mit dem einen Hauptabschnitt einleitenden כי (V. 4): Unterabschnitte werden mit einem אם eingeleitet (Vv. 5.7.14). Sie unterscheiden unterschiedliche Materialien, aus denen ein Opfer bestehen kann. Eine Deklarationsformel wie die am Ende von V. 6 מנחה הוא „Es ist ein Speisopfer" unterstreichen den priestlichen Charakter dieser Opferanweisungen. Weiter fällt die Erwähnung des Priesters in V. 8 in die Augen: Wieder ist es ein einzelner, nicht näher identifizierter Priester. Seine Rolle besteht darin, daß er das Vegetabilienopfer zum Altar bringt. Auch dieser wird nur mit dieser ganz allgemeinen Bezeichnung erwähnt und scheint nicht mit einem bestimmten Heiligtum verbunden zu sein. V. 9a setzt diese Ausführungen fort: Priester und Altar werden genannt. In den Versen 8 und 9 finden sich dann wieder jahwistische Bearbeitungen: V. 8a ordnet an, daß der Opfernde das Speisopfer JHWH darbringen soll, und V. 9b fügt die in den Kulttexten verbreitete[9] Formel an, die uns schon in V. 2 begegnet ist: ריח ניחוח הוהלי „[ein Feueropfer] ein angenehmer Duft für JHWH". Daran schließt sich V. 10 an, der feststellt, daß der von der Opfergabe übrig bleibende Rest „Aaron und seinen Söhnen" zufallen soll, offensichtlich ein Teil der jahwistischen Aktualisierung.

Mit V. 11 beginnt ein neues, bis V. 12 reichendes eingeschobenes Stück, das in 2. pers. plur. formuliert ist. Man hat den Eindruck, daß es sich um eine Bearbeitung eines älteren Stückes handelt, das eine Reihe von negativen Vorschriften enthielt (Verbot von Sauerteig und Honig als Opfer). Möglich ist, daß es ursprünglich eine Fortsetzung der in der 2. pers. formulierten Anweisungen enthielt und nachträglich in den Plural umgeformt wurde. Das wäre eine stärkere Anpassung an die umgebende jahwistische Aktualisierung.

In V. 13 wird die Fortsetzung deutlich sichtbar. Es wird wieder in die 2. pers. sg. übergegangen.[10] Jetzt geht es um die Vorschrift, alle Speisopfer

---

9 Cf. Ex 29, 18.25.41; Lev 1, 9.13.17; 2,2.9.12; 3,5.16; 4,31; 6,8.14; 17,6; 23,23.31.

10 LXX hat מנחתך und אלהיך in die 2. pers. plur. angeglichen, bei den Verbformen dagegen den Singular beibehalten.

zu salzen. Auffällig ist in diesem Satz die Formulierung „Salz des Bundes deines Gottes". Ob es sich hier ebenfalls um einen Bestandteil der Aktualisierung handelt oder einen Rest der älteren Vorlage, in der verallgemeinernd von einem anonymen Gott gesprochen wurde, muß offen bleiben.

V. 14 gliedert sich durch die Einleitung mit אם in die Reihe der Unterfälle des Formulars ein. Hier geht es zusammen mit V. 15 um das Erstlingsopfer, für das genaue Vorschriften erlassen werden. V. 15 endet noch einmal mit der deklaratorischen Formel מנחה הוה „ein Speisopfer ist es". In V. 16 taucht dann erneut der Priester (im Singular) auf, der Körner, Öl und Weihrauch verbrennt. Offensichtlich gehört das abschließende „ein Feueropfer für JHWH" zur jahwesierenden Überarbeitung.

Kap. 3 stellt sich von der Struktur her als die Fortsetzung von Kap. 1 dar.[11] Das Kapitel beginnt mit ואם „und wenn" und handelt vom Heilsopfer (זבח שלמים). Wie wir שלמים übersetzen sollen, ist umstritten. Die traditionelle Bezeichnung ist „Friedensopfer", aber charakteristisch für dieses Opfer ist, daß das Fleisch des geopferten Tieres von allen Teilnehmern des Opferfestes einschließlich des Opfernden gegessen werden kann. Deshalb ist auch die Bezeichnung „Gemeinschafts-Schlachtopfer"[12] sinnvoll.

Das Kapitel besteht aus drei Abschnitten: Im ersten Abschnitt (V.1-5) stammt das Opfertier (männlich oder weiblich) vom Großvieh (den Rindern). Die Hauptsache: es muß fehlerlos sein (V.1). Die Schlußworte יהוה לפני fallen deutlich heraus als jahwesierende Redaktion. Das weitere Vorgehen ist parrallel zu dem Opfervorgang in Kap. 1: V. 2a Der Opfernde stemmt seine Hand auf den Kopf des Opfertieres und schlachtet es. Zur „Tür des Zelts der Begegnung" (vgl. 1, 3. 5) treten im jetzigen Text „die Söhne Aarons", die aaronitische Priesterschaft in Funktion und sprengen das Blut rings um den Altar. Auch hier steht wieder als Apposition הכהנים „die Priester" dabei, vermutlich als Relikt einer früheren singularischen Textform zu werten, die aber, wenn Rendtorff recht hat,[13] nicht die ursprüngliche ist. V. 3 Am Anfang handelt wieder der Opfernde;[14] er bringt von dem Gemeinschaftsopfer ein Brandopfer[15] in Form der ver-

11 So u. a. auch Rendtorff, Leviticus, 9.17–18.117–118.

12 Rendtorff, a. a. O. 115.

13 Vgl. o.

14 Vgl. Rendtorff, Leviticus, 115–116 z. St., gegen die Plural-Lesung von LXX und Vulgata.

15 אשא dürfte zum ursprünglichen Text gehören, während ליהוה vom Inhalt her zur Bearbeitung zu rechnen ist.

schiedenen Fettbestandteile dar. Der konkrete Verbrennungsvorgang auf dem Altar wird im Endtext wieder den Aroniden zugewiesen. In der genauen Ortsbeschreibung fällt die Wendung „auf dem Brandopferaltar" auf, die in dem ganzen Kapitel nicht mehr vorkommt. Am Ende des Verses steht wieder die bekannte Schlußformel: „ein Feueropfer [eine Gabe?], ein angenehmer Geruch für JHWH". Die Zuordnung zu der jahwistischen Aktualisierungsschicht fällt nicht schwer.

Mit v. 6 beginnt der nächste Unterfall, mit ואם eingeleitet. Zunächst wird das Opfertier der Gattung ‚Kleinvieh' zugeordnet. Dann folgen die beiden Unterarten: Lamm (V. 7–11) und Ziege (V. 12–16). Die Einzelheiten sind hier – abgesehen von den durch die beiden unterschiedlichen Tierarten bedingten Abweichungen – weitgehend unter sich und zu dem ersten Abschnitt parallel. Besonders interessant ist aber ein Unterschied zu diesem: Während in V. 5 die Söhne Aarons den Auftrag erhalten, das Fett des Opfertieres auf dem Altar zu verbrennen, wird in V. 11 und 16 der Priester (im Singular!) als der diese Handlung Ausführende genannt. Das wiederum stimmt mit unseren Beobachtungen in Kap. 1 überein, wo wir zuerst an diesen Merkmalen die ältere Schicht aus dem Text herausgearbeitet hatten. Erst in der Überarbeitung zur Aktualisierung und Anpassung an die JHWH-Religion wurde der einzelne Priester durch die „Söhne Aarons" ersetzt und außerdem typische Züge wie das „Zelt der Begegnung" und ausdrückliche Verweise auf JHWH eingeführt. Der Altar, unspezifisch und im Singular, wird dagegen, wie wir schon in Kap. 1 sahen, zur älteren Schicht gehören.

Die Schlußworte von v. 16 „Alles Fett gehört JHWH" deuten die Vorschrift, das Fett von dem Fleisch abzutrennen und zu verbrennen, wie es in sämtlichen Einzelvorschriften vorkommt, von einem jahwistisch-theologischen Standpunkt aus. V. 17 betont abschließend die für alle Israeliten gültige Vorschrift, kein Fett zu essen. Hier ist die jahwistische Herkunft nicht so eindeutig. Die Grundlage bildet anscheinend ein apodiktisches Gebot in V.17b; typisch hierfür ist die Formulierung לא mit dem Imperativ.[16]. V.17a könnte zusammen mit V.16 zu der israelitischen Bearbeitungsschicht gehören.

Kap.4 hat große Ähnlichkeit in der Struktur mit den Kapiteln 1 und 3. Es handelt vom Sündopfer (חתאת). Die Gliederung des Kapitels wie auch von Kap. 5 erfolgt allerdings nach einem anderen Prinzip: Der Fall der unbeabsichtigten (בשגגה) Verschuldung und des jeweils fälligen Sün-

16 Vgl. W. Gesenius/E.Kautsch, Hebräische Grammatik. Leipzig 190928, Nachdruck Hildesheim und Darmstadt 1985, §7o.

dopfers wird aufgegliedert nach der gesellschaftlichen Stellung des schuldig Gewordenen. Zuerst geht es um den gesalbten Priester (V. 3–12), dann um die ganze Gemeinde Israel (V. 13–21), anschließend um den Fürsten (נשיא)[17] (V. 22–26) und schließlich um einen gewöhnlichen Menschen (V.27-35)

Die kasuistische Darlegung beginnt analog 2,1 in V.2 mit נפש כי: „Wenn jemand". Das ist die Oberüberschrift, die sich später in verschiedenen Unterfällen entfaltet. Voran geht nur der für P charakteristische doppelte Wortübermittlungsauftrag (JHWH-Mose; Mose-Söhne Israels), eine eindeutig sekundäre Einleitung. Wenn man den JHWH-Namen ausscheidet, könnte der kasuistische Einleitungssatz ursprünglich sein. Gegenüber den reinen Opferregeln, die in Kap. 1 und 3 herrschen, ist in Kap. 4 der Schuldbezug wichtig: alle darzubringenden Opfer sollen der Sühne dienen. Zu der ungewollten Versündigung des gesalbten Priesters wird sogleich gesagt, daß er damit auch das Volk in Verschuldung gebracht hat.[18] Der Begriff ‚Volk' (העם) fällt an dieser Stelle auf, der von den sonst meist in den Kapiteln anzutreffenden Begriffen עדה und קהל abweicht.[19] Der Begriff in seiner Allgemeinheit könnte der alten Grundlage entstammen. Speziell von Israel ist noch nicht die Rede. Der Kollektivschuldgedanke steht im Hintergrund: ein Repräsentant des Volkes wie der Priester kann seine persönliche Schuld auf das ganze Volk übertragen.

Es folgt die Vorschrift[20] für den liturgischen Ablauf einer Opferhandlung. Diese weist starke Parallelen im Ablauf zu denen in Lev 1 und 3 auf, ist allerdings stärker als dort jahwistisch aktualisiert worden. V. 3 ist nach Streichung des ליהוה anscheinend unverändert überliefert. Hier wird in Analogie zu Kap. 1 und 3 vorgeschrieben, daß der schuldig gewordene Priester einen fehllosen jungen Stier zum Opfer bringen soll. Der in V. 4a folgende aktualisierte Text nennt als Ort, wo die Darbringung geschehen

---

17 Zu seinen Funktionen vgl. H. Niehr, Art. נשיא in: ThWAT V (1986), 647–657 (Lit.).

18 R. Rendtorff, Lev, 137, übersetzt mit „sich seiner Schuld bewußt wird" und begründet dies ausführlich, 152–53. Obwohl er sich dabei auf Vorarbeiten stützt, ist diese Übersetzung nicht einleuchtend. Das Mitschuldigwerden als Realität geht dem Bewußtwerden dieses Zustandes voraus und muß deshalb an erster Stelle genannt werden. Nur dies entspricht auch der Bedeutung der Wurzel אשם. Außerdem setzt Rendtorffs Übersetzung voraus, daß die Tatfolge nur dann eintritt, wenn das Vergehen öffentlich bekannt wird.

19 Außer in Lev 4, 27 (s. u.) kommt der Begriff עם in Lev 1–7 nur noch in der כרת-Formel in Lev 7,20.21.27 vor.

20 Das ist das sinnvollste Verständnis des perf. cons. als logischer Folgesatz des eingetretenen Zustandes, vgl. GesK § 112p – gegen R. Rendtorffs indikativische Wiedergabe der Verben.

soll, wie in Lev 1,3b den Eingang des „Zelts der Zusammenkunft" vor. Die Parallele in Lev 3, 1 hat nur לפני יהוה. V. 4b regelt den nächsten Schritt des Rituals. Wiederum in Analogie zu Lev 1, 4 und 3, 2 wird von Handaufstemmung auf den Kopf desOpfers und seiner Schlachtung gesprochen, beides von dem Opfernden ausgeführt, der aber nicht in seiner Eigenschaft als gesalbter Priester, sondern als persönlich schuldig Gewordener handelt. Ein erneutes לפני יהוה ist leicht als Zusatz zu erkennen. Die Wiederkehr der Bezeichnung „der gesalbte Priester" in V.5 scheint zu besagen, daß es noch der Opfernde ist, der das Blut des Opfertiers an den heiligen Ort bringt. Eine besondere Frage ist, ob „das Zelt der Begegnung" hier eine ältere Bezeichnung verdrängt hat. Sicher ist jedoch offensichtlich, daß die eigentliche Bluthandlung nicht mehr von dem opfernden „gesalbten Priester" vollzogen wird, sondern von dem diensttuenden Priester, der hier wie in den früheren Vorkommen der Bezeichnung (Lev 1,7.9.12.17; 2,2.8.9.16; 3,11.16) mit dem einfachen Begriff הכהן bezeichnet wird. Er sprengt von dem Blut siebenmal in Richtung auf[21] den heiligen Vorhang. Die Wendung יהוה לפנה „vor JHWH" gehört eindeutig zu jahwesierenden Überarbeitung. Die Frage ist, ob der Vorhang auch in diesen Bereich zu verweisen ist, und damit möglicherweise der ganze Vers. Denn im folgenden V. 7 wird noch eine zweite Bluthandlung des Priesters genannt. Diesmal geht es darum, daß der Priester etwas von dem Blut an die Hörner des Räucheraltars streichen soll. Diese Anweisung scheint eindeutig zu der älteren Schicht zu gehören und ist an verschiedenen Stellen aktualisiert worden: wiederum durch ein לפני יהוה, diesmal ergänzt durch den Relativsatz „der im Zelt der Begegnung ist", welcher sich nur auf den Räucheraltar beziehen kann. In der zweiten Vershälfte wird die Anweisung durch die Bestimmung ergänzt, daß er das übrige Blut an den Sockel des Brandopferaltars schütten soll, aufgefüllt mit dem parallelen Relativsatz, daß sich dieser am Eingang des Zelts der Begegnung befinde. Wenn man diese Relativsätze zu der Aktualisierungsschicht rechnet, wird deutlich, daß sowohl der allein fungierende Priester wie die beiden Altäre aus der älteren Tradition stammen, welche diese typisch israelitisch-priesterschriftlichen Akzessoirs noch nicht kannte. Die Verse 8–9 beschreiben die Behandlung des Fettes des Opfertiers mit genauen Angaben, an welchen Stellen des Körpers es abgetrennt werden soll. Wer dies alles zu vollziehen hat, ist nicht gesagt. Nach dem Zusammenhang müßte es der amtierende Priester sein. Wenn man aber von der Parallele in Lev 1,

21 Gane, Cult and Character, 72–80, begründet ausführlich, daß את פני ‚vor' bedeute (vgl. auch die Übersetzung von Rendtorff, Leviticus, z. St.). Das ist nicht völlig überzeugend.

6.9 ausgeht, ist dies wieder die Aufgabe des Opfernden. Die Verse 8–9 beschreiben die Behandlung des Fettes des Opfertiers mit genauen Angaben, an welchen Stellen des Körpers es abgetrennt werden soll. Wer dies alles zu vollziehen hat, ist nicht gesagt. Nach dem Zusammenhang müßte es der amtierende Priester sein. Wenn man aber von der Parallele in Lev 1, 6.9 ausgeht, könnte dies wieder die Aufgabe des Opfernden sein. Dafür spricht vor allem V. 10b, der wieder mit neuem Subjekt dem amtierenden Priester den Vollzug des Brandopfers auf dem Brandopferaltar zuschreibt.

Es folgen noch V.11–12, in denen es um den Abtransport von Fell und Fleisch des geopferten Stieres handelt. In V. 12 wird kein Subjekt genannt. Nach dem Zusammenhang müßte es der amtierende Priester sein. Aber es handelt sich hier nicht mehr um eine Handlung im Vollzug des Opfers, sondern nur noch um die Beseitigung der Reste, da bei diesem Schuldopfer das Fleisch, anders als beim Gemeinschaftsopfer, nicht gegessen werden kann und auch den Priestern, weil der Opfernde selbst ein Priester ist, nichts zusteht. Vielleicht ist dabei auch die abschließende Wendung charakteristisch, welche die Aussage noch einmal wiederholt, diesmal aber mit einer passivischen (niph'al) Formulierung. Dies spricht eher für ein anonymes Subjekt.

In den übrigen Abschnitten von Kap. 4 werden die weiteren Fälle behandelt: Zunächst, angereiht mit dem typischen ואם, V. 13–21 das Opfer für eine fahrlässige Schuld der ganzen Gemeinde. Hier wird ausdrücklich festgestellt, daß es sich um eine Schuld handelt, welche die Gemeinde nicht bemerkt hatte, und die erst später aufgedeckt wurde (V. 13–14). In beiden Versen sind die Spuren einer israelitischen Überarbeitung sehr zahlreich. Der Begriff עדה (Gemeinde) ist typisch priesterschriftlich[22] und nach L. Rost[23] womöglich erst von P geschaffen. Älter ist der Begriff קהל[24], der mehrfach (V. 13.14) hier im gleichen Kontext auftaucht und offenbar der älteren Schicht angehört. Der Ablauf ist hier der gleiche wie im ersten Abschnitt, nur daß die Ältesten[25] der Gemeinde ihre Hände auf den Kopf des Opferstieres stemmen. Zusätzlich zum ersten Abschnitt erfahren wir hier auch, daß der Priester – er tritt auch hier im Singular auf

22 Noch V.15 und Lev 8, 3.4.5; 9,5; 10,6.17; 16,5; 19,2; 24,14.16; עדת ישראל noch Ex 12, 3.6; 19, 47; Num 16,9; 32,4.

23 Leonhard Rost, Die Vorstufen von Kirche und Gemeinde im Alten Testament (BWANT 76 = NF 24. Stuttgart 1938, Nachdruck Darmstadt 1967), 32.87. Vgl. auch Karl Elliger, Leviticus (HAT I, 4; Tübingen 1966), 70.

24 Vgl. Rost, a. a. O., 7–32.

25 In P äußerst selten (nur hier und Lev 9,1).

und ist deshalb zu der älteren Schicht zu rechnen – für die Gemeinde Sühne[26] erwirkt (V. 20). Neben dem Verbum כפר pi., dessen Subjekt der das Opfer vollziehende Priester ist, steht das Verb סלח im Niphal: Man muß sich Gott als Subjekt denken. Gottes Handeln passivisch zu umschreiben, ist eine ganz gängige Praxis. In V. 21 steht dann noch ein Satz über das Fortschaffen des getöteten Stiers und sein Verbrennen, wobei ausdrücklich auf die entsprechenden Aussagen im ersten Abschnitt verwiesen wird. Den Abschluß bildet eine deklaratorische Formel: „Dies ist ein Sündopfer der Gemeinde“. Wenn hier noch einmal der Begriff קהל auftaucht, ist das ein Zeichen, daß auch diese Formel zum alten Bestand gehört.

In dem folgenden kurzen Abschnitt V. 22–26, in dem als Opfertier ein Ziegenbock vorgesehen ist, der im übrigen aber dieselben Schritte des Rituals enthält, ist die umstrittenste Frage, wer mit dem נשיא gemeint ist.[27] Alternative Vorschläge lauten: Entweder die Stammesfürsten, die in Num 7 die Abgaben ihres jeweiligen Stammes zum Heiligtum bringen. Oder es handelt sich um eine Bezeichnung für den König, wie sie in Ez 40–48 für den Herrscher der Heilszeit gebraucht wird. Eine Entscheidung ist nicht leicht. Aber die zweite Möglichkeit scheidet, obwohl sie von den jüdischen Auslegern bevorzugt wird[28], aus. Ein eschatologischer Aspekt wie in Ez 40–48 liegt nicht vor. Wenn der (vorexilische) König gemeint wäre, würde man einen Artikel erwarten. Es sieht vielmehr so aus, als ob der נשיא einer unter anderen seines Ranges sei. Auffällig ist, daß er mit einem Ziegenbock ein im Vergleich mit den Stieren geringes Opfertier darzubringen hat. Elliger[29] schließt daraus, daß dies eine ältere Form des Opfers und das ganze Stück relativ alt sei. Allerdings sind das Spekulationen. Im Ganzen ist das Opferritual in diesem Abschnitt auffällig kurz: Es fehlt ein Blutakt, und der eine Akt, der erwähnt wird, das Bestreichen der Altarhörner (V.25), erfolgt nicht am Räucheraltar (V. 7.18), sondern am Brandopferaltar.

---

26 Zu dem Begriff vgl. neuerdings Jay Sklar, Sin, Impurity, Atonement: The Priestly Conceptions (Hebrew Bible Monographs, 2; Sheffield 2005). Es gibt noch eine große Menge weiterer Sekundärliteratur. BILDI zählt 213 Titel auf. Vgl. bes. Bernd Janowski, Sühne als Heilsgeschehen : Studien zur Sühnetheologie der Priesterschrift und zur Wurzel KPR im Alten Orient und im Alten Testament (WMANT; 55; Neukirchen-Vluyn 1982; 20002, mit Anhang); auch R. Rendtorff, Leviticus, Exkurs 6, 176–78.

27 Dazu Rendtorff, Leviticus, 181–82.

28 Rendtorff, a. a. O., nennt die wichtigsten Vertreter.

29 Leviticus, z. St.

Der letzte Abschnitt, der sich mit dem Schuldopfer eines beliebigen Israeliten einfachen Standes (der אחת נפש, V. 27) befaßt, ist noch einmal in zwei Unterabschnitte je nach dem verwendeten Opfertier geteilt: Entweder kann eine weibliche Ziege genommen werden (V. 28b–31) oder ein Schaf (V.32–35). In beiden Fällen wird der einfache Ritus wie bei dem נשיא vollzogen, und wie bei diesem wird das Blut von dem Priester an den Hörnern des Brandopferaltars verstrichen.

Es ist sinnvoll, an dieser Stelle die Einzelauslegung abzubrechen, da Kap. 5 ein anderes Gliederungssystem (kasuistisch auf einzelne Anlässe bezogen) aufweist und Kap. 6–7, wo die einzelnen Opferanlässe noch einmal vorkommen, eine andere Herkunft hat.

Wichtig ist nun, aus den bisherigen Beobachtungen die richtigen Schlüsse zu ziehen. Am wichtigsten ist zu erkennen, daß sich hinter der jetzigen Form des Textes, die an vielen Stellen ausdrücklich auf den JHWH-Kult, seine Priester nach der priesterschriftlichen Tradition, die Aaroniden, Bezug nimmt, eine ältere Entwicklungsstufe verbirgt, die sich nach Ausscheiden der vielen Zusätze als erheblich urtümlich darstellt. Für sie ist (1.) charakteristisch, daß die Person, die das Opfer darbringt (sei es nun ein Amtsträger oder ein Privatmann), einen wichtigen Teil der liturgischen Handlung selbst vollzieht: die Handaufstemmung, die Schlachtung des Opfertiers, während der amtierende Priester nur für die Blutriten und die Verbrennung der Fetteile, die der Gottheit gehören, zuständig ist. Auch die Beseitigung des toten Tieres in den Fällen, wenn das Fleisch nicht verzehrt werden kann (Lev 4, 3–12; 13–21) ist offenbar nicht seine Aufgabe.[30] Eine weitere Eigenart der offenbaren Urfassung (2.) ist, daß ein anonymer Priester die priesterlichen Aufgaben in der Liturgie vollzieht und nicht etwa Aaron und seine Söhne, die für die Priesterschrift die zuständige priesterliche Dynastie bilden. Alle ihre Erwähnungen erweisen sich als Hinzufügungen. Sie gehören meist zum Rahmenwerk, können aber auch im Inneren der Abschnitte auftreten. Außerdem (3.) gehören zu der ursprünglichen Fassung als Kultstätten nur zwei freistehende Altäre: Der Brandopferaltar und der Räucheraltar, die zudem einzeln gebraucht werden. Das israelitische Heiligtum des „Zelts der Begegnung“ (מועד אהל) mit seinen Einrichtungsgegenständen, in die auch die ursprünglich einzeln stehenden Altäre integriert werden, das Lager gehören in die den gesamten Text duchziehenden jahwesierenden Aktualisierungen.

30 Auch wenn die Form des Verbums in Lev 4,12. 21 zwischen den Versionen unklar ist (Singular oder Plural?) i.

Am wichtigsten ist sicherlich (4.), daß in der ursprünglichen Fassung kein Gottesname erscheint. Die zahlreichen Erwähnungen des JHWH-Namens sind spätere Zusätze, wie besonders in der Floskel לפני יהוה deutlich wird. Ganz deutlich ist (5.), daß die Stücke mit der Wortübermittlung von JHWH zu Mose und von Mose zu den Israeliten nicht zu den alten Traditionen gehören, sondern zu einem Gesamtrahmen, der in einem späten Stadium des Textes die priesterliche Gesamtdarstellung seit Ex 25 überspannt. Unter diesem Dach treten aber ältere Teilsammlungen hervor, wie die Kapitel Lev 1-3, die Abschnitte innerhalb Lev 4, 5, und dann wieder eine den vorangehenden Kapiteln in kürzerer Form entsprechende Sammlung in Lev 5-6 (die wir hier im Einzelnen nicht mehr besprechen konnten). Schließlich (6.) gibt es auch verbale Unterschiede zwischen den älteren Traditionen und der neueren Endfassung. Hier fiel uns insbesondere die Entwicklung von der älteren Bezeichnung קהל zu der jüngeren, typisch priesterschriftlichen Bezeichnung עדה für die Kultgemeinde in die Augen.

Für unsere Gesamtbeurteilung ergibt sich, daß die israelitische Glaubensgemeinschaft von ihrer Umgebung kultische Rituale übernommen und durch zahlreiche Ergänzungen jahwesiert, d. h. ihrer speziellen religiösen Tradition eingefügt hat. Über alle äußeren Übernahmen hinaus, von denen auf unserem Symposium die Rede ist, ist dieses Erbe besonders hervorzuheben. Offensichtlich war es das Kanaanäertum, das diese kultischen Rituale bereitgestellt hat. Ihre Anonymität, was das kultische Personal angeht und die verallgemeinernden rituellen Vorschriften, die sich nicht auf eine bestimmte Gottheit beziehen, sind anscheinend von ihrem polytheistischen Hintergrund her zu verstehen. Sie konnten im Rahmen eines Pantheons von den Anhängern verschiedener Gottheiten benutzt werden. Es ist schon seit langem bekannt, in wie weitem Maße Israel von seinen Vorgängern und Nachbarn im Lande abhängig war. Ich erinnere nur an den sog. „syrischen Tempeltyp", der u. a. auch dem Tempel Salomos in Jerusalem als Baumuster diente. Über diese äußere Form hinaus war der Kultus Israels, wie wir an unserem Beispiel sahen, in noch viel höherem Maße in seiner Ausübung von übernommenen liturgischen Abläufen bestimmt, die ihm in den vorjahwistischen Ritualen überliefert waren. Hierfür ließen sich weitere Beispielen bringen, aber schon die vorgeführten Texte lassen dies in reichem Ausmaß erkennen.

Einiges zu den altmesopotamischen Beschwörungstexten in sumerischer Sprache, besonders zu einer ungewöhnlich formulierten Beschwörung gegen die Folgen von Schlangen- und Hundebiss sowie Skorpionenstich

W.H.Ph. Römer, Baarn

I.

Vor etwa zehn Jahren hatte ich einmal versucht, eine in sumerischer Sprache abgefasste Beschwörung gegen die Folgen von Schlangen- und Hundebiss, sowie Skorpionenstich (VS 10,193) zu bearbeiten.[1] Auf diesen, wie es scheint, noch immer praktisch vereinzelt dastehenden Text möchte ich in diesem kurzen Vortrag noch einmal zurückkommen, nachdem inzwischen einige weitere Bearbeiter (N. Veldhuis; G. Cunningham; I.L. Finkel) sich ebenfalls an ihm versucht haben.[2]

Zusammenstellungen der auf uns gekommenen altmesopotamischen Beschwörungen in sumerischer, akkadischer und in anderen Sprachen aus dem Zeitraum von 2500–1500 v. Chr. verdanken wir P. Michalowski[3] und G. Cunningham in seiner unter dem einigermassen befremdenden Titel „Deliver me from Evil" erschienenen Dissertation.[4] Weitere Beschwörungen mit dreifacher Zielsetzung finden sich dort, falls ich richtig gesehen habe, nicht.

1 In: M. Dietrich; O. Loretz (Hg.), „Vom Alten Orient zum Alten Testament", (2.) Fs. W. von Soden, AOAT 240, Kevelaer; Neukirchen/Vluyn 1995, S. 413ff.

2 N. Veldhuis, ZA 83,161ff.; G. Cunningham, „Deliver me from Evil", StP(M) 17, Rom 1997, S. 79f.; 82; Z. 11–15: I.L. Finkel, in: T. Abush; K. van der Toorn (Hg.), Mesopotamian Magic, Textual, Historical, and Interpretative Perspectives, Ancient Magic and Divination I, Groningen 1999 (Abk.: 'Mes. Magic'), S. 231f.

3 In: P. Fronzaroli (Hg.), Literature and Literary Language at Ebla, QS 18, Florenz 1992, S. 322ff.

4 StP(M) 17, S. 40ff.; 64; 96f.; 131ff.

Verwiesen sei hier nebenbei auf den jüngeren Text KAR 233 m. Dupl, Z. 28.[5] Doch sind bei G. Cunningham eine Anzahl Beschwörungen mit zweifacher Zielsetzung aufgeführt und zwar gegen die Folgen von Verwundungen durch Schlangen und Skorpione,[6] Schlange und (tollwütigen) Hund[7] und sogar gegen Fliegen und Skorpione.[8] Bemerkt sei übrigens, dass in Z. 15 unseres Textes nur noch eine Schlange erwähnt wird!

Es hat sich N. Veldhuis, der, wie wir sahen, auch eine Neubearbeitung unseres Textes vorgelegt hat, gefragt, weshalb diese drei Tierarten so gefürchtet waren und offenbar als gleichermassen gefährlich betrachtet wurden.[9] Denn zwar sind Skorpionenstiche tatsächlich immer gefährlich, doch sind die meisten Schlangenbisse ungefährlich, während die meisten Hunde nicht tollwütig sind. Wie es die Strukturalisten gewöhnt sind versucht der Verfasser sich an eine Erklärung dieses Problems mit Hilfe von binären Oppositionen, wobei er auf die Arbeit der Anthropologin Frau M. Douglas, „Purity and Danger" verweist.[10] Er nennt die drei Tierarten ‚liminal' animals, d.h. Tiere, die sich an einer Grenze u.zw. zwischen „nature and culture, desert and town, danger and security" bewegen, indem sie zwar zum Reiche der wilden Tiere gehören, trotzdem aber in die bewohnten Gegenden eindringen, bzw. dort zu Hause sind.[11] Vielleicht kann man sich aber auch einfach fragen, ob unsere Beschwörung nicht nur für konkrete Fälle (einen Fall?), in denen Schlange, Hund und (oder?) Skorpion gefährlich waren (das letztere Tier immer!), dienen sollte. Es sei hier noch auf eine nüchterne Bemerkung von M.J. Geller hingewiesen: „The point is that an incantation is effective, not against snake-bite or prevention of snakes, but against the fear of snakes"![12] Schliesslich sei hier noch auf eine wichtige Stelle in der altbabylonischen Liste von Krankheiten aufmerksam gemacht, wo untereinander aufgeführt sind: x x šub-ba = *zi-qí-it zuqiqīpim* (G̃ÍR.TAB) / muš-zú-kur$_5$ = *ni-ši-ik ṣērim* (MUŠ) / gug$_6$.SAR = *ni-ši-ik kalbim* (UR.GI$_7$).[13]

5 Vgl. AOAT 240, S. 419; 41958.

6 Siehe StP(M) 17, S. 40.

7 StP(M) 17, S. 42.

8 StP(M) 17, S. 154.

9 ZA 83,166ff.

10 Ebd., 167.

11 Ebd. 167f.

12 ‚Mes. Magic', S. 55.

13 Siehe AOAT 240, S. 419 zu B. Landsberger, MSL 9, S. 78,97–99.

II.

Einleitend zur Deutung unserer Beschwörung VS 10,193 seien nun kurz an Hand von A. Falkensteins noch immer grundlegenden Leipziger Dissertation „Die Haupttypen der sumerischen Beschwörung literarisch untersucht“[14] einige Fragen der Serienbildung, der Textgeschichte, sowie der literarischen Formen (später unter IV.) der Beschwörungstexte der Ur III-Zeit und der altbabylonischen Periode erörtert, wobei wir zu der unten besprochenen Marduk-Ea-Formel (Typ c) auch auf die Bemerkungen von M. Krebernik in seiner Münchener Dissertation „Die Beschwörungen aus Fara und Ebla. Untersuchungen zur ältesten keilschriftlichen Beschwörungsliteratur“[15] eingehen.

Beschwörungen in sumerischer Sprache gehören zu den wenigen altmesopotamischen Literaturformen, deren Entwicklungsgang wir, wenn auch nicht ganz lückenlos, von der Frühdynastischen Periode (II: Fāra; III: Ebla) an bis zur neuassyrischen Zeit heute einigermassen verfolgen können,[16] nachdem jetzt M. Krebernik[17] und D.O. Edzard[18] die frühesten bislang bekannten aus Fāra und Ebla stammenden Beschwörungstexte philologisch zu erschliessen versucht haben.

Es hatte schon A. Falkenstein für die Beschwörungen des III. und II. Jhrt. zwei Hauptgruppen von Beschwörungstexten in sumerischer Sprache unterscheiden können, u.zw. eine ältere Gruppe, die bis in die Ur III-Zeit, d.h. in eine Epoche, in der das Sumerische wenigstens im Süden Mesopotamiens wohl noch gesprochen worden sein dürfte,[19] hinaufreicht und eine jüngere, altbabylonische, die uns meist aus Abschriften aus der späten Hammurapizeit überliefert ist.[20]

Bei der zuletzt genannten Gruppe handelt es sich erstmalig um stärkere Berührungen mit den späteren, in grosser Anzahl in Texten vor allem aus der Bibliothek Aššurbānipals in Nineveh überlieferten Beschwörungstexten.[21] Durch Zusammenstellungen der altbabylonischen Tafeln aus Nibru, wozu

14 LSSNF, Leipzig 1931.

15 Hildesheim usw. 1984, S. 211ff.

16 Vgl. etwa M. Civil; R.D. Biggs, RA 60,1ff.; P. Michalowski, QS 18, S. 305ff.

17 A.W.

18 ARET 5, Rom 1984.

19 Vgl. W. Römer, Die Sumerologie2, AOAT 262, Münster 1999, S. 4518; D.O. Edzard, Sumerian Grammar, HOr. 71, Leiden 2003, S. 173ff.

20 A.W., S. 7ff.

21 A.W., S. 8.

jetzt vor allem auf eine Arbeit von M.J. Geller[22] verwiesen werden kann, mit den genannten späten Texten aus neuassyrischer Zeit konnte A. Falkenstein den in der Ḫammurapizeit in etwa erreichten Stand der Serienbildung aufzeigen, die dann im 1. Jhrt. v. Chr. zu einer normativ gültigen Reihenfolge nicht nur der einzelnen Beschwörungen untereinander, sondern auch der zu Serien zusammengefassten Tafeln, einer Art Kanonisierung,[23] führen sollte.[24] Mit diesen zuletzt genannten Serien meint A. Falkenstein die grossen Sammlungen Udughulameš,[25] Saĝgigameš, Azaggigameš und Šurpu.[26]

Bei den älteren nichtkanonischen Beschwörungen, zu denen auch unser Text VS 10,193 gehört und bei denen man etwa von ersten Ansätzen zur Serienbildung sprechen könnte,[27] dürfte es sich nach der Ansicht von A. Falkenstein um solche handeln, die nur erst im Auszug aufgezeichnet worden sind, wie verschiedentlich aus dem Fehlen von literarisch an sich notwendigen Teilen und der Kürzung von Sätzen, z.B. im Ritual und Themen zu ersehen ist.[28] Erfreulicherweise sind den ‚kanonischen' Texten schon frühzeitig – wie in nachaltbabylonischer Zeit üblich[29] – akkadische Interlinearübersetzungen beigegeben worden, wodurch das betreffende sumerische Material vor allzu starker Entstellung geschützt wurde.[30]

III.

Als ‚nichtkanonische' Beschwörungen aus älterer Zeit in immer grösserer Zahl bekannt wurden, stellte sich immer dringlicher die Frage nach der Herkunft der Texte und den Zielen, denen sie dienen sollten. Die betreffenden Texte sind, wie J. van Dijk zeigen konnte,[31] nicht nur in sumerischer und

---

22 „Forerunners to Udug-ḫul. Sumerian Exorcistic Incantations", FAOS 12, Stuttgart 1985.

23 Vgl. zu diesem Begriff etwa H. Hunger, BAK, AOAT 2, S. 6; 61.

24 A. Falkenstein, a.W., S. 9f.

25 Vgl. etwa E.E. Knudsen, Iraq 27,160ff.; M.J. Geller, Iraq 42,23ff.

26 Siehe jetzt D. Linton, „The Series SAG.GIG.GA.MEŠ and Related Incantations", Birmingham 1975–'76; E. Reiner, „Šurpu. A Collection of Sumerian and Akkadian Incantations", AfO Beih. 11, Graz 1958 (vgl. zuletzt J. Bottéro, BÉHÉ, 4e Section [Sciences historiques et philologiques] 328, Genf, Paris 1985, S. 163ff.). Vgl. auch A. Falkenstein, a.W., S. 12ff.

27 Vgl. J. van Dijk, HSAO, S. 238f. (zit. LSSNF 1, S. 8ff.).

28 Vgl. a.W., S. 15; 152.

29 Siehe J. Krecher, RlA 5, S. 124ff.

30 Siehe A. Falkenstein, a.W., S. 17.

31 Vgl. VS 17, S. 7ff.; YOS 11, S. 1ff.; CRRA 25, S. 97ff.

akkadischer,[32] sondern auch in elamischer und ḫurritischer[33] Sprache überliefert. Unter den fremdsprachigen Beschwörungstexten in Mesopotamien scheinen die elamisch-sprachigen wohl am zahlreichsten vertreten zu sein. Es hat sich herausgestellt, dass diese Gruppe von Texten vor allem mit den Gefahren, denen Wöchnerinnen, sowie neugeborene Kinder[34] ausgesetzt sind, zu tun haben, während die Beschwörungen in ḫurritischer Sprache in erster Linie gegen gefährliche Tiere und die Folgen ihrer Bisse oder Stiche (vgl. oben I.) gerichtet sind.[35] Zur erstgenannten Gruppe zählen auch die uns schon lange durch eine Beschwörungsserie aus später Zeit,[36] aber auch durch ältere elamische,[37] akkadische[38] und sumerische[39] Texte bekannten Beschwörungen gegen die Dämonin Lamaštum,[40] bei der elamische Herkunft nicht nur durch sprachliche und inhaltliche, sondern auch durch archäologische Indizien[41] nahegelegt werden dürfte.

Die grosse Mehrzahl der fremdsprachlichen Beschwörungen in Mesopotamien stammt anscheinend aus den südbabylonischen Städten Larsam und Enegi,[42] einige aus Ešnunna, während weitere ḫurritische Beschwörungstexte aus Māri am mittleren Euphrat bekannt geworden sind.[43] Allgemein dürfte für die Herkunft der Tontafeln mit älteren nichtkanonischen Beschwörungstexten vielfach an das Königreich Larsam zu denken sein.[44]

---

32 Vgl. W. Farber, ZA 71,51ff.

33 Vgl. J. van Dijk, CRRA 25,99f. und siehe V. Haas; H.J. Thiel, AOAT 31,10ff., auch zur Frage der Bedeutung von ‚subaräisch'.

34 Siehe J. van Dijk, CRRA 25, S. 99.

35 Vgl. J. van Dijk, a.W., S. 99f.

36 Siehe D.W. Myhrman, ZA 16,141ff.; A. Falkenstein, LKU, S. 5ff.

37 Vgl. J. van Dijk, a.W., S. 100ff.

38 Siehe W. von Soden, Or. 23,337ff.; 25,141ff.; BiOr. 18,71ff.; W. Farber, ZA 71,52ff.

39 Vgl. etwa YOS 11,86,29ff. (s. J. van Dijk, ebd., S. 49); 88,89 (s. J. van Dijk, CRRA 25, S. 101f. [s. YOS 11, S. 15]).

40 Vgl. zu ihr W. Farber, RlA 6, S. 439ff.; ZA 79,223ff.; „Schlaf, Kindchen, schlaf! Mesopotamische Baby-Beschwörungen und -Rituale", Winona Lake 1989, S. 177; in: F. Rochberg-Halton, Fs. E. Reiner, AOS 67, S. 85ff.; F.A.M. Wiggermann, in: M. Stol, Birth in Babylonia and the Bible. Its Mediterranean Setting, CM 14, Groningen 2000, S. 217ff.

41 Vgl. J. van Dijk, CRRA 25, S. 104ff.

42 Vgl. J. van Dijk, YOS 11, S. 2; 29.

43 Vgl. J. van Dijk, CRRA 25, S. 106.

44 Siehe J. van Dijk, YOS 11, S. 2.

IV.

Was die literarischen Formen der verschiedenen Typen von Beschwörungen in sumerischer Sprache anbelangt konnte A. Falkenstein[45] auf Grund des ihm zur Verfügung stehenden Materials vier Haupttypen herausarbeiten, die jeweils mit bestimmten während einer Beschwörungshandlung oder mit zum Zweck ihrer Durchführung erforderlichen Tätigkeiten verbunden waren. Allerdings bleibt schwer zu ermitteln, ob bzw. wie die verschiedenen Beschwörungshandlungen, auf die die Beschwörungstexte Bezug nehmen teilweise oder insgesamt miteinander verbunden waren oder sein konnten, da wir über den Verlauf der Handlungen bei einer Beschwörung keine Auskunft erhalten. Auch der bekannte übrigens aus späterer Zeit stammende Text KAR 44 „Leitfaden des Ritualfachmannes (Beschwörers)"[46] hilft uns hier nicht weiter.

Die vier Haupttypen der sumerischen Beschwörung seien hier nur kurz angedeutet. Etwas ausführlicher beschreiben wir nur den ‚Marduk-Ea-Typ' (unten, c), da ihm unser Text VS 10,193 angehört. Es handelt sich um:

a) den Legitimationstyp.[47] Hier legitimiert sich der Beschwörer als Gesandter der Götter der ‚weissen Magie', wobei er verschiedentlich auch die Kultmittel erwähnt, die er bei der magischen Handlung bei sich führt. Nachdem die eben schon erwähnte Arbeit von M. Krebernik einen, wenn auch vorläufigen, Einblick in die frühen Beschwörungen aus Fāra und Ebla gewährt hat, wissen wir, dass die Selbstlegitimation des Beschwörers durch die Verweisung auf eine Gottheit, die ihn geschickt habe, etwa später Enki von Eridu, oder von der die Beschwörungsformel stamme, schon durch die in Fāra begegnende Aussage „Beschwörungsformel der (Göttin) Ningirima"[48] bezeugt ist;[49]

b) den prophylaktische Typ.[50] Er dient zum vorbeugenden Schutz von Laien, damit sie nicht bösen Dämonen zum Opfer fallen;

c) den Marduk-Ea (Asalluḫi-Enki-)Typ,[51] der zur eigentlichen Austreibung von Dämonen und Krankheiten dient.[52] Es gibt auch Nebenbildungen

45 LSSNF 1, S. 19ff.

46 Vgl. zuletzt J. Bottéro, BÉHÉ, 4e Section (s. Anm. 26), S. 65ff.; RlA 7, S. 225f. S. noch J. van Dijk, HSAO, S. 239, 2. Abs.

47 LSSNF 1, S. 20ff.; 83ff.

48 Siehe zu ihr M. Krebernik, RlA 9, S. 363ff. Art. Nin-girima I.

49 Vgl. M. Krebernik, BFE, S. 208ff.

50 LSSNF 1, S. 35ff.; 87ff.

51 LSSNF 1, S. 44ff.; 89ff.; J. Bottéro, RlA 7, S. 229ff.

52 Siehe E. von Weiher, SpTU 2, ADFU 10, Berlin 1983, S. 4.

zu diesem Typ; so kann die Marduk-Ea-Formel anders gestaltet werden, oder es können die anderen Themen umgebildet, oder der Beschwörung mythologische Erzählungen als Erweiterung beigegeben werden[53] – vgl. den Vortrag von M. Dietrich in diesem Kolloquium.

Der Aufbau des Marduk-Ea-Typs gestaltet sich normalerweise wie folgt:

1. Die zwei Einleitungsthemen: a) das präsentische, das das Treiben der Dämonen, ihre Herkunft, Aufenthaltsort, Aussehen und Handlungen an Mensch und Tier beschreibt, sowie b) das präteritale Thema, das über einen in der Vergangenheit erfolgten Angriff der Dämonen, durch den der Mensch erkrankte, berichtet. In den älteren Beschwörungen vom Marduk-Ea-Typ kann die Einleitung auch nur präterital gehalten, d.h. vielleicht gekürzt sein, sowie es in unserem Text VS 10,193 der Fall zu sein scheint.[54]

2. Die Marduk-Ea-Formel, in der der Gott Asalluḫi (später mit Marduk von Babylon gleichgesetzt worden) sich an seinen Vater Enki (Ea) von Eridu um Rat betreffs der am Kranken zu vollziehenden Behandlung wendet. Nach der Untersuchung von M. Krebernik[55] findet sich dieser Teil der Beschwörung in Fāra und Ebla in etwa vorgebildet, u.zw. in einer von ihm lú-gi$_4$-Formular genannten Formel. Dort treten aber merkwürdigerweise nicht Enki und sein Sohn Asalluḫi, sondern der Gott Enlil und die auch aus späteren Beschwörungstexten bekannte Göttin Ningirima (vgl. oben) auf, während Enki dort vielmehr die feindselige Rolle eines krank Machers zu spielen scheint![56]

3. Ritualanweisungen, die Enki seinem Sohn Asalluḫi auf dessen in 2. geäusserte Bitte erteilt[57] mit der Bemerkung, dies sei eigentlich überflüssig, weil sein Sohn genau dasselbe wisse wie er! Zu beachten ist, dass in älteren Beschwörungen in denen Asalluḫi verschiedentlich einen Boten zu seinem Vater Enki schickt mit der Bitte um Auskunft, Enki dann zum letzteren in 3. sg. über seinen Sohn Asalluḫi spricht wie es auch in unserer Beschwörung Z. 9-14 der Fall ist.[58]

4. Schlussthema, das den Wunsch äussert, dass die betreffenden Dämonen oder Krankheit den Heimgesuchten nunmehr verlassen mögen und

53 Vgl. LSSNF 1, S. 67ff.; 93ff.; J.S. Cooper, ZA 61,12ff.

54 Z. 2–3; vgl. auch Z. 6–7.

55 BFE, S. 211ff.

56 Ebd., S. 212.

57 Fehlen in unserem Texte.

58 Vgl. AOAT 240, S. 41736.

eventuell auch darum bittet, dass gute Geister an die Stelle der bösen treten mögen;

d) den Weihungstyp.[59] Dieser diente dazu, die verschiedenen für das exorzistische Ritual benötigten Dinge vor ihrem Gebrauch zu weihen, weswegen man auch von Kultmittelbeschwörungen spricht. Zu beachten ist, dass wir diesen Typ am wenigsten zu den Beschwörungen stellen würden; die alten Mesopotamier aber gaben auch diesen Texten die bei Beschwörungen übliche Überschrift é-nu-ru-Beschwörung" (én-é-nu-ru).[60]

V.

Der Beschwörer – man deutet manchmal auch „Ritualfachmann"[61] – der die Beschwörungen und die damit verbundenen Rituale durchzuführen hatte,[62] wird auf Sumerisch meistens (lú-)mu$_7$-mu$_7$ „Mann der Beschwörungsformeln" (auch lú-ka-inim-ma) oder maš(-maš)[63] genannt. In den Beschwörungstexten begegnet er vor allem im Legitimationstyp (oben a)). Er ist genau vom anderen Fachmann, der dem erkrankten Menschen zur Seite stand, nl. dem Arzte[64] zu unterscheiden. Den Unterschied zwischen beider Tätigkeiten haben etwa E.K. Ritter,[65] P. Herrero,[66] M. Stol,[67] J.A. Scurlock[68] und E. Reiner[69] näher herauszuarbeiten versucht, wir kommen unten zu VI. noch kurz darauf zurück. Die Tätigkeit des Beschwörers, wozu auch unser Text gehört, obwohl er ihn, wie übrigens beim ‚Marduk-Ea-Typ' üblich, nicht *ex-*

59 Vgl. LSSNF 1, S. 76ff.; 99f.

60 Siehe dazu besonders J. van Dijk, YOS 11, S. 4f.

61 Vgl. E. von Weiher, a.W., S. 4; 425 (zit. W. Mayer, UFBG, S. 59f.); W. von Soden, „Einführung in die Altorientalistik", Darmstadt 1985, S. 191.

62 Vgl. J. Bottéro, RlA 7, S. 225f.

63 Vgl. AHw. 1487f. *(w)āšipu(m)*; s. weiter AHw. 628; CAD M1 381 *mašma(š)šu*, vgl. auch *bārû(m)* (vgl. A. Falkenstein, „La divination en Mésopotamie ancienne et dans les régions voisines", Paris 1966, S. 5115; 52; 525) und AHw. 684; CAD M2 276f. *muš(la)laḫḫu* (mit letzerem ist der Schlangenbeschwörer gemeint, vgl. J. van Dijk, Or. 38,539ff.; I.J. Gelb, StOr. 46, S. 60ff.). Vgl. zum Beschwörer und seiner Diagnostik in den Beschwörungen vom Legitimationstyp neuerdings N. Heessel, Babylonisch-assyrische Diagnostik, AOAT 43, Münster 2000, S. 69ff.

64 Vgl. PSD A I 207f. a-zu.

65 AS 16, S. 299ff.

66 „Thérapeutique mésopotamienne", Paris 1984, S. 22f.

67 JEOL 32, S. 58ff.

68 ‚Mes. Magic', S. 69ff.

69 „Astral Magic in Babylonia", TAPS 85/4, Philadelphia 1995, S. 46ff.

pressis verbis erwähnt, bestand in exorzistischen und apotropäischen Handlungen. Im ersteren Falle handelte es sich um die Austreibung von Krankheit(sdämon)en zur Heilung eines Patienten, im letzteren Falle um das Fortaltenhalten von Dämonen. Dies hatte ein Beschwörer zwecks seiner eigenen Prophylaxe (vgl. oben, Typ a)) während seiner Arbeit zu tun.[70] Dabei konnte er sich auf den Besitz von Zaubermitteln berufen, die ihm von den Göttern Enki und Asalluḫi verliehen worden waren. Er konnte in dieser Weise unbekümmert ins Haus der erkrankten Person eintreten und den Patienten vor der Beschwörungshandlung untersuchen. Auch hatte er noch, wie wir sahen (Typ d)), die beim Ritual erforderlichen Gegenstände und Materialien vorher zu weihen.[71]

VI.

In letzter Zeit hat man sich mehrfach mit dem Problem der (medizinischen) Wirksamkeit der altmesopotamischen Beschwörungen befasst indem man sich die Frage stellte, was die betreffenden Handlungen für den individuellen Menschen bedeutet haben mögen und wie sie ihm in etwa geholfen haben könnten.

So hat vor einigen Jahren M.J. Geller in seinem Aufsatz „Freud and Mesopotamien Magic“[72] bei einem Versuch zur Klärung des eventuellen ‚psychological impact‘ der mesopotamischen Magie daraufhingewiesen, dass die mesopotamischen Beschwörungen tatsächlich bis zu einem gewissen Grade effektiv gewesen sein mögen „by defining or repressing fears“. Weiter bemerkt er: „Freud himself might agree with the proposition that the incantations are designed to help counter the patient's fear[73] which is represented by the demons, but not the demons themselves“.[74] Im Grunde ähnlich dachte P. Michalowski: „... Purposefulness is particularly vivid in the case of medical charms ..., which were utilized in ceremonies which were effective to a large degree because they must have led to certain psycho-somatic healing effects“.[75] Auch M. Stol[76] meint: „Several complaints and modes of behaviour

70 Siehe A. Falkenstein, LSSNF 1, S. 31ff.

71 Zu diesen kurzen Bemerkungen zur Tätigkeit des Beschwörers vgl. noch J. Renger, ZA 59, 223ff.; N. Heessel, AOAT 43, S. 69ff.

72 ‚Mes. Magic‘, S. 49ff.

73 Siehe besonders auch M. Stol, ‚Mes. Magic‘, S. 57ff.

74 Ebd., S. 55.

75 ZA 71,12; vgl. auch ders., QS 18, S. 308.

76 Ebd., S. 67.

have a psychosomatic origin; we tried to relate them to the ‚fears' of the patient". Verwiesen sei schliesslich in diesem Zusammenhang auf Ausführungen von E. von Weiher,[77] der auf die beruhigende psychologische Wirkung der Beschwörung auf Einzelpersonen, die sich durch Krankheit oder Zauberei getroffen fühlten, hingewiesen hat. Der erste Teil einer Beschwörung, die die Leiden, unter denen der Mensch leidet, beklagt, hätte ihm sozusagen die Möglichkeit gegeben, sich über sein Leid „auszusprechen", es sich „von der Seele zu reden".[78] Die Beschwörung hätte durch die Anteilnahme, die sie am persönlichen Schicksal des Leidenden nahm, diesem ein gewisses Gefühl der Geborgenheit und auch des Trostes vermittelt.[79] Auf der anderen Seite gibt es – so E. von Weiher – viele Beschwörungen, bei denen die Schilderung der Krankheitserscheinungen derart wirklichkeitsnah anmutet, dass sie uns fast als eine Art Vorläufer einer medizinischen Beschreibung vorkommt.[80] Dass man durchaus nicht jedes Leiden und Krankheit nur mit Hilfe von Beschwörungen bekämpft, sondern auch – mit der Zunahme der medizinischen Kenntnisse – immer mehr rein ärztliche Eingriffe durchgeführt hat – dazu verweisen wir hier auch auf einen Aufsatz der Medizinerin Frau M. Haussperger[81] – wurde schon bei der Andeutung des Unterschieds zwischen Beschwörer (*wāšipum*) und Arzt (*asûm*) oben unter V. kurz bemerkt. Die Beschwörung hätte nach der Ansicht von E. von Weiher manchmal dazu gedient, den Patienten auch seelisch in die richtige Verfassung für die ärztliche Behandlung zu versetzen.[82] Es hatte übrigens schon vor Jahren J. Renger festgestellt, dass der Erfolg oder Nichterfolg des Beschwörers bei der Behandlung von Kranken im Wesentlichen im Psychologischen begründet waren.[83]

VII.

Abschliessend bieten wir jetzt noch eine versuchsweise Übersetzung unseres Beschwörungstextes VS 10,193 (Transliteration: AOAT 240, S. 419f.), den wir schon mehrfach erwähnten und der Ausgangspunkt unserer Darlegungen war.

---

77 SpTU 2, S. 3ff.

78 A.W., S. 7f.

79 A.W., S. 6.

80 A.W., S. 7.

81 ZA 87, 196ff.; N. Heessel, AOAT 43, S. 69ff.

82 A.W., S. 7f.

83 ZA 59, 2291121 (zit. C. Lévi-Strauss, Strukturale Anthropologie, Frankfurt 1967, S. 192ff.).

1) é-nu-ru-Beschwörung.

1. 2) Dem Menschen hat eine Schlange ‚zugeschlagen' (?), hat ein Skorpion ‚zugeschlagen' (?), hat ein tollwütiger Hund ‚zugeschlagen' (?),
3) ihr Gift haben sie in ihm hineingebracht(!?).

2. 4) Asalluḫi
5) schickte jemanden zu seinem Vater Enki
6) (mit der Meldung:) „Mein Vater, dem Menschen hat eine Schlange ‚zugeschlagen' (?), hat ein Skorpion ‚zugeschlagen' (?), hat ein tollwütiger Hund ‚zugeschlagen' (?),
7) ihr Gift haben sie in ihn hineingebracht(!?).
8) Was ich dagegen machen soll, weiss ich nicht!"
9) Enki antwortet dem Boten:) „Mein Sohn — was weiss er nicht,
10) was soll ich ihm hinzufügen?"

3. 11) Er reinigte(!?) mit(?) seinem reinen a-lá-Gefäss.
12) Nachdem er auf das betreffende Wasser die Beschwörung geworfen hat,
13) das betreffende Wasser den gebissenen(?) Menschen dar(aus) hat trinken lassen,

4. 14) möge das betreffende Gift von selbst aus ihm herausgehen!
15) Einen Menschen hat eine Schlange gebissen. Das betreffende Wasser gehört zu dem(?), was der gebissene(?) Mensch trinken soll(?).

Einige zusätzliche Bemerkungen zu AOAT 240, S. 419ff.

Für die Z. 11-14 bietet jetzt I.L. Finkel einen eng verwandten Passus in Mes. Magic, S. 232: Nr. 8,1-3. Auch verweist I.L. Finkel, a.W., S. 232 für das Ritual auf die Stelle VS 17,2 (zit. J. van Dijk, VS 17, S. 10), die eine gewisse Verwandtschaft mit unseren Z. 11-14 aufweist.

Der Text wurde bearbeitet von W. Römer, AOAT 240, S. 413ff.; N. Veldhuis, ZA 83,161ff.; G. Cunningham, StP(M) 17, S. 79f. Z. 11-14 noch bei I.L. Finkel, a.W., S. 231, ebenso bei G. Cunningham, a.W., S. 82.

Die Beschwörung könnte aus der Ur III-Zeit stammen, vgl. N. Veldhuis, ebd. 161; 161[1], doch meint P. Michalowski, QS 18, S. 324: ‚perhaps OB'.
Die Nummern 1-4 im Rande der Übersetzung beziehen sich auf oben IV. c, 1-4 (Marduk-Ea-Typ).

Zusätzliches zum Kommentar in AOAT 240, S. 420ff., auf den hier laufend verwiesen sei:

Z. 2; 6: Sowohl N. Veldhuis wie G. Cunningham betrachten mu-ra als Relativsatz (< mu-ra-a-e), wobei der erstgenannte ‚biting‘ (schwierig, weil auch auf einen Skorpion bezogen) und der letztgenannte ‚wounding‘ deutet.

Z. 3; 7: N. Veldhuis, N.A.B.U. 1994, S. 55: Nr. 63 meinte nach Kollation der Zeilen statt ku$_4^!$ vielmehr sum-[m]a lesen zu können.

Z. 5: lú möchte ich nach wie vor als ‚jemanden‘ („einen Menschen“) verstehen (G. Cunningham: ‚a man‘; ebenso I.L. Finkel, in: S. Maul, Fs. Borger, S. 73/4, 17); N. Veldhuis, ZA 83,163: „obviously some ritual actor, not the patient“.

Z. 11: Die Verbalwurzel lesen sowohl N. Veldhuis wie G. Cunningham zalag; sie deuten ‚purify‘ bzw. ‚make shine‘. Nach N. Veldhuis, N.A.B.U. 1994 a.a.O. fehlt nach Kollation vor a-lá nichts.

Z. 13; 15: Hier deutet G. Cunningham ähnl. wie ich es mit J. van Dijk angenommen hatte: ‚the/a bitten man‘, während N. Veldhuis nach H. Vanstiphout eher ‚the infected person‘ (unorthographisch für lú-ku$_4$-ra) annehmen möchte. Dagegen möchte M.J. Geller, AfO 46/47,271 eher an das gewöhnliche lú-kúr(-ra) ‚foreigner‘ denken; es könnte s.E. sein, dass „the ritual was partly designed to have a foreigner drink poison as a form of symphathetic magic“ (er verweist auf StP(M) 17, S. 96: Nr. 51, worin er „occasional reference to ‚foreigners‘ in Ur III incantations“ sehen möchte. Zur zweiten Hälfte von Z. 15 hat N. Veldhuis eine andere Auffassung (bei ihm Z. 16). Dagegen nähert sich G. Cunningham „It is for making a bitten man — a man a snake has bitten“ in etwa mehr der von mir versuchsweise vorgeschlagenen Deutung.

Magier im Neuen Testament

Peeter Roosimaa, Tartu

Einleitung

Verschiedene übernatürliche Kräfte und Phänomene, darunter auch Magie, haben die Menschen schon immer interessiert. In Betracht des vorliegenden Themas, soll daran erinnert werden, dass während der Entstehungszeit des Urchristentums verschiedene Formen von Magie und Zauberei im Römischen Imperium üblich waren.

Ohne tiefer auf die Begriffe einzugehen, kann man sagen, dass Magie verschiedene Geheimlehren, vor allem aber Zauberei und Astrologie bedeutete. Ursprünglich war ein Magie beherrschender Magier (μάγος) ein medischer Priester, danach auch ein Priester des Zarathustra Glaubens. In der Geschichte Irans haben die Magier durch ihre Zugehörigkeit zum Priestertum eine wichtige Rolle gespielt. Während des hellenistischen Zeitalters, als die östlichen Lehren dem griechischen Glauben angeglichen wurden, hat man auch Zaubereipriester, Astrologen (Chaldäer), Wahrsager und andere östliche Weise (z.B. in der Geschichte von Jesu Geburt) angefangen als Magier zu bezeichnen. In die Religion Irans haben die Magier Lehrelemente von Mitlere Osten und hellenistische Lehrelemente eingefügt und spielten somit als herrschendes Priestertum eine wichtige Rolle in der iranischen Geschichte.[1] Wie man sieht ist der Begriff Magier keineswegs eindeutig und war es wahrscheinlich auch in neutestamentlicher Zeit nicht. Als Magier wurden auch Menschen mit übernatürlichem Wissen und Fähigkeiten genannt, Menschen, die mit den Seelen Toter kommunizierten, Träume und Omen deuteten, sowie diejenigen, die Reinigung und Versöhnung u.a. mit Zaubermitteln anboten.[2]

Persische, chaldäische und ägyptische Magier waren bekannt als Zauberei-, Alchimie- und Astrologielehrer. Wobei Zauberei in viele verschiedene Arten unterteilt werden kann: Bindungs-, Schädigungs-, Schutzzau-

---

1 Siehe Maagia; maag. – Antiigileksikon I, S. 330.

2 Siehe auch G. Delling ThWNT Bd. IV, S. 360ff.

berei (das Vertreiben böser Mächte mit Hilfe bestimmter Zauberformeln) sowie Heilungs- und Gunst-Zauberei, Wetterzauberei, Beschwörungen, Zauberformel, Verfluchungen u.v.a. Allgemein verbreitet war auch die magische Benutzung der Schrift (z.B. Buchstabenmystik).[3] Beispiele dieser Magier finden wir auch in dem Alten Testament, wie z.B. in einem Zitat aus Dan 2,2: „Und der König ließ alle Zeichendeuter und Weisen und Zauberer und Wahrsager zusammenrufen, dass sie ihm seinen Traum sagen sollten. Und sie kamen und traten vor den König."[4] In der LXX Übersetzung wird für das Wort Weisen der Ausdruck μάγος benutzt.

Im Blick auf die Magier aus Mt 2,1ff schreibt der estnische Theologe Elmar Salumaa: „Unter den ‚Weisen' soll man Sterndeuter oder Astrologen verstehen, die anhand Sternpositionen und Sternbewegungen die Geheimnisse der Geschichte, der Nationen und des Lebenslaufes einzelner Personen lüften sowie Zukunft vorherzusagen versuchten. Man dürfte sie schwerlich als Betreiber der ‚Zauberkunst' oder als heidnische Priester bezeichnen obwohl astrologische Beschäftigungen sich im Prinzip der Schwarzen Kunst annähern. Man soll bedenken, dass in der damaligen Kultur Astrologie als ernsthafte und notwendige Wissenschaft betrachtet wurde."[5] Man könnte wahrscheinlich damit einverstanden sein, dass unter den Magiern eine sog. Spezialisierung auf bestimmte Beschäftigungsfelder vorkam. Doch die Annahme, dass die Magier, die gekommen waren um das Jesuskind zu ehren nicht zu den Betreibern der Zauberkunst oder zu den heidnischen Priestern gehörten, scheint eher ein Wunschdenken zu sein. Bekanntlich war den Magier die Bindung zur ihrer Religion gerade wichtig.

Wenn man über Magier spricht, dann wäre es in diesem Zusammenhang richtig auch andere inhaltlich ähnliche Ausdrücke aus dem Neuen Testament zu erwähnen: γόης – der Zauberer, der Gaukler, an Dämonen Glaubende (2.Tim 3,13),[6] φαρμακός – der Zauberer[7] (Offb 21, 8; 22,15) und φαρμακέια – die Zauberei, die Magie[8] (Gal 5,20; Offb 9,21; 18,23). In den genannten Bibelstellen weist man nicht auf konkrete Personen, sondern allgemein auf solche Personen und auf deren Tätigkeit.

3 Siehe Nõidus. – Antiigileksikon II, S. 40.

4 Siehe LXX Text Dan 2,2; siehe auch Dan 2,10f.

5 E. Salumaa 2001, S. 48 (Übersetzung des Autors).

6 Siehe G. Delling ThWNT I, S. 737f; W. Bauer S. 327.

7 Siehe W. Bauer S. 1703.

8 Siehe *ibid* S. 1702.

Wenn man das oben genannte berücksichtigt, ist es leicht anzunehmen, dass auch die Christen mit Magie und Zauberei in Berührung kamen. Konnte dieses für Christen Probleme bereiten? Wie stellt das Neue Testament die Magier oder Zauberer dar und wie beurteilt es sie?

Textbetrachtungen

Im Folgenden betrachte ich neutestamentliche Texte, in denen von Magiern als konkreten Personen berichtet wird. Als ich unter den entsprechenden Stichwörtern nach Bibelstellen suchte, war ich ziemlich überrascht, dass im Neuen Testament so wenig über Magier erzählt wird. Deutet das darauf hin, dass die Christen Kontakte zu den Magiern vermieden oder dass sie hier kein besonderes Problem sahen, das einer besonderen Erwähnung bedurft hätte? Von den konkreten Personen, den Magiern (μάγος) wird nur in Mt 2 sowie in Apg 8 und 13 berichtet. Wie schon genannt, werden die Betreiber der Zauberei (γόης) in 2.Tim 3,13, Zauberer (φαρμακός) in Offb 21,8; 22,15 und Zauberei (φαρμακέια) in Gal 5,20; Offb 9,21; 18, 23 in allgemeiner Bedeutung erwähnt. Es ist möglich, dass man hier auch die falschen Propheten dazu rechnen soll, z.B. Mt 7, 15. Dieses könnte man damit begründen, dass in Apg 13, 6 Barjesus sowohl ein Magier als auch ein falscher Prophet genannt wird (τιηὰ μάγον ψευδοπροφήτην).

1. Die bekanntesten Magier sind wohl ohne Zweifel die aus dem Morgenland, die gekommen waren um den neugeborenen König der Juden zu ehren (siehe Mt 2,1ff). In Jerusalem erzählten sie, dass sie den entsprechenden Stern gesehen hatten. Daraus schließt man, dass sie Astrologen waren. Das wiederum war der Grund sie als Weise zu bezeichnen. In der ganzen Geschichte kann man eine wohlwollende und positive Einstellung gegenüber diesen Magiern sehen. Sie waren ja einige der ersten, die den gottgesandten Messias anbeteten. Diese positive Einstellung spiegelt sich auch in den Übersetzungen von Mt 2 wieder, wo sie als Weise aus Morgenland genannt werden. In den im Laufe der Zeit entstandenen Legenden werden sie sogar als Könige bezeichnet.

Doch war die Einstellung zu diesen Menschen damals, als das alles stattfand auch so positiv? Als die Magier aus dem Morgenland, entsprechend der Erzählung aus Mt 2,1f Jerusalem erreichten und nach Auskunft über den neugeborenen König der Juden suchten, erzeugten sie folgende Reaktion: „als das der König Herodes hörte, erschrak er und mit ihm ganz Jerusalem" (Mt 2,3). Die Bestürzung des Herodes könnte mit seiner Sorge um den Thronfolger begründet sein. Konnte aber das Erschrecken der

Einwohner Jerusalems nur aus der Angst, dass Herodes böse reagieren könnte resultieren? Ich denke, dass man hier auch damit rechnen muss, dass den Juden Magie, darunter Wahrsagerei nach den Sternen, grundsätzlich verboten war und dass die Ankunft der Magier in Jerusalem für die dortigen Geistlichen ein ernstes Gefahrzeichen sein sollte. Die negative Einstellung der dortigen Einwohner gegenüber den Magiern wurde ziemlich bald nach ihrem Fortgehen, durch die Tötung von vielen kleinen Jungen durch Herodes Soldaten in Bethlehem bestärkt (siehe Mt 2,16).

2. In Apg 8,9ff wird von einem Simon, Bewohner Samariens, berichtet, der zu den Magiern gehörte (μαγεύων). Was können wir über diesen Mann sagen, mit wem hat man hier zu tun? Sein Name Simon deutet auf seine hebräische Herkunft hin. Man kann daher vermuten, dass er an den gleichen Gott glaubte, wie auch andere Juden. Bei den Samaritern war wahrlich die Situation etwas komplizierter. Die Samariter waren eine Art Mischvolk. Dieses hatte sich aus den von der Deportation der Bewohner des israelischen Nordreiches, übrig gebliebenen Israeliten und aus dem eingewanderten assyrischen Kolonisten gebildet. Nach der Rückkehr aus der babylonischen Gefangenschaft, wollten die Samariter sich den zurückkommenden Juden anschließen, doch die gesetzestreuen Juden haben sich geweigert, und zwar wegen ihrer Vermischung mit Nichtisraeliten als auch wegen der Übernahme gewisser heidnischer Bräuche von den assyrischen Kolonisten[9]. Wenn man diesen geschichtlichen Hintergrund berücksichtigt, dann könnte man bei Simon mit einem Mann zu tun haben, der den Glauben an den Gott Israels mit heidnischen Glaubenspraktiken zu verbinden suchte.

Simon wird als ein Magier dargestellt, der Bewunderung im Volk auslöste. Sowohl die Kleinen als auch die Großen waren beeinflusst von ihm, da man annahm, dass die Kraft Gottes in ihm wirkte: „Sie hingen ihm aber an, weil er sie lange Zeit mit seiner Zauberei (ταῖς μαγείαις) in seinen Bann gezogen hatte“ (Apg 8,11). Wegen der großen Schar seiner Nachfolger hat man ihm bescheinigt: „Dieser ist die Kraft Gottes, die die Große genannt wird“ (Apg 8,10).

So hat also Simon eine Tätigkeit ausgeübt, die auf seiner Fähigkeit, übernatürliche Kräfte zu vermitteln, hinweist. Jürgen Roloff hält es für möglich, dass die ursprüngliche Form des Gesagten aus der Apostelge-

---

9 Siehe G. Kroll 2002, S. 193. Michael Heltzer lenkt die Aufmerksamkeit auf den Namen von Simon. Da der Name im Neuen Testament mit griechischen Buchstaben geschrieben worden ist, braucht es nicht unbedingt auf die hebräische Herkunft zu verweisen. M. Heltzer, mündliche Überlieferung.

schichte „ich bin die große Kraft“ heißen könnte (vgl. Apg 8,9f) und dass hier sowohl der jüdische als auch heidnische Gedanken zusammen fließen. Im Judentum war das Wort *Kraft* oder entsprechend *die große Kraft* ein oft angewendeter Ersatzausdruck für den Namen Gottes (siehe 5.Mose 9,26ff u.a.). In der hellenistischen Welt sah man Wundertäter und Magier als diejenigen an, die mit der Gottheit und ihren Kräften erfüllt waren, und sie einsetzten. So hat sich Simon möglicherweise als die Inkarnation des höchsten Gottes, als den *göttlichen Mensch* angesehen, in dem sich der Wunder tuende Gott erweist und der das Gottheits-Seligkeitswirken anbieten kann. Dieses Anbieten von Seligkeit entsprach der damaligen elementaren Sehnsucht der hellenistischen Welt nach Erlösung durch Anteilhabe göttlicher Kräfte. Darum ist es auch nicht wunderlich, dass Simon so einen großen Einfluss hatte.[10]

Als Folge der Missionsarbeit von Philippus sind viele Menschen Christen geworden und wurden getauft. Auch Simon wurde gläubig. Nach seiner Taufe blieb er bei Philippus. Aus der ganzen Geschichte kann man keine entstandenen Hindernisse erkennen.

Die Situation wurde erst dann kompliziert, als die Apostel Petrus und Johannes nach Samaria kamen um die Missionsarbeit zu unterstützen. Sie beteten für die gläubig gewordenen Samariter, damit sie den Heiligen Geist empfingen, was auch geschah (siehe Apg 8,15ff). Die Menschen empfingen den Heiligen Geist und dieses hinterließ bei Simon einen starken Eindruck. Es kann gut möglich sein, dass er in der Tätigkeit der Apostel eine Form der Magie sah, die stärker war als seine. So eine Fähigkeit wollte er auch haben. Anscheinend wollte er dafür das entsprechende Geheimwissen erwerben. Er meinte dies von den Anderen einfach käuflich erwerben zu können und bat den Aposteln Geld an. Daraus kann man schließen, dass Simon keine Erkenntnis über das Wesen der Kraft hatte, die in den Apostel wirksam war. Er hatte nicht verstanden, dass hier keine Menschen, sondern Gott am Wirken war.[11]

Auf das Geldangebot von Simon regierte Petrus scharf, in dem er die geistliche Situation von Simon und die ihn bedrohende Gefahr offenbarte: „Du hast weder Anteil noch Anrecht an dieser Sache; denn dein Herz ist nicht rechtschaffen vor Gott. Darum tu Buße für diese deine Bosheit und flehe zum Herrn, ob dies das Trachten deines Herzens vergeben werden könne. Denn ich sehe, daß du soll bitterer Galle bist und verstrickt in Ungerechtigkeit“ (Apg 8,21ff). Es ist bemerkenswert, dass Simon tatsäch-

10 Siehe J. Roloff 1988, S. 134.

11 Siehe *ibid*, S. 136.

lich Buße tat und wünschte, dass man für ihn betet. Ich neige zu der Meinung derer, die schon die erste Bekehrung Simons als ernsthaft,[12] doch nicht ausreichend ansehen.

3. In Apg 13,6ff wird berichtet, wie Paulus und Barnabas während ihrer ersten Missionsreise die Insel Zypern besuchten. Dort haben sie einen Magier und falschen Propheten Barjesus bei dem Statthalter Sergius Paulus getroffen. Diese Daten stimmen mit der historisch-geschichtlichen Situation überein. In der Antike war es weit verbreitet, dass Magie und Wahrsagerei synkretistisch vorkamen.[13] Auch außerhalb des Judentums gerieten die christlichen Missionare in eine religiöse Konkurrenz hinein, wobei die Kampfgrenzen nicht immer so deutlich waren. In dem hier genanntem Fall hatte man mit einem, für die Missionsarbeit des 1. Jahrhunderts, typischen Kontakt mit dem jüdisch-hellenistischen Synkretismus zu tun.[14] Da Barjesus als erster vor dem Statthalter genannt wird, kann man davon ausgehen, dass er derjenige war, mit dem Paulus und Barnabas zuerst zu tun hatten. Offensichtlich war er ein Hoftheologe und Hofastrologe, der bei allen wichtigen Fragen zu Rate gezogen wurde und der das Wohlwollen der himmlischen Mächte vermittelte.[15]

Wie die Einstellung von Barjesus zu der Tätigkeit von Paulus und Barnabas war, ist nicht bekannt. Man kann zumindest nicht sehen, dass er auf irgendeine Art versucht sie hätte zu verhindern. Ein andere Magier, Elymas trat indessen der Tätigkeit der Apostel entgegen. Scheinbar war er ebenso wie Barjesus bei Sergius Paulus angestellt.[16] So wie Barjesus, ist wahrscheinlich auch Elymas ein semitischer Name.[17] Jedenfalls nach der Meinung des Autors der Überlieferung, bedeutete dieser Name Magier. Elymas wollte also den Statthalter vom Glauben abbringen. Offensichtlich hat er in den neuen Missionaren eine Gefahr für seinen Einfluss und für seine Position gesehen und versuchte darum mit allen Mitteln seinen Arbeitgeber von der christlichen Botschaft fern zu halten.[18] Darum ist die scharfe Reaktion von Paulus verständlich. Paulus sagte: „Du Sohn des Teufels, voll aller List und aller Bosheit, du Feind aller Gerechtigkeit,

12 Siehe A. Weiser 1989, S. 121.

13 Siehe *ibid*, S. 178.

14 Siehe J. Roloff 1988, S. 196.

15 Siehe *ibid*, S. 198.

16 Nach der Meinung von z.B. G. Kroll sind Barjesus und Elymas ein und dieselbe Person Barjesus Elymas; siehe G. Kroll 2002, S. 234.

17 Siehe J. Roloff 1988, S. 198.

18 Siehe *ibid.*

hörst du nicht auf, krumm zu machen die geraden Wege des Herrn? Und nun siehe, die Hand des Herrn kommt über dich, und du sollst blind sein und die Sonne eine Zeitlang nicht sehen!" (Apg 13,10f).

4. Wenn man die Reaktion des Petrus aus der Schilderung von Apg 8 mit der des Paulus aus Apg 13 vergleicht, kann man große Ähnlichkeiten erkennen. Petrus hat z.B. dem Magier gesagt: „...dein Herz ist *nicht rechtschaffen vor Gott.* Darum tu Buße für diese deine *Bosheit* ... Denn ich sehe, dass du *voll bitterer Galle* bist und *verstrickt in Ungerechtigkeit*" (Apg 8,21ff). Der Vorwurf von Paulus gegen Elymas klingt ähnlich: „*Du Sohn des Teufels*, voll aller *List* und aller *Bosheit,* du *Feind aller Gerechtigkeit,* hörst du nicht auf, *krumm zu machen die geraden Wege des Herrn*?" (Apg 13,10).

Was war der Grund für so eine scharfe Reaktion der Apostel? Wussten sie, dass das Handeln dieser Menschen böse war, oder eher, dass sie Magier waren und daher einen solchen Ruf hatten. Selbstverständlich schließt das eine das andere nicht aus, doch anhand der Bibelstellen sowohl aus dem Neuen als auch aus dem Alten Testament könnte man eher das letztere folgern. Im Judentum hat sich eine negative Haltung gegenüber den Magiern herausgebildet und dies wurde auch von den Christen berücksichtigt.

Schlußfolgerungen

1. Berücksichtigt man die neutestamentlichen Bibelstellen, die sowohl in einem konkreten Zusammenhang mit Magiern stehen als auch verallgemeinernde Aussagen beinhalten, kann man sehen, dass die Einstellung der Christen gegenüber den Magiern – Zauberern und ihrer Tätigkeit allgemein negativ war. Die Magier wurden für Personen gehalten, die voll aller Bosheit, List und Betrügerei, verstrickt in Ungerechtigkeit und Feinde der Gerechtigkeit waren, die die geraden Wege des Herrn krumm machten und die das Volk von dem wahren Gott weg führten. Solche haben kein Anteil an dem ewigen Leben (Gal 5,19ff; Offb 21,8). Dies bedeutet, dass Magier für schlechte Menschen in der schwerwiegenden Bedeutung gehalten wurden.

2. Was die Magier aus dem Morgenland betrifft, gibt es keinen Grund zu meinen, dass die allgemeine Meinung gegenüber ihnen anders gewesen wäre, gleiches gilt auch Barjesus. Man kann nirgends herauslesen, dass sie zu den sogenannten guten Magier gehörten. Es wäre außerdem Zweifelhaft zu meinen, dass die Magier, die sich so gesehen ausreichend bekehrten, weniger Magier als die anderen gewesen wären. Gegenüber diesen

Magiern, die gegen die Missionare arbeiteten oder derer Bekehrung nicht ausreichend war, wurde deutlich eine negative Meinung geäußert.

3. Da Magier und Magie zu ihrem damaligen religiösen Umfeld gehörte, ist es ganz natürlich, dass die Missionsarbeit in Kontakt mit ihnen kam. Die urchristliche Mission war auf alle Menschen ausgerichtet, unabhängig von der heidnischen Glaubenszugehörigkeit. Wenn man das alles berücksichtigt, kann man sagen, dass die Bekehrungen von Magiern keine außergewöhnlichen Ereignisse waren. Es ist möglich, dass hier die Überlieferung von den Magiern aus dem Morgenland, die als ersten Heiden kamen um das Jesuskind zu ehren, einen ermutigenden Dienst leistete. So gesehen war das Magierdasein kein besonderes Hindernis. Alles hing von der Einstellung gegenüber Christus, sowie von der Buße des jeweiligen Menschen ab. Die, die aufrichtig Gott suchten, fanden Annerkennung und himmlische Hilfe. Und so konnten die Magier einige der ersten sein, die den Christus verehrten.

Literatur

Bauer, Walter, 1988: *Griechisch-deutsches Wörterbuch zu den Schriften des Neuen Testaments und der frühchristlichen Literatur.* 6., völlig neu bearbeitete Auflage, hgg. Von Kurt Aland und Barbara Aland. Berlin; New York: Walter de Gruyter.

Delling, Gerhard, 1966: γόης – ThWNT Bd. I; S, 737f.

Delling, Gerhard, 1966: μάγος, μαγέια, μαγεύω – ThWNT Bd.IV; S. 360–363.

Kroll, Gerhard, 2002: *Jeesuse jälgedel.* Tartu: Johannes Esto Ühing.

Maagia – *Antiigileksikon.* 1. A–MET. Tallinn: „Valgus", 1983; S. 330.

Maag – *Antiigileksikon.* 1. A–MET. Tallinn: „Valgus", 1983; S. 330.

Nõidus – *Antiigileksikon* 2. MET–YSE. Tallinn: „Valgus", 1983; S. 40.

Roloff, Jürgen, 1988: *Die Apostelgeschichte.* Übersetzt und erklärt von Jürgen Roloff. Berlin: Evangelische Verlagsanstalt. Reihe: Das Neue Testament Deutsch, Teilband 5.

Salumaa, Elmar, 2001: *Matteuse rõõmusõnum.* Tallinn: Logos.

Weiser, Alfons, 1989: Die Apostelgeschichte. Leipzig: St. Benno-Verlag.

Mündliche Überlieferung: HELTZER, Michail, Kommentare in Tartu, 26. April 2004.

Abkürzungen

LXX – *Septuaginta. Id est Vetus Testamentum graece iuxta LXX interpretes,* edidit Alfred Rahlfs. Stuttgart: Deutsche Bibelgesellschaft, 1979.

ThWNT – *Theologisches Wörterbuch zum Neuen Testament.* Begründet von

G. Kittel, in Verbindung mit zahlreichen Fachgenossen. Hrg. von G. Friedrich. Stuttgart: W. Kohlhammer Verlag.

Abkürzungen der biblischen Bücher

Apg – Apostelgeschichte
Dan – Daniel
Gal – Galater
Mt – Matthäus
Offb – Offenbarung
2.Tim – 2. Timotheus

Vergöttlichung der Könige von Akkade

Vladimir Sazonov, Tartu

Eine Einführung in die Problematik

Dieser Vortrag kann nur einen Versuch darstellen, das wichtigste Textmaterial zur „*Vergöttlichung der Sargoniden*" zusammenzufassen, um es daraufhin synchron zu analysieren.

Schon in meiner Magisterarbeit „*Herrschaftsideologie in der Sargoniden-Zeit (XXIV.–XXII. Jahrh. v.Chr.)*" habe ich mich mit dem Problem der Herrschaftsideologie und der -konzepte der Herrscher der Akkade-Zeit befasst, darunter auch mit dem Problem der Vergöttlichung der Könige von Akkade seit Sargon I. (2334–2279), der das Akkadische Reich gegründet hatte, bis hin zu den Regierungsjahren des letzen akkadischen Herrschers Šu-Dur-UL (2168–2154) und einige Aspekte von Herrschaftskonzepten detailierter erforscht.[1]

Schon bereits früher haben sich mit der Frage der Herrschaftsideologie der Könige von Akkade einige Wissenschaftler beschäftigt, doch nicht so sehr speziell mit der Frage der Vergöttlichung der Sargoniden.[2]

Die Vergöttlichung oder besser gesagt die kultische Verehrung der lebendigen Könige war für die frühe mesopotamische Gesellschaft des Frühdynastikums (29.–24. Jahrh. v.Chr.) bis zum Ende des III. Jahrt. überhaupt nicht aktuell und bestimmt fremd (vgl. dagegen Ägypten, wo es starke individualistische Könige schon seit sehr früheren Zeiten gab, die auch vergöttlicht waren, bzw. als Söhne der Götter dargestellt wurden).

---

1 В.Сазонов, *Идеология царской власти в эпоху Саргонидов (XXIV–XXII вв.)*, магистерская работа, Тартуский Университет, Философский факультет, Отделение истории, Кафедра всеобщей истории, 202 стр. / V.Sazonov, *Kuningavõimu ideoloogia Sargoniidide ajal (XXIV-XXII saj. eKr.)*, magistritöö, Tartu Ülikool, Filosoofia teaduskond, Ajaloo osakond, Üldajaloo õppetool, 202 lk.

2 Über Königsideologie der Könige von Akkade siehe zB. Franke S., Königinschriften und Königsideologie. Die Könige von Akkade zwischen Tradition und Neuerung, *Altorientalistik* 1, Münster – Hamburg 1995.

Vermutlich hat sich kein Herrscher des Frühdynastikums in Sumer selbst als Gott bezeichnet – darüber haben wir keine Belege gefunden. Seit der Herrschaft der Dynastie von Akkade (2334–2154 v.Chr.) und später besonders seit der Hegemonie von Ur III (2112–2004 v.Chr.) begann jedoch die Vergöttlichung der Herrscher in Südmesopotamien, und die Vergöttlichung der Könige veränderte sich zum Ende der Ur III Zeit zu einer erblichen Institution – das heißt: vom Vater auf den Sohn, wie z.B. von Šulgi auf Amar-Suen usw.

In diesem Artikel versucht der Autor, einen kleinen Überblick über die Vergöttlichung der Könige von Akkade darzustellen und besonders die Frage der Vergöttlichung Šar-kalī-šarrīs zu erörtern. Zuerst jedoch müssen einige Fragen gestellt werden, die mit der Vergöttlichung der Sargoniden verbunden sind:

1) Waren Sargon I und sein Sohn Rīmuš „inoffizielle Gottheiten"?
2) Hat Maništūšu einen Versuch seiner Vergöttlichung durchgeführt?
3) Wann beginnt man mit der Vergöttlichung von Nāramsîn und von Šar-kalī-šarrī?
4) War Šar-kalī-šarrī in Wirklichkeit vergöttlicht, wenn ja, warum sagte er später der Vergöttlichung seiner Person ab? Beanspruchte Šar-kalī-šarrī als „Sohn" Enlils den Status von Ninūrta, wie sich z. B. später im XX Jahrh. v. Chr Lipit-Ištar und andere Könige der Ur III bzw. der Isin-Zeit repräsentiert hatten?

Sargon I, Rimuš und Man-ištūšu – eine Tendenz zur Vergöttlichung?

Sargon I. oder nach richtiger akkadischer Schreibweise – Šarru-kîn (ca. 2334–2279 v.Chr.), was auf Altakkadisch „König ist treu" oder „wahrhafte König" bedeutet, beschäftigte sich während seiner Regierungszeit fast nur mit Eroberungspolitik. Schon in der ersten Hälfte seiner Regierung wurde Sargon ein sehr starker, militärisch orientierender König, der Besitzer und Herrscher des ganzen Landes von Sumer und Akkad, der fast absolute Macht in seinen Händen konzentrierte und sich *šarrum* nannte. Trotzdem aber blieb sein Reich bis zu seinem Tode relativ unstabil und in manchen Aspekten sogar schwach.[3]

Sargon I. war nun kein „ensi(k)" mehr, kein Vertreter und Statthalter der den Stadtstaat regierenden Gottheit wie es z.B. Ningirsu in der ED-Zeit in Lagaš und sein Vertreter Entemena von Lagaš waren. Auch Sargon

3 Glassner 2003, 200.

war nun kein „lugal" mehr in sumerisch-frühdynastischem Sinne – das heißt, nicht nur kriegerischer Heerführer und Führer einer Konföderation von kleineren Stadtsaaten wie z.B. Lugalzagesi von Umma, der sich mehr an der sumerischen Oligarchie orientierte.[4]

Überhaupt haben die Sargoniden altsumerische Traditionen der Herrschaftsideologie nicht nur deutlich unterbrochen, sondern auch einige verändert. So z.B. haben die Sargoniden den frühdynastischen, nordsumerischen Titel „lugal Kiš" sehr aktiv gebraucht, aber in einem neuen Verständnis.

Aus vielen synchronen, altakkadischen Quellen der Sargoniden-Zeit (Siegellegenden, Jahresdaten und Königsinschriften) kann man deutlich ersehen, dass die Sargoniden (Sargon I., Rimuš, Man-ištūšu, Narām-Su'en, Šar-kalī-šarrī) in Mesopotamien das erste „absolutistische" Königreich mit sehr starken Königen an der Spitze der Staatshierarchie geschaffen haben. Die Herrschaftsideologie der Sargoniden hat viele Unterschiede im Vergleich zum altsumerischen Herrschaftskonzept des Frühdynastikums (dies kann man ersehen aus großen Veränderungen in der königlichen Politik, in der königlichen Titulatur und der Vergöttlichung der Herrscher). Die frühdynastische ideologische Weltanschauung konnte nicht die Konzentration der ganzen Machtvollkommenheit im Staat in den Händen eines Individuums allein – „lugal" oder „ensi" anerkennen. Seit der Akkade-Zeit jedoch kommt die Idee des „absoluten" Herrschers oder Königs (*šarrum dannum, šar kibrātim arba'im*) – *„Mächtiger König", „König der vier Weltgegenden"* deutlich auf.[5]

Selbst Sargon I. nannte sich in seinen Inschriften und Datenformeln „lugal Kiš" oder in Akkadisch *šar kiššatim*, aber seit Sargon I. bekam dieser altsumerische Titel „lugal Kiš" eine ganz andere Bedeutung – nämlich: Sargon I. wurde als „König des Alls", „König des Universums", bezeichnet (akk. *šar kiššatim*, sum. lugal kiš). Der frühdynastische Titel „lugal Kiš", den die ersten Sargoniden – Sargon I., Rimuš, Man-ištūšu sehr aktiv gebraucht haben, war ein Titel in einem ganz neuen Verständnis. „Lugal Kiš" ist nun nicht mehr „Herrscher über Kiš" oder ein Hegemon über nördliche, sumerische Stadtstaaten, sondern ein „König der Welt", ein „König des Universums".[6]

---

4 ИДВ I, 235.

5 Sazonov 2005, 190–192.

6 Diakonov 1959, 222; Siehe auch Postgate 1995, 401; Siehe auch Artikel von S. Stadnikov „Universalism kui fenomen" (S. 93–142) in Stadnikov 1998, 132.

Ganz deutlich ist, dass die Nachfolger Sargons und selbst Sargon viele altsumerische Traditionen der Königsideologie nicht nur aufgegeben, sondern auch einige verändert und manche ideologische Aspekte der Königsherrschaft weiter entwickelt haben. Dieses wird sehr deutlich aus der neuen Politik, die die Sargoniden planmäßig durchführten:

1.) Die Könige von Akkade versuchten, die wichtigsten Heiligtümer und Tempel von Sumer mit Tempelwirtschaft unter ihre Kontrolle zu bringen. Dazu setzten die Könige von Akkade dort ihre Töchter und Söhne oder andere Verwandte ein, wie z. B. Enḫeduanna, Tochter Sargons I.[7]

2.) Sie haben Städte unter die Verwaltung eines *ensi* gestellt. Die lokalen *ensi* von Sumer wurden dabei als einfache Gouverneure (sum. ensi(k), akk. *išš(i)akku(m)*) eingesetzt.

3.) Die altsumerische Oligarchie von Städten, die früher unter den sumerischen Städten völlig unabhängig vorherrschte, verlor ihre frühere Position und Machtvollkommenheit.

4.) Im Laufe ihrer Regierungszeit versuchten akkadische Herrscher schon seit Sargon I. mehrmals ihre Macht zu legitimieren, wofür Propaganda in verschiedenster Art und Weise genutzt haben, um sich als legitime und treue Könige und manchmal sogar als vergöttlichte und kultisch verehrte Herrscher und Halbgötter zu zeigen. Selbst schon die Namen mancher Könige der alt-akkadischen Dynastie kann man als Propaganda und Legitimation ersehen, so z.B. bedeutet der Name *Šar-kalī-šarrīs* „König aller Könige". Der Name *Šar-kalī-šarrī* wurde später bei den Herrschern im Vorderen Orient als Königstitel gebraucht.[8] Auch die Namen Sargons I. und seines Enkels Narām-Su'ens wurden später von anderen

7 Siehe z.B FAOS, Bd.7 (1990), 64–65, Inschriften Sargon A1 und Sargon C 15, wo es zu Enhedu'anna aus Ur heißt: En-hé-du$_7$–an-na SAL.NUNUZ.ZI.-^{d}Nanna dam-^{d}Nanna dumu-⸢*Śar-ru*⸣-[GI] [lugal]-⸢KIŠ⸣ [é- ^{d}INANN]A.ZA.ZA [ŠEŠ.AB^{ki}-ma-k]a [bára-si-ga] [bí-dù] [bára banšur an-n]-a mu-šè bi-[sa$_4$] - „Enhedu'anna, die hohe Priesterin des Nanna, die Gemahlin des Nanna, das Kind des Sargon, des Königs des Alls, hat im Tempel der INANNA.ZA.ZA in Ur einen Altar errichtet (und diesen) „Altar, Tisch des An" mit Namen benannt. (Übersetzung bei B. Kienast und I.J. Gelb). Siehe auch RIME 2 (1993) (Sargon E2.1.1.16), 35–36; Über Enheduanna siehe auch Westenholz 1989, 549; Siehe auch Diakonov 1990, 267; und auch Hallo, van Dijk 1968; Siehe auch Emelianov 2003, 203–206.

8 Siehe den altpersischen Text der Inschrift von Bisutûn von Darius I, 1 Zeile (Übersetzung von F.H. Weissbach): „ich (bin) Darius, der große König, König der Könige ...", Weissbach 1911, 8.

Herrschern als eigene Personennamen benutzt.[9] All diese oben genannten Aspekte traten auch in späteren historischen Perioden in Mesopotamien auf, so dass man sagen kann, dass die Sargoniden zu einer „Musterdynastie“ oder ein Paradigma für spätere Herrscher wurden (assyrische, babylonische, altpersisch-achämenidische und sogar sassanidische) im Rahmen einer *translatio imperii*.[10]

Ein wichtiger Teil dieser neuen „absolutistischen“ Herrschaftsideologie und Politik der Sargoniden-Zeit war auch der persönliche Kultus des Königs von Akkade und dessen Vergöttlichung, die von den Sargoniden durchgeführt wurde.

Waren die ersten Sargoniden vergöttlicht?

Es ist wahrscheinlich, dass der erste vergöttlichte König in Mesopotamien Narām-Su’en war (das wissen wir sowohl aus dem Textmaterial als auch aus kunsthistorischen Quellen, vgl. hierzu die Stele von Narām-Su’en usw.), aber schon seine Vorgänger – Sargon I. und Rimuš haben inoffiziell Vergöttlichungselemente gebraucht. Seit der Zeit Sargons haben wir einige Belege, welche uns zeigen, das man möglicherweise schon in den Regierungsjahren von Sargon I. und Rimuš versuchte, Sargon und Rimuš zu vergöttlichen und kultisch zu verehren, aber das war wahrscheinlich inoffiziell. Manche Beamte oder Diener von Rimuš haben einen Namen wie z. B. „*ì-lí-Ri-mu-uš*“ (Mein Gott ist Rimuš) getragen.[11]

Man kann vermuten, dass Sargon betont hat, er sei von Göttern geschaffen worden. In der späteren Legende (*The Sumerian Sargon Legend*)[12], nach der Interpretation von B. Alster: „54.) lugal ^{d}Ur-^{d}Za-ba$_{4}$-ba$_{4}$ ^{I}*Šar-ru-um-ki-in* ⌜dingir-re-e⌝-ne šu-dug$_{4}$-ga-ar – 54.) King Ur-Zababa, for Sargon, creature of gods, ...“.[13] Auch aus der Zeit von Rimuš (ca. 2278 - 2270) haben einige seiner Diener solche persönlichen Namen mit theophoren Elementen wie „Ilī-Rimuš“ („Rimuš ist mein Gott“) getragen.[14] Vielleicht zeigt uns das, dass schon die ersten Sargoniden vergöttlicht waren.

---

9 Einige spätere (assyrische) Könige, so wie z.B. Sargon II. (721–705), nannten sich ebenfalls Šar-kali-šarrī (Edzard 2004, 78).

10 Westenholz 2000, 99–100.

11 Di Vito 1993, 144.

12 Cooper, Heimpel 1983, 67–82.

13 Alster 1987, 171.

14 Di Vito 1993, 144.

Später, nach dem Tode von Rimuš, versuchte wahrscheinlich auch ein anderer Sohn Sargons I., der ältere Bruder von Rimuš, König Man-ištūšu (ca. 2269–2255), seinen Kultus in Akkade einzurichten (einen lokalen Kultus), was ihm aber nicht gelang. Es gibt einen interessanten Text aus der Zeit Man-ištūšus – einer Siegellegende von Taribu, der Gattin von Lugal-ezen, wo zu lesen ist:

^{d}*Ma-ni-iś-ti-śu/Tá-rí-bu/* DAM Lugal-ezen/MU-NA-DÍM[15]
„(Dem) göttlichen Man-ištūšu hat Taribu, die Gattin von Lugal-ezen, (dies[16]) hergestellt".

Hier steht der Name Man-ištūšus (^{d}Ma-ni-iś-ti-śu), mit Gottesdeterminativ „dingir". War Man-ištūšu somit in Wirklichkeit vergöttlicht? Warum haben wir nur einen einzigen Text, wo Man-ištūšu als Gott genannt ist? Und warum im Text der Taribu? Bedeutet dass nicht, dass nur Taribu und Luga-ezen ihn vergöttlicht haben? Oder kam die Idee für eine Vergöttlichung von Man-ištūšu selbst? Wenn aber dies von Man-ištūšu kam, dann kann man vermuten, dass der Versuch, seine Vergöttlichung durchzuführen, gescheitert war.

Narām-Su'en als „Gott von Akkade" und „König der vier Weltgegenden"

Wir haben genaue Informationen, dass der allererste König, der vergöttlicht wurde, Narām-Su'en (Narāmsîn) war (ca. 2254–2218), der in Akkade seinen Kultus durchgeführt hat. Jedoch begann Narām-Su'en mit seiner Verehrung nicht ganz am Anfang seiner Regierung, sondern etwa in der Mitte – dies zeigen uns mehrere Königsinschriften und eine ganze Reihe von Datenformeln.

Erstens: in vielen alt-akkadischen Texten findet sich der Name Narām-Su'ens zusammen mit dem Gottesdeterminativ ‚dingir'.[17] Zweitens: in derselben Zeit trug Narām-Su'en den Titel *ilu(m) dannu(m) – „mächtiger König"*. Drittens: auch die berühmte Stele von Narām-Su'en (gefunden in Sūsa) zeigt uns, dass Narām-Su'en vergöttlicht war – der König ist ste-

15 RIME 2 (1993), (Man-ištūšu E 2.1.3.2003) 83; Siehe auch FAOS, Bd.7 (1990), (S-6), 40.

16 Siegel.

17 Blocher 1999, 262.

hend auf den Köpfen seiner Krieger dargestellt, 1,5 mal größer als andere Krieger und mit Hörnerkrone.[18]

Dazu haben wir auch Inschriften auf der so genannten Bāsetki-Statue (Bāsetki ist ein Dorf, das sich auf dem Wege von Mosul nach Zāhō befindet), wo geschrieben ist, dass der König Narām-Su'en in Akkade als Gott erwählt war.[19]

(1.-56.) *Na-ra-am-* ^{d}EN.ZU *da-núm* LUGAL *A-kà-dé* ^{ki} *ì-nu ki-ib-ra-tum ar-ba-um iś-te*$_{9}$*-ni-iś i-*KIR*-ni-śú in rí-ma-ti* ^{d}INANNA *tár-a-mu-śú* 10 LÁ 1 KAS.ŠUDUN *in* MU 1 *iš*$_{11}$*-ar-ma ù* LUGAL^{ri} *šu-ut i-śî-*<*ù*>*-nim i-ik-mi al ši in pu-uš-qí-mi* SUHUŠ.SUHUŠ URU$^{ki\text{-}li}$*-śu u-kí-nu* URU^{ki}*-śu iś-te*$_{4}$ ^{d}INANNA *in* É.AN-NA$^{ki\text{-}im}$ *iś-te*$_{4}$ ^{d}En-líl *in* EN.LÍL^{ki} *iś-te*$_{4}$ ^{d}Da-gan *in* Tu-tu-li ^{ki} *iś-te*$_{4}$ ^{d}Nin-ḫur-saĝ *in* Kèš *iś-te*$_{4}$ ^{d}En-ki *in* NUN^{ki} *iś-te*$_{4}$ ^{d}EN.ZU *in* ŠEŠ.AB^{ki} *iś-te*$_{4}$ ^{d}UTU *in* AN.UD.KIB.NUN^{ki} *iś-te*$_{4}$ ^{d}Nè-eri$_{11}$-gal *in* Gú-du$_{8}$-a *ì-lí-iś* URU^{ki}*-śu-nu A-kà-dè* ^{ki} *i-tár-śu-ni-iś-*<*śu*>*-ma qáb-li A-kà-dè* ^{ki} É*-śu ib-ni-ù.*[20]

(1.-56.) „Narāmsîn, der Mächtige, der König von Akkade, hat, als die vier Weltgegenden insgesamt gegen ihn rebellierten, durch die Liebe, die Ištar ihm erwiesen hat, neun Schlachten in einem (einzigen) Jahr siegreich bestanden und die Könige, die sich gegen ihn erhoben hatten, gefangen genommen. Weil er in d(ies)er Notlage die Machtbasis seiner Stadt gefestigt hat, haben (die Bürger) seine(r) Stadt bei Ištar in Eanna, bei Enlil in Nippur, bei Dagān in Tuttul, bei Ninḫursaĝ in Keš, bei Enki in Eridu, bei Sîn in Ur, bei Šamaš in Sippar, bei Nergal in Kutha zum Gott ihrer Stadt Akkade ihn (Narāmsîn) sich erbeten und inmitten von Akkade seinen Tempel errichtet."[21]

Auch dieser Text zeigt, dass in Akkade, in der Hauptstadt des Reiches, ein Tempel für Narām-Su'en gebaut und sein Kultus eingeführt war. Unter den wichtigsten Gottheiten von Sumer und Akkade, die Narām-Su'en als Gottheit anerkannt hatten, waren Ištar (*sum.* Inanna), die auch die Patron-Gottheit der Dynastie von Akkade war, Enlil, Dagān, Ninḫursaĝ, Enki (*akk.* Ea), Su'en (*akk.* Sîn), Šamaš (*sum.* Utu) und Nergal. Sie alle haben

18 Orthmann 1985, Abbildung 104.

19 Edzard 1989, 104.

20 FAOS, Bd.7 (1990), 81–82. / Siehe auch Al-Fouadi 1976, 70–73.

21 Die Übersetzung und Transliteration des Bāsetki-Textes in diesem Artikel ist von Gelb und Kienast (FAOS, Bd.7 (1990)), 81–82; Siehe auch RIME 2 (1993), (Narām-Sîn E2.1.4.10) 113–114; al-Fouadi 1976, 63–77; Farber 1983, 67–72; Espak 2006, 63–64.

Narām-Su'en als Gottheit akzeptiert. Außerdem haben wir mehrere Belege wie z.B. Siegellegenden über Narām-Su'ens Vergöttlichung. Wir finden auf einer Siegellegende folgenden Text:

^{d}*Na-ra-am-*^{d}EN.ZU /dingir-*A-kà-dè* ^{ki} /U-ki-in-ul-maš / DUMU-*šu*,
„Narām-Su'en, Gott von Akkade: Ukinulmaš, sein Sohn."[22]

Hieraus ergibt sich eine weitere Frage: Wann wurde Narām-Su'en zu einem Gott? Wurde er zu einem Gott ganz am Anfang seiner Regierung oder später, vielleicht in der Mitte oder am Ende seiner Regierung?[23] Es ist zu vermuten, dass Narām-Su'en nicht gleichzeitig mit seiner Inthronisation den göttlichen Status in Akkade bekommen hatte, sondern vielmehr später. Das zeigt uns auch das Textmaterial. Eine ganze Reihe synchroner, alt-akkadischer Texte aus der Narām-Su'en-Zeit nannten den Namen Narām-Su'ens ohne Gottesdeterminativ „dingir", wie z.B. die folgenden Königsinschriften – *Narāmsîn 10,*[24] *Narāmsîn A 1,*[25] *Narāmsîn B 2,*[26] *Narāmsîn B3,*[27] *Narāmsîn B 4,*[28] *Narāmsîn B* 9,[29] *Narāmsîn B 10,*[30] ebenso eine ganze Reihe von Datenformeln Narām-Su'ens: *D-8,*[31] *D-9,*[32] *D-10,*[33] *D-17,*[34] *D-18,*[35] *D-19.*[36] Jetzt kann man vermuten, dass Narām-Su'en nicht früher als im 10.–15. Regierungsjahr vergöttlicht worden war – das zeigen uns seine Datenformeln, wo der Name Narām-Su'ens ohne ‚dingir' steht. Aber vielleicht war Narām-Su'en auch erst später vergöttlicht worden. 9

22 FAOS, Bd.7 (1990), 41. Siehe auch Edzard 1969 (*AfO* 22), 15 (Text 21). Siehe Diakonov 1959, 236. Siehe auch die folgende Siegellegende in: FAOS, Bd.7 (1990), 40, 41, 42, 43.

23 Schon W.W. Hallo 1957 meinte, daß Narām-Su'en nur seit der zweiten Hälfte seiner Regierungszeit vergöttlicht war und nicht früher.

24 FAOS, Bd.7 (1990), 97.

25 Ebd., 102–103.

26 Ebd., 106–107.

27 Ebd., 107–108.

28 Ebd., 108.

29 Ebd., 111.

30 Ebd., 112.

31 Ebd., 50.

32 Ebd., 51.

33 Ebd., 51.

34 Ebd., 52.

35 Ebd., 53.

36 Ebd., 53.

Schlachten gegen revoltierende Länder, mehrere Kriege und Feldzüge, seine großen Verdienste für sein Volk oder besser gesagt, seinen Untertanen (das alles, was im Bāsetki-Text (Narāmsîn 1[37]) gemeint ist) – alle diese Taten haben viel Zeit gebraucht. Als Beispiel nenne ich hier nur eine altakkadische Siegellegende, deren Besitzer Lugal-ušumgal war, ein Funktionär Narām-Su'ens.[38]

S-13.[39] ^{d}*Na-ra-am-*^{d}EN.ZU/ *da-núm* /DINGIR *A-kà-dè* ^{ki} LUGAL / *ki-ib-ra-tim* / *ar-ba-im* Lugal-ušumgal / DUB.SAR / Ì[R/I⌜R$_{11}$-ZU⌝

„Narām-Su'en, der mächtige Gott von Akkade, König der vier Weltgegenden: Lugal-ušumgal, der Schreiber, dein Sklave."

Analoge Texte haben wir eine ganze Reihe.[40] Auch in der Akkade-Zeit trug man solche Namen wie ^{d}*Na-ra-am-*^{d}EN.ZU-*ì-lí* – *„Narām-Su'en ist mein Gott."*[41]

Vergöttlichter Šar-kalī-šarrī im Status eines Gottes Ninūrta?

Meiner Meinung nach war der Nachfolger und Sohn von Narām-Su'en, der König Šar-kalī-šarrī[42] (ca. 2217-2193), auch vergöttlicht, aber nur am Anfang oder spätestens in der ersten Hälfte seiner Regierungszeit. Erst dann hat er der Vergöttlichung seiner Person abgesagt. Die Texte zeigen uns, dass Šar-kalī-šarrī einer Vergöttlichung seiner Person nicht gleich nach seiner Inthronisation absagte, wie A. Westenholz[43] postuliert, sondern mindestens ein paar Jahre später. Dies zeigen uns einige Fakten, altakkadische Texte, die uns erhalten sind: 1.) Datenformeln von Šar-kalī-šarrī, 2.) Inschriften und Kopien von Inschriften Šar-kalī-šarrīs, 3.) Die

37 Ebd., 81–83, siehe auch RIME 2 (1993), (Narām-Sîn E2.1.4.10) 113–114.

38 Ebd., 42.

39 Ebd., 42.

40 Siehe z.B. Text S-16: ^{d}*Na-ra-am-*^{d}EN.ZU / dingir A-kà-dè ki / Śa-rí-iś-tá-kál / dub-sar / ir$_{11}$–zu „Narām-Su'en, Gott von Akkade: Šarištakal, der Schreiber, dein Diener", FAOS, Bd.7 (1990), 42.

41 Di Vito 1993, 144.

42 Šar-kali-šarrī trug nie die Titel *„König des Universums"* (Titel Sargons, Rimuš und Maništūšus) und *„König der vier Weltgegenden"* (Titel des Narām-Su'ens), sondern er nannte sich manchmal DINGIR UR.SAĞ A-kà-dè^{ki} – *„Held von Akkade"*. Siehe RIME 2 (1993) (Šar-kali-šarrī E2.1.5.2005), 201.

43 OBO 160/3, 56.

Siegellegenden und andere altakkadische Texte, die von Šar-kalī-šarrī verfasst sind oder von seinen Dienern und Beamten geschrieben wurden.

Paradox ist, dass Šar-kalī-šarrī, der Sohn von Narām-Su'en, die Tradition einer Vergöttlichung und Titulatur Narām-Su'ens nicht fortführte (Titel „König der vier Weltgegenden"), jedoch nicht am Anfang, sondern erst ein paar Jahre später nach seiner Inthronisation – nicht früher. Wahrscheinlich war dies mit der Verschlechterung der politischen und militärischen Lage in der Umgebung von Akkade eng verbunden (Schon Narām-Su'en fiel in der Schlacht mit den Guti). Doch auch die innenpolitische Position von Šar-kalī-šarrī in Akkade war für seine Königsherrschaft nicht mehr so günstig wie noch zuvor bei seinem Vater.

Datenformeln als Zeugnis der Vergöttlichung von Šar-kalī-šarrī

Dass Šar-kalī-šarrī vergöttlicht war, zeigen uns Siegellegenden seiner Hofbeamten, sowie seine eigenen Inschriften und Datenformeln. Wir wissen aus der „Sumerischen Königsliste", dass Šar-kalī-šarrī ca. 25 Jahre regiert hat,[44] und wir haben etwa 18-20 seiner Datenformeln, der Rest ist leider nicht erhalten. 2 Datenformeln nennen Šar-kalī-šarrī als ^{d}*Śar-kà-lí*-LUGAL^{ri} „göttlicher Šar-kalī-šarrī", wie z.B. die Datenformel D-39 zeigt: „*in* 1 mu ^{d}En-líl ^{d}*Śar-kà-lí*-LUGAL^{ri} SU ⌜x x x x⌝ SU"[45] „im Jahre, nachdem für Enlil, (göttlicher) Šar-kalī-šarrī…" und auch D-38.[46] Auch kann man vermuten, dass in den anderen nicht erhaltenen Datenformeln Šar-kalī-šarrī ebenfalls als Gott genannt war.

Die Inschriften als Zeugnis der Vergöttlichung von Šar-kalī-šarrī: Šar-kalī-šarrī, der erste König in Mesopotamien, der sich als Ninūrta, als Sohn von Enlil bezeichnet hatte?

In altakkadischen Texten kann man einige Belege finden, die zeigen, dass Šar-kalī-šarrī (vielleicht sogar schon sein Vater Narām-Su'en) vermutlich einer der ersten Könige in Mesopotamien war, der sich als Sohn von Enlil bezeichnet hatte und auf die Position Ninūrtas prätendiert war. Das beginnt nicht mit der Ur III-Zeit oder Isin-Larsa-Zeit, als z.B. Lipit-Ištar (ca. 1934 - 1924), König von Isin, den Status Ninūrtas beansprucht hatte.[47] Dies beginnt auch nicht mit Ur-Nammu, Šulgi und Šu-Su'en, sondern

---

44 Michalowski 2006, 84.

45 FAOS, Bd.7 (1990), 56.

46 Ebd., 56.

47 Siehe z.B. Westenholz A., Westenholz J.G., 2006, 90 (No. 3: Dedicatory Cone of Lipit-Ištar).

schon früher mit der Sargoniden-Zeit, zumindest mit Šar-kalī-šarrī. A. Annus zählt in seiner Doktorarbeit zu den Königen, die sich als Söhne von Enlil nannten, folgende: Narām-Su'en, Šulgi, Šu-Su'en, Išbi-Erra, Šu-ili-šu, Išme-Dagān, Lipit-Ištar und vielleicht auch Ur-Ninūrta.[48] In den Preisliedern auf Lipit-Ištar (1. Dynastie von Isin) steht:

1.) *Lipit-Ištar A,* Zeile 2: ^{d}*Li-pí-it-eš$_4$-tár* dumu ^{d}En-líl-lá-me-en, „Lipit-Ištar, der Sohn von Enil, bin ich."[49]

2.) in der Hymne *Lipit-Ištar D,* Zeile 39: $^{[d]}$*Li-pí-it-eš$_4$-tár* nun za-a-šè ĝál-la dumu ^{d}En-líl-lá-ke$_4$,[50] oder in 3.) *Lipit-Ištar H,* Zeile 6: /^{d}*Li*\-*pí*-/*it*\-*eš$_4$-tár* dumu ^{d}/En\-[líl]-lá-ra mí zi na-mu-[ni-dug$_4$].[51] Außerdem haben wir noch einen anderen Beleg über Lipit-Ištar (1934-1924), König von Isin, gefunden; nämlich ist in einer Inschrift Lipit-Ištars dieser König in den Zeilen 7 und 8 als *ma-ru* ^{d}*En-líl,* als „Sohn des Enlil" bezeichnet.[52]

Auch die Inschriften von Šar-kalī-šarrī zeigen uns, dass er vergöttlicht war und dass er Enlil als seinen Vater bezeichnet hatte. Z.B. in einer Kopie der Inschrift *Šar-kalī-šarrī C 2* gibt es ein folgendes Fragment: ^{d}En-líl LUGAL *ì-li* ^{d}*Śar-kà-lí*-LUGAL^{rí} ⌜DUMU *da*⌝ *-dì-śu* [*da-núm* LUGAL *A-kà-de* ^{ki}] [...] [...] [*maḫ-rí-iś*] [^{d}En-líl] *a-bí-śu a-na* EN.LÍL^{ki} *É-la-kam* ..., „Enlil, dem König der Götter, der (göttliche) Šar-kalī-šarrī, sein geliebter Sohn, der mächtige König von Akkade, ..., vor Enlil, seinem Vater, in Nippur ging ...".[53]

Besser erhalten ist die Inschrift *Šar-kalī-šarrī 2,* wo geschrieben steht: „^{d}*Śar-kà-lí*-LUGAL^{rí} DUMU *da-dì-śu* ^{d}En-líl *da-núm* LUGAL *A-kà-de* ^{ki} ...", „göttlicher Šar-kalī-šarrī, geliebter Sohn des Enlil, mächtiger König von Akkade ...".[54] Ähnliches kann man auch in *Šar-kalī-šarrī* C 3 finden.[55] Hier sehen wir, dass Šar-kalī-šarrī ‚Gott' genannt wurde, aber auch Sohn Enlils.

---

48 Annus, A., 2002, 18.

49 ETCSL c. 2.5.5.1; Siehe auch „*The Literature of Ancient Sumer*" 2006, 309, Zeilen 1–2.

50 ETCSL c. 2.5.5.4, Zeile 39.

51 ETCSL c. 2.5.5.8, Zeile 6.

52 Westenholz A., Westenholz J.G., 2006, 90 (No. 3: Dedicatory Cone of Lipit-Ištar).

53 FAOS, Bd.7 (1990), 279–281; RIME 2 (1993) (Šar-kalī-šarrī E2.1.5.6), 194–195.

54 ebd., 114–115, Siehe auch RIME 2 (1993) (Šar-kalī-šarrī E2.1.5.2), 188–189, wo nach der Übersetzung von D. Frayne (Zeile 1–12.) „Šar-kalī-šarrī, beloved son of the god Enlil, mighty, king of Agade and of the subjects of the god Enlil, builder of Ekur, temple of the god Enlil at Nippur ...".

55 Ebd., 281–282.

Dies lässt uns vermuten, dass Šar-kalī-šarrī mit Ninūrta identifiziert worden war.[56]

Šar-kalī-šarrī war in vielen Texten aber als „Held von Enlil“ und auch als „heldenhafter Gott von Akkade“ genannt - dingir-ur-saĝ / *A-kà-dè* ^{ki}.[57] Ninūrta, Sohn Enlils, war *„Krieger von Enlil“*, Ningirsu war z.B. seit der Zeit Eanatums als „ur-saĝ-^{d}En-líl-la“, als *„Held von Enlil“* bezeichnet.[58] Das alles zeigt uns, dass es eine Verbindung zwischen Šar-kalī-šarrī und Ninūrta/Ningirsu gab. Auch in anderen Inschriften war Šar-kalī-šarrī als Gott, als geliebter Sohn von Enlil und mächtiger König von Akkade, genannt – z.B. in *Šar-kalī-šarrī C 5.*[59] *Šar-kalī-šarrī 2,*[60] *Šar-kalī-šarrī B 4,*[61] nannten Šar-kalī-šarrī Gott. Vielleicht nicht nur *Šar-kalī-šarrī* - so kann man vermuten, sondern alle Sargoniden waren auf die Position Ninūrtas prätendiert. Dies bleibt aber nur eine reine Vermutung.

Was zeigen uns die Siegellegenden aus der Zeit Šar-kalī-šarrīs

Noch eine Art von Quellen, wo Šar-kalī-šarrī als vergöttlichter Herrscher gemeint ist, sind Siegellegenden. Das sind Texte auf den Siegeln von Funktionären Šar-kalī-šarrīs:

S-26.[62]

^{d}*Šar-kà-lí*-LUGAL^{ri}/ lugal / ⌜*A-k*⌝ *à-dè* ^{ki}/ *Ib-ni*-LUGAL/ dub-sar/ ir$_{11}$-zu „(Göttlicher) Šar-kalī-šarrī, der König von Akkade, Ibnî-šarrum, der Schreiber, dein Sklave.“

Auch der Text *S-34,* der praktisch ganz zerstört ist, nennt Šar-kalī-šarrī als Gott.[63] Aber bedeutender ist *S*-29:[64] ⌜*Šar*⌝-*kà-lí*-LUGAL^{ri} / dingir-ur-saĝ/ *A-kà-dè* ^{ki}/ Lugal-ĝiš/ dub-sar/ é⌜nsi⌝/ UD.[NUN^{ki}] ir$_{11}$⌜x⌝-zu – „Šar-kalī-

56 Die Rolle Ninūrtas in der Königsideologie hat A. Annus in seiner Doktorarbeit untersucht (Annus 2002).

57 FAOS, Bd.7 (1990), 46.

58 Annus, A., 2002, 10.

59 FAOS, Bd.7 (1990), 281–282.

60 Ebd., 114–115.

61 Ebd., 119.

62 Ebd., 45.

63 Ebd., 47.

64 Ebd., 46.

šarrī, heldenhafter Gott von Akkade: Lugal-ĝiš, Schreiber, Statthalter von Adab, dein (?) Diener." Das zeigt uns, dass auch seine Beamte und nicht nur in Akkade, sondern auch in anderen Städten, ihn verehrt haben. Schließlich im Laufe seiner Regierung hat Šar-kalī-šarrī von seiner Vergöttlichung abgesagt, warum wissen wir nicht, aber man kann vermuten, dass die innen- und außenpolitische Lage in Akkade stark verschlimmert war, daher bin ich nicht einverstanden mit der Hypothese von A. Westenholz (1999), der meinte, das Šar-kalī-šarrī von seiner Vergöttlichung absagte gleich zu Beginn seiner Regierungszeit, und nur der Statthalter von Adab hat ihn weiter als vergöttlicht verehrt.[65] Ich meine, dass es mir gelang zu zeigen, dass Šar-kalī-šarrī wenigstens 2-3 Jahre vergöttlicht war (und nicht nur in Adab), und vielleicht sogar noch weitere Jahre.

Skizzierung der Vergöttlichung der Könige von Akkade (Resümee)

Als Resümee habe ich eine Skizzierung zur Vergöttlichung der Könige von Akkade verfasst. Nach meiner Information hat bereits W.W. Hallo 1957 eine derartige erstellt, doch habe ich diese weiterentwickelt.[66]

1.) Von den ersten Sargoniden – Sargon I, Rīmuš, Man-ištūšu und zu Beginn der Regierungszeit Narām-Su'ens gibt es keine Information über eine offizielle Vergöttlichung der Könige von Akkade. (Man braucht aber nur inoffizielle Vergöttlichungselemente in den Namen der ersten Sargoniden wie z.B. das theophorische Element in dem Namen „*ili-Rīmuš*" u.s.w.[67]) zu betrachten. Wahrscheinlich versuchte schon Man-ištūšu seinen persönlichen Kultus einzuführen, was ihm aber nicht gelang.[68]

2.) Seit Mitte oder zweiter Hälfte der Regierungsjahre Narām-Su'ens begann dessen offizielle Vergöttlichung in Akkade (vermutlich nicht früher als 10.-15. Regierungsjahr; es ist aber möglich, das dieses Ereignis auch

65 A. Westenholz schreibt über Šar-kali-šarrī : „After his accession to the throne, he appears to have devoted most of his resources to the completion of the ambitious temple building program begun by his father. In that task, he showed himself as a devoted son. But he also soon recanted on the more excesses of his father. He was not 'King of the Four Cornes' but more modestly 'King of Akkade', nor did he claim divinity for himself." (Siehe OBO 160/3, 55–56).

66 Hallo 1957, 60.

67 Diakonov 1959, 235.

68 RIME 2 (1993), (Man-ištūšu E 2.1.3.2003) 83; Siehe auch FAOS, Bd.7 (1990), (S-6), 40.

später stattgefunden hat). Zu Beginn der Regierungszeit von Šar-kalī-šarrī ist dessen Vergöttlichung belegt.

3.) Die zweite Hälfte der Regierungszeit Šar-kalī-šarrīs und die letzen Jahren des Akkadischen Reiches unter den letzten Königen von Akkade, die aber keine Sargoniden mehr waren, gab es keine Vergöttlichung der Herrscher von Akkade. Bis jetzt wurde kein Beleg von den akkadischen Königen Dudu (ca. 2189 - 2169) und Šu-Dur-Ul (ca. 2168 - 2154) gefunden, welcher uns zeigen kann, dass diese beiden vergöttlicht waren.[69]

Zusammenfassend kann man sagen: es scheint, dass Šar-kalī-šarrī von seiner Vergöttlichung im Laufe seiner Regierungszeit abgesagt hatte – etwa zu Beginn oder in der Mitte. Vielleicht war dies mit einer innen- und außenpolitischen Instabilität des Akkadischen Reiches verbunden. Hinsichtlich Šar-kalī-šarrī ist wichtig, dass er in den alt-akkadischen Texten als Sohn von Enlil genannt war und wahrscheinlich hat man ihn im Status von Ninūrta/Ningirsu gesehen. Es scheint, dass er der allererste unter den Herrschern in Mesopotamien war, der sich mit dem Gott Ninūrta identifiziert hat.

Abkürzungen

AfO	Archiv für Orientforschung, 1923 ff.
FAOS 7	Gelb I.J., Kienast B., *Die alt-akkadischen Königsinschriften des Dritten Jahrtausends v.Chr.*, Freiburger Altorientalische Studien 7, Franz Steiner Verlag, Stuttgart 1990.
JAOS	Journal of the American Oriental Society, New Haven /Ann Arbor 1843 ff.
ИДВ I	Дьяконов И.М. (ред.), *История Древнего Востока, часть первая, Месопотамия,* Главная редакция восточной литературы, Наука, М., 1983.
OBO 160/3	Westenholz A., Sallaberger W., *Mesopotamien: Akkade-Zeit und Ur III-Zeit*, in: *Orbis Biblicus et Orientalis* 160/3, Annäherungen 3, P. Attinger - M. Wäfer (Hrsg.), Universitäts-verlag, Freiburg, Schweiz, Vandenhoeck & Ruprecht, Göttingen 1999.
OrNS 52	Orientalia. NS = Nova Series, 1932 ff.
RIME 2	Frayne D., *Sargonic and Gutian Periods (2334-2113 BC), The Royal Inscriptions of Mesopotamia, Early Periods.* Volume 2, University of Toronto Press, Toronto-Buffalo-London 1993.
ZA	*Zeitschrift für Assüriologie und Vorderasiatische Archäologie*, 1886 ff.

69 Hallo 1957, 60.

Bibliographie

1. Quellen

ETCSL: Black, J.A., Cunningham, G., Ebeling, J., Flückiger-Hawker, E., Robson, E., Taylor, J., and Zólyomi, G., *The Electronic Text Corpus of Sumerian Literature* (http://etcsl.orinst.ox.ac.uk/), Oxford 1998- .

Edzard 1969: Edzard D.O., *Die Inschriften der altakkadischen Rollsiegel*, *AfO* 22, 1969, 15 (Text 21).

FAOS 7: Gelb I.J., Kienast B., *Die altakkadischen Königsinschriften des Dritten Jahrtausends v.Chr.*, Freiburger Altorientalische Studien 7, Franz Steiner Verlag, Stuttgart 1990.

Michalowski 2006: P. Michalowski, *Sumerian King List* in: *Historical Sources in Translation: The Ancient Near East*, (ed. by.) M. Chavalas, Blackwell Publishing, 2006, lk. 81-85.

RIME 2: Frayne D., *Sargonic and Gutian Periods (2334-2113 BC), The Royal Inscriptions of Mesopotamia, Early Periods*, volume 2, University of Toronto Press, Toronto-Buffalo-London 1993.

The Literature of Ancient Sumer 2006: Black J., Gunningham G., Robson E., Zólyomi, G., The Literature of Ancient Sumer, Oxford University Press, 2006.

Weidner 1970: Weidner E., Die Inschriften Tukulti-Ninurtas I. und seiner Nachfolger, Archiv für Orientforschung, (Hrsg.) E. Weidner, Beiheft 12, Biblio Verlag, Osnabrück 1970.

Weissbach 1911: Weissbach F.H., *Die Keilinschriften der Achämeniden*, Leipzig, J.C. HINRICHS`sche BUCHHANDLUNG 1911, in der Reihenfolge des Erscheinens der Vorderasiatischen Bibliothek 3. Stück, unveränderter fotomechanischer Nachdruck der Originalausgabe 1911, Zentral-Antiquariat der Deutschen Demokratischen Republik, Leipzig 1968.

Westenholz A, Westenholz J.G 2006: Westenholz A, Westenholz J.G, Cuneiform Inscriptions in the Collection of the Bible Lands Museum Jerusalem, The Old Babylonian Inscriptions, Cuneiform Monographs (General ed.-s Abush T. - Geller M.J, - Maul S.M. - Wiggermann F.A.M.) vol. 33, Brill: Leiden-Boston 2006.

2. Sekundärliteratur

Al-Fouadi 1976: al-Fouadi A.H., Bassetki Statue with an Old Akkadian Royal Inscription of Naram-Sin of Agade (B.C. 2291-2255), *Sumer* 32 (1976), 63-77.

Alster 1987: Alster B., *A Note on the Uriah Letter in the Sumerian Sargon Legend*, *ZA* 77, 1987, 77 (1987).

Annus 2002: Annus A., „The God Ninurta in the Mythology of Ancient Mesopotamia“, State Archives of Assyria Studies, volume XIV, The Neo-Assyrian Text Corpus Project of University of Helsinki, Institute for Asian and African Studies, University of Helsinki, Finland 2002.

Blocher 1999: Blocher F., *Wann wurde Puzur-Eštar zum Gott?* in: BABYLON: Focus Mesopotamischer Geschichte, Wiege früher Gelehrsamkeit, Mythos in der Moderne, 2. Internationales Colloquium der Deutschen Orient-Gesellschaft 24.-26. März 1998 in Berlin, im Auftrag des Vorstandes der Deutschen Orient-Gesellschaft, (Hrsg.) J. Renger, GDOG, Band 2, Berlin 1999.

Cooper, Heimpel 1983: Cooper J.S., Heimpel W., *The Sumerian Sargon Legend*, *JAOS* 103, 1983.

Di Vito 1993: Di Vito R.A., *Studies in Third Millennium Sumerian and Akkadian Personal Names*, *The Designation and Conception of the Personal God*, Studia Pohl: Series Maior, *Dissertationes scientifiecae de rebus orientis antiqui* 16, Editrice Pontificio Istitutio Biblico, Roma 1993.

Diakonov 1959: Дьяконов И.М., *Общественный и государственный строй древнего Двуречья: Шумер,* Издательство восточной литературы, Москва 1959.

ИДВ I: Дьяконов И.М. (ред.), *История Древнего Востока, часть первая, Месопотамия,* Главная редакция восточной литературы, Наука, М., 1983.

Diakonov 1990: Дьяконов И.М., *Люди города Ура*, Главная редакция восточной литературы, Наука, М., 1990.

Edzard 1989: Edzard D.O., *Das „Wort im Ekur“ oder Perepetie in „Fluch über Akkade“* in: Dumu-É-DUB-BA-A, *Studies in Honor of Åke Sjöberg,* H. Behrens, D. Loding, M.T. Roth (ed-s.), Occasional Publications of the Samuel Noah Kramer Fund 11, Philadelphia 1989, 99-105.

Edzard 2004: Edzard D.O., *Geschichte Mesopotamiens, Von den Sumerern bis zu Alexander dem Großen*, Verlag C.H. Beck, München 2004.

Emelianov 2003: Емельянов В.В., Древний Шумер. Очерки культуры, Санкт-Петербург, Издательство «Азбука-классика», «Петербургское Востоковедение», 2003.

Espak 2006: Espak P., *Ancient Near Eastern gods Enki and Ea: diachronical analysis of texts and images from the earliest sources to the Neo-Sumerian period*, Master's thesis, Tartu University, Faculty of Theology, Chair for Ancient Near Eastern Studies, Tartu Ülikool, 2006.

Farber 1983: Farber W., *Die Vergöttlichung Naramsins*, *OrNS* 52, 1983, 67-72.

Franke 1995: Über Königsideologie der Könige von Akkade siehe zB. Franke S., Königinschriften und Königsideologie. Die Könige von Akkade zwischen Tradition und Neuerung, *Altorientalistik* 1, Münster - Hamburg 1995.

Glassner 2003: Glassner J.-J., *The Invention of Cuneiform*, Writing in Sumer, (transl.) Z. Bahrani and M. van de Mieroop, John Hopkins University Press, 2003.

Hallo 1957: Hallo W.W., *Early Mesopotamian royal titles: a philologic and historical analysis*, New Haven: American Oriental Society, 1957.

Hallo, van Dijk 1968: Hallo W.W, Van Dijk J.J.A., *The Exaltation of Inanna*, New Haven and London, Yale University Press, 1968.

Orthmann 1985: Orthmann W., *Der alte Orient,* in: *Propyläen Kunstgeschichte*, Frankfurt a.M. 1985.

Postgate 1995: Postgate J.N., Royal Ideology and State Administration in Sumer and Akkad. in: *Civilizations of the Ancient Near East*, (ed.) J. M. Sasson, Volume 1. New York: Charles Scribner's Sons, 1995, 395-401.

Sazonov 2005: Saznonov V., *Kuningavõimu ideoloogia Sargoniidide ajastul (XXIV-XXII saj. e. Kr.)// Идеология царской власти в эпоху Саргонидов (XXIV-XXII вв.)*, Tartu Ülikool, 2005 (trükkimata magistri-dissertatsioon).

Stadnikov 1998: Stadnikov S., Vana Egiptuse Kultuurilugu: valitud artikleid, tõlkeid ja esseid, Tallinn: Kodutrükk 1998.

Westenholz A., Sallaberger W., *Mesopotamien: Akkade-Zeit und Ur III-Zeit*, in: *Orbis Biblicus et Orientalis* 160/3, Annäherungen 3, P. Attinger - M. Wäfer (Hrsg.), Universitätsverlag, Freiburg, Schweiz, Vandenhoeck & Ruprecht, Göttingen 1999.

Westenholz 1989: Westenholz J.G., *Enheduanna, En-Priestess, Hen of Nanna, Spouse of Nanna,* in: Dumu-É-DUB-BA-A, *Studies in Honor of Åke Sjöberg,* H. Behrens, D. Loding, M.T. Roth (eds.), Occasional Publications of the Samuel Noah Kramer Fund 11, Philadelphia 1989, 539-556.

Westenholz 2000: Westenholz J.G., *The King, The Emperor, and the Empire: Continuity and Discontinuity of Royal Representation in Text and Image*, in: The Heirs of Assyria, Proceedings of the Opening Symposium of the Assyrian and Babylonian Intellectual Heritage Project Held in Tvärminne, Finland, October 8-11, 1998 Melammu Symposia, volume I, Sanna Aro, R. M. Whiting (eds.), Helsinki 2000, 99-125.

Sozialgeschichtliche Forschung am AT und ihr theologischer Ertrag

Gottfried Sprondel †, Osnabrück

I. Grundzüge der Sozialgeschichte Israels

Es mangelt nicht an wissenschaftlich hermeneutischen Zugängen zum Alten Testament. Jede Epoche der Auslegung hat von ihren Voraussetzungen her, also von ihrer „Gotteskonzeption" und ihrem Verständnis der Realität aus, Zugänge gesucht und erschlossen. Wo kritische Befassung mit Literatur und historische Fragestellungen die Szene beherrschen, entsteht eben eine historisch-kritische Wissenschaft von der Bibel, wie sie heute, filigran ausgearbeitet und gelegentlich auch einen erschöpften Eindruck hinterlassend, die wissenschaftliche Exegese charakterisiert. Wo die Größe „Religion" ins Blickfeld gerät, wird eine spezifisch religionsgeschichtliche Schule nach Israels Abhängigkeit und Originalität im Konzert der Religionen fragen. Wo die Epoche sich für ihr gesellschaftliches Substrat zu interessieren beginnt, entfaltet sie eine neue Aufmerksamkeit für soziale Strukturen, soziale Programme und soziale Wirkungen der biblischen Antike bis in die Gegenwart, je nachdem ob sie diese Gegenwart in der Kontinuität jenes Altertums sieht oder nicht. Die Texte, die ja nur gelegentlich die Denkvoraussetzungen der Fragesteller teilen, antworten in der Regel nur mittelbar, regen die Fragelust dadurch natürlich mächtig an und rufen ganze Literaturen hervor, die freilich eben wegen jener Indirektheit der Antworten nicht immer aus dem Halbdunkel der Vermutungen herauskommen. Dennoch: einige Grundzüge der Sozialgeschichte Israels haben sich vorläufig herausgeschält.

Israels Väter leben als Halbnomaden und Kleintierzüchter (Schafe, Ziegen, Esel) am Rande des palästinischen Kulturlandes, abhängig von Wasserstellen und bedroht von der Gefahr der Überweidung. Etwa halbjährlich wechseln sie zwischen Steppe und (gerade abgeerntetem) Kulturland. Ein allmählicher Übergang zu sesshafter Lebensweise mit Rinderzucht und Ackerbau ist schon in den Erzvätersagen zu erkennen. Man lebt in Gruppen, nämlich in Familien („Häusern"), Sippen und (später) in Stämmen. Stammbäume haben größte Bedeutung (Geschlechtsregister). Die Sippe und der Stamm dienen zugleich als Rechtsgemeinschaften nach außen wie nach innen. Der „Fremde", also das nicht der sozialen Einheit zuzurechnende Individuum, steht unter dem Schutz des Gastrechts.

Nach dem Übergang zur Sesshaftigkeit im Kulturland zwischen den kanaanäischen Stadtkönigtümern entstehen größere soziale Einheiten und ein neues Recht. Der Boden gilt als Jahves Eigentum, das er den Gruppen zuteilt, und zwar als Erbe auf Dauer. Der Mann, der eine „Nachalah" besitzt, besitzt auch die vier großen Rechte des Israeliten zur Ehe, zum Kultus, zum Krieg und zur Rechtspflege.

Die Staatsbildung und die Monarchie bewirken den einschneidendsten Wandel in der Sozialgeschichte Israels. Hofhaltung und Verwaltung, Söldnertruppe und Krongut bringen ganz neue, ständisch gestufte Klassen hervor. Eine städtische Bevölkerung bildet sich heraus, unterschieden von der Landbevölkerung. Die Wirtschaftsformen ändern sich, Großgrundbesitz legt sich auf die alte Ordnung des Sippenerbes, Binnen- und Außenhandel schaffen neue Vermögen, neuen Reichtum. Ausländische Vorbilder fördern Luxus und Ungleichheiten. Grosso modo lassen sich für die Königszeit vier Schichten unterscheiden:

1. Die Beamten, Militärs, Kaufleute und Handwerker in den Städten 2. Die freien Grundbesitzer auf dem Lande. 3. Die Leute ohne Grundbesitz, also die „Armen". 4. Die Sklaven.

Dieser Gesellschaftsaufbau wird durch das katastrophale Ende Judas und Jerusalems zerschlagen. Aus Israel wird zunehmend eine um den Tempel gescharte Gemeinde unter der Souveränität fremder Großreiche und deren Verwaltungsorganen. Darüber mehr im folgenden Kapitel:

II. Max Weber und das Alte Testament

Der Theologe, der Max Webers Studie „Das antike Judentum" 80 Jahre nach ihrem Erscheinen und mit der Entwicklung der protestantischen alttestamentlichen Wissenschaft im selben Zeitraum im Kopf, durcharbeitet, staunt. Sein Staunen betrifft zwei Dinge: a) Welch ein Meister sich hier eines gewaltigen Stoffs bemächtigt hat, bis zur völligen Beherrschung, niemals mit der Attitüde des von außen kommenden Besserwissers, sondern mit vornehmem Respekt vor seinem Gegenstand sowohl als auch vor der alttestamentlichen Forschung seiner Zeit, die er nicht nur gründlich kennt, sondern souverän zu würdigen versteht. b) Der andere Grund zum Staunen liegt darin, wie wenig dieses Meisterwerk in die Forschung der Theologischen Fakultäten hineingewirkt hat. Eine Fülle von späteren Neuentdeckungen mit durchaus sensationellem Beigeschmack klingt bei Weber bereits an, gelegentlich im Nebensatz, aber nie ohne Folgen für sein Gesamturteil.

Der dritte Band seiner Gesammelten Aufsätze zur Religionssoziologie, ein unvollendetes Werk, ist dem antiken Judentum gewidmet. Ihm geht es nicht darum, etwas zu beweisen, etwa die Offenbarungsqualität der alttestamentlichen Botschaft oder etwa die Minderwertigkeit des Jüdischen in der Menschheitsgeschichte beides Lieblingsthemen auch in der Wissenschaft des 19. Jahrhunderts -, sondern seine Absicht ist die „Betrachtung seiner Entwicklungsbedingungen" (S. 7) zur „universalhistorischen Wirkung seiner Religion an einem Angelpunkt der ganzen Kulturentwicklung des Occidents und vorderasiatischen Orients" (ebenda). Weber hat sich als „Mitglied der badischen Landeskirche" identifiziert (allerdings in einer ironisch gefärbten Anmerkung in seiner Protestantischen Ethik). Aber es gibt keinen Anlass, für sein Christentum und dessen Verhältnis zu seinem Forschungsgegenstand etwas anderes anzunehmen als für das geistige Band zwischen seiner politischen Leidenschaft und seinem Ideal einer wertfreien Wissenschaft von Politik und Gesellschaft.

Zum Zweck also jener „Betrachtung" wirft er über das ganze Alte Testament ein dichtes Netz soziologischer Begriffe. Diese gliedern die (in ganz anderer Absicht sprechenden) Texte neu. Sie machen Zusammenhänge sichtbar und begreiflich, präparieren verdeckte Spannungen und Konflikte heraus, arbeiten vor allem der Antwort auf eine Frage unaufhörlich zu, deretwegen Weber seine ganze Untersuchung anstellt: wie ist aus der Jahwe-Religion des kleinen vorderasiatischen Randvolkes Israel die weltgeschichtliche Kraft geworden, die einmal verhindert hat, dass dieses Volk sich im Orkus der Geschichte verloren hat wie zahllose andere Völker der antiken Welt, und andererseits Ursprungsenergie für die gesamte westliche Kulturentwicklung geliefert hat.

Weber ist – wohl in der Nachfolge Hegels – geleitet von der Grundüberzeugung, dass derartige universale Bewegungen mit der Analyse materiell-natürlicher Bedingungen niemals verständlich zu machen sind. Deswegen sein beharrliches und so ungewöhnlich fruchtbares Aufspüren der geistigen Wurzeln großer Bewegungen in der Geschichte, mit dem er der sozialgeschichtlichen Forschung am Alten Testament bei aller möglichen Kritik am Detail für immer den Weg gewiesen hat. Sein Interesse ist also nicht die gesellschaftliche Einzelheit, die den einzelnen Text transparent macht (nach Art von Themen wie „Der Fremde im Alten Testament", „Die Frau im Wandel der Geschichte Israels" etc.), sondern vielmehr: Was ist am Geist der Religion Israels und an historischen Gegebenheiten zusammengekommen, nicht nur um das Alte Testament hervorzubringen (ein Ergebnis, von dem Weber im Ton höchster Bewunderung spricht), sondern um einen Typus von Religion zu schaffen, dessen sozialgeschichtlich ungeheure Wirkung bis heute einen ganzen Kulturkreis beherrscht.

Webers berühmte These nun lautet: „Was waren, soziologisch angesehen, die Juden? Ein Pariavolk". Eine problematische Begriffswahl, die vor allem jüdische Kritiker auf den Plan gerufen hat! Der Begriff „Paria", der aus der hinduistischen Welt genommen ist, hat für Weber aber nichts Wertendes noch gar Abwertendes. Er erläutert ihn so: „ein rituell, formell oder faktisch von der sozialen Umwelt geschiedenes Gastvolk" (3). Dies Ergebnis der Geschichte Israels tritt natürlich erst mit Exil und Diasporaexistenz ans Licht. Aber es bereitete sich lange vor, vor allem in den beiden Hauptereignissen der vorexilischen Zeit, dem Entstehen der levitisch-deuteromischen Thorafrömmigkeit, und der Wirksamkeit der großen Propheten, die in erster Linie Unheilskünder sind, aber dennoch die Kontinuität Israels mit dem alten Jahve-Bund unbeirrt festhalten („heiliger Rest") und so am Ende bei eschatologischer Heilsbotschaft ankommen.

Dass die Vernichtung der politischen Existenz Israels 586 nicht das Ende dieser Geschichte mit sich bringt, verdankt sich der Leistung der babylonischen Exilsgemeinde, vor allem des großen Brückenbauers über den Abgrund, den wir Deuterojesaja nennen (d. h. wir wissen nicht einmal seinen Namen). Ein doppeltes Verdienst kommt ihm zu: nach der scheinbaren Auslöschung des Jahvebundes verkündet er reines Heil, Heimkehr der Verbannten und kosmisch-übernationale Zukunft des Heilsbundes, der nicht wieder „hinfallen" wird, mit dem der Prophet die Lethargie der ins geschichtliche Abseits gedrängten Exilsgemeinde durchbricht.

Zweitens aber schafft er schließlich sogar den „Idealtypus" der künftigen Geschichtsexistenz des Judentums in der Gestalt des stellvertretend leidenden „Knechtes Jahwes" (Jesaja 53). „Diese enthusiastische Verklärung des Leidens als des Mittels, der Welt zum Heil zu dienen, ist dem Propheten offenbar die letzte und in ihrer Art höchste Steigerung der Verheißung an Abraham, dass sein Name dereinst ein ‚Segenswort für alle Völker' werden soll" (S. 392). Der Sinn des ganzen Alten Testaments ist nach Weber die Verklärung der Pariavolkslage und des geduldigen Ausharrens in ihr. Von da ab gilt: die soziale, rituelle und personale Isolierung der Juden, dieses „Ghetto im innerlichsten Sinne des Wortes", ist nicht zu verstehen als ein lediglich erlittenes Joch, sondern „war primär durchaus selbstgewählt und selbstgewollt, und zwar in stetig wachsendem Maße" (S. 435).

Es war Max Weber nicht mehr vergönnt, diese Linien auszuziehen über das antike Judentum hinaus ins mittelalterliche und neuzeitliche. Fesselnd erschiene mir u. a. eine Darstellung des auf Emanzipation und Assimilation gerichteten jüdischen Liberalismus des 19. Jahrhunderst, der so grauenvoll in den Abgrund des Holocaust gerissen wurde. Die Provokationen, die für die christliche Theologie in Webers These stecken, liegen auf der Hand und fokussieren sich in der Interpretation von Deuterojesaja, vor allem von Jesaja 53, einem Text, der für die Christologie von fundamentaler Wichtigkeit ist. Aber dem nachzugehen, wäre ein anderes Thema.

III. Sozialgeschichte und Sozialismus

Bei Lichte gesehen hat es sozialgeschichtliche Forschung am Alten Testament immer gegeben, jedenfalls solange es eine alttestamentliche Wissenschaft gibt. Hermann Gunkels Grundfrage nach dem „Sitz im Leben" der jeweils analysierten Texteinheit bzw. nach ihrer ätiologischen Absicht wäre ohne sozialgeschichtliche Kategorien gar nicht denkbar und verständlich. Natürlich musste man fragen, auf welche Verhältnisse sich die Gesetzesüberlieferungen Israels bezogen, wer Über wen etwa in der Sippe zu bestimmen hatte, warum die Urteile über das entstehende Königtum so weit auseinandergehen oder welche sozialen Misstände die vorexilische Prophetie mit ihrer vernichtenden Kritik überzieht.

Weber, der Erzvater der Religionssoziologie, begnügte sich nicht mit der Aufhellung von Strukturen durch Einzelbeobachtungen, sondern griff gleich nach den Sternen. Seine Arbeit galt der Antwort auf zwei grundsätzliche Fragen: 1.) Wie ist die einzigartige Rolle Israels (er sagte: des Judentums) in der Weltgeschichte zustande gekommen und wie ist sie zu deuten? 2.) Was sagt diese Geschichte aus über die Gesetzmäßigkeit religionsgeschichtlicher Prozesse überhaupt? Auf die erste Frage antwortet er mit seiner These von Israel als „Paria-Volk" und dessen Vorgeschichte. Die zweite Frage ordnet er ein in sein Konzept von der Rationalisierung und „Weltentzauberung" im Okzident, die er bereits bei seiner berühmten Analyse der protestantischen Ethik bewährt hatte. Beides sind religionssozialogische Themen erster Ordnung (man denke nur an die Säkularisierungsdebatte), aber ebenso theologische Herausforderungen. Dass die Theologie sie so zögernd aufgreift oder ganz vernachlässigt, ist wahrlich Anlass zur Verwunderung.

Nun gibt es unter dem Einfluss der immer wichtiger gewordenen Soziologie und als deren Fernwirkung in der alttestamentlichen Forschung eine wachsende Zahl von sozialgeschichtlichen Studien ganz unterschiedlicher Tendenz. In den Vordergrund gedrängt hat sich dabei eine Betrachtungsweise, die versucht, „die Intentionen der Bibel auf methodisch unanfechtbare Weise im Handlungszusammenhang der Gegenwart zur Geltung zu bringen“ (W. Schottroff, S. 2). Mit Nachdruck wird der Anspruch der historisch-kritischen Methode auf das Interpretationsmonopol in Zweifel gezogen, weil dieser Methode die Tendenz zur Spiritualisierung der Texte zu „freischwebenden Sprach- und Gedankengebilden“ innewohne. Stattdessen wird der „garstige breite Graben“ zwischen damals und heute übersprungen in der Preisgabe der distanzierten Beobachterhaltung, in der Analyse der eigenen sozialen Lage und in der Aufdeckung von Herrschafts-, Unterdrückungs- und Ausbeutungs-verhältnissen damals wie heute.

Solche Bibelinterpretation qualifiziert sich selbst als Teil einer „Theologie der Befreiung”. Ich nenne aus der deutschen Debatte die Namen von Frank Crüsemann, Wolfgang Stegemann, vor allem aber von Willy Schottroff, dessen Arbeiten seit neuestem in dem posthum erschienenen Sammelband „Gerechtigkeit lernen“ (Gütersloh 1999) übersichtlich vorliegen.

Die knapp skizzierte Betrachtungsweise dieser Forschungsrichtung hat ohne Frage den Blick geöffnet für zahlreiche sozialgeschichtliche Erkenntnisse, die unser Verständnis der Texte bereichern, etwa was das israelitische Bodenrecht angeht, oder die Stellung der Witwen und Alten in der israelitischen Gesellschaft. Doch „deine Sprache verrät dich“, um mit der hohenpriesterlichen Sklavin zu sprechen (Matth. 26, 73). Der Sprung über den geschichtlichen Graben gelingt nur auf den Schwingen des Sozialismus Frankfurter Prägung. Wenn diese Schwingen erlahmen, kehren die alten Probleme zurück, etwa was die Übertragbarkeit der Fragen und Antworten eines antiken Volkes, bei dem überdies religiöse Bundesgemeinde („Eidgenossenschaft“ sagt M. Weber) und Volkszugehörigkeit sich decken, auf die Gegenwart mit ihren völlig veränderten religiösen, politischen und wirtschaftlichen Zuständen angeht, die zudem zu einem guten Teil Wirkungen jener biblischen Entscheidungen sind. Es wäre nicht das erste Mal, dass ein von außen kommender Reiz die Theologie zu Schritten stimuliert, die dann nur solange plausibel erscheinen, wie der Reiz andauert, um dann wieder zu verblühen. Freilich kann es sein, dass dabei gewonnene Einsichten auch ohne den ideologischen Zusammenhang überdauern.

Beobachtungen zur Entwicklung des Korpus lexikalischer Texte in Assur

Frauke Weiershäuser, Göttingen

Bereits unter den ersten keilschriftlichen Texten, die in der zweiten Hälfte des vierten Jahrtausends in Mesopotamien niedergeschrieben wurden, finden sich verschiedene Wort- und Gegenstandslisten. Im Verlauf des zweiten Jahrtausends entwickelte sich ein umfangreiches Korpus verschiedener lexikalischer Texte, deren Inhalt von einfachen Silben- und Zeichenlisten für den Schulunterricht bis zu komplexen thematischen oder etymologischen Listen reichte.

In der zweiten Hälfte des zweiten Jahrtausends finden sich lexikalische Texte im gesamten Verbreitungsgebiet der Keilschrift, nicht nur im mesopotamischen Kernland Assyrien und Babylonien, sondern an vielen Orten, an denen Keilschrifttexte in größerem Umfang zu Tage traten, darunter in Ḫattuša, Alalaḫ, Ugarit, Emar und Tell el-Amarna. Es fragt sich nun, auf welchen Wegen diese Texte verbreitet, den jeweiligen lokalen Bedürfnissen angepasst und erweitert wurden, bis sie im Laufe der ersten Hälfte des ersten Jahrtausends v.Chr. in einer standardisierten Fassung[1] in ganz Mesopotamien vereinheitlicht worden waren. Welche Unterschiede lassen sich nun zwischen den Überlieferungen einzelner lexikalischer Serien im Kernland und in der Peripherie in der mittelassyrischen Zeit beobachten? Wann, wo und unter welchem Einfluss wurden die standardisieren Fassungen erarbeitet, wie sie uns aus dem ersten Jahrtausend bekannt sind?

In diesem Artikel soll insbesondere der Frage nachgegangen werden, welche Stellung die Schreiber in Assur bei diesem Prozess einnahmen und welche Veränderungen sich in Assur selber zu Beginn der neuassyrischen Zeit beobachten lassen.

---

1 Zur Frage der Kanonisierung bzw Standardisierung siehe M. Civil, MSL 14, S. 168–169; F. Rochberg-Halton, Canonicity in Cuneiform Texts. JCS 36 (1984), S. 127–144; N. Veldhuis, Continuity and change in the Mesopotamian lexical tradition. In: B. Roest, H. Vanstiphout (Hg.): *Aspects of Genre and Type in Pre-Modern Literary Cultures. COMES Communications 1* (Groningen 1999) S. 112.

Herkunft und Datierung der Texte

Die lexikalischen Texte aus Assur datieren in die Zeit zwischen dem 13. und dem 7. Jahrhundert v.Chr. Bisher sind keine altbabylonischen oder altassyrischen Textvertreter bekannt. Doch das Korpus lexikalischer Texte aus Assur zeigt sich seit dem Beginn der uns erhaltenen Überlieferung voll entwickelt und es ist davon auszugehen, dass derartige Texte auch vor der mittelassyrischen Zeit in Assur verwendet wurden.

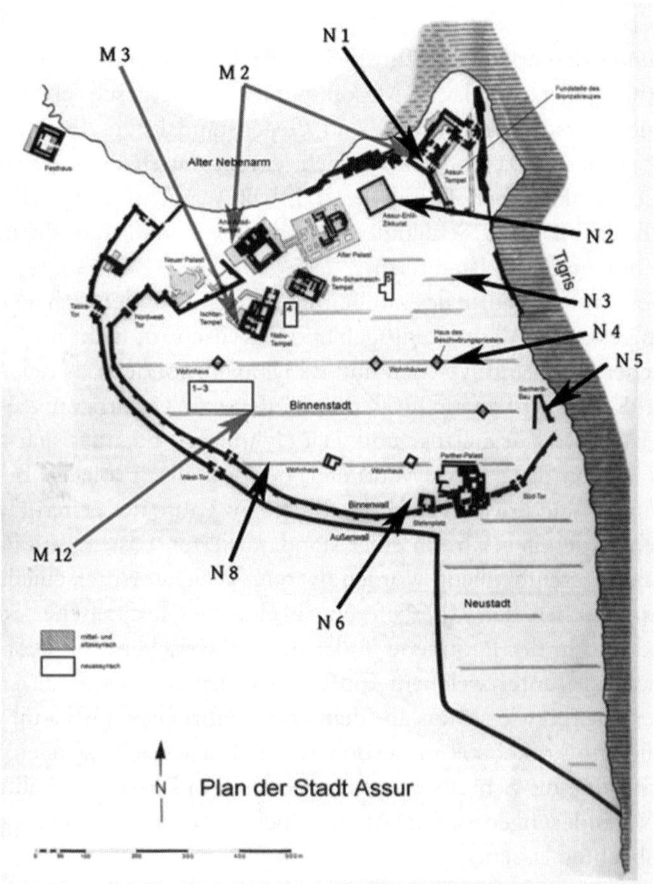

Abb. 1: Fundorte lexikalischer Texte in Assur
(aus Marzahn/Salje (Hg.): Wiedererstehendes Assur.
100 Jahre Deutsche Ausgrabungen in Assyrien,
Mainz 2003, Nachsatz.)

Bisher sind über 400 Texte und Fragmente lexikalischen Inhalts aus Assur bekannt, welche zu 18 verschiedenen Serien gehören. Die Tafeln stammen von unterschiedlichen Fundorten, die über das Stadtgebiet verteilt sind. Es fanden sich lexikalische Texte im Kontext offizieller Gebäude wie dem Anu-Adad-Tempel und dem Assur-Tempel e-benso wie in privaten Gebäuden. Pe-dersén hat in „Archives and Libraries in the City of Assur" die einzel-nen Tafeln nach ihren Fundkontexten zusammenge-stellt. Alle Fundorte, die Pedersén mit einer M-Nummer versah, stammen aus mittelassyrischer Zeit, Objekte aus Fundorten mit einer N-Nummer sind überwiegend neuassyrisch. In den Fundkomplexen N1/M2 fanden sich in einem spät-neuassyrisch erscheinenden archäologischen Kontext Tafeln sowohl aus mittelassyrische wie aus neuassyrischer Zeit (Abb. 1).[2]

Leider können nur ca. 25% aller lexikalischen Texte aus Assur präzise einem Fundort zugeordnet werden. Für alle anderen Tafeln ist der genaue Fundkontext nicht mehr zu rekonstruieren.

Die Datierung der lexikalischen Texte stellt eine gewisse Schwierigkeit dar, da der überwiegende Teil dieser Tafeln kein Datum trägt. Wenn die einzelnen Tafeln nicht aus einem gesicherten Fundkontext stammen, muss die Datierung auf inhaltlichen und paläographischen Kriterien beruhen, doch ist dabei nur auf einige wenige Zeichen zurückzugreifen, welche häufig genug vorkommen, um Vergleiche zuzulassen, und die deutliche Unterschiede zwischen ihrer mittelassyrischen und der neuassyrischen Zeichenform aufweisen[3]. Allein paläographische Unterschiede reichen

---

2 O. Pedersén, *Archives and Libraries in the City of Assur I, A Survey of the Material from the German Excavations.* (*Acta Univ. Upsaliensis, SSU 6*, Upsala 1985) S. 31.

3 Vgl. die Gegenüberstellung der Zeichenformen unter Tiglat-Pileser I. und jener unter Assurbanipal bei E. Weidner, Die Bibliothek Tiglatpilesers I, AfO 16 (1952–53), S. 201. Allerdings ist die Zuweisung der von Weidner zusammengestellten Texte zu einer „Bibliothek" des Tiglat-Pileser I. heute nicht mehr haltbar. Es ist davon auszugehen, dass die von Weidner zusammengestellten Texte zu verschiedenen Tafelsammlungen gehörten, die im Bereich des Assur-Tempels wie des Anu-Adad-Tempels aufbewahrt wurden. Die hier besprochenen lexikalischen Texte sind um etwa 50 Jahre früher zu datieren als die Akzession Tiglat-Pilesers I. Siehe H. Freydank, *Beiträge zur mittelassyrischen Chronologie und Geschichte.* (*SGKAO 21*, Berlin 1991) S. 75–78 und 94–96.

Vgl. auch die Zeichenlisten der in den letzten Jahren publizierten mittelassyrischen Textkorpora: S. Maul, *Die Inschriften von Tall Bderi. (BBVOT 2,* Berlin 1992) S. 56–62; E. Cancik-Kirschbaum, *Die mittelassyrischen Briefe aus Tall Šēḫ Ḥamad, Dūr-Katlimmu. Berichte der Ausgrabung Tall Šēḫ Ḥamad/Dūr-Katlimmu 4 (Texte 1)* (Berlin 1996) S. 73–87 und K. Radner, *Das mittelassyrische Tontafelarchiv von Giricano/Dunnu-ša-Uzibi. (Subartu XIV,* Brepols, Turnhout 2004) S. 55–61.

jedoch nicht aus, einen Text sicher zu datieren. Einige wenige Texte können über ein Kolophon datiert werden.

Dies ist der Fall bei Texten aus dem Fundkomplex N2, dem Archiv und der Bibliothek einer Schreiberfamilie. Der Name des Schreibers Šumma-balāṭ aus der zweiten in dem Archiv überlieferten Generation, findet sich auf mehreren lexikalischen Texten[4]. Andere Texte aus dem Archiv dieser Familie datieren in die Jahre 687 und 683 v.Chr. Somit ist die Datierung der Texte aus dem Fundkomplex N2 in die späte neuassyrische Zeit gesichert.

Eine Gruppe von Tafeln aus dem Fundkomplex N1/M2 ist über Kolophone teilweise zu datieren. Der Text VAT 10466 (Silbenvokabular A) trägt den Namen des Eponymen Bēlu-libūr, eines Beamten aus der Regierungszeit des Tiglat-Pileser I[5].

Ein weiterer Text aus dem Fundkomplex M2, VAT 9487 (Diri = *watru* Tafel 3), nennt den Eponymen Samnuha-ašarēd, der wohl in die Zeit des Aššur-dān I gehört.[6] Der Kolophon erwähnt neben dem Eponymen auch den Prüfer Bēl-aḫa-iddina. Dieser ist wahrscheinlich identisch mit einem Prüfer dieses Namens der im Kolophon zweier Texte des Marduk-balāssu-ēreš auftritt[7]. Aus dem Fundkomplex M2/N1 stammen die Tafeln der drei Brüder Marduk-balāssu-ēreš, Bēl-aḫa-iddina und Sīn-šuma-iddina[8], Söhne des Ninūrta-uballiṭ-su, Schreibers des Königs, von denen Marduk-balāssu-ēreš und Bēl-aḫa-iddina gegenseitig ihre Tafeln überprüften.[9] Die Tafeln dieser Schreiberfamilie sind über mehrere Kolophone mit

4 VAT 10262+12973+12956 (Erim-ḫuš = *anantu* Tafel 6), VAT 10270 (igi-du$_8$–a = *tāmartu*), VAT 9000 Uruanna Tafel 2 und VAT 10143+12966 an = *šamû*).

5 H. Freydank, *Beiträge zur mittelassyrischen Chronologie und Geschichte,* S. 125. C. Saporetti, *Gli Eponimi medio-assiri, (BiMes 9,* Malibu 1979) S. 153 und 160.

6 H. Freydank, *Beiträge zur mittelassyrischen Chronologie und Geschichte*, S. 76f Anm. 205. C. Saporetti, *Gli Eponimi medio-assiri*, S. 69.

7 VAT 9716 (Sig$_7$–alan = *nabnītu* Tafel IV), MSL 16, S. 73, 76–92 Textzeuge B und VAT 10383 (ká-gal = *abullu* Tafel B), MSL 13, S. 234, 236–237 Textzeuge C.

8 VAT 10172 (e-a = *nâqu* Tafel 1), MSL 14, S. 173, 176–195 Textzeuge C. Für alle drei Brüder werden hier nur die Texte lexikalischen Inhalts zitiert. Zu anderen Texten der Brüder siehe die Belegstellen unter den jeweiligen Personennamen bei C. Saporetti, *Onomastica Medio-Assira. (Studia Pohl 6,* Rom 1970).

9 VAT 9552 (*ana ittišu* Tafel III), MSL 1, S. 32–50 Textzeuge B und VAT 9592 (ká-gal = *abullu* Tafel A), MSL 13, S. 231–233 Textzeuge A. Zur wechselseitigen Kontrolle der Texte durch die Brüder siehe H. Freydank, *Beiträge zur mittelassyrischen Chronologie und Geschichte*, S. 95 Anm. 245.

Angabe eines Eponymen zu datieren, wobei die Namen Aššur-išmanni, Sohn des Abī-ilī, Aššur-aḫa-iddina und Ikkaru auftreten.[10] Diese Eponymen sind von Saporetti in die Zeit Tiglat-Pilesers I. gestellt worden.[11] Wie Freydank gezeigt hat, ist die Wirkungszeit der drei Brüder jedoch in die Zeit des Ninurta-apil-Ekur und wohl auch in die frühen Jahre von Aššur-dān I. einzuordnen.[12]

Die Tafel VAT 10457 (Ur_5-ra = *ḫubullu* Tafel 7A) ist ebenfalls in der mittelassyrischen Zeichenform geschrieben, der im Kolophon erwähnte Eponym Še'i-Aššur hatte dieses Amt im Jahr 909 inne.[13]

Aus dem Gesagten folgt, dass Texte mit mittelassyrischer Zeichenform im lexikalischen Korpus aus Assur in die Zeit zwischen 1200 und 900 v.Chr. zu datieren sind. In einigen wenigen Fällen kann die Datierung über einen Eponymen im Kolophon näher eingegrenzt werden. Wie im folgenden zu zeigen sein wird, ist es neben einer ersten zeitlichen Eingrenzung über die Paläographie und einer genauen Datierung über die Nennung eines Eponymen mitunter möglich, eine nähere zeitliche Einordnung aufgrund der Reihenfolge der einzelnen Einträge im Vergleich zur Abfolge der Zeilen in der standardisierten Fassung des ersten Jahrtausends vorzunehmen.

Standardisierung der lexikalischen Listen im 1. Jahrtausend

In altbabylonischer Zeit waren die verschiedenen lexikalischen Serien noch nicht so strikt standardisiert wie im ersten Jahrtausend. So sind aus Nippur verschiedene Textzeugen der Serie Ur_5-ra = *ḫubullu* bekannt, die sich alle in kleineren Details unterscheiden.[14] Im ersten Jahrtausend hatten die Schreiber einen Kanon der verschiedenen umfangreichen lexikalischen Listen entwickelt, der in Assyrien wie in Babylonien in nahezu gleicher Form in Gebrauch war. Mit der Herausbildung von standardisierten Fassungen einzelner Listen hatte sich auch die Funktion dieser Textgattung verändert, lexikalische Texte wurden nun nicht mehr primär als Übung für

10 Vgl. H. Hunger, *Babylonische und assyrische Kolophone. (AOAT 2,* Neukirchen-Vluyn 1968) Nr. 43. Neben lexikalischen haben auch literarische Texte ein derartiges Kolophon.

11 C. Saporetti, *Gli Eponimi medio-assiri*, S. 151–154.

12 H. Freydank, *Beiträge zur mittelassyrischen Chronologie und Geschichte*, S. 76–77 mit Anm. 205.

13 VAT 9487 (diri = *watru* Tafel III), MSL 15, S. 136, Textzeuge B. Der genaue Fundkontext dieser Tafel kann nicht mehr rekonstruiert werden.

14 N. Veldhuis, Continuity and Change in the Mesopotamian Lexical Tradition, S. 108–109.

Schüler angesehen, sondern galten selber als Teil des literarischen Erbes, das zu bewahren war.[15]

Kleinere Abweichungen der einzelnen Textzeugen untereinander kamen auch in dieser Zeit noch vor. Als ein Beispiel mögen hier die letzten 27 Zeilen (Z. 382-409) der 14. Tafel von Ur₅-ra = *ḫubullu* dienen. Jeweils zwei Textzeugen aus Babylon und aus Assur sind für diesen Abschnitt erhalten.[16] Die Datierung der Tafeln aus Babylon basiert auf der Fundsituation, jene der Texte aus Assur auf paläographischen Kriterien, da ihr genauer Fundort nicht mehr rekonstruiert werden kann.

Assur:	A: LTBA I, 40 (VAT 11517, babylonische Schrift)
	B: LTBA I, 44 (Const. 175f)
Babylon:	K: LTBA I, 49 (nur die letzten 14 Zeilen erhalten)
	L: LTBA I, 37[17]

Textzeuge A[18]

382	⌜a⌝-za-lu-lu	*nam-maš-ti*	Getier
383	MIN	*zer-man-du*	Kleingetier
384	MIN	*ni-du lìb-bi*	Fötus?
385	MIN	*bu-ul da-šú-uš*	sechsarmig? Bez. für Getier
386	MIN	*te-ni-še-e-ti*	Menschheit
387	ú	*ú-ma-mu*	Tiere
388	⌜ú⌝-kú	MIN	ditto
389	⌜ú⌝-ma-mu	MIN	ditto
390	⌜máš⌝-anše	*bu-ú-lu*	Vieh
391	⌜máš⌝-udu	MIN	ditto
392	[níg]-⌜úr⌝-límmu-ba	MIN	ditto

15 ebd. S. 112–113. Auch im ersten Jahrtausend wurden lexikalische Texte im Schulunterricht genutzt, wie die große Zahl von Schultexten mit Exzerpten verschiedener Listen zeigt. Vgl. P. Gesche, *Schulunterricht in Babylonien im ersten Jahrtausend v.Chr. (AOAT 275*, Münster 2000), sowie die Schultexte aus Assur VAT 8573, VAT 10071 und VAT 10756. Letztere sind kopiert bei W. G. Lambert, Babylonian Wisdom Literature (Oxford 1960) Pl. 73.

16 Die Texte wurden in MSL 8/2 unter den Sigeln A, B, K und L bearbeitet, der fragliche Abschnitt findet sich auf den Seiten 41–43.

17 Zu LTBA I, 49 siehe O. Pedersén, *Archive und Bibliotheken in Babylon. Die Tontafeln der Grabung Robert Koldeweys 1899–1917. (ADOG 25,* Berlin 2005), N22:4. Die Tafel stammt aus dem Bereich des Etemenanki. Zu LTBA I, 37 siehe O. Pedersén, ebd., N3:18. Die Schülertafel stammt aus dem Eingangsbereich der Südburg.

18 Die Zeilenzählung folgt hier wie in den anderen Beispielen der Zählung von MSL.

393	[níg]-⌜úr⌝-límmu-⌜ba⌝	*bu-lim* ^{d}GÌR	Getier des Šakkan
394/5	MIN : ⌜*nam-maš-šú-u*⌝	MIN-edin-na : MIN *ṣe-ri*	Wildtierherden der Steppe
396	MIN MIN	MIN ^{d}GÌR	ditto des Šakkan

397	níg-zi-gál	*nam-maš-šú-ú*	Getier
398	níg-zi-gál	*[a-šu-ú]*	Lebewesen
399	níg-zi-gál	*[šik-na-at na-piš-te]*	Lebewesen
400	níg-MIN	*[nam-maš-ti]*	Getier
401	níg-šu-úr	⌜MIN⌝	ditto
402	níg^{ni-qi}-ki	⌜*zir-man*⌝*-du*	Kleingetier
403	níg-ki-gar	*zir-man-du qaq-qar*	Kleintier des Erdbodens
404	níg-gír-ùz	*nam-maš-ti*	Getier
405	⌜anše⌝-ùz	MIN	ditto
406	mir-ùz	MIN	ditto
407	mir-⌜ḫul⌝	*ḫul-miṭ-ṭu*$_{4}$	Drache
408	mir-⌜ḫul⌝	*ḫul-ma-ḫu*	eine Schlange
409	[x] $^{⌜bu-lu⌝-ug}$da	*ṣe-e-ri*	Schlange

Fangzeile zu Tafel 15

Die Abfolge der einzelnen Zeilen ist bei allen Textvertretern weitgehend identisch, doch zeigen sich folgende kleinere Differenzen:

— Die Zeile 384 ist nur bei Textzeuge A vorhanden.
— Die Zeilen 394/5 sind bei den Paralleltexten nicht in einer Zeile zusammengefasst.
— Textzeuge B und L haben zusätzlich eine Zeile 401a (níg-ki = MIN) eingefügt.
— Auf der Schülertafel L ist zusätzlich eine Zeile 386a (a-za-lu-lu = *šik-na-at na-pi[š-ti])* eingefügt.

Neben diesen Unterschieden, die Einträge ganzer Zeilen betreffen, ergeben sich zwischen den einzelnen Textvertretern Differenzen bezüglich der genauen Schreibung einzelner Einträge[19].

In der Standardedition der lexikalischen Listen Mesopotamiens, der Serie „Materialien zum Sumerischen Lexikon“ (MSL), werden in der Regel

19 Siehe hierzu die Anmerkungen zu den einzelnen Zeilen in MSL 8/2, S. 41–43.

Textzeugen aus dem zweiten und dem ersten Jahrtausend aus verschiedenen Fundorten verwendet, um eine Standardversion der verschiedenen Listen zu rekonstruieren, M. Civil war der Überzeugung, die standardisierten Fassungen seien, basierend auf den altbabylonischen Vorläufern aus den großen Zentren Babyloniens, insbesondere Nippur, eventuell auch Babylon, in der kassitischen Zeit kompiliert wurden.[20] Aus Babylonien sind kaum Textzeugen aus dem späten zweiten und dem frühen ersten Jahrtausend erhalten, sodass die Annahme von M. Civil für Babylonien derzeit noch nicht näher verifiziert werden kann. Allerdings zeigt sich bei genauerer Betrachtung, dass die mittelassyrischen Textzeugen aus Assur noch nicht in das Schema der standardisierten Rezensionen passen. Immer wieder finden sich in mittelassyrischen Textvertretern Zeilen, die in späteren Rezensionen nicht mehr aufgenommen worden sind. Auch die Reihenfolge der einzelnen Einträge kann in dieser Zeit noch deutlich von jenen der späteren Zeit abweichen. Mitunter sind mittelassyrische Rezensionen jedoch auch über längere Passagen vollkommen parallel zu der späteren standardisierten Fassung.

Es stellt sich nun die Frage wann, wo und unter welchem Einfluss die standardisierten Fassungen der einzelnen lexikalischen Serien, wie sie von der neuassyrischen Zeit an in Gebrauch waren, kompiliert wurden. Das entsprechende Material aus Babylonien fehlt derzeit noch weitgehend. Dagegen sind eine Reihe von Textzeugen aus dem Norden, insbesondere aus Assur, aber auch aus Nuzi, sowie aus dem Westen, aus Alalaḫ, Ḫattuša, Ugarit und Emar bekannt.[21] Vergleiche von Textvertretern aus diesen Orten mit den entsprechenden Passagen aus altbabylonischer Zeit einerseits und mit der standardisierten Fassung des ersten Jahrtausends andererseits können Hinweise darauf liefern, wo und unter welchem Ein-

20 M. Civil, Lexicography. In: S. J. Lieberman (Hg.): *Sumerological Studies in Honor of Thorkild Jacobsen on his seventieth Birthday June 7, 1974*, (*AS 20,* Chicago 1976), S. 128.

21 M. Civil, Lexicography, S. 128–129. Für neuere Editionen siehe u.a. zu den Texten aus Emar D. Arnaud, *Recherches au pays d'Aštata. Emar VI/1–4* (Paris 1985–87), zu Texten aus Ugarit B. André-Salvini, Les Textes Lexicographiques. In: P. Bordreuil (Hg.): *Une bibliothèque au sud de la ville. Les textes de la 34e campagne (1973). (Ras Shamra-Ougarit VII*, Paris 1991) S. 105–126. Der überwiegende Teil der lexikalischen Texte aus Ugarit ist bislang noch unpubliziert. Zum Textbestand des lexikalischen Korpus aus Ugarit siehe W. van Soldt, Babylonian Lexical, Religious and Literary Texts and Scribal Education at Ugarit and its implication for the alphabetic literary texts. In: Manfred Dietrich, Oswald Loretz (Hg.): *Ugarit. Ein ostmediterranes Kulturzentrum im alten Orient. Ergebnisse und Perspektiven der Forschung. Band I: Ugarit und seine altorientalische Umwelt. (ALASP 7*, Münster 1995), S. 171–176.

fluss die verschiedenen Rezensionen einzelner lexikalischer Serien kompiliert worden sind. Ein Vergleich der Texte aus Assur mit jenen aus Emar ist dabei von besonderem Interesse, da beide Städte in direktem Kontakt zueinander standen, wohingegen direkte Kontakte zu Ugarit eher selten bezeugt sind.[22] Ob Schreiber aus der Stadt Assur selber in Emar gearbeitet haben, ist derzeit nicht festzustellen, jedoch ist der Fall des assyrischen Schreibers Kidin-Gula bekannt, der, wohl aus der Region am mittleren Euphrat oder aus dem Norden Babyloniens stammend, in Emar als Lehrer gewirkt und dort auch lexikalische Listen im Unterricht verwendet hat.[23] Die Tätigkeit assyrischer Schreiber außerhalb des Kerngebietes von Assyrien ist auch für Ugarit nachgewiesen.[24] Somit sind Kontakte der verschiedenen lokalen Schreiberschulen und -traditionen des mesopotamischen Kernlandes mit Gebieten im Westen nicht nur mittels Textvergleichen zu erschließen, sondern in einigen Fällen sogar für bestimmte Persönlichkeiten konkret zu belegen.

Vergleicht man nun die verschiedenen Rezensionen einzelner lexikalischer Texte des zweiten Jahrtausends untereinander sowie mit der Standardrezension des ersten Jahrtausends, lassen sich sowohl Parallelen als auch deutliche Unterschiede erkennen. Hier stellt sich die Frage, auf welchen Wegen diese Texte weitergegeben wurden und wann und wo welche Veränderungen vorgenommen worden sind. Weiter ist zu fragen, welche Position die Schreiber der Stadt Assur bei diesem Prozess des Kulturtransfers einnahmen. Es wäre sowohl möglich anzunehmen, Assur habe als Vermittler des Wissens Babyloniens an die Zentren des Westens gewirkt, wie es auch denkbar wäre, dass Assur seinerseits Impulse aus dem Westen erhalten und aufgenommen hätte, die später Eingang gefunden haben in die Standardrezension des ersten Jahrtausends.

Im Rahmen dieses Beitrags ist eine umfassende Behandlung dieser Frage nicht möglich, es soll aber anhand von zwei Beispielen im folgenden aufgezeigt werden, wie sich die verschiedenen Rezensionen im einzelnen unterscheiden und wo Parallelen bestehen.

---

22 B. Faist, *Der Fernhandel des assyrischen Reiches zwischen dem 14. und 11. Jh. v. Chr.* (*AOAT 265*, Münster 2001) S. 216.

23 Y. Cohen, Kidin-Gula – The foreign teacher at the Emar scribal school. RA 98 (2004) S. 89–92, 94.

24 W. van Soldt, Naḫiš-Šalmu: an Assyrian scribe working in the Southern Palace at Ugarit. In: W. van Soldt et al. (Hg.): *Veenhof Anniversary Volume. Studies presented to Klaas R. Veenhof oh the Occasion of his sixty-fifth Birthday* (Leiden 2001) S. 429–444.

Von altbabylonischen Vorläufern zur mittelassyrischen Rezension

Das erste Beispiel ist ein Auszug aus einer Liste von Gegenständen aus Holz, die in der Standardversion als Tafel 7A zu der Serie Ur5-ra = *ḫubullu* (Zeile 6-28) gehört. Für den zitierten Abschnitt, in dem verschiedene Waffen aufgeführt werden, sind altbabylonische Vorläufer aus Nippur und Sippar, eine mittelbabylonische Quelle aus Ur sowie mittelassyrische Textzeugen aus Assur, Emar und Ugarit erhalten. Es sind bisher keine neuassyrischen Textvertreter bekannt, weswegen in MSL die Quellen aus Ur und Assur zur Rekonstruktion der „Standardversion" herangezogen wurden. Dieses Vorgehen ist nicht unproblematisch, da die Rezensionen aus mittelassyrischer Zeit von den neuassyrischen deutlich abweichen können, wie im zweiten Beispiel zu zeigen sein wird.[25]

Der Textvertreter aus Ur ist in der folgenden Tabelle nicht mit aufgenommen, da er weitgehend parallel zu der Rezension aus Assur ist. Nur die altbabylonischen Texte sind einsprachig sumerisch, die Rezensionen aus Assur, Ugarit und Emar sind sumerisch-akkadisch, auf die vollständige Wiedergabe der akkadischen Einträge wurde hier verzichtet, um die Übersichtlichkeit zu wahren und aufgrund des schlechten Erhaltungszustands der akkadischen Einträge insbesondere des Textes aus Emar. Für den Text aus Assur ist nur die Zeilenzählung angegeben, die sumerischen Einträge sind weitgehend parallel zu anderen Textzeugen. Zu den Differenzen bezüglich der akkadischen Einträge siehe unten. Sind einzelne Zeilen in der Übersicht freigelassen, so sind diese nicht abgebrochen, sondern fehlen bei dem betreffenden Textvertreter.

Nippur:	Ni II, 127, Veldhuis, Elementary Education at Nippur, S. 162 Z. 496-502
Sippar:	Si 720, MSL 6, S. 149-150, Z. 78-83
Assur:	LTBA I, 17, MSL 6, S. 84-86 Textzeuge A
Emar:	Emar VI, 4 No. 545, S. 77 Z. 450'-461'
Ugarit:	RS 34.180,2, André-Salvini, Les Textes Lexicographiques, S. 107 No. 49 Z. 17-29

25 Ab der Zeile 17 liegt ein neubabylonischer Paralleltext vor (F. Thureau-Dangin, Notes Assyriologiques. XLIV. Fragment de vocabulaire RA 21, S. 140–141, siehe MSL 6, S 85–87, Textzeuge B), der jedoch nur bedingt parallel zu dem mittelassyrischen Text aus Assur ist, so hat dieser Text parallel zum Vertreter aus Ur die in Assur fehlenden Zeilen 18 und 20 sowie als einziger Text die Zeilen 21–22, es fehlen jedoch die in Assur vorhandenen Zeilen 28, 30 und 32–53, der Text aus Ur bricht nach Zeile 27 ab. Dieser neubabylonische Text ist in der untenstehenden Übersicht nicht aufgenommen worden.

Nippur	Sippar	Assur	Emar	Ugarit
^{giš}tukul	^{giš}tukul	6	(broken)	^{giš}tukul
^{giš}tukul-šu	^{giš}tukul-šu	14	min-[ ]	^{giš}tukul-šu
^{giš}tukul-úr-ra	^{giš}tukul-úr-ra	15	[min]-dingir-[ ]	^{giš}tukul-din[gir]-ú[r-r]a
^{giš}tukul-kun	^{giš}tukul-kun	24		
^{giš}tukul-dingir		10		
^{giš}tukul-gaz	^{giš}tukul-gaz			
	^{giš}tukul-ma-nu			
	^{giš}tukul-dingir-ra	9	[min-ding]ir-ra-vii-b[e]	^{giš}tukul-[dingir-ra]
			[x] min-lugal	^{giš}tukul-⸢lugal⸣
		16	[x]-min-^{d}Da-nu	^{giš}tukul-^{d}Da-mu
			kul-min-giš-ma-nu	$^{[giš]}$tukul-giš-⸢ma⸣-nu
			[x-min]-še	[^{giš}tuku]l-še
			[min]-min-še-giš-ì	[^{giš}tuku]l-še-ì-giš
			[min]-min-zú-lum	[^{giš}tukul]-zu-lu$_4$-⸢um⸣
		19	tukul-sag-n[a$_4$]	[^{giš}tukul]-sag-na$_4$
			tukul-giš	
				[^{giš}tukul]-sag
^{giš}sag-tukul	^{giš}sag-tukul	28		[^{giš}sag-du-tuk]ul
		29	sag-tukul-sag	

Die beiden altbabylonischen Textzeugen weisen nur geringfügige Differenzen auf. In der Assur-Rezension sind die meisten altbabylonischen Einträge übernommen worden, jedoch in veränderter Reihenfolge. Es fehlen der Eintrag ^{giš}tukul-gaz und der nur aus Sippar belegte Eintrag ^{giš}tukul-ma-nu. Gegenüber den altbabylonischen Vorläufern sind in der Assurrezension die Einträge ^{giš}tukul-^{d}Da-mu und ^{giš}tukul-sag-na$_4$ aufgenommen worden. Die Rezensionen aus Emar und Ugarit folgen in der Abfolge der Zeilen enger der altbabylonischen Vorlage, jedoch fehlen die noch in Assur enthaltenen Einträge ^{giš}tukul-kun und ^{giš}tukul-dingir. Neben den schon in Assur hinzugefügten Einträgen nehmen die Schreiber aus Emar und Ugarit noch eine Reihe neuer Begriffe in die Listen auf. Weitere Unterschiede sind bei den erhaltenen (oben nicht wiedergegebenen) akkadischen Einträgen zu beobachten:

— Zeile 19:
  Assur: *ḫu-tap-⌜pa-lu-ú⌝*
  Emar: *[ḫ]u-ut-[p]á-lu-u*
  Ugarit: *ša-gi-ia-ḫa-[ ]*
— Während die altbabylonischen Vorläufer jeweils nur einen Eintrag ^giš^sag-tukul aufführen, kennt der Assurtext zwei akkadische Gleichungen für diesen Eintrag[26]:
  Zeile 28: [ŠU]-⌜*ma*⌝ (=*sagtukullu*)
  Zeile 29: *[re-eš]* ⌜*kak*⌝-*ki*
  In Emar wurde offensichtlich der Eintrag der Zeile 29 aufgenommen – *[q]a-qa-[ad]*, wohingegen man in Ugarit die Gleichung der Zeile 28 listete – *ša-ga-du-t[u]*.

Die Textvertreter aus Assur, Emar und Ugarit sind nicht genau zu datieren. Der Assurtext stammt aus dem Fundkomplex N1/M2[27], in dem einige mittelassyrische Texte, wie oben besprochen, über ein Kolophon auf die Regierungszeit der Könige Ninūrta-apil-Ekur (1191-79) und Assur-dan I (1178-33) zu datieren sind. Die Archive von Emar enden um das Jahr 1187, im gleichen Zeitraum wie jene von Ugarit.[28]

Aufgrund dieser Datenlage ist eine Beeinflussung in beiden Richtungen denkbar, also ein Einfluss assyrischer Schreiber auf die Textkompositionen in Emar und Ugarit und umgekehrt. Für ersteres könnte sprechen, dass in den Rezensionen aus Emar und Ugarit die gegenüber den altbabylonischen Fassungen in Assur hinzugefügten Zeilen enthalten sind. Auffällig ist jedoch, dass die Texte aus Emar und Ugarit bezüglich der Zeilenabfolge den altbabylonischen Texten sehr viel näher sind. Denkbar wäre auch, dass die altbabylonischen Texte über die Route am oberen Euphrat den Weg nach Westen genommen haben, und dass im 13. und 12. Jahrhundert unter gegenseitiger Beeinflussung in den verschiednen Zentren von den Schreibern unterschiedliche Rezensionen einzelner Listen entwickelt wurden. Diese wichen teilweise noch deutlich von der späteren Standardrezension ab, wie das folgende Beispiel verdeutlichen kann.

---

26 Die Ergänzungen folgen der Edition in MSL 6.

27 O. Pedersén, *Archives and Libraries in the City of Assur II*, N1:17.

28 Zu Emar siehe M. R: Adamthwaite, *Late Hittite Emar, The Chronology, Synchronism, and Socio-Political Aspects of a Late Bronze Age Fortress Town. (ANES S 8*, Louvain 2001) S. XIX mit weiterer Literatur. Zu Ugarit siehe M. Yon, The City of Ugarit at Tell Ras Shamra. (Winona Lake, IN 2006), S. 21–25 mit weiterer Literatur.

Die Entwicklung der standardisierten Fassung von Ur$_5$-ra = ḫubullu Tafel 14

Für den folgenden Abschnitt sind neben den unten zitierten Tafeln noch weitere Textzeugen erhalten, die alle die standardisierte Fassung des ersten Jahrtausends wiedergeben.[29] Für den untenstehenden Abschnitt der 14. Tafel der Serie Ur$_5$ -ra = *ḫubullu*, in dem verschiedene Wildtiere aufgeführt werden, sind wir in der glücklichen Situation, aus Assur sowohl eine mittelassyrische Rezension wie auch mehrere Exemplare der Standardrezension erhalten zu haben womit sich Parallelen und Unterschiede des gleichen Textes aus einem Fundort studieren lassen. Etwa zeitgleich mit dem mittelassyrischen Text aus Assur[30] ist der Paralleltext aus Emar anzusetzen. Die Einträge dieser Rezension entsprechen weitgehend jenen der Tafeln aus Assur, weswegen hier für den Emartext nur die Zeilenzählung nach der Edition von Arnaud angegeben ist. Zu größeren Abweichungen siehe unten.

Einträge der mittelassyrischen Texte aus Assur und Emar, die nicht in der Standardrezension aufgenommen sind, werden im folgenden hervorgehoben.

Emar: Emar VI, 4 No. 551, S. 115 Z. 37'-54'
Assur: LTBA I, 42, MSL 8/2, S. 17-18 Textzeuge J (mittelassyrisch)
Assur: LTBA I, 40, MSL 8/2, S. 16-18 Textzeuge A (neuassyrisch)

neuassyrische Standardrezension			mittelassyrisch	Emar
120	az	*a-si*		37'
121	ug	*u$_4$-mu*		38'
				39'
122	ug-gal	MIN		
123	pirig	*lu-ú*		
124	pirig	*lab-bi*		41'
125	pirig	*né-e-šú*		40'
126	pirig-ka-du$_8$-a	*na-ad-ri*		
127	pirig-MIN	⸢*kat*⸣*-til-lu*		
128	pirig-ka-tab-ba	MIN		
129	pirig-ḫuš	MIN		

29 Dies sind nach den Sigeln von MSL 8/2 folgende Texte: B: LTBA I, 44 aus Assur; C: CT 14, 1 aus Kuyunjik; D: LTBA I, 45 aus Assur; F: LTBA I, 46 aus Assur; Schultexte S4: LTBA I, 45 aus Babylon und S7: Iraq 6, Nr. 72 aus Kiš.

30 Der genaue Fundort der Tafeln LTBA I 40 und 42 ist heute nicht mehr zu rekonstruieren.

130	pirig-šu-zi-ga	*na-ad-ri*			
131	pirig-ugu-dili	MIN			
neuassyrische Standardrezension			mittelassyrisch		Emar
132	pirig-ugu-dili	ŠU-u			
133	pirig-zag-3	*šul-⌜lu⌝-šú*			
134	pirig-$^{⌜\text{nim-ri}⌝\ (\text{radiert})}$-tur	*mi-ra-nu lab-bi*			
135	pirig-$^{\text{nim-ri}}$-tur	*⌜ni⌝-im-ri*			42‘
136	pirig-tur-bàn-da	MIN *ek-du*	(Anfang abgebrochen)		
137	ti$_8$	*a-ru-ú*	[ti$_8$]^{mušen}	*<a>-ru-ú*	
137a			[ti$_8$]-uš	ŠU	
137b			[ti$_8$]-uš	*na-ad-ru*	
137c			[ti$_8$-uš]-gu-la	MIN	
137d			[ti$_8$-uš]-gu-la	*ni-i-ru*	
138	nu-um-ma	*zi-i-bi*			
140[31]	téš-bi-kú	MIN			
141	téš-bi-kú	*a-ki-lu*			
142	[udu]-idim	*bi-⌜ib-bi⌝*			
143	⌜šeg$_9$⌝	*a-tu-du*	šinig	*du-ú-du*	43‘
144	⌜šeg$_9$⌝-bar	*sap-pa-ri*	šinig	*sa-ba-ru*	44‘
144a			a-lim	*di-ta-a-nu*	46‘
145	lu-lim	*lu-lim-mu*	lu-lim	*lu-lim-mu*	45‘
142			⌜udu-idim⌝	*bi-ib-bu*	*47‘*
144b			alim[32]	*ku-sa-ri-⌜ku⌝*	
146a			si-mul	*ia-a-⌜lu⌝*	48‘[33]
146	si-mul	*⌜a⌝-a-ri*	si-mul	*a-a-⌜lum⌝*	49‘
147	⌜dara$_3$⌝	*⌜tu-ra⌝-ḫu*	dara$_3$	*tu-⌜ra⌝-[ḫu]*	50‘
148	dara$_3$-⌜maš⌝	*a-a-lu*	dara$_3$-maš	ia-*[a-lu]*	51‘
149	dara$_3$-maš-⌜dà⌝	*⌜na⌝-a-a-lu*	dara$_3$-maš-dà	*[na-a-a-lu]*	52‘
150	⌜dara$_3$⌝-ḫal-ḫal-⌜la⌝	[MIN]	⌜dara$_3$-maš⌝-ḫal-	[MIN]	53‘

31 Die Zeile 139 (ur-idim-ma = MIN), die laut MSL 8/2, S. 17 nur auf diesem Textzeugen zu finden sei, ist nicht vorhanden. Die Kopie (LTBA I, 40) ist korrekt.

32 Das Zeichen ‚alim‘ ist hier geschrieben als A-IGI-GÌR statt GÌRx A-IGI, weswegen CAD hier alim$_x$ liest. nach R. Borger, *Mesopotamisches Zeichenlexikon* (*AOAT 305*, Münster 2003) Nr. 703 sind beide Schreibweisen jedoch als Variante eines Zeichens anzusehen.

33 Die Zeilen 48‘ und 49‘ der Emar-Rezension sind stark zerstört, nur der Beginn der sumerischen Einträge ist erhalten. D. Arnaud gibt in seiner Bearbeitung die Transliteration „ur[“ für beide Zeilen an, doch nach dem Paralleltext aus Assur ist eventuelle eher „si[“ zu lesen.

		ḫal-⌜la⌝	
151	⌜maš⌝	*[ṣa]-⌜bi⌝-[tu]*	54‘

Deutlich ist zu erkennen, dass nur ein geringer Teil der Zeilen 120–140 schon in der Emar-Rezension enthalten war. Nur in dem mittelassyrischen Text aus Assur sind die Zeilen 137a–d zu finden, wohingegen die Zeilen 144a und b sowie 146a auch in Emar bekannt waren. Zu der Zeile 144a ist anzumerken, dass sie auch in allen anderen Textzeugen, also sowohl in Assur wie auch in Ninive und Babylon, in der Standardrezension aufgenommen wurde, nur der hier zitierte Textzeuge A aus Assur lässt diese Zeile aus.

Die Zeilen 138–141 der Standardrezension sind offensichtlich erst spät in diese Liste aufgenommen worden, da sie weder in Emar noch in der mittelassyrischen Rezension aus Assur enthalten sind. Und Zeile 142 ist zwar in allen drei oben zitierten Versionen enthalten, wurde jedoch im ersten Jahrtausend weiter vorne in der Liste platziert als in mittelassyrischer Zeit.

Auffällig ist der Eintrag der Zeile 39‘ aus Emar: pirig-<gal> = *pi-ri-gál-lu-u*. Dieser Text aus Emar ist der einzige bisher bekannte Beleg für den Eintrag *piriggallu* in einer lexikalischen Liste. Neben dem Eintrag aus Emar ist dieses Wort bisher nur in Inschriften der neuassyrischen Könige Sargon und Sanherib bezeugt.[34]

Weitere Auffälligkeiten:

— Die Zeilen 124/125 und 144a/145 sind in Emar gegenüber den Texten aus Assur jeweils in umgekehrter Reihenfolge angeordnet.

— Zeile 143: Der mittelassyrische Schreiber aus Assur schreibt als einziger irrtümlich *du-ú-du* für *atūdu*. Der sumerische Eintrag in Emar lautet si SÌ.

— Zeile 144: Die Mehrzahl der Texte schreibt šeg$_9$-bar = *sap-pa-ri*. Der Schultext aus Babylon (S$_4$) hat dagegen den sumerischen Eintrag zà-bar, und der Schreiber aus Emar notierte sa-bar = *sa-pá-ru*. Hier wurde offensichtlich sa-bar = *saparru* „Netz“ mit šeg$_9$-bar = *sappāru* „Wildbock“ verwechselt[35].

— Zeile 144a: Alle Texte aus dem mesopotamischen Kernland haben

34 Siehe CAD P, S. 395b.

35 Siehe zu den beiden Lemmata CAD S 161 und 166a.

den akkadischen Eintrag *ditānu*, wohingegen in Emar *li-šá-nu* geschrieben ist.

Es zeigt sich, dass die beiden mittelassyrischen Texte aus Assur und Emar starke Ähnlichkeiten untereinander und noch deutlich Unterschiede zu der Rezension des ersten Jahrtausends aufweisen. Die verschiedenen Textzeugen für die spätere, standardisierte Fassung differieren dagegen nur in kleinen Details voneinander.

Zusammenfassung

Auf der Grundlage von nur wenigen kurzen Ausschnitten einzelner Tafeln nur einer lexikalischen Serie (Ur$_5$-ra = *ḫubullu*) sind Aussagen über die Wege gegenseitiger Beeinflussung und des Austauschs von Traditionen und Ideen kaum möglich. Es ist vorstellbar, dass die Schreiber der Stadt Assur eine Vermittlerfunktion bei der Weitergabe der lexikalischen Traditionen Babyloniens zwischen dem mesopotamischen Kernland und den Zentren im Westen eingenommen haben. Die Anfänge der Listentradition in Assur sind derzeit noch nicht bekannt, in mittelassyrischer Zeit findet sich ein vollständig entwickeltes Korpus unterschiedlichster lexikalischer Texte in Assur, das noch deutlich von der Standardrezension des ersten Jahrtausends abweichen kann. Im Vergleich der mittelassyrischen Texte zu jenen aus Ugarit und Emar zeigen sich Parallelen aber auch Unterschiede, sodass derzeit noch nicht zu sagen ist, in welche Richtung der Austausch an Wissen in dieser Zeit im vorderen Orient erfolgte. Angesichts der Tatsache, dass Schreiber aus Assyrien und Babylonien in den Städten im Westen als Lehrer tätig waren, kann angenommen werden, dass auf diesem Weg auch eine Verbreitung der lexikalischen Texte stattgefunden hat. Dies bedeutet jedoch nicht, dass dieser Kulturaustausch nur in eine Richtung vonstatten ging, sondern es lassen sich, wie das zweite Textbeispiel gezeigt hat, Hinweise auf eine gegenseitige Beeinflussung finden.

Die lexikalische Tradition in Mesopotamien war in der zweiten Hälfte des zweiten Jahrtausends offenbar noch nicht so uniform, wie bisher häufig angenommen wurde. Auf der Grundlage der altbabylonischen Vorläufer wurden die verschiedenen Listen überarbeitet und konnten den jeweiligen lokalen Bedürfnissen individuell angepasst werden.

Weitere Untersuchungen anhand der Vergleiche einzelner Listen aus unterschiedlichen Zentren und Epochen werden Aufschluss über die Verbreitung des lexikalischen Korpus und dessen Ausgestaltung und Entwicklung bis zu den standardisierten Rezensionen des ersten Jahrtausends geben können. Hier sind neben den Texten aus Emar[36] insbesondere die Parallelen aus Ugarit[37] und Ḫattuša von großem Interesse. Derartige vergleichende Studien können, so ist zu hoffen, auch tiefere Einblicke in die Rolle der Schreiber einzelner Städte bei dem Prozess der Standardisierung wie auch bezüglich des Transfers von Wissen und des Kulturaustauschs im zweiten Jahrtausend geben.

36 Vgl. M. Civil, The Texts from Meskene-Emar. AuOr 7 (1989), S. 5–25.

37 Vgl. W. van Soldt, Babylonian Lexical, Religious and Literary Texts, S. 171–176.

Indices

Personal Names

Aboud, J. 76, 88
Abusch, T. 281
Annus, A. S.V, 335, 340
Astour, M.C. 56, 57, 63, 67, 68, 70, 74, 88

Biggs, R.D. 305
Black, J. 9
Bonfante, L. 18
Bottéro, J. 306, 308, 310
Boustan, R.S. 12, 51
Bräuer, G. 136
Buchholz, H.G. 55, 58, 68, 77, 80, 88
Bulliet, R.W. 139
Butterworth, G.W. 35

Caplice, R. 103, 123
Caubet, A. 68, 88
Cavigneaux, A. 143
Chadwick, H. 12
Civil, M. 305, 349, 356, 365
Culianu, I.P. 8, 16, 23, 24, 50
Cumont, F. 1, 2, 8, 31, 32, 42, 50
Cunningham, G. 303, 313, 314

Dalley, S. 4, 49, 50, 51, 260
Day, J. 233, 244, 255
Deger-Jalkotzy, S. 62, 68, 88
Delitzsch, F. 243
Dellling, G. 315
Demandt, A. 194
Demargne, P. 68
Denzey, N. 8
Dhorme, E. 243
Diakonoff, I.M. 263
Diamond, J. 137
Dietrich, M. 41, 55, 56, 59, 60, 63, 64, 65, 67, 78, 81, 83, 84, 85, 88, 89, 95, 96, 97, 98, 99, 100, 102, 103, 104, 106, 108, 117, 124, 263, 303, 309
Dijk, J. van 95, 98, 125, 306, 307, 308, 310, 313, 314
Dodds, E. 8, 23

Edmonds, R. 42
Edzard, D.O. 305
Eller, K. S.V
Emerton, J.A. 233, 255
Espak, P. S.V, 331, 340

Falkenstein, A. 305, 306, 307, 308, 310, 311
Farber, W. 250, 307
Feldman, M.H.
Finkel, I.L. 303, 313, 314
Freu, J. 70, 73, 76, 87, 89
Freydank, H. 259, 351, 352, 353
Fronzaroli, P. 303

Galter, H.D. 257
Geller, M.J. 304, 306, 311, 314
George, A.R. 7, 10, 31, 33, 35, 36, 38, 41, 43, 51, 208
Gese, H. 228, 244

Pedersén, O. 261, 351, 354, 360
Pettinato, G. 96, 98, 99, 125
Pingree, D. 14, 27, 28, 51
Põlenik, A. S.V
Postgate, J.N. 260, 263, 264
Powell, M. 128
Prudentius 34

Rad, G. von 228, 280, 292
Reed, A.Y. 12, 51
Reiner, E. 306, 307, 310
Rendtorff, R. 292, 293, 297, 300
Renger, J. 262, 311, 312, 340
Robinson, W.C. 18
Roloff, J. 319, 320
Römer, W.H.Ph. X, 98, 104, 105, 106, 303
Römheld, K.F.D. 229, 244
Rüterswörden, U. 64, 91

Salonen, A. 145
Salumaa, E. 316
Sanmartín, J. 60, 89, 124
Sawyer, J.F.A. 278, 284, 285
Sazonov, V. S.V, X, 325, 327, 341
Schaeffer, C.F.A. 59, 70, 71, 72, 91
Schökel, L.A. 227
Schwiderski, D. 145
Scurlock, J. 281
Seifert, G. 142, 143
Seux, M.-J. 258
Sfikas, G. 208
Singer, I. 74, 76, 87, 91
Sommerfeld, W. 99, 106, 125
Steiner, R.C. 246, 263
Stol, M. 281, 307, 310, 311
Strumpe, J. S.V

Tadmor, H. 262
Talon, P. 125, 263
Teh, Wu Lien 142, 146
Tropper, J. 64, 91, 116, 125

Umming, M. S.V

Veede, R. S.V
Veldhuis, N. 303, 304, 313, 314, 349, 353
Volt, I. S.V
Vööbus, A. IX, 147, 148, 149, 151
Võsa, A. S.V

Watson, J.D. 145
Watson, W.G.E. 91, 227
Weiher, E. von 308, 310, 312
Weiser, A. 243, 320
Westenholz, A. 333, 336, 337
Wiesner, J. 71, 91
Wilamowitz-Moellendorff, U. von 210, 212, 214, 220
Williamson, H.G.M. 233, 255
Woolley, C.L. 11

Yadin, Y. 237
Yon, M. 58, 68, 88, 91, 360

Zimmerli, W. 233

Topo- and Geographical Names

God and Temple Names

Ancient and ANE Personal Names

Subject Index

Lugal 326, 327, 328, 329, 330, 332, 333, 336, 359